**MIMESIS
INTERNATIONAL**

PHILOSOPHY
n. 62

Hanz Gutierrez Salazar

BEYOND THE BIBLE, BEYOND THE WEST

The "Eros" of Interpretation

© 2023—MIMESIS INTERNATIONAL
www.mimesisinternational.com
e-mail: info@mimesisinternational.com
Isbn: 9788869774539
Book series: *Philosophy*, n. 62

© MIM Edizioni Srl
P.I. C.F. 02419370305

CONTENTS

Luisella Battaglia
PREFACE
MEANING AND LIFE:
FOR A POST-MECHANISTIC AND POST-ANTHROPOCENTRIC HERMENEUTICS   11

INTRODUCTION
THE "BEYOND" THE TEXT AND THE "ON THIS SIDE" OF INTERPRETATION.
FOR A HERMENEUTICS OF LIFE   17
   1. The "Beyond" the Text   19
   2. The "On this Side" of Interpretation   22
   3. The "On this Side" and the "Beyond" of Being   25
   4. The "On this Side" and the "Beyond" of the Meaning of Life:
      A Hermeneutics of the South   31

PART I
THE HERMENEUTIC CIRCLE: THE TEXT AND THE READER

I. WHAT IS HERMENEUTICS?   57
   1. A Theological-Cultural Look at Hermeneutics   61
   2. Reading the Bible   64
   3. Interpreting the Bible   66
   4. The Dual Hermeneutical Nature of Christianity   70
   5. The "Hermeneutic Circle"   73

II. HISTORY OF HERMENEUTICS   79
   1. A Theological-Cultural Look at the History of Hermeneutics   82
   2. Pre-Modern Period. A "Text-Centric" Hermeneutics   86
   3. Modern Period. A "Reader-Centric" Hermeneutics   99

    4. Interpretive Fragmentation. Pluralism and Hermeneutical
       Polytheism   115
    5. Interpretive Compactness.
       Sola Scriptura and Hermeneutical Monolithism   122

III. A "FORMATIVE TEXT"   127

    1. A Theological-Cultural Look at the Text   132
    2. The Text and its Autonomy   139
    3. The Text and its Multiple Recipients   141
    4. The Text and the Broken Referentiality   144
    5. Informational Texts and Formative Texts:
       The Why of Being "in Reading"   147

IV. A "VITAL READER"   153

    1. A Theological-Cultural Look at the Reader   158
    2. The Reader and his Rooting "Upstream" of the Text:
       Pre-Understanding   163
    3. The Reader and his Uprooting "inFront of" the Text:
       Self-Criticism   165
    4. The Reader and his Pro-Rooting "Beyond" the Text: Imagination   168
    5. The Obedient Reader and the Vital Reader:
       The Why of Creativity "in Reading"   170

PART II
INTERPRETED LANGUAGE AND INTERPRETING LANGUAGE

V. THE INTERPRETED LANGUAGE   191

    1. A Theological-Cultural Look at Biblical Language   196
    2. A Complex and Multifaceted Language   200
    3. Word and Scripture as a Tension that Grounds Biblical Language   213
    4. Plurivocity and Sobriety as Hallmarks of Biblical Language   218
    5. Centripetal and Centrifugal Dimensions
       as the Dual Vocation of Biblical Language   222

VI. THE INTERPRETING LANGUAGE   225

    1. A Theological-Cultural Look at Religious Language   232
    2. Hermeneutic Levels: Some Characteristics   243

3. Three Intra-Textual Hermeneutic Levels: From Event to Paradox 246
4. Three Extra-Textual Hermeneutic Levels:
   From Paradox to Paradoxes 253
5. For a Biblical Hermeneutics of Polyvalence and Paradox 258

VII. HERMENEUTIC ANOMALIES "BY EXCESS" OF TEXT.
TEXTUAL POSITIVISM 269
   1. A Theological-Cultural Look at Textual Reductionism 274
   2. Biblical Literalism: Formal Inerrancy 282
   3. Biblical Confessionalism: Confessional Inerrancy 285
   4. Biblical-Theological Rationalism: Ideological Inerrancy 288
   5. Modern Book-Centrism: Cultural Inerrancy 291

VIII. HERMENEUTIC ANOMALIES "BY DEFICIT" OF TEXT.
ANTHROPOCENTRIC SUBJECTIVISM 295
   1. A Theological-Cultural Look at Hermeneutical Individualism 301
   2. Biblical Subjectivism: Psychological Anthropocentrism 307
   3. Biblical Confessionalism: Ecclesiological Anthropocentrism 310
   4. Biblical Pragmatism: Experiential Anthropocentrism 312
   5. Modern Rationalism: Cultural Anthropocentrism 316

PART III
TRINITY, MYSTERY AND THE UNAVAILABILITY OF MEANING

IX. THE FATHER'S PASSION AND THE POSSIBILITY OF MEANING 331
   1. Theological Positivism: "Monarchianism" 332
   2. Monarchianism and Globalization 336
   3. The Father's Complexity:
      "The Good Shepherd and the Welcoming Housewife" (Sl 23) 340
   4. "The Heroism" of the Good Shepherd 343
   5. "The Anonymity" of the Cozy Housewife 344
   6. From Sheep to Commensal: An Anthropological Metamorphosis 346
   7. "The Exuberant and Sober Love of the Father":
      The Contingency of Meaning 348

X. THE GRACE OF THE SON AND THE GRATUITOUSNESS OF MEANING. 357
   1. Christological Positivism: "Christocentrism" 358

   2. Christocentrism and Pathologizing   365
   3. The Complexity of the Son: "Jesus and Emmanuel" (Mt 1:18-23)   367
   4. "The Purity" of Jesus   371
   5. "The Accompaniment" of Emmanuel.   372
   6. From Sinner to Person: Anthropological Rebirth   375
   7. "The Exuberant and Sobering Grace of the Son":
       The Vulnerability of Meaning   376

XI. THE VITALITY OF THE SPIRIT AND THE RESILIENCE OF MEANING.   383

   1. Pneumatological Positivism: "Sanctification"   385
   2. Sanctification and *Regulation*   390
   3. The Complexity of the Spirit:
       "The Holy Spirit and the Spirit of Life" (Rev. 11:1-11)   392
   4. "The Order" of the Spirit of Holiness   394
   5. "The Unpredictability" of the Spirit of Life   398
   6. From Saint to Vital: Anthropological Flourishing   402
   7. "The Exuberant and Sobering Communion of the Spirit":
       The Miraculousness of Meaning   404

XII. READING THE BIBLE FROM THE SOUTH. THE EROS OF INTERPRETATION   413

   1. Chronicity and Persistence of Hermeneutic Nihilism
      in Late Modernity   418
   2. A Dysfunctional Trinity: The Death of Things   426
   3. A Dysfunctional Bible: The Canon Against the Spirit   437
   4. *Auferstehung* and the "Pneumatological Turn":
      Against the Necrophilia of Sense   445
   5. Beyond the Bible. The Birth of a Third Testament   459
   6. Beyond the West. On the Possibility of Other Knowledges   467
   7. The Resonance of Meaning:
      Sabbath, Advent and *Unverfügbarkeit*   484

BIBLIOGRAPHY   519

INDEX   541

To the Ferretti (Mario, Francesca and Filippo)
Who have redeemed my life -- several times.

To Dave Larson, friend and colleague,
for the linguistic inculturation
to which he submitted me with rigor and cultural
empathy.

To my friends of "BIBLIA",
Agnese, Martina, Cristina,
Piero Stefani, Piero Capelli,
Enrico Norelli, Marinella Perroni,
and all the others,
for their vision, passion and diversity,
in reading in a culturally new way
an ancient religious book.

To Peru, land of ambivalence, paradoxes
And abundant life.

Luisella Battaglia
PREFACE
Meaning and Life: for a Post-Mechanistic and Post-Anthropocentric Hermeneutics

If -as Gadamer states- that what characterizes the emergence of the hermeneutic problem is the need to bridge a distance, to overcome an estrangement, it seems destined to flourish especially at times of crisis of established visions, when our experience of the world becomes increasingly problematic and complex. But is this not the experience we are dramatically having today before the challenges of the 21st century, in search of a cultural rebirth that promises a resurrection of meaning? We are indeed facing a kind of "necrophilia of meaning" that should urge us to think - to borrow Hanz Gutierrez's expression - about a "hermeneutics of life." Inspired by this project is his essay on theological hermeneutics whose central thesis concerns the nature of the Bible (text) and the nature of the interpreting act that takes it up (reader) from a reflection on the "hermeneutic circle," on its configuration and scope.

We are faced here with an oscillation between a traditional understanding of the Bible as a "king text," before which the reader can only bend in obedient listening, and a modern understanding of the "creative reader" as a producer of meaning that the Bible can only suggest. In this second perspective, interpretation is configured as an experience of toilsome clarification of a meaning that -as the Author reminds us- remains always and in any case a complex, plural and paradoxical meaning, precisely because it is a human meaning and because the whole interpretive process is rooted in an oral or written language that, though actualized, remains unavailable and mysterious.

Gutierrez invites us in his text to the awareness that reading can become the grave of meaning or the place of its resurrection. It becomes its tomb when meanings follow one another uninterruptedly, but automatically and predictably, and reading is pure ascertainment from which essentially nothing asymmetrical, no ruptures and no paradoxes pointing forward arise. It is the place of its resurrection, on the other hand, when meanings are intermittent, unpredictable and fragmentary and reading becomes like childbirth, an experience marked by fatigue and suffering, but in the expectation of something new and unique that depends in part on the reader but is not entirely his or her own. We could therefore say -following the suggestive metaphor suggested by the Author- that, like childbirth, every reading is a mixture of continuity and discontinuity, it is an end and a beginning, a place of hope par excellence, a space of waiting for a conversion and a change by virtue of a different, oblique and unplanned gaze. An other gaze, a gaze other, then, that demands a radical reformation of mind and spirit, what we might call the ek-static amazement of the new person who opens himself to the enchantment of what is. This is why reading, rather than precision and discipline, requires above all vision and passion: an erotic experience -as it is felicitously called- that sets the reader on the path to something that is seen and hidden, that creates movement in the imagination and awakens curiosity and passion for new meaning in the confidence of expectation.

One is manifestly placed here in a perspective far removed from the biblical positivism and ecclesiological positivism which corresponds to a parallel cultural positivism, across the board and widespread in our secularized societies. It should not be forgotten, in this regard, that the essay explicitly presents itself as a critique of both "textual positivism," which makes the univocity and clarity of a text the main goal of its task, and "cultural positivism," which elevates univocity and clarity to the ultimate and total paradigm of the system in which we live. Indeed, the Author's stated aim is to try to problematize the notion of "text" and that of "reader's interpretation" by wresting them from that hermeneutic positivism that conceives them both only as instances of clarity, thus preserving the dimension of mystery, ambivalence and paradox of life, without which meaning itself would be deformed and compromised. In the penetrating critical analysis proposed to us, cultural positivism is composed of two anomalies, being, on reflection, the perfect superposition of a "deficit" and an "excess," or, more precisely, a paradoxical mixture of a deficit of "enchantment" and an excess of "efficiency."

If the "excess" of efficiency, in its various possible forms, is given by the cult of precision whereby measurement has swallowed complexity, the "deficit" is the result of the now chronic inability to think and experience the symbol in its structural ambivalence and paradox. In this one might recognize "the disease of the West" marked by a chronic defect: the unmentionable inability to mythologize, to create living and transformative meaning, which far from being recognized as a cultural involution, is sublimated as a cognitive virtue. The result? One is forced to know more because in fact one knows less and poorly. Gutierrez defines in the pages of his essay this cultural positivism and the related biblical positivism as "hermeneutic nihilism," the end result of which is an apathy and symbolic illiteracy that forces the Western person to propose "empty forms" as solutions, which the Western person, however, erects as a universal parameter. It should be added that an eroticism of interpretation, such as the one proposed, compels us not only to go beyond the Bible but also beyond the West, which epistemologically, according to Gutierrez, has killed the world's other knowledge by imposing on other peoples its knowledge as the only possible one. The West, through sophisticated informational, educational and advertising strategies, wants to teach the peoples of the South, for example, how to make groups, how to relate to nature, how to believe in God, how to read texts or what symbols are. Hermeneutic nihilism, we might say, is thus emptiness presented as fullness, form as substance, quantity as quality, growth as development, complication as complexity, contract as gift or sense as meaning. And here we come to the really fundamental question.

How to regain the hermeneutic and cultural sense that has been lost in a historical period like ours, where everything must be immediately efficient and immediately usable? In the view of the Author a hermeneutic renewal is not enough but what is needed is a cultural metanoia, a cultural *Auferstehung*, a real rebirth of the Spirit accompanying what has been called the 'other gaze'. The overthrow of a positivist culture, which encloses life and meaning in the mechanism of a calculation and a rational equation, can only be overthrown -Gutierrez persuasively argues- by a culture of life, by a change of language, by a spiritual resurrection. For this reason, it is the Spirit of Life -to be understood as the inclusive and universal Spirit whose horizon of action is not the narrow horizon of a denomination, a culture, a historical period, but the horizon that includes every form of life, human and otherwise- that must once again become the center of a spiritual and cultural rebirth.

The renewal of hermeneutics, the recovery of the meaning of life and biblical meaning, and, in a broader perspective, also the recovery of meaning in general, pass through the "pneumatological turn," which invites us both to a change of language and, at the same time, to a revisitation and reinterpretation of the whole Christian message, forming the basis for renewing culture and opening up a new conception of meaning. One might still wonder why the Author resorts to such a strong metaphor as *Auferstehung*, displacing it from its natural biblical-theological context and applying it to the whole culture.

Among other reasons, it seems to me of great significance that suggested by philosopher Martha Nussbaum, who in *Upheavals of Thought* describes today's real change as an "earthquake of thought" whereby *Auferstehung is* configured as a typical relational experience with the totally Other. In other words, one is not resurrected on one's own, just as one is not born on one's own through an exercise of one's own will and awareness, but solely through reliance on the intervention of an Other who comes to us from outside.

Thus, the rediscovery of meaning in the West cannot take place through an internal refinement or innovation within the modern system that would lead to the perpetuation of the anomaly it seeks to correct. Instead, the system must be "broken" from outside, through alternative forms of thinking that provoke real telluric movements, epistemological shocks, and that have as their common denominator the motivational, perspectival and symbolic power of the emotions. These alternative strategies of knowing are typical and classic strategies of "Recognition" of the Other, which the West has not only misplaced but prematurely and cynically called superstition. If in the narrative of modern human beings, the drive for an orderly and growing future is exclusively seen as a virtue, in Gutierrez's reading the passion for an orderly and efficient world is the sign of an anthropological loss, the loss of the Other. A loss that appears marked by a structural ambiguity because it gave rise to an extraordinary organizational and creative dynamism underlying the West's progress, the dark side of which, however, is not only the minimization, discrediting and then oppression and exploitation of other peoples and other species, but even more paradoxically the attrition and alienation of its own project of civilization. The *Auferstehung of* the Other consequently requires the introduction of a new language since the Other cannot be discovered with current positivist language that anonymizes and neutralizes it.

The only way, then, to enrich meaning is to connect it to that which guarantees it, to life, to reality, to God. Indeed, it is in the connection with the Other, with Others and with Otherness, incarnated in cultural, social and religious irreducible and inassimilable systems, that meaning can return and begin again to live. Hence the call for a cultural resistance that allows us to overcome abstract universalism in order to achieve a universalism of differences by virtue of a cultural mediation articulated on two dimensions, the first anthropological and cultural, the second ecological and political. It is fundamentally about rediscovering the immeasurable value of connectedness, a value that, according to the Author, Europe should learn from other peoples by learning to interact with other cultures. This, in his view, is the way to overcome gnoseological nihilism -which seems to constitute the most explanatory figure of our civilization- and at the same time respond to the problem of social disintegration. However, it is necessary to emphasize, Gutierrez warns, that the connection with life, with others and with God, as a path to guarantee a living meaning, occurs only when that Other, that is life, I do not possess it but I contemplate it, listen to it and bless it, that is, I speak well of it without manipulating it and, above all, when in that Other I discover and recognize its unavailability. This is a notation of great importance which, in emphasizing the need to learn to think differently, leaving behind a conception of ethics based on narrowly anthropocentric criteria, highlights extremely significant implications for bioethical reflection.

The unavailability that marks not only the Other but also the possibility of meaning, is such only by virtue of its -it is reiterated once again- ambivalence and paradox, that is, its mystery and its capacity to surprise, by virtue of that intrinsic complexity that one learns to recognize and respect. This is why a hermeneutics of life, multicultural and ecological in an irreversibly plural world urges us to know how to look with love and respect at the complexity of the world by connecting life, pluralism, cultural specificities and community around the centrality of the work of the Spirit.

We now move in a post-mechanistic and post-anthropocentric epistemic context, in the transdisciplinary horizon of a global history. For this reason, if the encounter of hermeneutics with the human sciences and, in particular, with the life sciences, from ecology to ethology, takes place under the sign of complementarity, it proves particularly fertile, in my opinion, for bioethics recovered in its original meaning of "ethics for the world of the living," according to the vision of Fritz Jahr, the Lutheran theologian who first coined the word back in 1927. Hence the revival of a new ontology and a new anthropology at the center of which is the explicit recognition of openness to a renewed conceptual map and a planetary ethics in which -as bioethics inspired by complexity thinking teaches us- the languages of life are arranged in a relationship of mutual listening and vision.

Luisella Battaglia
University of Genoa
National Committee for Bioethics (CNB) - Rome

INTRODUCTION
The "Beyond" the Text and the "On this Side" of Interpretation: A Hermeneutics of Life

Our reflection here takes the form of an essay of ontological hermeneutics.[1] It is critical of "textual positivism," which makes the univocity and clarity of a text the main goal of its task. It is also critical of "cultural positivism," on which "textual positivism" depends and of which it is an expression. This cultural matrix, in focusing on the immediacy, efficiency and productivity of human processes (in the various and heterogeneous levels in which these are organized within a society and culture), elevates univocity and clarity to the ultimate goal of contemporary systems.

This essay will attempt to problematize the notion of "text" and that of "reader's interpretation" in order to wrest them from a certain hermeneutic positivism that conceives both only as instances of clarity. Hermeneutics is partially and only initially an epistemological and correct reading enterprise.

First and foremost, hermeneutics is an experience of ontological grounding that interdicts the manipulation of meaning. Sense is created only partially; it is essentially given. It is given not necessarily in a transcendent way but most often from below, in an immanent way, yet preserving the dimension of mystery, ambivalence and

---

1 The need to link interpretation to ontology is certainly not new. In hermeneutics we can trace it back to the reflections of Heidegger and Gadamer, but as Claude Geffré rightly points out, the hermeneutical and cultural situation has deteriorated even more since then. Hence the need to urgently recapture an ontological dimension of interpreting. In what sense? From what perspective? This is what we will try to articulate in this text. Cf. C. Geffré, *Credere e interpretare. La svolta ermeneutica della teologia*, ("*Believing and Interpreting. The Hermeneutical Turn in Theology*"), (Brescia: Queriniana, 2002), pp. 19-21.

paradox of life, without which meaning itself would be deformed, tampered with and compromised.

This manifestative and non-pragmatic dimension of meaning today is overwhelmed not by biblical fundamentalism but by a culture of clarity of which fundamentalism, and more generally contemporary Christianity across all the spectrum, is only one manifestation. Sense as unmanipulable sense, as incomprehensible sense, has become for us moderns and post-moderns an alien, unbearable and finally useless experience. This essay indirectly sketches a cultural critique and not only a theological one. Means, medium and guarantor of this ontological[2] indelible reserve, are ambivalence and paradox. We will try to follow the trace of these throughout the hermeneutic arc, and not only at its beginning.

This we will do starting from a reflection on the Bible. Ours is an essay on theological hermeneutics. The central thesis of this essay concerns the nature of the Bible (text) and the nature of the interpreting act that takes it up (reader). This is, then, a reflection on the "hermeneutic circle," its configuration and scope. That hermeneutics emerges and arises only when these two elements are recognized and legitimized structurally escapes no one, no discerning reader.

What is not at all evident, however, is the appropriate description of the nature of this particular text, the Bible, and the nature of the interpretive act that tries to gather its meaning. One oscillates between two options. One is a traditional understanding of the Bible as a "king text," with meanings already full because they are revealed, before which the reader can only bend in obedient listening and application. The other is a modern understanding of the "creative reader" as a producer of meaning that the Bible alone can suggest and introduce through the suggestion of certain revealed ingredients that, however, need the final touch, not only applicative, but also innovative, of the reader. Neither pole, neither the text nor

---

2   Hermeneutics, if it wants to promote meaning and guarantee it, must remain linked to ontology. Cf. L.A. Schökel, J.M. Bravo Aragon, *Appunti di ermeneutica. Comprendere e interpretare i testi biblici e letterari*, (*"Notes on Hermeneutics. Understanding and Interpreting Biblical and Literary Texts"*), (Bologna: Edb, 2014), pp. 154, 155.

the reader, disappears in these two perspectives. The hermeneutic circle would be guaranteed, in both cases and from a formal point of view, in the maintenance of a subordination. Most of the time is that of the reader, but sometimes it can also be that of the text. Could this formal observance of the hermeneutic circle be enough to speak of successful interpretation? Can it be said to be successful when meaning is achieved, when from various possible senses of an ambivalent text we move to an unambiguous, specific, precise and clear sense? Here is where our doubt becomes a contestation. We believe, and we will try to argue, that interpretation is never the linear process that goes from plurivocity to univocity, from mystery to clarity, from complexity to synthesis. It is par excellence the experience of a troubled and suffered clarification of a sense. While creating orientation and specific addresses, it opens up new horizons and perspectives of possible human path. But it remains though a complex, plural and paradoxical sense, because it is a human sense and because the whole interpretative process is rooted in an oral or written language that, although actualized, remains unavailable and mysterious.

1. The "Beyond" the Text

How can we ensure this double need for clarity and plurality, for specification and mystery, for fullness and tension of meaning, in the interpretive process that pushes us structurally beyond the text? In our view, this can and does occur only when we can understand the true nature of biblical language and the true nature of the interpreting act, which is given by ambivalence and paradox. Ambivalence and paradox[3] are thus, in our reflexive hypothesis, not two phenomena derived from unwanted interference in the uncontrollable communicative process, which must therefore be purified and neutralized. They are two structural and original situations that ground every linguistic process. If this is true for every human linguistic process, it is even more so for the

---

[3] "Ambivalence" and "paradox" are central to our analysis of the interpretive process and will be present, sometimes explicitly and sometimes implicitly, throughout our essay.

Bible. Contrary to what is thought, the Bible is not a clear book but an obscure book. This is because the Bible recognizes both ambivalence and paradox and perceives them in the deepest and most foundational layers of human experience. This is in faith and in God, to which it bears witness and of which it is a partial record.

Unlike most Christians, we start with the belief that the Bible is not a clear text. But contrary to what is commonly believed, this fact does not appear negative to us. On the contrary, it points to the greatness of this text. This lack of clarity founded in the polyvalence of biblical language guarantees the creation of a sense and mode of meaning that is typical of the biblical linguistic structure, and that is the plural sense. Therein lies its strength, for this plurality of meaning, which certainly slows down the interpretive process, actually enhances its inclusiveness. To say that the Bible is unclear is to recognize as structural its ambivalence, which not only makes interpretation possible but also defines it in the plural.

Ambivalence at its basis, the existence of various possible meanings of words and events, makes interpretation necessary. This principle, which applies to other texts similar to the Bible such as poetry or narrative, applies even more to the Bible, taking into account the object of its description: God himself, his action and his mystery. It is thus by virtue of this structural ambivalence that the Bible pushes beyond itself toward interpretation. The Bible itself demands its overcoming. Interpretation, as a going "beyond" the text, is a transgression that the Bible itself promotes and makes necessary by virtue of its linguistic configuration. It is the Bible itself that creates the "anti-Bible," thought as interpretations that go beyond it in creating new meanings that the Bible itself does not contain or contains only latently. Interpretations are the "anti-type" that the Bible, as "type," always makes possible.

Interpretation does not betray, does not jeopardize, but fulfills the biblical text. The ambivalence and structural paradox of the Bible makes it flexible and inclusive. It views interpretation not with distrust but as an opportunity to project out of the text what is only latent and dormant in it. It is what Umberto Eco[4] calls an "open

---

4   Umberto Eco clearly conceives of interpretation not as a moment of application, but as a moment of sense-making, in which the impulses that

text."⁵ An open text is one that not only legitimizes but requires the necessary participation of the reader in the recovery of a meaning that would otherwise remain not only unexpressed but in a sense even nonexistent or only at the level of a trace. Umberto Eco, regarding this openness of texts, through a reference to a sonnet by Baudelaire entitled *The Cats,* writes:

> "*Les Chats*" is thus a text that not only requires the cooperation of its reader, but also wants this reader to attempt a series of interpretive choices that, if not infinite, are at least indefinite, and in any case more than one. Why then not speak of "openness"? To postulate the reader's cooperation is not to pollute structural analysis with extra-textual elements. The reader as an active principle of interpretation is part of the generative framework of the text itself. At most there is only one objection to my objection and to Lévi-Strauss's objection: if even anaphoric references postulate cooperation on the part of the reader, then no text escapes this rule. Correct. The texts I then called "open" are just a more provocative example of exploitation, for aesthetic purposes, of a principle that governs both the generation and the interpretation of all kinds of texts."⁶

Here is where the second question emerges. If the first hermeneutical question is about the closure of the text and the possibility and duty of opening it up to interpretation, this second question asks instead how not to betray the text, not to stray from its essence while surpassing it in interpretation. Interpretation cannot be and cannot become a betrayal of the text, its vocation and its project.

---

undoubtedly come from the text are taken over by the reader to creatively complete a sense that would otherwise remain fragmentary and purely in a state of latency. Umberto Eco will criticize at this level C. Lévi-Strauss who, understandably, stopping at the structures of a text as a final register, contested the concept of "open text" with regard to a sonnet by Baudelaire entitled *The Cats.*

5 It is what Daniel Marguerat calls the structural incompleteness of a text. Cf. D. Marguerat, Y. Bourquin, *Per leggere i racconti biblici. La Bibbia si racconta. Iniziazione all'analisi narrativa,* ("*To Read Biblical Narratives. The Bible Narrates Itself. Initiation to Narrative Analysis*"), (Rome: Borla, 2011), pp. 130-133.
6 U. Eco, *Lector in fabula. La cooperazione interpretativa nei testi narrativi,* ("*Lector in Fabula. Interpretive Cooperation in Narrative Texts*"), (Milan: Bompiani, 2006), p. 7.

2. The "On this Side" of Interpretation

Interpretation while legitimate and necessary has a constraint. Will this constraint be the necessary clarification of meaning? No one could deny that interpretation requires a specification of meaning. Otherwise, what would be the interpretive benefit? More importantly, what would be the use of the reader's mediation if this affirmed meaning is not up to date with what the existential and historical circumstances of the reader and his or her community of reference are? Sense specification is thus necessary in interpretation; but will it be sufficient?

Here is our contention, which we formulate as follows: the specification of meaning is a necessary but insufficient criterion for describing the nature of any interpretive act. If this were the case, interpretation would in fact become a substitute for the text. This legitimate but radicalized and out of hand move would absolutize itself thereby breaking the balance of the hermeneutic circle. A balanced interpretation always maintains as valid "the interpreted text" of interpretation.

This "On this side" of interpretation is not surmountable, is not merely propaedeutic. It is not destined to disappear in a synthesis that absorbs it. It resists all interpretations as a guarantee of the interpretations themselves. It is a guarantee of the hermeneutic circle, preventing it from becoming a unidirectional and evolutionary line in which the text is buried by the interpretation and this in turn buried by further, newer interpretations.

This danger, which arises from a hermeneutical virtue, indeed obligation, has always been present. But today, in a cultural system like ours that is diffusely constructivist, it has become an almost unstoppable drift. Hence, for example, Paul Ricœur's constant call to limit this subjectivist drift of modern hermeneutics through the recovery of the notion of "textuality."[7] Ricœur writes with respect to this necessary textual mediation as a hermeneutic obligation:

---

7 Ricœur's entire hermeneutics can be described as a hermeneutics of the "text," certainly not to deny the orientation of an age such as ours with its emphasis on the centrality of the individual reader, an indelible tendency moreover, but only to balance it and try to limit its radicalization. P. Ricœur, *Dal testo all'azione. Saggi di ermeneutica,* (*"From Text to Action. Essays in Hermeneutics"*), (Milan: Jaca Book, 1994), pp. 133-154.

"In regard to hermeneutics I will adopt the following working definition: hermeneutics is the theory of operations concerning the understanding of texts in relation to the interpretation of texts. [The] guiding idea will thus be the effecting of discourse as text. The entire second study will thus focus on the elaboration of the categories of the text, to which it will pave the way by the attempt, offered at the end of the first paper, to resolve the central aporia of hermeneutics, namely the alternative, disastrous for me, between explaining and understanding. The search for a complementarity between these two attitudes, which hermeneutics of romantic origin is inclined to dissociate, will then express on the epistemological level the change of orientation imposed on hermeneutics by the notion of text."[8]

Behind the text and in the text itself, the instance that curbs this excessive subjective drift and the absolutization of interpretations that have become ends in themselves -what guarantees the plausibility and validity of this "On this side" of interpretations- is still the ambivalence and the paradox of the text. Ambivalence and paradox, maintained throughout all the interpretive arc and not only at the beginning, are the elements that guarantee a possible and desirable "beyond" of the text and also a "On this side" of the interpretation. They are unmistakable signs of a healthy interpretive process.

The ambivalence and paradox that the interpretive act maintains, and is required to maintain, is not the copy but the reproduction of that ambivalence and paradox of the interpreted text. The ambivalence and paradox that survive in interpretation are guaranteed by certain elements.

1. The transitoriness of the found sense. The sense found cannot be a definitive sense, otherwise the interpretation would become more important than the text it interprets.

2. The plurality of meanings elaborated by the same interpreter. The interpreter's interpretation should never be monolithic, and not only out of constraint with the subjective openness of the reader, but especially out of obligation to objective fidelity to the interpreted text (Bible). Every good interpretation creates its own alternatives.

3. The plurality of interpreters. The interpreter and his or her system of reference -the church, the community, an ideology- must

---

8 P. Ricœur, *Dal testo all'azione...,Op. cit.*, pp. 71,72.

recognize other systems and live with them and the different senses those other systems process and propose.

The first and second parts of our essay aim to describe the necessary permanence of ambivalence and paradox throughout the interpretive arc, at the level of the "Text" and at the level of the "Reader" who interprets that text. The biblical hermeneutics of paradox does not aim at the answer, but at the extension and enrichment of the question. Biblical hermeneutics is not and cannot be a synthetic and resolving instance of meaning. It is not a hermeneutic of clarity, but of complexity, indeed, of dynamic complexity, that is, of paradox.[9]

The hermeneutical problem is thus reversed. The question is not why more clarity is not achieved, but rather the opposite: why is there too much clarity? Instead, the assumption of most interpretive endeavors is fundamentally flawed, because in them interpretation is commonly conceived as the moment when this ambivalence is and must be overcome. The text, then, would be ambivalent only transiently, because interpretation would have the clear task of making it transparent.

Instead, we think that ambivalence (complexity) should also be maintained in interpretation and in all moments of the interpretive arc. The various chapters of the book argue for this hypothesis by describing as hermeneutic anomalies not those that prevent and hinder clarity, but those that promote and defend it, elevating it to the ultimate goal of reading.

This is what we call "textual positivism" and bibliolatry. Ignoring, neglecting, trying to erase the typical biblical ambivalence, gives rise to these varied forms of biblical reductionism that we call "textual positivism." The biblical fundamentalism and literalism are only one of its forms, and not necessarily the most widespread. Of this "textual positivism" Protestant Christianity, but also Catholic Christianity, is a refined religious expression, precisely because the basic secular cultural matrix, that of modern Western culture, represents and embodies its perfect prototype. The West is a linguistically and

---

9 U. Galimberti, *Orme del sacro. Il cristianesimo e la desacralizzazione del sacro*, (*"Footsteps of the Sacred. Christianity and the Desacralization of the Sacred"*), (Milan: Feltrinelli, 2000), pp. 35-61. See also, *Il corpo* (*"The Body"*), (Milan: Feltrinelli, 2002), pp. 11-27.

hermeneutically positivist culture because it has built the efficiency of its system on precision and compactness of meaning, on scientific and cultural univocity.[10] Of this linguistically positivist culture, "biblical positivism" is only a particular expression.

3. The "On this Side" and the "Beyond" of Being

The search for the hermeneutic ontological register has become not only a theological but also a cultural obligation. Hermeneutics cannot be just a way of knowing; it is a way of being. We are something more and better when we interpret a text which is beyond the more accurate information that texts convey to us. We find, thanks to that, a firmer grounding in the life that precedes every text (ontological "On this side") and also a confident thrust forward (ontological "Beyond") that goes beyond textual interpretation and places us in a perspective of hope.

Hermeneutic reductionism occurs not only when one of the poles of the hermeneutic circle is erased or tampered with, but especially when the interpretive act is dissociated from life[11] and becomes purely gnoseological. Language, oral or textual, aspires to be connected to Being. When this does not happen, hermeneutics is reduced to its pure epistemological dimension. This is the most common drift of our time, which we call "textual positivism." At this point, the Heideggerian call to resist the temptation to reduce hermeneutics to a purely cognitive

---

10   Umberto Galimberti believes that Western culture is massively built on unambiguity and clarity. From this fact derives its double destiny. On the one hand its strength and incredible dynamism, on the other its reductionism based on control. And dynamism, like its related control, was only possible, according to Galimberti, from the dismantling and erasure of "ambivalence," which is what characterizes reality, life and especially, the body. U. Galimberti, *Il corpo*, Op. cit., pp. 11-27; *Il tramonto dell'Occidente nella lettura di Heidegger e Jaspers*, ("*The Decline of the West in the Readings of Heidegger and Jaspers*"), (Milan: Feltrinelli, 2017), pp. 451-459.

11   From this connection with life comes the parallel term that we will use several times to designate the interpretive process in its most inclusive and best perspective and which we call precisely "hermeneutics of life."

experience remains ever valid and urgent, especially in our late-modern times where the cult of "transparency" reigns.[12] Such is the impetus and argumentative force of the Heideggerian ontological appeal that the philosopher identifies the hermeneutic experience not with the preservation of the text and its meaning, nor with the reader and the meaning it can create, both poles bearing from the hermeneutic arc. He assimilates the hermeneutics as such (text and reader) to the confrontation with Being. In the well-known seventh section on hermeneutics (*Auslegung*) of *Being and Time*, of which we quote here a long but clarifying paragraph, Heidegger articulates this ontological urgency as the central task of all hermeneutics, of hermeneutics as such.

> "The *logos* of the phenomenology of Dasein (Beingness) has the character of hermeneuein, through which the proper meaning of being and the basic structures of the very Being of Dasein are made known to the understanding of being that belongs to Dasein itself. Phenomenology of Dasein is hermeneutics in the original signification of that word, which designates the work of interpretation. But since the discovery of the meaning of being and of the basic structures of Dasein in general exhibits the horizon for every further ontological research into beings unlike Dasein, the present hermeneutic is at the same time 'hermeneutics' in the sense that it works out the conditions of possibility of every ontological investigation. Finally, insofar as Dasein has ontological priority over all other beings -as a being in the possibility of existence [Existenz]-, hermeneutics, as the interpretation of the being of Dasein, receives the third specific and, philosophically understood, primary meaning of an analysis of the existentiality of existence. To the extent that this hermeneutics elaborates the historicity of Dasein ontologically as the ontic condition of the possibility of the discipline of history, it contains the roots in what can be called "hermeneutics" only in a derivative sense: the methodology of the historical humanistic disciplines."[13]

---

12 According to Byung-Chul Han, our contemporary societies have become highly functional because they erase negativity as a disruptive and slowing element in communicative and cultural processes that they believe should instead be immediately profitable, efficient and clear. Cf. B.-C. Han, *La società della trasparenza*, (*"The Transparency Society"*), (Milan: Nottetempo, 2014), pp. 30-38.

13 This paragraph closes the seventh section and also the introduction to *Being and Time*. Section eight, which formally is the last section of the introduction, is in fact a short section where only the outline of the book

Following this Heideggerian call, in the third part of our text we connect the biblical interpretive process to God himself. We try to argue that the Bible's indelible complexity as a text, given its indelible ambivalence, characterizes God himself even more at the core. The disconnect between the Bible and God's Being is the first step in absolutizing both the text and subsequent interpretations, and thus giving rise to what we have called "biblical positivism." The connection between language and Being,[14] that is, between the Bible and God, is thus essential to unhinging all hermeneutical positivism. The Bible, because it is built on ambivalence as a value, is able to preserve the mystery that no interpretation can exhaust or drain, only in its connection to a mystery that precedes it. This is the mystery of God and the Trinity. Indeed, by virtue of this fact, interpretations do not exhaust but multiply possible meanings.

This biblical ineffability is based on the ineffability of God. The connection between the Bible and the Being of God does not reinforce the clarity but the mystery of both. This prolongs the ineffability of God in the ineffability of the Bible, as mechanisms not of sacralization but of dialogue. The appeal to God's Being as the foundation of the biblical hermeneutical process does not sacralize the Bible, as it might seem at first glance. On the contrary decentralizes it, flexibilizes it, and makes it relational, because it is mystery that makes qualitative knowledge of God and his Word possible. Where there is no mystery, where the ineffability of God and the text has become transparent, dialogue becomes manipulation.

The connection between language and Being has a dark side that is difficult to manage. It is a delicate and dangerous connection. Instead of

---

is set forth. See M. Heidegger, *Essere e tempo*, (*"Being and Time"*), (Milan: Longanesi, 1976), p. 58.

14 Between Being and language there is clearly a link, but the affirmation and defense of this link should not lead to reducing Being to language. There will always be an excess of Being over language. If premodern thought tended, despite everything, to preserve the surplus of Being over language, the modern world tends instead to absorb Being into language and make Being completely transparent to language. See V. Brugiatelli, *La relazione tra linguaggio ed essere in Ricœur*, (*"The Relation Between Language and Being in Ricœur"*), (Trento: Uni Service, 2009), pp. 15-58.

preventing the absolutization of the text, recourse to Being has frequently in history produced the opposite effect. It has ended up sacralizing texts and interpretations of them even more. This is why the connection between Bible and God, between text and Being, is a delicate passage that must be approached with prudence, wisdom and measure.

To say that God (Being) is the foundation of his Word (Bible) must lead one to relativize the text and its interpretations, for this fact reminds us that these will never exhaust God's Being. God is the foundation of his Word, so consequentially, it is God's communicative (relational) Being that grounds his Word as communication. The Bible is not a communicative strategy external to God. God is communication. God is there and He speaks, and because He speaks He is there.

The Bible represents for Christians the recognition and affirmation of three essential communicative principles concerning God. The Christian God is a God who wants to "communicate" (will and intention), wants to "reveal himself" (revelation) and wants to "inspire" (inspiration) those with whom he comes into contact: human beings. At the same time, he affirms meaning and ontological unavailability not as a limitation but as a guarantor of his own revelation.[15] God reveals himself by hiding and hides himself by revealing himself. This is *Revelatio*, showing and hiding. Total manifestation, fullness of light, complete openness (*Offen-barung*)[16] of the divine event and Being is something foreign to biblical thought.[17]

---

15 One should not confuse sense of language and language. God is revealed in language, not necessarily in judgment as an expression of language. Cf. L.A. Schökel, J.M. Bravo Aragon, *Appunti di ermeneutica...*, Op. cit., pp. 19-24.

16 This is, for example, Bruno Forte's critique of the Protestant concept of "*Offen-barung*" (revelation) where the sense of concealment and mystery inherent in the biblical conception of revelation is lost and which the Latin equivalent "Revelatio", keep instead intact. B. Forte, "Sacra Scrittura e Teologia", in, *Adventus,* no. 22/2012, Florence Adventist Faculty of Theology, pp. 30-42.

17 Christian theology is articulated between affirmation and mystery, thought and praise. It is forbidden to be a totalizing and definitive theology. The essence of theology is thus relation not only because it faces the All Other as referent but also because in that referent (God) it also connects to his mystery. This tension marks, according to Douglas Ottati, the method and

1. God is a "communicative God." In contrast to the God of Deism, the God of the Bible does not want us to solely acknowledge his existence. He wants to communicate with us. He desires that we recognize in him a God with his own will, intention and specific purpose for us humans. He is not a neutral God who hides behind a standard attitude that applies to everyone and then, ultimately, to no one. He wants to enter into relationship with us, and he makes this known because this intention is already part of his message. This communicative will characterizes not only him and his Word, but also the beings he created. God created us humans, in fact, as communicative beings because he is communicative in his essence. And we are made in his image and likeness.

The proof and guarantee of this structure and communicative possibility lies in the autonomy granted to us at the moment of creation. Contrary to popular belief, it is not proximity and symbiosis that creates communication. It is autonomy and differentiating detachment that makes communication possible. Two symbiotically united beings do not actually communicate, even though they can talk a lot, because there are not two but one fused and confused identity. Communication always involves otherness as a condition and detachment and differentiation as a necessary experience.

The Christian God is a relational God by nature. He is so because he has created independent creatures, which are not an extension of himself, with whom he seals a free and chosen commitment of frequentation that takes the form of communication. This creates rapprochement but not symbiosis, in convergent dialogue but does not take away the mystery of the autonomous entities that dialogue. He wants to be in contact with his creatures without controlling them, as his creatures know him without taking away his mystery. The Bible is only the expression of this communicative desire and respect.

2. God is a "God who reveals himself." That God reveals himself means that the initiative for the knowledge of God starts from him, not from us. This is revelation. He is not forced to reveal himself. Communication in God as in us humans, from the way we

---

perspective of all theology. Douglas F. Ottati, *A Theology for the Twenty-first Century*, (Grand Rapids: William B. Eerdmans, 2021), pp. 35-76.

are structured, is not a necessity. It is a contingent act. In the path of relationship with his creatures he will also be forced to reveal himself in certain forms, but revelation in and of itself, in its essence, is a free act of God.

The Bible is a revelation of God but it is not the whole revelation of God. The Bible is God's circumstantial revelation and, as such, it has been partially forced by circumstances and bears the limits of those circumstances. Revelation, as God's intended manifestation, precedes the Bible and has existed in God's being from all time. God's revelation is not an *a posteriori* and circumstantial fact. It belongs to God's being. From always, God is a God who reveals himself. He also reveals himself because he is constituted in a certain way such that he has creatures other than himself to be in contact with. God's revelation is a contingent act that is not necessary. At the same time, it is an *a priori* non-circumstantial act. It freely belongs to his being. God gives himself and offers himself in his word. At the same time, he always remains beyond our understanding. Revelation and God's unavailability are not contradictory but mutually interdependent.

3. "God inspires" human beings to be reliable witnesses of his revelation. Because of the way he created his creatures as autonomous though dependent beings, he could not fail to give them the capacity for communication. Inspiration is not God-centered even though it starts from God as a guarantor. In inspiration God makes himself a guarantor of human communication. He accepts human participation as necessary and positive. God's revelation is matched and followed by human revelation through inspiration.

Every creature is capable of revelation, so every human revelation is important because it is unique. If man were not capable of revelation, God could not have inspired him. Inspiration of humans occurs only if they are also capable of revelation. Inspiration guarantees God's revelation and recognizes man's revelation as positive. That revelation of the human, which God himself guarantees, he considers important and even akin to his own revelation, and so he decides to merge them both into a common destiny, the Bible.

Hermeneutics is that interpretive process where the free and polyvalent Word of God is taken up by the free and polyvalent human word. It conveys not only information and data about life, but life itself as an affirmative way of being in the world and feeling loved by God.

4. *The "On this Side" and the "Beyond" of the Meaning of Life: A Hermeneutics of the South*[18]

The understanding of meaning is inseparable from that which grounds it: Being. Sense is never orphaned, but is always made

---

[18] Philip Jenkins describes in his various texts the emerging strength of Southern Christianity. His work, important in pointing out this new phenomenon, is more descriptive than theological; this sometimes prevents him from seeing the innovative theological and cultural orientations being gestated and articulated in the Southern hemisphere. Our description of the hermeneutics of the South is of an entirely different kind and is culturally and theologically opposed to his reading. Ph. Jenkins, *I nuovi volti del cristianesimo*, (*"The New Faces of Christianity"*), (Milan: Vita e pensiero, 2007), pp. 37- 69. Our analysis of the South, of Southern hermeneutics, of their vitality, creativity and dynamism in proposing alternative and innovative perspectives, follows a different strand of thought. Some of the Southern authors, with whom we will implicitly dialogue continuously in this essay, are: A. Appadurai, *The Future as Cultural Fact. Essays on the Global Condition*, (New York: Verso, 2013); *Modernity at Large. Cultural Dimensions of Globalization*, (Minneapolis: University of Minnesota Press, 2010); A. Mbembe, *Critique de la raison nègre*, (Paris : La Découverte, 2013); B. de Souza Santos, *Epistemologies of the South. Justice against Epistemicide*, (London: Paradigm Publishers, 2014); A. Al-Azmeh, *Islam and Modernities*, (New York: Verso, 2009); S. Mahmood, *Religious Difference in a Secular Age. A Minority Report*, (Princeton: Princeton University Press, 2016); T. Asad, *Genealogies of Religion. Discipline and Reasons of Power in Christianity and Islam*, (Baltimore: The Johns Hopkins University Press, 1997); A. Chanady (ed), *Latin American Identity and constructions of Difference*, (Minneapolis: University of Minnesota Press, 1994); P. Gonzalez Casanova, *Las Nuevas Ciencias y las Humanidades. De la Academia a la Politica*, (The New Sciences and Humanities. From Academia to Politics), (Barcelona: Anthropos 2005); N. G. Canclini, *Hybrid Cultures. Strategies for Entering and Leaving Modernity*, (Minneapolis: University of Minnesota Press, 1995); W.D. Mignolo, *The Darker Side of Western Modernity. Global Futures, Decolonial Options*, (Durham: Duke University Press, 2011).

possible and accompanied by Being. Being itself, which precedes sense, is never inseparable from life, of all life, of life flowing and expanding and expanding in history and nature. That meaning and that life that guarantees it are not related purely to man, and less so to his awareness alone. They are also linked to and dependent on the sigh, intuition, figures, dreams, aspirations, prayers, visions, suffering, resilience, imagination, desire, body and nature that are the amniotic fluid in which meaning and life are born and flourish.

Life[19] that grounds meaning and Being is thus movement and pause, action and passion, imagination and contemplation, giving and receiving, reason and emotion, order and disorder, clarity and mystery, strength and vulnerability; in essence, history and cosmos. Meaning, like life, is necessarily tensional. It is not one or the other, but the one and the other of all these categories and registers mentioned. Meaning and life are slow, opaque, complex and paradoxical realities that one must learn to love in the sober

---

19   Hence the frequent use of the term "hermeneutics of life." From various theological perspectives, Catholic, Orthodox, Protestant and Evangelical, the theme of life as a framework for thinking about the meaning of Faith in particular and the meaning of existence in general, has been asserting itself forcefully and persistently for some years now. As, for example, in the case of the encyclical *Evangelium vitae* (March 30, 1995) where John Paul II contrasts a "culture of life" with a necrophilic thrust of modern culture, which the encyclical calls a "culture of death." The III Unity Commission of the Ecumenical Council of Churches deliberated in Larnaca in 1993 a program on the "theology of life." At the Ecumenical Council of Churches in Camberra, in 1991, Korea's Chung Hyun Kyung promoted a "culture of solidarity" based on and guaranteed solely by a "culture of life." In 1991 Moltmann published his book on the Spirit entitled, *Lo spirito della vita. Per una pneumatologia integrale, ("The Spirit of Life. For an Integral Pneumatology")*, (Brescia: Queriniana, 1994). In 1992 the same happened with M. Welker and his text, *Lo Spirito di Dio. Teologia dello Spirito Santo, ("The Spirit of God. Theology of the Holy Spirit")*, (Brescia: Queriniana, 1995); in 1993 G. Müller-Fahrenholz published, *Erwecke die Welt. Unsere Glaube an Gottes Geist in dieser bedrohten Zeit, ("Awaken the World. Our Faith in God's Spirit in this endangered Time")*, (Gütersloh: Gütersloher Verlagshaus, 1993). Cf. J. Moltmann, *La fonte della vita. Lo Spirito Santo e la teologia della vita, ("The Source of Life. The Holy Spirit and the Theology of Life")*, (Brescia: Queriniana, 1998), pp. 18-36.

and incomplete joy of non-possession and the non-bulimic hope of expectation. Rootedness and perspective, memory and expectation, inheritance and projection are the hinges within which meaning, Being and life are given and offered to all of us as gift and task.

Interpreted meaning is not just a way of knowing. It is a way of being in life, of knowing oneself preceded, of feeling overwhelmed and propelled forward, the true goal of any process of contemplation or sense-making.

The Being of meaning is always a Being in life, for life. It is life[20] the "On this side" and the "Beyond" of meaning. It is in life that meaning is born. That life we try to gather it into that meaning which we articulate and elaborate and which suddenly touches us tangentially making us witnesses but not possessors of that meaning. It is still in life that meaning grows and it is life that pushes and provokes it forward. The interpreter, individual or corporate, secular or religious, rich or poor, male or female, cannot control the sense and less still the life of which the sense is a sign. At most, the interpreter is a witness with a double task. On the one hand to contemplate and collect, and on the other hand to touch and tamper with the sense, for that sense cannot only be suffered and imposed. That sense not only bears well the intervention of the reader/subject, but even demands it. The vital sense is always an inclusive sense of people and events that I, as the reader, try to enlarge to others.

The problem with the hermeneutics that have emerged in history at the level of biblical interpretation or at the level of various cultural configurations has not been that they have offered or claimed a greater specification of the interpreted meaning. This claim is perfectly

---

20 This emphasis on the precedence and priority of "life" over "life reasons" or "life duties" we make it in implicit connection with the Aristotelian tradition of the "good" as the primary perspective of human action. Cf. W. Pannenberg, *Fondamenti dell'etica. Prospettive filosofico-teologiche*, (*"Foundations of Ethics. Philosophical and Theological Perspectives"*), (Brescia: Queriniana, 1998), pp. 35-48. In this sense with Paul Ricœur, not only for ethics but also for the search for meaning, we emphasize the category of "good" as a foundational category that precedes that of "duty." P. Ricœur, *Sé come un altro, ("Self as Another")*, (Milan: Jaca Book, 2005), pp. 266-275.

legitimate. The general sense can and must become specific. The problem is that that necessary specification of meaning, which all good interpretation introduces, has created unilateralisms of various degrees and forms that end up paralyzing meaning and disconnecting it from life, the true source and goal of all possible meaning. The enchainment of life to a particular sense is the continual temptation of all interpretation, especially since the redemption and promotion of life demands and requires that specification of sense, but always, only and still as a partial and transitory exercise. Interpreted meaning is never final goal, but merely stage and transition; that is, passage.

Following in this wake, we might note the greatness and limits of the claim of a new hermeneutical sense, that of "liberation theology," proposed fifty years ago in a geographical area, the Global South, more specifically Latin America. Taken symbolically, we would like to think of today as an alternative geographical and theological place to a hermeneutical positivism[21] that is transversal and rampant in our time precisely by virtue of its "meekness."

Today, the classical social and scientific positivism of the mid-19th century, with its purported objectivity and optimism, is not only challenged but also out of fashion. Across the board there is a belief in the historicity and relativity of everything we know; above all, we have lost the enthusiasm and optimism in the processes and results that in early modernity we considered instead linear and almost certain.

This is why the word "positivism," applied to hermeneutics, seems improper and anachronistic. Yet, our hypothesis is that, although it is yielding and limiting itself, indeed, although it has been forced to scale back, today positivism, as an obsession with clarity and unambiguousness, theoretical and practical, continues to be a transversely operating phenomenon. This is through a form of its own with a less compact profile that we call "mild positivism."

---

21 By "hermeneutic positivism," or by the parallel terms such as "textual positivism," "biblical positivism," or even "cultural positivism," we will refer throughout our text to a reductivist but efficient view of the articulation of meaning (reading, interpretation, cultural forms) that aims at clarity of meaning as the ultimate goal with the concomitant neutralization of mystery, complexity and paradox.

Introduction

"Mild positivism" is similar to "mild despotism", typical, according to Tocqueville, of democratic societies that challenge heteronomous authoritarianisms without realizing that they themselves, from below, create an authoritarianism with a kind face. It is more devastating in its effects. Although it is lighter, it is at the same time more chronic and transversal. Going unnoticed, it spreads without resistance precisely because it is created by ourselves.[22]

In 1971, Gustavo Gutierrez, a Peruvian theologian, published the text *Liberation Theology,* which would begin this hermeneutical initiative in the Global South. In contrast and close criticism with interpretations predominant in Northern Christianity which ran into blatant contradictions and anachronisms, he criticized the ambivalence of these efforts to safeguard the orthodoxy of Christianity. Gutierrez, in his critique of the orthodoxy of ideas that had become completely detached from life and no longer pushed toward its liberation, wrote the following:

> "Finally, the rediscovery in theology of the eschatological dimension has made it possible to see the central role of historical praxis. Indeed, if human history is, first of all, an opening to the future, it must appear as a task, a political operation; man, by building it, orientates himself and opens himself to the gift that gives ultimate meaning: the full and definitive encounter with the Lord and with other men. "Doing the truth," as the gospel says, thus acquires a precise and concrete meaning: the importance, for Christian existence, of action. Hence the recent use of the term "orthopraxis," which still shocks some sensibilities, and which does not pretend to deny the meaning that orthodoxy understood as the proclamation of statements considered true and as reflection on them can have. What is intended is to balance or even reject the primacy and near-exclusiveness of doctrinal fact in Christian life, especially the many times obsessive care of wanting an orthodoxy that, often, is nothing more than fidelity to a fallen tradition or questionable interpretation. In its positive development what is wanted is to assert the importance of concrete behavior, gesture, action, praxis in the Christian life."[23]

---

22 A. de Tocqueville, *La democrazia in America,* (*"Democracy in America"*), (Milan: Utet, 2019), pp. 810-815.

23 G. Gutierrez, *Teologia della liberazione. Prospettive, ("Liberation Theology. Perspectives"),* (Brescia: Queriniana, 1992), pp. 63, 64.

Paradoxically, we begin our relative valorization of the "Global South" as a new subject and as a new hermeneutical space -because in theology "the who" and "the where" matter as much as "the what"- with a critique of "liberation theology."

The critique of orthodoxy as a single register and the valorization of orthopraxis, strongly emphasized by Gutierrez, both appear limited to us today. While shifting the center of gravity from the church and faith to the world and concrete existence, they give the project of liberation theology a strongly anthropocentric, androcentric, pragmatic, overly linear and heavily history-centered profile.[24]

This is not a truly alternative project to the anomalies the West has created. Here the limitation of not seeing that the alienations are interrelated and dependent and that the liberation of economic alienation still means little if the others stand. Above all there is the limitation of having a linear reading of alienation, ignoring that in the complexity and paradoxicality of life a supposed liberation can easily turn into new alienation, and that solution strategies often do not heal but radicalize the problem. What is most missing in Gutierrez and liberation theology is a critique of history.[25] This critique is not of the history of the West but of the West as History. It is of history as the primal category and pivotal concept of the entire Western project, religious (biblical) and secular, around which all other primary proposals, strategies and goals revolve.

---

24 Despite this criticism of Gutierrez and liberation theology in general, the efforts of some liberation theologians to broaden their perspective in the search for a defense of life as a more inclusive reality should be acknowledged. Such is the case of Gustavo Gutierrez himself who published in 1992, twenty years after the publication of his book *Liberation Theology*, his book on life. Cf. G. Gutierrez, *Il Dio della vita*, *("The God of Life")*, (Brescia: Queriniana, 1992).

25 In this sense, our hermeneutical proposal (Hermeneutics of the South) has the contours of an ecological hermeneutics related to human life and all creatures. And this is not only for theological reasons, but also and especially for reasons of current cultural context. Cf. Ph. Descola, *Par-delà nature et culture*, (Paris : Gallimard, 2005), pp. 525-662; B. Latour, *Dove sono? Lezioni di filosofia per un pianeta che cambia*, *("Where Are They? Lessons in Philosophy for a Changing Planet")*, (Turin: Einaudi, 2021), pp. 23-47.

Liberation theology lacks a multicultural and ecological dimension,[26] two registers without which no project can be said to be fully relevant today, precisely because at the center of its project are liberation and freedom, not life. As Achille Mbembe well reminds us, in articulating a new "politics of life,"[27] decolonization cannot be limited to liberating oppressed peoples or the identity of imprisoned individual selves. It must reconnect to all life, to all beings and things that we disown, precisely because we have separated ourselves from them by trying to survive on our own.

Mbembe writes:

> "The desire for life must become the cornerstone.
> of a new way of thinking in politics and culture."[28]

The world has changed. The church and ourselves have also changed. Life, to which all meaning must refer, now expresses itself in other ways. It is threatened not only by new or updated instances, but also by once new senses that have become old and one-sided. "Orthopathy"[29] is he category we would like to redeem and exalt as

---

26 These two essential registers, multiculturalism and ecology, are described by Bruno Latour as the two most pressing issues on the political agenda. Cf. B. Latour, *Tracciare la rotta. Come orientarsi in politica,* ("Charting the Course. How to Orient Oneself in Politics"), (Milan: Raffaello Cortina Editore, 2018), pp. 129-136.

27 A. Mbembe, *Critique de la raison nègre,* (Paris: La Découverte 2015), p. 262.

28 A. Mbembe, *Ibid,* p. 260.

29 By "orthopathy" (from the Greek ρθός/orthos "correct" and πάθος/ pathos, suffering/passion) we are not referring to the alternative medicine movement called "Natural Hygiene" (NH), traceable to Isaac Jennings (1820) and which, representing an extension of the naturopathic movement, advocates a philosophy of "natural living" with the promotion of fasting, a sober and balanced diet and other natural lifestyle measures. Nor do we refer to the parallel term "normopathy," a psychiatric current that describes the "normopath," as opposed to the "borderline" personality, as the individual who seeks shelter from mental life by immersing the self in material comfort and a life of leisure. Cf. C. Bollas, *L'età dello smarrimento. Senso e malinconia, ("Meaning and Melancholy. Life in the Age of Bewilderment"),* (Milan: Raffaello Cortina Editore, 2018), pp. 95-

central to this process of metanoia and cultural and hermeneutical reorientation, without discarding the value of right ideas (orthodoxy) nor that of good practices (orthopraxis). Orthopathy[30] is the attitude that is not only true but, above all, healthy. Starting in a pre-rational level, but not by this i-rrational or a-rational way, from the center of a person's life, it leads us to perceive our incompleteness, vulnerability and dependence on what is external to us. By feeling that outside (neighbor, group, nature, cosmos or God) as our own, we aspire to reach out to it and to be touched, provoked and involved by it, without losing in this encounter either our specificity or autonomy, but giving both direction, motivation and desire for relationship.

Underlying this emphasis on orthopathy[31] is the valorization of bonding, relationship and alliance, the aspiration for the

---

104. The sense of "orthopathy," as we try to make explicit in these pages, is related to life as a perspective in which meaning is given and becomes more inclusive.

30 This third sense, not necessarily against but beyond the orthodoxy of ideas and orthopraxy of action, is the meaning Bruno Forte ascribes to beauty. Cf. B. Forte, *Dove va il cristianesimo?* (*"Where is Christianity Going?"*), (Brescia: Queriniana, 2001), pp. 75-83.

31 As is evident from what we have said so far, we connect the sense of orthopathy to the dimension of affections and feelings, as a complementary way of connecting with the external world. In this sense, our definition of "orthopathy" is closer to that in force in Pentecostal spirituality, where orthopathy indicates the relevance and indicative value of the affections in determining the quality of faith experience. Cf. D. Trementozzi, *Salvation in the Flesh. Understanding How Embodiment Shapes Christian Faith*, (Eugene: Pickwick Publications, 2018), pp. 157-205. In this sense, our definition of orthopathy fits fully into Friedrich Schleiermacher's definition of religion, when in the second of his five discourses on religion he defines it in these terms: "In this way religion, in order to take possession of what belongs to it, renounces all claim to what belongs to morality and metaphysics, gives back everything that has clung to it. It does not yearn to determine and explain the Universe in its nature, as metaphysics does; it does not aspire, as morality does, to develop and perfect it by virtue of man's freedom and divine will. Its essence is neither thinking nor acting but intuition and feeling." Cf. F. Schleiermacher, *Sulla religione. Discorsi a quegli intellettuali che la disprezzano, ("On Religion. Discourses to those Intellectuals who Despise it")*, (Brescia: Queriniana, 2017), pp. 72, 73.

recomposition of the whole. This is not by resorting to contractualist (rational and conscious) strategies that presuppose a strong and self-sufficient subject who resorts to the group only strategically and transiently. Neither is by resorting to identity strategies that presuppose the strength of the system/group as the guardian and guarantor of the well-being of individuals, which they cannot challenge and cannot even do without. It is by resorting to persuasion strategies that persuade individuals that, precisely because we are free, we are free for the sake of relationship. There is no freedom outside the relationship.

The loss of meaning is thus a loss of the other. There is no sense without the other, just as there is no freedom without the other. This strong relationship between freedom and the other[32] can be seen in the English words free and friend or in the German words *frei* (free), *freund* (friend) and *friede* (peace), all derived from the Indo-Germanic root *fri* meaning "to love."[33] To be free therefore means to belong to friends or lovers. One is free only in bonding and there is bonding only in vulnerability.

This bond, taken as a life perspective because it is not a totalitarian, homogeneous or subjugated bond, but a heterogeneous, desired and chosen bond, is the natural site of the ambivalence and paradox of which the Bible is a master. The Bible has these characteristics by virtue of the complexity of the life it is meant to witness. The Bible and life, therefore, cannot be grasped in their essence and perspective through exclusively analytical, immediate and purely descriptive processes.

---

32 Byung-Chul Han expresses himself in this sense, saying that one is free only in belonging and in the perimeter of ties. He writes, "One feels free in a relationship of love and friendship. The bond, not the lack of it, makes one free. Freedom is then a relational term par excellence. Without a retainer there is also no freedom," in B.-C. Han, *Il profumo del tempo. L'arte d'indugiare sulle cose*, ("*The Scent of Time. A Philosophical Essay in the Art of Lingering"*), (Milan: Vita e Pensiero, 2017), p. 41.

33 B.-C. Han, *Ibid*, p. 40.

Orthopathy,[34] which represents a slow and fast, complex and fragmentary, unitary and paradoxical way of arriving at meaning, aims to grasp the vision of totality without possessing it. It pushes toward the intuition of the whole without manipulating it. It promotes the imagination of the complexity of life by renouncing the compulsiveness that claims to order and organize it. Southern hermeneutics[35], therefore, are those hermeneutics that start from

---

34 Orthopathy, then, we think of it in Martha Nussbaum's sense (even though she does not use this word) when she speaks of emotions as "thought upheavals" with their own particular form of intelligence and ethical relevance. Cf. M. Nussbaum, *L'intelligenza delle emozioni, ("Upheavals of Thought. The Intelligence of Emotions)*, (Bologna: Il Mulino, 2004), pp. 37-116. In this sense we find today a revaluation of the correct emotions (orthopathy) that prolongs the insights of D. Hume and A. Smith's "Theory of Moral Sentiments," passing from the rediscovery of empathy (*Einfühlung*) in early 20th century phenomenological reflection as in the case of Edith Stein. Adding to this revaluation of feelings is the latest feminism that moves from feelings as empathy with the other to commitment to the other (J. Tronto, V. Held, E. Kittay, A. Baier) through a correction of the formal concept of Justice, which in the liberal tradition is overly dependent on a rational paradigm. We find in Nussbaum the recognition of an affective dimension of justice. She writes, "Justice is about justice, and justice is a value that men love and pursue." Cf. M. Nussbaum, *Le nuove frontiere della giustizia. Disabilità, nazionalità, appartenenza di specie*, (*"Frontiers of Justice: Disability, Nationality, Species Membership")*, (Bologna: Il Mulino, 2007), p. 106. This allows Elena Pulcini to speak of the "passions of justice" in regard to a reformulation of the liberal concept of justice, which rightly includes feelings as correcting and balancing elements of a justice that would otherwise remain excessively formal and rational. Cf. E. Pulcini, *Tra cura e giustizia. Le passioni come risorsa sociale, ("Between Care and Justice. Passions as a Social Resource")*, (Turin: Bollati Boringhieri, 2020), pp. 49-68.

35 "Hermeneutics of the South" (plural), which we also sometimes describe as "Hermeneutics of the South" (singular), in addition to indicating geographical location, indicates the rejection of a "substantiation" of the South into a monolithic whole. The South is not monolithic and that is precisely why we must speak of "hermeneutics of the South" in the plural. Moreover, hermeneutics of the South are not the only possible hermeneutics. That is why we sometimes use, following Raimon Panikkar, the term "diatopic hermeneutics" (see below in the following notes),

Introduction

the complexity of the interpreting reader (orthodoxy, orthopraxy, orthopathy) and the complexity of the interpreted object (Bible, life, earth, cosmos). It has the intention of becoming witnesses to the complexity of life in a plural interpretive dialogue that Paul Ricœur calls "The Conflict of Interpretations."[36] Raimon Panikkar, in an even broader, inclusive and cross-cultural sense, calls it "Diatopic Hermeneutics."

Panikkar writes:

> "I call it "diatopic hermeneutics" in that the distance to be bridged is not merely temporal, within one vast tradition, but the gap that exists between two human topoi, 'places' of understanding and self-understanding, between two (or more) cultures that have not worked out their own models of intelligibility. Diatopic hermeneutics starts from the basic consideration that we must understand the other without assuming that they have the same basic self-understanding as we do. The ultimate human horizon is at stake here, not just different contexts between them."[37]

---

which describes the cultural pluralism of hermeneutics in dialogue and tension, of cultural systems that are not only different but irreducible to each other. Southern (hermeneutics) or hermeneutics do not have a monopoly on either the meaning of the Bible or the meaning of life. Theirs is solely a valuable testimony, which we are trying to reevaluate in this essay, but which remains fragile and partial. For this reason we also use the term introduced by W. Mignolo "Pluritopic Hermeneutics," which in essence follows Panikkar, adding the specification that hermeneutics in tension include cultures from the periphery of the world that are not mere contestations of Western hermeneutics (called "monotopic" hermeneutics by Mignolo) within a single cultural system, but are affirmative of strong political, ethical and ontological projects. See W.D. Mignolo, M. V. Tlostanova, *Encounters*, vol. 1, no. 1, Fall 2009, pp. 10-27.

36 P. Ricœur, *Il conflitto delle interpretazioni*, (*"The Conflict of Interpretations. Essays in Hermeneutics"*), (Milan: Jaca Book, 1995), pp. 17-37.

37 R. Panikkar, *Mito, fede, ermeneutica. Il triplice velo della realtà*, (*"Myth, Faith, Hermeneutics. The Triple Veil ofRreality"*), (Milan: Jaca Book, 2000), pp. 18-36. "Diatopic" hermeneutics is a hermeneutics that goes beyond traditional "morphological" hermeneutics and beyond "diachronic" hermeneutics, in that it "takes as its starting point the realization that *topoi*, the sites of different cultures, cannot be understood through the tools of understanding of only one tradition or culture."

Southern hermeneutics are hermeneutics that are flexible not only internally, for various accents and directions (orthodoxy), but are also flexible externally in dialogue with different cultural projects. They are close to a diatopic hermeneutic as proposed by Panikkar, which attempts to bring together deeply opposed human horizons, different traditions or cultural places (*topoi*), in order to arrive at an authentic dialogue that takes into account different cultures (*diatopos*). This requires *mythos and logos*, subjectivity and objectivity, heart and mind, rational thought and freer spirit, to come into contact, transgressing unilateral patterns that cage life and thought.[38]

While Heidegger speaks of a necessary ontologization of hermeneutics linked to Being considered in its ineffability, we want instead to link hermeneutics to Being embodied in the complexity of life from a perspective of the cultures of the Global South. It is true that, as anthropologist Francesco Remotti reminds us, any cultural form is itself reductive of the complexity of life. He writes:

> "The limits of culture are given, in the first place, by the complexity of reality. No culture is in itself able to dominate the reality that surrounds it: an infinity of aspects inevitably elude it...to understand the meaning of a culture it is necessary to consider what it brings into focus and what instead escapes its gaze and its interventions. Indeed, any culture coincides with operations to reduce complexity...any culture is always decidedly poorer than the reality with which it comes into contact. The consideration of these limitations is absolutely necessary to understand the meaning of a culture, its direction, its scope."[39]

Any culture, being reductive in itself, necessarily embodies an impoverishment of reality and its complexity. So do the cultures of

---

Morphological hermeneutics deciphers the treasures (*morphe*, forms or values) of a particular culture, of a single tradition; diachronic hermeneutics represents the mediation between the temporal distances of human cultural history, but is also centered, usually, in a single reference tradition.

38 R. Panikkar, *Mito, simbolo, culto. Mistero ed ermeneutica, ("Myth, Symbol, Cult. Mystery and Hermeneutics")*, vol. I, (Milan: Jaca Book, 2008), pp. 85-97.

39 F. Remotti, *Cultura. Dalla complessità all'impoverimento, ("Culture. From Complexity to Impoverishment")*, (Rome: Laterza, 2011), pp. 281,282.

the Global South that we take here as a paradigm. These cultures have their own inconsistencies, unilateralisms and even contradictions. In spite of these limitations, they represent an alternative vision to the dominant culture and current hermeneutics. This is by virtue of two characteristics peculiar to them: a strong connection of them to life as a whole and an understanding of life[40] as connectedness.

With respect to the first element, Francesco Remotti points out how in non-Western cultures a "gestalt" view of life predominates over everything; their vocation is for a comprehensive look at it. This is why Remotti calls them "complex cultures" (complexity). Modern societies, called by him instead "complicated societies" (complication), tend, on the contrary, to erase complexity through the reduction of the diversity of life levels to the quantitative one of growth and efficiency.

In contrast, societies with a holistic, life-oriented vocation, which the West disproportionately calls archaic or primitive societies, try to keep together the various levels of life irreducible to each other (divinity, nature, group). It is from this fact that their slowness derives. They are slow not because they are lazy, but because they are rich in keeping together various levels of life that require different attention and care and that, while related, are not reducible to a single criterion.

---

40 This emphasis on life as a whole and as a bond picks up and coincides in part with the Aristotelian tradition of the good. Cf. S. Natoli, *La felicità. Saggio di teoria degli affetti, ("Happiness. Essay on a Theory of Affection")*, (Milan: Feltrinelli, 2017), pp. 11-50. In a more theological key, the priority of the question of good over that of duty is also emphasized by Dietrich Bonhoeffer in his Ethics. See D. Bonhoeffer, *Ethics*, (New York: MacMillan, 1965), pp. 214-262. And in a more multicultural key and from a point of view from the cultures of the South (South America), the same priority of life as a whole and as a bond is expressed in the *Aymara* (one of the languages of the territory of the Incas) concept of *Suma Qamaña* ("Good Living"). Cf. F. Huanacuni Mamani, *Vivir bien, buen vivir. Filosofía, políticas, estrategias y experiencias de los pueblos ancestrales*, (Lima: Caoi, 2010); P. Solon, *¿Es posible el Vivir Bien? Reflexiones a quema ropa sobre alternativas sistémica*, (La Paz: Solon, 2016); J. Medina, *Suma Qamaña. Por una convivialidad postindustrial*, (La Paz: PBCC, 2000).

These Southern societies are complex precisely because they are societies of equilibrium and not of unilateral growth. Complexity comes not from the quantitative increase of factors or their entanglement, but rather from the qualitative differentiation and interaction in an organic whole of the various levels of life.[41]

With respect to the second element, German philosopher and biologist Andreas Weber reminds us that the West embodies this typical example of cultural involution that has become chronic. It is manifested precisely in its inability to see bonding as the foundation of life. Indeed, it sees bonds as obstacles to life. On the contrary, the cultures of the South, called indigenous, see life in bonding; bonding as life. Andreas Weber writes:

> "Each individual can only exist because his existence is indebted to another. People need parents and a social environment to grow up healthy; they need the other beings that nourish them, the air, the earth. "I exist because you are there" is more important than the phrase "I am myself and you are you." Reality can remain fruitful only if this reciprocity is preserved, if others are sacred, and if what is given to me always gives rise to a gesture of gratitude."[42]

While we Westerners live by the pragmatic motto, "Try in every situation to survive at any cost," a typical individualist dogma, indigenous people live by a different motto that goes like this, "Everything lives, therefore try together with others to nurture life." This is what Weber calls *Indigenialität*[43] (indi-geniality). Andreas Weber writes in this regard:

> "Indigeniality (Indigenialität) is an attempt to turn away from the eternal navel of Western thought in an explicit gesture that frees the gaze, that detaches it from ourselves, that teaches us not to take ourselves too seriously, to find ourselves in the gaze of others. It is an attempt that aims to suspend the narcissism of the intellectual, who no longer admits anything foreign, but always only projections of his own cultural experiences. It is an overbearing gesture, however emancipatory

---

41   F. Remotti, *Cultura. Dalla complessità... Op. cit.*, pp. 186-194.
42   A. Weber, *Indigenialität*, (Berlin: NP & I, 2018), pp. 110, 111.
43   A. Weber, *Ibid*, pp. 10-23.

it may appear, that we are forbidden to take seriously the experiences of foreign peoples as real experiences, and their worldviews as possible worlds. We are trapped in our universalism."[44]

"We are all indigenous," says Weber, making it clear that our civilization has not only colonized indigenous people, but also our way of thinking. Indigenous does not mean savage or primitive, but having and cultivating the "genius" of seeing that life is a reality of relationships and relations. Life is relationship. He who says relationship says trust. Trust is not a psychological or moral virtue that autonomizes the subject more. It is the experience that breaks the arrogance of wanting to do everything on our own and orient us confidently toward the other. Life is relationship and relationship is trust.

The genius of indigenous and non-Western peoples would be, according to Weber, to see life in relationship and relationship as life. Non-Western peoples do not just think about this. They embody it in their way of life and relationship with others and with nature.[45] This is why their civilization is not a civilization of "progress," but a civilization of "balance." The abandonment of relationships as the founding principle of life is what actually makes progress possible. Progress as the apparent fulfillment of life, however, in fact represents its impoverishment and negation.

> "Perhaps all indigenous virtues can be expressed in one. Just as all the beliefs of the West are centered in the fear of dying, the central indigenous virtue is the belief in being alive."[46]

This vision and understanding of life as a whole and of life as a bond, typical of Southern cultures, will be presupposed in this essay and will partially emerge here and there in the first and second

---

44 A. Weber, *Ibid*, pp. 21-26.
45 Life understood not only as human life but also as nature. Philippe Descola writes, "The question about the relationship of human beings to nature is for all intents and purposes the most important question of the century in which we live," cf. Ph. Descola, *L'écologie des autres. L'anthropologie et la question de la nature*, (Paris : Quae, 2016), p. 77.
46 A. Weber, *Indigenialität, Op. cit.*, p. 110.

parts, In the third part it will find a more accomplished elaboration, until it takes shape as a specific proposal that we call "Hermeneutics of the South." It is from this theological *topos*, the relation as the very place of complexity and paradox, as well as of Latin American cultural belonging, that this hermeneutic reflection is articulated. It is configured as a "hermeneutics of life"[47] and of the earth,[48] in an ecological dimension as a perspective, where meaning finds its best and most promising articulation.

Meaning, the meaning of texts and the meaning of life, as Pearl S. Buck, Pulitzer Prize winner in 1932 and Nobel Prize winner for literature in 1938, writes in her novel *The Good Earth*, is manifested

---

47 This "hermeneutic of life," which according to our reading is the defining characteristic of Southern cultures, clearly has its theological foundation in the understanding of the Holy Spirit, the third person of the Trinity, not so much as the "Spirit of holiness," although this is clearly presupposed, but primarily as the "Spirit of life." This theme will be more fully developed in the third part of our essay. It is the Holy Spirit as the "Spirit of life" who is the guarantor not only of greater universality but also of greater religious and human complexity, paradoxicality, vitality and inclusiveness.

48 Cf. Pachamama (also Pacha Mama or Mama Pacha) means "Mother Earth" in the Quechua language. It is a deity worshipped by the Incas and other peoples inhabiting the Andean plateau. She is the great mother goddess, goddess of the earth, agriculture and fertility. We speak here of the earth in an ecological sense as a living space in which meaning is given and articulated. We do not consider the divinizing and idolatrous connotations attached to Pachamama, rather the ecological, symbolic and even enchanted dimension necessary to broaden the perspective of meaning related to life. Cf. L.L. Rasmussen, *Earth Community. Earth Ethics*, (New York: Orbis Books, 2000), pp. 175-180. The possibility of constructing a theology of Creation, in the sense also of reconstructing a new hermeneutical sense, passes, according to Moltmann, through a revalorization of the earth. J. Moltmann, *Dio nella creazione. Dottrina ecologica della creazione, ("God in Creation. A New Theology of Creation and the Spirit of God")*, (Brescia: Queriniana, 1986), pp. 346-348. Cf. E. M. Conradie, "What on Earth is an Ecological Hermeneutics? Some Broad Parameters," in, David G. Horrell, Cherryl Hunt, Christopher Southgate, Francesca Stavrakopoulou (Eds), *Ecological Hermeneutics. Biblical, Historical and Theological Perspectives*, (New York: T & T Clark, 2010), pp. 295-313.

and concretized in attachment to and love for the earth as the unique space in which to find meaning in what we are and what we do. Faced with the indifference of children and grandchildren who have lived off the land, but who do not love it, rather, want to sell it to procure new earnings and investments, and coupled with their concomitant disdain for books (the four books of Confucianism)[49] and for reading, Wang Lung, the novel's protagonist, in a last desperate plea, tells his family:

> "When you start selling the land, 'he said in a broken voice', it is the end of a family. From the land we came and to the land we must return. [...] If you keep your land you can live [...] no one can ever take it away from you. [...] Do you still read the Four Books? [...] At that point they laughed with clear, young mockery at that old man, saying, No, Grandfather, no one reads the Four Books anymore after the Revolution."[50]

Paraphrasing Wang Lung, we too can say, from the perspective of a hermeneutics of the South, that when we become detached from the earth, from rootedness and embodiment in the earth, life ends. So do the texts that are, in one way or another, in their complementarity and tension, all witnesses to this rootedness. Text and reader, meaning and perspective, reading and interpretation, other and others, Being and rootedness, bonding and autonomy, reason and emotions, world and things, orthopraxis and orthopathy, truth and sanity, earth and cosmos, complexity and paradox, mystery and wonder[51] here are the extremes of a "hermeneutics of life." It finds a possible and concrete trace in the fragile and vulnerable but real and concrete witness

---

49 The Four Books mentioned by Wang Lung are the texts of classical Chinese literature designed as introductory texts to Confucianism. The Four Books are: *The Great Study*, *The Right Middle*, *Dialogues* and *Mencius*. P.S. Buck, La buona terra, (*The Good Earth)*, (Milan: Mondadori, 2021), p. 329.
50 P.S. Buck, *Op. cit.* pp. 324, 329.
51 A "hermeneutics of life" presupposes the non-manipulation of the real through the discovery of wonder. Cf. K. L. Schmitz, *The Recovery of Wonder. The New Freedom and the Asceticism of Power*, (Montreal: McGill-Queen's University Press, 2005).

of the hermeneutics of the South.[52] This "hermeneutics of life" is strongly linked to the rediscovery of the Trinity[53] and the model of relationality that it presupposes and proposes as a horizon, and which finds its center in the action of the Holy Spirit (the pneumatological turn).[54] This "hermeneutics of life" generates and makes possible a new spirituality that is not focused on and limited to humans and less so only to their reason and awareness. With respect to this new spirituality, Jürgen Moltmann writes:

---

52 With respect to the churches of the South, see especially the entire fifth chapter of Ph. Jenkins' book, *La terza chiesa. Il cristianesimo nel XXI secolo, ("The Next Christendom. The Coming of Global Christianity")*, (Rome: Fazi, 2004), pp. 115-145. Jenkins interprets this new Southern Christianity as a dynamic, inclusive movement, but with a reductive, fundamentalist hermeneutic. Southern churches are very heterogeneous; indeed, in many this hermeneutic criticized by Jenkins predominates. If, however, one considers not only their reading of the Bible but their understanding of life, in general, the conclusions certainly differ. Cf. Ph. Jenkins, *I nuovi volti del cristianesimo ("The New Faces of Christianity. Believing the Bible in the Global South")*, (Milan: Vita e pensiero, 2007), pp. 13-35.

53 See the entire third part of our essay entitled "Trinity, Mystery and the Unavailability of Meaning."
Cf. V.-M. Kärkkäinen, *Trinity and Religious Pluralism. The Doctrine of the Trinity in Christian Theology of religions*, (London: Routledge, 2004), pp. 4-17.

54 "Pneumatological turn," an ongoing theological and cultural movement, in clear and radical contestation with the anthropocentrism of our culture, secular and religious, and in equal rupture with the confessionalism and ecclesiocentrism of faith communities across the religious spectrum, is the recognition of the centrality of the person and action of the Holy Spirit not only within the Trinity as an element that enhances the profile of the Father and the Son and their interaction (perichoresis) but also outside of the Trinity in human history and not only in the church, through its capacity to promote life, in its autonomy and differentiation, but at the same time in its convergence and communion, from a discrete and anonymous profile, all aimed solely at making others flourish and free for relationship and convergence (communion). See, for example, R. R. Rodriguez, *Dogmatics After Babel. Beyond the Theologies of Word and Culture*, (Louisville: Westminster John Knox Press, 2018), pp. 145-195.

Introduction

> "And it is precisely the spirituality of life that awakens us from our inner daze, penetrates the shell of hearts' indifference, reveals our insensitivity to others' suffering. Now we can again shout and cry, laugh and dance, because divine love has awakened us to life and God's Spirit has awakened our vital spirits. He who begins to love life -- not just his own -- resists his own death drives and the powers that death wields around him: now he engages in the struggle for the very future of life."[55]

This hermeneutics of life is an "erotic hermeneutics"[56]. It longs for life with passion and risk without pretending to control or manipulate it. The book of Psalms reminds us that without the Spirit everything not only perishes but is destined to nonmeaning. In outlining the broad context of life as a place of meaning in connection with the Spirit, the psalmist writes:

> "You hide your face, and they are lost; you withdraw their breath and they die, they return to their dust. You send forth your Spirit, and they are created, and you renew the face of the earth."[57]

---

55 J. Moltmann, *La fonte della vita*...Op. cit., pp. 107,108.
56 See the last chapter (XII) of our essay: "Reading the Bible. For an erotics of interpretation"
57 Psalm 104:29, 30.

PART I
TEXT AND READER:
THE HERMENEUTIC CIRCLE

The Mediation of Text: "Slowness" and "Plurality"

This first part of our essay is a reflection on textuality. We will underline two determining characteristics for the articulation and flowering of meaning: slowness and plurality. On the one hand, the text slows down the acquisition of meaning because it mediates it, forcing it to be embodied and articulated in the signs of a writing, the outline of a style and the codes of a literary work. On the other hand, this slowing down of the process of sense articulation introduced by the text expands the text by making it even more plural through what Paul Ricœur calls the process of "distantiation,"[1] which is a mechanism of sense expansion that transforms it from singular to plural.

There are three elements involved in the process of reading and interpreting the Bible: the text, the reader, and the hermeneutic circle. Of these three elements, the text is the most distinctive element but not necessarily the most important. As we will try to describe in the second part of this essay, hermeneutical anomalies arise from wanting to introduce a hierarchy between them. This incurs unilateralisms that, by improperly privileging one element over the other two, break and compromise the balance and interaction between them. The text is the most distinctive element because hermeneutics is the process of reflection and analysis that necessarily takes place in front of a text. Although there are reflective and analytical processes of various kinds, they are not called hermeneutic processes because they do not take place in front of a text. It is the text that is configured

---

1   P. Ricœur, *Ermeneutica filosofica*...Op. cit., pp. 53-78.

as the backbone of the whole interpretive enterprise. Through it the other elements are configured as such.

This does not mean that hermeneutic reflection and analysis are articulated only in full obedience to the text. On the contrary, hermeneutics envisions, through the reader, a certain surpassing and even transgression of the text. But that transgression will still be done starting from and in relation to the text before us. It is still the text that tells us in what that overcoming consists. With respect to this second element of the interpretive process, that is, the reader, it can be said that it is the text that qualifies it as such. The reader who interprets, while interpreting is also an individual, a thinker, an applicator. But he becomes a reader only in function of the text that defines him as such and gives him that status. The reader is an individual who, when he reflects, necessarily reflects in front of a text.

The same thing happens with the third element of the interpretive process, the hermeneutic circle. It is defined and articulated only as a function of the text. The hermeneutic circle describes the bilateral flow, the reciprocity between the text and the reader but it still does so from the text. It is still the text that is the central point of the hermeneutic circle and it is so through two different strategies. It does this sometimes by valuing the text absolutely, as for example in the text-reader relationship, and sometimes by relativizing it when the text is preceded by pre-comprehension as a prior act to reading a text. The text is the most distinctive element of hermeneutics within what is the hermeneutic circle. Let us pause to briefly describe two essential characteristics of the text: slowness and pluralism.

1. Through the text, the process in the elaboration of meaning slows down its pace. It introduces a set of alternative mechanisms in the articulation of the message which may be direct or indirect; in the elaboration of the author's profile, which may be explicit or implicit; and finally, in the connection with the recipients, which may be real or ideal.

All of these editorial strategies in the configuration of the text slow down the communicative process. This offers sense additional space for its verification, refinement and enhancement. Text, then, is not sense's enemy but its ally, provided one grasps the value of slowness and textual mediation.

Hermeneutics is a praise of the text as a mediator of better meanings. The text thus serves as a positive obstacle in the face of the craving and enthusiasm for immediate, clear, and functional meanings. Hermeneutics is a typical cognitive strategy that makes mediation a value. This mediation is provided by passing through the text. There is no immediate or automatic meaning. Meaning is the product of an effort that sometimes becomes a peripeteia. Meaning is an earned result and not a presupposed intuition. Meaning is not arrived at immediately through an intuition, a stroke of genius, an illumination. Meaning arises through the suffered, slow and demanding passage of reading and close confrontation with a text.

2. The other characteristic is pluralism. The text is an element of meaning expansion, not so much with a view to its homogenization and compactness but rather with a view to its fragmentation. By introducing alternative, indirect or opposing formulations, it increases the intensity of meaning by making it plural. Every text presupposes an indelible plurality of senses of which interpretative reading is only one expression. Hermeneutics not only defends the plurality of senses latent in the read text. It also defends the plurality of readings of those senses that it itself tries to articulate. Across all the process, hermeneutics is thus the bet on the value and benefit of the plurality of possible senses present in the interpreted text and the corresponding interpretive readings.

Hermeneutics is inseparable from pluralism of meanings. At the outset, it presupposes the pluralism of possible senses. Through interpretation, one tries to choose the most relevant sense in connection with the context, situation and needs of the one reading. Downstream, hermeneutics again imposes pluralism because, from various possible senses, that is, from the structural ambivalence of interpreted languages, interpretations can only be various. The single, monolithic interpretation would deny the presupposition of hermeneutics itself. This is the polyvalence of interpreted languages and texts.

Hermeneutics, through the interpretation of texts, validates and legitimizes a strong pluralism because this legitimate variety of possible interpretations is not always complementary, as one would like and expect. Often, those varied and different interpretations coexist in a structural and irreducible tension. This is what Paul Ricœur calls the natural state of hermeneutics as the "conflict of interpretations,"[2] which are always in the plural.

Hermeneutics is a defense of the text as an element of preservation and better processing of meaning. In this view of a strong text, the text is not limited to being a mnemotechnical support of the oral message. Its function is more central. The message itself is profoundly altered when it becomes text. The nostalgia for the spoken word and the belief that the best communication is verbal communication survives in all of us. It is as if text is only a necessary evil.

In hermeneutics the opposite idea subsists and imposes itself. The text is the best ally of meaning because by delaying and mediating it, it refines, articulates and emphasizes it better as a plurality of possible meanings coexisting in creative tension. From beginning to end, hermeneutics is the compact bet on the timeless value of the text as a space of slowing down and plurality of possible meanings.

---

2   In his book Ricœur reviews some of these hermeneutics as diverse and irreducible to each other as structuralism, psychoanalysis, phenomenology, symbolism and even religion. P. Ricœur, *Il conflitto delle interpretazioni*, Op. cit., pp. 13-24.

CHAPTER I
WHAT IS HERMENEUTICS?

Hermeneutics expresses a particular way of knowledge. This is knowledge through a text. The text is the element that qualifies a knowledge as hermeneutic. The center of hermeneutics is thus the act of interpreting a text.[1] While it is true that the obligation to go through a text slows down and problematizes the process of sense articulation, it is equally true that that sense gained becomes better. It creates the mechanism of its own verification and filter, which in this case is provided by the text itself, its projection and the "alternative and experimental world"[2] that each text tries to delineate and suggest.

There is no immediate or automatic meaning. Meaning is the product of a struggle, which many times becomes an open adventure. Meaning is an earned result and not a presupposed intuition. Meaning is not arrived at immediately through an intuition, a stroke of genius, an illumination. It is earned through the suffered, slow and demanding passage of reading and close confrontation with a text.

Hermeneutics is a praise of the text as a mediator of better meanings. The text serves as a positive obstacle in the face of the craving and enthusiasm for immediate, clear and functional meanings. Hermeneutics is a typical cognitive strategy that makes mediation a value and an obligatory step. This mediation is provided by the passage through the text.

Various conceptions subsist on the text. Essentially, there are two.

---

1   J.G. Zimmermann, *Hermeneutics. A Very Short Introduction*, (Oxford: Oxford University Press, 2015), pp. 1-18.
2   P. Ricœur calls the project that each text suggests, the "world of the text," and it represents for him the center of every interpretive act because it encloses the main axes of the proposition that each text articulates and carries. Cf. *Dal testo all'azione... Op. cit.*, pp. 121-125.

The first is a weak conception of the text. It considers the text merely as a supporting element to a thought or idea without touching them or even changing their essence.

The second is a strong conception of text. In this case, a text is not limited to being a mnemotechnical support of the oral message. Its function is more central. The message itself is profoundly altered when it becomes text.

There survives in all of us the nostalgia for the spoken word and the belief that the best communication is verbal communication. Writing, one is convinced, must still be surpassed by the warmth and immediacy of the spoken word. The word preceded the text and it is still the word which is redeemed by the reading of a text in the process of understanding and assimilating the message. Writing is cold, anonymous and too formal, one thinks. Instead, the Word behind it, which must be resurrected, carries the force and persuasion of a warm and immediate message. It is as if the text is only a necessary evil.

The idea is adduced that talking face to face, viva voce, avoids misunderstandings related to text mediation. The more direct the communication, the better. Clearly, the advantage of oral communication lies in its freshness and overwhelming immediacy. However, this does not erase misunderstandings. Indeed, at another level, oral communication, through speech, increases these misunderstandings. In oral communication, which necessarily takes place in real time, words and replies to words cannot be stopped. The communicative flow must be guaranteed because it is that flow in its immediacy and naturalness that is the strength of oral language.[3]

In the freshness and immediacy of this flow of orality, spoken words find their strength but also their limitation. That flow overwhelms them, overlaps them, jostles them, bumps them, halves them, exasperates them, accelerates them. Indeed, they are forced by this flow to become fast words, less thought-out

---

3   W.J. Ong, *Orality ad Literacy. The Technologizing of the Word*, (London: Routledge, 2012), pp. 5-15.

words, instinctive words, words that are easy and immediate but not necessarily the best.

The undoubted greater coolness of the text brings with it necessary corrective benefits The written word, which becomes text, can become a thought, verified and filtered word, that is, a text. The text is a written word, therefore thought, and for this reason balanced, becoming an objective sign that communicates better, even if more slowly, the intentions and will of the dialoguers. This is the bet of hermeneutics and its praise of the text as a tool for better communication.

Hermeneutics is not the only possible way of knowing. Life in general and religious life in particular continually confront us with a variety of ways of knowing. It is true that some specific experiences tend to privilege a particular kind of knowledge, that which is most akin, relevant and functional to the area involved. But the best human experiences are never monolithic and always introduce a diversity of approaches and perspectives. These various ways of knowing are not always complementary. Sometimes they are called to coexist in tension. For this reason, about the Bible and Christian knowledge, two basic principles should generally be kept in mind.

1. The approach to the Bible must be able to make room for a variety of ways of knowing. It would be reductive to want to exhaust the relationship with the Bible by limiting it to a single cognitive strategy. Nor can biblical hermeneutics alone ascribe this prerogative to itself. Various types of biblical hermeneutics[4] are possible, but there will be also strategies that will be critical of the hermeneutic cognitive model as such. It is well that it should be so, because hermeneutics, while representing an important mode of reading, in our opinion the best,[5] nevertheless does not

---

4   J. Grondin, *Introduction to Philosophical Hermeneutics*, (Yale: Yale University Press, 1994), pp.124-139.

5   In this sense we make our own the conviction, expressed by Claude Geffré, that in today's historical period, with the limitations and side effects that must be continually monitored, theological reason has become structurally hermeneutic. And it would become so in rupture with "speculative reason," which for centuries has characterized

have a monopoly on reading the Bible. In defending its own legitimacy, hermeneutic knowledge will also have to defend the legitimacy of this cognitive diversity in which it itself fits.

2. These various cognitive modes sometimes complement each other, sometimes they do not. They can create a tension which is given by their non-assimilability. This tension is not in itself negative. On the contrary, tension makes sense possible and guarantees it in its articulation. Sense emerges within that tension, which one must know how to keep alive. The arc that that tension creates must never disappear even when the final sense, which is always a provisional sense, has been achieved. Sense can occur and survive only within that tensional arc.

---

theology in clear connection with Greek thought. The distancing from this metaphysical reason prompted us to approach theology from a "historical understanding." To think of theology as hermeneutical would be uniquely to draw the consequences from this shift from a "metaphysical understanding" to a "historical understanding" of reality. Geffré writes, "When, however, the notion of order is challenged in the modern era, we necessarily move from a still axiomatic understanding to an empirical and historical conception of science that is defined by experiment: its object, in effect, is not eternal truth but history and the totality of phenomena. Since, by definition, God escapes the limits of reason, the object of theology will be transformed. Theology tends to understand itself not simply as a discourse about God, but as a discourse that reflects on language about God, language that speaks humanly about God. Everyone recognizes the prerogative that is now given to the humanities of religion in the study of religion, in particular, to a linguistic approach to religious language. There is no direct knowledge of reality outside of language, and language is always an interpretation." Cf. C. Geffré, *Credere e interpretare...Op. cit.*, pp. 19-21.

1. A Theological-Cultural Look at Hermeneutics[6]

Hermeneutics is not the only form of knowledge. To better identify its specificity, we will try to parallel it with a different and even opposite kind of knowledge. The opposition between different ways of knowing is classically expressed, for example, by Blaise Pascal in one of his most famous thoughts:

> "The heart has its own reasons that reason does not know."[7]

Human intelligence is not only analytical-discursive but also synthetic-intuitive. This intuitive capacity Pascal attributes it to the heart. It is obvious that, in this sense, the heart has its own reasons that reason must merely presuppose with respect and docility, because they are foreign to it. To honor the legitimacy of this cognitive diversity and try to understand its deeper meaning, we will try, in this introduction, to compare two kinds of knowledge: the hermeneutic way of knowing and the rational "intellectual" way

---

6   Reflection on the scope and validity of hermeneutics is part of the discipline that goes by the name "Theory of Knowledge," a philosophical discipline that deals with problems related to the nature, acquisition and growth of different forms of human knowledge. See G. Cevolanti, F. Di Iorio, E. Di Nuoscio, "Dalla filosofia alla scienza, e ritorno: l'analisi della conoscenza tra epistemologia e scienze cognitive", (*"From Philosophy to Science, and Back: the Analysis of Knowleder Between Epistemology and Cognitive Science"*), in, J.-M. Besnier, *Teorie della conoscenza*, (*"Theories of Knowledge"*), (Soveria-Mannelli: Rubbettino, 2013), pp. 5-14. Although the classical formula expressed in the "tripartite definition" of propositional knowledge formulated by Plato in the Theaetetus (206-208), as "a True and Justified Belief," has lately been the subject of criticism (E. Gettier, *Is Justified True Belief Knowledge?* JTB, 1963), the underlying questions all remain, and all of them directly concern the purported validity of hermeneutic knowledge. See T. Piazza, *Che cos'è la conoscenza*, (*"What is Knowledge"*), (Rome: Carocci, 2019), pp. 27-35; R. Audi, *Epistemologia. Un'introduzione alla teoria della conoscenza*, (*"Epistemology. An Introduction to the Theory of Knowledge"*), (Macerata: Quodlibet, 2016), pp. 8-24; D. O'Brien, *Theory of Knowledge*, (Cambridge: Polity Press, 2017), pp. 10-21; N. Vassallo, Teoria della conoscenza, (*"Theory of Knowledge"*), (Rome: Laterza, 2015), pp. 30-41.

7   B. Pascal, Pensieri ("The *Thoughts of Blaise Pascal"),* (Milan: Rizzoli, 1999), Thought 277.

that Plato calls *noesis*. We will try, by grasping the difference, to understand the specificity of each, particularly that specificity that distinguishes the nature and scope of hermeneutic knowledge.

Plato compares knowledge to a line.[8] This line is then divided into two segments, corresponding respectively to lower sensible knowledge (*dòxa*) and higher rational knowledge (*epistéme*), which are divided in turn into two other subspecies of knowledge. Four types of knowledge are thus delineated. At the lowest level we find sensible knowledge (*dòxa*), also called "opinion." On the one hand, it includes conjecture" (*eikasia*) or knowledge by images, which has for its object the shadows of things that remain unrelated to each other. On the other hand, again in an ascending sense, there is "belief" (*pistis*) or knowledge through visible objects, which aims at grasping sensible things in their mutual relations.

At a higher level, we have rational knowledge also called "science" (*epistéme*). This includes "discursive reason" (*diànoia*), which has mathematical ideas as its object, It also includes at the highest level, "intellectual reason" (*nòesis*) or philosophical intelligence, which has immutable ideas as its object and proceeds only through intuition.

Plato not only argues for the superiority of *episteme* (reason) over *doxa* (opinion) but also, within *episteme* itself, for the superiority of intellect (*nòesis*) over analytical reason (*dianoia*). Argumentative reason (*dianoia*) in use, for example, in mathematics, still finds too many footholds, according to Plato, in the sensible world, since it starts from unproven assumptions drawn through objects perceived by the senses. In contrast, intellectual knowledge (*nòesis*) is supreme precisely because it proceeds only by intuition and has no recourse to any kind of mediation. It is direct and immediate through contemplation.

We might call Platonic and ancient idealism "objective" because it does not make Ideas dependent on the knowing subject. This is different in kind from modern idealism, i.e., ours, which is instead a "subjective" idealism characterized by the dependence of Ideas on the knowing subject. This is why modern idealism is constructivist

---

8   Plato, *Republic,* Book VI, 509d-511e.

and pragmatic while Platonic idealism is a contemplative, intuitive idealism and does not resort to any mediation.

Hermeneutics, in comparison with the Platonic intellect, is of an entirely different nature. It rejects the immediate path of the intellect and deliberately chooses the path of sense mediated through a text. For Plato, hermeneutics is inferior and unreliable knowledge because it relies on mediation in a structural way. For hermeneutics, on the other hand, immediate knowledge, the contemplative knowledge of the mystics or the intellectual knowledge of Plato, is seeded with stumbling blocks and recurring risks. For this reason it introduces an additional step that serves as a corrective filter and a place of verification of the sense that is arising. This place of verification and filter is represented by the passage through the text.

Hermeneutic knowledge recognizes its own slowness in the construction of meaning, conditioned by an additional step in the cognitive process, which is that of the text. The text necessarily slows down the articulation of meaning. At the same time, hermeneutics articulates a claim. This is that it is able to offer a better sense because it is filtered by an additional passage. The passage through the text does not actually narrow the sense but enhances and expands it through what Paul Ricœur calls the mechanism of "distantiation."[9]

This mechanism creates separation and detachment between the author and his or her message, between the author and the original addressee, and between the dialogists and the immediate external reality (reference). These three forms of distancing are possible only because of the text. This detachment (distantiation), introduced at these three levels by the text is not a negative detachment (*verfremdung*).[10] It is a mechanism that guarantees the enhancement of meaning through a positive detachment of otherness (*entfremdung*).[11]

Hermeneutics bases its claim to validity on the bet of the text as "distantiation" as a sense-expanding mechanism. We now turn

---

9 P. Ricœur, *Ermeneutica filosofica...*, Op. cit., pp. 53-78.
10 *Verfremdung* is a German word, translated as alienation in the sense of estrangement.
11 Also translated as alienation but in the sense of otherness.

our attention to the validity of this claim of biblical hermeneutics which is founded on a mechanism opposite to that of the intellectual knowledge (*nòesis*) articulated by Plato.

Hermeneutics is the choice of mediation as a means of constructing the meaning of the Christian faith. Not only Catholic but also Protestant Christianity, with its strong reference to the Bible, is a religion of mediation. As such it requires a hermeneutics. What is hermeneutics?[12] Let us try to describe it through the path of some stages.

2. Reading[13] the Bible

Since it is a book, the Bible can be approached from two strategies that are complementary but different in nature. One is through reading, which leads immediately to application. The other is through interpretation, which, moving from reading, also reaches application, but more slowly. Those who choose the first option tend to be wary of interpretation and see it not only as a mechanism for slowing down the achievement of meaning, but also as a space of risk for meaning itself. Those who choose the second, on the other hand, will see the interpretive slowdown as a positive mechanism for verifying meanings, which from a simple reading almost always arrive one-sided and distorted.

---

12 P. Ricœur, *Dal testo all'azione...* Op. cit., pp. 11-34. M. Ferraris, *Storia dell'ermeneutica*, (*"History of Hermeneutics"*), (Milan: Bompiani, 1997), pp. 5-7.

13 In this section and throughout our text (see the last chapter, Chapter XII, entitled "Reading the Bible from the South. The 'Eros' of Interpretation"), we would assume two types of readings. One that is closed in on itself and the other that instead is open to interpretation. When this happens then we are talking about a successful reading, as Werner G. Jeanrond does. Cf. W.G. Jeanrond, *L'ermeneutica teologica. Sviluppo e significato*, (*"Theological Hermeneutics. Development and Meaning"*), (Brescia, Queriniana 1994), pp. 157-201.

These two moments should be sequential and complementary.[14] Today there is a large cohort of Christians, especially in the most dynamic and high-growth churches and groupings, who in reaction to an overly rational approach to the Bible choose the short route from reading to application. This hermeneutical choice, naïve though often well-intentioned (because even those who choose not to interpret are actually interpreting anyway), is doubly short-sighted. First, it accedes to and follows the implicit traditional interpretation, the least current and therefore the worst, which it mistakenly identifies with the Bible itself, illegitimately imposing it as incontrovertible fact. Second, it forgoes constructing a current interpretation, which is the one most likely to become the best by virtue of its respect for the addressee, the projection of the text, and the challenges present in the context.

The setting aside of interpretation in favor of reading and its immediate application unfortunately does not give birth to the best meanings whether those present in the text itself or those that could be created from the text in its interaction with the current context. Haste, which tends to become an obsession to achieve meaning quickly, prevents one from seeing the complexity of the text with its richness and variety of possible meanings. It is still the same haste in application that also drives the reader to overlook the opportunities offered by the external context as stimuli for looking at the text from different perspectives.

The intended self-sufficient reading to grasp the meaning of the text hides yet another more insidious and distorting anomaly. This is the presumption and certainty behind the rush for immediate meaning that the text is transparent and unambiguous. This is the most important error of disallowing the nature of the biblical text, of thinking that the biblical text is a clear text whose meaning is immediately and automatically within the reach of the reader's sincerity and zeal.

---

14   In this regard, W.G. Jeanrond put it this way, "Hermeneutics is most interested in the analysis of the dialectic between reader and text, and the effects of this dialectic on the self-understanding of the individual reader or groups of readers," Cf. *L'ermeneutica teologica...* Op. cit , pp. 17,18.

These readers presume that the only task to be accomplished is to assume an attitude of listening and waiting in the face of a text that alone gives itself and delivers itself limpidly to the sincere reader. The complexity and difficulty they think, comes not from the text but from the reader, from his or her laziness or prejudices. This is a very common hermeneutic fallacy. Unfortunately, very often, it is directly proportional to the sincerity and spiritual eagerness of the believer on duty.

This reductive gaze with respect to the text is subsequently prolonged and validated also in the reductive gaze with respect to reality itself. Even the external reality, with which the text always tries to compare itself (linguistic reference), becomes, in this kind of reading, a crushed reality because it is reduced to its clarity. It is a non-reality, a falsified reality. The result is the implicit and unconscious hermeneutic union and fellowship between a "textual reductionism" and a "reductionism of the reality." The path of sincere reading of the Bible with its immediate application does not offer a horizon of authentic growth. It represents at its base a paradoxical form of spiritual involution. "Read and apply" seems the best and most direct option. Certainly, it is the fastest. It is not necessarily the best.

3. *Interpreting the Bible*

Hermeneutics is the art of interpreting a text.[15] Every text represents an otherness, an obstacle, a challenge. If the Bible is the text par excellence, this means that the difficulty in confronting it will be even greater. This is probably why euphoric Christians in constant search of spiritual sugars of immediate assimilation not only tend to run away from the arduous path of hermeneutics. It often happens that they also end up calling it the very antithesis of truth. But it is easy to see which side is common sense and which side is the "chaff that the wind scatters."[16]

---

15 M. Ferraris, *L'ermeneutica, ("Hermeneutics")*, (Laterza, Rome 1998), pp. 3-31.
16 Psalm 1:4.

In the hermeneutic way, reading is not erased. It becomes a necessary but not unique step and, even less, a conclusive step. Rather, reading opens the reader to the complication of the relationship with an other text that is external to me and that I do not possess. It is as the presence of a person whom I find in my path and who in no way belongs to me. Indeed, the other person I find on my path offers me a difficult but more direct relationship than a text requires of me, because with the other person the relationship is articulated in the immediacy of verbal dialogue without interposition or mediation. Text, on the other hand, represents an even more indirect way of dialogue, and consequently slows down the communicative process more markedly. In this sense, the interpretation of a text is typically a mediated route to meaning.

This fact invites us to a different reflection on Protestantism. Various times Protestantism is described as the religion of immediacy in the face of the typically Catholic and medieval burdening of religious experience that tends instead to create countless steps. In reality, this is not the case. Protestantism, like Catholicism and like Christianity in general, is a typical religion of mediation, not immediacy. God is not reached directly. The mediator is Christ and with him his Word, the Bible.

The true religions of immediacy radically combat the idea that to get to God one must go through a book. Even those Christian forms of mysticism throughout history that have had a critical look at religious formalities have never been able to truly detach themselves from the foundational Christian text, the Bible. The difference between Catholics and Protestants, in their common defense of religious mediation as the foundational mechanism of Christianity, lies elsewhere. It concerns the nature and quantity of necessary mediations, not their denial.

This fundamental trait of the Christian religion emerges and becomes visible in the choice of interpretation as a way to approach the Bible. Biblical hermeneutics is the linguistic way of expressing the very essence of Christianity as mediation. Reading,[17] with

---

17 Reading is essential in the interpretive process, that reading which does not close in on itself but turns into a dialogue with the text. This reading

immediate application, on the other hand, represents a deformation of it. Wanting to limit oneself to only reading the Bible with the corresponding immediate application is not only a hermeneutical deformation. Even more fundamentally, it is a theological deformation, because it dispenses with and denies the structurally mediated character of Christian faith. The obsession with a reading and its immediate application is a typically modern deformation.

The rush to read, understanding just what's necessary, to apply it with a view to a visible and quick result, is a typical deformation of our times that is nefarious and dangerous. Besides being abnormal, it claims to be the model to follow. In addition to this harm, it represents also a mockery of the text. This interpretative dysfunction is typical of our times because of the pragmatism it expresses. We could call it the way of "practical mysticism." This oxymoron expresses well the two components of this modern anomaly. On the one hand, there is the desire for immediacy typical of any mysticism; on the other hand, there is the desire for concreteness typical of contemporary pragmatism. Biblical pragmatism, a plague of our time as much as biblical indifference is, is a phenomenon that we moderns have given birth to and cannot transfer to other eras.

The simplicity of access to the Bible certainly existed in other eras and was also widespread. But this simplicity of approach to the Bible in other ages was an enchanted and mysterious simplicity. The simplicity claimed by today's biblical pragmatism is disenchanted and manipulative. This introduces an immediacy without mystique that, as such, could only arise in our time.

This passage through the text is therefore central to hermeneutics.[18] Text is strictly defined as a writing produced by an author and intended for a reader. This does not mean that the meaning of the text is circumscribable only to the author's intention or that the scope of

---

embodies the essence of interpretation. Cf. L.A. Schökel, J.M. Bravo Aragon, *Appunti di ermeneutica...*Op. cit., pp. 83-102.

18 This shift from text is essential in hermeneutics. Not only in the sense that without text there would be no trace of what needs to be interpreted, but the text is the true goal of interpretation beyond the author who wrote that text and its intentionality. Cf. L.A. Schökel, J.M. Bravo Aragon, *Appunti di ermeneutica...* Op. cit., pp. 25-38.

the meaning conveyed is exhausted in the interpretive logic of the original recipient. On the contrary, the meaning of what hermeneutics is and what it implies is at stake in the extension of meanings beyond the original author's intention and in the broadening of the interpreting community into potential recipients not included in the primary addressee.

The guiding question is to try to understand what the text really is and what the reader in fact represents. Can a text, which tends to make itself autonomous from its original author, consult circumstantial readers not envisaged in the initial configuration of the primary recipient, remain such without distorting and altering its original perspective and configuration? Or is hermeneutics precisely the legitimization of this alteration?

For the Christian, understanding this process is vitally important because Christianity has tied its destiny in an irreversible and primary way to understanding a text, the Bible. Many religions reconnect with a text to recount their origin, to think about the reality around them, and to articulate their own response to it. Although many religions develop reflections from a sacred text, not in all religions does that sacred text have the importance and primary status that the Bible has for Christianity. Christianity is necessarily and across the whole spectrum of its manifestations, a hermeneutical religion from its inception and not by historical accident.[19]

The need to understand what interpretation is imposes itself on the 21st century believer not only from the essence of his own religion, but also from the profoundly changed external cultural context. Contemporary culture, modern and postmodern, has made the book the privileged mechanism for gathering information about reality and on this to build one's own way of standing before the world.

Today the Christian is forced to interpret not only his Bible but also all the texts that accompany the natural and secular development of his life. Within one's own faith community, Bible commentaries, community organization manuals, catechetical texts, institutional statements, newspapers, magazines and the various texts produced within it are to be read as well as the Bible.

---

19 C. Geffré, *Credere e interpretare*...Op. cit., pp. 11-43.

From this brief introductory description, the reader comes to a rather clear perception that hermeneutics, and the interpretation of texts, is not a secondary component of being a Christian today. It represents its central node. Without close confrontation with one's foundational text, the Bible, the resulting faith profile is already born deformed, although the effects will only be visible over time. It is therefore required of the believer to understand as best he can what is at stake when he reads and interprets a text such as the Bible. Let us pause now to consider some important implications that this wager on interpretation carries.

4. The Dual Hermeneutical Nature of Christianity[20]

A first element to be taken up and carefully considered is the extent of the interpretive dimension in the very structure of Christianity. Christianity is a religion closely linked to a book, the Bible; this fact necessarily sets in motion an interpretive process. We often hear that interpretation undermines the Word of God because, through interpretation, one would like to make the Bible say not what it really says, but what one thinks it says. Effectively, interpretation carries a risk. But it must not be forgotten that non-interpretation also carries with it other risks. On the balance of risks of interpreting and non-interpreting, the risks of non-interpreting probably weigh more heavily.

The risks of interpreting are essentially two. First, is weakening the Bible by making it an interpreted word. The Bible becomes a more relative and therefore less binding and definitive Word.

---

[20] This dual characterization of Christian hermeneutics is described by Jeanrond in the following terms: "The early Christians thus had a twofold hermeneutical problem: 1. Initially almost always of Jewish background, they reinterpreted their Hebrew scriptures in the light of their experience of Jesus, his proclamation, death and resurrection; 2. They themselves put together, as time went on, a second body of scripture - New Testament - which, as it became increasingly canonical, that is, normative, ended up requiring appropriate interpretive strategies as well." W.G. Jeanrond, *L'ermeneutica teologica... Op. cit.*, pp. 33-41.

Second, elevating to a binding word a word that is instead only an interpretation, replacing the Word of God with a human word. The risks of not interpreting are also essentially two. First, making it irrelevant by not updating it. Second, making absolute a relative interpretation of the past. The risks are certain in both cases. Fundamentally, through different mechanisms, they consist in elevating what is purely circumstantial to a binding word. In the case of non-interpretation, the problem is to make binding not only a human word that passes itself off as divine, but also a word that has in addition the sin of not being actual and relevant.

Interpretation cannot be replaced by pure application. This is not only because interpretation has the merit of making an ancient word present. It is also because interpretation becomes the true site of verification of relative words that want to pass themselves off as absolute. Beyond these undoubted benefits of the interpretive process, Christianity is a hermeneutical religion for two structural reasons.

First, because it starts from an ancient book that needs to be interpreted to ground a faith. Christian faith is not born in the individual and then needs legitimization from the Bible. On the contrary, it arises only from hearing the Word of God that finds a hook in the human being. There is no other way to give birth to faith except through the reading of that book called the Bible.

In this sense, interpretation is not an anomalous or intrusive act in the Christian faith. It is its true and proper fulfillment. Only in contact with that text does faith have the possibility of its birth. We will call this first mechanism "exogenous interpretation." It is the interpretation which arises outside the Bible in the Christian community, in history, as a legitimate experience of the arising of faith through contact with the foundational text. The second mechanism can be called "Endogenous interpretation" because interpretation in this case precedes the believer's interpretation. The foundational text of Christianity, the New Testament, is itself already an interpretation of the Old Testament, so from extra-biblical interpretation becomes intra-biblical.[21] Interpretation then is not only legitimate because we have to interpret a text to found our faith: it is also legitimate for a more structural reason. The text that grounds us, the Bible, is itself already an interpretation of an earlier text. We call this second mechanism "endogenous interpretation." This is because it arises within the Bible itself.

This double foundation of Christian hermeneutics allows us to assert that Christianity is thus doubly hermeneutical because it legitimately and necessarily generates an interpretation (exogenous), but also because it arises genealogically from an interpretation (endogenous). This double fact carries with it two consequences. On the one hand, it gives legitimacy to the interpretation and the interpreter. Interpretation, therefore, is welcome. It is structurally necessary. It needs to be there. When the Christian interprets, he does not commit a crime but honors his faith. The obligation to interpret is placed in the wake and logic of the Christian faith. No one can be born as a Christian if he does not interpret. Interpretation represents the way into Christianity. This is why no one within Christianity has to ask permission to interpret. This is required of them as an obligation.[22]

On the other hand, the Word of God is conceived in its relationality as a Word that deserves and needs interpretation. Being conceived as a revealed Word, the Bible was constructed relationally; therefore, it needs and strongly calls for interpretations. The Bible bears all possible interpretations well and does not wear out at all in the face of them. Interpretations only succeed in enhancing, empowering and highlighting its many latent meanings. If there were no interpretations, the Bible would easily become a shrunken and insignificant book.

Interpretations give it muscle and vigor. Interpretations make it flourish. In its typical perspective of gift and exchange, the Bible does not fold in on itself, but aims to make readers who approach it flourish, recognizing in them legitimate interlocutors, legitimate

---

21 Cf. J. Barr, *Old and New in Interpretation: A Study of the Two Testaments*, (London: SMC, 1966), pp. 103-148.
22 Cf. C. Geffré, *Credere e interpretare...* Op. cit., pp. 17-19.

interpreters. The Bible has deliberately chosen to depend, in the construction of meaning, on external readers. How is the interpretive process configured in its essence?

5. The "Hermeneutic Circle"[23]

Any hermeneutics presupposes that the starting point for a cognitive process or articulation of meaning is the presence of a text. Only the presence of a text guarantees the emergence of a true interpretive process. In the Christian context, biblical hermeneutics strongly and irrevocably affirms the necessity and obligation to move from the biblical text. There is no Christian faith that is not simultaneously a reading of the biblical text.

This first structural element of hermeneutics, the text, is actually connected to a second foundational element: the reader. This second element is less visible and even when it is made visible it tends to be considered more secondary. The reader is a reader only because he is qualified by the text that grounds him as such. If the text is a sacred text such as the Bible, the Word of God, this sub-valorization of the reader tends to be even greater. The more sacred a text is, the stronger the tendency to delegitimize the reader and not to grant him or her a full and relevant status.

In the hermeneutic process, the reader is just as important as the text. There is no reader without a text that qualifies him as such, but synchronically there is never a true text that is not written for someone.

Christianity is configured as a strongly legitimating religion of the reader because that foundational book, the Bible, though inspired by God, is intended and shaped by virtue of the human beings who read it. There is no hermeneutics without a reader who reads the text. Apparently this second hermeneutical claim takes away from the prominence of the Bible because it makes it overly dependent on the reader who reads it. That the reader-believer depends on the Bible as a text is understandable and theologically necessary.

---

23 Cf. W. G. Jeanrond, *L'ermeneutica teologica...* Op. cit., pp. 16, 17.

That, on the other hand, the Bible also depends on the reader, seems heterodox and appears a bit extreme. If we tried to understand the deeper meaning of this statement, we would find that it fully agrees with the nature and meaning of what the Bible claims to be.

The Bible, while being "Word of God," is first and foremost "Incarnate Word of God." It is Word addressed to man and incomprehensible without its ultimate recipient, the human being. The fact that it is relational does not make it more comprehensible. The absolute words, those "in and of themselves" (those without a recipient) are those which after all are reachable. Although they may be difficult, they are always attainable in their meaning.

Although they are the closest and the most familiar, relational words instead are truly unreachable in their total meaning because they are based on the mystery of the other. This structural unattainability and impenetrability is the guarantee of their relationality and, paradoxically, of their openness and gift. Every relational word is articulated in this systole and diastole of the presence of the other that offers and withdraws, delivers and subtracts.

The Bible is Word near and far. Word revealed and hidden, Word that comes and goes. The relational Word is never fully transparent. The Bible is *the* Word but it is also *a* Word. The Bible does not express all and every word of God. There are other words of God that are not included in the Bible. The Bible is *the* Word of God in that it is *a* Word of God. For us Christians it is the most important, but not the only one. It is the most important because it is a relational Word in a specific context of salvation.

Biblical hermeneutics is both the affirmation of the text and the affirmation of the legitimacy of the reader. Text and reader are the two structural elements of any sound hermeneutics. In the hermeneutical process, the reader does not arrive at the meaning of life except through that text (the Bible), but at the same time that text is meant to flourish only through the reader's interpretation.

Why is the relationship between text and reader not linear?[24] Hermeneutics speaks of "hermeneutic circle" and not "line" or

---

24 It is not, as Alexander S. Jensen points out, precisely because the connection between text and reader, can occur in various ways; hence the

"hermeneutic pair." We talk about the hermeneutic circle because entry to the interpretive process has various routes and this is not solely of quantitative and organizational importance. The hermeneutic circle qualitatively describes and justifies the multi-directionality of the interpretive process. The interpretive process can be accessed from the side of the text (the most common route), but also starting from the reader.

It usually begins with the text that the reader reads and then applies. In what he applies, he takes into account what the text tells him. This is the "epistemological" way that presupposes the division, in the cognitive process, between the subject (reader) who knows and the object (text) that is known. Subject and object are separate and, in the process of their approach, only a cognitive, epistemological, relationship occurs.

The interpretive process can also begin with the reader, before the reader reads the text. Is this possible? Certainly. The reader is never a tabula rasa when approaching the text. When the reader comes to the text with preconceived ideas, and these are rigid, then the relationship breaks down because the reader will not feel challenged by the text but will impose his or her own biases on the text. The text will only be a pre-text to legitimize their own thoughts. The text will not change or transform them. But not every prior idea is a prejudice. A prior idea that does not manipulate the text is what in hermeneutics is called "pre-understanding."

"Pre-understanding" is legitimate and necessary for correct interpretation. If we did not have a pre-comprehension about the text we are reading, that text would become alien, unfamiliar and incomprehensible. Pre-understanding is the affinity that binds us readers as humans to what the text describes as a human text. Pre-comprehension has not only an epistemological dimension. It has and presupposes above all an "ontological" dimension related to life, because it reminds us that before reading a text the reader is already rooted in the life and reality that the text tries to describe.

---

category of "hermeneutic circle." See A. S. Jensen *Theological Hermeneutics*, (London: SCM Press, 2007), pp. 4,5.

Between text and reader, pre-understanding implies not a separation but a belonging. This belonging or rootedness, which binds reader and text together, represents the dimension of being and the bond of life by virtue of which all subsequent analytical, informational and epistemological knowledge is possible. The text speaks of reality but is not the total reality. A good reader, in addition to paying attention to the text he or she is reading, must pay attention to its rootedness in life, which is a pre-textual experience that does not destroy but ensures a healthy relationship with the text.

In this sense, the hermeneutic circle adds two other important mechanisms to the valuable mechanism of mediation and interpretive slowdown.

1. The mechanism of balancing the instances at stake. Hermeneutics is not only the text, even though that text may be sacred. Hermeneutics is also the reader and what this represents in the articulation of meaning. The interpretive process is successful not when meaning is reached at any cost, but when the hermeneutic circle is balanced and manages to ensure the survival of these two poles in creative tension.

The tension between the two poles is a guarantee, not an obstacle, to the manifestation of meaning. We find in the hermeneutic circle a kind of balancing of powers in a hermeneutic key. The health and truth of meaning are given not only by the linguistic and operational result, but by the process by which it is arrived at. Neither the text is absolute king nor is the reader. Or, put another way, both are kings, but such that they know how to create convergence and consensus.

2. The hermeneutic circle corrects the excessive rationalization into which biblical interpretation can run, uniting subject (reader) and object (Bible) at the base in a pretextual partnership. This is the meaning of pre-comprehension. In it, the typical separation of subject-knower and object-known is overcome. It is preceded through the affirmation of a bond prior to the more linear relationship between reader and biblical text. This bond, reading will only enrich, orient and correct, but not create in the strict sense.

The Bible can direct faith and correct it, but it cannot create it. Or it creates it in the relative sense, that is, that correcting it is like bringing it into existence. If the Bible created faith in the absolute sense as a capacity and attitude, then it would be the product of a book, a by-product.

Even those who do not read the Bible, by virtue of this ontological link to life, which is a pre-textual link, understand, know and experience what it means to be human in a more immediate and spontaneous way. We first are born and live as human beings, then we learn to read and follow what the Bible points us to. There is an ontological priority of being human over claiming and justly defending the value of a book. This ontological priority is neither secular nor denominational; it is simply human. In Christianity it is guaranteed by the call to the Creator God.

Hermeneutics as a slow way, because it is mediated by interpretation, embodies and articulates a tension that is its own and which it cannot do without. Interpretation is realized and possible only within this tension. It is actually a threefold tension. It is at the intersection of these three tensions that hermeneutics is configured as such. Only within can meaning arise. The first is an "endogenous" tension, within the text. In the text a meaning coexists with other meanings that it cannot erase. There is never in the text an isolated meaning, much less a single imperial and totalizing meaning. A textual tension ensues.

The second is a tension exogenous to the text, in the reader. Conflicting and ambivalent attitudes to the text, conscious and unconscious, coexist in the reader. The result is a tension in the reader that is structural and indelible. When we desire the reader to be unitary and monolithic, we immediately move to the terrain of ideology. The third tension is a tension between the text and the reader. Neither pole can be erased in the intent to diminish the tension. Both are legitimate and necessary. The result is an interpretive tension that is the very guarantee of meaning.

Hermeneutics is not a monolithic process in the acquisition of meaning It is articulated in the tension of the "hermeneutic circle." It tries, on the one hand, to de-emphasize the arrogance of a reader who wants to be independent of the text. On the other hand, it equally tries to de-emphasize the claim of a text that wants to be full of meaning regardless of the reader.

This mechanism, open and tensional in the articulation of meaning, guaranteed by the "hermeneutic circle," has become structural for theology today. By virtue of this fact, theological hermeneutics is not a section, much less an appendix, of theological work. It is not reduced to the interpretation of the Bible. Today, all theology has become hermeneutics. Geffré writes in this regard:

> "It can be said that not only in the case of the humanities, but also in the case of the experimental sciences, the so-called natural sciences, any scientific knowledge today is interpretive knowledge. There is no learning, immediate approach of reality outside of language, and language is already necessarily a certain interpretation. Thus, there is a consensus that all sciences are interpretive sciences. In fact, we have distanced ourselves from positivism or a certain scientism. It is in function of this epistemological break that the relevance of a hermeneutic model in theology should be understood."[25]

---

25 C. Geffré, *Credere e interpretare...* Op. cit., p. 15.

CHAPTER II
HISTORY OF HERMENEUTICS

The history of biblical hermeneutics,[1] is at first a description of the various forms of interpretation that have followed one another over time according to various schools, denominations, territories and historical periods. As such, it aims to fulfill two important tasks.

The first consists in proposing a unified and integrative view of the different interpretative forms. It intends to create a certain sequentiality and organization of events which, were it not so, would appear excessively dispersed, disconnected and elusive to a comprehensive gaze, The value of this first synoptic glance is not immediate because the connection between interpretive schools does not necessarily follow either the criterion of their territorial or their temporal proximity. Only a trained and discerning gaze can identify familiarity or common directions beyond apparent differences and contrasts.

The second intends to propose a differentiated view of the various interpretive proposals, which would otherwise appear as mere repetitions or extensions of pre-existing patterns. The value of this second look is valuable because it allows us to differentiate interpretive proposals that seem to belong to a common historical or territorial strain and instead contain *in nuce* a specific and differentiating element. Only in the evolution of history will this become more explicit and evident, creating true interpretive alternatives.

---

1 A.S. Jensen, *Theological Hermeneutics*...Op. cit., pp. 9-37.

The history of biblical hermeneutics[2] is not a purely descriptive act. It is not reduced to the effort of registering and cataloguing, albeit well organized various interpretative forms of the past. The history of biblical hermeneutics is itself an exercise in theological reflection. No description is completely aseptic. Neither is ours. Assumptions, affinities, unconfessed and unconscious preferences condition the choice and manner of dealing with the chosen material.

The theological-reflexive component from which this brief historical synopsis starts, which we try to elaborate in this chapter, is summed up in a thesis that identifies the shift from a "strong text" to a "weak text" as the most significant event in the history of biblical hermeneutics. This transition corresponds to a very specific event: the birth of modernity.

This might appear as a far-fetched and overly compact thesis, for it escapes no one that there are no monolithic historical epochs. Within historical periods there are always positions that quantitatively and qualitatively are well differentiated. It would take little to point out this incontrovertible fact. Yet, there is a common trait that binds pre-modern interpretations. This is that they share, beyond even marked differences, a certain almost sacred respect for the "stability of meaning." This element has led us to call premodern hermeneutics "text-centered hermeneutics," because in them, through respect for the text, respect for the stability of meaning predominates.

The hermeneutics that arose with the emergence of modernity are of an entirely different bent. Here, too, there is no shortage of sometimes radical differences between opposing positionings. Yet, there is a common element that seems to link the interpretive proposals that arose in our historical period: the "fluidity of meaning."

This recurring element, present in different proportions, prompts us to call modern hermeneutics "reader-centric hermeneutics," because in them, through the emphasis on the fluidity of meaning, the centrality of the reader is made explicit as a destabilizing

---

2   W.G. Jeanrond, *L'ermeneutica teologica*...Op. cit., pp. 25-75.

element of traditional meaning. The reader is the one who, by virtue of the validity and relevance he ascribes to himself and his own projects, deconstructs, critiques, overthrows, dismantles without much scruple, and with a spontaneous glee and freedom, the meanings and texts that the past has catalogued as sacred and unchanging.

"Text-centric hermeneutics" and "reader-centric hermeneutics" represent, in our historical review of interpretive schools, two central categories. Our historical look is not neutral. It starts, as mentioned earlier, from a well-typed theological reflection. This does not take the form of an ironclad prejudice, but rather a flexible historical-theological hypothesis. This will allow us to describe, list, organize, and analyze the different interpretive proposals that have emerged in history, trying to give them a theological and cultural intelligibility.

What are the mechanisms that prepare, announce, and determine this epochal shift from the centrality of the text to the centrality of the reader? What are the effects, foreseen and unforeseen, expected and unexpected, that result from this shift? Does this shift have a purely historical significance? Does it mark a structural change in the interpretive enterprise itself? Do its effects also press upon theology and force it to alter its outlook on God, faith, the church, and the Bible? What is the history of hermeneutics? What is important in this history? How could it be organized? How could it be understood theologically? What category, perspective or event to choose as a starting point?

These are some of the theological questions that will be behind the scenes as we try to briefly list some of the most significant schools and hermeneutical perspectives in the history of Christianity.

1. A Theological-Cultural Look at the History[3] of Hermeneutics

We will take the theological key to read this story from a non-theological event. It is a non-theological moment of modernity to which we still belong. We will start from a historical figure, from Descartes. It will be a story told from our present, not in the exposition of the stages, as we will follow the traditional historical sequence. In this basic perspective, we will aim to grasp from the beginning the specificity of modern hermeneutics. To grasp it, we will necessarily look to the past but starting from the present, because, as Benedetto Croce well remembered, "All history is contemporary history."[4]

To be compact and direct, our historical reading hypothesis is articulated in the following way. Modern hermeneutics, both philosophical and theological, marks an important shift from a

---

3 The history of hermeneutics, not solely in a chronological sense but in a qualitative sense, can only be understood by connecting it to the nodes, transitions and ruptures of culture taken as a historical whole. This connection points out that hermeneutics in general, but also the particular hermeneutics related to the reading of the Bible, is always rooted in, and thus influenced and conditioned in the essentials of its emphasis and focus, by the culture in which it is embedded. Cf. W. Ong, *Orality and Literacy*...Op. cit., pp. 136-152. This was true for the medieval period where sense predetermined by the group predominates over sense created by the individual, as in a broader perspective the group predominates over individual consciousness. See W. Ullmann, *Individuo e società nel medioevo, ("Individual and Society in the Middle Ages")*, (Rome: Laterza, 1974), pp. 1-43; J. Le Goff, *La civilisation de l'occident médiéval*, (Paris: Flammarion, 2008), pp. 234-289. And the same thing happens with the advent of modernity, where the sense created by the individual will win out over the sense emerging in the community, as in a broader perspective the individual will take over from the group. See A.J. Gourevitch, *La naissance de l'individu dans l'Europe médiévale*, (Paris: Seuil, 1997), pp. 141-193; E. Cassirer, *The Individual and the Cosmos in the Renaissance Philosophy*, (New York: Angelico Press, 1963), pp. 73-122; A. Cavicchia Scalamonti, *La morte. Quattro variazioni sul tema*, *("Death. Four Variations on the Theme")*, (Santa Maria Capua Vetere: Hypermedium, 2007), pp. 9-56.

4 B. Croce, *La storia come pensiero e come azione, ("History as Thought and Action")*, (Napoli: Bibliopolis, 2002). See also M. de Certeau, *L'écriture de l'histoire*, (Paris : Gallimard, 1995).

way of connecting to the sense of a text, in this case the Bible, as a "stable" and already given sense, typical of the Middle Ages, to a "fluid" sense that has yet to be constructed, at least in its final form. The mediator of that sense to be constructed is the interpreter. The interpreter, the "reader," becomes in the modern world, the mainstay of the interpretive enterprise. Although philosophical hermeneutics will formalize this with F. Schleiermacher in the early 1800s, who gave birth to philosophical hermeneutics, the shift in perspective certainly took place earlier. We have chosen, somewhat atypically and symbolically, to trace it back to Descartes. In Descartes, the extremes of what will become the perspective, the nature and the paradoxes of modern hermeneutics are already found in synthesis, but in a very clear way.

This pairing is all the more unusual and strange when one considers that hermeneutics is par excellence an exercise in mediation. Though hermeneutics is mediation, in Descartes we find expressed the persistent effort to disassociate itself from any mediation, so that it can come to construct an immediate and transparent knowledge. This is a knowledge that chooses to disassociate itself, through systematic doubt, from any sensory mediation in order to make its certainty rest solely in the immediacy of the *cogito*. Only the cogito, by virtue of its own doubt, arrives at the only possible certainty, which is that of its own thinking. Only thus does one arrive at "clear and distinct ideas," the only possible basis for new and irrefutable knowledge.

How can Descartes be then the starting point for a cognitive enterprise such as hermeneutics that makes the mediation of the text its strong point? He does this through an atypical but quite clear shift in its extremes and address from the very outset. A new cognitive and anthropological perspective based on two pillars comes with the rationality introduced by Descartes.[5] First, there is trust in the autonomous individual who with his reason (*res cogitans*) makes reality and the world transparent. Reason, with its order, analytical power and organizational capacity, imposes itself for the first time in a massive way on external reality, erecting itself as an unquestionable

---

5   R. Descartes, *Meditazioni metafisiche*, (*"Metaphysical Meditations"*), (Rome: Laterza, 1997); see especially the first and second meditations.

guarantor over all that is real and true. The cogito as a cognitive instance detaches itself from the rest of reality that had hitherto contained, accompanied, limited, and even oppressed it. It claims the status of an autonomous subject capable of knowing only from itself, resting only on the power of its own reason.

Second, in order to give the cogito its power an operation necessarily had to be accomplished first. Like any mechanism of domination and hegemony, the external reality or thing to be known necessarily had to be neutralized and demystified. No domination is exercised in a vacuum. Every conquest carries the trophy of a conquered territory. In Descartes, the controlled reality that guarantees the domination and rational supremacy of the cogito is the external world, reality, the cosmos and even that cosmos closest to the cogito which is one's own body. Reason must be able to control the distant and external cosmos and the near and familiar body. In order to control it, it needs to neutralize it. Descartes neutralizes far and near external reality by reducing it to one of its dimensions: measure (*res extensa*). Thus reduced, reality becomes predictable. It has no motion of its own. It has become a machine, a disenchanted reality. In order to move, it needs an element external to it, that is, the cogito. Having to depend on an external element, nature then becomes easily controlled by it. Nature becomes a reality subservient to the cogito.

Thanks to a new anthropology that overvalues the thinking subject as the determining element in ordering reality with its omnipotent reason, and thanks to a new cosmology that devalues nature because it reduces it to one of its dimensions, and in so doing "disenchants" it, this new world is ordered. Here the order of the world expresses the measure of its disenchantment. The Cartesian scheme thus expresses two truths, two claims. On the one hand, there is the power of the knowing subject. On the other, there is the impotence and subservience of the known object. Because the object has lost its mystery, it appears devalued. Meanwhile, the subject has gained it beyond what it would be allowed. It intoxicates itself with an illusion that improperly overvalues it.

Here are the two extremes of the Cartesian system that we will later find at the heart of modern hermeneutics and its anomalies. The reader, the mainstay of modern hermeneutics, is a direct descendant of the Cartesian cogito (*res cogitans*) in an interpretive key, just as the text

History of Hermeneutics 85

deciphered and controlled in its meaning and emptied of its mystery (*res extensa*) is a direct descendant of the reality and nature neutralized by Descartes.

We have seen so far that Christianity is a radically hermeneutic religion. In Christianity, interpretation is not a concession. It is "required" by moral and theological obligation. It is urged as a hallmark of those who claim to be truly Christian. The Christian believer, even before being a witness or a morally reliable person, is essentially an interpreter whose legitimacy is grounded in a text he is asked to read and understand before he can apply it. The nature and destiny of the foundational word of Christianity, the Bible, is not to keep it pure and aseptic. It is rather to contaminate it positively and continually with innumerable and ever new interpretations. Christian Scripture for this reason is not "interpretation-phobic." It is structurally "interpretation-philical." It does not flee or distrust interpretation. It willingly accepts and seeks interpretation as something inherent in it. Interpretation is for the Christian believer his amniotic fluid. It is that vital space that nourishes him and keeps him alive and without which his spiritual life would begin to perish and contract. It is in interpretation that the Bible finds its fullness.

Christianity has given rise to a multiplicity of hermeneutics that would be impossible to present in a summary chapter such as this one. The history of Christianity is the history of different hermeneutics that have been inspired by and originated from the stimulus derived from its founding book. Christian communities may vary in adding accompanying elements external or internal to the faith in order to better understand the meaning of Scripture. At the base the common conviction that that text, and the divine event that grounds, it remains. This is the starting point of all Christian experience. This is why interpretation in Christianity has always existed abundantly.

Let us look broadly at how these interpretations have followed and articulated themselves throughout history and, most importantly, at what, if anything, is the trait in it that distinguishes contemporary hermeneutics[6] from premodern hermeneutics.[7]

---

6   P. Ricœur, *Dal testo all'azione...Op. Cit.,* pp. 71-95.
7   M. Ferraris, *Storia dell'ermeneutica...Op. Cit.*, pp. 5-14.

2. Premodern Period: "Text-Centric Hermeneutics"

The basic hypothesis we will try to articulate in this section is that all premodern hermeneutics, beyond their differences in school or methodology, are united in a common trait, which is that of "sense stability." Premodern hermeneutics, ancient and medieval, find this stability of meaning not only in the text but in life in general. Therefore, our hermeneutic hypothesis starts from a cultural hypothesis. The stability of meaning in life in general finds in the stability of meaning in the text its natural extension. This is why the text is the guarantor of this stability. The guarantor of this stability is not the reader in the focus of premodern hermeneutics. This is why we describe these hermeneutics as "text-centered" hermeneutics.

a. Jewish Hermeneutics

In contrast to Greek thought, which is articulated as philosophical interpretation and reflection on the logos, with secondary reference to texts, Hebrew hermeneutics instead starts from a written text that becomes the inescapable starting point of knowledge of God and his will, which, through that text, becomes binding on faith. The believer must assimilate and make that text his own through reading and understanding its message. The reader is recognized as the rightful recipient of that message. Jewish hermeneutics is thus configured as the reading experience that affirms on the one hand the centrality of the text and on the other the concrete historicity of the interpreting community.[8]

These two elements are discernible from the very first chapters of Genesis and will become transversal and recurrent throughout

---

[8] One should not project into the past categories that are of our time, such as those of *text* and *reader* as we moderns have conceptualized and described them from the central and primary category of the "hermeneutic circle." However, one should not disregard the affinities and similarities either. That of the *text* and that of the *community that reads* and hears that text are in Judaism two essential components that reconnect and foreshadow our own. Judaism is not a mystical or orgiastic community, but an interpreting community.

Scripture. One of the most characteristic passages in this perspective is the one that recounts the experience of Ezra who, as a spiritual leader, reconstructs the identity of the people after exile from the rediscovery of the Torah, its reading and interpretation:

> "He read the book on the square that is in front of the Gate of Waters, from early morning until noon, in the presence of the men, women and those who were able to understand; and all the people strained their ears to hear the book of the law. Ezra, the scribe, stood on top of a wooden box, which had been specially made; beside him stood, on the right, Mattitiah, Semaiah, Ananias, Uriah, Chilchiah and Maaseiah; on the left, Pedaiah, Misael, Malchiah, Casum, Casbaddana, Zechariah and Mesullam. Ezra opened the book in the presence of all the people, for he stood in the highest place; and as soon as he opened the book, all the people stood up. Ezra blessed the Lord, the great God, and all the people answered, "Amen, amen," lifting up their hands; and they bowed down and prostrated themselves with their faces to the ground before the Lord. Iesuah, Bani, Serebiah, Iamin, Accub, Sabbetai, Odiah, Maaseiah, Chelita, Azariah, Iozabad, Anan, Pelaiah and the other Levites explained the law to the people, and they all stood in their places. They read in the book of God's law in an understandable way; they gave the meaning, so that the people would understand what they read. Nehemiah, who was the governor, Ezra, priest and scribe, and the Levites, who were teaching, said to all the people, "This day is consecrated to the Lord your God; do not be sad and do not weep!" For all the people wept, listening to the words of the law. Then Nehemiah said to them, "Go, eat fatty food and drink sweet drink, and send portions to those who have prepared nothing for them; for this day is consecrated to our Lord; do not be sad; for the joy of the Lord is your strength." The Levites calmed all the people, saying, "Be silent, for this day is holy; do not be sad!" All the people went out to eat, drink, send portions to the poor, and make a great feast, for they understood the words that had been explained to them." (Nehemiah 8:3-12).

Jewish hermeneutics is condensed into the categories this passage introduces: read, explain, understand, listen, act, rejoice.[9] The goal is not a theoretical understanding, but a personal and existential understanding that leads to and puts us in touch with

---

9 M. A Throntveit, *Esdra e Neemia ("Ezra and Nehemiah")*, (Turin: Claudiana, 2011), pp. 104-108.

life. Understanding the text does not appear here as a speculative experience, nor is it limited to being a mere explanation of words. It includes all registers of human existence and leads the reader to action and joy. We find in this short narrative the perfect articulation and mutual referral between the sacred text (*Torah*) and the equally synchronic centrality of the reading community (Israel), in order to take advantage of the blessings that through that text and its reading God wishes to bestow on his people.[10] We have in this pair, text-reading community, the forerunner of what in our day will become the "hermeneutic circle."

It emerges very clearly in this paradigmatic biblical passage, that in this hermeneutic, despite the recognition of the relevance of the reading community, the predominant and determining dimension in the construction of meaning is given by the text. Since it is in addition a sacred text, traceable to God himself, this centrality comes out even more reinforced and consolidated. Biblical Hebrew hermeneutics is thus configured as a typical "text-centric" hermeneutic whose strength is grounded and guaranteed by God himself and the fact that he is an all-powerful God, Lord and Creator of the universe. To the majesty, greatness and lordship of God correspond the majesty, greatness and lordship of the text. The text is as sacred as the God whom that text refers.

Post-biblical Jewish hermeneutics will maintain the validity of the two elements that foreshadow the hermeneutic circle. Their connection will be maintained and enriched. It will also be so in a creative and miraculous way because the undoubted sacredness of the Torah, reinforced even more by the territorial loss and by the emergence of Christianity, will not obscure or erase the dynamic and involved participation of the reading people. The sacred text does not stop but stimulates the creativity of the people. Jewish hermeneutics subsequent to the biblical period will confirm and reinforce this orientation in the form of the legal-moral interpretation of the Law

---

10 C.F. Keil & F. Delitzsch, *Ezra, Nehemiah, Esther, Job*, (Peabody: Hendrickson Publishers, 1989), pp. 143-147.

(*Halakhah*),[11] and in the form of the religious-spiritual interpretation of Scripture (*Haggada*),[12] in the context of intense talmudic-rabbinic interpretive activity. Thus, Jewish hermeneutics is not locked into the worship of the foundational text. In both the biblical and post-biblical periods, the sacredness of the text did not block or paralyze readers' participation. Emmanuel Levinas highlights this fact well when he states that, for the Jew, understanding the text also means understanding what is "beyond the verse." To understand the text is to transcend it.[13] Jewish hermeneutics has always ensured the connection that grounds the hermeneutic circle, between interpreted text and interpreting community. Indeed, in the *Tanakh*[14] itself, the sanctity of the Torah does not act as an impediment to further interpretive takes but, on the contrary, makes them possible. The *Tanakh* is the story of the interpretive revival of the Torah within the sacred text itself, as evidenced by the continuous reformulation of the Torah in the prophets and other Writings; just as the formation of the *Mishna* and *Ghemara* highlights, outside the sacred text, the same widespread and recurring interpretive process.

Once again and despite the decided involvement of the reading community, Jewish hermeneutics remains a typical "text-centric" hermeneutic even in the post-biblical period, because the reading community is regarded only as the extension of an existing sacred sense, rather than true creator of a new sense. Premodern Jewish

---

11 *Halakhah* is the religious normative tradition of Judaism, codified in a body of scripture; it includes biblical law (the 613 *mitzvòt*) and subsequent Talmudic and rabbinic laws, as well as traditions and customs.
12 *Haggadah* is a form of narration used in the Talmud and some parts of Jewish liturgy and the *Midrash*. The term refers to homiletic and non-legalistic texts of exegesis in classical rabbinic literature . In general, the *Haggadah* is a compendium of rabbinic homilies that incorporate folklore, historical anecdotes, moral exhortations and practical advice in various fields, from business to medicine.
13 E. Levinas, *L'au-delà du verset. Lectures et discours talmudiques*, (Paris : Minuit, 1982), pp. 10-23.
14 The word *Tanakh* contains the three letters that make up the acronym to designate the three parts of the Hebrew Bible: Torah, prophets and other writings (*Torah, Nebihim, Ketubim*).

hermeneutics is a hermeneutics of a sense that remains stable and aims to create stability. The stability of the text and its sense simply prolongs and validates the stability of life and reality in general through a faithful reading that guarantees the continuity of a sense predetermined by God himself. The sacredness of God corresponds to the sacredness of the text.

b. Christian Hermeneutics

The New Testament will certainly introduce a radical break. This is a perspective from which to read the Scriptures in a new way, in a revolutionary way. This new point of reference, not only theological but also hermeneutical, will be Jesus, the Messiah. He is the concretization and center of the Scriptures and at the same time the one who opens new horizons of meaning. The features of this new hermeneutics are visible, for example, in the Emmaus episode.[15]

> "And he said to them, 'Foolish and late in heart to believe the word of the prophets! Was it not necessary for Christ to endure these sufferings in order to enter into His glory? ''". And beginning with Moses and all the prophets he explained to them in all the Scriptures what referred to him. When they were near the village where they were headed, he made as if he had to go farther. But they insisted, "Stay with us because it is getting to be evening and the day is already waning." He went in to stay with them. When he was at table with them, he took bread, said the blessing, broke it and gave it to them. Then their eyes were opened and they recognized him. But he disappeared from their sight. And they said to one another, "Did not our hearts burn in our breasts as he conversed with us on the way, when he explained the Scriptures to us?"(Luke 24:25-32).

Hermeneutics changes center. The new center is Jesus. It is the Risen One himself who, beginning with Moses and all the prophets, interpreted[16] for them in all the Scriptures what referred to him, thus presenting his figure as the fulfillment of all Scripture. He establishes

---

15 R. C. Tannehill, *Luke, Abingdon* New Testament Commentaries, (Nashville: Abingdon Press, 1996), pp. 352-358.
16 Cf. *Dierméneusen*, Luke 24:27.

an interpretation of Scripture that no longer passes through the interpretation of the Law, but through the understanding of faith in his person.[17]

The insertion of this new center, Jesus and his resurrection, does not give rise to a mystical religiosity, as one might expect given his high spiritual appeal and charismatic profile. His person and words will not alter the articulation of the text-reading pair, but will, on the contrary, produce a reinforcement of the two poles that conform this pair.[18] Indeed, the pole of the text will become even more central as the new reference text, the New Testament, will be built on an interpretation of the Old Testament. The founder of the new faith, who, like any founder could have said completely new words, chooses instead to take up and re-propose words from the Old Testament, offering only a new interpretation of them. He quotes them, comments on them again and again, and, especially at crucial moments, reconnects with them almost obsessively. In the new covenant, the connection with the textual pole is not diluted but strengthened. The textual bond becomes twofold. On the one hand, fidelity is demanded in the face of the new text created by the apostles; on the other hand, the other text, the Old Testament, from which the apostles elaborated theirs, is confirmed.

From the perspective of the reader, a revolution arises because the reader-corporate of the Old Testament is gradually replaced by the reader-individual promoted by the New Testament. This reader is asked for the first time for allegiance only to God through his conscience. No longer the ethnic, political or even religious mediation of the group. The increased value of the text, by virtue of the presence of Jesus' own words, does not at all obscure the dynamic role of the reader, but even seems to guarantee and demand it. What emerges is a legitimized and empowered reader. No longer will the people alone legitimately read and interpret the text. This privilege will be granted to each individual believer. In the new covenant, the reader will become the load-bearing pivot in

---

17 F. B. Craddock, Luca, (*"Luke"*), (Turin: Claudiana, 2002), pp. 365-374.
18 D. L. Bock, *Luke* (2) *9:51-24:53*, Baker Exegetical Commentary on the New Testament, (Ada: Baker Academic, 2010), pp. 1903-1924.

the elaboration of meaning. He is the instance on which the hold of the whole interpretive framework rests. He is given the mission to go and preach by interpreting, educating and contextualizing the message of Jesus.[19] Every believer has become a priest by virtue of the universal priesthood introduced by Christ, which provides that between the individual believer and God there is no mediation other than that of his own conscience. Yet even this revolution will not break the text-reader pair, for that reader will continue to be qualified only as the reader of a text that precedes him and imposes itself on him with supreme authority.

In Christian hermeneutics the new centrality of Jesus reinforces the connection between text and reader in a new and innovative way. But the "text-centric" tendency of Old Testament hermeneutics not only does not disappear but is reinforced, albeit with a different sign. And it is reinforced through two new mechanisms.

1. One is recognize in Jesus and his words the supreme revelation of God. Just as the apostles will ground their authority in connection with Christ, so hermeneutics will become "Christocentric" for the same reason. Every subsequent interpretation will find its validity in the affirmation and promotion of Christ.

2. The other is that the typical eschatological tension introduced by Christ between the *already* of his resurrection and the *not-yet* of his second coming will be resolved in favor of celebrating the *already* happened. Christian theology, in general, and Christian hermeneutics, grounded in the risen Christ and *Pantocrator*, will tend to accentuate the dimension of salvation and meaning already acquired because they are irreversibly guaranteed by Christ's victory. In New Testament hermeneutics, we are dealing with a typical "text-centric" hermeneutic guaranteed no longer by the community of faith around the Torah, as was the case in the first covenant, but by the victorious Jesus. The "text-centeredness" of the hermeneutics of the New Testament is christologically and eschatologically justified. The great attention given to the reader as an individual, introduced by the theological and hermeneutical revolution brought about by Jesus, will remain only in the state of latency. This individual

---

19   Matthew 28:18-20.

consciousness will not explode in full force because the cultural context did not allow it. That context remained transversely, inside and outside the church, a corporate context whose goal was the stability of meaning guaranteed precisely by the group.

c. *Patristic-Medieval Hermeneutics*

In the early Christian centuries, we see the emergence of important and well-differentiated schools of religious thought, both theologically and hermeneutically. Let us pause to briefly consider two of them because of their importance territorially and theologically.

- *The school of Alexandria*[20]

Especially with Origin,[21] Greek patristics elaborated a very refined dogmatic and scriptural hermeneutics, with the assumption of allegory as a distinctive hermeneutical method.[22] The difference between the "spiritual sense" and the "literal sense" of Scripture, corresponds for Origen to the difference between the soul and the body, and essentially determines all Alexandrian hermeneutics. In Alexandria, Platonism with its dualism is imposed. It is the "spiritual sense" that matters and is decisive in interpretive logic. Alexandrian hermeneutics is, to all intents and purposes, a spiritualist hermeneutics whose very medium and guarantor is allegory. The spiritualist theology that stands out in Alexandria does so by virtue of that specific kind of hermeneutics.

Between theology and hermeneutics, there is no purely extrinsic and instrumental relationship. Hermeneutics and its typification is

---

20 P. Tillich, *A History of Christian Thought. From Its Judaic and Hellenistic Origins to Existentialism,* (New York: Touchstone, 1972), pp. 84-88; T. Lane, *A Concise History of Christian Thought,* (Grand Rapids: Baker Academic, 2006*)*, pp. 53-58; L. Berkhof, *The History of Christian Doctrines,* (Grand Rapids: Baker Book House, 1992), pp. 70-76; J.L. Gonzalez, *Christian Thought Revisited. Three Types of Theology,* (Nashville: Abingdon Press, 1990), pp. 23-28.
21 K. Heussi, *Kompendium der Kirchengeschichte,* (Tübingen: J.C.B. Mohr, 1988), pp. 17-19.
22 Philo had previously set the school in Alexandria. His use of allegory had been central and massive.

already a theological exercise that is articulated according to very specific presuppositions. To every theology about God corresponds a very specific hermeneutic of the same sign. Likewise, every hermeneutic is always an extension of a conception of God that precedes and grounds it. A long line of territorial churches, especially but not only in the Middle Ages, would draw on this more spiritualist approach, taking the statements of this School of Alexandria in part or in full.

- *The school of Antioch*[23]

Theodore of Mopsuestia rejected Origen's allegorical Platonism, which saw all historical reality only as a symbol of a deeper and higher reality. Drawing on Aristotelian hermeneutics, he showed greater concern for an exegesis of a historical, grammatical and philological kind. Against the spiritualist idealism of the Alexandrian school, the Antioch school will assert the validity of history, concreteness and "literal sense." Antiochene hermeneutics is historical hermeneutics whose go-between and guarantor is the literal interpretation of the text. Once again we note, even for this theological school of Antioch, the strong solidarity that exists between hermeneutical strategy and theological orientation.

So strong is this connection that we could almost say that it is not theology that chooses its own hermeneutics, but it is hermeneutics that founds theology and typifies it in its distinctive features and main thrust. Unlike the school of Alexandria, the school of Antioch will not have many followers during the Middle Ages. In terms of its basic perspective, however, it will compensate for this diluted and sober presence with a strong and widespread presence in the early modern period.

The conflict between the Alexandrian and Antiochian schools had the positive effect of bringing out a plurality of possible meanings of Scripture and also gave the opportunity to formulate some criteria for reading and interpretation. The four senses of Scripture[24] and also the

---

23 P. Tillich, *A History...* Op. cit., pp. 80-84; T. Lane, *A Concise...Op.* cit., pp. 57-60; L. Berkhof, *The History...*Op. cit., pp. 103-108; J.L. Gonzalez, *Christian Thought...*Op. cit., pp. 28-33.
24 W. Jeanrond, *L'ermeneutica teologica...*Op. cit., pp. 27-30.

principle of the "rule of faith" were gradually imposed.[25] Between the "literal sense" and the "spiritual sense," patristic hermeneutics as a whole favored the latter. In patristics, it was not only the intra-biblical relationship between the various possible senses that determined the hermeneutical orientation. The second front arose in connection with extra-biblical instances and the relationship that the biblical text had to maintain with them. The patristic hermeneutic circle composed of the "rule of faith," "tradition," and "magisterium" found its most accomplished expression in Augustine.[26] This hermeneutic will become the interpretive model throughout the Middle Ages. For Augustine, only the "rule of faith" expressed by the articles of the *Creed*, together with *Tradition* and the *Magisterium*, leads to the understanding of the "spiritual meaning" of Scripture in all its fullness.[27] Thus the typical patristic paradox is configured, where a wealth of interpretation of the Bible in its various levels of meaning is, however, subordinated to the extra-biblical instances of which the Magisterium and Tradition possess a monopoly.

The patristic principle of the dual sense of Scripture, literal or historical, spiritual or mystical, will be developed by medieval authors in all its hermeneutical subtleties, as H. De Lubac's classic study shows.[28] In contrast to patristic hermeneutics, Scholasticism will privilege the "literal sense" without erasing the plurality of senses of Scripture. Thomas Aquinas will also value the literal sense, but it will not be identified or reduced to the univocal sense; and he,

---

25 W. Jeanrond, *Ibid*, pp. 19,20.
26 W. Jeanrond, *Ibid*, pp. 41-47. Cf. "De doctrina christiana" by Augustine of Hippo (354-430).
27 Augustine, Confessions, I, 1,1.
28 Cf. H. de Lubac, *Exégèse médiévale: Les quatre sens de l'Ecriture*, (Paris : Aubier, 1959). The first of the four volumes of *Medieval Exegesis* by Jesuit theologian Henri De Lubac (1896-1991) is devoted to the study of the four senses of Scripture. The best known formula is the one handed down to us by Nicholas of Lyra around 1330: "*Littera gesta docet, quid credas allegoria, moralis quid agas, quo tendas anagogia.*" The literal sense refers to the deeds or history, the allegorical sense goes in search of metaphorical meaning, the moral or tropological sense targets the transposition of the Word into concrete life, and the anagogical sense seeks mystical and spiritual meaning.

like the entire Middle Ages, will continue to defend the principle of the multiple senses of Scripture.[29] The separation of the literal sense from the other possible senses and, above all, the identification of the spiritual sense with the literal sense, will come later, with the arrival of Protestantism. Erasmus of Rotterdam, while agreeing, at least initially, with many of the theses introduced by the Reformers, will take a more critical stance in the face of this strong emphasis on the literal sense, defending the twofold sense, literal and spiritual, of Scripture.

The impression is that medieval hermeneutics, with the abundance of meanings it creates, especially through widespread allegorical interpretation and with its privileging of parallel avenues of spiritual meaning over the Bible, has finally accomplished and realized the shift toward a reader-centered hermeneutics. Instead, even medieval hermeneutics remains to all intents and purposes a "text-centered" hermeneutic, despite its innovations. Although it moves away from the Bible as the sole source of meaning, and although it departs from literal interpretation, the basic mechanism is still the same. Meaning is stable because it is already given in the foundational text and is stable in and through the church, which claims for itself the monopoly of its reading. The meanings produced in the Middle Ages are not new meanings, but mere extensions of what is already included in the text. In this case, the stability of meaning rather than from Christ (as in New Testament "text-centered" hermeneutics) will be provided by the church. It is the church that is the stabilizing element in the interpretive process. In the Middle Ages, a "text-centric" hermeneutic is configured, but one that is ecclesiological in nature. It is the church that guarantees the meaning of the foundational text of the Christian faith and makes it stable.

Despite the diversity of accents and angles, premodern hermeneutics, have maintained a common conception of the hermeneutic circle. The cross-cutting element that unites them is

---

29 W. Jeanrond, *L'ermeneutica teologica*...Op. cit., pp. 26-30. See also G. Mura, *Ermeneutica e verità. Storia e problemi della filosofia dell'interpretazione*, ("*Hermeneutics and Truth. History and Problems of the Philosophy of Interpretation*"), (Rome: Città Nuova Editrice, 1990), pp. 101-122.

embodied in the priority given to the text rather than the reader. It is the text that appears as king. The reader has only to apply what he reads. The strength of the text resides in its fullness and completeness. The meanings are already there. They are not to be invented. The reader can and must become active only in the application of the meanings discovered, but from the standpoint of meaning-making he remains passive. The text, and this is even more valid for the Bible, already has all the meanings ready. The text is sacred because it conveys stable, proven meanings. That the reader does not see them because he does not know them or because he has not yet made them his own, does not detract from the fact that they are already there, complete, defined and definitive. They are enshrined in the perfection of an unchanging text. The text bases its authority precisely on this. If it did not have the stable meanings, it would not be an authoritative text. Its authority is based on the completeness and definiteness of the meaning it offers.

Not only the Bible, but all pre-modern texts are sacred because they convey a meaning that is not to be twisted and questioned. It is already there and it imposes itself with its own weight. They possess the stable register of what life and the life of faith must be. That is why the mechanism of reading is a highlighting of what is already there, and that it is only a matter of discovering, revealing and bringing out through reading.

This understanding of the stability of meaning that the text guarantees is certainly not just a linguistic issue. It is part of a broader cultural vision and one that is typical of the Middle Ages[30] The hermeneutics of a historical period cannot be dissociated from its cultural matrix. It is always, with relative innovations and shifts, an expression of the cultural model that nourishes it. The cultural model of the Middle Ages and the entire pre-modern period, is the "holistic" not "atomistic" view of reality and the world. In this view, it is not the individual who can be the bearer of meaning but only the group. Between group, cosmos, family, church, God and text, there

---

30 Cf. J. Le Goff, *Le Dieu du moyen Âge. Entretiens avec Jean-Luc Pouthier*, (Paris : Bayard, 2003), pp. 24-32; *Pour un autre Moyen Âge. Temps, travail et culture en Occident*, (Paris : Gallimard, 1977), pp. 43-54.

is a compact and unbreakable sodality. The logic of that fellowship is embodied in the belief that the individual is preceded by a sense that is greater than himself and that he cannot create. This sense is guaranteed by these transpersonal demands. The reader is called upon to be not a "creator" but merely a "ferryman" of a sense that does not belong to him and that he can only undergo, grasp and transmit.

The stability of group life must necessarily be matched by a hermeneutic that reflects that stability. Whether the text is secular or religious, Catholic or heretical, it matters little. That is not where the foundational trait lies. All pre-modern texts, and the Bible all the more so, serve as stabilizing artifacts. A text cannot overturn the meaning and arrangement of a culture, but it is born and articulated within it. Every hermeneutic is a child of its time.

The individual, whether he reads a book or lives his life, has only to find his place in the world. This is a world that he did not create but that precedes him. The medieval reader, like the medieval believer, is a being preceded. Preceded by a world that already carries with it in a predetermined way the meanings of everything that exists. The text, like the world and the reality outside the text, is a stable reality ready only to be inhabited, not to be constructed.

Two realities par excellence embody this premodern stability: the group and the cosmos. The group, and only it in its backbone, offers safe haven and certainty to the individual, who by nature can only be lost, hesitant and adrift. Only inclusion in the group saves the individual from insignificance. It saves him precisely because it does not even offer him a choice. The free choice to belong to this or that group would already be the negation of the group. The group is not chosen. In the group one is born. The individual is already born into the group, and any formal choice can only be a confirmation, not a decision whether to belong or not. The group precedes the individual as stable sense precedes reading.

The same thing happens with the cosmos. The cosmos is the primary reality from where the group takes its stability. The order of the cosmos is predetermined and does not depend on the choice of individuals. This order is hierarchical as in nature, and salvation is realized only when in that order one knows how to find one's place. Premodern communities are essentially all cosmo-centric. They recognize that there is an order that precedes them and is found in the cosmos. This is a cosmos created by God for those who are Christians. It is an eternal cosmos independent of God for those who are not Christians. In either case, the cosmos has a complete, stable and ordered outline.

The text only prolongs, in the act of interpretation, the same structure of stability given by the cosmos and the group. At the cultural level Cosmos, group and text are parallel expressions of the same admiration and submission to the mesmerizing charm of the world's stability.

3. *Modern Period: "Reader-Centric Hermeneutics"*[31]

What changes with modernity? It changes the emphasis of hermeneutics. The centrality from the text gives way to the new and revolutionary centrality of the reader. The hermeneutic circle is turned upside down. The variations and modulations of schools and thinkers, important but secondary to this epochal change, should not make us lose sight of this essential and fundamental shift in perspective. Behind this shift of emphasis from the text to the reader lies something that is even more central. This is that is the focus no longer on "stability" but rather on the "fluidity" of meaning. Let us sketch a concise description of some moments that determine the lineaments of interpretation in modernity.

a. *Protestant Hermeneutics and Hermeneutics in "Early Modernity"*

Some particular features will characterize the arrival and establishment of modern hermeneutics, such as the innovation introduced by the Reformers in their approach to reading the Bible, which becomes a book available and accessible to all. These include emphasis on and defense of the individual believer as an

---

31 R.E. Palmer, *Hermeneutics. Interpretation Theory in Schleiermacher, Dilthey, Heidegger and Gadamer,* (Evanston: Northwestern University Press, 1969), pp. 33-45.

articulator of meaning; enfranchisement of secular hermeneutics from biblical hermeneutics; development and enhancement of research methodologies in related fields, such as philology, history, jurisprudence; the emergence of historical sciences and the formation of an autonomous hermeneutics of a philosophical character by F. Schleiermacher.

The affirmation of philosophical hermeneutics will be a long process that cannot completely disregard the links that even in modernity it had with biblical hermeneutics, partly because of the impetus received from the Reformation.[32] Luther elaborated a hermeneutics focused on the relationship between "word and faith" in antithesis to scholastic hermeneutics. He strongly united "spiritual sense" with "literal sense." Very early, in 1517,[33] Luther rejected the doctrine of the fourfold sense of Scripture for two reasons. First, to reject the explanatory and dogmatic allegorism of Scholasticism, and second, to abandon the strong partnership that Catholicism had built over time between the "rule of Faith," "Tradition," and the "Magisterium." For Luther, faith will be the only principle underlying the interpretation of Scripture.[34] We are faced with the birth and affirmation of a concrete and existential approach in biblical reading.

Luther will assign primacy in the interpretation of Scripture to practical application,[35] in sharp contrast to scholastic hermeneutics, which privileged the moment of explanatory analysis.[36] The Word of God must have real, actual and immediate efficacy in the life of the believer. The Pauline antithesis between Letter and Spirit[37] is radicalized by assigning to faith, the sign of the presence in the believer of the Spirit of Christ, the task of understanding the meaning of Scripture. Beyond exegetical methodologies and rational analyses, the understanding of Christ in faith will become decisive for the understanding of the historical Christ. The Council of Trent censured

---

32 A. S. Jensen, *Theological Hermeneutics,* Op. cit., pp. 64-77.
33 T. Lane, *A concise History...,* Op. cit., pp. 155-160.
34 S. Nitti, Lutero, (*"Luther"*), (Rome: Salerno editrice, 2017), pp. 229-255.
35 W. Jeanrond, *L'ermeneutica teologica...* Op. cit., pp. 30-34.
36 T. Lane, *A concise History...* Op. cit., pp. 103-144.
37 Cf. 2 Co 3:6.

Luther's hermeneutical principle as subjectivistic, contrasting it with the binding principle of Catholic hermeneutics, which assigns to Tradition and the Magisterium the task of establishing the true meaning of Scripture.[38] With Luther, the concrete and pragmatic approach of faith in reading the Bible is affirmed.

The innovative and propulsive force of this immediate approach to Scripture introduced by Luther introduced a limitation which emerged only over time. The "spiritual sense" favored by Luther needed a more solid foundation.[39] Thus a technical interest in languages and translation work gradually developed, initiating a process of textual improvement never known before. Philip Melanchthon,[40] humanist and disciple of Luther, introduced the canons proper to literary hermeneutics into scriptural exegesis. However, we owe the first edition of the Greek text of the New Testament (1516) to Erasmus of Rotterdam[41] who, completing the work begun by Luther, carried out intensive translation and editing of classical texts.

This pragmatic orientation of faith, which emerged in Luther and was consolidated by the pragmatic linguistic interest of the philologists, had further consolidation by the non-speculative and anti-metaphysical rationalism that would take over with the Enlightenment. This rationalism in the reading of ancient texts will be highly critical of the Bible but, paradoxically, will not change its register; rather, it will end up reinforcing the concretism and pragmatism in the reading of texts inaugurated by the Reformers. In the 18th century, at the height of the Enlightenment, the privilege and primacy of sacred hermeneutics will be challenged, and this will lead to the progressive and total emancipation of secular hermeneutics.[42]

---

38 K. Heussi, *Kompendium der Kirchengeschichte...Op.* cit., pp. 337-369. The fourth session of the Council of Trent (1546).
39 A. Prosperi, *Lutero. Gli anni della fede e della libertà*, ("*Luther. The Years of Faith and Freedom"*), Mondadori, Milan 2017, pp. 120-131.
40 T. Lane, *A concise History...*Op. cit., pp. 160-162. See A.S. Jensen, *Theological Hermeneutics, Op. cit.*, pp. 64-77.
41 T. Lane, *Ibid,* pp. 151-154. See A.S. Jensen, *Ibid*, p. 66.
42 A.S. Jensen, *Ibid*, pp. 78-89.

Already in the previous century, Baruch Spinoza,[43] starting from the principles of the new rationalism that upheld the universality of reason and its undisputed primacy over faith, had asserted that the norm of biblical exegesis can only be the light of common reason.[44] Gotthold E. Lessing,[45] also because of the rise of the new philological disciplines, capable of ascertaining with scientific rigor the authenticity and authority of a text, will declare in his book *The Christianity of Reason* that it is solely up to reason to determine the canons and principles of interpretation, even in the field of Scripture.[46] He explicitly replaces reference to faith and the Spirit, characteristic of Protestant hermeneutics, with reference to the only hermeneutical criterion now acceptable: that of universal reason, the only element that unites the text and its interpreter. The consequence was that, in the sphere of Scripture, a rationalistic and demythicizing interpretation will develop. In the secular sphere, texts with greater rational or cultural content will be privileged. But the anti-speculative and pragmatic orientation of both is the same.

At last, after a long and troubled process, hermeneutics will assert its philosophical autonomy, clearly distinguishing itself both from sectorial hermeneutics (exegetical, philological, legal) and from those attempts to elaborate an abstract universal hermeneutics still present in the 18th century. The affirmation of the centrality of reason, embodied in a new and autonomous subject (reader-centrism), and the anti-speculative direction of a concrete and efficient reading strategy (hermeneutic pragmatism) by now are already fully integrated into the structure and direction of modern hermeneutics. The formal birth of philosophical hermeneutics with Schleiermacher

---

43 H. J. Kraus, *L'Antico Testamento nella ricerca storico-critica dalla Riforma a oggi, ("The Old Testament in Historical-Critical Research from the Reformation to the Present")*, (Bologna: Il Mulino, 1975), pp. 102-108.
44 Cf. B. Spinoza, *Tractatus theologico-politicus* (1670).
45 W. G. Kümmel, *Il nuovo testamento. Storia dell'indagine scientifica sul problema neotestamentario, ("The New Testament. History of the Scholarly Investigation of the New Testament Problem")*, (Bologna: Il Mulino, 1976), pp. 102-107. Cf. A. S. Jensen, *Ibid*, pp. 78-89.
46 Cf. *Das Christentum der Vernunft* (1753).

will only take note of this situation and have the merit of making this address comprehensible in a philosophical program built all around the maxim "understanding the understanding." According to Paul Ricœur's historical description, this definitive affirmation of philosophical hermeneutics will take place in two related but distinct stages, in which especially four names will play a central and foundational role: on the one hand, F. Schleiermacher and W. Dilthey, on the other, M. Heidegger and H.G. Gadamer.[47]

b. *The Foundation of Philosophical Hermeneutics and the Transition from "Epistemolgical" to "Ontological" Hermeneutics*

- *Friedrich Schleiermacher*[48] (1768-1834)

Schleiermacher is credited with the foundation of modern hermeneutics. In addition to the first formulation of a philosophical hermeneutics understood as a reflection on the meaning of human understanding through language, Schleiermacher is also credited with some central hermeneutic notions, foremost among them that of the "hermeneutic circle." With this, Schleiermacher also establishes a second hermeneutic principle: the principle of intuition (*einfühlung*), by which he indicates that beyond external rules and methodological canons, hermeneutics is characterized as a process of identification with the author's interiority. To truly understand a text, it is necessary to understand all that cultural, poetic, religious, literary and spiritual world that presided over its creation. It is necessary in a sense to descend, through a process of identification and intuition, into the interiority of the author of the work, so as to inwardly relive all that spiritual process that presided over his literary creation.

Schleiermacher[49] was driven initially to elaborate his hermeneutical philosophy by a pastoral concern. He was a theologian with a strong motivation to communicate the gospel in its essence and

---

47 P. Ricœur, *Ermeneutica filosofica...* Op. cit., pp. 13-52.
48 A.S. Jensen, *Theological Hermeneutics...*Op. cit., pp. 90-104; R.E. Palmer, *Hermeneutics...*Op. cit., pp. 84-97; J. Grondin, *Introduction to Philosophical Hermeneutics...*Op. cit., pp. 63-75.
49 A.S. Jensen, Op. cit. pp. 90-104.

in language persuasive to contemporary man.⁵⁰ He aimed to make 19th-century men formed by an Enlightenment culture understand the message conveyed by ancient texts written by authors formed by a predominantly mythical culture.

Schleiermacher introduced a strong point of rupture. This rupture is articulated not so much at the level of a radical rationality, but rather in tying interpretation to the individual interpreter and not to the group. It is at this level that the criticism made of him by Catholicism resides. This is disregarding tradition. He who says tradition says group. In Schleiermacher, in fact, it is no longer the group nor tradition, but only the individual that guarantees the articulation of meaning in the interpretive act. It will later be Gadamer, too, from a more secular perspective, who will make the same criticism of him, recalling that tradition is an indispensable horizon in the articulation and understanding of meaning. Gadamer and the "new hermeneutics" will understand the interpretive process as an intersubjective relationship.

The most severe criticism of Schleiermacher has come from the Protestant side. This critique was articulated by Karl Barth⁵¹ in his famous commentary on the Epistle to the Romans,⁵² where he contests Schleiermacher⁵³ (and all Protestant defined liberal theology that is inspired by his hermeneutics), of turning the Word of God into human words, thus faith into culture, Revelation into philosophy. Referring to the theses of S. Kierkegaard, Barth considers it fundamental for the theologian and the Christian to make a radical choice between the Word of God and the word of man, because faith does not come from a cultural exercise of interpretation. The Word of God is a sign of contradiction for every culture, because it

---

50 F. Schleiermacher, *On Religion,* Op. cit.; especially important is the first of the five speeches (pp. 41-63) where Schleiermacher describes his interlocutors; in the second speech he describes the essence and nature of religion.
51 W. Jeanrond, Op. cit. pp. 127-137.
52 Cf. K. Barth, *Der Römerbrief,* (Zürich: Theologischer Verlag, 1922), pp. 261-276.
53 K. Barth, *Protestant Theology in the Nineteenth Century. Its Background and History,* (Grand Rapids: Eerdmans, 2001), pp. 411-459.

contradicts every worldly and philosophical attempt to speak about God. This is why Barth aims to free theology from the "Babylonian bondage" represented by philosophy, particularly in the form of Schleiermacher's hermeneutics.

In the work *Fides quaerens intellectum*,[54] Barth argues that the absolute and unconditional starting point for speaking about God is not philosophy or the cultural categories of one's time, but God Himself, whose Revelation is the foundation of faith, which is pure initiative of grace. Faith is a sign of a pre-choice by God, and not a human choice due to efforts of interpretation. Barth's critique of Schleiermacher's hermeneutics[55] and of theology as "human discourse about God," could not be more direct. His criticism is also directed at Catholic positions based on *analogia entis*, to which Barth contrasts an unconditional *analogia fidei*, with which he wants to emphasize the infinite distance between the Word of God and the human word, between the free gift of faith, the absolute starting point of theology, and all forms of culture and theological hermeneutics.

- <u>Wilhelm Dilthey</u>[56] (1833-1911)

Dilthey will continue the foundational work of philosophical hermeneutics through the specification of its nature, beginning with the distinction between explaining and understanding, between the sciences of nature and the sciences of spirit. Together with Schleiermacher, Wilhelm Dilthey[57] equally represents the first stage of a hermeneutic philosophy, which opposes the traditional "art of interpretation" to the study and analysis of the very fact of "understanding," and indeed conceives hermeneutics primarily as a reflection on the meaning of understanding and interpreting. It is with regard to a philosophy of understanding that Dilthey sets up the distinction, which later became classical, between

---

54 Cf. K. Barth, *Anselm: Fides Quaerens Intellectum. Anselm's Proof of the Existence of God in the Context of His Theological Scheme*, (Pittsburg: Pickwick Publications, 2004).
55 K. Barth, *Der Römerbrief,* Op. cit., p. 225.
56 A. S. Jensen, *Theological Hermeneutics.* Op. cit., pp. 105-114; R.E. Palmer, *Hermeneutics. Interpretation...*Op. cit., pp. 98-123; J. Grondin, *Introduction to Philosophical Hermeneutics,* Op. cit., pp. 76-90.
57 A.S. Jensen, *Op. cit.* pp. 105-109.

explaining (*erklären*) and understanding (*verstehen*), between natural sciences (*Naturwissenschaften*) and spiritual sciences (*Geisteswissenschaften*). "We explain nature, but we understand spiritual life" was Dilthey's motto. [58] While it is the task of the natural sciences to make evident, through the protocols of scientific explanation, the laws that govern physical and natural events, the spiritual sciences have the arduous task of understanding the whole vast world of man's spiritual expressions, from art to religion, from philosophy to culture, products of the spirituality of man who is essentially a historical being, not reducible to an entity of nature and not explicable through the protocols of the natural sciences.

The notion of life (*leben*), as well as those of vital experience (*erleben*) and lived experience (*erlebnis*), will become important and fundamental concepts in the context of later developments in vitalistic and phenomenological hermeneutics. Lived experience takes on in Dilthey the meaning of the link between an author's work and his life, in the sense that to truly "understand" a work one must understand the "lived experience" expressed in it. This does not coincide with the author's external life, but rather with his existential experience, which is the "life project" that qualifies his existence and constitutes the most valid context of reference for its interpretation and understanding.

To the various currents of historical positivism in the 19th century, Dilthey contrasts a hermeneutic notion of history as the creative work of subjectivity, and one that cannot be understood without an understanding of the radically historical character of man. Human essence is not determined a priori, but is determined historically through the creative process of his freedom. Hermeneutic understanding, as historical understanding, is therefore temporal, historically determined. Beginning with Dilthey, the hermeneutic problem of understanding thus becomes the problem of "historical understanding," because of the historical character assigned to man, thus also to his interpreting and understanding.

---

58 M. Ferraris, *Storia dell'ermeneutica,* Op. cit., pp. 162-183. Cf. W. Dilthey, Die Entstehung der Hermeneutik, (Berlin: 1900), p. 144.

For Schleiermacher and Dilthey, at the center of the interpretive process, albeit with important nuances, is the interpreter (Reader) and his or her "understanding." We are faced, in essence, with two "Reader-centric" hermeneutics. This determines the epistemological orientation of interpretation in their project. Here, at this level, lies the strength and limitation of their enterprise. The strength lies in this focus on understanding and in the rigor of describing it with technical and formal categories of high precision, equal to those used in the natural sciences. It is also here that their great limitation emerges, which also becomes the limitation of all modern hermeneutics in its first phase.

This hermeneutics suffers from a major ontological deficit that neither Schleiermacher nor Dilthey was able to correct. According to P. Ricœur's reading, only with Heidegger and Gadamer will this deficit be filled, but in a bad way. In their solution of the ontological problem both will create a new one. It is the problem of minimization and trivialization of the critical instance, which every hermeneutic must always be able to integrate into its own project. Let us briefly describe the ontological corrective of the hermeneutics proposed by Heidegger and Gadamer.

– _Martin Heidegger_[59] (1889-1976)

Martin Heidegger shifted the central problem in his philosophical hermeneutics from the interpretation of texts to ontological understanding.[60] He regarded this as a direct being-in-the-world, not mediated by texts or other symbols, thus a more authentic being and not simply as an empirical presupposition for knowledge. Hermeneutics becomes analytic of the conditions of existence, no longer as one of the possible ways of understanding or knowing through authentic interpretation. It is the essential feature of existence itself, since man is a continuous self-interpreting being.

When we read a text and interpret it, we do not accumulate important information to know better how to move and orient

---

59 A.S. Jensen, _Theological Hermeneutics,_ Op. cit., pp. 115-134; R.E. Palmer, _Hermeneutics,_ Op. cit., pp. 124-139; R.E. Palmer, _Hermeneutics,_ Op cit., pp. 140-161; J. Grondin, _Introduction to Philosophical..._Op cit., pp. 91-105.
60 M. Ferraris, _Storia dell'ermeneutica,_ Op. cit., pp. 237-263.

ourselves in life. Understanding is a sign that we are already rooted in life, before we can develop reasoning on that belonging. The typical division between the knowing subject and the known object, which presupposes any kind of cognitive approach, is preceded in Heidegger by a prior state of binding and belonging that represents his ontological extract. Hermeneutic understanding cannot be reduced to knowing more. It articulates more at the base, a presence in the world, a mode of being.

In the second Heidegger, the Heidegger of the *Kehre* (turning point), this ontological dimension will become even more substantial. The question of being has been flawed from Plato onward because it is Plato who thinks of being as an entity. This is where the misplacement of the ontological difference between being and entities comes from. For Plato it is the subject who sees truth and goes in search of it, but he ends up tampering with it because he makes it an object. This is quite the opposite of what happened with the pre-Socratic philosophers, for whom truth is not grasped by the understanding gaze, but is itself revealed by itself (*aletheia*). It is not the subject that reveals truth. Heidegger follows the pre-Socratics in the non-objective definition of Truth. Truth is an unveiling and a hiding. This means that Heidegger decenters the focus of reflection from the subject to being.

Man is not the center, he is only a conduit of being. It is being that takes the initiative to reveal itself. In response to a text by Sartre entitled *"Existentialism is a Humanism"*, in which he asserts that at the center of the action of a reality, in which there is no god, is man, Heidegger responds with his *Letter on Humanism*,[61] in 1947, in which he asserts that for him at the center is not man, who is only a vehicle of being; at the center is being that manifests itself. Heidegger is thus one of the most important figures of anti-humanism. Heidegger's philosophy can be said to be "post-humanistic," because it places other structures of ontological character as priority and before man.

---

61 M. Heidegger, *Basic Writings,* David Farrell Krell (ed.), (San Francisco: Harper, 1992), pp. 213-265.

– *Hans-Georg Gadamer*[62] (1900-2002)
Gadamer would follow in the same wake begun by Heidegger and aim, like him, to correct the risk of a cognitive drift in modern hermeneutics.[63] From the very first pages of his major work, *Truth and Method*,[64] he made it clear how his hermeneutic reflection aimed, more radically, to reveal the universal and ontological character of the phenomenon of understanding. In this sense, Gadamer's attention, in the wake of Heideggerian teaching is directed primarily to the figure of pre-comprehension (*Vorverständnis*). Pre-comprehension is the event where meaning is attributed to Being. Knowing here is a sense to some extent pre-conceived. This is not entirely arbitrary, since it reflects a dimension of belonging that precedes and founds a subsequent relation of knowing.

The focus on the necessary character of pre-understanding in all forms of knowledge leads Gadamer to distance himself from the traditional Enlightenment gnoseological view, according to which knowledge consists in holding that the subject is quite distinct from the object, so that knowledge is all the more adequate the sharper the mutual autonomy of the two terms. Indeed, according to Gadamer, if every researcher begins his typical activity only from a pre-understanding of the meaning of what he proposes to know, then it must be agreed that no original separation can be given between the two terms and, ultimately, that they exist from the beginning within a single dimension.[65]

The criticism that P. Ricœur makes of Heidegger and Gadamer, beyond the undoubted benefit of having given an ontological

---

62 A. S. Jensen, *Theological Hermeneutics*, Op. cit., pp. 135-160; R.E. Palmer, *Hermeneutics. Interpretation...* Op. cit, pp. 162-193; R.E. Palmer, *Ibid*, pp. 194-217; J. Grondin, *Introduction to Philosophical...*Op. cit., pp. 106-123.
63 M. Ferraris, *Storia dell'ermeneutica*, Op. cit., pp. 265-276.
64 H.-G. Gadamer, *Verità e metodo*, *("Truth and Method")*, (Milan: Bompiani, 2000).
65 As Gianni Vattimo points out well, in reference to Gadamer, every interpretation is given within an Überlieferungsgeschehen (a historical tradition), which in Vattimo's case is that of the Catholic church, to which he explicitly refers. G. Vattimo, *Essere e dintorni*, (*"Being and Surroundings"*), (Milan: La nave di Teseo, 2018), pp. 325ff.

foundation to understanding, is that of skipping too easily the dimension of cognitive and analytic verification that any hermeneutics must instead always be able to protect and guarantee. Gadamer and Heidegger's position cannot be described as "reader-centric," however, the extreme, anti-critical ontological corrective they propose leaves the "reader-centrism" of modern hermeneutics intact and, by leaving it intact, paradoxically reinforces it. Even after Heidegger and Gadamer, the "reader-centeredness" of contemporary hermeneutics has not diminished. It has even increased. The only difference is that today it coexists with a parallel ontological direction inspired by, among others, Heidegger and Gadamer. This does not correct it but paradoxically keeps it alive.

What really changes with the arrival of modern hermeneutics in its various moments and manifestations compared to ancient and medieval hermeneutics? Our reading hypothesis is that modern hermeneutics produces a radical shift that essentially marks the transition from the realm of the "strong text" (text-centrism), typical of the pre-modern period, to the "creative reader" (reader-centrism) typical of contemporary hermeneutics. Modern hermeneutics is not only a chronological event. It represents the site of a new foundation; the foundation of the subject capable of standing rationally before the known object. Beyond Schleiermacher's specific contribution in introducing new hermeneutic categories, this new foundation is the same foundation that is also articulated in other parallel modern disciplines, such as sociology, psychology, This includes all the other modern disciplines that often retained the old name, but were in fact already taking shape as strongly rational disciplines having the subject as their center.

This centrality of the reader as a rational subject was not and is not always evident, because modern hermeneutics is also simultaneously the period in which textual criticism was born and thus attention, care and obsession with the accuracy of the text was established. Modernity is the period when scientific attention to the text is enhanced and refined. For the first time, there will be critical texts of ancient works, including the Bible. Yet, the implicit and primordial assumption does not decay. All modern hermeneutics, despite its enormous attention to the text, remains a "reader-centered" hermeneutic.

This fact will not leave the hermeneutic circle intact. While preserving it, the status of the text itself will undergo profound change. The definition of the text as a stable text could not survive. The text becomes fluid. This is a system that offers the reader only a set of initial ingredients and suggestions, which it will be up to the omnipotent reader to complete in a new and original project. Although we physically read the same Bible, in reality, our Bible is different from what the apostles and even the Reformers read. Our constructivist understanding of reality and the Bible leads us to see in the Bible only the inspired ingredients of a "cake" that is not given in advance but that we must create ourselves. Even those who refuse to adapt to the current worldview in biblical interpretation are actually already widely applying a constructivist approach in all other levels of life.

This is understandable only if we analyze modern hermeneutics in the context of modern culture. Modern culture introduces a radical shift from a "cosmocentric" view, based on the stability of the world, to an "anthropocentric" view of life, based on movement and change. In this new perspective, the world, life, identities, events and meanings do not exist as finite and fixed realities. They are merely ingredients that each individual is called upon to use in the construction of a particular chosen project. The world, the family, the state, etc. are not houses to be inhabited, but materials to be used in new constructions. The modern and its twin brother, the postmodern world, are "constructivist" in spirit and intention. Hermeneutics could not escape this fate of the culture in which it was born.

c. *Hermeneutics in the "Second Modernity"*

This new phase of modernity is sometimes called postmodernity and sometimes second modernity or late modernity. At the hermeneutic level we will use them as equivalent terms, even though they represent different understandings of this historical period. One would hope that with the arrival of postmodernity the centrality of the reader would diminish or disappear. But this is not what has happened. Postmodernity is an important phenomenon that marks and describes today a new way of standing in front of life and that, in a break with modernity, deconstructs the validity and relevance of the meta-narratives foundational to the various spheres of our contemporary culture. This makes them on the one hand partial, thus no longer transversal and universal, and on the other hand, relative and thus objectively non-binding in the way they were in early modernity.

Modern culture, in its early Enlightenment period up to the first half of the 20th century, despite its secularism, would not have changed course with respect to the explanatory and realizable confidence of human reason. It would still have believed in the possibility of explaining and, consequently, changing the world from an objective, rational and totalizing human perspective. Today, however, ideology, any kind of ideology, has entered a crisis by implosion from within and not solely from external causes. This would be the logic that marks the advent of postmodernity or second modernity.

Something important has also happened in hermeneutics. We are no longer dealing with the same hermeneutics. The problem is to specify what has changed and what has remained as before. Our reading hypothesis is that the distinctive feature of modern hermeneutics has not gone away. The typical "reader-centered" character of modern hermeneutics has not changed with the arrival of postmodernity. Only its justification has changed.

Here we need to pause briefly to describe the true scope of postmodernity so that we can then connect it with hermeneutics. There is a diatribe about how much has really changed with the arrival of postmodernity. In Anglo-Saxon circles and in philosophy people more willingly speak of the arrival of a new era, postmodernity. In European circles and in the social sciences, especially in sociology, people prefer to speak of a second modernity to identify this new historical period, which took over roughly from the 1970s onward. Sociologists speak of late modernity (Giddens), second modernity (Beck, Tourraine) and hypermodernity (Sebastien Charles).

They wish to affirm two things. First, that something has indeed changed since the beginnings of modernity. What has changed is not easy to say. Some speak of the demise of the great ideologies, others of fragmentation, still others of the loss of institutionality, etc. All of these are descriptive of an undeniable change. The psychological-anthropological attitude must also be taken into account. The great confidence of early modernity seems to have been succeeded by an across-the-board distrust. One wonders, however, what came before. Have we lost confidence and as a consequence also lost confidence in the great ideas that were previously evident and imposed themselves on us with their force? Or did the great explanatory systems first collapse and then did human self-confidence also fail?

Anthropological change is just as visible as ideological change. Yet, in the essential data, nothing has changed. If we take some specific areas and elements of modernity, we not only find that these still subsist, but that they have become even more radicalized. This is the thesis of Sebastien Charles[66] regarding four typical characteristics of modernity: individualism, democracy, economics and techno-scientific development. Let us take only one of these four elements as an example: individualism. This has not disappeared, in the so-called postmodernity, but has even gained more ground. Today, in postmodernity, we are even more individualistic. Only the format and perspective of its foundation has changed. The typical pragmatic and optimistic individualism of early modernity has been overlaid by the typical aesthetic and uncertain individualism of late modernity.

What implications does this have for hermeneutics? Basically two. First, the status of the text has changed. The text is neither definitive nor final. The text has become, in its status, even more fluid. It is only a starting point, a kind of initial ingredient that requires new elaboration. Second, the reader has reinforced his presence. This becomes decisive for the elaboration and construction of meaning that without him would remain unconcluded. All contemporary hermeneutics tends to be even more "reader-centric" than it was in Schleiermacher's time.

It is in this light that the rise of the most recent methodologies in textual analysis and exegesis must be seen. For example, the

---

66 S. Charles, *L'hypermoderne expliqué aux enfants*, (Montréal : Liber, 2017), pp. 15-22.

school of "Reader Response Criticism"[67] has shifted the center of gravity completely to the reader's side. The reader becomes an active agent in the creation of meaning, as he or she contributes to the "real existence" of the work and completes its meaning through interpretation. This school of thought argues that literature should be viewed as a performance art in which each reader creates his or her own performance related to the text. Although literary theory has long paid some attention to the role of the reader in creating the meaning and experience of a literary work, it was not until the 1970s, and particularly in the United States and Germany, that this approach became established through the work of Norman Holland, Stanley Fish, Wolfgang Iser, Hans-Robert Jauss, Roland Barthes and others.[68]

We must include Umberto Eco in this list of authors. He will give this new centrality of the reader its most accomplished and articulated form, speaking of the "open" text. The text in his view allows multiple interpretations in a different qualitative sense. This is the sense of creation and not just application of meanings. Here truth is never unambiguous, but is constituted by an infinite interpretative process of objects in which there remains only a "shaping form" that the subject must continually interpret. The work of art itself, meaning both "high" art and mass and popular artistic productions, is never bound to a single and permanent meaning. It needs a continuous interpretive integration of both critics and the common user. The "open" work is a text that allows multiple interpretations. In contrast, a closed text leads the reader to only one interpretation. Later Eco will complete his theory by arguing that the "novel" is a "lazy machine" that must continually renew itself in its meaning through readers' interpretation. Eco says that a text requires and needs someone to help it function, since it is a product whose interpretive fate must be part of its own generative mechanism.[69] Postmodern hermeneutics has radicalized even more the "reader-centeredness"

---

67   A.S. Jensen, *Theological Hermeneutics...Op.* cit., pp. 192-206.
68   P. H. Fry, *Theory of Literature*, (Yale: Yale University Press, 2012), pp. 68-81.
69   U. Eco, *Lector in fabula...Op.* cit., pp. 52-54.

that was already present in modern hermeneutics from the time of its founding.

This fact has qualitatively introduced two new opposing phenomena that mark and condition the landscape of current biblical hermeneutics. On the one hand, there is the exponential multiplication of interpretations that are not always convergent and that create a strong hermeneutical fragmentation. On the other, there is as a reaction to this fragmentation, a trend that aims instead to defend the compactness of the Bible and its interpretation.

We will provide from a predominantly descriptive and an nonevaluatative point of view a description of the "hermeneutic fragmentation" and "hermeneutic monolithism" that mark our present in the next section. In Part II, in Chapters 7 and 8, we will pause to consider instead the change of these tendencies into real hermeneutic dysfunctions or even hermeneutic pathologies. We will also explain why we choose to use strong and categorical terminology (pathologies) regarding these interpretive deformations.

4. *Hermeneutic Fragmentation. Pluralism*[70] *and Hermeneutic Polytheism*[71]

Let us begin by briefly describing the first of these two phenomena. A great diversity of interpretations has always existed in Christianity. However, this diversity was embedded in a context of basic stability and was given by an understanding of God, reality and the group as ordered and stable systems. Unlike the past, in addition to the increasingly radical dynamism of reference systems, the diversity of

---

70 V.-M. Kärkkäinen, *Christian Theology for a Pluralistic World*...Op. cit., pp. 1-8.
71 Hermeneutical pluralism, which has become structural today, is prolonged, according to C. Geffré, into a religious pluralism typical of our time. What has caused what? Was it religious pluralism that flexibilized the hermeneutics of sacred texts or the flexibilization of the hermeneutics of sacred texts that opened the profile of religious communities? It is difficult to say. In any case, the final effect, hermeneutical and religious pluralism, is now a cross-cutting fact that stands out. Cf. C. Geffré, *Credere e interpretare*...Op. cit., pp. 104-126.

interpretations that exists among us today possess some new features that we would like to briefly highlight. We mention four of them.

1. Interpretive diversification is markedly more widespread and cross-cutting. What was the exception in the past has now become the rule. One does not have to go very far to confront an interpretation different from one's own. It is close to us, next door. It has become familiar to us and is part of the territory we inhabit. While in the past the territories were "hermeneutically" more homogeneous, today they are very fragmented and diverse. Unlike in the past, today, when there is no interpretive diversity, there is a spontaneous feeling of being in a dogmatic and totalizing system. This proves that diversity has become structural.

2. This hermeneutical diversity is widespread and structurally more tolerant and open to dialogue. There is not necessarily a sustained dialogue and a constant exchange between these differentiated hermeneutical positions but while they were on the warpath in the past, they now coexist side by side without too much conflict. Tolerance today is demanded as a virtue for all. It is no longer only a desirable attitude as in the past. From an abstract value it has become a moral task: everyone, indifferently, is called upon to cultivate it. Without tolerance comes a lack of the familiarity with diversity that today is a prerequisite for making any aggregative system work.

3. This fragmentation occurs not only between communities or between faith systems. It occurs within the same communities and within the same religious systems. In order to confront hermeneutical diversity, one only needs to remain within one's own group and try to take note of the dynamics that occur within it on a regular basis. Interpretive diversity today, unlike in the past, does not loudly and explicitly claim its legitimacy. It simply exists and precedes the typical recognition mechanisms that were instead the norm in the past. More than a choice, it is a fact. So spontaneous is its establishment that it can be embodied by the same person who just before fought it. Not only communities, but individuals themselves are traversed by different stances according to the times and levels of life involved.

4. We should note that an implicit legitimization of this fragmentation has taken over, given by a hermeneutic relativism that

seems to be the most natural and appropriate response to this new situation. There is a tendency to explain this diversity according to a preferential scheme. The hermeneutic choice seems no longer to be the object of truth or falsehood, but only the result of a personal sensibility and as such always legitimate. Loving blue or yellow or reading this way or that way is neither true nor false, but is the product of simple subjective preference. This legitimization from below is more implicit than explicit, less compact and less overbearing. Paradoxically, it is more effective and more durable. More effective because, although slower, it spreads more transversally. More durable because, being preferential, there is no argument that can deconstruct it.

What to do in this situation? At first, one must simply take note of it as an irreversible fact, and then try to adjust. We need to introduce a hermeneutic realism that recognizes not what we would like to be there, but takes simply note of what is there. Several times the ideal prompts us to turn our backs on reality and live in an illusory world. This test of hermeneutic realism is not necessarily a renunciation of truth, as it might seem. On the contrary, it might be a way of welcoming a different truth that we do not yet know. It might be a truth that knocks on our door from an atypical place that is unfamiliar to us. It would not be the first time that truth comes in unexpected and unusual forms. Is this not a characteristic of truth since time immemorial? This indicates to us that taking serious note of the diversification taking place is not an improper act. It is suggested by the widespread presence of this differentiation in other areas.

Such is the case, for example, in ethics. In modern-day ethics we find the same fragmentation with the corresponding widespread relativization resulting from it. Could we really say that the undoubted relativization of contemporary ethics, a product of its marked differentiation, is completely negative? Certainly not. It has freed us from bullying, false values, rigidity, obsessions and millenarian ethical arbiter. Hasn't this ethical relativism, in certain areas, made our faith and our lives more humane?

The best way to respond to this diversification and fragmentation is not to suffer and accept it as an event of fate. Neither is it to oppose it to the bitter end and on principle. One must learn to understand what reality offers us. Understanding already implies a first degree of acceptance. At the hermeneutic level this is what Paul Ricœur suggests to us when he speaks of the inescapable fragmentation of contemporary hermeneutics of which we must take note. It is what he calls "conflict of interpretations,"[72] multiple and unassimilable, as a structural fact of our age, with which we must learn to live, because they are not only legitimate but also irreversible.

Since Ricœur wrote about the diversity of possible interpretations as a fact of our time, diversification and fragmentation have become even more radicalized, to the point that what was sporadic and sectorial has now become the rule, not only at the level of interpretation, but also at a cultural level. Diversification has become a defining feature of today's societies. Today we live in multicultural societies that must learn to live together with diversified paradigms. Not only between interpretations but also between different cultures, actually living together on the same territory or in the same church. Pluralism has become not only a fact but also a moral duty.

A theological element must be added to this fact of simple descriptive ascertainment. This diversity of interpretations and cultures is not yet the greatest stumbling block. This is only the manifestation and extension of a deeper diversity, of a basic theological diversity. Theological diversity, however, which is not, necessarily and always, the result of either petty quarrels or short-sighted unilateralism. That combative, quarrelsome, petty and deeply ideologized religious diversity we are not considering here. We are talking about conscious, balanced and respectful theological diversity.

This diversity is not the dazzle of an out-of-control theological euphoria, nor the mirage of a lost conviction. This diversity, at least in part, stems from deep convictions and long and suffered spiritual journeys. It arises from a fidelity to and passion for truth itself. It arises from and in respect for it. At the same time, we note that the other, besides and in front of us, dignifiedly and respectfully claims the same validity, the same relevance for an alternative conviction of his or her own to ours. The diversity of theologies is certainly not a

---

72 P. Ricœur, *Il conflitto delle interpretazioni*, Op. cit., pp. 10-33.

new factor. Diverse theologies have always existed, but they tended to exist in different systems. Today the new fact is the existence of diverse theologies within the same faith system.

For this reason, the time has perhaps come to build a new, more inclusive theological paradigm that keeps in balance a necessary convergence of theological diversity in the same system, but does not downwardly homogenize this diversity that is not and cannot always be complementary. This fact creates a tension given by the non-assimilability of the parties involved. So, how are we to articulate a new theological paradigm that includes and tolerates, without becoming paranoid and obsessive, a healthy tension that this irreversible theological diversity necessarily creates?

Our response is that of the introduction of what could be called a *"hermeneutic polytheism."* Beyond the seemingly provocative impact of the term, let us try to look at the substance. It is not the term itself that matters. It can be this one or another. It is the underlying mechanism that seems necessary to us. "Religious pluralism," as a category so far used to describe a certain degree of diversification, while useful at certain levels, is not sufficient today to explain this theological diversity. We are facing a new phenomenon. Increasingly, different views of God are being compared within the same faith community, creating de facto "interpretive polytheism," where none of the parties involved can claim a monopoly on right understanding. At the same time, however, neither can it renounce the validity of its own position.

At stake are not assertions about secondary aspects of faith. At stake are assertions about God himself, one's own understanding of who God is, the true foundation of a faith experience. Real different understandings of God coexist without being able to assimilate them into a final synthesis. We are faced with a strong "polytheism of ideas" about God. This is a fact that one must learn to understand without automatic purist jerks. One should not proceed by cliché, but by analysis of substance. Fundamentally, at the heart of this phenomenon is articulated the double claim. On one hand, it consciously claims to assimilate one's idea about God to God himself. On the other hand, it unconsciously assumes that God is reducible to the idea we have about him. In both cases there is a lack of awareness of a gap between my ideas and God. If I can think and feel God close to me through my ideas -one thinks- how can my ideas be wrong and coexist with other ideas opposite to mine? The automatic conclusion is that my ideas are true and others' ideas are necessarily false, thus unacceptable. This conclusion ignores the fact that God reveals Himself to us, despite the partiality and anomalies of our ideas, and that God in Himself is ineffable, thus beyond any of our ideas.

One cannot demand that one's ideas about God do not aspire to express Being or reality. At the same time, one cannot demand that one's ideas about God truly and exhaustively speak about God. Two incommensurabilities are compared here. These are the legitimacy of human incommensurability in saying God, and the divine incommensurability that challenges that of man. "Hermeneutical polytheism" can offer an alternative in that, by working on the gap between God and the human understanding of God, on the one hand it legitimizes the human claim in saying God, and on the other hand it challenges it by imposing a constraint of plurality on it.

The polytheist paradigm is being revived as an innovative cultural form because it enacts both the recognition of faith and the relativization of that faith itself. This is why the return of the polytheist paradigm would not be a negative thing, from a cultural point of view, comments anthropologist and philologist at the University of Siena, Maurizio Bettini in his book *In Praise of Polytheism*.[73]

That polytheism is back and has taken hold in the West is a fact. The Christian world certainly cannot accept this as a religious alternative. Notwithstanding we would be shortsighted if we did not see, as Christians, that this polytheism, as cultural pluralism, already exists even in Christian communities as "*polytheism of ideas,*" precisely as "hermeneutical polytheism." This is what we mean when we speak of the need to create a new theological paradigm for this diversity, which is not only linguistic, ethical, interpretive or cultural. This expresses also an irreversible theological diversity

---

73 M. Bettini, *Elogio del politeismo. Quello che possiamo imparare dalle religioni antiche*, ("*In Praise of Polytheism. What We Can Learn From Ancient Religions*"), (Bologna: Il Mulino, 2014), pp. 5-16.

that needs to be understood and within certain limits accepted. This is what the term "hermeneutical polytheism" tries to do.

It is therefore not a matter of "ontological polytheism"--as Christians this we cannot but deny-- but of "interpretive polytheism." This is important to recognize, because the terms "diversity of hermeneutics" and "religious pluralism" still do not express the intensity of these differences. We are not just dealing with different readings but with different ideas of God. It is still the same God, but grasped differently, and none of these interpretations can claim to have the most correct understanding, much less the most total understanding of God. It is a true "interpretive polytheism" that must be acknowledged and handled with wisdom and tolerance.

Here the lesson of Max Weber can be helpful. In one of two well-known lectures on the *Beruf* (vocation/profession) as an attitude in times of crisis, that of "Science as a Profession," he introduces the concept of "polytheism of values."[74] Weber sees a revival of the polytheism of the ancient world in a new sense, after a centuries-long dominance of a grand rationalism sprung from messianic prophecy that is reductive of reality. Rationalism and Christian enthusiasm share the same obsession: reducing everything to the one, to explain and save the world with a unified scheme and paradigm. Especially in times of crisis, we are always called to choose among multiple and conflicting values, knowing that no value can be an absolute normative criterion and that there can be no completely rational argumentation of choice.

The introduction of this paradigm on diversity could lead us to increase the degree of uncertainty. Actually, the inclusion of a limited dimension of uncertainty, determined by a "hermeneutical polytheism," would not be new. In fact, we already find it in the Bible. This is more so in the Old Testament than in the New Testament, because with the clear diversification of God into three persons that is affirmed in the New Testament, a nominal homogenization of God also takes over. In the Old Testament, on the other hand, the affirmation of the one God is synchronic with the plurality of

---

74 M. Weber, *La scienza come professione,* (*"Science as a Profession"*), (Turin: Einaudi, 2004), pp. 5-44.

his denomination. To the "compact monotheism" of Islam and the "trinitarian monotheism" of Christianity, the Old Testament contrasts its "differentiated monotheism" given by a "hermeneutic polytheism" that is embodied in the plurality of its denomination.

There is no one way to name God. The Old Testament is the example of a "nominal polytheism." God cannot be named in a single way, on pain of impoverishing his nature. This nominal polytheism, visible for example, in the contrast between Yahweh (Ge 2) and Elohim (Ge 1), enriched the Old Testament because the same person, God, is called and thought of in such different perspectives that at times it would seem as if we were dealing with two different persons. It is still the same person, but described in his complexity from two different interpretive perspectives.

5. *Interpretive Compactness.*[75] *Sola Scriptura and Hermeneutical Monolithism*

Now let us go on to consider the second contemporary phenomenon alluded to in this last section: "biblical monolithism." This counter-movement is singular because it is certainly not new. Reactionary movements are common in history: one exaggeration is answered by another of the opposite sign. This is what happened in the 16th century. Although it might not seem so to us Protestants, the original Protestantism is, in fact, an exaggerated and radical movement. Radicality is often necessary, otherwise paradigm shifts would not occur. The new paradigms that Thomas Kuhn[76] would like to see more gradual and sequential actually come most often

---

75 The hermeneutical and religious pluralism just described is paradoxically accompanied by an opposite movement, which is that of a religious fundamentalism. Again, it is not easy to understand whether religious fundamentalism has prompted the adoption of a fundamentalist hermeneutic or whether the opposite has happened. In any case, the obvious fact is not only the resurgence of a religious and hermeneutical fundamentalism, but also the concomitant and parallel hermeneutical pluralism. Cf. C. Geffré, *Credere e interpretare,* Op. cit., pp. 60-103.
76 T. Kuhn, *The Structures of Scientific Revolutions,* (Chicago: University of Chicago Press, 1996), pp. 6-18.

by radical rupture. Protestantism is proof of this. The reaction, however, is equally disproportionate and exaggerated; in this case it is the Counter-Reformation that is the proof. But in provocation and counter-reaction there is a mutual loss. Protestantism, in some areas easily discernible today, was born already a loser, because it was precisely exaggerated and one-sided. As did Tridentine Catholicism, precisely because it allowed itself to be excessively conditioned by the radicalism of the Reformers, it responded in a counter-reactionary and radical way, impoverishing the richness it had hitherto had within itself.

It also happened in the early 1900s, first in the U.S. and then around the world: in reaction to the strong impetus and dynamism of a rational reading of the Bible, embodied in the "historical-critical" method, many second- and third-generation Protestant churches instead chose the opposite path of biblical literalism.[77] And this is what is still happening at the beginning of this 21st century: to the widespread interpretive fragmentation just described, there corresponds and follows a counter-reaction of churches and groups that instead emphasize the compact, objective, and unambiguous authority of the Bible, invoking, in a strong if one-sided and restrictive way, the noble, misinterpreted principle of *sola Scriptura*.[78]

---

77 They are also called *"revival"* (*Revival*) churches and in the early 1900s, in various ways, reconnected with the Protestant tradition but introducing some elements of rupture, including a stronger adherence to the biblical text in contestation of the historical-critical method that dominated in those years among the mother Protestant churches. For a description of this biblical hardening in one of these churches, namely Adventism, see: M.W. Campbell, *1919: The Untold Story of Adventism's Struggle with Fundamentalism*, (Nampa: Pacific Press Publishing Association, 2019); G. W. Reid (ed), *Understanding Scripture. An Adventist Approach*, (Hagerstown: Review and Herald Publishing Association 2006). R. Cole, P. Petersen (eds), *Hermeneutics, Intertextuality and the Contemporary Meaning of Scripture,* (Cooranbong: Avondale Academic Press, 2014).

78 This is the phenomenon that Philip Jenkins describes in this 21st century and which sanctions the shift of Christianity to the south, giving birth to a new Christianity characterized by a fundamentalist hermeneutic though different from that of the early 1900s. Ph. Jenkins, *The Next Christendom. The Coming of the Global Christianity*, (Oxford: Oxford University Press, 2002); *The New Faces of Christianity. Believing the Bible in the Global*

It would be wrong to read this new form of biblical and hermeneutical fundamentalism in the present as a reminiscence and resistance of the biblical literalism of a century ago. Here we have a hypermodern phenomenon that is not of the past but of the future and that needs to be read and understood properly.

Already in describing this counter-reaction, the existing terms seem inaccurate and limiting. Propaedeutically we assign to it the name "biblical monolithism." It does not describe, as the name might suggest, that radical band we know by the name of "biblical literalism" or even "biblical fundamentalism." We are not talking about fanatical or bigoted Christians who use the Bible as a compact instrument of truth against a world warped by sin and which must be saved by the power of the Bible. In biblical fanaticism everything is out of whack: the conception of truth, of the world, of sin, of salvation, of power. We will not stop on this.

Instead, in "biblical monolithism," we have a noble, balanced and even dynamic religiosity, but one that tends to have a strong idea of the Bible. The Bible would articulate a clear and immediate message. In this tendency toward a "biblical monolithism," which is present in the intermediate and non-fanatical segments of Christianity, there seem to be two leading features.

1. One is the intent to conceive of the Bible as a compact and homogeneous unity. Continuity is preferred to discontinuity, complementarity to tension, synthesis to fragmentation, because God and truth are identified as unitary realities. If this is so, the Bible must also bear the same traits within itself. The most recurrent phrases to affirm this first conviction are "The Bible never contradicts itself"; "any contrasts are only apparent" or "the apparent contrasts belong to the human part of the Bible."

South, (Oxford: Oxford University Press, 2006), pp. 8-25. This new phenomenon of hermeneutical hardening corresponds to a larger sociological one, which is the bet on strong and compact reference group identity (*Communitarianism*) and which Elena Pulcini describes as "endogamic communitarianism." E. Pulcini, *La cura del mondo. Paura e responsabilità nell'età globale,* ("*Caring for the World. Fear and Responsibility in the Global Age*"), (Turin: Bollati Boringhieri, 2009), pp. 31-112.

The most distinctive feature of this first belief is the thought that the Bible is structurally clear. There would be no opacity in the Bible. Its meaning would be perfectly transparent and clear. It is the reader, by the vices he automatically brings with him, who introduces these opacities that must be dismantled through interpretation.

2. Another is an intent to conceive of the Bible as an autonomous reality. The Bible would come into being and subsist by virtue of a purely internal mechanism of faith. At this second level of relationship with the external, the opposite is chosen: discontinuity over continuity, tension over complementarity, rupture over integration. The Bible would not depend on any human reality. It is the pure product of divine revelation. The mantra of this second conviction is the *sola Scriptura* principle: the Bible is sufficient unto itself. To understand faith, and the way it struggles to survive, nothing else is needed. One understands the *sola Scriptura* principle in its most exclusionary, exclusive and self-referential dimension.

Biblical monolithism thrives on the belief that the Bible is to be protected and preserved from all manipulation and distortion. A purist view of Scripture is outlined. The longer the Bible remains in contact with realities foreign to it, the greater the risk of contamination. Anything from the outside can only contaminate the sacred Word. If the external is considered in any usefulness, it is only to the extent that this allows itself to be transformed by the pure Word of God.

The Bible therefore must be protected, guarded, safeguarded in its compactness, for it is precisely this consistency that would represent the sign of its truth and divine inspiration. This new biblical monolithism fits into the larger context of the rediscovery of identities, which have become strong bastions of refuge and resistance against a commodification of life expressed in the implicit manifesto of globalization.

Certainly faith, together with the Bible, must resist this homogenizing and widespread tendency of the economy and a consumerist culture expressed in globalization, while being careful not to create a polarization that ends up favoring it. Faith is alternative, not escape; critique, not demonization. For this reason, biblical faith must not isolate itself, but enter into critical dialogue with its own time. When this does not happen, the Bible comes out deformed. In fact, the Bible becomes monolithic when it is detached from everything else, from life itself, from the world, from culture; in other words, when it becomes abstract. Conversely, when the Bible becomes monolithic it becomes detached from everything. The more monolithic an entity is, the more abstract it becomes; similarly, the more abstract a reality is, the more monolithic it becomes.

CHAPTER III
A "FORMATIVE TEXT"[1]

Biblical hermeneutics is an applied hermeneutics and, as such, it uses in its work the categories introduced and established by philosophical hermeneutics. The "text"[2] is one of them. Indeed, it is the first category of hermeneutics, the most important one. In the application of this category, after Paul Ricœur, a reversal of perspectives takes place.[3] By virtue of the originality of biblical hermeneutics, progressively the category "biblical text" from application becomes a model. The ideal text presupposed by the Bible would enrich with additional data what the text in general and as a cultural category should be. And from an applied hermeneutic it becomes a leading hermeneutic category. What this originality

---

1   D. Marguerat, Y. Bourquin, *Per leggere i racconti biblici. La Bibbia si racconta. Iniziazione all'analisi narrativa ("To Read Bible Stories. The Bible is Told. Initiation to Narrative Analysis")*, (Rome: Borla, 2011), pp. 130-133.
2   The text, the mainstay of hermeneutics, can be described from different angles. Jeanrond emphasizes the stability dimension of the text by speaking of "written text." We chose a more dynamic dimension by speaking of "formative text," which, in essence, emphasizes less the reader's adaptation to the text's indications than the text's investment in the reader as a creative reader. Cf. W.G. Jeanrond, *L'ermeneutica teologica*...Op. cit., pp. 134-156.
3   "An entirely opposite relationship between the two hermeneutics appears, on the other hand, precisely when we consider theological hermeneutics applied to a certain type of texts, the biblical ones: it reveals such original features that it causes a progressive reversal of relationship, so much so that philosophical hermeneutics remains subordinate to theological hermeneutics and becomes an organon of it," in, P. Ricœur, *Ermeneutica filosofica*...Op. cit., pp. 79-80.

consists of we will try to describe in this chapter, but in the meantime we distinguish two types of texts.

What is a text?[4] Not all texts have the same status and nature. Regardless of the content of which texts are the means and medium, we can distinguish two major groups. A first group of texts is marked by *precision*. These texts are characterized on the one hand by the detailed and specific description of the individual elements of the information they convey, and on the other by the completeness and exhaustiveness of all that information provided. Put in another way, these texts describe well and say a lot. Their accuracy lies precisely in the attention to detail and the accuracy of the data provided. Reading them requires a parallel and corresponding diligence in assimilating that data.

In contrast, the second group of texts is marked rather by the "horizon" it opens and suggests to the reader. These texts are characterized on the one hand by the approximation and inaccuracy in the description of individual data, and on the other by the incompleteness and partiality of the total information delivered. Put in another way, these texts describe poorly and say little. These texts lack the attention to detail and comprehensiveness that characterize "precision" texts instead. This deficit does not stand though as an anomaly, because this is precisely where their strength emerges. Thanks to this fragmentary and incomplete nature of the information offered, on the one hand a horizon is outlined, only suggested and sketched that requires completion through participation, and on the other hand this very incompleteness awakens the reader's imagination and creative participation.

We will call the first group "informative texts," the second "formative texts."[5] And the main difference lies not in the

---

4   P. H. Fry, *Theory of Literature*...Op. cit., pp. 53-150. For not only a literary but also a cultural definition of a text, see M. McLuhan, *The Gutemberg Galaxy. The Making of Typographic Man*, (New York: Signet Books, 1969), pp. 5-21.

5   A. Rizzi, *Pensare dentro la Bibbia*, (*"Thinking Within the Bible"*), (Rome: LAS, 2010), pp. 19-27.

comprehensiveness of the material conveyed, but in the attitude they generate and arouse in the reader.[6]

The group of "informational texts" aims to take the best possible picture of reality and convey an already complete representation of it, proving the reliability of the author and producer of that text. The result is a type of readers who are precise and accurate in the transmission of the already complete representation, but not necessarily in the creation or elaboration of that same representation.

The group of "formative texts,"[7] on the other hand, not aiming for completeness, merely hints at the reality it is meant to describe. In "formative texts," however, partiality and incompleteness are not to be counted as laziness and carelessness. On the contrary, not saying everything is the result of arduous and careful work and not the result of chance and improvisation, it takes more wisdom and technical skills to "say less" than to say "more." It is more complicated to limit oneself to, by only suggesting something, being able to say the whole, than to abound in descriptive data because one is incapable of limiting oneself to only suggest something by hints and allusions. The descriptive bulimia of informational texts so many times is mistaken as a virtue, failing to recognize that, underlying it, there may be a compulsive mechanism that aims to control reality through the exhaustiveness of description.

Every common description aspires to say everything but never really succeeds, while successful descriptions are those that find the right formula to suggest the whole without saying it. The result is a type of readers who are provoked and even compelled to actively complete the suggestions that the text and its author only sketch but refuse to complete. This incompleteness of information is transformed from a negative to a positive datum because it provides the right space for the reader to become a participant in the creation of meanings that the text wisely only

---

6   This is what Ricœur will say about texts that "prompt thinking." P. Ricœur, *Esprit*, 27/7-8 (1959), pp. 48,59.
7   Jeanrond calls these kinds of texts "boring" because, despite the important information they can convey, they make the reader passive from the point of view of sense-making. Cf. W.G. Jeanrond, *L'ermeneutica teologica*, Op. cit., p. 18.

suggests. Therein lies their formative dimension. They train the reader to think for himself and not to be pure receptacle of meanings elaborated elsewhere.

To which group of these two does the Bible belong? Many Christians complain that the Bible is not clearer and more comprehensive and would gladly place it in the first group. The Bible is certainly a complex book. And as such it belongs in the two groups. But the predominant and distinguishing dimension is the "formative" one. Without neglecting the importance of certain information central to life and faith, which the Bible conveys accurately, the biblical text has chosen instead sobriety and description by tracts, not only because the themes it presents are complex and would be difficult to exhaust with precise schemes, but also because it aims to make the recipients of its message not only attentive and coherent readers, but above all visionary and creative.

That is why it is not easy for the believer himself to understand what is the status and function of the text before him, the Bible. And the proper concern that drives the Christian to focus on and attend to the content of that text must never lead him to neglect its form. In the biblical text, not only the *what* but also the *how* is central.

But this is not the end of the story; rather, reflection on the nature of the Christian reference text, the Bible, has just begun. What it entails to have a text in front of one is neither a foregone nor superfluous question. With the text one must certainly create a relationship of learning and discipline. Care, attention, rigor and constancy seem to be the characteristics that a text requires to open its meaning to the reader. If then the text is the Bible, this will only increase the proportion and intensity of those requirements. Can, however, the relationship with a text be solely cognitive? Certainly not. When confronted with the text, a connection with life also emerges that goes beyond the text itself. Indeed, it precedes it. Even when we learn nothing new from an informational point of view, a text can still contribute to the emergence of a closer relationship with life itself to which the text is merely a witness. At this level, the attitudes needed are of a different nature. No longer discipline, constancy and rigor, but willingness, intuition and listening are needed to grasp beyond the text the voice of Life that speaks and palpitates in the text.

This is why it is important to reflect more on what it implies for us as Christians to have a text as a reference point. Does it represent a pure form that we could do without losing anything of the message? Does the fact of transcribing the message in a text such as the Bible change the message itself and orient it toward a certain kind of understanding? That the message is conveyed through a text provokes and requires a particular attitude in us? Are we Christians also transformed not only by the content of our reference text, but also by its form? I believe that we have not yet given enough thought to the anthropological, ontological and theological implications for us Christians of having to confront a text in such a close, continuous and massive way. And especially we Protestants, who have made the appeal to Scripture a strong point, must be aware that this virtue also opens the door to side effects that can be devastating. It is neither free nor painless to erect a relationship with a text at the center of one's religious experience. There are benefits, but there are also possible drifts, which we need to monitor and manage wisely and with foresight.

For example, the mere fact of conceiving the relationship with the Bible at a tendentially cognitive level--a very common fact today--introduces a type of impoverishment not only of the experience of reading, but also of the experience of faith. And the integration of a more "ontological" dimension (of human growth), to correct this formal drift, many times does not solve but aggravates the problem by creating a polarization here that we would like to briefly pause to grasp, through consideration of the "cultural" dimension of the text, the elements that intervene to condition our human relationship with the text in the reading experience.

1. A Theological-Cultural Look at the Text[8]

The acceptance of text as a communicative route has posed some problems from the very beginning. Text as a cultural form introduces the typical problem of mediation. In cultures with an oral tradition, the word made by direct contact is privileged over mediation through writing. Hence the resistance, from the very beginning, to recognize the claim of the text to be relevant not only in *what* it says, but in *how it* says what it says.[9] The text, as a particular form of communication, makes the claim and cultural provocation that it wants messages to be better on the one hand when they are mediated by writing, and on the other hand when the fragility of the word is overcome by the reliability of a text that supports it.[10] Even when text was finally introduced and its validity recognized, cultures, however, remained primarily oral cultures for a long time. The text served only as a support, but not as a social transformer. It is with the arrival of modernity that the situation changes: from

---

8   Text as a cultural artifact has posed a specific problem from the very beginning. That of the ambivalence of mediations. For Plato (Symposium 202-210) Hermes is the messenger of the gods who interprets language and texts and who, by clarifying their meaning, at the same time opacifies and tamper with it. The text is thus a source of both clarity and deception. For this reason, while initiating a revolution, the introduction of Scripture and texts arouses admiration and distrust from the outset. The dynamism of the text will not explode in pre-modern cultures because the communicative and social structure of the oral tradition will remain strong and transversal. This is what Carlo Bordoni calls, taking up the nomenclature introduced by Walter Ong, the strength of "primary orality." Cf. C. Bordoni, *Società digitali. Mutamento culturale e nuovi media*, (*"Digital Societies. Cultural Change and New Media"*), (Napoli: Liguori Editori, 2007), pp. 7-9; W.J. Ong, *Orality and Literacy*...Op. cit., pp. 5-15. Everything will change with the arrival of modernity and the democratization of texts after the invention of the printing press. The text not only imposes itself quantitatively through its massive dissemination, but also qualitatively through the development of a new anthropological model. Cf. P. Ricœur, *Dal testo all'azione*, Op, cit., pp. 177-203; W.J. Ong, *Ibid.*, pp. 77-114; pp. 115-135.
9   Plato, Symposium, pp. 202-210.
10 M. Ferraris, *L'ermeneutica*, Op. cit., pp. 3-5.

being a cognitive support, text becomes a social transformer. And this happens in two ways.

a. From a "quantitative point of view". From elite texts, texts will become affordable to all and for all. They will become democratized. And they will do so thanks to a technological invention: typography. With typography, texts will increase their draft, decrease in price, and multiply their dissemination to the nth degree. This is what Marshall McLuhan describes in his analysis of the phenomenon created by the introduction of typography in the West. His text, *The Gutenberg Galaxy. The Birth of the Typographic Man*,[11] tells how typography, then the introduction of the book in massive form, changes European culture. Text becomes "central" and no longer peripheral and ancillary. According to M. McLuhan, the text imposes itself and becomes the tool for building a different culture and society.[12]

b. From a "qualitative point of view", which is even more important than the quantitative one, it changes the status of the text itself and consequently also that of the reader. The text will no longer be an artifact of "social stability," but will become an instrument of "social change and mobility."[13] The text will become lighter and more flexible and, as such, will be conceived as the beginning of a chain whose fulfillment will no longer be in the text itself, but in the reader's creative take on it.[14] Thus the text becomes a fundamental

---

11   M. McLuhan, *La galassia Gütenberg. La nascita dell'uomo tipografico*, (*"The Gütenberg Galaxy. The Birth of the Typographic Man"*), (Rome: Armando Editori, 2011), pp. 8-26.
12   *Ibid*, pp. 14-34.
13   This is the conclusion of anthropologist A. Cavicchia Scalamonti. *La morte...* Op. cit., pp. 9-58.
14   Moreover, the priority of the individual over the group or stable text is what marks the birth of true modern individualism. Marcel Gauchet says, clearly and unequivocally, what the choice of modernity has been: "By taken party of the anteriority of the world and the law of things; or by taken party of the anteriority of men and their creative activity. Either submission to an order integrally received, determined in advance and beyond our will; or responsibility for an order that is believed to emanate from the will of individuals pre-existing the bond that holds them together," M. Gauchet, *Il disincanto del mondo*, (*"The Disenchantment of the World"*), (Turin: Einaudi, 1992), p. XIII.

but insufficient ingredient in the creation of meaning, because the meanings it suggests cannot deliver them either as definitive or as unique. The text is only a starting point. It is the birth of a powerful new cultural conception that, by relativizing the traditional text, in some ways desacralizes it.[15] And precisely because it desacralizes it, it also makes possible the birth of a new world through the active participation of a reader who has become creative and co-participant in the articulation and formation of meaning.[16]

The text is not determinative only as a "literary form" (narrative, poetry). How important the Bible is in its literary forms, we will consider that in Part II, Chapter V.[17] So many religious and secular authors have described this specificity and greatness of the Bible. This is the analysis, for example, of one of the great hermeneuts of our time, Paul Ricœur, who continually reiterates, as a philosopher and not a biblical scholar, the greatness of biblical "literary forms" even in the sense of a formal contribution to philosophical hermeneutics.[18] Few stop to consider though the importance of the biblical text as a "cultural form." It is not the same text that is read in modernity. Regardless of the content and regardless of the literary form, there is a new cultural format that arises and will be instrumental in creating a new culture. The material text of the Bible will remain the same today than in the Middle Ages. Nor will the extraordinary development in the critical analysis and elaboration of the biblical text[19], with the scientific preparation of manuscripts, change much about the materiality of the biblical text, which will remain essentially the same. It is the cultural concept of

---

15   Walter Benjamin will describe this same mechanism with regard not to the text but to the work of art, characterizing modern time not only as the time of individualism but of what he calls the rise and multiplication of "expository value" at the expense of "cultic value." See W. Benjamin, *L'opera d'arte nell'epoca della sua riproducibilità tecnica*, ("*The Work of Art in the Age of its Technical Reproducibility*"), (Turin: Einaudi, 2014), pp. 11-14.
16   A. Cavicchia Scalamonti, Op. cit., pp. 87-91.
17   See Chapter V of this text, "The interpreted Language".
18   P. Ricœur, *Ermeneutica filosofica...* Op. cit., pp. 79-85.
19   B.M. Metzger, *Il testo del Nuovo Testamento*, ("*The Text of the New Testament*"), (Brescia: Paideia, 1996), pp. 235-271.

the text instead, the new epistemological status entrusted to it with modernity, that will be revolutionary and will change the structure and rhythm of daily life and faith itself.

We have here a typical example of *cultural homonymy*. The word "text," like other pivotal words (God, family, authority, church, work, bond), will be the same for the medievals and for us moderns, but the content will be completely different. This change will not affect, for example, biblical authority, as some complain. The Bible, in modernity, is authoritative in another way. It will be authoritative not *in what it says* but in what it *suggests*. This hermeneutical shift is not only essential from a theological point of view, but also from a catechetical and pastoral point of view. It is important not only for progressive Christians, but also for more traditionalist Christians, because being a cultural mechanism, like all structural cultural mechanisms it will be marked not only by its transversality, but also by its unconsciousness and ethical neutrality. Being modern or medieval precedes our choice and ethically it is neither better nor worse. Just as there is no ethical virtue to being ethnically black or white, Peruvian or Italian. It is the address chosen and the use given to that cultural mode that will become important and consequently the object of moral evaluation.

The text as a modern cultural mechanism will not only become an instrument of cognitive and social mobility, but will also serve, unfortunately, paradoxically, as an imprisoning mechanism of meaning. Necessity or contingency? Determinism or innovation? Which of the two is the emphasis of textuality inaugurated by the moderns? This ambivalence, moreover, does not belong only to hermeneutics. Carlo Galli identifies it also in the foundation of the modern state proclaimed by Hobbes.[20] Hobbes is the prophet of a new vision of politics, the one who inaugurates the typically modern view of the state as a social convention sealed through a contract. And this innovation also concerns anthropology and the way human groups are conceived in a total break with the Aristotelian axiom

---

20 C. Galli, *Contingenza e necessità nella ragione politica moderna*, (*"Contingency and Necessity in Modern Political Reason"*), (Rome: Laterza, 2009), pp. 38-71.

of man as a social being.²¹ With Hobbes, the typical atomism of modernity is imposed, which is the anthropological presupposition of the social contract that drives individuals to converge together artificially in the face of a common benefit to be gained. Coexistence has become contingent, so much so that it must be made necessary of a second necessity. Indeed, between contingency and necessity, Galli replies, "the Hobbessian state" is a state of order and necessity. The same conclusion we could apply to modern textuality. It is born under the banner of fluidity of meaning versus the text guarantor of stability of the Middle Ages, but it ends up imprisoning not only meaning but all culture. Modernity, which reads, develops a one-sided way of seeing the world as it has learned it from its texts. In modern texts, in fact, meaning is linear, sequential, ordered and analytically rational, as will become the thinking of the moderns. It is not the moderns who created the modern texts. It is the modern texts that created the moderns and their linear, mechanical, sequential, and ultimately reductive mindset of the world.

Hobbes' political ambivalence about how much freedom or how much ordering order should prevail in the modern state and society does not only apply as a parallelism of a historical or political dilemma in which biblical interpretation can find a correlate for its own interpretive ambivalence. Hobbes' modern ambivalence is in a direct way also a hermeneutical ambivalence. Hobbes was a diligent interpreter of the Bible. *Leviathan*²² , his main work, but also for example *De cive*²³ , which precedes it only by a few years, are true exegetical-theological treatises. The hermeneutical ambivalence of a modern text, which radically innovates but paradoxically imprisons the new found meaning, is perfectly visible in these two books. On the one hand Hobbes gives birth to a new Christianity based on an innovative reading of the Bible (Old and New Testaments) while

---

21   Thomas Hobbes breaks down the classical aggregative anthropology formulated by Aristotle (*Zoon politikon*) and which had dominated the entire Middle Ages to establish an atomistic view of society. T. Hobbes, *De Cive. Elementi filosofici sul cittadino*, (*"De Cive. Philosophical Elements on the Citizen"*), (Rome: Editori Riuniti, 2014), I,2.
22   T. Hobbes, Leviatano, (*"Leviathan"*), (Milan: Rizzoli, 2013).
23   T. Hobbes, *De Cive*. Op. cit.

on the other hand that same new found sense almost immediately becomes a prison for the overall sense expressed in the biblical text. The political contract that liberates and oppresses has its perfect parallel in the hermeneutical contract that innovates and imprisons meaning. The Bible read by Hobbes,[24] with the Christianity derived from it, are both a strange mixture of freedom and imprisonment. Hobbesian biblical hermeneutics, breaking with the deterministic logic of medieval hermeneutics, actually creates a groundbreaking interpretation regarding anthropology and the modern state, but it ends up shackling them both to the contract of a sense that can only be placed in the service of the State. Bible interpretation is doomed to pander to Leviathan and to absolutely and exclusively legitimize both its monopoly of political force and its monopoly of interpretive force. The modern hermeneutic contract liberates and imprisons meaning at the same time. And all modern texts since Hobbes have become true sense contracts. A sense free but imprisoned. Free to imprison and imprisoned because it is excessively free.

We describe, in this chapter, the biblical text in its positive function. The negative dimension of the text, as the imprisonment of meaning, we will analyze in Chapter 7 of Part 2. We want to affirm and show that the positive function of the biblical text, which will be enhanced and liberated with modernity, lies in its "formative" capacity.

Text certainly does not limit itself to being a mnemotechnical support of the oral message. Its function is more central. Indeed, the message itself is profoundly altered when it becomes writing. Although our culture today is transversely marked by writing, there survives a nostalgia for the spoken word and a belief that the best communication is verbal. Writing, it is convinced, must still be surpassed by the warmth and immediacy of the spoken word. The word preceded writing and it is still the word redeemed by reading that must replace writing in the process of understanding the message. Writing is cold, anonymous and too formal. Instead, the word behind it, which needs to be resurrected, carries the force

---

24 T. Hobbes, *Leviathan*. Ibid, cf. 3rd and 4th parts. Cf. *De Cive*. Ibid, *cf.* part 3 on religion, chapters 15 to 18.

and persuasion of a warm and immediate message. It is as if writing (text) is only a necessary evil. As soon as one can, in fact, one is called to overcome it to get to the word that is hidden in it. In this view, only the word, and not the text itself, is the bearer of meaning and significance.

It is argued that speaking four-eyed, viva voce avoids the misunderstandings associated with mediation such as writing. The more direct the communication, the better this would be. Clearly, the advantage of oral communication lies in its freshness and real immediacy. However, this does not erase the misunderstandings. Indeed, at another level, oral communication, through speech, increases these misunderstandings. In fact, in oral communication, which necessarily takes place in real time, words and responses to words cannot be stopped. The communicative flow must be guaranteed because it is precisely that flow, in its immediacy and naturalness, that constitutes the strength of oral language. But it is precisely here, in the freshness and immediacy of this flow of orality, that spoken words find their strength, but also their limitation. That flow overwhelms them, overlaps them, jostles them, bumps them, halves them, exasperates them, accelerates them. For they are forced by this flow to become fast words, words that are less thought out, instinctive, easy and immediate, but not necessarily the best.

The undoubted greater coldness of writing and text then brings with it corrective, necessary benefits. The written word, which becomes text, can indeed become a thought-out, verified, filtered word. A balanced word that communicates better, even if more slowly, the intentions and will of the dialoguers. But the benefit of a text does not lie only in the greater precision of the written form. Writing (text) causes three kinds of "formalizations" (distantiation[25]) that in the interpretive process increase the meaning of the message.[26] This is precisely where its strength lies.

---

25 "Distanciation" is the technical word used by Ricoeur to describe this formalization introduced by text and writing. Cf. P. Ricoeur, "The Hermeneutyical Function do Distanciation", in, *From Tex to Action. Essays in Hermeneutics, II*, (London: Continuum, 1991), pp. 72-85.
26 P. Ricœur, *Philosophical Hermeneutics*, Op. cit., pp. 80-95.

2. The Text and its Autonomy

To exemplify these three types of "distantiation" (distancing) and their outline within what we call the levels of textuality, we will refer to the prologue of Luke's Gospel, which we quote below to facilitate understanding of the explanation.

Luke 1:1-4

> "Since many have undertaken to order a narrative of the facts that have been fulfilled among us, as they have been handed down to us by those who from the beginning were eyewitnesses to them and who became ministers of the Word, it has seemed good to me also, after I have been thoroughly informed of everything from the origin, to write to you by order, most excellent Theophilus, so that you may recognize the certainty of the things you have been taught."

The first[27] "distanciation" is that which the text creates between the author and his initial project. It is as if at some point the text becomes autonomous and independent of its creator. The text has in its genes the articulation, reinforcement and assertion of its otherness from the author who created it. This fact might seem anomalous and unnatural. In reality, the estrangement of a text from its author is a natural and beneficial act. And as such, it triggers a process that is inversely proportional to the presence of its author. In the beginning, in fact, the text is the text of an author. The author is everything and his text is only a part of the author's potential. It is the author who ensures the success of the text. One knows and respects a text only because of the guarantee given by its author. Subsequently, however, it is the author who is known through his text. One knows that author only through that text; everything else he has done, most of his life, does not count. It is the text that saves its author from oblivion. The text is everything and its author has become only an accompanying element.

---

27 P. Ricœur writes: "Writing first of all makes the text autonomous from the author's intentions, because the text, once fixed through writing, no longer coincides with what the author intended to say" in, *Philosophical Hermeneutics*, Ibid, pp. 68-70.

This mechanism of replacing the author with his text has not only a temporal logic and historical wear and tear. Underlying it is a semantic fact that grounds hermeneutics precisely. It is the fact that the meaning of a text is always greater than the meaning that intentionally prompted its author to write it. The author is never fully aware of the meanings his text carries. For this reason, once given birth (written), a text begins to have a life of its own, and the meaning that seeks interpretation is no longer limited to the author's intention, to seeking what the author intended to say. The goal is the meaning of the text itself, a meaning that transcends and goes beyond the author's awareness. The author's intention does not lapse, but is simply embedded in a larger goal that ennobles and completes it. Opposed to this broader view of the meaning of a text are on the one hand the romantic hermeneutics, based on intuition, and on the other hand the pragmatic hermeneutics of many evangelical Christians, based on concreteness, which in opposite ways try to link interpretation only to the sometimes mythologized intentionality of the author.

Take, for example, the Gospel of Luke.[28] While it was in the process of construction, the text belonged directly and completely to the management of its author. Luke tells us this directly in the prologue (1:1-4), stating that it is he, after investigating, studying, sorting, and cataloging the material concerning the life of Jesus, who manages and determines the final configuration of that text.[29] Indeed, Luke's imprint on Jesus' biographical data is not secondary. He did not limit himself to being a transcriber or a copyist. The author's imprint in reporting objective data, concerning the life of Jesus, is very strong, even to the point of appearing selective and even distorting. It is precisely that selectivity and arbitrariness that actually ground the literary and theological style of Luke's Gospel. Had he confined himself to passing on objective data about Jesus, his Gospel would have been a copy of Mark's or John's and, as such,

---

28 J. Nolland, *Luke* 1-9:20, Word Biblical Commentary, (Dallas: Word Books, 1989), pp. xxvii-xlvii; R. Fabris, Luca, (*"Luke"*), (Assisi: Cittadella, 2003), pp. 21-34.
29 J. Nolland, *Ibid*, pp. 3-12.

useless. This fact simply indicates that the author, in this case Luke, is the true father of that text, because he imparts to those narrated data an outline, an organization and an interpretation that is a true contortion of objective meaning. Therein lies precisely his undoubted authorship and the persuasive force of his text.

Yet, the text breaks that authorship. It breaks that closeness. For gradually that text will have a life of its own, independent of Luke its author and what he intended to say. Meanwhile it will survive unscathed while the author is gone. The very meaning of that Gospel will be changed by Luke's disappearance and its autonomous permanence. The central question will no longer be, "What did the author mean?" Instead, the hermeneutical question will become, "What does that text mean?" And the two do not coincide, because there were from the beginning meanings in that text that even Luke was not aware of. This distancing that apparently plays against, because we can no longer ask Luke what he meant, actually plays in favor because it endlessly enhances, increases and multiplies the meaning of that text.

3. *The Text and Its Multiple Recipients*

The second "distanciation"[30] that the text creates is the disconnect between the given birth text and the initial recipient. There is no text that is born in the abstract. A text is always addressed to someone. And even when the author does not have a nominal addressee in mind, which is very rare, guiding the design and articulation of the text is always an ideal addressee. A text is not based only on the coherence of its author's reasoning. The horizon of the addressee is essential for the completion of the very architecture of a text. The consubstantial, and not merely applicative, work that the reader will further introduce in relation to the text, and which consists precisely

---

30 Ricœur writes, "The liberation of the text from the author corresponds to a parallel detachment of the text from the reader. Whereas in dialogue the very condition of discourse determines confrontation, the written text can attract an audience that includes virtually anyone who can read" in, *Ermeneutica filosofica,* Op. cit., p. 69.

in creating together with the text the meaning that it has masterfully only introduced, actually begins even earlier, precisely at the level of the original recipient.

The addressee, nominal or ideal, is the instance between the text and the reader that is still too often read only in its passivity. Without in any way detracting from the author to whom the design, ideation and audacity of enacting the strategy of meaning belong, the addressee, as the reader will later further do, actively contributes to the creation of meaning. Not only the extension of meaning in the text, but also its precision and nuance would remain crude and approximate if the addressee were to be absent. The fact that in texts, more often than not, we are not delivered abundant information about the addressee the author has in mind does not mean that the author does not include it nor that we, readers, can do without it. Data about the initial addressee would weigh down the text. For this reason, the reader's active participation is articulated not only at the level of reconstructing the text's message, but also at the level of imagining the addressee, which the text presupposes and which is imposed only in hints. Delineating the profile of the addressee is a primary hermeneutic obligation.

Even this essential component in the construction of meaning is broken by the text. The text interrupts it by imposing a discontinuity on it. Ostensibly, this interruption seems to compromise meaning. Instead, it does not. Paradoxically, not only is the sense not tampered with, it miraculously comes out enhanced. At some point in the process, the message for a specific recipient becomes a message potentially for everyone. It is the text that performs this miracle. The mechanism of expanding the message through multiple recipients is not just a mechanism of dissemination. It is not "one meaning," the specific one to that message, that reaches more people. It is the plurality of added recipients that allows latent meanings in the text to be surveyed and brought out that a single recipient would not have been able to bring out. Even at this second level of the chain of meaning, the text has performed a miracle, which is the miracle of expanding meaning from the text itself and without manipulating it.

Again taking Luke's Gospel in the prologue as an example, we find that, according to the evangelist himself, the initial addressee played a predominant role in choosing, organizing, and editing the material collected about Jesus. Luke's Gospel was written for him, for that specific recipient, which is in this case is a certain Theophilus (1:3,4).[31] Few words explicitly describe and name him, but these are decisive in signaling the centrality of his presence. Theophilus is just as important in structuring the message, even if mentioned only briefly, as is the subject of the story itself, Jesus. This may appear exaggerated, but literally and textually it is not. Theophilus is insignificant in the architecture of Jesus' life and teaching. Instead, he is central to Luke's account of Jesus' life. Between *life* and *life narrative there* is no equivalence. They are two close but different things.

What is binding and canonical for us Christians is the *life narrative* and not the *life of* Jesus himself. The life of Jesus is very important to us but not binding, mainly because we do not know outside the gospels what it was like. What is instead binding for us is the canonical account that the gospels have given of Jesus. Even if we were to find a writing made by Jesus himself, this would be very important but not binding (non-canonical). The account of Jesus made by Luke, on the other hand, is unthinkable without Theophilus. The Theophilus element, insignificant in the biography of Jesus, becomes instead binding as an element of the account about Jesus that is a canonical account. The historical and objective life of Jesus is filtered, for us Christians, not only by the gaze of Luke, who is the author, but also by Theophilus as the recipient of that text. All the material has been gathered and organized according to him.

The weight of this filter, imposed by the recipient, is perfectly visible in the structuring of the genealogy[32] in chapter 3, which is even presented after the baptism, whereas in Matthew it appears before Jesus' baptism. Even the configuration of the genealogy, which in Matthew is descending (beginning with Abraham), precisely by virtue of what Theophilus represents, Luke makes it ascending

---

31 D. L. Bock, *Luke* (1) 1:*1-9:50*, Baker Exegetical Commentary on the New Testament, (Grand Rapids: Baker Academic, 1994), pp. 51-67; H. Schürmann, *Il Vangelo di Luca* (1) *1-9:50*, (*"The Gospel of Luke* (1) *1-9:50"*), (Brescia: Paideia, 1983), pp. 53-67.
32 D. L. Bock, *Ibid,* pp. 80-91.

(beginning with Joseph) and leads it back, unlike in Matthew, not to Abraham but to Adam. Luke's constructed genealogy, with some literary and historical license that we could not afford today, is more universal and inclusive than Matthew's precisely by virtue of its recipient being Theophilus, a non-Jew. Luke's Gospel is therefore incomprehensible in some of its essential registers without its immediate addressee, Theophilus.

Here, too, the text breaks and introduces a clear discontinuity. Theophilus does not disappear, but by virtue of the autonomy of the text, which will be increasing over time, he takes a back seat. His place will be taken by all those addressees who in the initial form of the Gospel were instead only latent addressees. The obscuring of the initial addressee should lead to an impoverishment of the text. Instead through the mechanism of "distanciation" or breaking, the continuity between author and addressee, this does not happen. This fact not only does not reduce meaning, but even enhances it. For, having become text, that narrative is potentially addressed to everyone. Not only Theophilus, but any human being of Theophilus' period and of our own day becomes a legitimate eventual recipient of that narrative.

4. *The Text and the Broken Referentiality*

The third "distanciation"[33] is that which the text creates between the message and the reality hinted at. The reality hinted at by the author is no longer the same reality to which the reader will connect. However, in either case, one is asserting that the truth of the event or message described does not lie in the coherence of the elements within the message, but solely in the connection of these with the external world. The message of a text is articulated on two planes,

---

33 Ricœur writes, "The world of the text to which we now refer is not that of everyday language, but constitutes a new kind of distancing that we might call distancing the real," in, *Ermeneutica filosofica*, Op. cit., p. 74.

which Frege[34] called the "Sense" and the "Reference."[35] "Sense" expresses a linguistic truth that is immanent to the literary form and is essentially given by the differentiation and gap between elements within a given system. This is a technical truth and, as such, a truth with a lower "t". We might call it a descriptive truth. It does not change life, much less the world. It merely describes and affirms what reality is at a certain point in time. It is as if the truth of sense becomes small precisely because it is possessed and contained completely in sense. The result is a domesticated truth that produces neither change nor emotion nor imagination.

Instead, "Reference" expresses a claim to reach external reality and is articulated only as a leap from the system to what is outside of it. This going outside the system can succeed or fail. But in reference, it is no longer the linguistic system that is the factor or scenario where meaning occurs and is given. The linguistic system, in the reference, decenters itself and accepts that truth occurs outside of it, in connection with external reality. Beyond the fact that the proposed reference may then be true or false, that path is already a path of truth. It is the "reference" and not the "sense," strictly speaking, that is the locus of truth with a capital "T." This referential truth (reference) is a truth that escapes. It cannot be contained or even possessed in language. Language alone can act as a witness to reality, alluding to it tangentially, in hints. This is precisely why referential truth sets in motion, passion, imagination and is a promoter of change.

Between "sense" and "reference" is the distance that exists between "language" and "discourse." Speech like reference, have the claim to connect with external reality. "Sense" and language, on the other hand, do not. The "linguistics of language"[36] (structuralism, F. de Saussure, L. Hjelmslev) atemporally processes meaning without subject or intentionality and for that very reason without "reference." The "linguistics of discourse"[37] (E. Benveniste, P. Ricœur), on the other hand, temporally elaborates a meaning with

---

34 P. Ricœur, *Ibid*, pp. 70-72.
35 G. Frege, A. Bonomi (eds.), *La struttura del linguaggio*, (*"The Structure of Language"*), (Milan: Bompiani, 1973), pp. 9-32.
36 P. Ricœur, *Ermeneutica filosofica,* Op. cit., pp. 56-58.
37 P. Ricœur, Ibid.

subject and intentionality whose goal is given by reference. The text as distanciation does not take the side of a "linguistics of language" but is on the side of a "linguistics of discourse" because the text, in this its third distanciation, cannot renounce reference. The text must not be conceived as a transcription of "language," but as the freezing of a "discourse" in which reference is present even if dormant.

Here, too, the text introduces a break. It breaks a continuity with the initial reference in order to construct a new one. This rupture of referentiality is the defining characteristic of the text, because through it the text does not photograph reality as it is, but reconfigures it as a possible reality. Every good text, in the face of the given reality, always proposes an alternative reality. The great benefit of broken reference (third distanciation) is the enlargement and enhancement of the referential and truthful capacity of the text. Every text in this sense is a poetic text and a text of fiction, because it proposes a reconstruction of reality that is never the one that is already there. Proceeding in this way, affirms the possibility of thinking alternative and different realities from the present one. Poetry and fiction, as literary forms, only radicalize this artificial element found in all texts. By alluding therefore to a fictitious reality, which is not there, each text becomes critical of the present reality and, as an alternative to it, proposes possible realities through imagination. In this lies the revolutionary dimension of the text.

Taking up Luke's example, we find that the reality to which he relates[38] is a complex reality but one that can be framed in two typifying perspectives. On the one hand, from the socio-political point of view, the Jewish people appear in a position of weakness, while Romans and Greeks in a position of strength. On the other, from the religious point of view, the situation is reversed: the privileged are the Jews who had revelation and the disadvantaged are the Romans and Greeks who did not have access to this revelation. It is with reference to this reality that Luke's Gospel articulates its proposal. It does so by overturning the patterns and parameters of

---

38 R.C. Tannehill, *Luke,* Op. cit. , pp. 33-35; K. H. Rengstorf, *Il Vangelo secondo Luca,* (*"The Gospel According to Luke"*), (Brescia: Paideia, 1980), pp. 31-36.

the reality of the time through this broken referentiality. Reminding us that in the face of the political-social reality or in the face of the religious reality of the present, which impose themselves with their force, Jesus introduces possible alternative realities by virtue of his messianic and interpretive power. Starting with Jesus as a new criterion, on the one hand, the religious advantage of the Jews easily becomes a disadvantage and a reason for stumbling (this is in fact what happens), on the other hand, from the socio-political point of view, the advantage of the Gentiles becomes a religious disadvantage, but, as such, it will become an opportunity for salvation. This is what happens: it is the pagans who nurture the ranks of the first Christian communities, not the Jews.

Here, too, the text breaks the linearity of the connection with reality. When we read Luke, we no longer see the Jewish religious context and the Roman socio-political context, but we see our own context. It is no longer in connection with that referentiality that we construct the meaning we derive from reading Luke's Gospel, but in connection with our modern referentiality. The focus on that initial context is purely transient, because its reading and consideration actually aims to make us more aware of our context. The initial referentiality broken down through the text actually enhances the meaning of that text and those experiences that connect back to that text in the present.

5. Informational Texts and Formative Texts. The Why of Being "in Reading"

What is a good text? This not always easy to figure out, despite appearances. Venturing a somewhat atypical and in some ways even provocative hypothesis, we think we can confidently state that a good text is not the one "that says all," but rather the one "that does not say all." With this apparently atypical answer to a seemingly obvious question, we take up the initial difference we introduced with respect to the two types of texts considered, to add a further clarification. "Informative" texts, we said, are those that add knowledge and data to our cultural background. Contrary to what it seems, they do not require our active participation in the creation of meaning itself. At the level of meaning creation, the reader still appears too passive. This certainly is not so at all levels. At the application level, for example, the reader here is very much involved. We could say, therefore, that "informational" texts tend to create with the reader a relationship of an epistemological type, that is, of knowledge. One reads to know more, to be more informed and to apply assimilated knowledge.

Behind this cognitive relationship, however, an anthropology of certainty is articulated that easily becomes manipulative of meaning. The subject, as reader, does not define his essential profile by virtue of the text. He is independently of the text already a subject. As such, with a certain pre-textual identity, he chooses a text or texts to read only to learn and reinforce things he already knows. That new information does not ground his being but only enriches it. The epistemological type of interpretation that one articulates in the face of "informational" texts, but can also articulate in the face of "formative" texts -in this case deforming them through reductive reading- tends to downsize the texts, making them pure objects of cognitive grasp. The separation "knowing subject"/"known object," presupposed by informational texts, carries within itself from the beginning the seed of manipulation. A subject separated from the object can approach the object - texts - only by com-prehending them, by taking them in their sense, that is, by manipulating them, by appropriating their content.

In contrast, "formative" texts are sober and incomplete about information. But from the point of view of sense-making, precisely because they are incomplete, they require the reader's participation. Their limitation becomes an opportunity for the reader. If they were complete they would not be formative because they would not require his or her participation. These texts are slow texts because by articulating a deep dialogue between what they propose and the reader, the process of signification necessarily slows down. This slowing down represents their virtue, because the reader's involvement is no longer only cognitive. His whole being participates in it. A formative text forces the reader to an investment of his being and not only of his knowledge. In participating with its being, it is perfected and comes out, in this relationship, enriched. With formative texts there is an enhancement of the reader's being. The hermeneutics of formative texts is thus an ontological hermeneutics that can take place, at least partially, even in the face of informational texts, if the reader so desires. A typical example of this category of text is poetry. Poetry structurally is fragmentary, approximate, not precise, pluriform, which is precisely why in order to grasp its meaning, which is not immediate, the reader must actively participate with his being and imagination.

This allows us to say that it is not easy to understand the nature of the biblical text. The true greatness of the Bible does not lie in its exhaustiveness nor in its analytical description. The Bible's greatness must be sought by placing it in the category of those texts that we have called "formative" and that have basically two characteristics.

a. *Partial Texts*

First, "formative texts" are partial. They do not say everything and do not mean to say everything. In this order of ideas, we can say that the Bible does not say the last word, does not say everything and does not monopolize the word. On the contrary, it requires, stimulates and demands a human word and wants to be supplemented and enriched by it. Its (the Bible's) search for the human word is not a hidden strategy to then force and smuggle its meaning. The sense of God's Written Word is not a sense already made elsewhere and embodied in human history to pretend and simulate an approach and involvement of mercy. No, the sense God offers in his Written Word is an incomplete sense, because he cannot and will not complete it on his own. That would be irreverent toward the human. He halves his Written Word because every procreating Word, as in the meiotic reproduction of germ cells that must halve their genetic and chromosomal makeup to pass on life, must be a halved Written Word. A full Word can only create nothingness. Halving oneself is the condition for guaranteeing life. And if the Bible is the Written Word of life, it can only be so by becoming a halved Word. A sober, partial and incomplete Word.

When God speaks, it is said, we humans must be silent. This is only partially true. For from a more fundamental point of view it is the other way around. When God speaks, we, from being silent that we were, begin to speak, dare to articulate a thought, a prayer, a praise. God does not act as a paralyzing or castrating element but, on the contrary, as a promoting and stimulating element. As an incomplete text requiring completion, through the Bible the human word becomes a valued, welcomed, promoted, requested word. Of this God and his Written Word are not jealous. The Bible is not jealous if other texts say better what the Bible says only in summary, only as a draft. The Bible functions, as a text, as a collection of ingredients, which it is then up to each age to amalgamate into a final proposal, into a blueprint. The final interpretation is ours by virtue of the biblical incompleteness that has driven us to go beyond itself.

b. *Plural Texts*

Second, "formative texts" are also plural texts. They are structurally polyform. They are so not only by necessity, but also by choice. In the first instance, formative texts are plural "by necessity," because the truth is too big, too multifaceted, too much in flux to expect to embrace it from a single point of view, with the gaze of a single text. It is in the order of things that formative texts recognize their impotence and limitations in approaching truth, and that from this comes the search for a plurality that better tells life and truth. This necessary plurality is not only within one system (intra-community plurality) but also of different systems (inter-community plurality). This is why the homogenization of the Bible, that is, the denial of its internal plurality, almost automatically leads to closure "in the Bible," that is, the denial of external plurality. The Bible is not plural because it is strong, but it is strong because it is plural, with a plurality that breaks its own claims and necessarily opens to others. By opening to others, it automatically becomes vulnerable. The vulnerability of the Bible is expressed in its plurality. It is the open plurality of a vulnerable text. Plurality for the Bible is not a strategy of conquest, it is an ontological trait. The Bible, as a formative book, is plural by necessity.

On the other hand, formative texts are plural "by choice." They do not suffer plurality as a fate, because it cannot be done otherwise. On the contrary, formative texts choose to be plural out of conviction, even if many times this does not suit them. Chosen plurality opens an arduous, laborious, slow, unpredictable path of seeking difficult consensuses, of promoting laborious convergences. The plurality "by choice" of formative texts is not a plurality of strength and certainty, but a plurality of vulnerability and uncertainty that presupposes the unavailability of truth and life.

Precisely because life and truth are unavailable and even less so to the gaze of a single text, the Bible at its core gives voice to various versions of a single event, but also to various events uncontained in a single version. It is incomprehensible that those who perceive plurality in the Bible then reject the plurality of Bibles. Of Bibles there is not just one. There are a variety of them. And This variety is not the variety of different translations and even less the quantitative variety of different specimens. Every human word is a Bible; it is sacred. Sacred not canonically (canon) in its form, but certainly in its essence.

One is the canonical Bible, it must be remembered, but many are the non-canonical Bibles. One must resist the temptation to overestimate the canonical Bible and underestimate the bibles of men. Every human story, with its successes and failures, with its joys and sufferings, sometimes prolonged indefinitely, is a sacred story and is configured as a bible that God reads with emotion and attention. We need to resist even more tenaciously the temptation that makes the Bible precisely that instrument that undervalues and minimizes the history of men. That is not its task. The vocation and task of the canonical Bible is to recognize and appreciate the value of men's bibles. And the biblical canon is not a boundary of bullying, of excluding other texts, but of self-limitation, of relinquishing control of others. Through the biblical canon, God renounces invading human speech and gives Himself the task of dialoguing with it. The canon is not a limitation on human speech to prevent it from contaminating the divine word. The canon is a limit that God imposes on himself, on his Word, to prevent it from engulfing the human Word. The biblical canon expands the human word because it makes it possible by simply reminding him that the human word, desired and willed, is a preceded word. Preceded by God's (canon). The biblical canon[39] is a sign of openness and not closure. It is the sign that ennobles everything outside the Bible. This recognition of the value of all that is extra-canonical and extra-biblical, that is, human, becomes visible and articulated in the choice of human plurality of which the Bible is only a part. To the intra-biblical plurality is added by divine design choice the extra-biblical plurality, without which the Bible would be limited to being just a sad piece of museum and history.

The Bible, as a "formative text," says little (first characteristic) and that little it says in a plural way (second characteristic). The Bible is a collection of books not only in the sense of having various styles, but especially in the sense of giving voice to various projects, not always equivalent and complementary. We do not have in the Bible the plurality within "one homogeneous system", but the plurality "of different systems" living together in tension. This might appear as a problem for those who try to read the Bible in a unified and homogeneous way. The Bible was intended to be constructed in this way. Different versions of faith experiences find in it not only recognition but also a fine appreciation. What is even more striking is the fact that, after presenting them, the Bible does not overcome them through a final summarizing synthesis. It leaves them in tension and merely creates scaffolding mechanisms to make them convergent but not symbiotic. The purpose is to bring them together without confusing them. This is what creates that typical biblical mechanism of paradox. That is why in the Bible we can find a proposition and further on its opposite: both must and can remain in tension, without distorting the inclusive perspective of the larger meaning.

---

39   B.M. Metzger, *Il canone del Nuovo Testamento. Origine, sviluppo e significato*, (*"The New Testament Canon. Origin, Development and Meaning"*), (Brescia: Paideia, 1997), pp. 200-215.

CHAPTER IV
A "VITAL READER"[1]

Every text presupposes the profile of an ideal reader[2] It belongs to the logic of the interpretive process to conceive together with the text also a structural correlate of it, the reader. Even the Bible, as a text, presupposes a particular kind of ideal reader. Whereas in the previous chapter we stopped to consider what grounds the reader and makes its reading possible, that is, the text, in this chapter we will stop to describe and defend the relevance of the reader as a correlate of the text. As stated from the very first pages of this essay, the "hermeneutic circle," which is the central category of the interpretive act, requires us to have this dual fidelity which is fidelity and respect for the text and fidelity and respect for the reader.

The defense of the ideal reader, as a correlate of the text, cannot be limited to the defense of the one who reads the text. The profile of the ideal reader has a broader scope that we find not only "downstream of the text," that is, in the process of reading that tries to understand the text and its message. It is also "upstream of the text," that is, in the very creation of the text at the time of its construction and writing. The description of the complete profile of the ideal reader is necessary because there is a tendency to attribute to the reader a purely subsidiary and external task. This tendency to disregard the relevance and centrality of the reader is directly proportional to the sacredness of the text in question. The more sacred the text read

---

1   D. Marguerat, Y. Bourquin, *Per leggere i racconti biblici...*Op. cit., pp. 143-148.
2   Every text presupposes a certain kind of reader. There are various types of readers. We will describe two of them. What we call a "vital reader" is similarly described by Jeanrond when he speaks of a "transformative reading," meaning the vitality of a dynamic reader. Cf. W.G. Jeanrond, *L'ermeneutica teologica,* Op. cit., pp. 157-201.

becomes, the stronger the tendency to consider the reader irrelevant and unnecessary in the creation of meaning. In this perspective, every discovery of the Bible as a sacred book, thus every Christian moment of spiritual awakening that is based on this discovery, carries with it the danger of distorting the hermeneutic circle. It does this by distorting and vitiating the interpretive process conceived as a primary and continuous interaction between text and reader, through the fetishization of the sacred text at the expense of the relevance of the reader.

The correlation between text and reader is neither purely applicative nor related to reading, as the term "reader" seems to suggest. The reader is not someone who emerges only later. The reader is actually present from the beginning; he is not only someone who uses the text, but also someone who founds and composes the text. He founds it because at the time of writing and construction of the text the author shapes, cuts out, discards, chooses, organizes his material already having in mind the ideal reader. This ideal reader, a kind of original archetype, heavily participates and affects the construction of every text. Every text is always a text for someone. If the Bible is innovative with regard to the philosophical status of the text as the first hermeneutical category, according to what Paul Ricœur stated[3], it will also necessarily be so in the status of the reader. The Bible more than other texts presupposes an ideal reader with a central, substantive profile. The Bible is to all intents and purposes a text written for someone, not in the limited sense of someone who must read it, but in the sense that this someone, the ideal reader, is present from the beginning, in the construction and drafting of the sacred text.

The impact of the ideal reader presupposed by the Bible does not end there. Its scope is even greater. How the biblical text is

---

[3] "An entirely opposite relationship between the two hermeneutics appears, on the other hand, precisely when one considers theological hermeneutics applied to a certain type of texts, the biblical ones: it reveals such original features that it causes a progressive reversal of relationship, so much so that philosophical hermeneutics remains subordinate to theological hermeneutics and becomes an organon of it," in, P. Ricœur, *Ermeneutica filosofica...Op.* cit., pp. 79,80.

defined is the reason the Bible, as a text, is characterized not by its completeness and exhaustiveness, as is commonly believed, but by its fragmentary nature and incompleteness. It alludes and suggests rather than determines and completes. The task of the ideal reader becomes decisive not only in the reading or foundation of the Text, but in the creation of the Text "downstream." The moment of reading becomes not solely a moment of assimilation or application, but of sense-making through the reader's creative action from the ingredients and perspective suggested but not completed by the Text itself.

Here is what we call in this chapter the "vital reader." The vital reader is the one who takes on three tasks: 1. The task of downstream reading of the text; 2. The task of ideal presence in the upstream creation of the text; 3. The task of sense-making in the moment of reading, from the potentialities and senses latent in the text as ingredients, but not yet as completed and finalized meanings.

Not all readers are equivalent. We can delineate two reader profiles. On the one hand, there is the "diligent reader"[4] in applying the meanings gathered in reading, but who remains neutral in creating and processing them. This reader limits his role to gathering existing meanings and then making them his own and applying them as best he can in his own life journey. If hermeneutics is the locus of the creation of meanings in the interaction between the text and the reader, then we are faced here with a passive reader. This reader undergoes a meaning that he or she did not help create and simply accepts as a gift from others. Whether these others are God, the group or one's own church, at this level it does not matter much. The sense here does not belong to the reader. It becomes so solely in a derivative and secondary sense, in that only later does he make it his own by assimilating it.

On the other hand, there is the reader who participates in the creation of the sense suggested by the text, the "vital reader". That

---

4   Jeanrond calls him an "apathetic reader," because despite the important diligence and application in the act of reading, from the perspective of sense-making this type of reader is perfectly "apathetic." Cf. W.G. Jeanrond, *L'ermeneutica teologica.* Op. cit. , p. 18.

the reader actively participates in the creation of the sense does not mean that he alone creates all the sense. If he alone were to create all the sense then the text he reads would be completely useless, because he would not take it into account in the elaboration of the sense he tries to create. This is not what is meant, then, when it is stated that the active reader creates meaning without passively undergoing it. It is meant only that the active reader creates meaning as an ally, as a co-participant.

The "vital reader" is the ideal, creative and innovative reader that the Bible presupposes, promotes and creates.[5] It creates him through its language. It is the narrative-symbolic language used by the Bible that converts the reader from passive to active. Since it is not a book of casuistry nor of rules to be mechanically applied, the reader of the Bible is called and compelled first to perceive, then, subsequently, to choose among the various possible meanings that the text offers him. It is the kind of language the Bible uses, a plurivocal language, that requires the reader's creative participation. Plurivocal is said of language that can mean more than one thing. Reader participation intervenes at this very level. And it occurs in two ways.

The first occurs because the active intervention of the reader becomes absolutely necessary in order to choose, among the various possible meanings, the one that best suits the situation in which he or she finds himself or herself. At this level, the reader cannot be subjected to the standard meaning. Especially when the meaning claims to be the right one. That meaning is right once and in other circumstances, but may no longer be right today in new circumstances. This requires discernment from the reader. The reader must be able to perceive the plurality of possible meanings latent in the text. He must also discern the meaning best suited to his own context.

Second, the reader must simultaneously be able to look outside the text into the extra-textual reality. He must be able to read and understand it well. This ability to be able to read, outside the text, even the external reality, seems to be a nontextual task. But it is not, because understanding the external context does not serve solely as

---

5   U. Eco, *Lector in fabula.* Op. cit., pp. 50-66.

an application space where meaning, which would have been arrived at from a simple analysis of the text, can be poured out. Context also serves to choose well the best meaning that comes from the text and is in the text, to create meaning, in the sense of determining which of the possible senses is the most suitable. But understanding the context is key and central also before the upstream meaning-making, and not only in the application moment.

We will call the first type of reader the "obedient reader," and the second type the "vital reader." The Bible presupposes both, but the one the Bible particularly prefers and promotes is the "vital reader." We call him vital because on the one hand he gathers from the Bible the "life" that is articulated in it through those textual forms, and on the other hand because this same life he knows how to extend it, through his interpretation, into the reality outside the text.

Certainly the Bible recognizes anyone who approaches it as a reader and does not discriminate against anyone. Anyone can read the Bible and also possibly with any kind of attitude. And always he will get a benefit from it. However, the reader that the Bible prefers, aspires to and pushes to form is the "vital reader" who does not suffer meaning but becomes a co-creator of meaning. This feature of the Bible, which is to create active readers, did not materialize to its full potential before modernity for two reasons.

1. Because the Bible was materially uncommon, it was not read assiduously or easily. It was not read widely in general. If people had been able to read massively even at other times as we read today, the mechanism perhaps would have been triggered earlier.

2. Because even when there were books they tended to be read within stable cultures; therefore, people read the Bible as a stabilizing element. This does not mean that before modernity there were no creative and vital readers, just as it does not mean that all readers in modernity are creative and vital. In fact, it may be just the opposite; but at the structural level the historical periods before modernity did not privilege the "creative reader", but the "obedient reader". It is modernity that will structurally privilege the creative reader, because it will assign him or her a role in social transformation that he or she was denied before.

1. A Theological-Cultural Look at the Reader[6]

The centrality of the creative reader and instrument of social transformation came, according to anthropologist Antonio C. Scalamonti, only with modernity, because it is she alone who will bet on a new subject: no longer the group but the individual. It is the individual who will be the mainstay of the new epoch.[7] In what sense? In the sense that the individual could not be born in a world, such as the medieval world, where the focus was on stability. To truly give place to the individual was to destabilize the world. Opening up the world and reality, consequently, involved recognizing both as incomplete. The declaration of their completeness is synonymous with the denial of the individual, just as the declaration of the birth of the individual is synonymous with the denial of the completeness of the world and reality. If the world is complete, the individual becomes essentially unnecessary and superfluous. Conversely, if the world is declared open, then the individual is declared essentially

---

6   What it means to read and what status to entrust and acknowledge to the reader does not only recall a theory of communication, but an anthropology and sociology of cultural processes. See L. Sciolla, *Sociologia dei processi culturali*, ("*Sociology of Cultural Processes*"), (Bologna: Il Mulino, 2007), pp. 231-244; R. H. Robbins, *Cultural Anthropology. A Problem-Based Approach*, (Belmont: Wadsworth, 2013), pp. 131-175. But it is not only cultural macro-passages, such as that of orality to writing, that profoundly alter the profile and functionality of the reader, but also those micro-passages within the same historical period that introduce important ruptures and orientations regarding precisely the profile and meaning of the reader. This had been the central point of Ferdinand de Saussure's reflection, according to which the transition from a linguistics of "word" to a linguistics of "language" entails a radical downsizing of the status of the reader. See F. De Saussure, *Corso di linguistica generale*, ("Course of Linguistics") (Rome: Laterza, 2009). As well as the transition from structuralism to post-structuralism or deconstructionism implies once again and radically a major shift in the status of the reader. See W.J. Ong, *Orality and Literacy* Op. cit., pp. 136-152; J. Lewis, *Cultural Studies. The Basics*, (London: Sage, 2008), pp. 109-143; C. Barker, E. A. Jane, *Cultural Studies. Theory and Practice*, (London: Sage, 2016), pp. 21-24.
7   A. Cavicchi Scalamonti, *La morte...*Op, cit., pp. 43-56.

an agent[8] necessary to complete it and give it a new profile and configuration.

The birth of the individual in modernity is not the birth of its discrete presence. If the individual is there, it must be there in a strong way. This is individualism. Individualism is not born as an accompanying element, but as the central element of a new historical period. Individualism is not the limited sign of an ethical and personalistic change. Individualism is modernity and modernity is individualism. Individualism is the cultural mechanism that transforms an era, the sign that guarantees the establishment of a new world. With individualism comes a new cosmology, a new politics, a new religion by virtue of a new hermeneutics. The individual is first and foremost an individual who interprets the world and reality from himself.

Hermeneutics with a performing reader, recognized as central to the elaboration of meaning, could only arise in modernity. Indeed, hermeneutics with a "strong-reader" or "reader-centric" emphasis is just the application or extension of modern individualism in the area of Bible reading. But the reader, in modern hermeneutics, not only becomes central, he also becomes a creator of meaning. All modernity is constructivist.[9] Constructivism means that reality is not given to us beforehand, but we construct and design it. These ingredients certainly exist before us, precisely as pieces to be assembled, but not as a finished reality. It is the individual who assembles the new world. The world comes from our hands. We become creators of our world. "Reader-centered" hermeneutics is but the extension of this modern individualistic axiom into the realm of reading texts.

This constructivist soul is visible in all modern hermeneutics, as for example, in that of Umberto Eco. For him, the reader is the true creator of meaning,[10] consequently we will speak of an "open" text as a characteristic of all texts, precisely because of the necessary creative intervention of the reader. The text is so because it requires

---

8   Cf. W.J. Ong, *Orality and Literacy*...Op. cit., pp. 31-76.
9   C. T. Fosnot, *Constructivism. Theory, Perspectives and Practice*, (New York: Teachers College Press, 2005), pp. 11-21.
10 U. Eco, op. cit.

multiple and continuous interpretations by virtue of the reader's innovative power. It is the creative reader who makes a text open. In contrast, a closed text reduces interpretations because it claims to offer the reader a ready-made meaning. The reader has become the agent that makes a text what a text is; an open work.[11]

U. Eco actually only enhances what modernity already carries in its bosom from the very beginning. This centrality of the meaning-creating subject is in fact already at the heart of the Kantian program. Kant elaborates a conception of knowledge that constitutes a real revolution, because at the center of the cognitive process he no longer places the object (text or reality), but the subject (reader or thinking mind) with its capacities and activities. Knowledge consists in the activity by which the subject organizes the data provided by experience, ordering them, processing them, unifying them through the intervention of certain mental functions. Therefore, knowledge is configured as the result of an activity, a human construction. The object of knowledge is not a datum but a product of its activity. Knowledge certainly does not create its own objects; Kant in this sense is very critical of Berkeley's extreme idealism. At this level the Kantian project is more modest. It merely seeks to give form to the material of knowing gathered from sensible intuition. But by organizing the material given to him by experience, which is presented as formless, disorganized and chaotic material, it is as if the subject were creating reality. The mental organization of reality is almost equivalent to creating that reality. The change is radical: we are faced with a new perspective.

Until Descartes or Kant, the definition of truth to which Western philosophical culture had adhered was that of Aristotelian-Thomistic derivation, that is, of the "adaptation of the intellect to being".[12] Now, on the other hand, it is argued that it is reality that must adapt to the ways in which the subject knows things. From this perspective,

---

11 U. Eco, *Lector in fabula...* Op. cit., pp. 52-54.
12 "*Adequatio rei et intellectus*" (correspondence between reality and intellect), a classic formula that goes back to Aristotle and was taken up by Thomas Aquinas. Cf. *Somma contro i gentili. Libro primo e secondo*, (*"Sum Against the Gentiles. Book One and Two")*, (Bologna: Edizioni Studio Domenicano, 2000), p. 46.

knowledge, for Kant, is configured as a synthesis between a subject of knowing and a form by which the knower organizes it. Indeed, Kant states in a famous phrase, "Everything begins with experience, but not everything is derived from experience."[13] Kant argues that forms and structures operate in knowledge that do not come from experience and are a priori. A cognitive field is constituted common to all men, precisely because common are the criteria for organizing the material of experience. Each of us has a way of organizing sensation that rests on conditions common to all men. These conditions are the a priori forms of knowledge. It functions independent of experience and is possessed by us "before" sensory experience. It belongs to our way of perceiving and thinking.

"A priori" constitute the conditions of possibility of experience itself. The investigation of such forms constitutes Kant's "transcendental philosophy." In this sense, the term "transcendental," referring to the "a priori" forms by which experience is constituted, has a different meaning from the term "transcendent," which instead concerns a sphere that lies beyond (transcends) experience itself. Only by admitting the presence of those a priori forms and structures can the existence of universal and necessary knowledge be explained. That is why it can be said that "We of things do not know a priori except what we ourselves put into them."[14] This breakthrough in the field of knowledge theory is called a "Copernican revolution" by Kant. This is the essence of the synthetic-a-priori knowledge articulated by Kant, in which the central role becomes that of "the observer," that is, the man who, by investigating nature, structures and orders it through the organization of collected data.

Modern and postmodern hermeneutics is nothing but the extension in the interpretive sphere of the Kantian transcendental subject. It could not be otherwise simply because of cultural contiguity and proximity. This is why the apparent one-sidedness and exaggeration in describing contemporary hermeneutics as "reader-centric," which

---

13 I. Kant, *Prolegomeni ad ogni futura metafisica che potrà presentarsi come scienza*, (*"Prolegomena to Any Future Metaphysics That Would Be Able To Present Itself as a Science"*), (Rome: Laterza, 1996), pp. 95-167.
14 I. Kant, *Ibid*, pp. 25-41.

has been our reading hypothesis since Part I, is not ultimately as improbable as it may seem at first glance. The reader is the linchpin of the modern hermeneutic project.

The value of the reader is not solely related to the instrumental value of his or her act. If there were no readers, who would read texts? The reader's contribution is deeper and has a great impact on the text itself. The reader is an indicator of an essential characteristic of the text: its openness to the world. Through this openness of the text, we understand that the reader is not so foreign to the text. Therefore, although there is a risk that the reader will alter the scope of meaning of the text, and distort it, structurally we can say that there is no text without a reader. The reader is the correlate of the text, the one who brings the text to its fullness. It is as if the text remains, without the reader, in the state of an unexplored latency. This latency manifests itself and becomes real only with the reader. Through the mechanism of reading and interpretation it is the reader who unfreezes the dormant potential of the text. A text cannot unfold its full signification until it is exposed by him. The reader embodies two important attitudes in the face of the text: 1. He must submit to the text and, almost annihilating himself, allow the text to unfold its full potentiality of meanings independently of him; 2. The reader must bring to bear in the face of the text his own specificity, which, while being the least textual thing, becomes the most suitable element for bringing out the latent meaning of the text.

Even more typically, the reader represents an opportunity for the text. In this the reader is a challenge to the text, and a good text knows how to welcome this challenge. A good text does not demand from the reader its flattening or passive subordination. There are four claims of the reader to the text.[15]

To better exemplify these four dimensions of the ideal reader's profile, we will refer to the prologue of Luke's Gospel, which we quote below to facilitate understanding of the explanation.

Luke 1:1-4

---

15 P. Ricœur, *Ermeneutica filosofica*...Op. cit., pp. 95-100.

"Since many have undertaken to order a narrative of the facts that have been fulfilled among us, as they have been handed down to us by those who from the beginning were eyewitnesses to them and who became ministers of the Word, it has seemed good to me also, after I have been thoroughly informed of everything from the origin, to write to you by order, illustrious Theophilus, so that you may recognize the certainty of the things you have been taught."

2. The Reader and his Rooting "Upstream" of the Text: Pre-Understanding[16]

Before anything else, the reader reminds the text that it is not first but second: every text is always preceded by life. If the first human experience were a textual experience, life would be reduced to a written formula. Even when a text is well written or the text in question is the best possible text, as might be the case with the Bible or another religious text, that written formula does not have sufficient consistency to replace and precede life. A true text recognizes its derivability and dependence on something that precedes it: life. The true reader is the one who finds, recognizes and claims his or her "rootedness" in the life upstream of the text. While it is true that the text informs the reader about things he does not know, it is also true that the reader learns from the text only details of experiences that are familiar to him, before the text and apart from it.

This is the meaning of the pre-comprehension included or presupposed in any reading of a text. The text tells me about things that are already familiar to me because I am already grounded in life. The text is only a deepening of things that are not new to me. The text is not life but a mapping of it. Useful and necessary, but subsequent to a pre-textual grounding in life. A text is great not when it claims to know more about life from the fact that that life has organized it around a successful cognitive schema. A text, even

---

16 Ricœur writes, "The theory of knowledge must be preceded by the recognition of the situation of rootedness in the world from which the anchorage of the whole linguistic system, and therefore also of books and texts, is assured," in *Ermeneutica filosofica*, Ibid. p. 38.

when it succeeds, fails because it is never able to contain life, all of life. Life will always be more than a text, just as life is always greater than any rule about life. That is not why the text lapses and loses its relevance. The relevance of a text is not to replace life, but to bear witness to it. That persuasive testimony, if constructed well, induces the reader to be interested in the text and even to go beyond the text. A good text, therefore, is always preceded by life and, at the same time, is surpassed by life. The good reader is one who is anchored in life and who, by virtue of this anchoring, is driven toward texts as expressions of life, but without becoming trapped in them.

We take up the passage from Luke's Gospel (1:1-4), which we used in the previous chapter, to describe the three types of "distanciation" that constitute the essence of the text and, in this new context, to illustrate now the profile of the reader. Theophilus,[17] as Luke's friend, is not born out of reading the text Luke writes for him. Just as their friendship is not born because of that text. Rather, that text will be the product of the life of which that friendship, that emotional bond, that human affinity, is an expression. Luke's text is not first but second to a life-relation and belonging that sees Theophilus and Luke already connected. Regardless of the gospel, there is a bond between the two of them that the writing of the gospel will come to enrich, illuminate, enhance, but not create. And even when relationships arise at the root of a reading, motivated by a text, in reality the reading of that text is always preceded by an excerpt of life with which the reader is familiar before knowing the text. If we did not know love, no text about love would be understandable to us. If we did not know intuitively and from life experience what friendship is, no text on friendship could ever break through to us. In other words, there is a grammar of life that we carry within us in an immediate way that highlights the fact that we are already in life, and only after that do intentions arise to improve it through the information conveyed to us by the texts. But those texts with new information about life are already an expression of life itself.

---

17 J. Nolland, *Luke 1-9:20*, Op. cit., pp. xxvii-xlvii; R. Fabris, *Luke*, Op. cit., pp. 21-34.

The friendship between Luke and Theophilus, or the desire to know the truth, is not born with the text Luke writes. That text enhances that life that already exists, giving it an opportunity for growth and reinforcement. This is the meaning of belonging, which, as such, is the condition and starting point for good interpretation.

3. *The Reader and his Uprooting "in Front of" the Text: Self-Criticism*[18]

The second moment the reader must assume is to put himself "in front" of the text and accept that that text upsets him.[19] Making sure that he feels and accepts the criticism that, starting from the text, comes directly to him. Being in front of the text thus causes a double effect. In a first moment the text reminds us that we are rooted in life. In a second moment the text tries, on the other hand, to uproot us from life through a critic of that rooted life. Not to destroy that rootedness, but to improve it. Improving it sometimes means deconstructing it, dismantling it, subjecting it to scrutiny in order to rebuild it as best we can. This second effect, which takes over after the primary process of rootedness in life, is a process of critique that becomes necessary because the connection with life so many times is given in an abnormal and deforming way. It easily becomes misleading ideology. Not all certainties are real and true certainties. When that rootedness in life has become symbiotic and uncritical, the text bursts in as a salvation because it produces, if there is willingness and flexibility in the reader, a radical self-criticism of that anomalous symbiosis that one wants to pass off as necessary and beneficial.

---

18 Ricœur writes, "The metamorphosis of the ego just alluded to implies a moment of distancing even in the relationship with the self, as a result of which understanding is appropriation as much as expropriation. Self-understanding can, indeed must, consequently, include both a Marxist and Freudian critique of the illusions of the subject," in *Ermeneutica filosofica*, Op. cit., pp. 77,78.
19 It is what L.A. Schökel calls, "The primacy of the question." Cf. L.A. Schökel, J.M. Bravo Aragon, *Appunti di ermeneutica...* Op. cit., pp. 92,93.

This verification exercise, starting from the text, should not be directed only at those elements that seem anomalous, arouse doubt and whose consistency must be verified. Critical verification must be applied to all elements in play, even those seemingly healthy and beyond doubt, because ideology easily creates appearance of truth and similarity of functional path in all departments and lanes of interpretive experience. Self-criticism is always an uncomfortable and apparently an unnecessary and an inappropriate exercise. It is never in time but out of time, never programmable but extemporaneous, starting with something unexpected that the text suddenly suggests. It must be realized by virtue of the fact that unfortunately not every "grounding in life" is necessarily a grounding that promotes self-affirmation and self-realization. There are purported rootednesses that actually are not.

The critique of false "rootedness" in life, advanced by the shrewd reader, does not reverse the relationship between "rootedness" (belonging) and "text" (distanciation). Structurally, first there will always be rootedness and then later the text, which generates criticism because it is only by virtue of the positive that the negative can be revealed and criticized. If this were not the case, criticism would be the grounding and would take precedence. Instead, it is the other way around: criticism, as a derivative event, is only possible if first there has been the affirmation of life to which the text bears witness.

Anomalous entrenchments in life, unfortunately, are not only common and widespread, but tend to perpetuate themselves precisely by virtue of texts that support them. Structurally anomalous texts or good texts read roughly and one-sidedly. These anomalous entrenchments are not always visible precisely because they stick to the reader like a second skin. For this reason, the critique that generates being "in front" of the text must always be a self-critique, not a critique of what is distant and peripheral; not a critique of others or of application strategies, but a critique of oneself, of the reader in his or her innermost essence. It is the reader himself who is the bearer of anomalies of which he himself is unaware. Self-criticism before the text is an exercise that partially corrects these anomalies because it at least highlights what tends to remain hidden.

Anomalous entrenchments are often presented as pure evidences. But they are not. They take the form of ideologies and as such resist any critical analysis. They exist at the collective level as well as at the individual level. Criticism that arises within groups or in individuals themselves, as internal corrective mechanisms, beyond apparent effectiveness, is often unsuccessful because it tends to maintain ideologies through updating them. This is why the text, as an external element, represents a unique opportunity for critique, for self-criticism. Not to deny belonging, but to correct it and, by correcting it, reinforce it. Before proceeding to the application of what I have read, I must be able to critique myself "in front" of the text. If this does not happen, diligent application of the text risks reinforcing existing ideologies in the reader. Instead of being a tool for liberation, the text becomes a justification for maintaining those anomalies.

In Theophilus' example, Luke's Gospel serves, before becoming a push toward application, as a space for self-criticism.[20] Theophilus, as his name indicates, was by nature a man sensitive to religion and God. *Theo* (God), *philo (to* love) "friend of God, lover of the things of God, inclined to religion, sensitive to faith, vulnerable to transcendence," all these meanings and paraphrases of the name Theophilus are the spontaneous extension of what this name bears at its core. It is a theophore name par excellence because it encloses at its center the need for God. In ancient times, and not only in Israel, the name carried a distinctive characteristic of people. People recognized themselves in their name and their name was a strong expression of who they were in reality.

Theophilus, by virtue of this natural inclination toward religion, which his name embodies, could have remained as he was, cherishing this connatural and structural attitude of his temperament and enriching it only with what Jesus offers to every human being. That is not what happens. That text that his friend Luke is offering him as a gift, instead of validating that natural religious virtue in him, ends up criticizing it, dismantling it, overturning it. That text serves as a space for self-criticism. Reading that text, which Luke writes for him, Theophilus finds the best part of himself, his belief, contradicted. For that text will tell him that much of what he believes is pure superstition.

---

20 D.L. Bock, *Luke,* Op. cit., pp. 51-67; H. Schürmann. *The Gospel of Luke,* Op. cit., pp. 53-67.

We do not have records of Theophilus' reactions, however, we can well imagine them. To a man who is very religious, Luke's Gospel says that to a great extent his religiosity is false or, at the very least, superstitious, because true religion consists only in recognizing Jesus as the Christ. This is the Christ whom Theophilus does not know and must struggle to know and accept as savior. That text thus represents a harsh critique of Theophilus' religious and human ideologies. Luke's Gospel is not condescending to Theophilus. It does not mold a Christ to his measure, for the use and consumption of his natural religiosity. That text, written by Luke, will complicate his human and religious journey, because it will introduce into the center of his life an obstacle, a stumbling block, an element of scandal. We know, however, indirectly, that Theophilus, on the other hand, is open to such criticism. And that is why Luke will dedicate a second book to him.[21]

This self-criticism "before" the text the Spirit accomplishes, at first, through the unhinging of our certainties. The text must create in us an awareness regarding our own anomalies. If the reader does not first correct his or her own anomalous and improper assumptions, which he or she often holds up even with biblical justifications (racism, machismo, speciesism), it is clear that direct application would only end up reinforcing them. In the moment of self-criticism, the reader distrusts his or her deepest beliefs and allows himself or herself to be unhinged by the text.

4. *The Reader and his Pro-rooting "Beyond" the Text: Imagination*[22]

In a third moment and before application, the text pushes us forward in an unusual way: it pushes us to go beyond it through

---

21 Acts 1:1.
22 Ricœur writes: "If, in other words, a fundamental dimension of the referentiality of the text is its fictional character, so too is it in regard to the subjectivity of the reader. As a reader, only when I lose myself do I find myself; from reading I am introduced into the imaginative variations of the ego; in accordance with play, the metamorphoses of the world are also playful metamorphoses of the ego," in *Ermeneutica filosofica*, Op. cit., p. 77.

imagination. Not to escape and run away from belonging, but to create new ones and, by creating them, reinforce them through their renewal. A good text always promotes a possible beyond. The text always has a latency. It proposes meanings just by suggesting them, by introducing them as possible, indirectly, almost without mentioning them, but only alluding to them. Instead, these incomplete and sketchy meanings from the text explode only through the reader's imagination. It is the reader who brings these insights to fruition and concretizes them into alternative visions, outlines and forms to the text through imagination. With imagination, the reader, starting from the text, goes beyond it through the creation of alternative worlds, practices and realities. The reader has a revolutionary vocation in the interpretive process.

Reading cannot become the place where the reader's passion dies. On the contrary, every good reading gives birth to passion through imagination.[23] Through the text, the reader imagines[24] worlds that do not yet exist, but can exist if we begin to perceive them as possible. If application took over immediately without this explosion of meaning, which is the moment of imagination, reading would become a place of imprisonment, not only of meaning, but also of the reader. We could say that imagination represents true self-criticism. In some ways, imagination comes before self-criticism and grounds it. Self-criticism is an unconcluded imagination and imagination is a fully realized self-criticism.

Reconnecting with Theophilus and Luke,[25] although we do not find an account of how the moment of imagination takes place in Theophilus, it is clear that the reading of that text prompted

---

23 Imagination on the other hand is not a pure distractive and consoling mechanism but transforms reality the most concrete and leads it toward freedom and personal flourishing. Willie James Jennings, *The Christian Imagination. Theology and the Origins of Race,* Yale University Press, Yale 2011, pp. 21-32.
24 Imagination is that attitude that exploits the potentialities latent in the text and brings them to fruition. Cf. L.A. Schökel, J.M. Bravo Aragon, *Appunti di ermeneutica...* Op. cit., pp. 94-97.
25 R.C. Tannehill, *Luke,* Op. cit., pp. 33-35; K.H. Rengstorf, Il vangelo secondo Luca, Op. cit., pp. 31-36.

Theophilus to look at the world, his life, and reality differently. The change in behavior was preceded, thanks to the gospel text, by a change in vision, in mindset. This is *metanoia*. Metanoia as conversion is, before being moral, a conversion in imagination. It represents a change in thinking. A different way of standing before the the world, a going beyond what we perceive. Metanoia as conversion is an imaginative process at the basis of salvation, because only through it can the believer perceive a new world. In the present he does not see it; he can only imagine it. Faith itself is a strong imaginative process, making visible what is not yet there in the present. It introduces a horizon that includes that reality which, according to the criteria of the present, is not real but becomes so through imagination. It is precisely this flight of imagination that becomes reality in the life of Theophilus, of which we have no explicit record, but which is undoubtedly there, for it is by virtue of that and the great transformations it produced that Luke dedicates a second text to him, the book of the Acts of the Apostles.

5. *The Obedient Reader and the Vital Reader: The Why of Creativity*[26] *"in Reading"*

In a fourth moment, the reader remembers and claims before the text his "grounding" in life downstream of the text. While it is true that the text tells the reader things he does not know, it is also true that the reader, in the application of what he learns from the text, tests how much of what he has learned from the text is true or false, relevant or irrelevant, functional or illusory. In application, the reader takes note of the latent meanings of the text and extends them into concrete life.[27] Every application always goes beyond the text and adds things to the text that it does not say. The guarantor of this passage is precisely the reader. The text is not an authoritarian

---

26 Ricœur writes, "I rightly said imagination and not will, because the power to allow oneself to be seized by new possibilities precedes the power to make a decision and choose," in *Ermeneutica filosofica*, Op. cit., p. 99.
27 In this sense any hermeneutic application is necessarily creative. W.G. Jeanrond, *L'ermeneutica teologica*...Op. cit., pp. 157-201.

king who says what reality must be by decree; rather it is reality that offers and initiates a path and opens to a new reality. Of this larger reality beyond the text, the reader is the ambassador. The true reader is the one who does not feel obliged to pay an eternal tribute to the text that has guided him for a stretch of his path. The true reader is transgressive in his essence. He is so because of the text itself. The text itself, if it is true and noble, is the element that impels the reader to go further.

This space of transcending the text, which we call the space of application, is not a subordinate stage. It represents an important place of realization for the reader and also for the text. It is as if, in application, the text itself rejoices in being transcended. Application is not the place of flattening the reader who prolongs the text in its fullness. The moment of application is not the pure reflection of a sense of the text applied to perfection in the reality of life.

The word application easily misleads, because application suggests the complete replication of the text and its pattern in real life through the diligence of the reader. Instead, diligence is not the central point in application. It is necessary and essential, but at the same time insufficient. Application,[28] more than being a space of diligence, is a space of creativity. This is because a true text does not want the subjugation of reality to its mapping, but rather the opposite. A true text desires to be a map that the reader uses as a point of departure, not as a point of arrival, because, if that were the case, the text and its mapping would become mechanisms of bewilderment. The map should serve to explore the territory, not to confuse it and replace it with the map. It is only the reader's creativity that allows that mapping (text) to be used well in the moment of real confrontation with the territory.

Only after the recognition of "rootedness in life," "self-criticism" and "imagination," does "application" become a corrective and constructive path because it outlines a possible process of redemption and growth. There is nothing magical about application, but it opens

---

28 Application does not only have to do with an external realization. It includes a personal and internalizing dimension. See L.A. Schökel, J.M. Bravo Aragon, *Appunti di ermeneutica...*Op. cit., pp. 97-102.

up possible worlds because it becomes the natural sequential stage of a prior work that takes and prolongs positive life thrusts from the text. Application structured in this sequence is transformed from repetition of the past to fidelity to the future, from validation of the already happened to the not-yet of the project. Verification changes into promise.

Reconnecting once again with Theophilus,[29] we can only imagine how the moment of application becomes the final stage of this interpretive journey. We are told nothing about how Theophilus applied what he learned from the text before him, the Gospel of Luke. Yet, much is suggested to us. That the book of the Acts of the Apostles, also dedicated to Theophilus is a sign of the greatness of his application. Indeed, the whole missionary turn of Christianity, which from centripetal will become centrifugal, precisely by virtue of its decentralization to foreigners, to pagan peoples, is placed in the perspective of what Theophilus represents. He is the pagan who became a Christian. The prototype of the new believer is not the unbeliever who begins to believe. This profile will be a profile of modern times. The profile of all nascent Christianity, which, beginning with the obsession with purity of faith (typical of the Judaism of Jesus' time) will become a Christianity in search of new inculturation, is embodied in Theophilus and put as the incipit of the book of the Acts of the Apostles (1:1). This is the typically ancient profile of a man already a believer who corrects that belief by orienting it toward Jesus. The Christian preaching of which Theophilus is the prototype is in its essence only a reorientation of faith, not its creation. The ancient man who converts is already a believer, like Theophilus, because that is how the anthropology and culture of that time is structured. Different will be the profile of contemporary man who, being secularized to varying degrees, must, in order to recognize Jesus as his Savior, learn to believe anew.

Let us take up the initial question of this chapter: who is the real reader? Let us problematize the situation by answering it atypically in this way to give an additional but decisive step in identifying that

---

29 D.L. Bock, *Luke*, Op. cit., pp. 51-67; H. Schürmann. *The Gospel of Luke*, Op. cit., pp. 53-67.

characteristic that qualitatively distinguishes the reader. The true reader is not "the one who reads everything" but "the one who does not limit him or herself to read everything." This atypical answer to a seemingly obvious question will allow us to specify further. The best reader seems to be, at first glance, the disciplined, knowledgeable, purposeful, and attentive reader of the text he or she reads. The problem is that the attention and awareness of that kind of careful reader already presupposes two anomalies.

The first consists in the fact that the text, implicitly, has already become an "object" for him. An object he needs to focus on, grasp, conquer in order to finally possess. The text seems to have become the object of an obsession with possession. This desire for possession presupposes the disenchantment of the text and its reduction to a primary source of information. The text is reduced to its informational dimension, its quantitative component. As if a text is valuable solely on the condition that it possesses new information. A typical textual reductionism is outlined in this view.

The second consists in the fact that this careful and determined reader not only embodies the greed of wanting to possess the object he lacks (the text) but upstream, also betrays a lack of his own, a primary emptiness. He starts already impoverished because he appears disconnected from the object he greedily seeks. That reader is orphaned and as such missing an essential connection. Here between reading subject and read object (text) there is a rupture, a detachment, a deprivation. This detachment, this initial non-attachment, creates a compensatory mechanism that is expressed in the attentive and disciplined greed of compulsive desire and conquest. The discipline and attentiveness of this attentive reader in front of the text, hides a non-binding that is intended to be corrected and is an expression of it. The noble intent to overcome that anomaly through reading, which aims precisely at the reconnection of the subject (reader) with the object (text), only adds to that rupture because it delivers to the greedy and orphaned reader a disenchanted text, a text that has become an object.

The best reader cannot be recognized in this careful and disciplined, decisive and determined reader. In this reader there is a hypertrophy of intention that translates a poverty and obsession. The true reader is more relaxed, but not because he already possesses the text. On the contrary, not only does he not own it, he is aware that he will never own it. This is because the text is not an object to be owned.[30] This reader, of type two, has a desire that is the telltale sign of his incompleteness. By this desire he is driven forward. His is not an obsessive incompleteness. His is a light incompleteness that leads him not to a desire to possess but to a courtship of the text, knowing that it will never be his completely. With that text that will never be his he already feels connected and therefore desires it. He is not orphaned by what he seeks. With what he seeks there is already a connection, a memory, a belonging. This reader, by virtue of that presupposed connection with the text, can do without possessing that text because he is already unconsciously connected to what that text is about, that is, life. The true reader is the one who is already connected to the life to which the unobjectified text bears witness. And he is connected to life for two reasons.

First, precisely because he is connected to life, he has no problem reading that text without the obsession of possessing that life that is expressed in the text. His is not an obsession with the text because he does not escape from life. Obsession and escape are not opposite experiences that often create an ironclad partnership. One tends to insistently seek what one is fleeing from, but is unable to take in without possessing. Too much reading easily becomes escape from life. Not escape as detachment and disinterest, but escape as obsession and attachment. It is all or nothing, so why nothing, then everything. Symbiotic attachment is the most refined type of escape because there is no estrangement but its opposite. Attachment is rapprochement in form but estrangement (escape) from the substance of life. A controlled life is no longer life. The greedy subject, who seeks attachment to the object through reading, actually turns away, despite approaching life, because he seeks a controlled life, a life made object, a manipulated text. This triggers a real mechanism of addiction and, like any addiction, it drives away that which it wants

---

30 In this sense Jeanrond speaks of "an ethics of reading" that is not one that stops at the letter of the text, but grasps its perspective and makes it its own. Cf. W.G. Jeanrond, *L'ermeneutica teologica*, Op. cit., pp. 196-199.

to approach. That thing that one approaches and feels the need for has become a dead thing, which one possesses quantitatively but escapes qualitatively. The best reader, on the other hand, is the one who, being rooted in the life that unites subject and object, does not read in order to have life, but reads because he is already connected to life. Reading does not become a sublimation, but an expression of life that dismantles the gluttony of wanting life by aiming to control it. Even the apparent and legitimate pursuit of the "meaning of life" through reading actually conceals the perversion of having life by trying to control it, by controlling its meaning.

The second reason for the connection to life is explained by the fact that only this rootedness in life sparks the imagination. Imagination is what distinguishes the creative reader. The creative reader is not the one who transcends text and life to jump into the void and chaos. On the contrary, he is the one who is rooted in life and the text and, by virtue of this rootedness, flies to the beyond, to new forms of life. He is an heir who receives and transforms, listens and innovates. Rootedness and listening to the text does not stop him, but nourishes him and propels him forward. The creative reader is not a loose cannon. The creative reader is the one who empowers life and this creates new spaces of expression. He gives life new forms by virtue of the very life that animates him. Only life creates life. This is the imagination.

The best reader is not the one who wants to com-prehend (take) meaning by making it his obsession through assiduous reading of texts. This kind of reader, who appears as a model to many, is actually a bad model because he or she is a reader in "withdrawal." The best reader is one who is well before reading and is well because he is rooted in life, so he does not aim to possess it. And being in life means being aware that you can lose it. Approaching life must always elicit an attitude of vulnerability. If we want to enjoy it, we must know that we cannot possess it. If we owned it, we would immediately kill it. Life embodied as an object in the sense of a text ultimately turns out to be a poor life that does not convey life. As readers in reading, we must seek not a strength but the discovery of our vulnerability. True reading of a text is the discovery of the unavailability of life and its meaning. In reading we look at a goal (life) that we cannot have, but if the desire animates us it means that that life is already in us and it is by virtue of it that we are moved by the desire to read. It is when that life is not there, because there is no rootedness in it, that paradoxically the obsession to have it is triggered; but as soon as we have reached it, it slips from our grasp and we are left with only its carcass.

Let us now briefly return to the differentiation introduced at the beginning of this chapter between the "obedient reader" and the "vital reader." The obedient reader -we said- is a reader who is very active in the application but not in the creation of meaning, while the vital reader is not obsessed with the application of the meaning of the text but is the one who seeks, desires, acts and actually participates in the creation of meaning. Let us add a specification to this differentiation. An important specification that concerns the reader's being and not just his knowledge. For it is primarily at this level, and not only at the level of sense-making, that the most important difference between these two types of readers manifests itself.

The obedient reader is the one who receives from the text the meanings already made that he only has to apply. In this he takes no risks. He does not assume the price of freedom, so he prefers security in the paths established by what precedes him, whatever that may be: tradition, family, church, God or text. We might say that his obvious activism and application efforts may well be a compensation mechanism for not being able to create new meanings. He compensates his lack of creative capacities at the level of meaning by hyper-presence in the dissemination of that meaning he did not create. The dirigisme that requires him to apply the meanings he has just collected extends to imposing on him who he is to be. The obedient reader accepts for himself a norm that does not feature him and which he suffers as an obligation. Interpretive obligation becomes ontological obligation. This is the dimension of ontological laziness that delineates the contours of his profile. What he owes, can or simply is, he does not derive from himself, but receives from others, from elsewhere. He suffers his being, so he avoids the beneficial suffering of those who instead seek to be themselves by creating what they are. The obedient reader is one who bends before the text without asking the text questions that its historical grounding would require. He is incapable, in confronting the text (even more so if this text is sacred), of claiming as legitimate what he is, of expressing his anxieties, of giving space for doubts and questions. The sacredness of the text before him instills fear and paralyzes him.

Instead, the *vital reader* is a demanding reader who claims for himself the active right to question the text from the legitimacy of its historical grounding. In this new perspective, the reader is a co-creator of meaning: he assumes and understands that the world, life, identities or events do not exist as finite and fixed realities. They are only ingredients that each individual is called upon to use in the construction of personal projects, chosen according to what the text indicates and suggests, but also according to what we perceive our world to be and should be. The world, the family, the state or the texts are not imposed entities. They are not houses and places waiting to be inhabited, but materials to be used in new constructions. The *creative reader* does not allow the agenda of his actions to set the text alone. He must be a co-participant in determining what he is to do. Not only that: even in what concerns himself, his being, he is not submissive and compliant. While he is not the sole instance in determining what he is, he believes, in determining who he should be, that his own questions, anxieties, doubts and vicissitudes count as much as the text's suggestions.

He receives life and transmits it. It is a ferryman of life because there is meaning only if there is life. A life without meaning is empty knowledge. And the two characteristics that distinguish the vital reader are the force of "individualization" and the force of "participation."

a. *The Force of Individualization*

By "individualization" we mean the capacity for autonomy and the tenacity to mark a detachment in the face of the whole. The whole can be the family, the group, the city, the nation, the church or a foundational text. There is individuality when the person is able not to think of himself only in relation to a system and according to rhythms and deadlines that are not his own. Life must be able to be single life, to claim its own specificities, the ability to express and own its own registers without having to apologize for it. Life is single or it is not. In this sense, the process of achieving one's autonomy is always a transgression. Reading is always a transgression. Without transgression there is no life. And the first transgression is birth. Life begins with an ontological transgression. I go beyond the limit of an organ, the womb, that has nurtured and welcomed me perfectly. But that space that welcomes me perfectly can easily become my grave if I am not born into my autonomy as a singular being. In this sense reading can become unfortunately the grave of meaning. The symbiotic bond that connects us to a group, to a text or to an entity larger than ourselves is a human and legitimate bond if it provides for its own termination, if it expires at a certain moment. If it recognizes itself as an accompanying and promoting element of singular life. At some point, however, it must yield and be valued by its capacity to give freedom to the single life. The noble single life is the one that is affirmed as specific.

There is also the parallel concept of "individuation" developed in the field of analytical psychology by Swiss psychiatrist Carl Gustav Jung,[31] in the 1920s. The concept of individuation aims to emphasize the affirmation of the individual as a specific and coherent reality. It does so more on an internal level. In fact, individuation, according to Jung, is synonymous with that unique and unrepeatable psychic process of each individual that consists in the rapprochement of the ego with the self, that is, with an increasing integration and unification of the various elements that make up the personality. When this does not occur, the individual has the deconstructive experience of psychological dispersion.

"Individuation" is thus a process of integrating and harmonizing forces and instances within the individual. While "individualization" is a claim to autonomy from external forces; individualization is

---

31 C.G. Jung, *Phychologische Typen*, (Dusseldorf: Walter-Verlag, 1995), pp. 13-25.

what Paul Tillich calls, "the courage to be."[32] The courage of one's autonomy, of one's "singularity."[33]

In hermeneutics, it means that the individual capable of individualization is the reader, who through reading is able to affirm himself. He becomes in reading, capable of transgression. Capable of going beyond, Capable of creating new life. Reading and interpretation nurture and create him. It is in the text itself that the vital reader is able and learns to find reasons to affirm himself, to be autonomous, to forge his individuality. Interpretation generates and regenerates him. The text ceases to be a guilt mechanism for the individual who decides to go beyond it. It is the text itself that deconstructs his sense of shame at having decided to be different from the group. The reading and interpretation liberates him and suggests reasons for him to be himself at the cost of being different from others.

b. *The Power of Participation*

Here we are dealing with the opposite path with which the individualization process must learn to live in tension. In participation the individual recognizes himself as part of a whole. The vital reader knows how to live in company of texts and with these texts to live in communion and continuous dialogue. Life is always a life together with others; it is recognizing connectedness as a guarantee of survival. In participation we can identify two perspectives. On the one hand, participation as a condition; on the other hand, participation as a choice.

Participation as a condition means recognizing that participation precedes us. We are preceded beings, we do not choose it: it is already there before we are aware of it. It is a condition of life that makes life possible. It is becoming aware that we are born and attain an autonomy of our own by virtue of and because of a grounding in being. This is the version of participation according

---

32 P. Tillich, *The Courage to Be*, (Glasgow: Collins, 1979), pp. 4-19.
33 P. Tillich, *Ibid,* pp. 114-151.

to Paul Tillich,[34] which he calls "ontological rootedness." Every other activity undertaken by the individual in the course of his or her existence-epistemological, pragmatic, ritualistic, etc. - presupposes this rootedness in being that one must learn to recognize.

Participation as choice, on the other hand, is that which takes over after experiencing the dispersion of one's life and then arouses the need to create bonding. Bonding between the parts and centrifugal forces of one's life, but also bonding between this life and other lives. Here participation appears not as a foundation, but as a goal, as a task to be accomplished in order to guarantee the individual life a chance of survival. This is the perspective of Erich Fromm,[35] for whom the necessary autonomy of the individual, which at first enables him or her to overcome symbiotic bonds, enables him or her, at a later stage, to direct them and place them in the service of a noble and ennobling bond, without which autonomy itself would easily become destructive. Love as chosen participation, which places life in a context of bonding that guarantees it, has four characteristics: care, responsibility, respect and knowledge. Autonomy does not disappear; on the contrary, it becomes the guarantee of possible bonding. Active love is precisely this vocation to a participation that is not suffered, but freely chosen in virtue of life.

In hermeneutics, it means that the individual capable of participation is the reader who, through reading, is able to recognize a dependency. Reading helps him to think of himself as a derivative being, someone who is preceded. Reading ceases to be a sophisticated and clumsy exercise in self-foundation. In and through the text the reader finds compelling reasons to understand that his life is a response to something that precedes him. Interpretation integrates it to something. First to life itself, then to a community that precedes and welcomes it and to which the text bears witness. The text ceases to be an object of study that he tries to com-prehend and use to solely reinforce his own sufficiency. The text becomes the site of an epiphany of being together. In the text, life happens and is

---

34　P. Tillich, *Ibid*, pp. 89-113.
35　E. Fromm, *L'arte di amare*, (*"The Art of Loving"*), (Milan: Mondadori, 1996), pp. 29-40.

contemplated in the witness of which that text is a medium. Reading and interpretation complement him and suggest reasons for him to feel connected to and preceded by things he did not create.

Moving to a more theological realm, we can ask how far the Bible reader has preserved its revolutionary character, especially in Protestant circles, where the relevance of the individual believer was claimed by the Reformers, from the very beginning, as the primary reality of faith experience.

In fact, Protestantism has not only produced "reforms" but, after some centuries, unfortunately also some "deformations." Some anomalies, derived from the Protestant approach relating precisely to the status of the reader of the Bible, are, for example, the conformist reader, the obedient reader, the ethically reliable and morally predictable reader, which tends to impoverish and dent the profile of a curious, innovative, dreamer, transgressive reader, which is the profile of reader that the Bible presupposes and that we have called "vital reader." The reading of the Bible is not validated by a formal appeal to it, as Protestantism tends to do, but by the quality of reading and reader that that appeal produces. Protestantism was revolutionary in proposing the Bible as a criterion of faith when faith was impoverished by a scattershot appeal to secondary instances of religious experience. This same recall to that sacred book as final instance of truth risk today to become the tomb of meaning. The call to this centrality of the Bible cannot substitute for the qualitative effects that that centrality should produce, namely, a reading and a reader who flourish in the articulation of meaning making and innovation.

PART II
INTERPRETED LANGUAGE
AND INTERPRETING LANGUAGE

The Mediation of Language: "Pre-comprehension" and "Referentiality"

This second part of our essay is essentially a reflection on language, not directly but indirectly, as a presupposition of the interpretive process. We will redeem two features of language that are crucial to the articulation and flowering of meaning: the ontological anchoring of language upstream and the referentiality of language downstream. On the one hand, language is grounded in and preceded by an extralinguistic element, by the grounding in life and being, of which language then speaks. In this sense language is not first reality but second reality. This is why it is inseparable from being. Language speaks of being in which it is grounded and of which it gives a version and interpretation. On the other hand, language is forward movement. It is a going beyond, beyond itself, to reconnect with an alternative reality, a new reality by virtue of what Paul Ricœur calls "the world of the text",[1] which in its essence is the expansion of meaning that, from an intra-linguistic perspective, becomes a possible extra-linguistic reality. Language aims to connect itself to the external reality of which it speaks.

We will therefore consider language as presupposed by hermeneutics and the dysfunctions that arise in its regard. The text and the reader, elements that configure the hermeneutic circle, basically are linguistic events. The meanings that configure a text as text and the interpretations that configure the reader as reader are all linguistic realities before which one must ask: what kind of language

---
1 P. Ricœur, *Ermeneutica filosofica...*, Op. cit., pp. 53-78.

do they presuppose and what kind of language do they refer to? There is no single conception of language.

Language was conceived by the ancients as a reflection and mirror of reality. In their "naive realism" they still believed in the neutrality of language and its possibility of being able to tell being and express itself about it. Theirs was not an age of suspicion about the deforming and alienating capacity of language. For them between language and being there was a strong closeness and convergence. Despite this closeness, they still maintained a differentiation between language and being, for it was still being that decided the validity of a language and not the other way around. Language was subordinate to being. The affirmation of this priority of being over language, scholasticism inscribed and embodied it in the formula *Adaequatio rei et intellectus*,[2] namely, that the relevance of a linguistic-conceptual representation is validated only by the correspondence it has with external reality. Only if language describes external reality well, so that what it states corresponds to what it is, then language can be said to be true.[3]

The modern world has reversed this relationship by developing on language, beyond the great differences and contrasts between schools and thinkers, a rather coherentist view of language and truth from two strategies. On the one hand in questioning direct and immediate access to external reality, and on the other by privileging the subjective perception of reality rather than reality itself. Language has completely absorbed being, as Feuerbach denounced with respect to Hegelian rationalism.[4] That absorption of being into thinking and language is not only a Hegelian problem, but a problem

---

2 T. d'Aquinas, *Somma contro I gentili*...Op. cit., p. 46.
3 This is, for example, Feuerbach's description of the ancients: "Ancient philosophy still lived in the difference between thinking and being; for them thinking, spirit, idea was not the reality that everything contains, that is, the one, the only, the absolute reality. Ancient philosophers were still savants who had worldly knowledge - physiologists, politicians, zoologists," in L. Feuerbach, Fondamneti della filosofia dell'avvenire (*"Foundations of the Philosophy of the Future"*), (Forli: Clinamen, 2020), pp. 98,99.
4 Feuerbach writes about Hegel's philosophy, "Hegel is a realist, but a purely idealistic or, rather, abstract realist, a realist in the abstraction of all reality... According to him, philosophy has for its object only 'what is,'

of all modern philosophy, which differs within itself as a matter of degree and not of basic address and horizon.

Modern language, which recognizes its own limits which should have led it to sobriety, instead ends up swallowing external reality overbearingly. This is what happens with Kant's transcendental philosophy, for example. It criticizes reason that wants to talk about everything, even the "noumena," imposing on it an insurmountable limit that, however, legitimizes it when it gives it almost absolute power in the construction of "phenomena." Kant's transcendental reason does not create phenomena, but by ordering them through the categories of synthetic a priori judgments it is as if it created them. Thought has absorbed reality. This tendency to distance itself from external reality, or to speak of it only as a function of the language that describes it, will be a constant of modern episteme across the spectrum, as Foucault will also try to say.[5]

If a "correspondentist" view tends to mystify reality as ineffable, a "coherentist" view tends to reduce reality to language as a closed system. Neither of these approaches is actually nefarious in itself. Ancient and modern language both have a record of validity and legitimacy in relation to their own historical context. At the same time, they carry with them important drifts. The main one of modern language is to disavow reality and especially to reduce it to the order of thought and concept. This is the cultural positivism we are trying to describe in this essay.

---

but this 'is' is itself only something abstract, something thought," in L. Feuerbach, *Ibid.* p. 102.

5 Foucault writes, with respect to the modern tendency to move away from reality and swallow it up in closed systems, "It (the word) obeys a certain number of strict laws that similarly govern all the other elements of the same language; so much so that the word is no longer bound to a representation, except insofar as it is first and foremost part of the grammatical organization by which language defines and founds its coherence. In order for the word to be able to say what it says it is necessary that it belongs to a grammatical totality that, with respect to it, is configured as primary, fundamental and determining." in, M. Foucault, *Le parole e le cose. Un'archeologia delle scienze umane,* (*"The Order of Things: An Archeology of the Human Sciences"*), (Milan: BUR, 1978), pp. 303,304.

In this second part we will try to revisit the hermeneutic circle and thus the interpretive process from the perspective of language, calling the text "interpreted language," and the reader "interpreting language."

We have already mentioned the fact that the kind of language to which we connect the interpretive act is a language open to being. Hermeneutics, if it wants to win over textual and cultural positivism, could not do otherwise. It must modify its relationship with language, conceiving it not as a set of meanings within a closed system, such that meaning is grounded only in the differentiation and opposition of elements within the system. The ontological dimension of hermeneutics must dare to relate language to an extra-linguistic element, connecting it on the one hand with life, thus with being, and on the other hand with external reality through its referential dimension.

Living language is not the autonomous and self-referential language that closes in on itself, but that which recognizes itself as a means and a medium. Language is passage and mediation. It is a ferry that goes from life and leads to life. Language recognizes itself as dependent on the life that precedes and grounds it and of which it speaks. Living language does not speak of itself but of the life in which it is founded and of which it is an expression. There is thus a prelinguistic element that grounds language, as Gadamer tried to describe in his well-known work *Truth and Method*.[6]

The language that accompanies hermeneutics is not just any language, an average, standard language. Nor is it a refined and elitist language. Both pragmatic language and sophisticated language do not meet and match the vocation of hermeneutics. Cultural positivism, which unfortunately also traps interpretation, is satisfied with these languages of precision. The language of hermeneutics is a particular kind of language that has in its openness to Being and reality its main vocation. It is the connection with this kind of ontological language upstream (with Being) and downstream (with

---

6 Moreover, Gadamer describes this prelinguistic element that grounds all language, in regard to both language and history and aesthetics. H.-G. Gadamer, *Verità e metodo,* Op. cit., pp. 9-21.

reality) that gives interpretation its typical opacity embodied in its structural ambivalence and paradoxicality. The complexity of Being and reality that imposes on language, which wants to connect to them, a constraint of mystery that manifests itself in its polyvalent and paradoxical character. It is a sign of the unavailability of a meaning that refuses to be grasped and imprisoned by the messianic arrogance of univocal and transparent languages.

This living dimension of language presupposed by hermeneutics would seem to be found only in the reader and not in the text. In the text we would have a language reduced to a system of meanings that only the reader would resurrect. Instead, no, because text and reader both presuppose a living language, open to being and reality.

The difference that exists between interpreted language (Bible) and interpreting language (religious languate) is not that between language and word, as it would seem at first glance, according to the classic distinction elaborated by Ferdinand de Saussure.[7] Nor is it that between "schema" and "use," according to Louis Hjelmslev's equally well-known distinction.[8] "Interpreted language" and "interpreting language" are both on the side of speech and use, and not of language or schema, because they fit into an intentional and temporal linguistic pattern. The Bible and its interpretation resurrect and bet on an actualized linguistic project. They are living words. Text and reader presuppose a living and actualized language.

This distinctive feature of interpreted language and interpreting language prompts Paul Ricœur[9] to choose a better, more inclusive and far-reaching category to express the actuality and intentionality of the biblical project. This is the category of "discourse" which he

---

[7] De Saussure defined Language as an anonymous and timeless system or structure and Word, as the intentional and temporal actualization of that system. See F. de Saussure, *Course in General Linguistics,* Op. cit.

[8] L.T. Hjelmslev established like Saussure a basic linguistic differentiation between a structural element, however, which he called "schema" and a fluid, intentional element which he called "usage" instead. Cf. *Essais linguistiques*, (Copenhague: Cercle linguistique de Copenhague, 1959).

[9] P. Ricœur starts from a linguistics that presupposes instead an actualized language, in *Ermeneutica filosofica...*Op. cit., pp. 56-61.

borrows from the linguist Emile Benveniste.[10] He, perhaps more than other linguists, has worked in this direction, which takes as its linguistic unit of reference not the phonological or lexical sign (system language) but the "sentence" (living and actualized discourse). The sentence is a set of words that expresses even better than the word itself what distinguishes actualized language, namely, intentionality and design. The three characteristics that distinguish discourse, thus interpreted language (Bible) and interpreting language (interpretation of the Bible), are spatio-temporal specification (referentiality), source intention (author) and target intention (addressees). Speech is a historical event and, as such, is opposed to language, which remains, instead, a virtual reality, anonymous and outside of time.

---

10 É. Benveniste, Problemi di linguistica generale ("*Problems of General Linguistics*"), (Milan: Il Saggiatore, 1973), pp. 10-26.

CHAPTER V
THE INTERPRETED LANGUAGE

We will consider in this chapter what we believe the scope and nature of biblical language means and represents. For many, biblical language is simply a hindrance and an impediment to understanding the spiritual message it underlies. This is because that language, which is indirect, imprecise, approximate, confusing and contradictory, belongs to other historical times when mankind, due to inexperience and lack of linguistic and cognitive means, was forced to work with and use a kind of language that we today, with a bit of superiority and a dash of cultural contempt, call mythical language. That mythical language, which the Bible uses with full hands, is no longer suitable for understanding God and his meaning for us in our time. Neither is it adequate for understanding our contemporary world, shaped by science and precision languages, which serves as the context for experiencing God today.

Demythologization,[1] then, understood as the correction of that inadequate language, as proposed for example by R. Bultmann[2] (but certainly not only by him), would be a hermeneutical obligation. It arises from the intent to update and bring within our grasp the essence of the biblical message. Left as it is, it not only fails to reach us moderns. It also deforms the essence of its own message. Bultmann's proposal will appear radical[3] to many from the outset, but its basic

---

1 Cf. W. G. Jeanrond, *L'ermeneutica teologica,* Op. cit., pp. 240-244.
2 R. Bultmann, *Foi et Compréhension. Eschatologie et démythologisation* (2), (Paris : Seuil, 1969), pp. 101-111.
3 Criticism of the Bultmannianproposal actually comes from various fronts. In the "evangelical" world, the rejection is categorical. Cf. D.G. Bloesch, *Holy Scripture. Revelation, Inspiration & Interpretation, Christian Foundations,* (Downers Grove: IVP Academic, 1994), pp. 223-254; M.J. Erickson, *Christian Theology,* (Grand Rapids: Baker Academic, 2013),

logic cuts across, through the sharing of a double presupposition, even by those who oppose the Bultmannian program.[4] This double presupposition considers that the only noble and reliable languages are the languages of precision, anti-mythological languages. On the other hand, it holds that the texts that use mythological language, including the Bible, must necessarily be filtered to try to redeem what in them has a universal but hidden value.

With regard to the value and relevance of biblical language, we do not stand against the rational analysis which is present in the demythologization program. We stand against the one-sided conclusions of Bultmann and also of those who oppose him. In both positions, although for opposite reasons and with opposite mechanisms, there subsists an obsession with the univocity of languages of precision, theoretical or practical. In this we make our own, at least in part, the more measured and differentiated analysis made by Paul Ricœur[5] of the program of demythologization. He

<blockquote>
pp. 69-71. A similarly critical position, but for different reasons, is expressed, for example, by Oscar Cullmann when he challenges the Bultmannian program, not so much for the necessary linguistic updating, but for the process of "de-escatologization" that demythologization triggers. O. Cullmann, *Le salut dans l'histoire. L'existence chrétienne selon le Nouveau Testament*, (Neuchatel : Delachaux et Niestlé, 1966), pp. 35-37. Also critical is the position of Armido Rizzi who, however, prefers to speak of "de-Hellenization." Cf. C. di Sante, *Dentro la Bibbia. La teologia alternativa di Armido Rizzi*, (*"Inside the Bible. The Alternative Theology of Armido Rizzi")*, (Verona: Gabrielli Editori, 2018), pp. 17-42.
4   This is, for example, the opinion of Eugenio Trias, aSpanish philosopher and careful analyst of modernity and postmodernity, who in a fair way recognizes the uniqueness of modern thought unparalleled in its dynamism, but also categorizes it as reductive thought. And the limitation of this thought lies in its inability to mythicize, which it sublimates, however, by presenting itself only as enlightened thought (*Enlightenment*). The symbolic and mythical deficit is sold by modern and postmodern thought only as a virtue. In the inability to mythicize is evidenced the chronic symbolic deficit typical of the West, which Trias describes as the "disease of the West." See E. Trias, *Pensar la religion*, (Barcelona: Galaxia Gutenberg, 2015), pp. 99-111.
5   Much more sober, fair and relevant in this regard is Paul Ricouer's analysis of the program of demythicization, grasping its limitations on the one hand but also highlighting its relevance. Ricœur emphasizes a double
</blockquote>

manages to grasp the Bultmannian intention and also to defend it, without, however, sparing it a harsh criticism, because, at its basis, there would be in Bultmann a double misunderstanding. On the one hand, Bultmann fails to grasp that even in the Bible there is a program of demythologization. Demythologization does not arise only with modernity but, to a certain extent, it is already an integral part of biblical language. On the other hand, because in the biblical language, along with a demythologization thrust, we synchronically find also a mythicizing thrust of a positive sign. Myth also serves, in part, as an unparalleled tool for describing and referring to complex and paradoxical realities that could not be said well with precision languages, and for that reason use the typical descriptive strategies of symbolic language of which myth is an expression.[6]

When we talk about biblical language we are still not talking about content, but about container. The Bible is important not only because of what it says but especially because of how it says it. That biblical language is important escapes almost no one. Most of the time, however, this attention is reduced to its consideration as the medium of a sacred content that we must preserve with care and attention. There is a widespread belief that biblical language is only a medium, a channel. As such, that it has a deadline. The deadline usually given to it is the attainment of meaning. Once meaning is found, biblical

---

level of relevance in the word demythicization. The second level is not only positive, which even does not belong only to the modern spirit, but is already present in the Bible itself, in the Old and New Testaments. Cf. P. Ricœur, *Il conflitto delle interpretazioni*...Op. cit., pp. 400-405.

6   Realities such as the ambivalence of freedom between action and passion, between voluntary and involuntary in decision-making processes, the union of necessity and contingency in the explanation of the cosmos and nature, are unspeakable outside symbolic languages. Hence Ricœur's defense of this kind of language. For a more anthropological description of the value of symbolic language regarding the paradoxes and complexity of the human, see: *Le volontaire et l'involontaire. Philosophie de la volontè*, (Paris: Aubier, 1988), vol. I. For an appreciation of symbolic language instead at a more cosmological level, consider some sections of the second volume, "Les mythes du commencement et de la fin," in *Finitude et culpabilité. Philosophie de la volonté,* Idem, vol. II, pp. 309-477; «La simbolique du mal,» in *Ibid*, pp. 167-306.

language would automatically become fallen and unnecessary. Instead, in our view, and according to our analysis, biblical language is a structural and timeless part of biblical truth itself. Considering what the Bible says, stopping merely subsidiary to consideration of the language it uses, inexorably ends up distorting the profile and scope of the content itself. Without its language, biblical truth becomes progressively distorted, even when the meaning has already been achieved. It is the *how* (language) of the Bible that actually guarantees from beginning to end the nature and scope of the content of its message. Biblical content and language are certainly not identical, but neither are they disjointed, on pain of deforming the meaning derived.

At this level, the myopia of Christians seems to have become chronic and almost irreversible. The tendency of both Christians and non-Christians is, more often than not, to look intently, if not obsessively, at the content, considering biblical language purely as incidental. Thus one easily arrives at a double distortion. On the one hand, the reduction of biblical language to a pure medium takes over; on the other, the parallel and symbiotic reduction of the content to a univocal sense. In reality, it is not sense, or at least it should not be sense alone, that usurps the totality of the content of revelation. This would be pure biblical positivism. God is not revealed in the sense of content alone. That content, at the very least, has other possible senses, so the sense is always in tension with other latent senses. The content of the message also includes nonsense. Unmeaningful nonsense is one thing, but non-sense as meaning not yet understood is for all intents and purposes part of the content of the biblical message. So many times the Word of God has appeared to its hearers as non-sense. Yet, behind that non-sense was simply hidden an alternative sense not yet understood. This is why the formula "God reveals Himself in language"[7] is different from the formula "God

---

7   Schökel makes the difference between "inspiration in the key of judgment" and "inspiration in the key of language." The former leads to abstraction, to privileging "the idea of God," thus to theological monolithism and finally to exclusion and war over ideas. The second, on the other hand, leads to communicative relationship, thus to privileging "the Word of God" as a plural, inclusive and un-obsessed meeting place with a

reveals Himself in sense." Certainly God reveals himself in the sense. This fact is difficult to dispute. But does God reveal Himself only in the sense? In the intelligible sense? Certainly not.[8] It is contestable to make the connection between God, or the content of the biblical message, and an absolute sense. Sense is only one part of God's revelation. To say that God reveals Himself in human language is not remotely reducible to saying that God reveals Himself in the unambiguous sense of that language. Language is something larger, and it is in that larger container that God has decided to become incarnate. God became verb, language, and the sense we can grasp and give to that language does not exhaust either that language or God. This specific fact is preserved by "biblical language," and that is why it is just as important as the biblical content, so it needs to be preserved with care and attention.

Biblical language is not and cannot be only a temporary means. It is not and can never be surmountable, either at the beginning, during or at the end of the interpretive process. To leave it out is to lose even the content and to distort it partially or totally. The interpretive resumption must be able to transfer, as is necessary for it to do, the content but also the rhythm and scope of the biblical language into other contexts and linguistic forms, but without omitting it along the way.

This attention to biblical language brings with it another benefit: that of also making us aware of the scope and limitation of the language of the interpreter. Failure to perceive this difference leads us to impose on the Bible, as if it were our own, while assimilating its content, a language that is instead ours. On the one hand we impose on the biblical content a language that is not its own, thus devaluing it; on the other hand we advance as biblical a language that is not biblical, thus overvaluing a language, ours, that is instead relative.

---

monolithic truth. L.A. Schökel, J.M. Bravo Aragon, *Appunti di ermeneutica*...Op. cit., pp. 19-24.

8   The language in which God reveals himself is not traceable to his verbal communication, much less to the intelligible sense of that communication of his. Cf. W.G. Jeanrond, *L'ermeneutica teologica,* Op. cit., pp. 19,20.

1. A Theological-Cultural Look at the Biblical Language[9]

Our reflection is mainly articulated therefore at this second level, that is, of *how* (language) the Bible says what it says. It is articulated on two dimensions, one synchronic and one diachronic.

---

9   *Biblical language* must be related to but also differentiated from, on the one hand, the "biblical text," *and on the* other hand, the "biblical interpretation." The biblical text is the mediating but not foundational element, just as biblical interpretation is the resulting but not foundational element. Cf. R. W. Funk, *Language, Hermeneutic and the Word of God*, (New York: Harper & Row, 1966), pp. 10-25. The common element is given not only by content but also by form, which is determined by narrative and discursive "plurivocity." This common element is found in different proportions in the three instances, but it is greatest in the foundational instance, that is, biblical language. Cf. P. Ricœur, *Interpretation Theory: Discourse and the Surplus of Meaning*, (Dallas: Texas Christian University Press, 1977), pp. 24-37; *Hermeneutics and the Human Sciences*, (Cambridge: Cambridge University Press, 2016), pp. 54-69; R. Alter, *L'arte della narrativa biblica*, ("*The Art of Biblical Narrative"*), (Brescia: Queriniana, 1990); *L'arte della poesia biblica*, ("*The Art of Biblical Poetry"*), (Milan: San Paolo Edizioni, 2011). The foundational element of *biblical language*, taking into account that it is biblical language that grounds the biblical text and the biblical text that grounds biblical interpretation, is given and determined by its exuberance or "plurivocity." Schökel and Bravo emphasize this exuberance of biblical language by making the distinction between "judgment" and "language." The former is more precise but less inclusive, while the latter is more general but more inclusive. They apply the second criterion to the Bible, not the first. L.A. Schökel, J.M. Bravo Aragon, *Appunti di ermeneutica*...Op. cit. , pp. 19-24. Ricœur will not only describe this exuberance as the structural and characterizing center of biblical language, but will expand it to all kinds of language. Loretta Dornisch, regarding what language is for Ricœur, writes: "At the same time language is distorted; it is equivocal, it has multiple meanings, it means more than it says. Since men are born in the sign of language, it is not so much spoken by men as spoken to them. Ordinary language has an incredible ambiguity, an amphibological construction and confusion inherent in idiomatic expressions and metaphor."-L. Dornisch, "Symbolic Systems and the Interpretation of Scripture: Introduction to the Work of Paul Ricœur," in P. Ricœur, *Biblical Hermeneutics*. Op. cit. , p. 12. On the "plurivocity" and exuberance of biblical language, see: D. Marguerat, Y. Bourquin, *Per leggere I racconti biblici*...Op. cit. pp. 112-128. For "plurivocity" in a general sense related to narrative, see: M. Kundera, *L'arte del romanzo*, ("*The Art of the Novel"*), (Milan: Adelphi, 1988).

The Interpreted Language

On the synchronic dimension, which aims to take the Bible as it is, without investigating its historical evolution, we have privileged two themes. The theme of "textuality," in chapter three of part one, and the theme of "linguistic form," in this chapter. Textuality and linguistic form are certainly related but not identical phenomena. We will try, in this chapter, to separate the linguistic form, which in our opinion distinguishes the Bible, from the fate of its form as a text, having reserved the theological-cultural analysis of the text for a longer reflection in the aforementioned chapter.

The historical investigation of the kind of interpretations that have followed one another over time fits on the diachronic dimension of the *how of the* Bible. We, have, instead, developed a hypothesis on the uniqueness of the modern period which is presented in chapter two of part one. Chapters seven and eight of this second part are on this dimension of diachronic analysis. This is where we will discuss hermeneutic anomalies of our time.

We come, then, to the subject of this chapter: the nature of biblical language. The characteristic feature of biblical language would consist, according to some, in the fact that it embodies a transcendence, an other Word, so as to exclude its identification with purely human mechanisms. For others, the strong point is instead the humanization of the religious message: the fact of finding in the Bible a divine Word embodied in human language. Today, for most Christians, the characteristic of biblical language lies above all in its concreteness, as opposed to the more speculative language of other books and especially philosophy. The Bible would not be interested in the gratuitous motion of either thoughts, concepts or words because it would point to the immediacy of the application of God's unambiguous will for us. The Bible articulates a language of salvation that offers itself to the reader in an immediate, concrete and unambiguous way.

This pragmatic view, which is quite prevalent especially in the more dynamic and zealous sections of Christian communities fails to grasp the characteristic of biblical language. It even proposes a model of it that is opposed to it and has nothing biblical about it. On the contrary, it is inspired by and stems directly from modern pragmatism. There is nothing perverse about modern pragmatism itself, provided we do not elevate it to an ideology above criticism and, above all, do not identify it with biblical language. In today's interpretive pragmatism, one merely transfers typical technical univocity, articulated as precision, from theory to spiritual practice. In divine transcendent language or divine language embodied in human language, the important thing would be its univocity and compactness. This is the opposite of what distinguishes the Bible and its language. It is the unavailability of meaning, its mystery, and its polyvalence what characterizes biblical language.[10]

This is the thesis Erich Auerbach expresses in his book *Mimesis. Realism in Western Literature*.[11] He was as a German Romanist of Jewish descent, a professor of Romance Philology at the University of Marburg. In 1936, due to Nazi racial laws, he was forced to leave Germany and take refuge in Turkey, where he was offered the same professorship at Istanbul University. Between 1942 and 1945 he wrote *Mimesis*, his masterpiece.

In the first chapter of the book, titled *The Scar of Odysseus*, he makes a comparison between the Odyssey and the Old Testament, specifically between Book XIX of the Greek text and Chapter 22 of the book of Genesis. The particularity of biblical language, in this case in the description of Isaac's sacrifice, becomes clearer when it is compared with an ancient text such as the Odyssey. Homeric description is characterized by precision and exactitude. Nothing is left to chance. For Homer, it is intolerable to see the scar emerging from a dark and elusive past. He abounds in specification data. His characters speak, they are circumscribable in their action, proceeding and destiny.

No description in Homer appears incomplete or interrupted for lack of clear and orderly logical and linguistic articulation. Conjunctions, adverbs, particles, and other syntactic devices clearly delineate people, things, and events from one another, while at the same time creating a fluid and continuous connection. In this way there is a

---

10 A. Rizzi, *Pensare dentro la Bibbia*...Op. cit., pp. 28-37.
11 E. Auerbach, *Mimesis. Il realismo nella letteratura occidentale*, ("*Mimesis. The Representation of Reality in Western Literature*"), (Turin: Einaudi, 2000).

sequential and rhythmic chaining of well-defined phenomena and events into a plot with a clear and distinct outline.

In Homer we find, according to Auerbach, detailed descriptions, connections without gaps, transparent close-ups, accompanying elements with evidentiary clearness. At the same time we have though, limitation and greater superficiality in perceiving historical development and the depth, complexity and paradoxicality of human issues and related human characters.

In the biblical account instead, the beginning already surprises us. Abraham says, "Here I am." But where do the two dialogues stand? This is not mentioned. The reader knows that the two dialoguers are in different places. Where does God address Abraham from? It is not mentioned. God's reason for putting Abraham through such an extreme test is also not mentioned. The intense inner travail that such a question necessarily arouses in the heart of any parent is neither specified nor described. The God of Abraham and the Hebrews is fixed neither in a figure nor in a place. Although present and close, he remains a mysterious God. We come to him only by hints, by informative elements that even do not depend on us, but on his self-revelation, which seems to conceal more than it manifests.

God's enigmaticity is matched by Abraham's enigmaticity. Where is Abraham? We do not know. His "Here I am" stands only to signify his positioning in relation to a mysterious God. As such, he remains in an undecipherable, open-ended position because he is still in the making. Abraham is more describable as a function of what he may be than as a function of what he is in the present. Everything else is of no interest to the narrator. Nothing is known about his past or even about the inner baggage he carries with him.

Biblical language, according to Auerbach, elaborates a fragmentary description, proposes a broken style, offering, more often than not, only clues. The biblical narrative proceeds by summaries, sowing here and there only suggestive traces, where the implicit and the unspoken are part of the discourse that has multiple backgrounds. This gaunt, minimalist and dried up style becomes though pretentious and exuberant in describing the historical evolution and change of characters, situations and human interactions. Its descriptions purport to be universal and are ambitious in proposing qualitative, important, though fragmentary insights into problems and conundrums essential and central to human living in their sequentiality and historicity.

2. A Complex and Multifaceted Language[12]

The Bible is certainly a unique book. Some of the data concerning it are quantitatively impressive and give a clear idea of its size. It consists of 66 books written over a period of 1,500 years on three different continents (Asia, Africa and Europe), by more than 40 authors. There are to date more than 5,000 manuscripts of the New Testament alone (between those with capital and lowercase letters) dating from the first four centuries after Christ. For classical antiquity the situation is much more precarious. For example, the oldest manuscript of the work of Aeschylus (525-456 B.C.) dates from around the 11th century A.D., and the situation for Plato or Aristotle is almost identical.[13] These numbers confirm the extraordinary evidence of the integrity of the biblical text, the first known book to be translated, the first to be printed in the West, and the first to be spread so widely and in so many languages that 95 percent of the current global population is able to read it.

Can the uniqueness of the Bible and its language be traced solely to this quantitative fact? I believe not. The uniqueness of the Bible is not related to the quantitative extraordinariness of its composition and dissemination or even only to the strength of its content. Let us briefly describe some characteristics that distinguish the qualitative greatness of biblical language.

---

12 Richness and complexity of biblical language is analyzed from "formal" and "literary" perspectives, for example, by J. Barr, see *The Semantics of Biblical Language*, (London: Xpress, 1983), pp. 1-8. But it is also so from a different, more "theological" perspective, by B.S. Child, *Biblical theology of the Old and New testaments. Theological Reflections on the Christian Bible*, (London: Xpress, 1996), pp. 11-29.

13 O. Cullmann, *Il nuovo testamento*, (*"The New Testament"*), (Bologna: Il Mulino, 1968), pp. 13-20.

a. *Biblical Language and Literary Form*[14]

A first characteristic of biblical language is the close link it claims between form and content. The Bible claims to be relevant already in its literary form, in its language. Its literary form is already part of its message. It is message. That is why the literary form is neither incidental nor surmountable. It is not accessory because it does not represent an exchangeable form that can be replaced by other forms. It is not surmountable because when meaning is achieved this form does not decay. Biblical literary form is related to the beginning of the message, to the middle and to the conclusion of the process of articulating meaning. If we tried to transcribe the biblical "content" into other "linguistic forms," it would be deformed. It would be deformed not necessarily in the sense of its destruction, but in the sense of its impoverishment and depowerment.

The validity of form is true not only for the Bible but also for any other communicative process. This close link between form and message, which biblical language claims for itself, has helped us to understand how this mechanism is widespread and actually characterizes all processes of transmitting meaning. Between content and communicative medium (form), in its various modes, the link is much closer than what we might think at first glance. This is what Marshall McLuhan had in mind when he introduced his well-known phrase: *The Medium is the* Message (The medium-the instrument, the form-is the message).[15] This means that the narrative, the poem or the parables in the Bible, as its internal and specific linguistic forms, as much as the external forms and channels of transmission that that message uses -such as the voice, the book, the television or the telephone- expresses already, even before the content and to some extent independently of it, a truth that precedes its content. This truth, forms and shapes its content by granting it its own specific validity through a formal structure.

---

14 P. Ricœur, *Ermeneutica filosofica...Op.* cit., pp. 80-85.
15 M. McLuhan, *Understanding Media. The Extensions of Man*, (New York: Signet, 1964), pp. 9-23.

This is what Paul Ricœur perceives and describes in the Bible even more specifically when he reiterates the equal validity of the forms of biblical language and the content in what he calls "the profession of faith."[16] It is not possible to grasp the meanings of faith without going through the explanation of the forms of discourse it uses. Attempts to translate the contents of faith into other forms have come to a half-truth. The necessary translation of the biblical message into Greek, for example, has resulted in the deformation of the identity and profile of the biblical God. The Greek language, and the modern languages that relate to that kind of thinking and rationality, describe God as foundation, as cause or essence. This is a God who is abstract and non-interactive because he is presented as a foundational and primary element at the beginning of a chain of events that guarantees, as a first principle in its own right, uncontaminated. Biblical language instead places God in an interactive story (salvation history) by describing him through narrative. This makes him concrete and relational, to the point of being touched, influenced and even enriched by the reaction of human beings.[17] All this is only through the use of the narrative form.

b. *Biblical Language and Ambivalence*[18]

A second characteristic of biblical language is its structural ambivalence. This is where a profound misunderstanding arises.

---

16 Ricœur writes, "The fundamental point to focus on is the following: in the biblical documents a "profession of faith" is expressed that is inseparable from the relevant "forms" of discourse, i.e., for example, the narrative structure of the Pentateuch and the gospels, the oracular structure of prophecy, parable, hymn, etc. Each form of discourse provokes not only a style of profession of faith, but the comparison between these forms of discourse promotes, within the same profession of faith, tensions and contrasts not without theological significance." in P. Ricœur, *Ermeneutica filosofica...* Op. cit., pp. 80,81.
17 P. Ricœur, *Ibid*, p. 83.
18 J. Jeremias, *Gesù e il suo annuncio*, (*"Jesus and His Proclamation"*), (Brescia: Paideia, 1993); *Teologia del Nuovo Testamento. La predicazione di Gesù*, (1), (*"New Testament Theology. The Preaching of Jesus"*), (1), (Brescia: Paideia, 2000); *The Parables of Jesus*, (New York: SCM Press, 1963), pp. 23-114.

The Bible's ambivalence, becomes especially in modern and contemporary Christianity the anomaly to be demolished, the spurious element that needs to be dismantled and erased. A new paradigm, that of "clear and distinct ideas," which extends to religion and consequently also to biblical language, is the reason why Western Christianity, Catholic as well as Protestant, has focused heavily on clarity. This typical obsession of modern times, has made the biblical message clear and unambiguous while deforming and impoverishing it. The greatness of biblical language, mistakenly, has been identified with its clarity. The Bible has gained in quantitative value what was functional to a certain kind of conquering religiosity; however, it has lost its qualitative value by giving up complexity and mystery.

That biblical language is structurally ambivalent means that it can mean several things at the same time. This fact does not diminish its impact or its relevance. On the contrary, it increases and augments them, because this finds correspondence with the heterogeneity of life itself, which cannot be reduced to just one of its dimensions. Just as a point of view does not exhaust the richness of life, similarly a meaning does not exhaust the richness of biblical description. This is why the linguistic form of the Bible expresses itself through ambivalence, and makes this its starting point and its ending point.

This is Joachim Jeremias'[19] description of the language of the Gospels. Because it can be remembered more easily and is therefore less manipulable, the language of the parables, for example, is metaphorical, exuberant, allegorizing. It is characterized by its surplus of meaning and by its unavailability. Speaking of the art of sense intensification as the defining element of biblical language. Robert Alter proposes the same description [20] for the language of Hebrew narrative and poetics. This exuberant sense underlies ambivalence as a linguistic mechanism that refuses to consign itself

---

19 J. Jeremias, *The Parables of Jesus, Ibid*, pp. 23-114.
20 R. Alter, *The Art of Biblical Poetry*, (Edinburgh: T&T Clark, 2000), pp. 62-84; *The Art of Biblical Narrative*, (London: George Allen & Unwin, 1981), pp. 3-22.

to a single, monolithic meaning. Biblical language, structurally creates alternative meanings.

c. Biblical Language and Inclusiveness[21]

Inclusiveness is a third characteristic of biblical language. The ambivalence described above is not an end in itself. It does not only express a dimension of descriptive plurality. More fundamentally, it connects with and guarantees a radical inclusiveness. The biblical form does not aim at self-sufficiency but at interaction with the other. It aims at dialogue with the other through the search for a convergent point that does not erase difference. Difference is the basis of dialogue. Difference guarantees dialogue. Difference makes dialogue possible. For this reason the ambivalent biblical language is the specific linguistic form that corresponds to the relational theological vision of the Covenant. This is a typical biblical focus and motif which recurs in both the Old and New Testaments. Biblical language gives it this dialogical and inclusive form

The theological inclusiveness of the Old and New Testaments, which is obligatory because it aspires to universality, is hooked on and preceded by this linguistic inclusiveness. It is this inclusiveness that disappears or fades when instead the Bible is reduced to its clarity. Ambivalence and linguistic inclusiveness are closely linked in the Bible and determine the degree of theological inclusiveness that churches, at some point in their journey, are forced to introduce if they do not want to become purist sects. Forgetting this simple linguistic principle, leads the inordinate and unshrewd spiritual ambition and excessive pragmatism of many of today's religious communities to distort the indelible inclusiveness of the gospel. The more precise a language is, the more exclusionary it becomes. The more ambivalent a language is, the more inclusive it becomes. This is why it often happens, especially in evangelical churches, that the all-out defense of the Bible and its clarity, through, for example, a one-sided emphasis on the *sola Scriptura* principle, actually causes its impoverishment and ineffectiveness.

---

21 C. di Sante, *Dentro la Bibbia*...Op. cit., pp. 53-56.

From a formal point of view, the Bible's inclusiveness is also founded on another trait of its language: sobriety. The Bible does not build its greatness on the ashes of other books by denigrating the goodness and wisdom expressed in other texts of humanity. The Bible is not jealous of human wisdom and does not claim exclusivity of good thoughts. The fact that the Bible is unique does not exclude that there are other valuable books, religious or secular. This inclusiveness of its form is linked to its linguistic sobriety, in the fact that it does not say everything. It does not want to say everything. It renounces saying everything. Its silences are as important as its statements. Only this generous sobriety is able to open a space for other books to make their statements, for men not to be ashamed of their babbling words. The greatness of the Bible is its relational greatness that leads it to rejoice not when it speaks on its own, but also when the few words it expresses, those essential words, do not dumb down others but motivate them and move them to speak. The Bible is God's motivating Word, God's inclusive Word.

d. *Biblical Language and Biblical Authority*[22]

A fourth characteristic of biblical language is its authoritativeness. Two questions are important at this point for understanding the nature of biblical language and its recovery in interpretation. The first concerns its authority and authoritativeness. The second concerns how this authority is articulated and manifested. Both are important, but they must be distinguished. Responding well to the first does not imply responding equally well to the second. On one side, there are people who answer the first question well, so they recognize the value and authority of the Bible, however, unfortunately, they do not answer the second question well. They give authority an inadequate, reductive and approximate reading, which does a disservice to their testimony about the Bible. On the other side, there are people who do not answer the first question because they are not believers;

---

22 Cf. B.M. Metzger, *Il canone del nuovo testamento*... Op. cit. , pp. 232-245. See also B. S. Child, *Biblical Theology of the Old and New Testaments*...*Op* cit., pp. 70-79.

however, they can better grasp the particular way in which the authoritativeness of the Bible is manifested.

There are objective and subjective criteria which pertain to the first question. The objective criteria that are usually listed --such as fulfillment of prophecy, age and antiquity of the texts, plurality of authors and forms, important cultural effects attached to it-- are not absolute and should be used and mentioned with caution. We find the same ambivalence in other dimensions as well. The validity, regarded as objective, of the phenomena one wishes to assert, sometimes turns out to be less conclusive than it might seem. The more incontestable, objective and absolute the authority of the principle that is advanced as certain is, the less guaranteed is the attitude of deep faith and conviction. These are ultimately the ones that count. In a context of absolute and objective authority, not faith but compulsion to believe arises which is pressed by external or internal constrictions. But faith in essence is not a compulsion but rather an unnecessary and contingent act. It presupposes relative, soft, persuasive authority. If the authority it proposes were not relative, faith would be necessary, so it would no longer be faith. It would become perfectly useless because it has become mechanical and automatic.

This is why subjective criteria, which are not relativistic and for this reason to be discarded a priori, are more decisive in establishing and recognizing the authority of a foundational entity or event. Relative criteria are such because they are structurally incomplete. Incompleteness is the element that gives rise to conviction. Provocation and listening, recall and response, are intertwined in those missing spaces. The conviction that freely recognizes an authority arises. It is affirmed not in the face of force, but only in the face of persuasion.

Applied to the Bible, all this means that we Christians often err strategically because we aim to make authority necessary when it should instead remain relative. This relativity gives rise to the best affirmation mechanism, which is that of conviction. Subjective, individual and communal criteria are the ones that arise from conviction, the ones that affect the most in the recognition of biblical authority. This is not a bad thing because it confirms for us, from another perspective, that the truth and authority of the Bible are historical and relational in nature. Only through faith do we accept the bond of the Bible's authority over us. All objective evidence, if any, is such for those who have already believed. The second question concerns *how* the authority of the Bible is structured. This is about how the kind of linguistic form the Bible is, becomes a more objective fact that can be analyzed through literary, formal and historical investigation even independently of faith. Here another great misunderstanding arises: people often want to answer the second question with the answer to the first. Actually, positively answering the first question about whether the Bible is an expression of God's will is not equivalent to answer the second question well. It is about how one believes and thinks that authority is formally articulated and expressed in the Bible.

The misunderstanding lies in thinking that the Bible expresses its authority in an *unambiguous* form, choosing the dimension of clarity and precision. An authority that expresses itself in a dispersive or ambivalent way would lose its compactness, thus its strength. This way of answering the second question is insufficient, superficial, and irrelevant. Considering it ancillary and secondary, it fails to grasp the specificity of the form and nature of biblical language. This distorts the authority of the Bible, making it an iron, inflexible, monolithic and intransigent authority. On pain of distorting it, the nature of biblical authority cannot be dissociated from the literary form in which it is expressed. And this literary biblical form, constructed on its ambivalent and paradoxical language, doesn't articulate a direct but rather and indirect form of authority based on persuasion.

e. *Biblical Language and Truth*[23]

A fifth characteristic of biblical language is its vocation with truth. The dissociation between biblical authority and the literary form in which it is expressed has led to making it the locus of truth. Those who care about the Bible, those who read it most assiduously, are especially likely to distort it in this way. The Bible becomes for them par excellence the perimeter within which God's indubitable

---

23 Cf. G. Mura, *Ermeneutica e verità...Op. Cit.,* pp. 11-27.

and compact truth reigns unchallenged. They claim that the Bible is the religious book that enables us to distinguish truth from falsehood with certainty. It is the only antidote against error and heterodoxy. This belief, openly expressed, represents one of the most important misunderstandings in the history of Christianity.

The Bible "is not the place of truth."[24] Pilate's pertinent question - "What is truth? " - is not a bewilderment of either spirit or thought. It is the only possible question; it is the essence of a possible truth. Truth always adopts the form of a question. Doubt about what is truth is the central and most pertinent question of spirit and thought of all life. Doubt about truth is the pilot light that points to the true horizon of that truth. The truth of the Bible is then a truth mixed with doubt. This is both, a truth as a path and a path of a searching and doubting truth. The question "what is truth" then, is not a stupid or a useless question. We cannot delegitimize it by attributing to it ambiguous psychological traits related to Pilate's careerism and moral cynicism which are often present in us as well. Our moral or human smallness does not delegitimize our question about truth; on the contrary, it guarantees it. The question about truth always arises, as in Pilate, in a dirty ground. The ground must be dirty, otherwise what real question would there be about truth?

This question should be asked especially to those who claim to have understood the truth. It is easy to confuse truth with my own truth. We can do this by not recognizing that in its fullness truth goes beyond our understanding of it. We can also do this by identifying truth with a partial manifestation of it. Truth can only give itself in the form of a question. Truth that no longer questions itself decays from the weight of its own presumption. The true Christian, the true believer in that final scene of the Gospels is Pilate and not the crowd. He doesn't represent the indifferent people who are elsewhere that day worried and occupied with the little material things of life and who don't believe. Neither is he the over-believing crowd which believes in everything else except in the only believable person,

---

24 E. Cerasi, *Dire quasi la verità. Per una filosofia del linguaggio religioso*, (*"Saying Almost the Truth. For a Philosophy of Religious Language"*), (Rome: Città Nuova Editrice, 2014), pp. 11-21.

Jesus. Neither of them, neither the indifferent nor the over-believing, question anything. He who flaunts the truth and has his own zeal and attachment to it already sets himself up as a prophet of the false. Ours, if we claim to believe in truth, can only be an attitude of witnessing, not possessing, much less identifying with truth.

Christian churches cannot be places of truth. They can only be places that allow themselves to be crossed here and there, tangentially and sporadically by truth. They can only aspire to be witnesses to truth. This is not renunciation. This is the path of truth. Truth is a path. We cannot tell the truth or live in the truth all the time. Our lives would be cluttered with too many certainties that would prevent us from walking. We would become unbearable as well as paranoid. A church that is always in the truth is an idolatrous church. Reductive binary thinking which perceives error when there is not an immediate truth, has led Bible-reading Christians to be obsessed with truth. Obsessed with truth, we have become monsters. Truth, that truth, has not saved us. It has alienated, destroyed and deformed us. It has consumed our best energies. It has isolated us. It has made us distrustful and conceited, selfish and even cynical. It has taken away our humanity, which is one of the most distinctive features of truth. Truth, on the other hand, is connection. It is desire for the other. It is trust in the other, in the different. It is accepting the challenge of difference. Truth does not want to control the Other. Truth wants to be enriched and instructed by him. You desire the other only if you are incomplete, only if you are broken and fragmented, only if you lack something. A being who claims to be full or someone who claims a truth without fractures, a compact and homogeneous truth, becomes detached and isolated from others. He also ends up being left with a carcass of truth, with a shrunken truth.

Between truth and error there is an interstice, a median territory, an intermediate space that is essential for life. It is life itself and, as such, it is already truth. This is a different truth. It is unconscious, unchosen, flowing without obsession, even mingling sometimes with error. It is, however, the error of a seeking truth. It is not error in the perspective, although it may be in circumstantial fact, in a fraction of time. That intermediate space, of an implicit and unconscious truth, is neither true nor false; it is the space of the church. Flee from the churches, Catholic or Protestant, which worship on Saturday or Sunday, that give up living and articulating that intermediate space and destroy it by having it invaded by massive truths. It is there, in that in-between space, that life grows and faith is strengthened. That is a space beyond "truth and error." That is our amniotic fluid. There a life is neither true nor false, it simply is, and if it is, it is already in the truth. It is in the path of truth.

The Bible is par excellence that in-between space, it is the perfect prototype of that living space that is neither true nor false. This is so because it is neither one nor the other. It is a welcoming space for any life that grows and develops trying to find its own North. If the Bible were the space of that declarative truth, it would be an exclusionary and exclusive book, suitable only for a few, or for no one. Because it is not obsessed with truth, the Bible is the Word where anyone feels at home. This is its truth. This is not a truth that sanctions and declares. It is a truth that welcomes and includes. It is so by virtue of the language it uses even before it articulates its content. It is that space that refuses to qualify itself as true. It knows that when truth reigns massively in life, all life becomes impossible. The Bible cannot be the place of truth. It is the place of the suspension of truth. When we are really in the intermediate space of the Bible, we do not have the anguish of being in error. Consequently, we are not obsessed with the truth. This intermediate space has another kind of grounding in the truth. It is the non-conscious and unconscious grounding. We are in the truth mostly when we do not know and do not realize it. If we inhabit that intermediate space, we are more likely to be in the truth without knowing it. Truth is only partially a matter of awareness and choice. Truth is linked to an unconscious grounding in life, in God and in others. It is the truth that welcomes us, not we who choose it. It is the truth that chooses. It chooses us in that in-between space that is the Bible. It is prolonged in the church and in life. It is where that obsession with truth has been given up.

Is the Bible, then, a place of truth? Certainly not of that truth to which the churches are accustomed. It is not that conscious, chosen, consistent, militant, missionary, clear, unambiguous, functional, immediate, decisive, diriment and certain truth. That truth[25] seems authentic, but it is not. It is not because it is authentic for too few people. It is truth only for that person who claims it for his group, for his tribe, for his church. How could such a partial and narrow truth be the truth? That truth is actually a counter-truth. The Bible cannot be a relative or accomplice of that truth.

This is why the seemingly clear formula which describe the Bible as truth is misleading. It seems correct but it is not. It is not for several reasons: first, because the Bible is the locus not of one truth but of several truths. True truth is always plural. Second, because the Bible is the place of a truth on the way, not of a final and ultimate truth. Third, because most of the Bible is beyond "truth and error," because only there, in that interstice, in that neutral ground, can life flourish. Fourth, because the Bible does not just say what life should be, but more simply describes and welcome life as it is.

f. *Biblical Language and Diversity*[26]

A sixth characteristic of biblical language is its structural diversity.

It is here that biblical language teaches us another logic. A logic that includes tension and incompleteness as part of meaning. Much religious and theological reasoning, on the other hand, is too dependent on an univocal logic that stigmatizes diversity or grasps it only to overcome it. This is the logic of the West and its religion, which at this level have assimilated, in different ways and degrees, the univocal perspective of Aristotelian logic. We owe to Aristotle the full understanding of the importance of three principles of our

---

25 P. Gisel, *Verité et Histoire. La théologie dans la modernité. Ernst Käsmann*, (Paris: Beauchesne, 1985), pp. 12-35.
26 Erich Fromm compares and contrasts two positions with respect to what is truth. The first ties it to Aristotle and the development of Western rationality that is related to it, including the development of religious thought, which he believes would be overly dependent on univocal rationality. Of a different character would be what he calls the paradoxical logic typical of Eastern cultures. See E. Fromm, *L'arte di amare*, Op. cit. pp. 71-84.

common reasoning: the principle of identity, non-contradiction and the excluded third.[27]

1) The principle of identity, states that given A, A is A.

2) The principle of non-contradiction holds that we cannot affirm and deny a subject predicate at the same time and in the same sense. We cannot say that Mario is greater than John and at the same time, say that he is not. We could do so only if the temporal relation changed.

3) The principle of the excluded third states that in a statement is either true or false: a third possibility is excluded.

These three principles are interdependent and traceable to each other, and basically define things, people, ideas or events in a compact and homogeneous way. A thing is well understood only when it becomes clear and with well-defined contours that allow us to differentiate and separate it from everything else. This grand Aristotelian formula was great for what it aimed to describe: how things are and can be classified. Aristotle certainly used it better than we do. This is because he was a shrewd and sharp philosopher. It is also because he was not obsessed with the obsessions of us moderns.

This Aristotelian logic of clarity and unambiguousness is not only legitimate but also necessary. It is useful for understanding and organizing a part of our human experience. It is also useful for our faith experience. But its indiscriminate use has become a transversal reductive model. This creates a major theological-hermeneutical problem. Its implicit and unconscious elevation as a biblical model creates a major misunderstanding. Legitimacy (acceptance) should not be confused with legitimization (absolutization).

We read the Bible with this logic, misused and misapplied, filtered into our modern languages and reinforced by the parallel univocity of contemporary technology. The result is unequivocal: a clear, homogeneous and compact faith is born. By this logic, with the intention of wresting more and more clarity from it, we force the Bible to tell us things that it itself does not want to tell us. The Bible, by virtue of this univocal logic, improperly assigned to it, has become

---

27   Aristotle (*Metaphysics* IV, 1005b, 19-20).

a typical industrial machine of sense-making. A homogeneous and compact sense, little differentiated. An overbearing sense. There is no question of delegitimizing such human language as the conceptual language typical of our time. However, one can neither reduce biblical language to that sectional language nor elevate that partial language to general biblical language. It is not a problem of recognition and legitimacy but of extension. Any human language, representative of a culture and a community, is legitimized to receive the biblical message, but it cannot replace biblical language. How to recapture the true dimension of biblical language? Let us pause to consider three levels of relevance.

3. Word and Scripture as a Tension that Grounds Biblical Language

The first level of relevance and richness of biblical language is manifested in the Word-Scripture polarity. There is a tendency in all theology, but also in faith practice, to make them equivalent. They would both be perfectly superimposable and interchangeable, structurally aligned synonyms. This is not the case because these two terms, while complementary, are different. They are opposed. They create an insuperable tension that brings out the structural richness of biblical language.

The tension that this polarity articulates is even more crucial because it actually expresses an upstream rupture, a more basic differentiation, a differentiation in God himself. This is between the God who speaks and the God who "writes".[28] We are clearly dealing here with anthropomorphic metaphors of God. That God writes may sound excessive, not least because it would derive from this image a reinforcement of the already strong tendency to sacralize the biblical text itself, thus contributing to the affirmation of biblical literalism and inerrancy and place it at a foundational level, at the level of

---

28 These are metaphors we use to talk about God. Cf. G.A. Lindbeck, *The Nature of Doctrine. Religion and Theology in a Postliberal Age*, (Philadelphia: The Westminster Press, 1984); G. Lakoff and M. Johnson, *Metaphors We Live By*, (Chicago: Chicago University Press, 1981).

God himself. This is not the intention here. On the contrary[29] the intention is to distance, through this image, the biblical message from manipulation, not only from inerrantism but also from what we have called "textual positivism."

Not only the category of Scripture but also the category of Word attributed to God create criticalities and raise problems and objections. We therefore take them as metaphors that help us to understand partially God's communicative intentionality. Consider also the fact that they also introduce hostile elements to thinking. The term Word, as metaphor applied to God's revelation, with its limitations and criticalities do not prevent its massive use in theology. The same can then happen with the parallel category of Scripture. God's revelation is only partially represented by both terms. What remains irrefutable is what the two categories underlie and this is that the God of the Bible expresses himself, wants to communicate and makes his will explicit. The biblical God is not neutral or silent like the God of deism. He makes his will known and expresses his ideas and plans. To say that he does so by speaking (Deut. 5:4,5) or writing (Ex. 24:12) is tantamount to expressing metaphors that concretize his desire to express himself and to make his will known to men. These are to be taken, one and the other, as metaphors. They are metaphors that symbolically describe attitudes, ways of being of God and we take them as such with their specific limits.

The linguistic structure of the Bible, in its two forms, Word and Scripture, would be preceded by a double dimension in God himself and in his way of being. While they should appear in their convergence and complementarity, this apparent pair is not an equivalent pair. It is a polarity that introduces a linguistic and ontological tension which is central to understanding the structure of biblical language and its richness.

There has always been a tendency in the history of Christianity, which prevails to this day, to privilege the Word over Scripture. This

---

29 We take Scripture (God writing) here not in the sense of a full manifestation of Being, thus absolute and final, but on the contrary as a trace that one must always take up again and that creates a "difference" that is never conclusive nor final. J. Derrida, *Della grammatologia*, ("Of Grammatology"), (Milan: Jaca Book, 1968).

fact is understandable but cannot be justified because it leads to a one-sided and unbalanced look at the Bible. The Word is privileged to Scripture because it conveys dynamism, life, immediacy and warmth. Scripture, on the other hand, seems like a cold medium. It is as if it were a necessary evil, a surmountable sign. The true message cannot reside in the form of Scripture. It cannot depend on a material structure. Consequently, the message must involve overcoming and transcending scripture. Christian theology therefore tends to articulate itself as a theology of the Word beyond Scripture. This should not be so because there is instead a dialectic between the two terms that guarantees not only a greater but also a better sense of God's Revelation.

The term Word, used to refer to the Bible, indicates the dimension of "assimilability" of God's message. As the Word, the Bible has the vocation and form of the message that we can make our own. From the human point of view, the Word of God presents itself as warm communication that penetrates our being and reaches our innermost being. It becomes part of us. It is the personalized, direct and immediate Word that we make our own. That external Word becomes an internal Word. The divine message as Word aims at becoming part of us. There is here in perspective the experience of fusion. God becomes part of us and we become one with him through his Word.

From God's point of view, his Word expresses something particular about God himself; about what he is; how he is; his intimacy; what he cares about; what his intentions, passions and fears are; and not just his ideas. In his Word God unbalances himself and speaks to us not in the abstract language of what he thinks, but in the involved language of what he feels. He tells us that he is dialogical, well-disposed and available. Through it he conveys to us not something external to him, but himself, that which represents him most, his essence, his love. In his Word God unbalances himself, expresses his intention, gives himself to us in what represents him most. The Word thus expresses God's uniqueness and vulnerability, his mobility and emotional dynamism in a direct, immediate and spontaneous way. God expresses the best and most intimate part of himself and offers it to us who are able to assimilate it and make it our own.

The term Scripture, on the other hand, when used to refer to the Bible, indicates the dimension of "non-assimilability" of God's message. If the Bible were only assimilable, it would be easy to be manipulated to the point of making us gods ourselves, because God's Word, by becoming ours, would come to reinforce not God and his otherness, but us and our interpretation. This is why the term Scripture is a specific and contrasting term if it's used as a complementary term that emphasizes the fact that the divine message represents a reality that is hostile and resists our understanding and manipulation. Scripture is God's revelation that cannot be assimilated and stands as an immovable rock. From the human point of view, this means that Scripture will always be and remain foreign and external to us. It will never be fully ours. We will never be able to feel it close and familiar. It expresses God's otherness on a linguistic level, which we must attend continuously, not by relying on what we remember of it, but by going to it as it is expressed in that external *Scripture*.

To us humans, the Bible, as Scripture, always appears and will always appear as an external, formal, cold sign, especially since it implies and requires effort. The Bible, as Scripture, will never appear immediate and spontaneous to us. It embodies an effort that it is up to us to make. It is a challenge. To encounter it we must always move. In the Word, on the other hand, it is God who comes to us. In Scripture we toil and go toward God. We are not spared this toil. That external sign we must learn to know it and read it again and again, but it will never be ours. Although we have internalized that sign, that sign will always escape us. The memory we have of it does not represent God, but because it is our memory, it is our sign. It represents us while referring to God. The memory of that external sign, even if true, grows old and easily becomes inappropriate because it is out of date. Every memory of it is past memory that easily leads us to illusion. It is like a photo taken that ages every day even if it is true. Every photo is true and is false because it easily becomes out of date, a past memory. So it happens with Scripture. We can approach it and take a picture (an interpretation), but that picture can never exhaust the otherness of Scripture as an inassimilable external sign. That is why we need to revisit that external sign, Scripture, again and again, even when we already seem to know and have grasped and understood it in the past.

Considered instead from God's perspective, Scripture conveys to us something more, something different about who God is and how God acts. If the Word conveys to us God's immediacy and assimilability, Scripture conveys to us God's resistance to becoming ours. God as Scripture remains a distant sign, opaque and mysterious, resistant to our inquiry. As Scripture, the Bible expresses the fact that this kind of communication even to him costs effort. Scripture is not an automatic and standard communication for God. Having to write requires, even for him, an act of patience and dedication. It requires of him time, focus, differentiation, specification. It is not an automatic experience. No writing is immediate and quick. Neither is it for God. Through Scripture God agrees to toil for us, to make an effort for us. He agrees to learn how to modulate his thought and word for us, working in a specific, unique and purposeful way. He is like a craftsman who through toil and perseverance imprints on the worked object an intention of his own. This is not spontaneous but filtered through toil, effort and imagination. For him, for God, that effort even involves going through the Scripture of men.

Scripture demands that we stop and try to bring out the best in each other. In a sense, it is more personalized than the Word. The Word is more immediate for the other, but that is why the other does not have time to think it through and perceive it well. Scripture, on the other hand, by implying toil for God Himself, guarantees that that toil will help God to think better about both the recipient of that Scripture and His own intentions. It is the fatigue of Scripture that expresses even better the fatigue of the incarnation. The true incarnation of God is the incarnation in Scripture. Jesus is the incarnate Scripture of God. He is God's excellent and noble toil for us.

4. Plurivocity and Sobriety as Hallmarks of Biblical Language[30]

The second level of relevance and richness of biblical language is manifested in its two primordial characteristics: "sobriety" and "plurivocity." These characteristics give the Bible its profile without which it would be a lesser book. The problem is that these characteristics are not immediately visible. They emerge slowly over time and it is only a certain kind of reading that is able to highlight them. It is as if they appear in their fullness only gradually and after an intense and shrewd reading exercise. The hasty, zealous and presumptuous reading of a certain religious pragmatism, unfortunately widespread today, not only disregards these two essential features but even "snubs" them. Because this way of reading the Bible is not even able to perceive them, it ends up reinforcing and articulating reductive reading strategies that flatten the scope of biblical language. Let us consider them briefly.

a. A "Sober" Language

A first characteristic of biblical language is sobriety. The Bible, even for the number of pages it actually has, says little about the events it narrates. It is very sober and succinct. It is essential. The sobriety of the Bible is not only related to the essentiality of its descriptions. It also relates to the number of topics it touches upon. The Bible does not say everything. It does not want to say everything. Even what it does say, it says as if it did not say it. This mode of expression is not a defect, not an abdication. It is the sign of an alternative and ancient wisdom that one must recognize and learn to appreciate. If the Bible said everything, it would leave no room for human speech.

This is why the Bible is articulated as minimal language. Most of the time, it is only circumstantial because, through the little it says, it aims to engage the human being and urges him to speak and externalize. The Bible is not a book that paralyzes the human

---

30   C. Di Sante, *Dentro la Bibbia...* Op. cit., pp. 17-42.

being. On the contrary, it continuously motivates and urges him. A Bible that said everything and well in an exhaustive sense would intimidate the human and force him into silence. The best way to prompt us humans to speak is to articulate not a Word that says it all, but a dialoguing, inviting Word which says just the essentials.

The Bible is a sober and incomplete Word that also wants to be instructed by its hearers. Through his sober Word, God accepts our words and takes them seriously, makes them his own and rejoices because, through their words, his creatures enrich him and make him happy. This is the essence of praise. In this the Bible is the sober and limited Word of God who says, about life and the world, only essential and initial words to make dialogue and even life possible. Because God does not want to come alone with his conclusions, many topics and themes are only sketched out. In the Bible God comes to conclusions with us. God's sober and free Word provokes and gives rise to free and spontaneous words of praise. The essence of the Bible is praise.

The complexity of the biblical text is not only given by its heterogeneity. It is also given by its intentional narrowness. First, the Bible intentionally renounces saying everything. If it said everything, it would immediately become not a better text but a plethoric and heavy text, insignificant and anonymous because it claims to say too much. Great texts are great because they renounce the obsession with comprehensiveness and completeness. A good text says more when it says less. This is the magic of poetry but also of short, powerful texts such as that of some great political constitutions.

The sobriety of the Bible is also related to the character of its readers. To engage and include the reader, a good text must remain evocative only. Only a partial description of reality, such as is typical of evocative texts, is capable of awakening the imagination in the attentive reader. Without imagination, it is impossible to guarantee any learning process, ethical or religious. The Bible is limited and partial because it aims to make the reader participate in the creation of meaning. This is what the understanding of the "hermeneutic circle" really means. Text and reader go together. A perfect and exhaustive text would actually be a bad text because it would tend to exclude the reader by making him or her inessential and superfluous. A good text, on the other hand, like the Bible, makes the reader necessary, not only as a repository of an existing meaning, but as a participant in the creation of new meaning. This is perhaps what Gregory the Great was trying to express in the 6th century when he wrote, "The Word of God (Bible) grows along with those who read it."[31] In this he expressed an incredible understanding of the meaning of what the "hermeneutic circle" really implies.

b. *A "Plurivocal" Language*

The second characteristic of biblical language is plurivocity. The Bible says "little" (sobriety) and that little it says in the "plural" (plurivocity). In Hebrew thought a cross-cutting and ubiquitous mechanism is that of "reformulation." These reformulations are not as usually believed, mere repetitions that confirm by hammering on the same key of thoughts already expressed. They represent the diversified, elaborated look, from various angles, of the event being described. Neither reality nor the language that captures it can be monolithic. This structural compromise with the pluralism of life is already seen upstream, in the structure of language itself. Unlike European idioms, Hebrew lacks vowels, so the structure of the language allows for various shades of possible readings and interpretations that coexist together. The Bible does not choose the concept form as its linguistic form.

Whether on the side of ideas or on the side of norms, pointing to the clarity of the message, the "conceptual" reading of the Bible represents a mode of reading typical of Western Christianity, Catholic and Protestant. It does not, however, represent the biblical perspective. The distinction that is constantly made between biblical and non-biblical almost always stops at a difference in content. The real difference is seen on the side of linguistic form in which its theological specificity is best expressed. This difference results in

---

31 "*Scriptura crescet cum legente.*" G. Magno, *Commento morale a Giobbe 20,1,1*: Ogm I/3, 86-87, ("*Moral Commentary on Job 20:1,1*: Ogm I/3"), 86-87. Cf. I. della Stella, *Sermoni*, ("*Sermons*"), vol. II, (Milan: Edizioni Paoline, 2007), p. 25.

"plurivocity" (various meanings) as a descriptive mechanism of reality. This implies that there is no single possible meaning to say what people and events are.

People and events are always ambivalent, and this expresses their complexity. This way of describing reality could have recourse only to those forms that structurally compromise most deeply in expressing the complexity of life, that is, symbolic, narrative or poetic forms and all other forms related to them (metaphors, parables, prophecies, etc.). The Bible has a direct, non-speculative, but not unambiguous language. It privileges ambivalence. It could not be otherwise. If the Bible aims to describe the concrete reality of us humans, which is a complex reality, it could only choose a complex language, such as the symbolic one in its various declinations.

This plurivocity of biblical language is structural. It never wanes even when circumstantially we privilege one meaning over others. The biblical text is structurally heterogeneous because it is plurivocal. It necessarily has several possible meanings. Interpretation chooses one among the various possible meanings, but only temporarily. At that precise interpretive moment, the text is invested with only one meaning. This is necessarily so in order to personalize the meaning and make it applicable. The other possible meanings are not abolished though by this reading procedure, but are only bracketed. The heterogeneity expressed in this latent plurivocity of the text remains intact throughout. The various meanings are not transient or merely preparatory to the final meaning, but the opposite. The final synthetic meaning is transient and circumstantial. The various possible meanings remain because they alone express the essence of the text. This is why the literary form of the Bible is not that of the "univocal" form of mathematics or philosophy. It is the multifaceted and polymorphic form of symbolic linguistic forms, such as that of poetry, narrative, metaphor or prophecy.

The biblical text is doubly heterogeneous because, through a literary artifact, it seeks to preserve the different and even conflicting views of the same event. Whereas in the Quran the various stories are succinctly told by a single narrator, the Bible preserves the various versions of the various authors that the final editor has just put together with some linking mechanisms. This fact is visible, for example, in the two creation narratives in Genesis 1 and 2, but it is, present throughout the Bible. That is why truth in the Bible does not become multiple and differentiated only with later interpretations. It is already multiple and differentiated from within, in the Bible itself, at its origins. Biblical truth is never monolithic or compact because it always includes alternative versions from within.

5. *Centripetal and Centrifugal Dimensions as a Dual Vocation of Biblical Language*

The third level of relevance and richness of biblical language is manifested in its dual "centripetal" and "centrifugal" dimensions, which emphasize the open, flexible and inclusive character of its structure.

a. *The Centripetal Dimension*

The centripetal dimension of the Bible is best expressed in the concept of authority. The Bible does not give up being the authoritative Word of God. If this dimension of authority were amputated from it, it would automatically cease to be God's Word. In this sense, the Bible is not a necessary suggestion or an opportune consideration, but God's commandment with the strong bond of obedience. It claims to speak God's truth and it requires everyone and everything to bend to its demands. She is the (centripetal) center toward which everything else must converge. This indelible dimension of the Bible can be said in various ways. Ways that are good in one historical period are no longer necessarily good in others. The traditional wording "supreme authority," suitable perhaps in other times, is counterproductive today because it does not express the kind of authority the Bible represents. Supreme authority today designates an authoritarian, a non-dialoguing and inflexible instance.

The authority of the Bible is not only one of command, but also one of teaching and service. It is hardly identifiable in a total and compact way with a vertical and totalizing authority. Another term used to express the authority of the Bible is that of *sola Scriptura*.

The idea and intention is legitimate insofar as it expresses the sense of absolute priority and precedence that the Bible has over any other human instance. Today, unfortunately, even this formula expresses a sense of arrogance, non-dialogue, insensitivity and arbitrariness that cannot be descriptive of what the Bible and its language are. The authority of the Bible is expressed mostly indirectly. It is not a frontal authority. Evidence of this is the kind of language it uses. The Bible is basically narrative, poetry, symbol. This kind of language is essentially authoritative, not authoritarian. It expresses a mediated, indirect, broken authority. This is even more effective because it maintains a fixed point in substance, but in form it is articulated in a less confrontational and polemical way. The Bible is authoritative without being authoritarian, motivating without becoming constraining, orienting without ever being deterministic.

b. *The Centrifugal Dimension*

The Bible has a second dimension, the "centrifugal" dimension, which is most often overlooked and forgotten. In this dimension, the center is not given by the Bible, but by the word and the human reality it aims to reach and engage. Here the Bible has no problem in "decentering," in making itself subordinate, in listening others. In this dimension, the Bible is not interested in asserting its authority, but rather in making others authoritative. In order to do this, the Bible sets itself aside. It does not disappear, but makes others the protagonists. This is the dialogical word that does not block the word of others, but makes it possible. When the Bible is there, when the word of God is expressed in its centrifugal dimension, human beings overcome, through it, the paralyzing fear and silence and begin to speak, sing and witness. Here the Bible is a motivating word, a facilitator of others' speech because it enhances it. In this sense, the Bible gives space for human speech and, in order to truly do so, she herself is silent, silent so as not to block and intimidate the hesitant human being. Rather, she listens and learns, because the Bible is not the only source of wise and relevant words. It allows itself to be complemented by the human word. It is not a jealous word. It does not claim to have exclusive rights to what is right and good. It rejoices if others say better what is in its intentions. In this sense it does not want to say everything nor does it claim to be the last word. The Bible is not God's logorrheic word, compulsively articulated to say everything and more and to silence others.

Through the Bible, the Word of God, expressed in its centrifugal dimension, human beings overcome the paralyzing fear that frightens them. With it and in it humans learn to speak. The Bible gives space to human speech and, to achieve this, it makes silence. The Word of God is made up of silence. It is silence. This is not a self-referential silence selfishly articulated to meditate on one's own wisdom. It is a relational silence. It is silence to appreciate the gifts and witness of others who use that silence as a place of manifestation.

It is not difficult to understand that the Bible claims to be authoritative and prescriptive (centripetal force). But it refuses to become and be reduced to a purely descriptive formula of what the world and the human are. It is not difficult to understand also that the Bible has a strong vocation for updating (centrifugal force). It presents itself as a designer of perspectives rather than specific strategies. Its words and suggestions have been applied, supplemented, blended, inserted into the most diverse contexts and with incredibly heterogeneous formulas. Beyond the recognition of these two undoubted biblical characteristics, it is still difficult and obstructive today to say when one is in the presence of one and when the other. Which parts, which categories, which motives are centripetal and which are centrifugal? How do these two dimensions interact? We will try to explore this dimension in the next chapter on hermeneutical levels.

CHAPTER VI
THE INTERPRETING LANGUAGE

In this chapter we will talk about interpretation (interpreting language), trying to keep it in connection and tension with the interpreted object (interpreted language). "Biblical language" is the interpreted object (previous chapter) and "biblical hermeneutics" is the interpreting act (this chapter). Between these two hermeneutical moments there is a continuity and discontinuity, but they never abandon their specific linguistic dimension, given by plurivocity and ambivalence. The foundational text, the Bible, is expressed in a linguistic event with its own characteristics and the reading of that text -the interpretation- is still expressed in a linguistic act with equally typical and proper characteristics.

The difference between interpreted language (Bible) and interpreting language (Bible interpretation) is not that between language and word, as it would seem at first glance, according to the classic distinction elaborated by Ferdinand de Saussure.[1] Neither is that between "pattern" and "use," according to Louis Hjelmslev's well-known distinction.[2] "Interpreted language" and "interpreting language" are both on the side of speech and use, because they fit into an intentional and temporal linguistic pattern. The Bible and its interpretation resurrect and bet on an actualized linguistic project.

---

1 Ferdinand de Saussure defined language as an anonymous and timeless system or structure and speech as the intentional and temporal actualization of that system. See F. de Saussure, *Course in General Linguistics,* Op. cit., pp. 12-24.
2 L.T. Hjelmslev established, like De Saussure, a basic linguistic differentiation between a structural element he called "schema" and a fluid, intentional element he called "usage" instead. Cf. *Essais linguistiques*, Op. cit.

They are living words. This distinctive feature of interpreted language and interpreting language prompts Paul Ricœur[3] to choose an even better, more inclusive and larger category to express the actuality and intentionality of the biblical project. This is the category of "discourse" which he borrows from the linguist Emile Benveniste.[4] He is the one who perhaps more than other linguists has worked in this direction. It takes as its linguistic unit of reference not the phonological or lexical sign (system language) but the "sentence" (living and actualized discourse). The sentence is a set of words which expresses, even better than the word itself, what distinguishes an actualized language, namely, intentionality and design. And the three characteristics that distinguish discourse,[5] thus interpreted language (Bible) and interpreting language (interpretation of the Bible), are spatio-temporal specification (referentiality), source intention (author) and target intention (recipients). Speech is a historical event as opposed to language, which instead remains a virtual reality, anonymous and outside of time.[6]

Besides the sacred and canonical value, in the case of the Bible, from a purely linguistic point of view, the only difference between interpreted language and interpreting language is that the former is delivered to us as text. It is as if we have in the Bible an actualized "discourse," frozen in a textual structure, but that frozen text is on the side of discourse, not language. Instead, the interpreting language (interpretation of the Bible) can be written or oral.

---

3   Paul Ricœur starts from a linguistics that presupposes an actualized language instead. Cf. *Ermeneutica filosofica...* Op. cit., pp. 56-61.
4   É. Benveniste, *Problemi di linguistica generale,* Op. cit., pp. 21-32.
5   Referring to Plato's Theaetetus and Sophist, Ricœur says that for Plato the word itself is neither true nor false. The bearer of meaning is the "sentence" (discourse), not the words. Ricœur writes, "Error or Truth are 'affections' of discourse, and discourse requires two basic signs -a noun and a verb-, which are connected in a synthesis which goes beyond words" in P. Ricouer, *Interpretations Theory.* Op. cit., pp. 1,2.
6   Ricœur also attributes to Aristotle the same connection of meaning with the phrase. Ricœur writes, "Aristotle says the same thing in his treatise on Interpretations. A noun has a meaning and a verb has, in addition to its meaning, an indication of time. Only their conjunction bring forth a predicative link, which ca be called logos" in P. Ricouer, *Ibid.* p. 2.

This common element (actualized living word) and differentiation (eventual written text) conceals an even more important feature which is that of the inexorable ambivalence typical of actualized languages. The word or speech, as actualized language, would seem to overcome the typical neutrality of the language system that possesses, because it is not actualized, multiple possible meanings. It would therefore belong to the word and discourse a greater precision, thus a natural aspiration to univocity. It is in fact the opposite because non-actualized systems, (such as language, which possess in latency various possible uses given by their within a system) tend to obliterate ambivalence, thus to behave as programmable and predictable signs.

The behavior of actualized linguistic realities such as speech and discourse is quite different. They reduce the possibilities of linguistic use because they introduce intentionality, which by nature is a restrictive and specifying mechanism but at the same time are also, by nature, typical ambivalent instances. The more language is actualized through speech or discourse, the more ambivalence grows. And if this datum is present in all actualized languages, it is even more so in the biblical interpretive chain, both on the side of interpreted language (Bible) and on the side of interpreting language (interpretation). The most characterizing element of interpreting language (the theme of this chapter) is not orality or textuality per se. It is rather its strong and marked ambivalence, which interpretation derives and gathers from the language it interprets, that is, from the Bible, which by its very nature is articulated and structured as ambivalent language.

Therein lies the greatest misunderstanding. If it is conceded, still with great difficulty, that the Bible carries with it various possible meanings, that it is ambivalent in a structural way, it is nevertheless asserted with great conviction that the interpretation of the Bible must be characterized by overcoming this ambivalence.

The interpretation of the Bible must be clear, must be able to decisively and possibly definitively settle the knots of human and spiritual reality, which in the Bible still appear intertwined and confused. Our thesis moves in the opposite direction because we consider that, if interpretation is to remain biblical or biblically based, it must necessarily prolong, albeit in other terms and with different strategies, that primary ambivalence. Good interpretation certainly orients better but by not surrendering to clarity, much less idolizing it as a fetish. It keeps standing that distinctive feature of the Bible which is ambivalence. It is the ambivalence of biblical language, dutifully preserved in interpretation, that is the true center of Revelation itself and the language that describes it, and the only category suitable for preserving the mystery, complexity and pluralism of complex realities such as faith, love, relationship, community, God or the world.

This strong constraint of fidelity to ambivalence, which the Bible imposes on all interpretations that refer to it, does not invalidate the creative, experimental and innovative vocation that every interpretation is called to have. On the contrary, it makes it possible. The right of every interpretation to add things that the Bible does not say is preserved to all intents and purposes by this fidelity to ambivalence. The structural ambivalence of the Bible represents a limitation for the interpretation itself, as for any kind of sacred discourse, bulimic with power and a desire to perpetuate itself. At the same time, it represents the most obvious guarantee for making possible ever new interpretations.

In this sense, the Hellenization of the reading of the Bible that took place in the first centuries of Christianity, often criticized by biblical purists as undue, is not only legitimate but also necessary, by virtue of the fact that it is biblical ambivalence that requires and grounds it. Had this not been the case, the situation would have been even worse because, what was there before and instead of a Hellenizing interpretation -which was still an interpretation and as such relative and not foundational- would have been improperly taken and described as biblical. In this sense modern demythologization is also legitimate because it is still the structural biblical ambivalence that allows and necessitates it. All modern interpretations of the Bible, not just the Bultmannian program, are demythologizing in essence. The Bible and its ambivalence allow but at the same time impose on new interpretations three constraints. First, that those new interpretations not be canonized as Bible, but solely biblically inspired. Second, that while legitimate they should not become final and definitive.

Third, that they must remain as ambivalent and plural as the model from which they are inspired.

The innovative and experimental interpretation of the Bible is thus guaranteed by the Bible itself. The Bible puts constraints on all interpretation, not to stop it but to make it always possible. And the basic constraint is the maintenance of plurality. Interpretation can go beyond, experiment, add, but it is its primary task to preserve plurality and ambivalence.

What is the continuing temptation of legitimate and necessary modern interpretation? That of underestimating the biblical text and with it its structural ambivalence. This is arrived at through two errors to be avoided. On the one hand, it is the overlapping of Bible and interpretation. On the other hand, it is their disjunction. The first error, their overlapping, leads to making binding (sacred) what is only relative, that is, the interpreter's interpretation. The second error, their disjunction, leads one to making binding (sacred) only the reference text (the Bible). Yet this is nevertheless filtered by the interpreter's reading, so the interpreter and his interpretation is imposed on him, even if indirectly and covertly. We can say that the one who comes out reinforced, tends to be, at least in the current economy of sense-making, always the reader's interpretation, that is, the interpreting language. On the other hand, if we did not interpret the message of a text, in this case the Bible, it would never reach us. To what extent then is interpretation legitimate? To what extent is this even an obligation, a necessity? To what extent does this instead become illegitimate, anomalous and misleading?

This imbalance in favor of the reader and his or her interpretation begins very early. It begins before the reading itself, already in the reductive understanding of biblical language and its status. Reducing, implicitly, biblical language to our current language of faith represents the first overestimation of the reader. Then this overestimation of the reader and his language is further reinforced in the first interpretive take. For even when one differentiates one's interpretation from the Bible per se, if that interpretation, beyond the content, does not maintain in form the complexity of the biblical text, overvaluation of the reader's language at the expense of the biblical language again occurs. The most suitable interpretation, at the level of content, often becomes the one that denies and kills the richness and distinctiveness of biblical language. This is because it does not prolong its structure of meaning by deeming it surmountable.

The task of biblical hermeneutics is not only to grasp the content of faith, but also to maintain the essentials of its linguistic form and never make it fallacious. This is what the "hermeneutics of paradox" that we are trying to articulate in this reflection tries to do. The "hermeneutics of paradox," marked by its "plurivocity" (complexity), is merely the extension of biblical language and its corresponding plurivocity at the level of the interpreter. It is the plurivocity (complexity) that characterizes the two terms of the "hermeneutic circle." The plurivocity of the text must also remain as plurivocity of the reader who reads that text called the Bible. The plurivocity of the text cannot be resolved in the univocity of the reader and the interpretation he or she elaborates. The reader is not the locus of the ultimate epiphany of meaning. The legitimate transport that each reader experiences in discovering a sense of the text, but certainly not of the totality of possible senses, is and must remain a partial and transitory transport. Hermeneutic messianism is not a reality that is consummated in the present, but always postpones forward and describes a sense that is always on the way.

The reader is not an endpoint of the text but a continuation of it and as such must prolong the essential datum of the text, which is its plurivocity. For this reason, hermeneutics as an interpretive act must necessarily be as paradoxical as the text it reads is. Interpretive resumption cannot limit itself to resuming only the content. Along with it it must also take up and prolong the form in which that content is expressed in the text. That is, its plurivocal form.

It is true that every interpretive revival must add a clarification that the text does not have, otherwise that interpretation would remain a tautology of the text. That clarification legitimately added by the interpreter, however, cannot liquidate and make caducous the formal plurivocity of the text. This is the challenge. The plurivocity of the read text must be able to be transcribed into the new language that the interpreter uses to express what he has taken from the read text. In other words, the interpreter must be able to ensure the transcription of the content in a new context, but at the same time also be able to prolong the plurivocal linguistic form of the biblical text into the new languages in which the interpreter transcribes the collected message.

That plurivocity in interpretation is given and guaranteed by certain elements. The first is the impermanence of the found sense. The sense found cannot be a definitive sense, otherwise the interpretation becomes more important than the text it interprets. The second is the plurality of meanings worked out by the interpreter himself. The interpreter's interpretation should never be monolithic: not only out of constraint to the subjective openness of the reader, but especially out of obligation to objective fidelity to the interpreted text (Bible). Every good interpretation creates its own alternatives. And finally, the plurality of interpreters. The interpreter and his or her system of reference (church, community, ideology) must recognize and coexist with other systems and the different senses that those differentiated systems have worked out.

The biblical hermeneutics of paradox does not aim at the answer, but at the extension and enrichment of the question. Biblical hermeneutics is not and cannot be a synthetic and resolving instance of meaning. It is not a hermeneutic of clarity but of complexity. Indeed, of dynamic complexity, that is, of paradox.[7] It is so in the two linguistic levels described. The first, at the intra-textual level, or of what we have called the interpreted language (Bible), bringing out in the text itself the articulation of paradox as the center of all meaning. The second, at the extra-textual level, in what we have called interpreting language, that is, in the extension and superimposition of the biblical paradox with the paradoxes of life, outside the text, through the reader.

---

7 U. Galimberti, *Orme del sacro... Op.* cit., pp. 35-61. See also, *Il corpo,* Op. cit., pp. 11-27.

1. A Theological-Cultural Look at Religious Language[8]

Has Christianity succeeded in expressing in history, along with the content of biblical revelation, the characteristics of its language? The answer is not encouraging, as it concerns our specific historical period: the verdict by some scholars is very harsh and drastic. Eugen Drewermann,[9] for example, speaks of the exegesis

---

[8] Religious language is in Christianity an interpreting language, because it arises from a reprise of the biblical text. But at the same time it is something more, because it tries to articulate the experience of faith from other stimuli and contexts. Is biblical language marked by "plurivocity" while religious language "by univocity"? Or must religious language also remain "plurivocal," both in fidelity to the Bible and in fidelity to the complexity of life? Ricœur attributes to "religious language" the same poetic and plurivocal vocation with which he characterized "biblical language." He writes: "It is on the basis of poetics that religious language reveals its specific character... Religious language modifies (enriches) poetic language by various procedures such as intensification, overstepping or transgression, pushing to the limit, which make it, according to Ian Ramsey's expression, an original, singular language," in P. Ricœur, *Biblical Hermeneutics*...Op. cit., p. 117. Cerasi like Ricœur considers that religious (theological) language is not characterized by univocity; not only because the object of religion is a complex object both as it relates to God and as it relates to life, but in addition, because the language of precision is necessarily exclusive and exclusionary, while religion has the opposite vocation. E. Cerasi, *Dire quasi la verità*...Op. cit., pp. 23-120; E. Cerasi, *Il mito del cristianesimo. Per una fondazione metaforica della teologia*, (*"The Myth of Christianity. For a Metaphorical Foundation of Theology"*), (Rome: Città Nuova Editrice, 2011), pp. 165-220; *Il mito del cristianesimo, Ibid*, pp. 221-249. This had also been Lindbeck's innovative contribution to a more inclusive description of religious language. G. A. Lindbeck, *The Nature of Doctrine. Religion and Theology in a Postliberal Age*, (Philadelphia: The Westminster Press, 1984), pp. 30-45. In a similar vein, Umberto Galimberti expresses himself by describing ambivalence as an essential and irrevocable feature of all religious language, in *Orme del sacro*...Op. cit., pp. 37-43. See also, J. Hillman, *Re-visione della psicologia*, (*"Re-vision of Psychology"*), (Milan: Adelphi, 2008), pp. 117-121.

[9] E. Drewermann, "La verità delle forme," in, *Psicologia del profondo e esegesi. La verità delle forme. Sogno, mito, fiaba, saga e leggenda*, 1, (*"Depth Psychology and Exegesis. The Ttruth of Forms. Dream, Myth,*

of our time, referring especially to the historical critical method, as a structurally atheistic enterprise even when it speaks of God. Because the rationalistic imprint, which permeates Bible study in its various fields, would be bewitched by obsession with *objective facts,* completely leaving out the true spiritual dimension, which for him is essentially an inner, psychic reality. Biblical interpretation would be irreligious because, with the language it uses, it restricts itself to objectively describing "the Word" and is no longer able to "let speak" the world of images, dreams, and metaphors, which represents the true place where every truly religious word is born. The "univocity" of the objective word has taken over from the "plurivocity" typical of biblical language.[10]

Beyond the somewhat one-sided solution proposed by Drewermann, which may or may not be shared, his diagnosis, which is not the only one, seems to us, on the other hand, pertinent. It captures a trait that is not only distinctive but also constant and widespread throughout a historical period such as ours, which reads the Bible only in this way. Drewermann, is still too soft and generous. He essentially includes the specialized work of exegetes and one school of thought: the historical-critical method. It is not only the exegetes. It is the great mass of the faithful believers who have collapsed before the allure of biblical objectivism in its various forms and degrees. The paradox is that the same Christian conservatives, avowed enemies of the historical-critical method, prolong and promote, unbeknownst to them and better than others, the same agenda of biblical objectivism typical of liberals. Their opposition is an opposition of form not substance. Liberals and conservatives remain, complementarily and with different strategies and purposes, prisoners of the fascination with the univocity of religious objectivism.

The even greater paradox is that the typical rational "reductionism" of moderns, of which biblical objectivism is only one expression,

---

Fairy Tale, Saga and Legend, 1"), (Brescia: Queriniana, 1996), pp. 27-120. E. Drewermann, *Wozu Religion? Sinnfindung in Zeiten der Gier nach Macht und Geld. Im Gesprach mit Juergen Hoeren,* (Freiburg: Herder, 2012), pp. 203-213. E. Drewermann, *Heilende Religion. Uberwindung der Angst,* (Freiburg: Herder, 2013), pp. 8-21.
10 E. Drewermann, *Psicologia del profondo e esegesi...*Op. cit., pp. 12-25.

is no better in anything than the much-criticized superstitious religiosity of the Middle Ages. Both express hermeneutical anomalies. The medieval one "by excess" and the modern one "by deficit" of religious sense. Rational objectivism and fascination with univocity is not only a problem of biblical reading, but a broader cultural problem. On the one hand, it synchronically involves the whole of a historical period such as ours; on the other, diachronically, it highlights a structural limitation in the face of other epochs. The undoubted gain in precision of moderns, compared to Bible readings in earlier historical periods, would be ominously accompanied by a structural contraction of meaning. This realization should prompt us to historical humility.

If all historical periods, in this case the pre-modern and modern periods, have structural limitations and anomalies, how do we ensure the possibility of appropriate and relevant meanings? From the Christian perspective, we answer by saying that life and God are generous and wise. They do not wait for the correctness of either religious ideas or practices to pour out gifts and blessings on humans. This does not imply that life and God consider the superstition of premoderns or the reductionism of moderns right and proper. It only means that, despite them, life and God are generous to humans. Put more hermeneutically: God did not fail the premoderns, just as he does not fail us modern or post-moderns, of his presence and mercy despite the countless hermeneutical anomalies that they and we entertain and cultivate. Hermeneutical correction must not become hermeneutical purism. The attainment of meaning is not a mechanical matter. Like any qualitative experience, it can never be guaranteed at the outset by the precision of the interpretive tools put in place. The attainment of meaning is always an unknown because all true meaning, by definition, is unavailable and does not depend on the interpreter's efforts, discipline and reading strategies.

At this level, the interpreter's hermeneutical monolithism, unfortunately, is reinforced or is conditioned at the outset by the monolithism of contemporary religious language. The reductive hermeneutics of the Bible is already the effect and cause of a religious language that resembles it. Religious language is not that which speaks of God but that which makes God possible. Today's religious language, of which hermeneutics is only one manifestation, tends to be non-religious, irreligious or even atheistic. More than others, those who would kill religious language or compromise it in its essence would be Christianity itself.

Christianity has demystified not only religious language, but also practices, rituals, symbols, and God himself. Initially, Christianity applied this strong demystifying, iconoclastic and demythologizing thrust to other religions, and with great success. Without realizing that it was preparing its own demise. The same tools that Christianity used to neutralize other religions were then used internally, to neutralize Christianity itself. Indeed, not others, but Christians themselves were the mediators of this hollowing out of their own religion.[11]

The slaughter of meaning that the univocity of objectifying language, typical of modern Christianity, has caused in today's religiosity, however, would not be an accident of the way, but would be inscribed, according to Slavoj Žižek, in the very genes of Christianity from its birth.[12] This would represent the "perverse heart" of Christianity. Certainly Žižek is not the only one who thinks this way. Hermeneutical iconoclasm and the desacralization of myth would be part of the Christian project all along. And this is why we Christians must be even more careful today in dealing with this iconoclastic genetics of ours for two reasons. First, for an "immunological" reason. That is, to prevent the destruction of what

---

11 This reductionism, which has found a home within religious language itself, is part of a more transversal tendency that Graham Ward identifies in the cultural logocentrism typical of the West. Graham in the face of this drift proposes a renewal of religious language that he finds possible to do from an Augustinian perspective that links knowledge and faith, reason and culture, with the intention of uniting what has been excessively fragmented by a structurally nominalist culture. Together with John Milbank and Catherine Pickstock, they have shaped a "radical orthodoxy" movement that aims to recast religious language from this perspective. Graham sees in Karl Barth and Jacques Derrida the extremes for proceeding in this direction. G. Ward, *Barth, Derrida and the Language of Theology*, (Cambridge: Cambridge University Press, 1998), pp. 53-78.
12 S. Žižek, *Il cuore perverso del cristianesimo*, (*"The Perverse Heart of Christianity"*), (Rome: Meltemi, 2006), pp. 7-17.

is still religious in Christian churches from happening through the use of our own uncontrolled and drifting Christian mechanisms. Second, for an external "contagion" reason. This is that parallel reigning cultural reductionism, which offers undoubted functional benefit in some areas because of the clarity and dynamism it creates, does not become a model that religions uncritically follow and use full-handedly in an effort to compete with highly productive socio-cultural and techno-political systems that are at the forefront of data and event management and organization.

The interpretation of the Bible today must be able to perceive this drift and try to stem the damage. It must maintain, along with the validity of the biblical content, the perspective and nature of its language that finds in exuberance and sobriety its main characteristics. What is at stake here is not only the validity of biblical language, but the validity and specificity of religious language in general.

What distinguishes the religious language of which every biblical interpretation is a part? According to Slavoj Žižek, it is the obsession with orthodoxy that has led Christianity to destroy the sense of the religious. For Umberto Gallimberti it is the loss of ambivalence,[13] as a distinctive feature of all sacred discourse, that has caused this nihilistic drift. Galimberti describes this reductive drive not only at the level of religious language. He transversally attributes it to the entire Christian culture. The whole West, as a cultural-historical phenomenon, would be impregnated at its roots with this reductive virus, because, again according to Galimberti, everything in the West is Christian, including atheism. Christianity had the great merit of having given life and form to the West. At the same time though, the West would rip the authentically religious heart out of Christianity by particularly affecting its language.

Talking about the essence of religious language, of which Bible interpretation is a part, is not easy because two needs must be taken into account. 1. The need for clarity. If religious language did not bring greater clarification of what God, life, and the world are, this language would be superfluous and useless to many. 2.

---

13 U. Galimberti, *Cristianesimo. La religione del cielo vuoto, ("Christianity. The Religion of the Empty Sky")*, (Milan: Feltrinelli, 2012), pp. 139-208.

This language cannot be reduced to clarity alone because it would immediately lose its ability to speak of realities that are by nature ineffable, i.e., unclear, such as God, life and the world. The added problem is that the undeniable need for clarity has often led not only to distort the object of faith. It has also made religions belligerent and aggressive. Reductionism and belligerence are the devastating side effects of a religious language identified with clarity. These are the two deformations that Slavoj Žižek has in mind when he speaks of the "perverse heart of Christianity."

Strategies for flexibilizing religious language have been proposed to limit these two side effects. One of them is that proposed by George A. Lindbeck.[14] He rails against religious language that is intended to be nonnegotiable. He divides religious language models into three groups. The first is what he calls, "informational propositional" language. The advantage of this type of language lies in clarity. The disadvantage is that if the truth of religious statements is propositional or cognitive, the only possible outcome is the compact conviction that sets out on crusade against all those who take value away from those propositions. If this is the starting point, religious communities can hardly come to an agreement. This kind of language underscores what differentiates religions.

The second model is what he calls "experiential-expressivist." This type of language is a non-informative symbolic language that emphasizes the similarities between religions. This type of language is typical of liberal theologies and can be traced back to, for example, F. Schleiermacher. The advantage of this type of language lies in offering ample space for religious negotiation and convergence. Its disadvantage lies in its limitation in explaining differences between religions and especially in not recognizing religious claims as substantive.

The third model tries to bring together both the propositional and symbolic dimensions of religious languages and takes the form of a hybrid model. This type of language is, for example, preferred by some Catholic theologians with an ecumenical vocation, such as Karl Rahner or Bernard Lonergan.

---

14 G. A. Lindbeck, *The Nature of the Doctrine...* Op. cit.

Lindbeck essentially disagrees with these approaches and regards religions as languages and doctrines as grammatical rules. He writes:

> "Put in more technical terms, a religion can be seen as a kind of cultural and/or linguistic scheme or medium that shapes the totality of life and thought. It functions somewhat like a Kantian "a priori," although in this case the "a priori" consists of a set of acquired capacities that could also be different. Religion is not primarily an unfolding of beliefs about truth and good (although it may include them) or a symbolism that expresses basic attitudes, sensations or feelings (although it creates them). Rather, it resembles a language system that makes possible the description of realities, the formulation of beliefs and the experience of inner attitudes, sensations and feelings. Like a civilization or a language, a religion is a communal phenomenon that forms the subjectivities of individuals rather than being a manifestation of them. It comprises a vocabulary of discursive and non-discursive symbols and a distinctive logic or grammar that makes this vocabulary work by giving it meaning. Finally, just as a language (or "language game," to borrow an expression from Wittgenstein) is correlated with a form of life, and just as a culture has a range of both cognitive and behavioral dimensions, so it is also with religious tradition."[15]

Doctrines, for Lindbeck, opposing the liberals, are authoritative. At the same time, against the traditionalists, they are neither eternal nor unchangeable. The reference to Wittgenstein is certainly not accidental. Wittgenstein's philosophy has had a great impact in our time also for religion by remodelling more generally our understanding of language itself, its nature and function.

Wittgenstein's contribution cannot be limited to the concept of "language games." Wittgenstein is also the author of the "Tractatus logico-philosophicus"[16], one of the most influential books in 20th century philosophy. He wrote much more at the level of notebooks and notes. To these various and other writings belongs the text *Philosophical Investigations*,[17] published in 1953, two years

---

15 G. A. Lindbeck, *The Nature of the Doctrine*. Ibid, p. 51.
16 L. Wittgenstein, *Tractatus Logico-Philosophicus*, (*"Tractatus Logico-Philosophicus"*), (Milan: Feltrinelli, 2022).
17 L. Wittgenstein, *Ricerche filosofiche*, (Philosophical Investigations"), (Turin: Einaudi, 2021).

after his death. This posthumous book probably exerted an even greater influence than the *Tractatus*, outlining an entirely different philosophy. In the *Philosophical Investigations,* the notion of a plurality of languages emerges, each and with its own relevance and validity within its own specific life context. It is as if the idea of a single universal essence, valid for all, is to decay, and with it the idea of a single foundation of language and the world.

In the *Tractatus* it was as if, with language, only one game was being played: the fundamental game of representing the world. No, language instead possesses various other features and possibilities. Its most specific value lies in its use. It can certainly have a use through representation, but that does not exclude other uses. The uses of language can be as varied and contrasting as that of religion, art or politics. In each of these areas a specific use will impose itself that cannot be confused or compared with other uses in different areas. One can even be able to give a metaphysical or spiritual use to language. The important thing is not to make incorrect uses of the different language games. Do not apply the language of one domain to another.

In Wittgenstein we actually find a double reflection on language,[18] valid for the tension it creates. On the one hand, there is the need to share a unique linguistic space through which mutual, clear and specific dialogue and understanding is made possible (*Tractatus*). On the other, Wittgenstein outlines the need to grant particular areas the possibility of saying their own specificity, which is essentially unspeakable in the languages of others (*Philosophical Investigations*).

Wittgenstein's most innovative contribution, with the concept of "language games," lies in the fact that he broke the monopoly of an abstract universalism, which Europe in particular has used not only to stigmatize and minimize the language of other peoples, but also to impose its own rationality as the sole measure of what is true

---

18 A. Massarenti, *Il filosofo tascabile. Dai presocratici a Wittgenstein. 44 ritratti per una storia del pensiero in miniatura,* ("*The Pocket Philosopher. From the Presocratics to Wittgenstein. 44 Portraits for a History of Thought in Miniature"),* (Parma: Ugo Guanda Editore, 2010), pp. 227-232.

and real. This contribution should not hide though the problem it has created, which is that of the limit of all linguistic and cultural incommensurability. If incommensurability, which Wittgenstein defends, is absolute, then not only dialogue becomes impossible, but also criticism and correction of the anomalies that each system brings with it. If, on the other hand, incommensurability is understood in a relative sense, then the dual possibility exists: to allow each system its own internal coherence and at the same time to leave the possibility of interaction, dialogue and comparison between different systems.

The West has nevertheless persisted in the reductivist tendency of its cultural framework.[19] This has happened also at the level of religious language. This religious reductionism can be seen, for example, in the reduction of religion to ethics. Christianity, oblivious to Kierkegaard's reminder that the religious[20] stage transcends the ethical stage, has reduced the religious dimension to a moral issue. If there is a possibility for Christianity to recover a relationship with the sacred, this possibility comes through Christianity's renunciation to become a *legislating morality*. There is no commensurability between human knowledge and divine knowledge, so God's judgment cannot be forced into the rules by which humans have organized their reason and packaged their morals. The sacred is somehow beyond true and false, just as it is beyond good and evil.

The historicization and embodiment of faith itself triggers, according to Galimberti, this reductive process. Christianity is the religion of the empty sky, the religion that desacralized the sacred. Dealing fully with the world, it would be transformed into a "diurnal event," an event of conscious and chosen meaning. We would be faced with unambiguous meaning, with a religion of clarity. By producing itself in discourses that any civilized society can safely make for itself, Christianity would abandon the management of the "undifferentiated night of the sacred" to the solitude of individuals or to the madness of groups.

---

19 U. Galimberti, *The Decline of the West...* Op. cit. , pp. 451-459.
20 S. Kierkegaard defends the specificity of the religious dimension, which in no way can be reduced to ethics. Cf. *Timore e tremore*, (*"Fear and Trembling"), (*Milan: Mondadori, 2016), pp. 9-24.

Man has always felt, as superior to himself, powers that he has placed in another region, called sacredness. Sacredness is an ambivalent word that means, at the same time, blessing and curse. All words that transcend the human are ambivalent words. On the one hand, man fears the sacred,[21] as one can fear that which one considers superior and is unable to master. On the other hand, he is attracted to it as one is attracted to the origin from which one is one day emancipated. The sacred is an enduring dimension in the human condition. Although it can be removed or even forgotten, it operates nonetheless. If we want to define this sacred dimension, we must give it a definition by default, a definition in the negative because with definitions we are already in the restricted human sphere of reason. Man tries to define, specify and delimit. While the sacred is the undifferentiated and the undifferentiated is that scenario within which it is not possible to find differences, distinctions.

To defend us from the sacred, religions were born, which are not dimensions that relate us to the sacred, but rather defend us from it. The word religion means to relegate, to enclose, to contain, and religions have done a great operation of containing the sacred dimension, because contact with the sacred is a contagion, it is something extremely dangerous, with basically unpredictable effects. Christianity has carried out this project of religions to perfection. It has become the model religion. It has created a dynamic and performing religiosity, introducing a strong element of control over the sacred. It has done so especially at the level of language, reducing the typical "ambivalence" of the sacred to the "clarity" of faith. Difference, distinction, is what allows us to name things and treat them according to an unambiguous meaning. This allowed Christianity to introduce a stabilizing dimension from this neutralization of ambivalence, and extend it to all religious experience. Indeed, this linguistic order reduced distress but made behaviors predictable.

One may well disagree with this radical description by Galimberti, but in its essence it captures the complaint we have been trying to articulate from the beginning. This concerns the profoundly

---

21 R. Otto, *Il sacro*, *("The Sacred")*, (Milan: Se, 2014).

reductive character not only of Christian hermeneutics interpreting the Bible, but also of Christians' own conception of their Bible. One of the limitations of Galimberti's analysis is that he does not differentiate between Christian interpretation and the Christian text, which he seems to know little about and poorly. But pressed by his examination, which in essence seems pertinent to us, we might say that it is not ancient paganism, the polytheistic and mythicizing paganism, that threatens us most today. It is the new univocal paganism of technology, material or linguistic it matters little, that is destroying Christianity, its language and its basic text. We Christians do not see the effects modern paganism of the univocal, of equivalence, of precision, of efficiency is producing today. We have even made it an ally of the faith. We have substituted it for the God of the Bible. The Bible itself has become a spreading instrument of this modern idolatry. Although it might seem paradoxical and extreme, the complexity of the Bible and its multifarious language have more in common with classical paganism than with today's orthodox Christianity. We cannot dialogue with paganism -it would seem surreal- and it is not necessary to come to that. We can be challenged though by the problems that paganism raises and faces and that it is perhaps facing better than Christianity. After several centuries of intemperance, counter-senses, idolatries, one-sidedness, perversions, we cannot think that Christianity has remained untouched. It is not certain that paganism cannot partially regenerate itself and make itself persuasive again. Marc Augé, along with others, believe that this is happening. In his book *The Genius of Paganism*[22] he describes the cultural strength of the new paganism of which the relevance of its more inclusive and more concrete language is a part. Christianity does not have a monopoly on truth as much as paganism is not compactly a set of perversions. Today we must analyze theme by theme, according to the relevance of each individual register, and not automatically consider a system in its totality as true or false, good or bad, correct or incorrect.

---

22 M. Augé, *Genio del paganesimo*, (*"Genius of Paganism"*), (Turin: Bollati Boringhieri, 2002), pp. 9-14.

2. Hermeneutic Levels: Some Characteristics

The Bible is a generous book. It does not presuppose or establish preconditions to its reading. Anyone can approach it and find benefit in it. In this sense it is an immediate and democratic book. This does not mean that those who benefit from it always get the best or all possible benefit from it. Every reading of the Bible leaves us with something, but it does not disclose the fullness of its design. Every reading of the Bible is legitimate, but it is not necessarily representative of what the Bible embodies and wants to communicate. For this reason, we want to list briefly in this section some characteristics of the six hermeneutical levels that we will describe more specifically in the next section. These features are the articulation of the plurivocity and complexity already present at the level of biblical language, but which we now find at the level of the interpretation of that language.

a. *Intensity*

Hermeneutic levels are in the first instance an instrument of sense intensification. They are so in a twofold perspective. On the one hand, they are in a quantitative perspective in that they re-propose, through repetition, a rearticulation of meaning with the integration of an added element. A repetition here is never a tautology. That added element, though minimal, sometimes given only by a synonym, expands the sense by reconfiguring it in a new perspective. On the other, they are at the qualitative level, because the repetition of a specific element, even without adding anything more, taken up simply at a higher level, automatically changes the whole articulation of meaning. The element in question could remain the same. Nothing has been added. But it is the new placement that doubles the intensity of meaning through new contextualization.

b. *Sequentiality*

The hermeneutic levels mark not only a layering of meaning that properly determines an enrichment of it. This differentiation of them also creates a progression, which does not necessarily imply the annulment or overcoming of the previous levels. All levels are necessary and are necessary because of the complementarity they create but also because of the tension they introduce. These various hermeneutic levels are not always immediate. That is what interpretation is for: to highlight them. To census the various levels in the offered text and make them manifest is the task of hermeneutics. Hermeneutics does not aim to capture only the most immediate sense or the most convergent sense; its task is also to illuminate the mechanisms, the extracts, the differentiations, the knots that are articulated in the processes and progressions of meaning. This is sequentiality: it does not only create continuity and complementarity of meaning. Often sequentiality is a guarantor of ruptures and discontinuities that at first seem to destabilize meaning but, in the long run, enrich it.

c. *Complementarity*

These various levels brought to light by hermeneutics in their diversity create a convergence. This convergence acts as a multiplier of meaning. One thing is an element with its particular meaning in isolation, another is that same element together with other meanings. The result is not a sum but a multiplication. At the level of meanings, one plus one does not make two; it can make four, five or ten. The combination of hermeneutic levels enhances the meaning of words and events, expanding them into unsuspected horizons through interaction and convergence. Any lucid hermeneutics must aim to build bridges between the various elements that at first glance may appear distant from each other. This convergence is not always visible, this is why the complementarity of levels is not automatic. It must be sought and sometimes imagined. It is the nature of biblical language that pushes toward this. Thus, one only needs to be drawn by the impulse of the text itself to create links and convergences that intensify the scope of the meaning being worked out in the interpretation.

d. *Complexity*

These hermeneutic levels that intensify meaning and give it sequentiality and complementarity are not to be understood in a linear or evolutionary sense. Their differentiation and progression does not intensify meaning in the sense of greater precision, thus greater effectiveness. The richness of meaning is of a different nature. It is also given by the slowing down or complication of a meaning that gets stuck, by the emergence of an alternative meaning or even a counter-sense. Not every obstacle of meaning is nonsense. Sense, in order to become noble, must always confront one of its paradoxes or opposites. This alternative element to sense, which is now contrasted, serves as a stimulating and reinforcing element because it pushes sense. On the one hand, this brings out its potentialities in an effort to tick it off. On the other hand, it coexists with other different senses. This is the complexity presupposed by hermeneutic levels.

e. *Tensionality*

These hermeneutic levels do not always create convergence and complementarity, but stand before each other in a tense relationship. When this happens, the temptation to harmonization is strong. But it must not happen, on pain of dismantling and neutralizing one of the most important hermeneutic mechanisms in the creation of meaning: hermeneutic tension. It is not given by a text that is clear and a reader who, being external and unrelated to that text, tries to approach it, inevitably creating an interpretive tension. No, the hermeneutic tension is internal to one's text and remains there even when the reader is not there. The reader reproduces and maintains in his or her interpretation this tension internal to the text. Interpretation in this sense does not represent an unambiguous final synthesis that breaks down the tension. In some ways, it is the opposite. This is because interpretation prolongs and enriches this tension, introducing an added and supplementary component that does not resolve the prior alternatives but takes them up. It strengthens them and makes them dialogue with a new interpretation, a product of the singularity of the interpreter on duty. The complexity given by different hermeneutic levels should not be conceived as surmountable. Meaning is not situated beyond. It occurs within the tension that creates that complexity. It is within that complexity that convergence must be sought, not the other way around. That complexity is the guarantee of both the functioning of meaning and the opening of the text forward to other possible meanings.

f. *Circularity*

These hermeneutical levels create a sequentiality and progression and, in a sense, even a hierarchy. The third intra-textual level, characterized by "paradox" -and which we will describe next- is undoubtedly a culmination of meaning and, as such, represents the goal of any reading of the biblical text. To stop earlier is to fail to understand the meaning in its fullness. The same thing happens at the extra-textual levels. It is the articulation of the paradox in the paradoxes that represents the pinnacle in the articulation of meaning. Yet, the prevoius levels can never be surpassed. In a "circular" configuration of hermeneutic levels, not only are the previal and initial levels not erased. They can serve, in the interpretive process, as additional spaces where the fullness of meaning occurs in an inverted and nonlinear way. Sometimes meaning is evinced in the text itself and its paradoxes, and sometimes in the reader and his paradoxes.

These six hermeneutical levels that embody and articulate the complexity of the biblical text are nothing more than the specification of the hermeneutical circle. The first three relate back to the text pole and the last three to the reader pole.

3. *Three Intra-Textual Hermeneutic Levels: From Event to Paradox*

In addition to demarcating and defining each of these hermeneutical levels from a descriptive and sequential point of view, in this section we will briefly give an application example from Psalm 23, which we then quote below to facilitate understanding of the explanation.

> PSALM 23
> *Psalm of David.*
> 1 The Lord is my shepherd: nothing I lack.
> 2 He maketh me to lie down in green pastures, He leadeth me beside the still waters.
> 3 He restores my soul, He leads me by paths of righteousness for His name's sake.
> 4 Even when I walk through the valley of the shadow of death, I will fear no evil, for you are with me; your rod and staff give me security.
> 5 For me you set the table, before the eyes of my enemies; you sprinkle my head with oil; my cup overflows.
> 6 Surely, goods and goodness shall accompany me all the days of my life; and I will dwell in the house of the Lord for long days.

a. *Hermeneutics of the Event (Literal, Intra-Biblical Interpretation)*

This hermeneutic is characterized by its immediacy. I read what is written and apply it directly. This immediacy presupposes a continuity between biblical times and our times. The Bible is perceived as a unified document and the reader as a purely supporting component in the articulation of meaning.

Here the meaning is already given. It is only necessary to unveil it. This kind of hermeneutics represents an essential moment. It gives immediacy and concreteness to the meanings contained in the Bible. Interpretation, by the interpreter, gathers only the already full and total meaning contained in the biblical text. This does not mean that the interpreter is passive. On the contrary, the interpreter, with the collected interpretation, can be very active, not at the level of the creation of meaning though, but at the level of its application.

This level cannot be skipped. It will always remain valid. We are faced here with a literal and immediate hermeneutic. Literal does not mean literalist. The difference lies in the fact that the former is a concrete, but open hermeneutic, while the latter lacks this openness and this leads it to reduce it to the dimension of the letter. The Bible must be able to offer itself immediately to those who read it, and those who read it will always find a first meaning at hand. This first meaning is true because it is offered by the text itself. That this first level is necessary does not mean that it is sufficient. It is not sufficient because it does not grasp the knot of the text that is always expressed in a paradox and depth not visible to an immediate and superficial glance. Until one grasps that paradox that grounds every text and expresses its structural complexity, interpretation remains incomplete and insufficient. Incomplete and insufficient does not mean false. It means that it is an important first step but that it cannot become final and definitive.

Taking Psalm 23, *The Good Shepherd,* as an example, we can say that the literal hermeneutics of this psalm puts us in immediate connection with the central message of this passage, which is articulated in God's top-down heroic guidance of us as "shepherd."[23] The figure of the shepherd who is secure and firmly at the helm by virtue of his knowledge and skill in leading the sheep immediately conveys and instills a sense of trust and confidence. Even for someone who does not grasp other crucial nodes of the psalm or grasps only part of it, this first message of confidence comes through smoothly and immediately. This interpretation of the good shepherd protecting us is true, legitimate, and captures an essential address of the psalm. It certainly does not exhaust the total meaning of the psalm expressed in the other hermeneutical levels. Even beyond its undoubted relevance, this first meaning falls short of the perception of that "paradox" that we believe is the constitutive and central element of this text.

---

23 The classical reading of this psalm stops at this first metaphor and captures it in its literalness. This is the approach of Luther, who emphasizes the power of this clear and direct scripture that proclaims God's uncontested sovereignty. Indeed, the reformer links this psalm to the third commandment. M. Luther, *Reading the Psalms with Luther*, (Saint Louis: Concordia Publishing House, 2007), pp. 59-60; G. Ravasi, *Il libro dei Salmi. Commento e attualizzazione*, (*"The Book of Psalms. Commentary and Actualization"*), vol. I, (Bologna: Edizioni Dehoniane, 1999), pp. 425-446; L. A. Schökel, C. Carniti, *Salmos,* vol. I, (Navarre: Verbo Divino, 1992), pp. 396-407.

b. *Hermeneutics of the Principle (Ideal, Intra-Biblical Interpretation*

This hermeneutic is characterized by its clarity. It is no longer an immediate hermeneutic like the previous one because, behind the events, rules and narratives, we are called to grasp the universal principle that does not wane and transcends the circumstantial forms it takes in that passage. This hermeneutic is characterized by the perception of an inevitable difference between biblical times and our time, but it continues to regard both as homogeneous and transparent times. The perception of biblical unity prevails over the perception of its diversity and pluralism. The reader emerges only as the circumstantial custodian of universal and eternal principles. Interpretation and the interpreter here emphasize a greater grip on the text given by the ability to go beyond the primary and immediate, formal and theological forms to a more hidden but nevertheless evident meaning in the text.

This hermeneutic marks an important step because it opens the text to a universal constant that is not necessarily immediate and visible but is nonetheless present. The universal constant, embodied in the universal principles, is hidden. It is the nobility of the hermeneutic of the principle that brings them out and affirms them as central. This hermeneutic level introduces an important qualitative shift in the understanding of both the text and the role of the reader. This element lies in the positive distance that the reader introduces with respect to both the text and himself. The goal of interpretation is neither the first glimpse of the text nor what the text provokes in the reader. It is the universal constant that is always hidden and must be sought with insistence, perseverance and intelligence.

This hermeneutical level, while legitimate and necessary, and while representing an advance over the previous hermeneutical level, still does not discern, in the found meaning, any asymmetry, rupture, or tension that expresses the complexity that every biblical text has. The meaning found and linked to a universal principle that does not coincide with an immediate reading of the text appears though as a compact, homogeneous and absolute meaning. The compactness of meaning has only been transferred from the primary and initial event to the hidden universal principle. For this reason, in this second hermeneutic level, we do not yet find the confrontation with what Ricœur calls "the thing of the text,"[24] which is given by the figure of paradox. We have not yet arrived at the central and foundational knot of every text that is expressed in a paradox. This is why the hermeneutics of the "principle" is necessary but still insufficient.

Connecting to Psalm 23,[25] we might say that the reasoning within this second hermeneutical level prompts us to consider important not the country and peasant form that care and guidance take in this psalm, but the principle of care and guidance itself, which in our time will be expressed in other forms. The peasant and country form was essential for the primary recipients of that text, but that form to us moderns no longer says anything or says too little, because we have all become urban individuals, bound to cities, to the rhythms and deadlines that the city imposes on us. Instead, the principle of care and guidance expressed in the psalm is still valid, however, it will be embodied in other forms that correspond better to our new urban context. And this is what the hermeneutics of the principle does: it tries to grasp the mechanism behind it, which has not changed, but from the ancient forms in which it was expressed, it tries to embody it in forms that are appropriate to the reality of today's readers.

---

24 Ricœur actually uses various expressions to describe the center of a text. One of these expressions is "the thing of the text." Only after perceiving "the thing of the text" can one say that one has understood a text. P. Ricœur, *Ermeneutica filosofica...Op.* cit., pp. 89-95. We, , are more of a guarantor because we grant that even when the interpretation lies on this side of this discovery, that is, of the "thing of the text," the interpretation is not only legitimate but also true. To this concession we add only one condition: that a legitimate and also true reading of a text does not yet mean having understood the text in its centrality.

25 This is what Calvin captures in Psalm 23. The principle of guidance from God even when this is expressed in different ways today. Cf. J. Calvin, *Commentary on The Psalms*, (Carlisle: The Banner of Truth Trust, 2009), pp. 125-128; G. Ravasi, *Il libro dei salmi,* Op. cit.; L. A. Schökel, C. Carniti, *Salmos,* Op. cit., pp. 396-407.

c. *Hermeneutics of Paradox (Pluralistic, Intra-Biblical Interpretation)*

This hermeneutic is even less immediate. It notes the existence of a knot that is not external to the text but at its center. Meaning then is given only at the center of this knot and by the tension it creates. This hermeneutic is characterized by the perception of an inevitable difference between biblical times and our own and considers them both heterogeneous and opaque. The Bible is perceived in the tension of its different, heterogeneous patterns, categories and narratives. The perception of the Bible's internal "complexity" mirrors the parallel "complexity" of external reality. At this level, the interpretation and the interpreter no longer function only as immediate collectors and applicators, because the perception of this paradox creates in them a pause, a surprise, an unexpected contrariety that allows and requires reflection as a necessary complement in understanding that asymmetry of meaning.

This attitude of surprise and even perplexity, because the clarity of meaning appears broken in the text itself, leads not only to reflection on the text but also triggers a second mechanism that will be to push to go beyond the text. This third hermeneutical level of paradox is central to understanding the vocation of the text, which is always a vocation to point beyond it, toward external reality. Every good text highlights this internal limitation that de-emphasizes its potential and by doing so forces it to look beyond, at reality itself. Every good text is a referential text that does not exhaust its vocation within a purely intra-linguistic and immanent sense. Every good text, by virtue of this third hermeneutical level based on paradox, is and necessarily becomes a transgressive text, a text that always goes beyond a linguistic form to land in reality itself.

This is why the perception of the intra-biblical paradox is essential for hooking up with extra-textual reality. Without this paradox, the connection with extra-textual reality would become more difficult, perhaps not impossible, but certainly flatter and more linear, more orphaned of that complexity to which paradox is flame, driver and witness. It is only at this hermeneutic level, and by virtue of the perception of the paradox foundational and present in every text, that we can speak of successful interpretation. This is the minimum goal. Before this level, interpretations can help, guide, orient but they do not do so from the centrality of the text, but from its periphery. Without grasping this center, which is expressed in the paradox, interpretations, while true, remain insufficient without being false for that reason. The perception of paradox is not immediate. One must search for it and exercise, in addition to patience and perseverance, a good dose of curiosity, imagination and relational analysis.

The main paradox, the one around which the central perspective of a passage is articulated, is also always hidden behind a more immediate and more superficial paradox. The paradox is sometimes given in the same verse, sometimes in a chapter itself. Other times only within a section or book and sometimes only comparing the text with what is outside the text. In the case of Psalm 23 it is given not in one verse but in the logic and within the whole chapter.

There is a fundamental paradox in Psalm 23: only in case one grasps it does the psalm disclose its fullness.[26] Only when this level is reached can it be said to grasp the full meaning of the biblical text. Its true horizon, is described by Ricœur as "the thing of the text."[27] Here the text expresses and unveils its essence, its purpose through a paradox, a rupture. In this text the pastor's metaphor is only one part. The other part is more hidden and is given by a second metaphor, that of God as a housewife preparing a table for her guests. That of the shepherd is a "theocentric" metaphor; that of the housewife is instead "anthropocentric." In the first metaphor God leads and is the protagonist. In the second God follows and indulges, but the protagonists are the guests, the humans whom God, as the housewife, serves by enriching them.

Psalm 23, like any other biblical text, changes after grasping its paradox, its central fracture. This is why we can say that this

---

26   G. Ravasi captures this paradox in Psalm 23 which is given essentially by not one but two metaphors; the metaphor of the "shepherd" and the metaphor of the "house," creating a sense-creating tension. G. Ravasi, *Il libro dei salmi, Op. cit.,* pp. 434-438; L. A. Schökel, C. Carniti, *Op. cit.,* Ibid.

27   Cf. He also calls it "The World of the Text," P. Ricœur, *Ermeneutica filosofica...*Op. cit., pp. 89-95.

third hermeneutical level is the one that represents the pinnacle of biblical hermeneutics. How to grasp it, however? We will see that, surprisingly, this center, this paradox that grounds every text, is best grasped by relating the text to the extra-textual element, to the reader and his world. The extra-textual reality is not secondary to the creation of meaning and should not be taken only as an applicative realm of the meaning found in the text. The extra-textual sphere (reader) is functional and essential to the creation of meaning itself; hence the need to consider the other three hermeneutic levels, which are extra-textual but not extra-hermeneutic levels, since the hermeneutic is given not only by the presence of the text but also by its correlate, which is the reader as an extra-textual instance, but nevertheless connected to the text, not only because he reads it, but because he is anchored in life itself, of which that text he reads is an important, though not unique, register and witness.

4. Three Extra-Textual Hermeneutic Levels: From Paradox to Paradoxes

In profiling each of these three extra-textual hermeneutical levels, we will again refer to Psalm 23 as a starting application example and to facilitate understanding of the explanation.

a. Reader's Hermeneutics (Biographical Extra-Biblical Interpretation)

The reader becomes, at this level, the protagonist in deciphering the interplay, overlap and tension of the various biblical levels and in making the decision as to which of these is more significant. Here the hermeneutic proceeds through the subjectivity of the reader, who becomes the filter for better looking at the text. The reader is not an intruder, someone who asks uncomfortable and impertinent questions. On the contrary, it is the reader with his questions, anxieties, perplexities, doubts, who gives the text the opportunity to express itself and bring out the best of its latent meanings. Without the reader provoking the text, it would remain unexplored, locked in its latent meanings and semantic potential.

The reader is not the one who undergoes the text by passively receiving meanings that are already complete and ready for their application. Without the reader there are no relevant meanings, for it is in connection with the situation in which he finds himself and it is in relation to his mediation that the meaning of a text completes its configuration as such. However, the reader does not create meaning by himself, but articulates it from the ingredients that come to him from the text and its context: he is the one who does this mediation. Thus, the reader's mediation is twofold because on the one hand, through his existential and historical position, he provides the text with extra-textual outlets for connection and application; on the other hand, he highlights in the text itself the various possible meanings that often emerge only from the text's confrontation with the extra-textual element, and forces the interpretive gaze to review the text not only to survey those hidden latent meanings, but to evaluate and choose them in accordance with not only intra-textual but also extra-textual relevance.

Reconnecting with Psalm 23[28] we find that taking seriously the status of the reader not only illuminates this psalm differently but also introduces a new reading of the reader himself. The intent to understand the reader's situation and profile leads us to see, behind this typically theocentric psalm (because it speaks primarily of God and his guidance), a profound and relevant description of the human being as well. We discover that this is not only a psalm about God, but also about the reader-man. So behind the two foundational metaphors of this psalm, those of the "shepherd" and the "housewife," which the hermeneutics of the third level has helped us to discover and focus on, lie two implicit images of man. The first is the image of man as a "sheep," related to the first metaphor of the shepherd; the second is the image of man as a "diner," related to the second metaphor of

---

28 This sense of connection with the situation of the present reader is emphasized, for example, by Bonhoeffer. D. Bonhoeffer, *Pregare i salmi con Cristo. Il libro di preghiera della Bibbia*, (*"Praying the Psalms with Christ. The Prayer Book of the Bible"*), (Brescia: Queriniana, 2019), pp. 29-32; L. A. Schökel, C. Carniti, *Salmos, Ibid.*

the "housewife." Thus, reflecting on himself, the reader discovers that his ideal profile is not monolithic, but that he, like God, has a differentiated and heterogeneous profile. He is asked not only for "obedience" as a sheep, but also for "freedom and creativity" as a diner invited around the table by the housewife. Final destiny of the believer's vocation is thus not only obedience, but becoming free people. And this complexity, found at the level of the reader, prompts him or her to reread the text differently, later finding ingredients and stimuli that already orient toward a diversified understanding of human beings in the horizon of their complexity.

b. *Hermeneutics of Reality (Contextual Extra-Biblical Interpretation)*

The reader is only a part of this reality external to the text, not all of reality. This hermeneutic is characterized by the tension created not by an internal diversity, but by an external one, introduced by reality itself without which it is impossible to perceive and understand the Bible. The serious consideration of "external reality" does not intervene to diminish the value of biblical meaning, but to amplify and enhance it, because the main feature in the Bible is to describe the external complexity of life and reality. The Bible is amplified in its meaning and scope by external reality, and the mediator of the interaction between the text and reality is the reader, who has become an active interpreter. But the interpreter-reader does not exhaust that external reality. It is only a first dimension. That reader enters into a network of relationships, human and non-human, of events and places, which represent the historical world on which the biblical text aims to say something.

But as in the previous hermeneutic level, there is a double referral between reality and text in this fifth level. On the one hand, understanding our present historical reality prompts us to reread the text in a different way, highlighting details that previously escaped us; on the other hand, the text itself prompts us to read the external reality in a way that is destabilizing because it is new. This new reading of the text, starting from our historical and not just individual reality, is not immediate. It is not reducible to the first impression. Just as the appropriation of the biblical message requires years of attendance, learning new linguistic tools, care in gathering data, organizing the categories surveyed -- rhythm, familiarity and intuition in the handling of meanings -- in the same way knowledge of external reality is not immediate. It is not reducible to slogans. It requires the same effort and time, perhaps even more. But there is no alternative. Non-knowledge of extra-biblical reality condemns one to fail to grasp the stimuli latent in the biblical text.

Reconnecting with Psalm 23, we can say that to understand it well, it is necessary to know well the present time in which we live.[29] Every historical time wrests new meaning from the Bible. But knowledge of our present is not immediate. Understanding our present requires significant reflective effort. Is our time a time of moral, anthropological and institutional rigidity, or is it rather a time of ethical dispersion and social disintegration? It could be one and the other, and more. Depending on the answer we give to this question, the psalm will be read and applied differently. And neither of the resulting readings from the "shepherd" or "housewife" metaphor will be true or false. At a more essential level, the biblical meaning is more relevant, not very relevant or not relevant, but not necessarily false. One must be careful about labeling as false what is actually only a latent sense of the text, which at some point is not the most corresponding and appropriate sense for a given situation. The alternative views of reality given by the metaphor of "pastor" or "housewife" can be matched, overlapped, contrasted, ordered in various ways. And it corresponds to the reader to innovatively choose, without betraying the essence of the text but going beyond it, the most meaningful combination. The openness of the text and the nature of its language do not allow establishing a single combination. The reader will be able to emphasize the firmness of the pastor's interventionist leadership or the soft, subdued, purposeful leadership of the housewife. He or she may focus on the obedience of the sheep

---

29 This is the dimension that Bernd Janowski emphasizes. The psalms would not only be texts of spirituality but would refer to an anthropology of which those texts would be just one component. B. Janowski, *Konfliktgespräche mit Gott. Eine anthropologie der psalmen*, (Neukircher-Vluyn: Neukirchener Verlag, 2003), pp. 1-35; L. A. Schökel, C. Carniti, *Psalmos, Ibid.*

or the freedom and creativity of the diners. The text offers all these various possibilities, but it will be up to the reader to semantically exploit them and apply them according to the relevant context.

c. *Hermeneutics of Imagination (De-contextual, Extra-biblical Interpretation)*

This sixth hermeneutical level introduces an uncomfortable question. What is the true reality? Is it the one that is there now or the one that could be there? A good text is never a validation of what is there. It is not merely descriptive. Certainly a fictional text is more creative than a historical text. But all texts, if they are such, are partially fiction texts because they implicitly critique what is there from what could be there. Present reality is always shorter than future possible realities.

In other words, hermeneutics cannot be used to validate the world and reality that is in the present even though they, being the object of reflection in the previous hermeneutic level, are essential steps in the interpretive process. Hermeneutics, with the interpretations it gives birth to, tries to open new realities through imagination. The true reality is always the one that is being created. And it is interpretation that has to create this opening process. It represents the art of exploring, intuiting, creating new trails of meaning from a text that propels us forward through the imagination that categories, forms and paradoxes create in us. This is why we could also say that the legitimate intent of contextualization, which breaks and opens up a hermeneutic that would like to stop only at the reader and his or her self-referential search for meaning, is in itself insufficient, because it is part of the hermeneutic process of de-contextualizing our present perception of reality in order to imagine a context that is not yet there but is possible. This further step is fostered by the text itself and the reader's present imagination. If the biblical text has from the beginning fostered a beyond-itself, opening to the extra-contextual element, it is still the text that pushes toward a beyond-present context and points to an extra-contextual reality that is not yet there but can be there by virtue of the power of interpretive imagination.

In connection with Psalm 23, the imagination[30] can find marginal elements that, however, with its exercise then become central. The theme of guidance, of trust, is strong and recurrent in the psalm. The motif of inclusiveness is almost absent. The sense of the flock in the metaphor of the shepherd, or of the family in the metaphor of the housewife, emphasize the sense of the exclusiveness of the group, which is best articulated in the exclusive circle of their intimacy. Yet, this psalm, through imagery that exploits, in and out of the text, seemingly secondary elements, has great potential for inclusiveness. And this can start with the exploitation of the "enemies" motif. That enemies are also seated at that table[31] is suggestive. So the home, quintessentially a sign of intimacy, can actually become a place of welcome and inclusion not only for one's own group, but for anyone. That table is actually the place where anyone can find a place, enemies included.

If interpretation is only there when there is interaction between "text" and "reader" (hermeneutic circle), only levels 4, 5 and 6 deserve to be called hermeneutic in the strict sense. Levels 1 and 2 still remain sophisticated forms of readings without yet configuring themselves as true hermeneutics. Levels 1 and 2 tend to neglect, underestimate and disregard the structural necessity of true interaction between the Bible and the believer's historicity. The central hermeneutical level remains level 3 because it is the one that signals, through paradox, both the incompleteness of the text without reality and the partiality of a reality without a text.

5. *For a Biblical Hermeneutics of Ambivalence and Paradox*

In the previous chapter, we considered some load-bearing features of the

---

30 This component of imagination is very present in W. Brueggemann's interpretive takes with respect to the Psalms in general and Psalm 23 in particular. W. Brueggemann, William H. Bellinger, Jr., *Psalms*, New Cambridge Bible Commentary, (New York: Cambridge University Press, 2014), pp. 122-126; L. A. Schökel, C. Carniti, *Ibid.*

31 The reference to enemies is an explicit one and we find it in verse 5. "For me you set the table before the eyes of my enemies."

biblical language: sobriety and exuberance. This creates a double movement of contraction and expansion of meaning within which any interpretive revival must fit. Interpretation is not the repetition of biblical language and its message as the reader found them. That would be pure tautology and, as an interpretive event, perfectly useless. No, interpretation adds specification to the Bible read. The interpreter does not stand there before the biblical message as a purely decorative element, as an ornamental hermeneutical element with no real impact on the process of meaning formation.

The interpreter is required to leave his or her own imprint on the biblical language. Indeed, to add to that language something it does not have. Through his intervention, the interpreter ennobles the Bible because he converts its latency of meaning into something specific. The interpreter is not only a potential deformer from which to protect the sacred text, he is also a necessary enhancer of the sacred text. And he does so as a ferryman of a sense that, from latent, becomes explicit by virtue of extra-textual events that allow one to look at the Bible from new perspectives. In this sense, it is as if the Bible awaits the creative hand of the interpreter to deliver to the world meanings that, without this hand, would remain purely potential and in a state of latency.

This is what we mean by a hermeneutics of ambivalence and paradox. Among ambivalence and paradox, the common element is given by the synchronic existence of various possible meanings. Both are thus declensions in the plural. In ambivalence and paradox, plurality does not wane but becomes the hallmark of the interpretive act in all its stages. The interpreter is required to maintain and reproduce in his interpretation the plurality he has found in the Bible and which is not to be overcome in the new found meaning.

The sense derived does not mark the demise or exhaustion of biblical language and its plurality. How then to maintain the biblical message and language without being tautological and without denying the necessary addition of the interpreter and his creative intervention? The challenge is therefore daunting and can be summed up in this maxim: the exuberance and sobriety of biblical language must be prolonged in the interpretation that the interpreter constructs from the Bible.

Ambivalence and paradox, while similar, are not completely identical. Ambivalence refers to a plurality of senses that coexist together and may eventually converge until they somehow overlap. In paradox, on the other hand, there is a plurality that does not assimilate but remains in tension. In paradox the senses present remain asymmetrical and unassimilable, but it is this structural tension that provides the space where the senses occur and confront each other, thus opening up a horizon of meaning. Ambivalence and paradox are thus two looks at the plurality of meaning, similar but different.

New meaning, thanks to this preserved or repurposed plurality with equivalent strategies, remains mysterious. A statement by clues and fragments. There is never complete epiphany of meaning. The sense derived can never be definitive. True interpretation is prohibited from totalizing synthesis and clarification. It is testimony, not explanation. That is why it offers not only answers but increases questions. It refuses to convert into a doctrinal casuistry of confessional orthodoxy, to become meditation and prayer.

The Bible truly becomes a guide when the characteristics of its language are preserved in the interpretations it gives birth to. Interpretation is successful when the exuberance and sobriety of biblical language are prolonged and survive in new faith formulations that draw on the Bible.

What does it mean to preserve, in interpretation, the sobriety and exuberance of biblical language?

1. They must not become totalizing or definitive. They must remain like the Bible, indicative and circumstantial. They must elaborate prospective and guiding indications. They must remain sober, for if they were full they would not tolerate alternative interpretations or even further updates. They would present themselves as concise and definitive definitions. The Bible and its language, as indeed any religious language, necessarily expresses an inclusive intent, not of a synthetic but a tensional inclusiveness. This means that the accepted meanings will never be surmountable in an unambiguous synthesis, but will always coexist in a creative tension.

2. They are and must always remain "exuberant," that is, "multiple" as is the Bible they interpret. The fact that interpretations are also multiple means that they cannot create a final synthesis, thus claiming to close the rushing stream of meanings that biblical language typically provokes. Each interpretation must create possible alternatives. If an interpretation instead becomes compact and monolithic, it is not good because it has not taken from the Bible the openness of its language. Good interpretations are those that always create alternatives.

This is the essence of a hermeneutics of paradox. A hermeneutics that aims at prolonging questions rather than closing them with final, resolving answers. The biblical hermeneutics of paradox does not aim at a final and resolving synthesis of meaning. It does not identify with a hermeneutic of transparent clarity. It remains, from the beginning to the end of the interpretive process, linked to the complexity and productive tension it can create.

This dynamic complexity, i.e., of paradox,[32] is expressed at three levels.

1. At the intra-textual level, bringing out in the text itself a tension of meaning that is the birthplace of all meaning.
2. At the extra-textual level, highlighting that even in the life of the one reading the text there are paradoxes that create existential tensions parallel to those found in the text.
3. At the level of linkage, the non-synthetic comparison and juxtaposition between paradoxes inside and paradoxes outside the text: it is in the tensional space between inside and outside the text that meaning occurs and is given.

Biblical hermeneutics is not only complex in the sense of its plurality. That plurality is not always complementary. Sometimes it presents itself as irreducible. It does not integrate but resists synthesis. Paradox is thus a guarantee of truth. The Bible works with a structural tension that does not wear it down, but makes it possible. This is in essence a hermeneutic of paradox.

---

32 U. Galimberti, *Orme del sacro...* Op. cit., pp. 35-61. See also, *Il corpo*, Op. Cit., pp. 11-27.

But paradox is not easily identified. Therefore, a hermeneutics of paradox cannot be immediate. It presupposes legitimate prior levels of interpretation that cannot claim to express the main perspective of the text. Only when one discovers the paradox that grounds a text can one claim not to exhaust the text, but to follow its horizon. A text unveils its message and offers itself to the reader only from its central paradox. This is why all texts of the Bible are difficult, because the paradox that grounds them cannot be traced immediately. We list below four levels where paradoxes can emerge.

a. *Proximal-Immediate Paradox*

The proximal-immediate paradox emerges in proximity, in the same verse, but it does not mean that its understanding is instantaneous. It just means that the paradox is closer spatially than we might imagine. It is found in the same verse. An example is Psalm 119:105:

"Your word is a lamp to my foot and a light to my path."[33]

The message of this verse is that when we take God and his Word seriously, we immediately experience clarity and certainty in our life journey through the illumination of his Word. In this first interpretation, however, the proximal-immediate paradox, because in the same verse, has not yet been grasped. The paradox here is twofold. The first paradox is given by the light of the lamp that goes, not, as we might naturally expect, to illuminate the path but the foot. Almost suggesting that the light, initially at least, is not to be applied to the path but to the walker, that is, the one who walks, so it is an introspective light.

The second paradox, on the other hand, is invisible if we limit ourselves to modern translations. This only emerges when reading the original, because the word used for light, in the second part of the verse, in Hebrew *ohr*, means "little light." Thus suggesting that we do not have here an illumination of the whole path, of the whole

---

33 Version NR.

of life as we would like, but a circumscribed illumination, more problematic than decisive, because it is small in scope. A limited enlightenment that constantly needs to be refocused, readjusted and only according to the next step that is to be taken. It does not allow a planning, a filing, a synopsis of the path as a whole. The paradox lies in the fact that this light of God illuminates by hiding and hides by illuminating. That is why it is not on the light itself that one must rely, but only on the God of that light.

b. *Proximal-Deferred Paradox*

The proximal-deferred paradox emerges not in the same verse but within the entire passage or entire chapter of reference. This means that reading, much less hasty application, is not enough to grasp the central address of the passage. Because it is deferred, this paradox is grasped only later, after much reading and reflection, which, however, must not create habit or habituation. The challenge is to maintain a repeated and recurring reading without erasing the imagination. An example of this kind of paradox is found in Psalm 23.

> *Psalm of David.*
> The Lord is my shepherd: nothing I lack. He maketh me rest in verdant pastures, He leadeth me along still waters. He restores my soul, He leads me by paths of righteousness, for His name's sake. Even when I walk through the valley of the shadow of death, I will fear no evil, for you are with me; your rod and staff give me security. For me you set the table, before the eyes of my enemies; you sprinkle my head with oil; my cup overflows. Surely, goods and goodness shall accompany me all the days of my life; and I will dwell in the house of the Lord for long days.

The immediate message of this psalm is the Shepherd's skill, care and attention in guiding his children. When we choose God as our shepherd, we immediately experience the confidence, consolation and assurance that his guidance communicates to us. This message is immediate and perceptible in the first reading and runs throughout the psalm from beginning to end. But the paradox is not so obvious: it emerges only when we grasp the second metaphor, that of the "table" with which the first metaphor of the "shepherd" is in structural tension, because the shepherd is a metaphor external to the house, while the table is a metaphor internal to the house.

It is as if this psalm describes two modes of being: not only ours as humans, but of God Himself as the supreme Being. We do not behave outside the home as we behave inside the home. Attitudes, emotions, strategies are different. The believer, consequently, is not monolithic in his attitudes but has structurally diverse ways of being; therefore, flexibility is required of him as an essential characteristic of a shrewd and wise faith. He needs to know how to live wisely inside the church but also outside in the world. This double emphasis on the complexity of the believer's profile and his actions emerges only when we grasp this proximal-deferred paradox and the tension it introduces into the reading through these two metaphors.

c. *Distal Intra-Textual Paradox*

The intra-textual distal paradox does not emerge in the same verse nor in the same chapter, but at a distance (distal), either in other chapters of the same book or in a different book of the Bible. This means that reading, much less hasty application, is not enough to grasp the central address of the passage being read. Because it is distal one grasps it only later, after several readings not only of the passage in question but of the whole book in which the passage is found. Reading the whole of a book should be neither scattershot nor monolithic, because it is a matter, through familiarity with style, typifying themes and imagination, of finding connections and highlighting them. An example of this kind of paradox is found in the thematic parallelism of these two verses:

> "If anyone comes to me and does not hate his father, mother, wife, children, brothers, sisters and even his own life, he cannot be my disciple" (Lu 14:26).

> "Children, obey in the Lord your parents, for this is right. Honor your father and mother (this is the first commandment with promise)" Eph 6:1,2.

The immediate message of Luke's passage is that when one chooses Jesus, one must be willing to leave everything behind, including such fundamental ties as family. This renunciation, difficult in the immediate moment, turns out to be compelling later, because we see that, despite this loss, life with God gratifies us in other ways, and eventually it is possible that the family itself, over time, will understand the goodness of our choice of faith. Immediately we see, however, that there is a difficulty in this interpretation and also the danger of a drift in our faith. We note that this passage can easily be interpreted one-sidedly, thus misinterpreted. For if someone is already in dispute with his or her family, he or she finds in this gospel request the perfect alibi to break with it permanently.

Therefore, this passage should not be read alone. One must read other passages, in other books of the Bible (distal) that give a different look at the same topic. The Ephesians passage suggests a completely different attitude, introducing a tension that is difficult to resolve. There we are asked to adopt a less radical, more guarantor-like, more sober attitude, reminding ourselves that faith and faithfulness to Jesus is not played out, most of the time, in breaking with the family but remaining there, as the text suggests, because if there is one place where it is possible to test the consistency and validity of our faith, it is precisely the family. Only by knowing how to live the family, with the family, in the family, do we show that our faith is mature. Breaking with the family, even for reasons of spiritual choice, many times is an escape from reality and true faith. The way to live faith and family is not given only by the verse in Luke, but in the comparison of the verses detached and inserted in different (distal) passages that we have to tie together through the Spirit's guidance.

d. *Distal Extra-Textual Paradox*

The extra-textual distal paradox emerges not in the same verse nor in the same chapter or even in the Bible, but at a distance (distal) and in connection with a non-biblical fact or event that occurs in reality itself. This requires us to make a different kind of effort. A different reading of the Bible. A knowing how to read not only the

Bible but also reality and everyday common life. This extra-textual distal paradox reminds us that the Bible cannot be read alone. We must, along with it, know how to read reality and the world. Because it is distal, this paradox is grasped only later after various readings, which include non-Biblical readings.

The Bible is not the whole of reality, but only an important part of it, so in order to grasp its message, we cannot escape but must confront the reality to which the Bible is a witness, guide and reflection. It is the Bible itself that pushes us toward reality. If this does not happen, it is a clear sign that we are reading the Bible wrongly. The Bible is a map of reality, not reality itself. And this extra-textual distal paradox reminds us of this very essential fact. To read the Bible well we need to read it together with and not instead of reality. An example of this kind of paradox is found in the thematic parallelism of the passage in 1 Corinthians 14:34,35 with the world today.

> "As is done in all the churches of the saints, let the women be silent in the assemblies, for they are not permitted to speak; let them be submissive, as the law also says. If they want to learn anything, let them question their husbands at home; for it is shameful for a woman to speak in the assembly."

The immediate message of this passage is clear for pre-modern, hierarchical, patriarchal communities that did not know what individual freedom and the right to self-determination was, much less that referring to women. This is not to say that their social and cultural configuration did not have merits and did not express guarantees that today, for example, we do not have and are unable to offer people. It was simply a different historical configuration. The immediate message of this text is rather clear. Belonging is to be preferred to individual or to minority rights. It is to be favored, even with the support of faith, order, authority, stability, continuity, and verticality of relationships, because those were the guarantee of the balance of a faith community in that epoch.

We note at once that there is a difficulty in this interpretation and also the danger of a drift in our faith. We note that this passage can easily be interpreted one-sidedly, thus misinterpreted. We cannot find verses in the Bible that really offer alternatives to that religious understanding. We can find individual verses that allude to certain minority experiences where the woman showed initiative and resourcefulness even then. But, on the whole, we will not find in the Bible, as some would have it, either the defense of the individual as such and detached from the value of the group, or even less, consideration of the woman herself, beyond and outside the group or her family.

The Bible could not anticipate the times, nor was it necessary. Not only for the family, but also for the conception of politics or science: the Bible, while correcting some excesses and elements, is a child of its time. But its greatness is in introducing, not completing, reflections valid for all times. Then again, this is true not only for the Bible, but also for the so-called great classical texts, which have a timeless and current value because they only suggest, introduce and outline universal perspectives but don't give specific recipes. So this passage from 1 Corinthians, though harsh and provocative for us contemporaries, should be read and grasped in its perspective, which is eventually partially valid but can't be taken as a recipe for dealing with women today. The extra-textual distal paradox is not created by the Bible, but by comparing the Bible with the external world of today's reality which is a reality that defends the choice and self-determination of single individuals, women included.

CHAPTER VII
HERMENEUTIC ANOMALIES
"BY EXCESS" OF TEXT
Textual Positivism

In this chapter and the next, we deal with some interpretive dysfunctionalities. These anomalies are perfectly possible and more common than we think. They emerge and are chronically present where they are least expected. Reading the Bible, unfortunately, does not cause only benefits and blessings, as we would like. It also causes anomalies and sometimes real hermeneutical pathologies.

Most believers think that it is only failure to read the Bible causes spiritual anomalies. This belief is vitiated by two assumptions. First, that reading the Bible, because it is the product of an authentic and personal search, always produces a benefit. Second, that the Bible itself is transparent and immediate and that it is enough to read it to understand its various propositions. The first is an anthropological error that overestimates the value of personal conviction. The second is a theological-cultural error that disregards and downplays the complexity and difficulty of every communicative process, including the religious one.

The problem of hermeneutics, that is, of reading and assimilating meaning, is faced by those who read the Bible, that is, believers. It is not faced by those who do not read it, that is, non-believers, as most Christians believe. Those who do not read the Bible have eventually other kinds of problems, including possible spiritual problems, but not hermeneutical ones. This is because they do not make attending and reading the Bible their priority or their life commitment. Hermeneutical problems arise within that segment of Christians who are more committed and more involved in faith experience and Bible reading. It is this spiritually militant majority, noble and committed band of people in the various Christian communities, only a fraction of whom meet the criterion of fanaticism and radicalism, that we will be concerned with in these two chapters. It represents the reservoir where these various hermeneutical dysfunctionalities are cultivated and articulated.

With a synoptic intent, we will say that this group of committed Christians basically incur two kinds of hermeneutical dysfunctions. We will call the first, anomaly "by deficit," the second anomaly "by excess." The anomalies are not all of the same sign, they do not enact the same dysfunctional mechanism and, consequently, they do not all require the same kind of corrective intervention. It is not the quantitative differentiation that is most important, but rather the qualitative one. This double differentiation between anomalies by deficit and anomalies by excess is, in its essence, a qualitative differentiation. We will define them both by a qualitative relation to the text, which is the basic hermeneutic category. Hermeneutical anomalies by deficit are those that neglect, underestimate, theoretically or practically, the importance of the biblical text. Those by excess instead overemphasize and affirm the centrality and foundational priority of the biblical text in any interpretive process.

Although this simple division into two groups seems clear and fairly obvious, it actually implies a series of stances, assumptions, relationships and effects. In their intersection and interaction, they well exemplify the nature of the relationship with the Bible. They also exemplify some more hidden cultural assumptions that heavily determine the interpretive act. The theoretical and practical implications arising from this differentiation are of vital importance in properly directing the interpretive process

Hermeneutical anomalies due to a deficit of biblical reading will require a certain kind of pastoral and theological intervention. The corrective hermeneutic intervention must here focus on the mechanism of "stimulation" at both the level of supply (biblical persuasion) and demand (personal motivation). Hermeneutical anomalies due to a excess of biblical reading, on the other hand, will require another kind of intervention. The valid mechanism here is no longer that of "stimulus" but that of "cooling" (tempering) the supply, demand or at least proposing a different and alternative configuration of them.

Two important descriptive-diagnostic confusions emerge at this level.

First, churches seem to possess and offer only one kind of hermeneutical strategy. It aims to push everyone to read the Bible, because it is naively believed that the most widespread anomaly consists in not reading the Bible and that, as a result, everything is solved by reading it. Unfortunately, this is not the case: sometimes reading the Bible can make the situation even worse. If someone does not read the Bible, it is good that he reads it. But if someone reads it badly, we make the situation worse if we stimulate more assiduous (abnormal) reading.

Second, churches seem to think that the most damaging anomaly is that by a deficit of biblical reading. This possibly is the most widespread anomaly but not necessarily the worst. We might say that those who read the Bible little at least know that their problem lies in not reading it enough. The more insidious, more hidden hermeneutical problem, lies rather with those who read the Bible assiduously. The Christian who is most committed and involved in the faith is the most susceptible to developing a hermeneutical anomaly that is difficult to correct. Reading the Bible has become for this Christian complicit in a mechanism that reinforces the anomaly one wants to correct.

In this chapter, we will consider anomalies by excess and in the next chapter those by textual deficit. The first group we will also call "textual positivism" or "biblical positivism." Textual positivism thrives on a double affirmation. On the one hand, the importance and absolute priority of the biblical text is affirmed. On the other hand, and as an automatic correlate, there is a tendency to minimize and neglect the reader's questions, situation and anxieties. They are considered inappropriate or even unnecessary. From this perspective, the text is king and the reader has only to comply and submit to the absolute directions coming from the text. We use the word "positivism" because like scientific or social positivism, typical modern cultural forms, "biblical positivism" also lives by the same basic assumption. This is that the reality in question, in this case the biblical text, is completely transparent, measurable and clear.

This emphasis on the sacred and absolute character of the text would seem to contradict the overriding tendency of the hermeneutics of our time that we have described as "reader-centric." On a second level, however, this paradox is perfectly possible. It is so because the text presupposed and defended by those who incur this anomaly by excess of text is certainly not the premodern text characterized by its stable meaning. It is an all-modern text. The premodern text was not only characterized by its stability, but also by its mystery. It was an enchanted text.

The text that is defended and elevated here is a fluid text, made artificially stable by modern biblical positivism and, above all, without mystery. It is a disenchanted text, characterized only by the functionality and correctness of shared information, typical form and configuration of modern texts. Those who defend the sacredness of the biblical text today think or are under the illusion that they are defending an ancient text when they are defending a clearly modern and "positivist" understanding of that text. It is firm only at a point of modernity elevated to a sacred schema through the disguised, albeit unconscious, recourse to the authority of the biblical text.

The text defended from this perspective is actually an indirect defense of the individual and the typically modern individualism that underlies it. It is a kind of referred symptom. In medicine, pain cannot always be directly linked to the place of its manifestation. Referred pain is pain shifted to a territory derived from the place where it originates and which only a trained clinical eye can decipher well in its genesis and manifestation. A headache does not always originate in the head but could be caused by a metabolic and functional problem residing elsewhere. This is our hypothesis about biblical positivism, consisting of a radical defense of the biblical text. It is a mediated defense, a "referred symptom" of the centrality of the reader that one wants to affirm and maintain even through indirect mechanisms.

It is as if a typical dissimulation mechanism occurs in biblical positivism such as, for example, occurs in the "reactive formation"[1]

---

1 Cf. N. McWilliams, *Psychoanalytic Diagnosis. Understanding Personality structure in the Clinical Process*, (New York: The Guilford Press, 2019), pp. 140-142.

described by Freud. In this secondary defense mechanism, an unmentionable thought is sublimated through the creation of a virtuous thought. It is hidden, unknowingly, behind extreme purism and moral rigor, a marked unmentionable sexual weakness. Similarly, the unmentionable modern individualism that has reinterpreted the Bible for the individual's use seems sublimated, in biblical positivism, behind a great respect for the Bible. It is not very complicated to show that many biblical ideas, passionately defended by many biblical fundamentalists in the present day, rather than being biblical are typically modern ideas, sclerotized and stationary at one point in modern history.

With respect to hermeneutic anomalies, another specification must be introduced. This one concerns the word "anomaly." What kind of dysfunctions do anomalous readings of the Bible embody? Are they just alternative looks? Fallacious techniques? Simple misreadings? Interpretive asymmetries? Or are they real hermeneutical pathologies? Two brief considerations can help us to understand the dimension of the problem.

1. All reading, including biblical reading, presupposes the existence of errors, but these do not compromise either the reading effort or the final result of the reading. In some ways these errors are necessary, perhaps even beneficial, and one should guard against stigmatizing them. That would be like expecting a child to grow up well and healthy without ever disobeying a rule. Perhaps the attitude of a child who always obeys would be more abnormal, just as a reader who always reads well and arrives at the meaning without any peripatetic reading would become suspect. No, errors in reading and interpretation should not be demonized, but should be welcomed as natural stages in the long and winding process of interpretation.

2. There are, however, reading errors that not only undermine the result of reading, but also warp the reader's motivation and interpretive attitude at the outset. If we are vouchers for the first type of errors, we are instead critical of this second type, for which we will use a strong term: "hermeneutic pathology." Yes, there are and frequently exist real hermeneutic pathologies.

Although this may seem excessive, we defend this terminology for two reasons. On the one hand, it is because these errors contaminate not only the reading, but also the resulting theology and its communal, ethical and cultural extensions. On the other, it is because some hermeneutical anomalies unfortunately become chronic and, becoming so, also resistant to corrective strategies. There is no way to correct them, also because the biblical dimension is itself sensitive and of first importance. It is what is good from the point of view of religious mobility and functionality, but not from the curative and therapeutic point of view. Those who think they read God's Word out of conviction and obedience are unlikely to be corrected in the hermeneutical anomaly they embody. They perceive the correction as a sacrilegious intent to destroy their faith. This fact determines that these anomalies take the form of true hermeneutical pathologies.

1. *A Theological-Cultural Look at Textual Reductionism*[2]

The description of these hermeneutic anomalies is not done on neutral territory. We do so within a historically precise world: the

---

[2] Textual reductionism, which is the phenomenon that claims to reduce the complexity of reality and life to the reduced dimensions of a piece of writing (text), is certainly not only a linguistic or literary phenomenon. Cf. L. Zoja, *Contro Ismene. Considerazioni sulla violenza*, (*"Against Ismene. Considerations on Violence"*), (Turin: Bollati Boringhieri, 2009), pp. 99-116. More underlying is a cultural phenomenon that Heidegger describes as the obsession to rationally control being, confusing it with beingness. U. Galimberti writes, "The West is the time of the epoché of being... Underlying all the initiatives of Western man is indeed the overt or covert attempt to dominate being, to lord it over," in, *Il tramonto dell'Occidente*...Op. cit., pp. 282-283. However, this cultural and not just textual reductionism is not negative. On the contrary, it underlies modern efficientism and is part of its DNA and conscious project. Cf. S. Toulmin, *Cosmopolis. The Hidden Agenda of Modernity*, (Chicago: University of Chicago Press, 1990), pp. 89-137. If this had not brought undoubted benefit, modernity, greedy for results, would not have chosen and maintained it at all. But what modernity had not calculated are the adverse side effects of this reduction, which essentially occur in the ambivalence of reason and its undoubted vocation to nihilism. See T. Adorno, M. Horkheimer, *Dialectic of Enlightenment*, (New York: Verso, 2016), pp. 3-42; U. Galimberti, *Il tramonto dell'Occidente... Op, cit.*, pp. 411-416.

contemporary world. This first type of hermeneutical anomalies, which we group under the name "biblical positivism," needs to be specified in two senses. One is an "intensive" sense, in that this anomaly is much deeper and more deeply rooted in the Christian sphere than we think, and cannot be circumscribed only to so-called biblical literalism. A second is in an "extensive" sense, in that biblical positivism, beyond its deep hold in all strata of Christianity, is actually the extension and Christian form of a much more widespread cultural phenomenon that precedes it and that Christianity perfects with its own categories.

This cultural phenomenon, which Christianity presupposes and perfects, we could call "textual reductionism". It is a typical phenomenon of the contemporary world. Textual reductionism is that cultural configuration, born in the West, which tends to enclose complex and polyform reality in books, and in the knowledge and concepts that books contain and pass on. It positively causes a great dynamism in and of the reference system, depending on the order it introduces at the level of the reading of reality. At the same time, it falsifies reality itself because it reduces it only to what the reference books say about it. We are faced with the reduction of reality to the description of reality, of the world to the representation of the world, of life to the concept of life. In the reality-writing (written thought) pair, everything is to the advantage of writing. Writing, of which modern books and texts are the form and medium, replaces true reality. From reality is considered only that which is thinkable and writable.

This textual reductionism as a typical deformation of the West has three characteristics: 1. It tends to confuse the representation of reality with reality itself; 2. It has become an across-the-board and widespread phenomenon in our time to the extent that it is implicitly enacted by all of us automatically and without questing it, in everything we know and undertake. 3. It seems difficult if not impossible to stop. Any intent to correct and to balance it merely updates and reaffirms it in an even more sophisticated way.

Cultural anomalies have a long genesis. This positively allows them to protect themselves against untimely and abrupt mechanisms and changes. Unfortunately, they also have the disadvantage of requiring long periods of time in the application of corrective mechanisms. This manifests itself in their chronic resistance to change. Cultural anomalies tend to become chronic and difficult to correct. Many times cultural anomalies, as in this case textual reductionism, are not dysfunctions that take over later at a later period of a group's historical journey. They are co-present, in an incipient form, since the birth of cultural phenomena. This anomaly of "textual reductionism" is congenital and synchronous to Western cultural greatness, hence the difficulty of its containment.

This is the diagnosis of Luigi Zoja, who speaks of pervasive and persistent cognitive patterns arising from apparently decentered or marginal cultural sectors as could be for instance the psychoanalysis. Zoja, and before him Jung himself, and with Zoja a large cohort of analyst as James Hillman for instance, all of them raise to modern culture, of which contemporary biblical hermeneutics is a part, not only a psychological question about the state of inner being, but above all an epistemological question. This question and critic concern the pervasive presence of a reductive way of knowing and of approaching life and reality. Their question and contestation focus on this point. The undoubted inner decay and the clear emotional and psychological fragility of our time, which, as Philip Rieff well reminds us in his book *The Triumph of Therapy*,[3] occurs and results in the massive spread of psychotherapies, is rooted and conditioned, in a deeper level, by a epistemological problem. Not only existential and inner disruptions, which have always existed, cause the psychological withering that exists today. The cause is a type of knowledge that, having become excessively rational and objectifying to the bitter end, can no longer nurture people's inner selves.

This substantive problem is not only psychological but also epistemological. James Hillman speaks of a radical linguistic and psychological nominalism that underlies contemporary culture and

---

3   Ph. Rieff, *The Triumph of the Therapeutic. Uses of Faith After Freud*, (Wilmington: ISI Books 2006), pp. 23-45.

its malaises.[4] This is a distortion not at the level of inner being, but at the level of the way of knowing the real. It underlies the inner attrition of modern and postmodern man. Jungian psychoanalysis, through the massive use of images, metaphors and archetypes, proposes, before psychological therapy, an epistemological reconversion.[5]

Zoja calls this reductivist orientation and drift of all Western culture, of which biblical hermeneutics is a part, the "disease of the West."[6] This reductionism emerges not only in modern technology. It is a strong idea throughout the history of the West and it is widespread in all levels of cultural expression. Reductionism is a cognitive experience that replaces multifaceted experiences and diverse and complex points of view with one. The result is not immediately negative. On the contrary, it results in great functionality and efficiency. Everything becomes mobile and the quantitative grows. The obvious loss in this process is the known object, that is, reality.

In this process the object is "objectified." It is made a thing, an inert and immobile reality, therefore manipulable. One knows a depowered, essentially dead reality. The depowered object of knowledge, because it is rendered a "thing," automatically takes over the depowering of the knowing "subject." The subject's strength and vitality depend on the kind of knowledge it has of the external world. Contemporary man myopically and short-sightedly traded the life-giving force of images and metaphors that nourish the inner life for depowered images (concepts) that cannot nourish him. They can give him only the fleeting impression of knowing and powering more. The modern subject finds in his hands a depotentiated (disenchanted) world that is a perfect copy of his own depotentiated being. The subject itself comes out depowered because what nourishes it and makes it alive (powerful) cannot be self-nourishment and pure self-care. It must be life that comes from outside, from others and from otherness. The modern subject is a subject that has shut itself in. It has erased the idea and actual reality of the other. It moves solely in the world of the equal and the same.

---

4   J. Hillman traces this reductionism to the nominalism that has corroded the strength of our language for centuries. *Re-visione della psicologia*, Op. cit., pp. 117-131.
5   Cf. J. Hillman, *Ibid.*
6   L. Zoja, *Contro Ismene. Considerazioni sulla violenza, Ibid.*

This is the diagnosis of several authors. Among others is that of Byung-Chul Han, who writes:

> "The time when there was the Other is gone. The Other as mystery, the Other as seduction, the Other as Eros, the Other as desire, the Other as hell, the Other as pain disappears."[7]

Still on textual positivism related to calculus as one of its most direct manifestations Byun-Chul Han writes further:

> "Thought has access to the totally Other. It has the power to interrupt the Equal. In this consists its character as an event. Calculus, on the other hand, is an endless repetition of the Same. Unlike thought, it cannot give rise to a new state of affairs. It is blind to the event. Instead, a true thought possesses the nature of an event."[8]

Zoja, in this regard, argues that Jungian psychoanalysis was born in opposition to this tendency. It was born in opposition to Descartes and his rationalism that wants to reduce psychic existence to the ego of clear and distinct ideas. It was also born in opposition to Freud who wanted to reduce the unconscious to a layer of confused and contradictory existential and linguistic anomalies and blocks, which must be resolved and overcome by clarity of thought. Jungian psychoanalysis shares this corrective element and resistance to reigning reductionism with other cultural forms that resist this reigning thinking. At this point in the description, the question is also about hermeneutics. Is hermeneutics part of the resistance or the empowering group of this cultural reductionism?

How does "textual reductionism" settle and form at the level of biblical interpretation? Beyond the fact that cultural processes are multifactorial, slow and unconscious and therefore difficult to diagnose, certain attitudes help to reinforce it. We mention three of them: unilateralism; compact conviction; and lack of counterbalancing instances.

---

7   B. -C. Han, *L'espulsione dell'altro. Società, percezione e comunicazione oggi*, (*"The Expulsion of the Other. Society, Perception and Communication Today"*), (Milan: Nottetempo, 2017), p. 7.
8   B.-C. Han, *Ibid*, p. 11.

Let us start with unilateralism. The indelible selectivity of every faith experience carries from the beginning the seed of reading unilateralism. Every choice presupposes the necessary narrowing in one's perspective in order to choose and identify with one option and leave out the others. There is no choice without this narrowing. Choice is narrowing. Every reading of the Bible must wear by moral obligation the cloak of humility. It enables us to be aware of the benefits of this narrowing, but also of the anomalies that this almost automatically creates. Every reading of the Bible, especially the most involved ones, is inexorably joined to a parallel process of stiffening and one-sidedness. They necessarily articulate this process of focusing. They do it by virtue of the misrecognition of other possible senses that are legitimately present in the text and that cannot be erased completely, but only bracketed transiently.

Anyone who reads the Bible actually reads it badly because he or she abandons the totality of possible senses. This seemingly drastic opinion has relevance. In a more general sense, we can say that every reading, by introducing a focusing mechanism, introduces an element of arbitrariness. Thus, unilateralism settles very early in the reading and does so mainly under a guise of legitimacy. Reading the Bible reductible does not necessarily mean reading it wrongly. Unilateralism is not lacking in the best readings. Yet, reading the Bible unilaterally is enough to misread it. It is to elevate a partial reading to a total reading. One-sided reading of the Bible is that reading which reads well, but does not read the whole. By not reading the whole, it automatically reads the whole badly. This is the essence of the unilateralism that leads to textual reductionism.

The second attitude is compact conviction. When humility is lacking, unilateralism is not only not perceived but even reinforced by compact and overly certain conviction. Conviction is always necessary to begin a reading. This is a sign of commitment and involvement but an excess of conviction is certainly not necessary. It easily alters and damages the interpretive process. Asking conviction to self-limit is like asking someone who has been fasting for a few days to stop only at the first forkful of an inviting and appetizing dish. This is very unlikely to happen. Because this does not happen, unbalanced conviction changes from being an ally to becoming an enemy that does not allow us to see well. The convinced reader, almost automatically, loses clarity about the whole. He can no longer read well the overall situations and the interconnection of the various latent senses.

When God, therefore, blesses us in spite of our unilateralism, the compact conviction leads us to presumption. For in that undeserved blessing, and only granted by grace, we sometimes find inappropriate validation of our unilateralism. If God has blessed us, we conclude, then our reading is correct. Not only do we fail to see our limitation, we even legitimize it. It is by virtue of that limitation of reading, we think, that God has blessed us.

It is easy to cultivate and maintain prejudices and misconceptions about things. We know this from human experience. But the same thing happens with the Bible. Prejudices and crooked ideas about the world, life and ourselves not only do not go away with Bible reading. They are often entrenched by it. In order to maintain and perpetuate some sloppy and unhealthy preconceptions, it is enough to read the Bible with consistency and conviction that avoids enacting the critical instance that the Bible wants to introduce both at the level of the content of ideas and at the level of attitudes and ways of thinking. Consistency and conviction in reading the Bible, without wisdom, whose main characteristic is the pursuit of interpretation as a place of questioning, easily become destructive virtues.

Our history shows how diligently consistent, good and well-prepared Christians with the help of the Bible and a firm conviction have supported in the past, and continue to support in the present, the current exploitation of labor, racial discrimination, gender stigma, asymmetrical occupational recognition, hierarchical authoritarianism and self-destructive religious attitudes. Just as food is not only a pleasure but also includes a long list of eating disorders, so, too, biblical reading is not only a blessing but also includes a long list of dysfunctions and real hermeneutical pathologies.

It is not enough to claim to be biblical in order to be truly biblical. Those who claim to be biblical, because of the inevitable unilateralisms we have briefly described, easily become today hermeneutically dangerous. There is a need to temper scriptural zeal. It is not zeal that we lack today, but the moderation that can dampen overly compact and monolithic attitudes. We need wise and less zealous readers. Just "being moderately biblical" would be enough to give a better testimony on behalf of the Bible. This formula is not very convincing to many. It seems renunciatory, accommodating and minimalist. Yet it is a wise as well as realistic suggestion. In medicine, anomalies are not only those "by deficit, " but also those "by excess" of functionality. While those by deficit tend to be the most prevalent, it is also true that those by excess, which may be the least prevalent, turn out to be the most complicated and the more resistants. A call for "biblical restraint" is never out of place.

This is the call of psychoanalyst Bruno Bettelheim in another sensitive area, as parenting can be. He says, and this is the title of one of his books, that the best goal for parents is not to be perfect but only *"A Good Enough Parent"*.[9] One must aim more soberly to be only "Good Enough." That is not completely perfect. Total perfection, from apparent advantage, turns into nightmare. So also with the Bible. It would be sufficient to be "Good Enough Bible readers" or "moderately Bible readers." This would be a guarantee. On the other hand, those who want to be very biblical, zealously biblical, do not realize that within that "very biblical" are unknowingly hiding many unbiblical things. In addition to being unbiblical, they are improperly smuggled in as though they were.

"Being biblical enough" is not a status but a pilgrimage. Having been biblical in the past does not ensure being biblical in the present and future. Claiming to be biblical can be the most sophisticated way to be idolatrous and religiously static. Being biblical or appealing to the principle of *sola Scriptura* is only tangentially and peripherally related to reading the Bible on a daily basis. The Bible is more concerned with our becoming than with what we are or read in the present. The goal is to connect with the vitalizing perspective of the Bible so as to give it the space to correct and reorient our lives. This is only possible if we fit properly within the interpretive arc in all its stages, as these are articulated in the "hermeneutic circle." If our biblical reading only confirms our existing deep convictions and structural spiritual orientation, whether personal or communal, this is a sufficient sign to

---

9   B. Bettelheim, *Un genitore quasi perfetto*, ("A *Good Enough Parent. A Book on Child-Rearing")*, (Milan: Feltrinelli, 2013), pp. 5-16.

start worrying. This beneficial spirit of iconoclastic renewal can only exist within the interpretive experience, not in the mere reading of the Bible.

We come to the third point: the lack of balancing instances. If unilateralism had, from the outset, balancing instances, it simply would not be unilateralism. Here it is important to distinguish between two levels: the functional and the structural. If unilateralism is only at a functional level, the interpretive enterprise as a whole is not necessarily compromised. On the other hand, when unilateralism is situated instead at the structural level, it drifts and becomes more irrepressible. It is the tracks themselves and no longer just the train that have an anomaly.

The element that best guarantees structural harmony and most averts the threat of textual reductionism is the hermeneutic circle. It almost automatically brings in not one but two criteria in every process of reading and interpretation. Only this double confrontation, which the hermeneutic circle imposes by obligation on every reading, actually halves the risk of any kind of unilateralism and textual reductionism.

Let us now turn to consider some forms of textual reductionism as they take shape at the level of Bible reading. We will choose the term "biblical positivism" to designate these dysfunctions. At a first level, biblical positivism, in the form of "inerrantism," will be a problem related to a limited group of Christians. At a second level, biblical positivism will instead, through a central concept of theology such as *sola Scriptura*, invest a more substantial swath of Christianity. At a third level, biblical positivism will remain limited to a small band of Christians, although intellectually very active and refined. And at a fourth level, biblical positivism will be reinforced through a cultural form, thus becoming a mass cultural phenomenon.[10]

2. Biblical Literalism: Formal Inerrancy[11]

The first form of biblical positivism comes from the proponents of biblical inerrancy. To better understand its scope and nature, we compare

---

10 L. Zoja, *Contro Ismene. Considerazioni sulla violenza*, Op. cit., pp. 99-116.
11 Cf. Position of M.J. ErickSon, *Christian theology*, (Grand Rapids: Baker Academic, 2013), pp. 188-209.

it with the classical view of most Christians. Christians, across all the spectrum, assert that the Bible is inspired by God. They believe that those who materially wrote its text acted under divine influence. Most Christians believe that what it states is completely reliable, useful and true. At the same time, the vast majority of Christians, maintain that the historical or scientific data and details of the Bible are less important or even irrelevant to faith and conduct, and that it may contain formal errors of varying degrees that do not affect the essence of the message.

The inerrantists or literalists, on the other hand, claim that even the scientific, geographical and historical details of the Bible are completely true and free from error. They also believe that the apparent contradictions or errors that we seem to find depend on our subjective perception or knowledge, which is inadequate or distorted. The Protestant churches and even the Catholic church, which teach the total absence of doctrinal errors from Holy Scripture, nevertheless reject any literalist interpretation of it.

To this first form of biblical positivism we add the qualification of "formal inerrantism." Let us specify the two terms more. "Biblical positivism" is that orientation, we said, which tends to make the Bible unambiguous, transparent and clear. "Formal inerrantism" is that attitude that tends to see the literary, grammatical form and historical-scientific content of the Bible as free from any kind of error. Formal inerrantism is the most extreme form of biblical positivism because it places clarity, transparency and unambiguousness of the Bible at the most visible, immediate and material level of the interpretive chain, that is, at the formal level.

Formal or literal inerrantism represents a minority part of Christianity, although it is the most targeted by criticism and stigma. It represents in the spectrum of biblical positivism the most extreme position, but not necessarily the most harmful one, despite appearances. In this band of Christianity there subsists a tendency to regard the Bible as a compact instrument of truth against a world warped by sin, which must be saved by the power of the Bible. The two distinguishing elements are an extreme emphasis on biblical clarity and a belief in the structural self-sufficiency of the Bible.

Regarding the first element, we can say that for the inerrantist the Bible appears as a unified and compact reality. In the Bible everything is important, which is why everything must be true. There are no secondary parts, negotiable sections, negligible elements. Everything in the Bible is central and, consequently, everything is imbued with truth. It is not the idea of perfection that necessarily leads the inerrantist to read the Bible compactly. On the contrary, it is the compact view of the Bible and of reality in general that, by preventing him from introducing differentiations of levels, channels and layers, forces the inerrantist to regard everything in the Bible as true and without error. If there is truth, it must be everywhere. It is the theorem of the indivisibility of reality and the Bible that compels the literalist to give a status of truth even to secondary elements.

This textual compactness is matched by a psychological compactness. At first glance the reader seems to be forgotten completely, by virtue of this hyper-attention given to the perfection of the text. At a second glance it becomes clear that the compactness given to the text is only an extension of the reader's own psychological compactness to the text. It is the mind of the literalist that is totalizing and compact. Its compactness is transferred to the text.

The inerrantist carries with him the limitation that he cannot distinguish between what is primary and what is secondary. For him there are no minor battles. All battles are final and decisive. This unnecessarily leads to extreme consumption of energy, triggering radical battles in defense of the Bible over completely trivial issues. The inerrantist lacks discernment. In the end, this costs him a high price, because he loses his strength in futile and secondary points.

Regarding the second element, the inerrantist sincerely believes in the absolute autonomy of the Bible. It depends only on divine revelation. No contextual element, historical or moral, and even less religious, can condition its birth and development. It is autonomous from any historical conditioning. It even gives true meaning and significance to all historical events clearly and directly. It is not reality that has to say what is true or what is false. It is the Bible that says what is true or false in the outside reality.

The map (Bible) has completely replaced the territory. The map is the territory. The Bible is the reality. The emphasis on the perfection of the Bible, perfection without error, is heavily conditioned by this detachment from reality. Because the Bible is detached from reality, all the weight and presence of truth falls on the Bible and invests it massively. Since the territory has disappeared, all truth has and must reside only in the map.

In the biblical fanaticism of the literalist, everything is out of whack: the conception of truth, of the world, of sin, of salvation, of the church. The "formal" inerrantist lives completely in a parallel world.

3. Biblical Confessionalism: Confessional Inerrancy[12]

A larger part, indeed, the numerically largest part of Christianity, disassociates itself from "formal inerrantism," but continues to

---

12 Adventism is a typical example of what we mean by "denominational inerrancy." Formal, literalist inerrancy has been overcome on an exegetical and biblical level, but it survives on a denominational and communal level. However, the overcoming of biblical literalism is not synonymous, in Adventists as in many other non-fundamentalist religious denominations, with a balanced hermeneutic. There remains a tendency toward a hermeneutic that is closed, ecclesiocentric, and especially for specific themes (Sabbath, lifestyle, eschatology) also highly ideologized. Cf. F.M. Hasel, M. G. Hasel, *How to Interpret Scripture*, (Oakland: Pacific Press Publishing Association, 2020); M.W. Campbell, *1919: The Untold Story of Adventim...,* Op cit. The characteristics of Adventist hermeneutics can be summarized in four statements recurring in all official documents, including even the most recent ones:
1. Scripture arises independently of its context through its own, internal logic.
2. The Bible has no contradictions and presents a unified outline.
3. Scripture interprets itself.
4. The meaning of Scripture is clear and immediate.
Cf. R. M. Davidson, "Biblical Interpretation," in, R. Dederen (Ed), *Handbook of Seventh-day Adventist Theology*, (Hagerstown: MD, 2000), pp. 58-104; J. Crocombe, *Hermeneutics, Intertextuality and the Contemporary Meaning of Scripture*, Avondale Academic Press, Adelaide 2014, pp. 234-237; G.W. Reid (ed), *Understanding Scripture. An Adventist Approach*, Vol. 1, (Silver Spring: Biblical Research Institute, 2005); see also the more recent volume that takes up and reinforces the same claims and primordial axes of Adventist hermeneutics. See F. M. Hasel, *Biblical Hermeneutics: An Adventist Approach,* Vol. 3, (Silver Spring: Biblical Research Institute, 2021).

attribute to the Bible a dimension of infallibility at the doctrinal level. Trust in the Bible as a source of truth remains intact, although it has changed in form.

A strong emphasis on biblical exclusivity, through, for example, the determined and all-out defense of the principle of *sola Scriptura*, characterizes this stance. The Bible would be self-explanatory, essentially understandable and transparent in itself. Most importantly, it would require no substantive connection or interaction either with the outside world or with society or culture to fully articulate its message. It would connect to society and culture only within the circle of a historical-temporal framing.

To this second form of biblical positivism we add the qualification of "confessional inerrantism." The "positivist" tendency to identify the meaning of faith in an unambiguous, clear and transparent way has not disappeared; faith and the Bible are reduced to sense. Only sense gives meaning to faith. Faith cannot have a double sense, a broken, seemingly senseless, mysterious sense.

Faith must be clear by nature. The desire for clarity and the obsession with unambiguousness have not disappeared. They are always there. The tendency to erase the possibility of error (inerrancy) from faith has not disappeared either. Inerrancy is still there. Clarity and inerrancy have simply been transferred from the form of the text (letter) to one's "confession" of belonging, to communal faith. We are here in face of a biblical confessionalism. The community, to legitimize its authority, resorts to the Bible, through the principle of *sola Scriptura*. It is not Scripture itself that is taken into consideration. It is *sola Scriptura* as interpreted by that church. That Bible is made completely dependent on the community that reads it, and the community implicitly claims to have the only legitimate reading of the Bible. Thus a strong partnership arises between church certainty and biblical certainty. A strong fusion is created between them that prevents one from seeing and evaluating the truth claim of the other independently.

"Confessional inerrantism" represents a substantial part of Christianity and it has a greater religious impact. This is the part that contributes most to the establishment of the biblical positivism we are describing as anomalous. It is anomalous for two basic reasons.

One is its intent to conceive of the Bible as a compact and homogeneous unity. Continuity is preferred to discontinuity, complementarity to tension, synthesis to fragmentation, because God and truth are identified as unitary realities. If this is so, the Bible must also bear the same traits within itself. The most common phrases to affirm this first conviction are "the Bible never contradicts itself"; "any contrasts are only apparent" or "apparent contrasts belong to the human part of the Bible." The most distinctive feature of this first belief is the thought that the Bible is structurally clear. There would be no opacity in the Bible. Its meaning would be perfectly transparent and clear. It is the reader, by the vices he automatically brings with him, who introduces these opacities that must be broken down.

A second is the intent to conceive of the Bible as an autonomous reality. One prefers and chooses in the relationship of the Bible with the external element discontinuity over continuity, tension over complementarity, rupture over integration. The Bible is not dependent on any human reality. The mantra of this conviction is the principle of *sola Scriptura*. One understands this sound principle in its most exclusionary, exclusive and self-referential dimension.

"Biblical confessionalism" lives on the conviction that we must protect the Bible, preserve it from all manipulation and distortion, starting from the assumption of a supposed purity. The longer the Bible remains in contact with realities foreign to it, the greater the risk of contamination. The Bible must be protected, guarded, safeguarded in its compactness, because it is this that represents the sign of its truth and divine inspiration.

The Bible appears in this view monolithic and homogeneous because it has been detached from everything else, from life itself. But also vice versa: the Bible is detached from everything else because it has become monolithic, compact and inflexible. The more monolithic an entity is, the more abstract it becomes. The more abstract a reality is, the more monolithic it becomes.

4. Biblical-Theological Rationalism: Ideological Inerrancy[13]

Another part of Christianity disassociates itself from "formal inerrantism" and from "confessional inerrantism," arguing that these forms of "religious positivism" are excessively schematic and reductive. Here it is important to grasp, beyond biblical and confessional forms, the universal principles that ground not only faith but life as such. Those historical forms, biblical text or faith community, are not the truth. They cannot be the truth. They are only a concretization, an application, an intent to embody universal principles in structures close to us so that they give us a sense of familiarity and closeness. We cannot confuse universal principles with historical forms. These principles, which lie behind the forms, are rational and self-evident. They are not always immediate, because one must, behind appearances and beneath the surface, search for them even with effort. This is what causes most believers, who are content with what is more immediate and requires less effort, to remain on the surface of forms and confuse biblical and confessional forms with the substance of faith. If, on the other hand, one perseveres and resists this fascination with immediate forms and puts forth an attitude of rational search, he or she will find that the true principles behind them are the foundations of faith and must be safeguarded. And those principles, once found, are clear and obvious.

To this third form of biblical positivism we have added the expression "ideological inerrantism." The "positivist" tendency to identify the sense of truth with an unambiguous, clear and

---

[13] An example of this type of more sophisticated positivism are the representatives of the liberal Protestant movement who lived at the turn of the nineteenth and early twentieth centuries, such as Friedrich Schleiermacher, Albrecht Ritschl, Adolf Von Harnack, and Wilhelm Herrmann. Cf. W. Pannenberg, *Storia e problemi della teologia evangelica contemporanea in Germania. Da Schleiermacher fino a Barth e Tillich*, (*"History and Problems of Contemporary Evangelical Theology in Germany. From Schleiermacher Until Barth and Tillich"*), (Brescia: Queriniana, 2000), pp. 9-51; K. Barth, *Protestant Theology...O*p. cit., pp. 1-15.

transparent sense has not disappeared. Truth and principles are reduced to sense. Only sense gives meaning to truth. Truth cannot have a double sense, a broken sense, a seemingly senseless sense, a mysterious sense. Truth and principles must by nature be clear and distinct.

The desire for clarity and the obsession with unambiguousness have not disappeared; they are always there. Nor has the tendency of truth and principles to erase the possibility of error (inerrancy) disappeared. Inerrancy is still there. Clarity and inerrancy have simply been transferred from the form of the text (letter) and the "confession" *of* belonging, to the rational form of conceiving truth and principles.

"Ideological inerrantism" is a sophisticated and refined form of "biblical-theological positivism" because clarity, transparency and unambiguousness are placed no longer at the level of the textual form nor the community, but at the level of the abstract theological reason that interprets the Bible.

In this ideological inerrantism, a principle cannot carry both clarity and error at the same time. Every principle must be compactly true. If it is not compactly true it is not true, therefore it is false. The Bible, even if understood no longer according to its form but according to its eternal principles, would thus be the book of faith par excellence, because it enables us to distinguish truth from falsehood. The Bible would be the place of truth.

The distortion lies in this. If the Bible is the book of truth then it discards, unmasks, rejects and excludes falsehood and error. This would be its vocation and main function: to unmask the false. This is how the Bible is viewed and read in most Christian denominations, even the liberal ones. This has led us to make two mistakes. The first is to consider true only what is Christian, and the second is to consider false everything that is not Christian.

This hermeneutical disease of truth as exclusion does not belong only to inerrantists. It is the disease of all Protestantism. The problem that we impute to inerrantists (fundamentalists) of constructing on the Bible a truth that is expressed in forms also manifests itself at a more transversal level in Protestantism when it thinks that the Bible is a book of truth.

There has only been a level shift. The grammatical truth of the inerrantists has become the doctrinal truth of the evangelicals and the ethical truth of the liberals. The mechanism has not disappeared; it has only been shifted. Protestantism is traversed in all its components by this biblical positivism that has reduced the Bible to a place of clear and unambiguous truth.

The Bible is not a place of truth when it is read to exclude. A truth that excludes cannot be truth. Even worse, it excludes truth. There is probably more truth in the excluded than in the one who excludes. The Bible cannot best be read with the criterion of truth and error. Not only does it come out an exclusionary book but also a paranoid one. If everything must be sifted and verified, then we are far from life and truth. The truth that has been created in the Bible, and around those who so read it, is a "small" truth. That is a "confessional" truth. A confessional truth is always a small truth that cannot claim to embody the larger truth.

The greatest truth is always inclusive. This is the criterion for differentiating between different types of truth: inclusiveness. Truth, according to biblical positivism, at any level of manifestation, cannot be inclusive. Truth, by nature, distinguishes, clarifies, excludes. It is unambiguous and clear. It tends to defend itself from others. It cannot be contaminated and must create distance. This distinguishing feature alone is sufficient to unmask it and describe it as untrue. The truth of biblical positivism, positivism of the letter, confession or principle, is a small truth. Big and true truth is always inclusive because it creates life. And life is bonding.

5. Modern Book-Centrism: Cultural Inerrancy[14]

As we pointed out in the opening of this chapter, the West has identified itself from the very beginning of its historical emergence with clarity as the goal of all knowledge. This is visible in Descartes, in the Enlightenment: from then on this tendency has only been reinforced. This has then been compounded by the spread and use of the book as the privileged promoter and support of this clarity. Books and rational clarity have created an incredibly productive and efficient mixture, which have radically transformed the contemporary world.

The same sequence occurred in Christianity. In Western Christianity, which is the one that spread everywhere, the book (Bible) and rational clarity made a winning combination. This changed Christianity from within and from without and made it dynamic until it spread to all latitudes. What came first, the book-centered rationality of Christian clarity or that of modernity? It is difficult to say. Such is the interpenetration of these two phenomena that the contours of one and the other cannot be well defined. Between Christianity and modernity there seems to be a symbiosis. This is a paradoxical symbiosis because clearly there are very marked differences. Western Christianity is one thing, Western culture is

---

14 This positivist tendency to conceive of modern rationality as the only possible rationality, embodied in his books, is what Giacomo Marramao calls "identity universalism," which he proposes to change to an inclusive and polycentric "universalism of difference." Cf. G. Marramao, *La passione del presente. Breve lessico della modernità-mondo*, ("*The Passion of the Present. A Brief Lexicon of Modernity-World*"), (Turin: Bollati Boringhieri, 2008), pp. 187-205. See also the harsh critique of exclusionary cultural positivism as expressed by postcolonial studies. Cf. D. Chakrabarty, *Provincializing Europe. Postcolonial Thought and Historical Difference*, (Princeton: Princeton University Press, 2000), pp. 8-14; H.K. Bhabha, *The Location of Culture*, (London: Routledge, 2007), pp. 23-35; G. Chakravorty Spivak, *A Critique of Postcolonial Reason. Toward a History of the Vanishing Present*, (Cambridge-Massachusetts: Harvard University Press, 2003), pp. 25-41. And in a more radical and provocative tone is expressed by B. de Sousa Santos, *Epistemologies of the South*...Op. cit., pp. 9-23.

another. More than in the past, when culture and religion were more structurally linked, today the register of rupture has been chosen. The most obvious sign is the process of secularization which puts religion in parentheses. This is something that has never happened before.

Yet, we probably live in the age when culture and Christianity are more similar than ever. They are not similar in form but in substance. In some ways contemporary culture, in its essential registers, is completely Christian. Contemporary Christianity is all for the use and consumption of modernity. The shaping of Christianity according to modern culture is masterful. So is the way in which modern culture has gained strength by virtue of certain essential Christian categories. This is not new. It is present in the great founders of modernity. This is the case with Hobbes, for example, who creates a new contract culture by legitimizing it with the Bible. He goes even to the point of conceiving all of Christianity functioning as Leviathan, that is, the modern state. One of the most important points of convergence in substance between Christianity and modernity is this textual positivism, this book-centrism of clarity, this reductionism of knowledge.

Life, reality, nature, others, for the modern and postmodern West, is a matter of truth or falsehood. Technique has reinforced to the nth degree this univocal orientation of the entire West, and then imposed it as the only pattern valid throughout the world. The truth of instrumental, human or organizational technique has become even more perverse. Everything is filed, ordered, catalogued, differentiated, specified. It is the absolute realm of clarity and order. The alternatives of mystical meaning, accompanying sacredness or spiritual escapism continually emerge. We would otherwise be swallowed up by the overwhelming flow of linear technique. In reality, these alternatives change nothing. They serve only as moments of pause and respite to continue in the compulsive rhythm of univocal and flattened production toward consumption.

Faith and market have become, in seemingly alternative forms, homozygous twins. There has been no real secularization in this respect. There has been a secularization of forms, not of substance. Even secularization strictly applies to all levels of life the same criterion of efficient univocity that faith applies within the church. Secularization has as its prototype the same clarity of books, of reasoning, of action, of life whether religious or secular.

To this fourth form of biblical positivism we add the qualification of "cultural inerrantism." The "positivist" tendency to identify the meaning of life with an unambiguous, clear and transparent sense has not disappeared. Life has been reduced to meaning. Only sense gives meaning to life. Life cannot have a double sense, a broken sense, a seemingly senseless sense, a mysterious sense. Life must be clear by nature. The desire for clarity and the obsession with unambiguousness have not disappeared. They are always there. Inerrancy is still there.

In this univocal drift of the West and current theology, the predominant, though not exclusive, model is the univocal model of Aristotelian logic. We owe to Aristotle the full understanding of the importance of three principles of our reasoning: the principle of identity, non-contradiction and the excluded third.[15]

These three principles are actually traceable to each other and form the backbone of univocality. Inside the church, we read the Bible this way. Outside the church we read the newspaper and other books the same way.

Modern exegesis and hermeneutics arose as critical strategies in the face of sloppy and exuberant (allegorical) medieval reading. The typical rationality that characterizes across all modern hermeneutics stigmatized immediate readings as superstition and fideism. For a long time, modern hermeneutics was right to curb through its rationality the unwarranted excess of meaning derived from the Bible. But the Bible can be distorted not only by excess, according to a typical human mechanism of distortion, but also by deficit.

Modern hermeneutics thus sins from what represents its true strength, rationality. The same rationality that corrected the excess of superstition, has over time caused the deficit of mystery. Cultural positivism in all its forms expresses, in a not so veiled way, its allergy to mystery. Modern hermeneutics is to all intents and

---

15 Aristotle (*Metaphysics* IV, 1005b, 19-20). Cf. E. Fromm, *L'arte di amare*, Op. cit., pp. 71-84.

purposes a hermeneutics of the deficit. A disenchanted, reductive hermeneutics.[16] Moreover, this mechanism of "rationality" and "disenchantment" increase proportionally. Max Weber sees it in action not only in hermeneutics, but in all modern culture. It has constructed itself as a rational culture and in a directly proportional way, it has become also a disenchanted one.

This is what we call "cultural inerrantism." The inerrancy of biblical literalism, religious confessionalism, and theological rationalism, which focus on the clarity and unambiguousness of concepts and events, has simply moved out of the church and out of faith to be situated in culture, in technology, in the most essential registers of contemporary living.

---

16 Cf. Introduction to the book by E. Drewermann, *Psicologia del profondo e esegesi...* Op. cit., pp. 7-19.

CHAPTER VIII
HERMENEUTIC ANOMALIES "BY DEFICIT" OF TEXT
Anthropocentric Subjectivism

Although eating is a pleasure, it also includes a long list of eating disorders. Likewise, although reading the Bible is a blessing, it also includes a long list of anomalies, deviations and even real hermeneutical pathologies. In the previous chapter we described some of the most frequent anomalies related to the "text." In this chapter, again following the structure of the hermeneutic circle, we will instead consider some anomalies related to the "reader" pole. While those related to the text tend to be more visible, structural and direct anomalies, those related to the reader tend to be more invisible, rather functional and indirect anomalies. Both introduce operational short-circuits and one-sided applications of the categories that ground the hermeneutic circle. Between "structural" and "functional" anomalies there is the same parallelism, contrast and conditioning that exists in the field of medicine between "anatomical" and "physiological" anomalies.

The former involves disproportion and asymmetry in structure and architecture, while the latter involves imbalance and one-sidedness in practical operations and strategies in the process of reading and interpretation.

It is not "textual positivism" (described in the previous chapter) but rather "textual subjectivism" (described in this chapter) that is the basic, frequent and characteristic form of the anomalies that have a strong hold today and often end up unbalancing the interpretive process. This is our basic thesis that we have been articulating since the first part. In reality, hermeneutic anomalies, as in the physical organism, always involve all sectors and all components of the system and, as such, are always systemic anomalies. As is also the case in medicine, at some point in the process, pathologies as systemic anomalies always include an anatomical-structural and a physiological-functional component. This fact does not prevent a pathology, although conditioned and related to these two dimensions, from depending on and involving more of one of them. The same thing happens in hermeneutics. When the hermeneutic circle is unbalanced by an excessive weight given to the text, synchronically the other pole, that of the reader, will also be deformed, will suffer a deficit. Conversely, when it is the reader who is given excessive attention, synchronically the text will also be deformed and will suffer a deficit of attention.

As we mentioned in the previous chapter, text-related anomalies are common currency in our time. These depend on an even more central, primary and basic anomaly: "biblical subjectivism." Our hypothesis is even more paradoxical because it advances the idea that "biblical subjectivism" is actually at the root of biblical fundamentalism (biblical literalism), which instead appears and presents itself as a real anomaly related to the biblical text. Even the most extreme forms in defense of the Bible as a sacred text (biblical inerrancy) are actually produced by a basic "biblical subjectivism" typical of modernity. "Biblical subjectivism," however, is expressed on various levels. Let us briefly consider some of these levels.

At a first level, between "textual (biblical) subjectivism" and "modern individualism" there is a clear relationship of contiguity and belonging. Both bet on the individual as subject. At this first level, textual subjectivism appears as an extension and application of socio-cultural individualism, as a more global and generic phenomenon, characteristic of our time. To the question, "How came "biblical subjectivism," in its various forms, to be so widespread among Christians today? ", the answer is straightforward and immediate: "Because 'biblical subjectivism' is the child of modern individualism." It could not be otherwise. The trends and orientations of a historical epoch influence and affect by determining, in the short or long range, all manifestations, all levels and all processes within that culture. Modern individualism could not spare or leave untouched our way of reading and interpreting. Biblical subjectivism is thus a direct and emblematic manifestation of modern individualism, which is one of the most characteristic features of our historical period.

At a second level, the degree and nature of the implication and dependence that exists between "textual subjectivism" and "modern individualism" not only varies but is reversed. From another perspective, we could say that "modern individualism" is actually the child and extension of "textual subjectivism." In other words, "modern individualism" is born as "textual subjectivism." The equation behind this statement is as follows. Faced with strong, stable texts that were the embodiment of group power, including the Bible itself as a sacred book, the first locus of assertion of an autonomous subject was the claim of prerogative to introduce new, unique, innovative meanings into the reading of those traditional texts. This de facto claim automatically relativized the power of those texts and their claims on the individual. At the same time it pointed to a new locus of affirmation of the individual that originated in the realization of free readings and innovative experiments in meaning.

This second-level implication not only highlights the real engine of modern individualism, which is not, at least initially, pragmatic and applicative, but ideational and theoretical. It is when the individual is able to think, through new readings, new scenarios and alternative worlds to the existing one, that individualism is truly born. Individualism is not born, then, when one finally arrives at a serious and rigorous application of things that one already knows and that the individual merely concretizes. It is born from the introduction, through a new way of reading and thinking, that has the individual as the undisputed protagonist, of new worlds in rupture with the traditional texts of the past.

This revolutionary vision of individualism as a creator of new horizons we see applied to the modern book and texts. Modern texts are the first examples of the force of modern individualism, even though it would seem the opposite. It would seem that texts limit, hinder, moderate modern man's endless drive for freedom. Our age is the age of books. There have never been so many books for all ages, for every subject and of every nature. These pose a challenge to contemporary man in that they highlight the limitation of his knowledge, the arbitrariness of his choices and the partiality and one-sidedness of the information he possesses. This is partially true because books represent indeed this challenge to modern man. On the other hand though, these very books, which highlight the limits of modern man, are at the same time a production of modern man. Conceived in this way, they did not exist before. The status and social role that we contemporaries attribute to books is not the same status and role that premodern cultures attribute to them. As mentioned in the previous chapter, the modern book is a different kind of book, all produced by the dynamism of the modern individual. Even the ancient books that we read today, because they are for us classics that we respect and accept as cultural reference points, including the Bible, we read them as if they were modern books, fluid and partial in their meaning that we individuals are called upon to complete. They do not in the least represent absolute mandates, much less complete mandates of what needs to be done today. Premodern books were highly prescriptive and connected to a fixed and stable reality. The books we moderns create and the classical books we read are books best conceived as suggestions scattered within a highly experimental and deliberative individual reading process, where the emphasis is on choice, not on the application of various possible meanings. This is modern individualism incarnated in our current way of reading and interpreting.

This implicitly new understanding and definition of ancient processes and categories occurs not only for the book, but also, for example, for science. Modern scientific knowledge, which purports to be objective, is actually anthropocentric. It is this subjectivist, anthropocentric orientation, hidden and sublimated at the root of the environmental crisis, which is an anthropocentric anomaly from beginning to end. The same thing can be said of modern totalitarianisms. We would like to think that they are the reminiscences of past, pre-modern and primitive eras which we would minimally consider related to an age of freedom such as ours. Actually, they are typical modern phenomena that did not and could not exist in the Middle Ages. Similarly, biblical positivism, even in its most extreme forms, such as biblical inerrancy, which we would think of as reminiscences of past, obscurantist eras, is actually a typical modern phenomenon related to and giving birth to a subjectivist and individualist age like ours.

This textual subjectivism, which characterizes our age, at first involves the Protestants, because they are the ones who have made *sola Scriptura* their cardinal principle, but still making it pass through the filter of the conscience of the individual believer. Actually, in *sola Scriptura* Protestantism, despite appearances, it is not the text (the Bible) that predominates, but the individual who reads that text, because the alternative is not between Bible and individual. In this case Bible and individual are at the same level. The alternative is between church and individual. The Bible will actually be found in both cases, on the side of the church if I choose the church, as in the Middle Ages but also on the side of the individual, if I choose the believer, as in the case of Protestantism. Protestantism is not in the first instance a religion of the book. It is only secondarily so. Protestantism is primarily a religion of the individual. Biblical subjectivism is not a late drift in Protestantism. It is present from the beginning in its basic structure.

In a second moment, textual subjectivism involves all of Christianity, because Christianity has tied religious experience to a text read and metabolized by the believer. Faith comes through the continuous and diligent reading and study of that book. The believer is responsible for understanding and applying that meaning. Modern Christianity has only radicalized this tendency. It has emphasized the reliability of that text more than in the past. It has also made its reading one that is more related to the awareness, freedom and self-determination of the subject.

In a third level, the West has invested heavily in the subjectivity of the individual and his autonomy and self-determination. This strongly anthropocentric project has radicalized the role of the subject even more.[1]

---

1   C. Taylor, *Il disaggio della modernità*, (*"The Malaise of Modernity"*), (Rome: Laterza, 2003), pp. 5-21.

Textual subjectivism is not just a hermeneutical trait or just the expression of a widespread tendency in present-day Christianity. It represents the direction of our entire historical period. Historical periods are never monolithic. Like other historical periods in the past, ours manifests a diverse and contrasting set of phenomena that compose and determine it. But textual subjectivism is undoubtedly a hallmark of the historical period in which we live and of which biblical subjectivism is an extension.

Finally, we come to a last introductory consideration regarding hermeneutic anomalies in general, which applies particularly to modern individualism. There is a tendency to regard anomalies as deviations that take over later and, more importantly, to regard them as the result of misapplication of the virtuous criteria of the system. More often than not, this does not hold up to thoughtful analysis. Often the deviations are present from the beginning and are latent in the system's virtuous categories themselves because of their one-sidedness. The same unilateralism of vision prompts one to consider the onset of the anomalies as the product of misapplication of the categories that ground the system. This causes the anomalies to worsen as, in order to solve them, the same categories that caused them are more convincingly applied. This is what happens with individualism. Extreme subjectivism, self-referentiality, narcissism, or anthropocentrism do not take over later, at a later time, but are from the beginning present in the modern project. They are so not tangentially but structurally, because they arise from the same virtues that found modern individualism. The analytical gaze cannot stop at considering only the anomalies. It must also consider, describe and know best the virtues and the very structure of modern individualism.

1. A Theological-Cultural look at Hermeneutical Individualism[2]

Interpretive reductionism, which we have also called "textual positivism" and which widely involves all of Christianity and all of contemporary culture, creates, at some point, its own alternative. This alternative is identified and built around the subject. Textual positivism, in its natural evolution, pushes, almost naturally, toward "textual subjectivism" as a kind of obligatory alternative. These are those typical ping-pong movements of history where it proceeds by

---

2   Hermeneutic individualism (hermeneutic subjectivism), which is the phenomenon that claims to reduce the complexity of (written) texts to the narrow and preferential registers of individual subjectivity, is certainly not only a linguistic or literary phenomenon. See C. Taylor, *Il disagio della modernità,* Op. cit., pp. 65-81; *Sources of the Self*, (Cambridge-Massachusetts: Harvard University Press, 1989), pp. 285-302. More underlying it is a cultural phenomenon that Louis Dumont describes as the ideology of modernity. He writes, "(Individualism)... moves from individuals, as is natural for moderns, and only later sees them brought together in society; sometimes it even gives rise to society from the interaction between individuals," in, *Saggi sull'individualismo. Una prospettiva antropologica sull'ideologia moderna*, (*"Essays on Individualism. An Anthropological Perspective on Modern Ideology"*), (Milan: Adelphi, 1983), p. 14. However, this social and not just hermeneutical individualism is not negative. On the contrary, it is the basis of modern efficientism, part of its DNA and conscious project. Referring to the *Oratio de hominis dignitate*, a passage by Pico della Mirandola, the starting point of modern individualism, A. Cavicchia Scalamonti writes: "This oration seems to be a manifesto in which it is clearly established that man's dignity is no longer to be found in the place he had been assigned in the pre-established cosmic order, but, as the oration demonstrates, in his ability to self-define himself autonomously," in, *La morte...* Op. cit., p. 10. If this had not brought undoubted benefit, modernity, greedy for results, would not have chosen and maintained it at all. But what modernity had not calculated for are the adverse side effects of this social and hermeneutic individualism, which occur not only in the isolation and uprooting of the subject, but also in its implosion and, , also in the manipulation of everything external to it; the world, reality and, consequently, texts as well. Cf. C. Taylor, *Il disagio della modernità,* Op. cit., pp. 3-16; A. Finkielkraut, *Noi, i moderni*, (*"We, the Moderns"*), (Turin: Lindau, 2006), pp. 251-259; E. Pulcini, *La cura del mondo...* Op. cit., pp. 31-112.

provocation and counter-reaction. An excessive emphasis on the text is naturally followed by a radical claim to the relevance of the subject-reader. We shall see that, in reality, the relationship between these two phenomena is more complex and that textual subjectivism not only follows, but precedes and grounds textual positivism in a kind of hermeneutical somersault.

For the time being, however, let us try to describe the importance for biblical hermeneutics of contemporary (modern and postmodern) individualism and how this conditions it. Textual subjectivism and modern individualism appear as two different and parallel processes. Looking more closely, they are instead very related. On the one hand, textual subjectivism is but an extension and application of modern individualism to the reading of texts. On the other hand, social individualism arises from the claim to create new meanings that arise only in the subject. Modern individualism from the beginning is hermeneutic and cognitive.

There is much more proximity, coincidence and interdependence between these two phenomena than one might see at first glance. Actually, they are essentially the same thing. It could not be otherwise. A cultural tendency, as in this case individualism, hardly spares areas of a culture. It tends to be cross-cultural and widespread. There is much more solidarity than one might believe among the diverse spaces of a culture in a given historical period. The characteristic social individualism of our times could not spare hermeneutics.

Our reading hypothesis (already in chapter two of part one, in the brief historical review on hermeneutics), was clear and specific in its basic direction. The tendency of contemporary hermeneutics, we said, is not the centrality of the "text" but the centrality of the "reader." Contemporary hermeneutics is "reader-centric." Here, the "reader-centeredness" typical of today's hermeneutics is simply the extension of social individualism into the interpretive area. This tendency is not so much hidden in the founding manifesto of hermeneutics made by Schleiermacher. His motto was: philosophical hermeneutics aims at understanding "the understanding," that is, the reader in his understanding. The understanding takes place not in the text but in the reader's head.

Antonio C. Scalamonti[3] further specifies the solidarity between individualism and modern knowledge. Reversing the terms, he says that individualism is first and foremost a theory of knowledge, the claim that knowledge is guaranteed by the individual who innovates and not by the group that preserves it. Social individualism was only possible because of this cognitive and interpretive individualism. The relationship in favor of the group, consolidated for millennia through a knowledge that from the group imposed itself as destiny on the individual, who had to limit himself only to repeating and passing on, is now overthrown in favor of the individual. This occurs when the individual claims for himself and asserts his ability to create new knowledge (readings), solely from himself. It is when the individual is recognized as having the ability to introduce new knowledge that individualism is truly born. The relationship between social individualism and interpretive individualism is much closer than what it might appear at first glance.

Let us pause to briefly consider individualism as a mass cultural phenomenon, as, for example, Charles Taylor describes it. Taylor thinks that individualism is the defining characteristic of the contemporary world.[4] For centuries and centuries man lived with a self that he calls a "*porous" self (Porous self)*, but recently the self has become a "shielded" self (*Buffered self*). Until about 500 years ago, man felt confronted with external events having mysterious dimensions beyond him: natural disasters, good or bad spirits, magic

---

3   A. Cavicchia Scalamonti, *La morte...*Op. cit., pp. 39-47.
4   Taylor writes: "The buffered, disciplined self, seeking intimacy (although discipline and intimacy can be in tension), also sees him/herself more and more as an individual. We saw this clearly reflected in the understanding of society implicit in what we called the Modern Moral Order. The social orders we live in are not grounded cosmically, prior to us, there as it was, waiting for us to take up our allotted place; rather society is made by individuals, or at least for individuals, and their place in it should reflect the reasons why they joined in the first place, or why God appointed this form of common existence for them. These reasons in the end come down to the good of human beings, not qua fillers of this or that role, but just simpliciter, a human good which is that of all of them equally, even if they don't achieve it in equal measure." in C. Taylor, *A Secular Age*, (Cambridge: Harvard University Press, 2007), p. 540.

formulas and potions, vital fluids and relics, miracles in current daily events. A colorful "enchanted dimension" easily and unhindered penetrated that "porous" self, which, being nurtured from the outside, identified with it. Between self and external world there was absolute continuity; they were one and the same. The natural world represented the self well, just as the self was also perfectly describable in natural terms. Meaning filtered from the world outside to us automatically. Everything changed with the arrival of modernity, helped in this by Christianity in its Latin-Western version and, above all, Protestantism, as Weber suggests. What counts now is inwardness, personal faith, living prayer hidden in the intimate, in the heart. Soon after, with the Enlightenment the same rejection takes on a new face: the world, which had been obvious to porous man for centuries, is condemned as a false world. The external world, described by the pre-modernists, is the enchanted and illusory production of a world that is not there and is forged by a still immature interiority. Such a diagnosis marks the victory of the new well-shielded self, that is, by a self that is critical and distrustful of all exteriority. Thus individualism is born. It carries with it the idea, obvious to us, of history as development or progress. Western man perceives himself as superior to that of other ages and cultures. He declares himself autonomous and finally free from the ancient fears that bound him to nature. One of the great differences between us and our precursors is that we live with a much firmer perception of the boundary separating the self from the rest (i.e., the non-self). We are *shielded* selves. The perception of ourselves and the world has totally changed.

According to Taylor, the individualism that is born with the shielded self has a positive but also problematic trait. He thinks that the unease that marks our period is connected with individualism because this social attitude has become a moral task in what he calls the birth of the ethics of authenticity.[5] Individualism has become not only a fact, but a moral task. The social fabric is gradually crumbling because of the erosion, at its base, of the very matrix that guarantees the survival of every individual. This is the strength of the bond. We

---

5   C. Taylor, *Il disagio della modernità, Ibid,* pp. 31-36.

will try to see how this individualist tendency has also taken the path of contemporary hermeneutics.

Suddenly, however, a paradox appears, for not one but two would be the trends in contemporary hermeneutics. On the one hand, there is cognitive reductionism, visible in "biblical-hermeneutical positivism." On the other hand, there is social individualism, with its extension in "biblical interpretive subjectivism." Which of the two is more important? Is it the more decisive or the more visible? It is both. We have a concomitance of cultural dysfunctions. How are we to understand this polarization of two opposing but mutually sustaining phenomena? How are we to grasp the hidden complicity between objectifying reductionism and relativizing subjectivism, which characterize our age and our hermeneutics? Let us follow philosopher Giacomo Marramao's description of this.

He holds that the present time[6] is characterized by two socio-cultural trends. One is the techno-economic-consumerist homogenization which destroys differences and particularities. The other is, especially in more recent times, the defense and proliferation of differences. It is the flight from universalism. It is the feeling of strongly belonging to communities that promise to safeguard a strong and particular identity.

Universalist homologation and identity differentiation, in other words universalism and particularism, according to Marramao, are not two alternatives. They are the two sides of the same coin. At the center we find the paradoxical short circuit of both the global and the local (glocal). The globalization process and localization process, coexist together. The more technology tends to standardize ways of living in some respects, the more cultural differences seem to deepen. This is at least the demand for differential treatment, the rediscovery of small homelands, small communities.

The idea of the historical becoming on the image of a scientific reason, of a rationality, which gradually and progressively extends to all spheres of life, parallels the emergence of thrusts to the claim of one's own cultural specificity, thrusts even going in the direction of the demand for a cultural autochthony. The return of

---

6   G. Marramao, *La passione del presente...Op. cit.*, pp. 56-86.

community, is produced not only through the rebellion of cultures other than Western culture. It is also generated within where it results in a denunciation of Western democratic institutions which have become cold institutions. These are reduced to being purely technical-procedural institutions. They are incapable of motivating individuals, social groups, social aggregates. They are cold, insensitive institutions which are indifferent to communal warmth. The most conspicuous aspect of this critique turns out to be that of the claim for a democracy. Democracy seems today to overlook important needs. For this reason demands emerge for forms of life and forms of association which in some way claim the rights of a warm and human coexistence against the coldness and anonymity of current democratic procedures.

Democracy in the postmodern era, with its obsession with formal procedures and rules, appears unable to account for and respond to its members' need for symbolic identification. According to the critique of communitarians, for example, the element of belonging cannot be entirely resolved in the logic of citizenship. Individuals cannot find symbolic identification simply in the fact that they are citizens, equal before the law, having, along with other fundamental rights, the right to vote. They must somehow also be regarded as socially and culturally specific subjects, subjects who live a real life and for whom it is necessary to feel part of a cultural community.

With Marramao, we realize that opposing cultural dysfunctions which may coexist as such on the surface, are on a depeer level instead similar. They keep alive, albeit in different ways, the same underlying mechanism. Similarly, textual positivism, described in the previous chapter, and "biblical subjectivism" that we will describe in this chapter, on the surface appear to be opposites. Further investigation reveals that at their base they are instead similar. They feed off each other and represent two sides of the same coin. Our reading hypothesis is to bring together these two phenomena, the cultural and the hermeneutical. The description of a cultural polarization (see Marramao), which characterizes our time, is not only an example of how this is possible. That description has a hermeneutic significance. This is because the opposition between textual positivism and textual subjectivism is an extension of that cultural polarization into the sphere of reading texts. We think that biblical positivism is actually the religious transcription of the cultural tendency to defend closed identities. It seeks to compensate the objectifying homogenization of our time with the defense of closed and ideological communities. On the other hand, biblical subjectivism is the religious transcription of the technical-efficient, consumerist and homogenizing tendency of rampant and unlimited individualism, as described by Marramao.

2. Biblical Subjectivism: Psychological Anthropocentrism[7]

Understood in a philosophical sense, subjectivism is the characteristic of a doctrine that denies the existence of criteria of truth and value independent of the thinking subject. A corollary of this assumption is the extreme and radical denial of what is real and objective. In this sense, subjectivism is a relativist view. In ancient philosophy, which aimed at the search for an objective foundation of knowing, subjectivism was a rare phenomenon. It is found, for example, in the thought of the Sophists. It is present in Protagoras, who elaborates a philosophy based on the useful, where man becomes "the measure of all things." There are for him no criteria other than human sensations to distinguish the true from the false. But subjectivism, not only as a philosophical current but also as a widespread anthropological attitude, took over only with modernity.

---

7   Christopher Lasch gives a pertinent reading of psychological anthropocentrism, calling it "narcissism," and moves it from a purely personal dimension to a cultural tendency. Cf. C. Lasch, *The Culture of Narcissism. American Life in an Age of Diminishing Expectations*, (New York: Warner Books, 1979), pp. 71-103. Still on narcissism, but from the point of view of an individual, at a later stage, who is more vulnerable because he is over-exposed and over-stressed, Alain Ehrenberg has made some very pertinent observations from a psycho-social perspective. A. Ehrenberg, *The Weariness of the Self. Diagnosing the History of Depression in the Contemporary Age*, (Montreal & Kingston: McGill-Queen's University Press, 2016), pp. 15-19.

Modern philosophy takes its cue from Augustine's affirmation of the value of interiority as the starting point for understanding God and the world, which in him still remained in an initial and non-pervasive state. Later on, beginning with Descartes, an increasingly positive value to human subjectivity emerged. It resulted in Berkeley attributing the entire macrocosmic reality to thinking consciousness. Kantian criticism with its "Copernican revolution" gave the transcendental activity of the subject itself a central role. This paved the way for subjectivism and its affirmation of self-consciousness as the absolute principle of reality. Depending on the areas, one can further distinguish ethical, aesthetic or religious subjectivism, in which the sole norm of the right, the beautiful or the religiously true is attributed to the individual.

In biblical subjectivism the same shift occurs. The reader becomes the determining element in the creation of meaning. The connection to the text does not lapse because Christian hermeneutics would hardly go as far as total denial of the text. But the consideration and reading of the text is completely conditioned by the situation, goals and motivations of the reader. Since this is not moral but textual subjectivism, there is no lack of reference to the text. One always returns to the text. It is quoted, it is consulted. One talks about it, one comments on it. One praises the text and glorifies it. The text is always the center of attention. Yet it is not the text itself that one has in mind. One projects in the text one's own image, one's own situation, one's own experience. The text does not exist as otherness. It does not possess its own consistency. The text must limit itself to reflecting the reader's issues. If it contradicts it or if it simply does not talk about it, the text does not count, it does not exist. The text, in textual subjectivism, must be a pure reflection of the reader. This is what we call "psychological dogmatism." It is the decisive and peremptory character of the subjective component in Bible interpretation. A double weakness emerges here. It is that of the text, which in this view is justified only by the reader. It is also that of the reader, because in order to claim the value and relevance of his agenda he must resort to the authoritativeness of the text.

In biblical subjectivism what really creates the problem is not the presence in itself of personal motives, even in their most extreme subjective form. A biblical reading must be able to make room for these kinds of elements as well because these are part of the life we want to illuminate from the gospel. The problem arises when these subjective elements become the filter that conditions the whole substance of the Bible and imprisons its meaning, no longer allowing the perception of its broader horizon. Subjective motives are not only legitimate, they are also necessary and powerful for the articulation of meaning. But here, in biblical subjectivism, they have taken over everything else.

The legitimate precomprehension that the reader carries within and cannot do without becomes prejudice and imposition on the text. The text no longer intervenes as an element of confrontation, much less provocation. There is no longer any surprise, except solely the obsession with noting and verifying that the text reflects the reader's agenda. Pre-understanding has disappeared and has become prejudice and manipulation of the text. The reader, like Narcissus, in the water of the pond, sees only his own reflection. The text has been reduced to a mirror, embodying no otherness and carrying no message. Textual subjectivism, by ignoring the text, neutralizes it and finally kills it. By killing the text, however, it also neutralizes the reader, for it condemns the reader to feed on a lifeless object with no real and alternative meanings. Neutralizing the text becomes depowering the reader himself.

3. Biblical Confessionalism: Ecclesiological Anthropocentrism[8]

On a more political and social level, confessionalism is that system in which members of a certain religion are advantaged over others. On the more religious and internal level, confessionalism represents that intent to unify the faith and make it compact. It embodies the peremptory intent to reduce the "sense of faith" to the "sense of one's own faith." It proceeds by privileging the compactness and homogeneity of religious experience. Confessionalism is an intent to domesticate faith. Confessing one's faith and convictions is a natural and even necessary exercise in the economy of religious experience. In the confession of one's faith we are faced with a testimony of faith. In religious confessionalism, this testimony becomes a peremptory affirmation that is intended to be universal, valid for all, from a form that is instead particular and relative. In confessionalism the true confrontation with any external reality is skipped. This is what drives faith communities to modulate the profile and substance of their doctrinal statements in a excluding and exclusive sense.

There is a hermeneutical version of confessionalism. We could even say that every religious confessionalism is initially a hermeneutic confessionalism where the positively pluriform sense of the Bible is reduced to the univocal compact sense of one's own

---

[8] In biblical confessionalism we find hidden an individualism expanded to community and elevated to a primary criterion. Apparently the emphasis on community breaks down and criticizes individualism; it criticizes it at a first level and defends it at a subsequent level. And it defends it in two ways: first, because with communitarianism individualism does not disappear but is maintained through its radicalization and opposition to the group. Second, because communitarianism, like the individualism to which it is opposed, stops the reality of what matters only at the reference identity, which in this case is the group and no longer the individual. Communitarianism appears to many as group individualism. Both are and remain heavily anthropocentric realities and claims. Cf. A. Etzioni, *The Spirit of Community. The Reinvention of American Society,* (New York: Touchstone Book, 1993), pp. 163-206. See also, M.J. Sandel, *Justice. What's the Right Thing to Do?* (New York: Farrar, Straus and Giroux, 2009), pp. 244-269; A. MacIntyre, *Whose Justice? Which Rationality,* (Notre Dame: Notre Dame University Press, 1988), pp. 349-369.

group. That every religious group and community needs to interpret the meaning of the Bible from and within a view that reinforces its own faith profile is not only legitimate. It is also inevitable. The problem does not lie here. The problem arises when the meaning of the Bible is imprisoned in the profile of one's own confession of faith, when one too candidly identifies one's understanding of Scripture with Scripture itself.

In biblical confessionalism the same shift occurs. The reading community becomes the determinant of meaning-making. The connection to the text does not lapse: Christian communities cannot openly deviate from the text of Scripture. But the consideration and reading of the text is completely conditioned by the situation, motivations and goals of the reading community. Since this is a Christian community, reference to the text is not lacking: one always returns to the text; one quotes it, one consults it. It is talked about, it is commented on. One praises the text and even glorifies it. The text is always the center of attention. Yet it is not the text itself that one has in mind. Rather one projects in the text the image, the situation, the experience of one's community. The text does not exist as otherness, does not possess its own consistency. It must reflect only the issues of the community. If it contradicts them or if it simply does not talk about them, the text does not count, it does not exist. The text, in biblical confessionalism, must be a pure reflection of the community. This is what we call "ecclesiological dogmatism." It is the decisive and peremptory nature of the community component in the interpretation of the Bible.

In biblical confessionalism, we are faced with a collective biblical subjectivism in which the objective sense of the Bible is lost. Furthermore, it does not give the diversity within the group its due. This, we have seen, reduces the possibilities for qualitative growth of the group itself. Reading the text is nothing more than reading itself by validating its own certainties and anomalies. Biblical confessionalism creates an undue symbiosis between group and Bible. It also creates this undue symbiosis within the group, between member and member. Bring an alternative to the group, within the group, no longer exists. The voices have been reduced to one. A mutual resolidification is articulated between a text and the group that no longer says anything new. The text has simply become the mirror of the group. This is a group that, reading that kind of text, no longer creates alternatives within it.

In hermeneutical confessionalism there appears to be an objectivity of faith. Yet, by virtue of being a purely internal objectivity, it is nothing but group subjectivism. This objectivity of faith is too narrow. The true objectivity, the broad and universal one, transcends each individual group. The call, then, for an objectivity of faith based on the Bible, which claims to be the steadfast truth on which the group is founded, is a false objectivity because it is too narrow. That purported objectivity is actually subjectivism in disguise. A group reality speciously elevated to the status of objective universalism. Biblical confessionalism, in its various versions, is a sophisticated version of modern subjectivism.

4. Biblical Pragmatism: Experiential Anthropocentrism[9]

Pragmatism is a philosophical current that emerged as a reaction to the intellectualism of the nineteenth century. In the face of the failure of reason to solve metaphysical problems, it made practice

---

9   Pragmatism has various faces and manifestations. However, it represents the trend of an era and not just a school of thought. As such it still presents itself today in sublimated and refined guises. The typical efficiencyism of our contemporary societies is an example of this. The triumph of technology is another. Cf. U. Galimberti, *Psiche e techne. L'uomo nell'età della tecnica*, (*"Psyche and Techne. Man in the Age of Technology"*), (Milan: Feltrinelli, 2004), pp. 293-304. In the victory of pragmatism as an anti-humanist phenomenon, Günther Anders sees not a moment, but a constant in modern culture. G. Anders, *L'uomo è antiquato. Considerazioni sull'anima dell'epoca della seconda rivoluzione industriale*, (*"Man is Outdated. Considerations on the Soul of the Age of the Second Industrial Revolution"*), vol. 1, (Turin: Bollati Boringhieri, 2003), pp. 55-120; pp. 84-90. On pragmatism and its hold on all contemporary societies, which Byung-Chul Han calls the "performance society" (*Achievement Society*), the Korean-German author pauses to consider mainly the nefarious effects in what he calls pragmatism in the period of late modernity. Cf. B.-C. Han, in, *Società della stanchezza*, (*"Society of Weariness"*), (Rome: Nottetempo, 2012), pp. 5,6.

the criterion of verification. Pragmatism developed between the late 19th century and the first two decades of the 20th century, particularly in the American and Anglo-Saxon cultural area. In a more cultural and anthropological sense, pragmatism, understood as attention, care and obsession with the practicality of life, is an accompanying and distinctive feature of modernity and postmodernity. According to this pragmatism, which is more anthropological, what matters in what we do and how we live is the efficiency and result achieved. Everything must be able to give and guarantee results. If the results are not there we are faced with something unnecessary and useless that can easily be eliminated or skipped without compromising the health and survival of the system.

This view of the world and life, in different proportions and forms, is the most widespread form today of cultural and hermeneutic subjectivism. The extent of its imprint, even on churches, is visible in the typical "managerialization" and "technification" of life. It includes not only the more objective and quantitative aspects, but also the more subjective, qualitative and intimate dimensions of human living.

The prototype of this anthropological orientation is given, according to Hannah Arendt, by the obscuring of the different forms of human activity that in the past it was possible to distinguish. She mentions three of them: labor, work, action. If in the past, for example in the Greek world, action (activity) in any of its forms was preferred to contemplation, nevertheless there remained an awareness that the noblest activity was "action." "Work" represented the least noble activity because it was too closely tied to need and necessity. The free man, on the other hand, was capable of "action" among his peers and left the strenuous work to the slaves in the *oikos* (home). In the modern world, and precisely because the spread and force of pragmatism, this differentiation tends to disappear and everything becomes work. From being a despised activity, work becomes the only worthy activity. This, according to Arendt, marks the birth of the anthropological pragmatism of the moderns. One of the prophets of this pragmatic revolution was Karl Marx. He elevated the model of *Homo Faber* to an anthropological model. The basis and justification of modern pragmatism is the prototype of *Homo Faber*.

The social and public dimension of this pragmatic shift is provided by the emergence of the economy as the central dimension of modern politics. For the Greeks, Arendt continues, this would have been a contradiction in terms. What is political belongs to the dimension of free and creative action; economics, on the other hand, is the domain of the necessary, of the *oikos* (home), of work not action. Pragmatism is not a school of thought, and neither is the practical orientation of a part of the population. It represents the matrix of thought and action of the entire modern world. Pragmatism is a disenchanted, mechanical though very functional expression of modern subjectivism.

Pragmatism, involving an entire era, did not spare biblical hermeneutics. It has taken hold as reading pragmatism. It probably represents the most widespread form of hermeneutical anomaly. Not the speculative subjectivism of the liberals nor the aesthetic subjectivism of the charismatics, but the concrete subjectivism of the pragmatists today threatens to obscure more the nature and scope of the Bible by reducing it to an application strategy.

Biblical pragmatism discharges as unnecessary and superfluous all those interpretive passages that ground and articulate meaning in its various nuances. This is especially because they are guilty of dilating the time of meanings. The pragmatic reader has no time; he is always in a hurry. According to his thought pattern, it must be so, on pain of unnecessarily burdening the sense. Sense must be light, functional and immediate. Consequently, the slowness of true sense, that which characterizes its establishment and manifestation, appears to the pragmatist as a waste of time. All sense must be applicable. It must serve only to construct and elaborate on a sense that can be applied. Everything else has no justification. The typical exuberance of sense, given by plurivocity, is a dead and useless burden. If we have, in our interpretation, accompanying meanings that we do not use, then what good are they? Better not to have them. The pragmatist's is a thrifty, essential, war economy interpretation. The pragmatist thinks he knows the only sense that matters. He dispenses with the other possible senses. He destroys them if they already exist. He does not create them because they waste resources on meanings that would remain unused. They dissipate the energy that is needed to promote the only valid sense.

In biblical pragmatism the same shift occurs. It is the practice that becomes the determining element in the creation of meaning. The connection with the text does not lapse because Christian communities cannot openly depart from the text of Scripture. But the consideration and reading of the text are completely conditioned by the concreteness and practicality of the situation. Since it is a Christian community, reference to the text is not lacking. One always returns to the text. It is quoted, it is consulted. It is talked about, commented on. One praises the text and even glorifies it. The text is always the center of attention. In reality it is not the text itself that one has in mind.

The benefit, the result, the effect expected by the pragmatic reader is projected into the text. The text does not exist as otherness. It does not possess its own consistency. The text must limit itself to offering the concrete results that the reader expects. If the text does not accomplish this, then it does not count, it does not exist. The text, in biblical pragmatism, must be a pure guarantor of results. This is what we call "experiential dogmatism," because of the decisive and peremptory character of the pragmatic component in Bible interpretation.

This pragmatic view fails to grasp the characteristic of biblical language. Going further, it proposes a model of biblical language that is actually opposed to it. This model is a child of modernity. There is nothing biblical about it. It, too, is not perverse in itself as long as one does not elevate it to an ideology above criticism. Above all, as long as one does not identify it with biblical language. In modern interpretive pragmatism, the typical technical univocity is transferred to the reading of the biblical text. In divine transcendent language, or divine language embodied in human language, for pragmatism the important thing is its univocity and compactness. Very differently, what characterizes biblical language is its unavailability of meaning, its mystery, its polyvalence.[10]

---

10   A. Rizzi, *Pensare dentro la Bibbia*, Op. cit., pp. 28-37.

Hermeneutic pragmatism is a fast track that distrusts mediations. It distrusts them because they slow down any interpretive process. But this is not the most problematic element of hermeneutic pragmatism. The bigger problem is the clearance of plurivocity that leads to an obsession with accuracy and clarity in the Bible. Hermeneutic pragmatism dismantles biblical complexity and its language. It cages biblical plurisense in a clear, monolithic, and immediate sense.

5. *Modern Rationalism: Cultural Anthropocentrism*[11]

Anthropocentrism is the tendency to regard the human being, and everything about him, as central to the universe. Originating very early, it is clearly visible as early as the Renaissance in a marked way. From a medieval theocentric view, where man's destiny and positioning was predetermined by God, the group and the cosmos, we move to a view where man is the determining factor of his own destiny. This implies that the precondition for being able to affirm himself lies in the autonomy and detachment he claims vis-à-vis God and all that is transcendent. Man becomes the ultimate goal and, at the same time, the starting point for considering, looking at,

---

11   That social subjectivism, together with interpretive subjectivism, are dependents of a structural anthropocentric tendency of all contemporary culture is a fact that can hardly be disavowed today. And the word-category that best expresses the drift of this modern subjectivism and individualism even in its non-human effects, on nature and the cosmos, is the word "anthropocene." Cf. P.J. Crutzen, *Benvenuti nell'antropocene. L'uomo ha cambiato il clima. La terra entra in una nuova era*, (*"Welcome to the Anthropocene. Man has Changed the Climate. The Earth Enters a New Era")*, (Milan: Mondadori, 2005). On the genesis and a broader description of the anthropocene also at the cultural and political level, G. Pellegrino and M. Di Paolo have proposed a recent work, see G. Pellegrino, M. Di Paola, *Nell'antropocene. Etica e politica alla fine di un mondo*, (*"In the Anthropocene. Ethics and Politics at the End of a World")*, (Rome: Habitus, 2018). On the more immediate problems of the Anthropocene and the constraint they impose on today's politics, Bruno Latour has devoted important pages. Cf. B. Latour, *La sfida di Gaia. Il nuovo regime climatico*, (*"The Gaia Challenge. The New Climate Regime")*, (Milan: Meltemi, 2020), pp. 73-116.

describing, evaluating and determining everything else. It is here that the defense of human exceptionalism is born and articulated. All other species and entities that make up the cosmos are lesser realities because they do not possess the rationality, awareness, elective will and determination to guide human and historical processes to their fulfillment.

This radical bet on man conceals two reductions. The first is an anthropological reduction: man becomes detached from the cosmos that until then had been the guarantor of his survival. The second is an individualist reduction: it is no longer the group, which until then had been the extension and prolonger of the stability of the cosmos, that determines man's place and role in the world. It is the individual, alone, through his freedom and self-determination.

From being an elitist vision, anthropocentrism will become fully democratic and expand across all strata of contemporary societies. The various crises that have occurred in recent years - environmental, demographic and multicultural crises - have given rise to a strong contestation of the validity of this humanist claim. Post-humanism or transhumanism embody these contestations and claims some success. But looking at the data, results, and orientations, it can be said that anthropocentrism has not disappeared. It has even been reinforced. It has changed in some of its traits, replacing, for example, its initial optimism with a cynical pessimism, which continues in the scene to determine the main rhythm and direction of our age.

The problem of anthropocentrism does not lie in the consideration of human beings as part of the ecosystem that we must consider. This is legitimate, necessary and inevitable. The problem is that thinking of life from our own gaze has become the only possible gaze which we have imposed on all other species. Anthropocentrism has triggered in chains other reductivisms such as Eurocentrism, speciesism, and machismo, which still heavily condition our globalized reality. It is what we call "cultural dogmatism," because of the decisive and peremptory character of the anthropic component in the formation and articulation of today's culture, which then has a strong spillover effect on the way we interpret the Bible.

All these distortions have taken hold in biblical hermeneutics. We find readings today that are, unbeknownst to them, specist, masculinist, Eurocentric Bible readings. Today most Christians continue to read the Bible in these terms. Today's Bible readings tend to be almost exclusively anthropocentric readings. The paradox is that intentions to correct, balance or refresh Bible readings, several times, resort to new anthropocentric motives. The result is the reinforcement of biblical anthropocentrism through its updating. The effect of renewal is short-lived and deceptive, because the attrition that was merely delayed by the apparent novelty soon resurfaces. More importantly, is not perceived as the product of that anthropocentrism, so they try to curb it with what actually produced it.

PART III
TRINITY, MYSTERY
AND THE UNAVAILABILITY OF MEANING

The Mediation of a Kenotic Trinity: "Affirmation" and "Flexibility"

This third part of our essay is a reflection on the Trinity from the perspective of the relationality that distinguishes it. We will redeem two characteristics of this relationality that are crucial not only to the relationship of persons within the Trinity, but also to the articulation and flowering of meaning in the Bible: affirmation and flexibility.

Each person in the Trinity must be able to be the protagonist of his or her own story, through the affirmation of his or her own identity and will, his or her own values and ideas, his or her own distinctiveness and specificity. Without these a person would appear completely subordinate and subservient to the other persons within the Trinity.

This this necessary personal affirmation must then be extended as a possibility to the other triune persons, which can only happen through one's own flexibilization. This flexibility, through the downsizing of one's own profile, appears at first glance to be opposed to one's own affirmation, insofar as it limits it and makes it negotiable; however, it is actually complementary to the affirmation of all other triune persons. It is only from the space I cede (flexibility) that affirmative spaces can be opened for other persons as well, in dialogue, through what Paul Ricœur calls the discrete force "of attestation."[1] This is a sobering mechanism of self-affirmation within an inescapable coexistence and confrontation between different persons, even if united by the same nature, as occurs in the Trinity.

---

1 P. Ricœur, *Sé come un altro*, (*"Self as Another"*), (Milan: Jaca Book, 2005), pp. 411-415.

In the three chapters, which open the third part of our essay, we will pause to consider the theme of the Trinity in connection with the interpretation of the Bible, with the intention of giving an ontological and not only an analytical-explicative dimension to the act of interpreting. We have described, in the second part, an interpretive anomaly typical of our time, which we have called "biblical positivism." In its various forms it reduces the complexity of the interpretive process to one of its dimensions. More fundamentally it dissociates the "explaining" of the text from its "understanding."[2] This makes alternative a necessary analytical dimension in the interpretive process and a dimension of rootedness in life (Being). This is a pre-textual condition which precedes our relationship with the text. These should survive together in a structural tension.

The act of reading always involves more than simply assimilating and handling new information. There is always a risk of remaining on the side of what the interpretive process requires and demands. This risk is even greater when reading the Bible, even though it might appear otherwise. Those who read the Bible, one would think, are already by definition interested in a spiritual dimension. But spiritual, especially in the modern sense, does not necessarily mean ontological. The purely analytical, managerial and calculating attitude typical of instrumental reason has today extended to spiritual research as well. We are in an age of ontological deficit where the instances that should be able to guarantee our ontological grounding in life and reality, among them reading the Bible, do not solve the problem. They increase and radicalize it. Biblical positivism is the embodiment of this paradoxical dysfunction.

The most distinctively theological way to try to restore this ontological dimension to the act of interpretation is not to root interpretation in a pre-textual human dimension, as, for example,

---

2   Alternative that persists even in those who have tried to redefine what interpretation is and represents. As is the case with W. Dilthey who ends up creating an even greater gap than the one he wanted to correct between "explaining" (Erklären) and "understanding" (Verstehen). Cf. P. Ricœur, *Dal testo all'azione... Op. Cit.,* pp. 77-83.

Hans Georg Gadamer does.³ It is to connect the complexity (ambivalence and paradox) that characterizes the entire biblical hermeneutical circle, text and reader, to the Trinitarian complexity that precedes and grounds the Bible as text as well as us humans as readers. This Trinitarian reflection will not be an end in itself. It will be articulated in function of and in connection with the "possibility of meaning," as a hermeneutical condition.

With the word "meaning" taken up in the title of each of the chapters in this third part, we will try to show that its recovery can only take place from an ontological visitation of what grounds it. In the case of Christian hermeneutics, we think of refocusing on Trinitarian thought. In speaking of meaning, we refer to the classic distinction made by Gottleb Frege⁴ between "sense" and "meaning."⁵ According to Frege, "sense" (*Sinn*) differs from "meaning" (*Bedeutung*) in that "sense" is the linguistic mode in which the object of reference is presented. "Meaning" is the nonlinguistic factor to which the spoken or expressed linguistic expression refers.⁶ We have argued at various points in our essay in favor of the referential dimension

---

3   Hans G. Gadamer describes this pre-textual connection at three levels. At the level of aesthetic experience, history and language. In each of these experiences we have a life connection and prerational belonging that then makes analytic knowledge possible. The three parts, then, of his book *Truth and Method* are built on this basic thesis. H.-G. Gadamer, Verità e metodo ("*Truth and Method*"), (Bompiani, Milan 2000). On Gadamer consult P. Ricœur, *Dal testo all'azione...Op. Cit.*, pp. 91-95.

4   G. Frege, *Über Sinn und bedeutung,* (Herasugegeben von Uwe Voigt), (Ditzingen: Reclam Philipp, 2019). In Italian, "Sense and Denotation," in, A. Bonomi (ed.), *La struttura logica del linguaggio*, (Milan: Bompiani, 1973), pp. 9-32.

5   On "sense" and "meaning" see also: D. Marguerat, Y. Bourquin, *Per leggere I racconti biblici...Op. Cit.* pp. 153, 154.

6   A. Bonomi translates *bedeutung* not with "meaning" but with denotation. P. Ricœur, like E. Benveniste, translates *bedeutung* as "reference" (*référence*). See P. Ricœur, *From text to action... op. cit.,* pp. 108-111. Beyond the difference in the translation of *bedeutung* these various authors by *bedeutung* mean the nontextual element, thus, the reality to which the sense refers. See also a more complete description between sense and reference made by Brugiatelli from Ricœur's work. V. Brugiatelli, *La relazione tra linguaggio ed essere in Ricœur,* ("The

of text and human languages. In these three chapters on the Trinity, we will connect not to "referentiality," that to which language refers (*Bedeutung/signified*), but rather and more fundamentally to the possibility of "sense" (*Sinn*) that is articulated in human language. We will try, from another perspective, from the perspective of the Trinity, to discover the relevance of the linguistic forms we use to connect to external reality. These ways of articulating "sense" or making sense possible, in our view and according to the hypothesis articulated from the very first pages, is that biblical sense is not univocal (mono-sense) but plurivocal (pluri-sense). It is representative of a sense that coexists structurally with ambivalence and paradox. These traits characterizing the Bible we think we can also find in the Trinity. We think of the Trinity not as the reference to meaning, but as its condition.

By "unavailability of meaning," guaranteed by the Trinity and its mystery, we refer in this third part to the non-manipulable dimension of both the Trinity and the Bible, embodied, in either case, in ambivalence and paradox.

We have seen so far how ambivalence and paradox characterize the whole interpretive process and not only its initial stage. These two traits define both the pole of the text and the pole of the reader in their various layers. The task of biblical hermeneutics is to trace and monitor the presence of these two features at all levels of the interpretive chain. It is also to make sure that ambivalence and paradox, while interpreted, rearticulated or updated, never leave the scene.

Interpretation is never the linear process that goes from plurivocity to univocity, from mystery to clarity, from complexity to synthesis. It is par excellence the experience of a troubled and suffered clarification of a sense that, while creating orientation and direction, and while opening new horizons and perspectives of specific human path, always remains a complex, plural and paradoxical sense. Because it is a human sense and because the whole interpretive process is rooted in oral, written, actualized and polyvalent language.

Relation Between Language and Being in Ricœur"), (Trento: Uni Service, 2009), pp. 93-152.

If the hermeneutics of ambivalence and paradox were grounded only in the paradoxicality of the text or/and the reader reading that text, we would have in hermeneutics a great cognitive theory and a high-level linguistic-semantic program. Instead, a text like the Bible and the interpretations that take it up are also connected to an extra-textual reality. They find articulated in it the same ambivalence and paradox that are hallmarks not only of the text but also of life itself. We have tried in our reflection to perceive and compare, to place in dialogue, the ambivalence and paradox of the biblical text with the ambivalence and paradox of human reality, especially in the historical period in which we live.

Can biblical-theological hermeneutics limit itself to being only a reading strategy or a simple application of that meaning to practical life? We believe not. Therefore, in this third part, we would like to try to investigate the pretextual dimension of ambivalence and paradox, to try to ground it in God himself.

The first divine form that immediately imposes itself on us as a complex reality, similar and parallel to the complexity of the Bible, is the Trinity. The Bible, as we have said, is a complex linguistic reality, just as the Trinity is a complex ontological reality. Complexity is thus given by the impossibility of reducing the whole to a single element and the refusal to conceive of the relationship between the parts as purely linear and unidirectional. Bible and Trinity express the same paradigm, that of complexity, with all that this implies, albeit at different levels.

We cannot establish, between the Bible and the Trinity, a purely linear relationship or even a simple overlap. The Bible is not God to us. That would be bibliolatry. The Bible is the revelation and thus the testimony that gathers the being of the triune God and his action of grace and mercy toward humanity, in a partial and imperfect way. The triune God expresses a complexity which is greater and more foundational than the Bible. If the Bible is God's word, even in the indelible difference between the two, the Bible must be able though to convey and ground itself in that Trinitarian complexity that precedes it.

The link between the complexity of the Bible and the interpretive process and the Trinity is not fortuitous and random. The Bible is, represents, depends on and prolongs, albeit relatively and imperfectly, the essence of the Trinity. This parallelism between the Bible and the Trinity[7] does not aim to sacralize and deify the Bible as much as the opposite. It aims to make the Bible more relational, open and flexible. It parallels the Trinitarian multidimensional complexity that makes the persons within the Trinity more relational, open and flexible.

Trinitarian complexity is not given solely by the number of divine persons within. The interaction or, in technical terms, the so-called "perichoresis" is what makes Trinitarian life complex. Each person of the Trinity in interacting within the Trinity necessarily exhibits a necessary "exuberance," that is, a richness of its own that it is called upon to express as a specific trait of its identity profile. It also exhibits an equally necessary "sobriety," that is, a self-restraint, in order to allow the other persons within the Trinity to express themselves.

Even in sharing the same nature (monotheism), the persons and actions of the triune persons are differentiated, thus not equivalent despite their synergy and convergence. This specificity of persons and their corresponding actions creates the Trinitarian life with the character of this possible and differentiated interaction. Affirmation and flexibility, word and silence, action and passion, exposure and retraction, "exuberance" and "sobriety": these are the characteristics that, declined in various ways and articulated in different configurations, express in their tension the possibility of intra-trinitarian life and interaction.

It is possible to parallel the "exuberance" of each person within the Trinity with the "polyvalence (ambivalence)" of the Bible. We can also parallel the "sobriety" of Trinitarian persons with the "paradoxicality" of the Bible. In chapter five, the one on biblical language, we already pointed out "exuberance (plurivocity)" and "sobriety" as the two characteristics that best distinguish biblical language.

---

7   V. -M. Kärkkäinen, *Trinity and Revelation. A Constructive Christian Theology for a Pluralistic World*, vol. 2, (Grand Rapids: Eerdmans, 2014), pp. 11-29.

Typical of the Bible, in the communicative process it establishes, is "saying little" (sobriety/fragmentarily) and, that little said, saying it in the "plural (plurivocity, exuberance). This biblical linguistic mechanism is radically inclusive because its vocation is to elicit, through sui generis language, recognition of the other and dialogue with the other.

We find in Trinitarian "perichoresis" the same mechanism. This is possible only because of the "exuberance" and the linguistic and ontological "sobriety" of the Trinitarian persons. Thus "sobriety" and "exuberance" are fundamental not only to understanding the profile of the Bible, but also that of the Trinity as typical relational realities. Let us pause briefly to describe the nature of these two characteristics of Trinitarian relationality, mentioned earlier, which are also the two characteristics of the Bible itself: "flexibility" and "affirmativity," which we also call "sobriety" and "exuberance," as essential traits of a relational entity.

On one side the other finds an opportunity to be able to speak only in the sobriety of one's words. If we were always speaking, the scene would be full, but full only of our words, words that would stifle the other's desire to speak. Only one would be doing the talking, not two. There would be no dialogue, only the compact affirmation of a soliloquy. The apparent quantitative abundance of words would actually express a scarcity of words. For words are plural not when they are many, but when, though few, they are spoken by many. It is the plurality of speaking subjects that makes a language rich. There is plurality of speaking subjects when there is such sobriety as to allow fluidity and rhythmicity of exchange in each of the participants in the dialogue. The Bible is the "sober" Word of God which by virtue of its being partial and incomplete, ennobles and makes human speech necessary.

On the other side, only the "exuberance" of our speaking can drag and persuade the other person, motivating him or her to speak. If our speaking were empty, disengaged or detached; if we did not put into what we say what we are, the fullness and complexity of our lives, what we say would lack the compulsive force of involvement. Ours would be a disenchanted word, a linear and mechanical word, unimpressive because it is lifeless. It would be word without charm and without attraction, ghostly, a word with a deadline. Complexity of a life expressed in language propels a word forward and makes it persuasive and attractive to the other. The Bible is the "exuberant" Word of God by virtue of the fact that God puts all his being into it. His complexity, his fullness, becomes in every place and time capable of attracting and intriguing the human.

The problem lies right here. If a word is sober and dry, how can it be exuberant? If a word is exuberant and complex, how can it be sober? One cannot accelerate and brake at the same time. One cannot say little and a lot at the same time. Although the dilemma seems unsolvable, in the Bible the limitation of one's words does not at all mean a narrowing of the qualitative "exuberance" of language. The restriction of one's words (sobriety) makes that kind of exuberance possible.

The sobriety of the Bible is not that of a disenchanted and cold sobriety, just as its exuberance is not the plethoric exuberance of full and self-sufficient words. Not monolithism and compactness of meaning, but rather the opposite emerges when biblical sobriety enters the picture. When I have to say little, I am actually driven to speak better and use language that can say much with little. The symbolic language of narrative and poetry, sober and exuberant language par excellence, comes to my aid. That kind of language, which is the language of the Bible, says much with little and little with much. The exuberance of language does not arise, as is commonly believed, from bulimic and plethoric words. The exuberance of language arises from the sobriety of words. Because they cannot say everything, they choose to say a little through the exuberant but discreet language of the symbolic imagination.

In the three first chapters of this third part of our reflection, we will read three biblical texts. We will not develop, in reading these three passages, a theology of the Trinity in the full sense. We will simply propose, of the Trinity and its connection with the Bible, a reading by clues, by hints, by summaries. Of the three persons of the Trinity we will pause to consider, in the light of what these three passages suggest, their complexity and sobriety. We will try to outline the forms of connection between these two characteristics as they appear both in the Trinity and in the Bible.

Exuberance and flexibility are hallmarks of a kenotic identity. Christ is a kenotic being,[8] but so are the Father and the Spirit, and, as the Trinity is kenotic, so is the Bible. Because the foundation of Christianity, the Trinity and the Bible, are chenotic, everything that arises in Christianity must bear the same traits.[9]

This Trinitarian and biblical *chenosis* does not bracket the question of truth. On the contrary, it makes it possible. As Salvatore Natoli says[10] referring to Gianni Vattimo, "weak thought", understood as a chemotic form of thinking, has captured well the dimension of "flexibility" but not that of truthful "affirmation." A well understood category of chemosis, applied to the Trinity or to the Bible, doesn't cancel the affirmative moment of a entity but rather makes if possible through sobriety.

---

8 Philippians 2:5-11.
9 This is also the sense that G. Vattimo gives to the term "weak thought." "Weak thinking" is a chenotic thinking that Vattimo attributes to the essence of Christianity. G. Vattimo, Credere *di credere,* (Milan: Garzanti, 1999), pp. 25,26.
10 Natoli believes that all modern thought is "weak," but that therein lies one of its limitations. S. Natoli, Il linguaggio della verità. Logica ermeneutica, (*"The Language of Truth. Hermeneutic Logic"*), (Brescia: Morcelliana, 2014), pp. 21 ff.

CHAPTER IX
THE FATHER'S PASSION[1] AND THE POSSIBILITY OF MEANING[2]

Regarding the first person of the Trinity, the Father Creator,[3] the subject of the reflection in this first chapter, we will ask: How does the Father make meaning possible?[4] How is the meaning of life, and consequently also the meaning of a text, which tells us about human life, produced by the Father's action?[5] The answer is: through his "passion." Only the passion of the God who interacts

---

1   V. -M. Kärkkäinen, *The Doctrine of God: A Global Introduction,* (Grand Rapids: Eerdmans, 2004), pp. 15-34.
2   In discussing sense we will start from the distinction made by Gottlob Frege between "sense and meaning," (*Sinn und Bedeutung*) meaning by "sense" a linguistic reality that can be expressed in various ways and by "meaning" a reality beyond language that is instead unambiguous, that is, specific as an intended object.
3   J. Moltmann, *Trinità e regno di Dio. La dottrina su Dio, ("Trinity and the Kingdom of God. The Doctrine on God"),* (Brescia: Queriniana, 1983), pp. 30-71; J. Moltmann, *Nella storia del Dio trinitario. Contributi per una teologia trinitaria, ("In the History of the Trinitarian God. Contributions for a Trinitarian Theology"),* (Brescia: Queriniana, 1993), pp. 25-48.
4   In this sense we will privilege for the Father (and for the whole Trinity) the question not of existence (*An sit*), but that of his identity and relationality (*Quid sit*), thus taking up an important emphasis of more recent theology. Indeed, A. Dondeyne says: «On a l'impression d'assister à un déplacement du centre de gravité de la problématique de Dieu. Tout se passe comme si la question «quid sit» (le problème de la nature et des attributs de Dieu), prenait le pas sur la question «an sit» (question des preuves de Dieu). L'important pour l'homme est de préciser en quel sens il faut penser l'absolu,» in *Ephem. Theol. Lov.,* No. 37, 1961, pp. 462,463.
5   A. Geshé similarly emphasizes the question of meaning rather than the question of God's existence. A. Geshé, *Dieu,* (Paris: Cerf, 2010), pp. 24-29.

and takes risks in history, and not his apathy, as the supreme being, who keeps himself away from history or uses it solely as a space for manifestation, breaks the mechanicity of the exchanges between God and us humans, and makes meaning possible. The possibility of meaning arises from an ontological rupture given by God's creation. If God had not created, there would be only ontological and communicative tautology, and not a new and living sense exchanged by those who participate in the dialogue. The Father is not only the Creator but also the facilitator and the mediator of meaning by making otherness possible through his creative action.

Meaning always arises from a rupture, a differentiation, and creation represents the rupture of the continuity of God's being. God's being in creation welcomes and creates the surprise of another being who is the creature, the created. The possibility of meaning, as new meaning, thus requires an anthropology of the freedom of a new being and a theology of the risk of a Creator who decides to create new beings by challenging his ontological tautology.

1. *Theological Positivism: "Monarchianism"*

We will try to read the complexity that characterizes the being of the first person in the Trinity, God-the-Father, in connection with the complexity expressed in the Bible. We find ourselves before an interplay and tension between affirmation and flexibility, word and silence, action and passion, exposure and retraction, "ambivalence" and "paradox," "exuberance" and "sobriety." These ways are ways of expressing two characteristics of any complex identity that breaks with linear, atomistic and unidirectional logic and replaces it with the circular, relational, multidimensional and multidirectional logic typical of complex systems.[6]

---

6   We have introduced the theme of complexity from the very first pages of this essay. The hermeneutic exercise is an expression of a type of complex thinking. But complexity thinking is certainly not new and can even be traced back to the very moment of the birth of modern rationalist thought. However, at that time the euphoria of nascent thought was too strong and its successes covered the anomalies that were already latent and became

We can begin to look at the complexity of God's being from the anomalies that have emerged to repudiate and dismantle it. Just as biblical positivism tends to obliterate the complexity of the Bible, historical Christianity, while introducing a revolutionary conception about the complexity of God, that is, the Trinity, also introduced an anomaly from the very beginning. This was by making God monolithic and by depriving him of his complexity. This was the intent of monarchianism at an early stage in the development of Christianity.[7]

Monarchianism (from Greek μονος - mone, unique and αρχεω - arché, principle) is a Christian theological movement that flourished in the second and third centuries. It was the all-out defense of the unity of God, which consequently involved the denial of the Trinity and the partial denial of Christ's divinity. The word "monarchians" was first used by Tertullian to describe a type of monarchianism, the so-called patripassians.[8] Monarchianism was in fact of two types, both of which were aimed at defending the unity and monolithic nature of God's being.

The first was called "adoptionist Monarchianism." It had Paul of Samosata, bishop of Antioch of Syria, as its typical representative. He claimed that the *logos* (Christ) was indeed consubstantial

---

flags, albeit of minority groups and thinkers. In the 20th century, above all, the limitations and anomalies of modern rationalism emerged more clearly, and it was only then that the protests, once minority and reduced to the stage of draft, took shape and, while not overturning the supremacy of the still transversal modern efficientist model, nevertheless consistently proposed alternative models. And it is there, at that moment, that a more articulate proposal of complex thinking makes its way. Edgar Morin represents one of the thinkers around whom complexity thinking is best coagulated. Cf. M. Ceruti, *Il tempo della complessità. Prefazione di Edgar Morin*, (*"The Time of Complexity. Preface by Edgar Morin"*), (Milan: Raffaello Cortina, 2018), pp. 29-85. Important in Italy for the dissemination of complexity thinking is the Edgar Morin Center for the Study of Philosophy of Complexity at the University of Messina. Cf. G. Gembillo, A. Anselmo, *Filosofia della complessità*, (*"Philosophy of Complexity"*), (Florence: Le Lettere, 2017), pp. 19-33.

7   L. Berkhof, *The History of Christian Doctrines*, (Grand Rapids: Baker Book House, 1992), pp. 77-80.
8   Patripassianism affirmed that God the Father Himself became incarnate and thus suffered with Christ. Cf. L. Berkhof, *Ibid*, p. 79.

(*homoousios*) with the Father, but not a distinct person within the Trinity. Paul of Samosata and his followers denied that there were distinct persons within the Trinity. Theirs was thus a typical reductionist movement that wanted to impose a monolithic paradigm on God and on the church.

The second type of monarchianism, was called "modalist monarchianism." This was known as "patripassianism" in the West and as Sabellianism in the Christian East. "Modalist monarchianism" asserted that the persons in the Trinity were simply distinct "modes" through which the one God manifested Himself. Although modalists also affirmed the unity of the divine nature, they effectively denied the existence of the triune persons as such. "Monarchianist adoptionism" tended to deny Christ's divinity or grant it only later and with restrictions. "Modalist monarchianism," on the other hand, recognized Christ's full divinity from the beginning.

Three effects of monarchianism eventually dismantled the structural complexity that the Trinitarian doctrine of God sought to introduce and maintain as the primary configuration of faith.

The first effect was ecclesiological. Monarchianism introduced a vertical type of ecclesiastical authority in the management of church life and, especially, in the management of internal conflicts. Just as the voice of God, "monarch," who is unique and unified in his entity, is compact, clear, direct and absolute, similarly the voice of the church leaders who represent him must possess the same characteristics. No space is guaranteed for dialogue that yields and concedes, for consensus that is the result of negotiation, for compromise that tries to create convergence. What the monarch says is law.

Minority groups or alternatives are accepted internally only transiently while they align with directives from above and understand that differences are obstacles to be torn down. Anything that does not align with the direction that descends from above is declared deviant, heterodox, heretical. Theological monolithism serves as a legitimizer for authority and compact power is unbreeched. This monolithic model of ecclesiastical governance, as J. Moltmann reminds us,[9]

---

9   J. Moltmann explicitly refers to Carl Schmidt's "political theology," which centuries later still used the monarchchianist model in an updated

will also become a political model. Theological monarchianism will serve as a model and legitimating mechanism for political power.

The second effect was theological. Though it was declared heretical, Monarchian theological monolithism, imposed itself over time in its essence which embodied the diffuse aspiration to have a compact, clear and homogeneous God. And this is the concept of God that still prevails to the present day. The arrival of modernity, which was beneficial on some levels, on this theological level radicalized the reductive tendency even more. Modern pragmatism and rationalism are, in their essence, an extraordinary form of worship to cultural monolithism. This theological effect was not limited to reinforcing the unity of God. It also erased God's vulnerability.

The typical medieval conception of "Supreme Being"[10] gave way to the typical modern conception of God as "Absolute Subject."[11] Although different, these two models share the common trait of erasing the dimension of vulnerability in the definition of God. In both cases God is an a-pathic being, who cannot be lacking in anything, otherwise his perfection would be in jeopardy. He is thus a God without passion. The dogma of the apathetic God, who bases his greatness in this apathy, sublimated, however, into an impeccable management of salvation, has not been questioned. It has become a substitute for a more relational understanding of God.

The third effect is socioeconomic. The Christian West copied the same vertical model and set itself up as the master of the world, the guardian of other cultures. Instead of fostering the enculturation of Christianity in other cultures as it had been enculturated in the West, the Christian West imposes by visible forces (infrastructure) and, even worse, by invisible forces (superstructures) its own cultural interpretation of Christianity. It decided what other peoples were supposed to be. The idea of the monarch God, secularized to a cultural paradigm, became cultural imperialism rather than an instance of dialogue and healthy tension.

---

way.
10   J. Moltmann, *Trinità e regno di Dio* ...*Op. Cit.,* pp. 20-22.
11   *Ibid*, pp. 22-25.

There is a clear historical parallelism between biblical monolithism and theological monolithism with regard to the conception of God. In the first centuries this religious monolithism was manifested mainly at the level of the conception of God. It was predominantly a theological (God) but not a biblical monolithism. Around the Bible still predominated at that time a great ferment and plurality of references which found greater stability only in the closing of the canon in the fourth century. Modern religious monolithism is instead twofold.

On the one hand, it expresses a theological monolithism, typical of our time, which is given by a transversal though hidden modalism. On the other hand, it has become to all effects also a biblical monolithism. And it is given not only by biblical fundamentalism, which still remains a limited phenomenon, but by what we have called "biblical positivism" as a transversal phenomenon throughout contemporary Christianity. The effect of this theological monolithism, rooted in monarchianism, did not end when Christianity was secularized. In its secularized form this monolithism has become also a powerful cultural conditioner in our days.

2. *Monarchianism and Globalization*

Globalization, as a typical modern process of standardization and homogenization, by indirect routes, by distal complicity, lies in the wake of ancient monarchchianism. It updates its spirit by radicalizing and secularizing it and imposing it as a cultural obligation for every individual. The secularization of monarchchianism does not relativize it. Secularization ends up empowering it. While religious monarchchianism was limited to a few, secularized monarchchianism (globalization) influences everyone. Monarchchianism has won in its secular form by imposing an authority that is even more difficult to challenge because it is more invisible and anonymous but it is no less real.

The effects of secularized monotheism are much more decisive and widespread. Theological monarchchianism was heteronomous. It was more easily defined and delimited because it imposed itself from the outside. Globalization, coming from below, exerts its influence without our knowledge and by mechanisms that we ourselves set in motion but no longer control. Like monarchchianism, globalization introduces a pattern of homogenization. In the face of central power, entities and individuals are made equal in their common condition of subservience and subalternity. It is a mechanism imposed on them that escapes control and verification. The end result is the dismantling of diversity. It is especially the imposition of linear and unidirectional mechanisms of interaction.

This authoritarianism from below is more difficult to diagnose and neutralize because it is forged by ourselves. According to Tocqueville,[12] it arises from the same democratic system that granted us freedom. According to Tocqueville's genealogical reading, this "mild despotism"[13] is not later and posterior, but is the basic premise of current democratic systems. Despotic drift does not arise from a secondary and later anomaly, but from a foundational virtue of democracy itself.

Tocqueville focuses on the concept of passion. The passion for equality, which in democratic systems drives the individual to not accept differences, triggers a process of homogenization. Equality of conditions tends to result in conformity, in social massification, with a strong normative drive that comes not from above but from below. Alongside the passion for equality, the "passion for possession" also develops. Equality as similarity, as the rejection of differences, plus greed, create a dimension unto itself. This is a new social configuration, a "mistaken individualism," which is contemporary and synchronous with virtuous individualism. That mistaken individualism does not come later, because of the errors

---

12 Tocqueville develops this analysis mainly in the second volume of his classic work on America, especially in the fourth part of this, especially in chapter six. Cf. A. de Tocqueville, *La democrazia in America*, Libro secondo, (*"Democracy in America*, Book Two"), (Milan: Utet, 2019), pp. 810-815.
13 Tocqueville writes: "If despotism were to take hold in today's democratic nations, it is to be assumed that it would have other characteristics: it would be more extensive and milder and would demean men without tormenting them," *Ibid.* p. 811.

of the system, but from its own virtues. Democratic systems create atoms that lack social consistency. They tend to withdraw from all that is the common and public good. Unbeknownst to them, they generate, along with a welfare system, a despotic system as well. Tocqueville writes:

> "Let us imagine under what new aspects despotism could be produced in the world: I see an innumerable crowd of like and equal men who do nothing but revolve about themselves, in order to procure small and vulgar pleasures with which they satiate their souls. Each of these men lives on his own and is as if estranged from the destiny of all the others... Above them stands an immense and tutelary power, which alone takes charge of securing for them the enjoyment of goods and watching over their fate. It is meticulous, systematic, prescient and mild. It would resemble paternal authority if, like the latter, it had the purpose of preparing man to manhood, while it seeks only to arrest him irrevocably in childhood; it is content for citizens to amuse themselves, so long as they think of nothing but amusement. He gladly works for their happiness, but he wants to be its sole agent and arbiter; he provides for their security, foresees and guarantees their needs, facilitates their pleasures, guides their main affairs, directs their industry, regulates their successions, divides their inheritances, why should he not totally take away from them the trouble of thinking and the toil of living? ".[14]

This ambivalence characterizes democratic systems that facilitate sovereign power albeit with different mechanisms. Tocqueville continues:

> "Our contemporaries are constantly troubled by two conflicting passions: they feel the need to be guided and the desire to remain free. Unable to rid themselves of either of these contrary instincts, they try to satisfy both simultaneously. They imagine a single, tutelary, all-powerful, but citizen-elected power; they combine centralization and popular sovereignty. This gives them some relief. They take comfort from the fact that they are under tutelage, thinking that they have chosen their guardians. Each one endures being held in a noose, because he sees that it is not a man or a class that holds the head, but the people themselves."[15]

---

14 A. de Tocqueville, *La democrazia in America*, Op. cit., p. 812.
15 *Ibid*, p. 813.

Along the same lines, Charles Taylor also refers to this mild despotism that from below, as in globalization, imposes a sovereignty that is more difficult to challenge and criticize than the sovereignty of God or the emperor, which, while absolute, was nevertheless visible and with a sharper and clearer profile. Taylor writes:

> "A society in which human beings are reduced to the condition of individuals 'locked up in their hearts' is one in which few will want to actively participate in self-government. The majority will prefer to stay at home and enjoy the satisfactions of private life, at least as long as the government in office, whatever it may be, produces the means of these satisfactions, and makes a wide distribution of them."[16]

Modern individualism thus serves only to challenge heteronomous authority, but not to take the *governance of* civic life into its own hands. Taylor continues:

> "This raises the danger of a new, specifically modern form of despotism, which Tocqueville calls 'soft' despotism. It will not be a tyranny of terror and oppression, as in times gone by. The government will be mild and paternalistic. It may even retain democratic forms, with periodic elections. But in fact, everything will be governed by an "immense and tutelary power," over which men will have very little control. According to Tocqueville, the only defense is a vigorous political culture that places a high value on participation (at a multiplicity of levels) in the structure of government, and also on voluntary associations. But the atomism of the self-absorbed individual militates against this hypothesis. When participation declines, when the lateral associations that were its vehicles dissolve, the individual citizen is left alone in the face of the giant bureaucratic state, and feels, not unreasonably, powerless. This demotivates the citizen even more, and we thus arrive at the vicious circle of soft despotism."[17]

How does this affect sense-making at an interpretive level? It does this simply by blocking meaning. If meaning is the dialogue between different voices, exchange and confrontation between opposing entities, where there is monolithic identity instead, divine or

---

16 C. Taylor, *The Malaise of modernity...op. cit.,* p. 12.
17 *Ibid*, p. 13.

human, religious or cultural, meaning becomes sum, measurement, calculation. The calculation of instrumental reason necessarily becomes senseless. Let us read Psalm 23 as an experimental moment to rediscover the lost complexity of God-the-Father as the foundation of a new meaning.

3. The Father's Complexity: The "Good Shepherd" and the "Welcoming Housewife"[18]

> Psalm 23
> *Psalm of David.*
> The Lord is my shepherd: nothing I lack.
> He maketh me to lie down in green pastures, He leadeth me beside the still waters.
> He restores my soul, He leads me by paths of righteousness for His name's sake.
> Even when I walk through the valley of the shadow of death, I will fear no evil, for you are with me; your rod and staff give me security.
> For me you set the table, before the eyes of my enemies; you sprinkle my head with oil; my cup overflows.
> Surely, goods and goodness shall accompany me all the days of my life; and I will dwell in the house of the Lord for long days.

We pause now to consider the Father's being from a narrative point of view beginning with Psalm 23. In the previous section we briefly noted that the description of the Father's nature, profile and work is not clear or even complete in the Bible. We saw how this has prompted both Judaism and Christianity to come up with

---

[18] G. Ravasi, *Il libro dei salmi. Commento e attualizzazione*, ("*The Book of Psalms. Commentary and actualization*"), vol. I, (Bologna: Edizioni Dehoniane, 1999), pp. 425-446; L. A. Schökel, C. Carniti, *Salmos*, vol. I, (Navarre: Verbo Divino, 1992), pp. 396-407; D. Bonhoeffer, *Pregare i salmi con Cristo. Il libro di preghiera della Bibbia*, ("*Praying the Psalms with Christ. The prayer book of the Bible*"), (Brescia: Queriniana, 2019), pp. 29-32; B. Janowski, *Konfliktgespräche mit Gott. Eine anthropologie der psalmen*, (Neukircher-Vluyn: Neukirchener Verlag, 2003), pp. 1-35; W. Brueggemann, W. H. Bellinger, Jr., *Psalms*, New Cambridge Bible Commentary, (New York: Cambridge University Press, 2014), pp. 122-126; J. Moltmann, *Nella storia del Dio trinitario...Op. cit.*, pp. 49-64.

further reflections to complete the profile. The Bible proceeds and describes by clues and partial and incomplete hints, almost only suggesting themes but never expounding them in a comprehensive, synoptic and linear way. This way of proceeding depends on the object described, in this case God the Father. It is also a function of the addressees who must be from all ages and cultural affiliations. A further perspective and direction must be given that includes them all and is applicable to various contexts. This kind of discourse, in its fragmentary nature, was sufficient to nourish faith and inform it of what is essential and central. It necessitated the interpretive intervention of the faith community.

The intervention of the faith community, which was made necessary by the partial information about God the Father, simultaneously solved and complicated the challenge. Every interpretation made the figure of God clearer and it also distorted it by interpreting it one-sidedly. The difference between the descriptions deemed heretical about God and the orthodox ones many times was more a matter of proportion than of nature. Even the orthodox confessions were one-sided, though they were shared by many. They tampered with the biblical material about God the Father by tending to make it uniform and homogenous.

Those justified clarifications and necessary specifications of the community on the being of God the Father should have never lost their provisionality and partiality. Yet this is what happened. From being provisional, they became definitive, from partial they became totalizing. A return to the biblical sources becomes necessary. This is not to deny the validity of these actualizations. On the contrary, it is to legitimize them through a flexibilization of them. This is what Psalm 23 will enable us to do. It by itself will not solve the theological problem of who God is, because it will deprive it of necessary specifications. It will nevertheless show us something that no historical theological formula can do without. This is the preservation of the complexity of the Father. Every theological interpretation and formula must know how to safeguard it.

Psalm 23 is a Psalm of David that belongs to the first collection of the Psalter called the *Jahwist* (3-41). The Jahwist collection of psalms includes the first, fourth (90-106) and fifth (107-150) books.

With a total of ninety-nine psalms, it represents two-thirds of the overall collection and it is characterized by the invocation to God by the name of Yahweh.[19] The second collection of psalms, called the *Elohist*,[20] includes the second and third books and is characterized by the invocation to God by the name of Elohim. In the first book of Psalms (3-41), all the Jahwist psalms are attributed to David except Psalm 33. In the fourth and fifth books (90-150), only seventeen are attributed to him. Most of them are anonymous. This diverse naming of God in the psalms alone is neither accidental nor improvised. It is a clear defense of God's complexity. It is an invitation to embrace it.

The name Elohim tends to emphasize God's majesty, power, and transcendence. The name Yahweh tends to emphasize his closeness, vulnerability, and immanence. These specifics are even more evident in the second creation account (Ge 2). This is where Yahweh creates the human being by soiling his hands with mud and through the breath of his intimate breath that reaches directly into the nostrils of the first man and gives him life. In the first creation account (Ge 1), Elohim creates the world transcendentally, from above, from the power of his word alone.

The first book of Psalms (chapters 3-41), to which Psalm 23 belongs, is characterized by certain essential features. First, God is invoked as Yahweh. Second, all the psalms are signed by David. Third, all these opening psalms are individual prayers in contrast to the psalms in the latter part of the psalter, which, while also being Jahwistic psalms, tend to be communal and anonymous prayers. This fact should not mislead us. The complexity of the psalms is not related only to the type of author, individual or collective, or to the liturgical form, lament or hymn. The formal and thematic compactness of Psalm 23 suggests that it is a persuasive psalm. We are not dealing with a lament but with a psalm marked by the confidence that would derive from its simple and direct formula.

This psalm prompts us to elaborate a complex reflection on God the Father. The first thing to note, is that we are dealing with a

---

19   A. Lancellotti, *I Salmi*. Versione, introduzione, note *("The Psalms.* Version, introduction, notes")*,* (Milan: San Paolo, 1987), pp. 71-81.

20   *Ibid*, pp. 289-296.

heterogeneous psalm. It is heterogeneous because it is built not on a single metaphor but on two. One is the "shepherd," who leads his sheep with heroism and courage. The other is the "housewife" who prepares a table for her diners with care and emotional involvement. Monolithism is thus broken by the use of these two different metaphors. One of them refers to a context outside of the home to talk about God (the shepherd metaphor). The other refers to a context inside the home (table) to introduce a different discourse about God. Psalm 23 is a psalm that makes possible the sense, not only the literary sense, but especially the ontological sense of a differentiated God. Let us pause to consider this dual scenario.

4. *"The Heroism" of the Good Shepherd*[21]

This psalm represents a great page in the Bible and in the history of Christianity because it has instilled peace and consolation in the hearts of all those who have approached it. It has drawn them to a friendly God and his gentle and empathetic character. God is described here as a kind and comforting shepherd who takes the time to devote himself to his sheep with care and passion, leading them into the green and soft meadows and quenching their thirst at abundant fountains of water at the most crucial moments of their journey. The "good shepherd" prevents his sheep from being overwhelmed by the aggressiveness, unpredictability and rawness of the dangers and threats sown along the way. He also instills in them a feeling of tranquility and confidence right in the midst of the recurring vicissitudes of life.

Behind the gentleness and goodness of the "good shepherd," the metaphor presupposes something more important that common reading has too often overlooked. This is the contrasting profile of a shepherd who is courageous and ready for action, without fear or dread, even a little reckless. A reliable shepherd could not behave outside the home, exposed to the elements, in the woods or in the mountains, as he would behave inside the home in the tranquility

---

21   G. Ravasi, *Il libro dei salmi, Op. cit.*, pp. 434-437.

of his living room or in the familiarity offered by his kitchen. At home, one is relaxed and does not wear fancy clothes. Everything is familiar and cozy. Dangers and threats are not introduced on purpose or intentionally sown in the halls to harm those who live there.

Outside the home is a different story. One must dress differently; one must wear the appropriate shoes, possess the necessary tools to protect one's sheep. One must have eyes wide open and have constant attention. One must be on the alert to perceive the slightest risk, the most insidious danger. This is a different attitude, one of utmost attention, constant vigilance, great responsiveness. All of this is embodied in determined leadership. The "good shepherd" is such not because he is kind and good, almost as if he were trapped in these virtues. On the contrary, the "good shepherd" is good because he is stubborn and obstinate. Everyone knows, enemies and wild beasts alike, that to approach his sheep, to steal or mistreat them, would immediately trigger such a reaction in him as to make him unapproachable. He is a fierce, cunning shepherd; jealous of his sheep, he is a roaring lion. The shepherd appears, in this metaphor, large and majestic. He is the protagonist. The sheep simply have to follow him. They find themselves completely overshadowed by the shepherd's presence, his greatness and prowess, his heroism.

The image of God that this metaphor conveys to us is that of a God who is in control of life and history. He is the Lord and will lead his people to the expected goal. Nothing can stand between his sheep and his plan, which will be realized inexorably by virtue of his mighty hand. The security and tranquility that this psalm describes in believers does not come from their moral prowess or diligence. It depends solely on the heroic trustworthiness of the God of history.

5. *"The Anonymity" of the Cozy Housewife*[22]

The chapter does not stop with the first metaphor. In the second part, a second metaphor is proposed, contrasting with the first. This is that of God as a "welcoming housewife." The strong, visible and

---

[22] G. Ravasi, *Il libro dei salmi, Op. cit.,* pp. 437-438.

heroic masculine role of the first is limited and replaced in this second stanza, by the discreet, generous and anonymous feminine role attributed to him. God in the guise of this "welcoming housewife" does not devote to this her remaining time, a time gap, a pause interval. She gives the best part of her time to prepareng an inviting table to best welcome her guests.

Her intervention is not heroic and exceptional in a time of emergency. Her is a discreet and customary intervention in a regular, daily rhythm of life. To achieve it, she must leverage not only her organizational skills but also her spontaneity, instinct, and creativity, because a real celebration cannot be prepared by hard work or great planning alone. Passion and imagination are needed. The housewife is able to invest energy and time generously, without expecting anything in return. She is unlike many males who bring home the mentality of outside work, characterized by efficiency and profit. Hers is a radical nonprofit attitude: it is pure generosity. She doesn't mind "wasting time" in preparing a delicious food that she knows will be devoured in minutes, and perhaps without even receiving a thank you, as is often the case in our homes.

The housewife enthusiastically and passionately chooses colors, plants, and precious objects to make the atmosphere and sharing of that essential moment pleasant and magical. Above all, she is not focused on herself, self-centeredly, on her heroic act of preparing food. In her anonymous and reserved attitude, she only wants and desires to give and make full and abundant satisfaction to the people around her table. God, in this second metaphor, is not the main protagonist; on the contrary, he is happy to make others, the human beings present at his feast, sitting around his table, the protagonists. He does not think of his house as his property which he must preserve. He thinks of it as an open and inclusive place, offered to all, guests and enemies alike.

God, according to this psalm, is not monolithic. He does not have a single face. This fact is not a matter of inconsistency, but of richness and abundance. A uni-dimensional God, though strong and powerful, would be a poor God. This is the complexity and paradox found in God himself. At the same time and in parallel to this exuberance of images relating to God, there synchronically emerges the presence of a sober God, who under the guise of a discreet but joyful housewife, and portraying himself in the background, rejoices in making his friends the protagonists.

6. From Sheep to Commensal: An Anthropological Metamorphosis[23]

A new image of God, such as the one this psalm conveys to us, cannot remain harmless and inoffensive. It also overwhelms the outline of what human beings are called to be. This psalm also has a double metaphorical language to describe what human beings are to become. We are sheep, says the first metaphor. It does not belong to us to choose the way, the strategy, the place to rest. All this is entrusted to the shepherd. We need only to listen and follow, sometimes without even understanding, moved only by complete trust in the shepherd. This fact seems scandalous and disturbing for a rationalist and individualist mentality as ours is today. For the modern gospel of our day, no one can ever follow without understanding. The metaphor presses, provokes, disturbs. Sheep are not characterized by their ability to reason, but by their instinctive reaction of trust. This means that at least at one level, which has its importance in any case, the essence of religion is not rational or voluntarist. It is attitudinal. It is made up of trust and a prerational involvement of one's whole being.

The second metaphor requires the sheep to undergo a radical, surprising and unexpected transformation. Believers must learn to be sheep, but not to remain sheep. The sheep experience a metamorphosis, a complete transfiguration. In the second metaphor, the sheep become people. They become honored guests of the God-homemaker, who motivates them and requires courage from them to speak, to think, to share, to celebrate. The housewife asks them to go beyond an attitude of pure obedience and become courageously creative through imagination. The transformed sheep begin to talk, to propose, to create, to the point of enriching God himself. The housewife is curious, attentive, involved in what her sheep, having

---

23 G. Ravasi, *Il libro dei salmi, Op. cit.*, pp. 425-446.

become human beings, man and woman, can offer her. They are now the protagonists, in God and through his stimulating presence. The housewife listens and is enriched by what her guests create. Human beings, according to this psalm, are not monolithic. They never have a single face and in this they reflect the image of their own God. This psalm emphasizes, in parallel with the description of God, the complexity, paradox and contradictions of every human reality, of churches and individuals. This is something which our theology should never forget.

This anthropological metamorphosis affects the creation of meaning in several ways. First, the sheep is characterized by obedience but the diner, with the inter-acting presence of the guests, is characterized by the creation and sharing of multiple senses: poetic, humorous, moral, emotional, ideational. The sheep who becomes a person is someone who plays with senses. It is sensible. It receives and produces new senses. It metabolizes and dares to introduce unique senses by virtue of its creativity. The possibility of new senses emerges with the metamorphosis of the shepherd into a housewife and the metamorphosis of the sheep into a guest.

Second, as reiterated in the previous sections, meaning is not only a linguistic issue. More fundamentally it is an anthropological experience. Sense, and sense-making, require a ferryman, because sense is not descriptive of what is there, but of what can be there. Sense is not tautological. It thrives on the risk of saying something new about the world and life. Sense is always actualization made by someone. The same thing happens in the field of ethics: the ameliorative intervention of action finds its limitation if one does not take the side of the ethical agent. Only if the ethical agent is "happy" will the action it gives birth to be likely to be a successful action. Similarly, in hermeneutics, the nobility and greatness of meaning can only be guaranteed by the agent giving birth to that meaning. If the agent is poor, it is most likely that the sense will also be poor. Anthropological metamorphosis is essential to the improvement of meaning.

7. "The Exuberant and Sobering Love of the Father: The Contingency of Meaning

(2 Co 13:13)[24]

At this point, after amazingly describing God and the human being, this psalm reminds us that it is theology itself that comes out revolutionized by this reading. Theology cannot remain the same if man and God have changed. A healthy theology must have a differentiated spectrum of tools, categories, perspectives and languages.

While the first metaphor, that of the "good shepherd," *is a* theocentric metaphor, the second is anthropocentric. In the first God is at the center, in the second at the center is the human being. This change of the human is possible only if we perceive a different face in God himself, that of the "welcoming housewife." In the first metaphor the heroism of faith predominates, but it is not necessarily the case that Christianity has sinned more through negligence than through the impetuosity of faith. Christianity that refers only to the heroic God has unfortunately sown history with excessive certainty and religious dirigisme and intolerance and destruction.

God is also able to be a happy woman, able to think, feel and act in the shadow and without leading. In essence, God is capable of caring and not only leading. As a housewife, she is able to add to linear intelligence the benefit of circular intelligence. Being capable of care means going from things to people, from programming to intuition. It is to be able to introduce decentralization from strategies to people and from one's self to the people one cares for. That is why, in the second metaphor, in this exercise of decentralization that care implies, the evaluation of the event, process and outcome is not given to the housewife but to the diners. God hands over the evaluation of himself not to himself but to humans.

---

[24] R. P. Martin, *2 Corinthians,* Word Biblical Commentary, (Dallas: Word Incorporated, 1991), pp. 490-507; H.-D. Wendland, *Le lettere ai Corinzi,* (*"The Letters to the Corinthians"),* (Brescia: Paideia, 1976), pp. 472-476; F. Lang, *The Letters to the Corinthians,* Paideia, Brescia 2004, pp. 446-448; E. Best, *2 Corinthians,* (Torino: Claudiana, 2009), pp. 143-145.

This is the essence of love that, according to Paul, distinguishes God the Father. "The love of God the Father ... be with you all" (2 Co 13:13). In this classic Trinitarian formula, love is not the ability to love, not a merit badge, not a virtue of one's character. Love is the transitivity of a gesture, a word, a thought that by decentering us elevates the other. If God the Father is like this, the Bible as his word cannot be any less. The Bible, through its sobriety and complexity, aims, like the Father, not to make itself great, but rather those who read it. This is the essence of a biblical hermeneutic of paradox. Between the complexity of the Creator God and the complexity of the Bible as the word of God, there is a close relationship of similarity and interpenetration.

In the specific case of the first person of the Trinity, the Father Creator (which was the subject of reflection in this first chapter), we asked ourselves: how does the Father make possible the meaning of life and, consequently, also the meaning of a text that tells us about human life and God's life? The answer is through his "passion," his love. The title of this chapter is "The Passion of the Father and the Possibility of Meaning. It indicates that it is only the passion of God interacting in history, and not the apathy of God as a supreme being, that breaks the mechanicity of exchanges between God and us humans, and makes meaning possible.

The possibility of meaning arises from an ontological rupture given by God's creation. If God had not created there would have been only ontological tautology and communicative tautology, not new and living sense. Meaning always arises from a rupture, a differentiation, and creation represents the rupture of the continuity of God's being. God's being, in creation, welcomes and creates the surprise of another being who is the creature, the created. The possibility of meaning, as new meaning, thus requires an anthropology of the freedom of a new being and a theology of the risk of a Creator who decides to create new beings.

This can be perceived in the action of the Creator Father through two characteristics of the Creator that then parallel the two characteristics that, in our hypothesis, also mark the word of God (the Bible), and which are "exuberance" and "sobriety."

a. *The Father's Exuberance as Contingency*

First, we want to reaffirm that creation is an "exuberant" act of God. This fact is neither immediate nor obvious because the idea of a solemn God who creates has been imposed in theology transversely and now has force of a dogma. How, indeed, can creation be the result of levity? The common answer is, "No, it cannot be"; on the contrary, creation is God's most solemn act. Already Heraclitus, in Fragment 52, gave a different version of the origin of the world.

"Eternity is a child playing with tiles: of a child is the kingdom."[25]

This means that origin, according to Heraclitus, has the characteristics of exuberant play. Moltmann retorts by saying, in the wake of Heraclitus, that actually creation must be read in an aesthetic key, as the moment of greatest joy, lightness and freedom, not only of God, but also of the first creatures who, reproducing God's lightness, experience creation as exuberant and liberating play.[26]

The Father's exuberant joy not only marks the work of creation, and distinguishes all his work. Everything the Father does expresses this exuberant joy. Even his Word is exuberant, confident and joy-filled. As Isaiah writes in chapter 55:10,11:

> "As rain and snow come down from heaven and do not return to it without watering the earth, without fertilizing it and making it sprout, that it may give seed to the sower and bread to eat, so it is of my word, which went forth from my mouth: it does not return to me empty, without having accomplished what I will and brought to fruition that for which I sent it."

---

25 Heraclitus, *Fragments*, Francesco Fronterotta (ed), (Rizzoli, Milan 2013), fragment 52.
26 J. Moltmann speaks of Adam and Eve as "the first creatures released from the game of creation" (*Die ersten Freigelassene der Schöpfung*). See the whole of chapter III of the book, J. Moltmann, *Sul gioco. Saggi sulla gioia della libertà e sul piacere del gioco*, (*"On Play. Essays on the Joy of Freedom and the Pleasure of Play"*), (Brescia: Queriniana, 1971).

This exuberance of the Father reaches its climax in a dramatic moment in the ministry of the Son that will end with the cross. At that moment of handing over the mission to the Son, which implies for God the Father yielding the baton and stepping aside to make the Son the protagonist, at that very moment the Father expresses his greatest joy. In this particular episode, in the version of Matthew 3:17, the exuberant Father says of his own Son, "This is my beloved Son, in whom I am well pleased."

We are confronted here with an exuberance that goes so far as to abandon the Father's sacred composure. In his participatory enthusiasm, the Father is out of himself. He lets himself go and be carried away by the joy of the event and shouts in his exuberance, "This is my beloved Son." God's greatness and the power of his passion reside in his willingness to appear as an unhinged God. This capacity to invest in joy and to allow himself to be traversed by it is present from the very beginning, in the foundational act that is the act of creation. In creation the Father is out of himself, overwhelmed by the joy of creating beings with whom to enter into a dialogue of love. Creation is an act of exuberance and trust in others.

Creation does not happen out of mechanical and automatic necessity or even boredom. God's exuberant character is manifested in his biophilia that drives him to create life and to create it not through the security of a mechanism that he will completely control, but through the risk that each new life implies and sets in motion. God is not a self-folded being. "Creation," as opposed to the concept of "Emanation", wherein divinity only prolongs itself in the new being that is born and of which it has full disposition, implies the birth of a true otherness. While subordinate, creation cannot be arbitrarily reabsorbed without committing an ontological crime of arrogance. The Creator's exuberance is embodied in the introduction of "contingency." The cosmos, understood as a necessary reality by other religions, in which the visible grandeur of their deities is manifested, is instead made a contingent reality by the Creator.

Creation is freedom and exuberance of the Creator and this involves taking a necessary risk. This risk commits God to respect the autonomous life that is being born, of which God cannot arbitrarily dispose. Every new, therefore autonomous, ending created life needs an argument, a judgment, an explanation from God. Every new life is a place and a reason for questioning God himself, "Where did that life go?" Creation implies and sets all this in motion. The same does not happen in the world of emanation, where divinity is accountable to no one. By virtue of its very nature, emanation does not create. It only prolongs out of itself something that is ultimately only appearance. God's life-creating exuberance is not just cheerful and uninhibited exuberance. It is responsible exuberance, willing to interact with the other than itself in full mutual recognition and respect.

In creation God introduces contingency, which is a guarantee not only of a possible humanity but also of a possible meaning. Sense without contingency and without risk is no longer sense but pure calculation. Sense emerges when there is risk. Risk that something is not there. When something is there by necessity, sense is gone.

b. *The Father's Sobriety as Contraction*

Besides possessing the trait of exuberance, creation is a "sober" act of God. Everything God does He does with discretion. The Father works behind the scenes, as a guarantor not a protagonist, so that human beings can flourish. If the Father always occupied the whole stage, he would become a cumbersome and hypertrophic figure. He would paralyze all human initiative. The possibility of human action depends on God's ability to stand aside, thus on his sobriety. In Psalm 1's description of the "blessed one," comparing him to a luxuriant tree, the Father's presence does not disappear as a guaranteeing presence but becomes a presence in the shadows, a presence that retreats and hides. Psalm 1:3, in fact, says that

> "He shall be like a tree planted by streams, which yields its fruit in its season, and whose foliage does not wither; and all that he does, he shall prosper."

While God is mentioned explicitly in v. 2 through reference to his law, it seems that v. 3 is instead just a description of man flourishing. We actually find an allusion to God in the metaphor of the stream. The Father does not disappear, but he does not encumber. In the tree scene, the Father is a secondary figure, a side element that works in the function of the human's prominence.

God can back off. John says in his Gospel:

> "Moreover, the Father judges no one, but has entrusted all judgment to the Son, so that all may honor the Son as they honor the Father. Whoever does not honor the Son does not honor the Father who sent him" (Jn. 5:22-23).

This sobriety is even more visible in creation. Contrary to what is commonly thought, creation is not a monolithic act of a powerful God. It is a mixed act of God, where power and vulnerability coexist. There is a more loaded registry of vulnerability behind the obvious manifestation of power, as it appears especially in the "Elohist" version of creation (in Genesis chapter 1), where God creates, atypically when compared to traditional cosmogonies, through the word alone as a sign of his immeasurable power. If that new being is to be other and not a mere extension of God, that other being must receive and have its own specific and particular space.

Without that space and place of its own, that new being would be no one. It would be a mere fiction, an idea, a prototype, but not a real being. God, in creating a new being other than himself, must "surrender" a part of his divine space. Strictly speaking, God is no longer "omnipresent" in the sense of exercising full and total control over all the space in the universe. Over that space that belongs to that other and created being, God has only an indirect prerogative. By creating he has delegated to that new being the management of his own space.

Creation is thus an act of "sobriety" through which the Creator renounces the fullness of his prerogatives in order to give real and concrete space to his creatures. Creation more fundamentally presents itself, for all intents and purposes, not as an act of power but as an act of humility. It is a true kenotic act.[27] *Kenosis* is not only a Christological act and does not only have Christ as its protagonist.

---

27 From the Greek word κένωσις, "to empty oneself, to strip off." The most representative verse of *chenosis* is from Philippians 2:7 in which "emptying" (lowering) is applied to Jesus in his incarnation. "But he

Kenosis is a Trinitarian act that corresponds to this double movement which distinguishes the entire Trinity. Each of its persons is able to "affirm itself" (exuberance), and "empty itself" (sobriety) to allow the emergence of the other. If the Creator were not capable of *Kenosis*, the Son would hardly be. *Kenosis* is thus an ontological movement of shrinking of self that is visible, prior to the incarnation of the Son, in the creation of the Father.

This is Isaak Luria's reading of creation which is known as the doctrine of *Zimzum*.[28] This is a Hebrew term that means the "concentration," the "contraction," the "retreating" of God into an attitude of humility and *Kenosis*, in order to truly interact with humanity within the covenant framework. Gershom Scholem[29] took this Isaak Luria's version of this concept and elevated it to one of the fundamental concepts of Judaism. He used this kenotic version of creation[30] as a corrective to the Jewish rational doctrine of the Middle Ages, as expressed for example in the 12th century by Maimonides.[31]

The "contraction" of God's being, according to A. Heschel, is present in creation and in all of God's action as a condition of the covenant. Kabbalah also took up some themes from this perspective. The doctrine of Schekinah is one example among others. In this doctrine, as in the doctrine of creation, God is described in his "self-limitation" that makes possible the relationship with his people. Three concepts coexist in the Schekinah. They are the present "indwelling" of God, the "anticipation" of the glory of the coming Messiah, and the "lowering" (*chenosis*) of the Eternal.[32]

---

stripped (*ekenosen*) himself, taking the form of a servant, becoming like men."
28 Cf. J. Moltmann, *Trinità e regno di Dio... Op. cit.*, pp. 120-123.
29 G. Scholem, *Die jüdische Mystik in ihren Hauptströmungen*, (Frankfurt: Suhrkamp, 2009), pp. 285 ff; G. Scholem, *Schöpfung aus Nichts und Selbstverschränkung Gottes*, (Eranos-Jahrbuch, 1956), pp. 87-119.
30 G. Scholem, *Concetti fondamentali dell'Ebraismo*, (*"Fundamental Concepts of Judaism"*), (Milan: Marietti 1820), 1986, pp. 43-73.
31 *Ibid*, pp. 4,21.
32 A.J. Heschel, *Il messaggio dei profeti*, (*"The Message of the Prophets"*), (Rome: Borla, 1993), pp. 221-230. Cf. J. Moltmann, *Trinità e regno di Dio... Op. cit.* pp. 36,37.

c. *The Contingency of Meaning*

This "shrinking" (sobriety) of the Creator is the condition for the existence of the other and the possibility of meaning. "Exuberance" prompts the Creator to desire the other and its "sobriety" makes it possible. Without the other, there is no meaning: the other is indispensable for meaning. Sense is therefore not given in a monolithic, closed, tautological system. Sense presupposes otherness, something new that is, however, inseparable from the actual presence of the other as creation guarantees. Creation is the introduction of a concrete "other" for God. In this perspective, meaning is given only when there is an other. The other is given only when there is a narrowing of my own identity that makes it possible. Creation, then, makes sense possible. It is for all intents and purposes a creation of sense. The passion of the Father, through the risk of creation, in the investment in the other, downsizing his own identity, makes sense possible.

CHAPTER X
THE GRACE OF THE SON[1] AND THE GRATUITOUSNESS OF MEANING

As we did with God the Father in the previous chapter, we shall try in this chapter to read the complexity that characterizes the second person of the Trinity, the Son,[2] in connection with the complexity expressed in the Bible. We find ourselves in both cases before an interplay and tension between affirmation and flexibility, word and silence, action and passion, exposure and retraction, "ambivalence" and "paradox," "exuberance" and "sobriety." These are ways of expressing two characteristics of any complex identity that breaks with the linear, atomistic and unidirectional logic and replaces it with the circular, relational, multidimensional and multidirectional logic that typical of complex systems.[3]

In the case of the second person of the Trinity, we will ask: How does the Son make possible the meaning of life and consequently also the meaning of a text that tells us about human life and God's life? The answer is: through his "grace." The title of this chapter is "The Son's grace and the gratuitousness of meaning." It indicates that it is only the Son's grace that, through forgiveness, sets in

---

1   V.-M. Kärkkäinen, *Christ and Reconciliation. A Constructive Christian Theology for a Pluralistic World,* vol. 1, (Grand Rapids: Eerdmans, 2013), pp. 9-28.

2   J. Moltmann, *La via di Gesù Cristo. Cristologia in dimensioni messianiche, ("The Way of Jesus Christ. Christology in Messianic Dimensions"),* (Brescia: Queriniana, 1993), pp. 125-133; J. Moltmann, *Nella storia del Dio trinitario...Op. Cit.,* pp. 65-80; J. Moltmann, *La via di Gesù Cristo... Op. cit.,* pp. 91-174; O. Cullmann, *The Christology of New Testament,* (Philadelphia: The Westminster Press, 1963), pp. 1-10.

3   G. Gembillo, A. Anselmo, *Filosofia della complessità ("Philosophy of Complexity"),* (Firenze: Le Lettere, 2017), pp. 19-33.

motion again a relationship between God and the human that had become jammed. It breaks with the determinism of guilt and sin. It is the Son's forgiveness that revives the aspiration for life and thus the possibility of meaning, for meaning is life-affirming. It is the Son's grace that recovers meaning and gives it a new opportunity.

Every sense, in the natural course of its evolution, goes through a blockage, its jamming. There is never a linear sense. Calculus is linear by nature: it is automatic, it has no hesitancy or interference, no vicissitudes that interrupt its progressive and necessary manifestation. Sense is always threatened, stumped, hesitant, partial, and sometimes failed. Sense is always by nature a redeemed, forgiven sense. It is a resilient sense. Every sense is always a sense reborn. The jamming of sense is not only a possibility, but a reality. Sense is not necessary. It is the contingency of sense that makes its failure possible. Failure is possible. Sense can become senseless; however, right there, where sense has jammed irreversibly, grace redeems it.

Sense is always a sense that, through grace, one has overcome a failure, a serious threat, a fixation, a compulsion. The reborn sense is a sense reconciled by the grace of the Son. There is no sense without grace. Sense is not an achievement, the product of an equation. It is not even the summation or multiplication of what is there, a calculation that empowers the existing. Grace reaches us by arising out of the unexpected. It is manifestation, not production of the self. The possibility of meaning, as new meaning, requires an anthropology of vulnerability and a soteriology of grace, from the perspective of a reconciled life.

1. *Christological Positivism: "Christocentrism"*

We can begin to observe the complexity of Christ's being from the anomalies that have emerged to deny and dismantle it. This scenario is somewhat different from what we would expect because Christology can be warped by subtraction or by overloading it.

"Arianism"[4] is a typical anomaly by subtraction. It ascribes less divinity to Christ than He is entitled to. "Monophysitism"[5] is a typical anomaly by overload because it grants Him more divinity than He is entitled to. Christological deformations by overload have prevailed over subtractive ones. A set of cross-mechanisms that had to do with the relationship between Christ and the Holy Spirit caused this. Christian pneumatology has been deformed through a subtractive or "deficit" mechanism because Western Christianity has failed to conceive of the Holy Spirit, in theory and even less in practice, as equal to the other two persons of the Trinity.[6] The complexity of Christ has been tampered mainly by an overloading mechanism, by an "over-investment" in him. This gave rise to a deformation that has gone beyond ancient monophysitism. It has been embodied in the transversal Christocentrism of Christianity today.

Christianity in general, and modern Christianity in particular, have become strongly "Christocentric."[7] While the monophysitist Christocentrism of the early church still remained an enchanted Christocentrism, i.e., full of mystery, modern Christocentrism is instead pragmatic and without mystery. Moreover, this strong Christocentrism is not only visible in Protestantism, but also in medieval Catholicism. It is true that, in the old debate between Christology and Ecclesiology, Protestants have always criticized the subtle subordination of Christology to Ecclesiology that occurred in Catholicism very early, but continued contextually until its most

---

4   Doctrine of Alexandrian Arius (4th cent.) that denied the divinity of Christ, as he would not be of the same nature as the Father; condemned at the Council of Nicaea (325).
5   Theological doctrine that denies the dual nature, divine and human, of Christ, recognizing in him the absolute presence and predominance of the divine nature alone. This doctrine was elaborated in the 5th century by the Byzantine monk Eutyches, and condemned as heretical by the Council of Chalcedon (451), which proclaimed in Christ the hypostasis of the divine nature with the human.
6   Western Christianity has always given expression to a pneumatological subordinationism that modern Christianity has even radicalized.
7   This is, for example, the opinion of Geshé. A. Geshé, *Dio per pensare il Cristo, ("God to Think Christ")*, (Milan: San Paolo, 2003), pp. 20-27.

renewed and best version, in Vatican II.[8] On the other hand, as we suggested earlier, even in Protestantism one can legitimately wonder whether it is really Christology that predominates or rather the individualist anthropology that acts as a go-between in defending the centrality of Christ. Each community ultimately develops its own way of tampering, albeit unwittingly, with the universal reach of Christ.

The question remains whether in the end this is actually the means of exalting his identity (the church for Catholics or the individual for Protestants) that finally prevails to the detriment of Christ himself. Beyond this possible drift, which acts in a more hidden way, we can certainly say that all Christianity, ancient and modern, Catholic or Protestant, with different modes and paths, has become strongly Christocentric. It could not have been otherwise. Christian consciousness, not only in its self-assertion but also in its revolutionary missionary thrust, was founded from the very beginning on the power of Christ, risen and raised as *Kyrios*. Christianity could not have been born with a weak Christology; however, the necessary Christic affirmation got out of hand and stiffened into an imperial Christocentrism. From the start, it has created exclusion and separation.

The Christology of the two natures could have been a sign of discovering and maintaining the complexity of the Christian faith. It was not. This monolithically Christ-centered Christocentrism as *Kyrios*, reinforced from the fourth century onward by imperial support for the pursuit of strong symbols, dismantled the complexity of the Christian faith. This caused three negative effects.

The first effect occurred at the ecclesiological level in Christianity's break with Judaism. It was a Christocentrism that had become radical. It thought that it could split the relationship between the Christian Christ and the Old Testament. Although the break with Judaism had

---

8 Cf. the Constitution, "Lumen Gentium" of the Second Vatican Council and Vittorio Subilia's commentary on it. Cf. V. Subilia, *La nuova cattolicità del Cattolicesimo. Una valutazione protestante del Concilio vaticano Secondo*, (*"The New Catholicity of Catholicism. A Protestant Evaluation of the Second Vatican Council"*), (Turin: Claudiana, 1967), pp. 5-75.

various causes and depends on various conditioning, the euphoria, which later became arrogance, of Christian Christocentrism fostered and radicalized it. In early Christianity, there coexisted, albeit with tensions, misunderstandings and clashes, a Jewish-Christian community and a pagan-Christian community. This indirectly prompted Christianity to reflect on the necessary openness and flexibility of its own identity and to keep its relationship and dialogue with Judaism firm.

This dialogue was maintained from a biblical-hermeneutical point of view, despite some lone voices urging otherwise (Marcion). At an ecclesiological level, it simply ceased to exist in two ways. For one thing, Christianity stopped looking at Judaism with respect and engaging in dialogue with it. In addition, within Christianity itself, the Jewish-Christian community, that served as a stimulus for memory by pointing to the continuing need for dialogue with Judaism, disappeared.

Christocentric Christianity could have maintained complexity if it had preserved, with the tension and humility that this implies, dialogue with Judaism. Unfortunately, one cannot even console oneself by saying that separation from Judaism was only the banner of a minority, led, at times, by dubious and radical figures like Marcion.[9] All of Christianity in the early centuries went in the direction of its estrangement from Judaism. With this there was also, for example, the abandonment of the Sabbath.[10] This separation gradually became structural and radicalized. It took radical religious and political forms, together with more nefarious and more perverse forms, such as anti-Judaism and anti-Semitism. From time to time, these came down heavily on the Jews in the name of Christ. The main cause of turning away from Judaism, at least nominally, was

---

9 Marcion, a second-century Greek bishop, not only put the New Testament in antithesis to the Old Testament, but in his ideal biblical canon, he heavily retouched the New Testament and completely erased the Old Testament.
10 See in this regard the work of Samuel Bacchiocchi, *From Sabbath to Sunday. A Historical Investigation of the Rise of the Sunday Observance in Early Christianity*, (Rome: The Pontifical Gregorian University Press, 1977), pp. 11-25.

the accusation that it had rejected Christ, thus its structural and implicit anti-Christocentrism.

The great theological paradigm shift that took over and was introduced with Protestantism in the 16th century, once again in the name of a renewed Christocentrism, did not correct this reductive drift to the detriment of the complexity of the faith. Neither Luther[11] nor centuries later Arnold von Harnack did this.[12] Von Harnack catalogued the Old Testament not as a set of false or useless books. He saw them as a set of irrelevant books in the view of the radically new and innovative Christ of the gospels. He did this in the name of typical modern Christian Christocentrism.[13]

The second effect of this uncontrolled Christocentrism occurred at a theological level. Christian Christocentrism did not act as a guarantor of complexity, as might have been expected. It was a reductive element of the Christian faith itself, as Yves Congar already lamented.[14] Christology itself became unbalanced through its functionalization with the arrival of Protestantism. Compared to the speculations of the first centuries and the Middle Ages on the being of Christ, Protestant Christology brought a legitimate and beneficial breath of freshness, immediacy and lightening. This was visible, for example, in the classic formula used by Philip Melanchthon, *Christum*

---

11   Cf. M. Luther, *Degli ebrei e delle loro menzogne,* ("*Of the Jews and Their Lies*"), (Turin: Einaudi, 2008).
12   Cf. A. Von Harnack, *Marcione. Il vangelo del Dio straniero,* ("*Marcion. The gospel of the foreign God*"), (Turin: Marietti 1820, 2008).
13   Adolf Von Harnack constructed his argument not in contrast but by starting from Marcion and suggesting that at the limit the Old Testament books, in their relative pedagogical and historical value, were possibly part of the apocryphal books. A. Von Harnack, *Marcione...Op. cit.*, pp. 6-15.
14   Yves Congar is a critic of this widespread Christocentrism not because he disagrees with the emphasis on this central element of the Christian faith, but rather because, through a one-sided emphasis on it, other dimensions of the faith that guarantee the health of Christology itself come to disappear. Cf. Y. Congar, *Jésus-Christ,* (Paris : Edition du Cerf, 1965), p. 12.

cognoscere hoc est beneficia eius cognoscere.[15] With the passage of time this Christological functionalism became Christological pragmatism. Today this pragmatism is almost uncontainable. It is especially widespread in Protestant evangelicalism but not only there. This pragmatic deformation of Christology has led to the annihilation of differences, tensions, alternatives and asymmetries, within Christology itself. It has taken away its complexity. It has flattened Christology to the overriding and ubiquitous category of salvation, as we shall later try to describe. The category of salvation has absorbed all other Christological categories. It hides Christology behind the unstoppable force of Soteriology.

The third effect occurred at a sociocultural level. Christian Christocentrism failed to serve as a mediating tool vis-à-vis the non-Christian world in maintaining intra-Christian and inter-human complexity. It did this only transiently for proselytizing purposes. It conceived the Christian churches not as an embodiment of God's kingdom but as the only embodiment of it. Its form and articulation were imposed by divine mandate on all peoples, even by force, with a view to their good and eternal salvation.

We know that the backbone of the true Christian faith is not Christian ecclesiocentrism disguised as Christocentrism. It is only a decentralized and centrifugal Christocentrism in the direction of the kingdom of God. It was conceived and announced only as an inclusive and polycentric reality by Jesus himself in the gospels. Christian Christocentrism is justifiable only from this perspective. This is not the Christological version, ancient or modern, Catholic or Protestant, that has been predominant in history. This kind of inclusive Christocentrism articulated in the Gospels did not occur in ancient and medieval Christianity and not even with Protestantism. It happened even less so with the explosion of culturally biased and purely proselytizing missionary movements. It does not happen today in the desperate rush of churches which are focused only on trading their survival through myopic rejection of an unstoppable

---

15 Ph. Melanchton, *Loci Communes*, 1521, Werke, R. (Gütersloh: Stupperich, 1952), p. II, 7. Cf. J. Moltmann, *La via di Gesù Cristo...Op. Cit.*, p. 75.

post-confessionalism.[16] The only religious form capable of shifting emphasis from partial (denominational) goods to a common good is the one reflecting the universal and inclusive perspective of God's kingdom.

This failed mediation with respect to the non-Christian world, in a sociocultural sense as well, also depended on the fact that Christian Christocentrism grew and became stronger at the expense of the "power of the Spirit."[17] In Christocentric Christianity, Christ has obscured the Spirit, making it purely subsidiary to his program. This has produced a double impoverishment. To begin with, Christianity has become ecclesiocentric and folded in on itself. In addition, the element that could have limited this drift and made it culturally inclusive with a universal vocation, that is, the Spirit, has been downgraded. It has been made to become the guarantor of this closure, with the clear subordination of Pneumatology to this kind of centripetal Christocentrism.

---

16 On the inevitability of the demise of religious denominations as socio-theological phenomena Luca Diotallevi has elaborated an incisive reflection and analysis. L. Diotallevi, *Fine corsa. La crisi del cristianesimo come religione confessionale*, (*"End of the Race. The Crisis of Christianity as a Confessional Religion"*), (Bologna: Edb, 2017), pp. 5-63. Diotallevi's analysis does not stop at the theological implications of this demise. Christian confessionalism is certainly dependent on a strong Christocentrism. If the former decays, this cannot leave the latter unscathed and intact. Thus indirectly the demise of Christian confessionalism, at least in Europe, runs on par with a crumbling of typical centripetal Christian Christocentrism. This does not mean the end of either Christianity or even less of Christ, it only serves to correct that centripetal Christocentrism with a centrifugal one, as Jesus himself outlined in the gospels.

17 According to the title J. Moltmann gives to his reflection on the Christian church. Cf. J. Moltmann, *La chiesa nella forza dello Spirito. Contributo per una ecclesiologia messianica*, (*"The Church in the Power of the Spirit. Contribution to a Messianic Ecclesiology"*), (Brescia: Queriniana, 1976).

2. Christocentrism and Pathologizing

Perhaps it is not this secularized Christocentrism[18] and ally of the strong powers, that continues to exert a cross-cutting influence in our world today. It is instead, much more likely, that moral and psychological Christocentrism, in its soteriological version, which the West has internalized and which is embodied in what Ruth Benedict[19] calls a "society of guilt,"[20] which sees in every human action an error to be corrected. Even when the notion of sin has been completely unhinged and made obsolete, its secularization, in the category of error, has flourished and multiplied. Never mind that in error the sense of seriousness has diminished because error is a purely human event. No longer something one experiences before a judging God, the impact of error has multiplied.

Although the sense of seriousness was greater in sin as a relational event involving God, it tended to be more circumscribed because it was limited to the spiritual realm. When secularization turned sin into error, this relational dimension was lost, along with the intensity of guilt. Error ended up being broadened to the entire spectrum of human life. This increased its effect because it became more widespread and more chronic.

---

18 The connection between Christocentrism and modern individualism (*Buffered Self*), which we assume in this section, is strongly suggested by Taylor, albeit from a cultural rather than theological reflection. Taylor writes, "Buffer, discipline and individuality not only interlock and mutually reinforce, but their coming can be seen as largely driven by the process of Reform, as I have been describing it here. The drive to a new form of religious life, more personal, committed, devoted; more Christocentric; one which will largely replace the older forms which centred on collective ritual," in, C. Taylor, *A Secular Age*, (Cambridge: Harvard University Press, 2007), p. 541.

19 Ruth Benedict, in her book *"The Chrysanthemum and the Sword"*, describes Japan in contrast to American society. Japanese society is described as a culture of *shame (shame culture)*, while American society is described as a culture of guilt (*guilt culture*).

20 R. Benedict, *Il crisantemo e la spada. Modelli di cultura giapponesi*, (*"The Chrysanthemum and the Sword. Patterns of Japanese Culture"*), (Rome: Laterza, 2010), pp. 10-29.

Ruth Benedict says that "shame societies" dispose of discomfort by externally metabolizing it to others. "Guilt societies" internalize discomfort through a process of introspection. Guilt is more suffered than chosen because in individualist societies the other simply disappeared. Guilt becomes not a virtue but a destiny. I am forced to impute responsibility to myself. I cannot impute the error to someone from whom I have detached myself and of whom I have lost track.

A "society of guilt" is a society of internal discomfort. More importantly, it is an individualist society. In addition to assuming discomfort as one's own, one assumes it individually. Guilt is typically an individualistic process. It disassociates me from others and forces me to experience guilt only in the personal register. Although this seems far from Christocentrism, and in some ways it is, soteriological Christocentrism and guilt have two things in common. One is the strong sense of internal discomfort. The other is this individual and personal register that Christianity, by virtue of its Christology, has opened and inaugurated since its inception. Individualism and guilt are structural to Christian Christology. This is especially so in the further developed Christocentrism which by various ways we find in the secularized Western societies of late modernity.

Secularized Christocentrism, by insisting on culpability, leads to excessive cultural purism. Society wants to save individuals from every error. As a result, common situations, existential asymmetries, anthropological uncertainties, decision-making ambivalences are pathologized. Everything must be univocal, functional and effective. Our society is, according to James Hillman,[21] a society that pathologizes normal life. Although secularized guilt turned into discomfort into needs to be alleviated, secularized soteriology expands it through the cult of performance. As Byung Chul Han points out,[22] compromise with achievement, a typical feature of modern society that discovers rational organization in view of certain outcomes, was in early modernity imposed from outside in what Foucault called "a

---

21 J. Hillmann, *Revisione della psicologia...*Op. Cit., pp. 111-201.
22 B. -C. Han, *La società della stanchezza*, ("The *Burn out Society"),* (Rome: Nottetempo, 2012), pp. 5,6.

disciplinary society." The discipline required, from heteronomous became autonomous. God no longer imposed it. Human society guaranteed it through its own organizational mechanisms. In the disciplinary society of early modernity, the demand is apparently diluted by the fact that it no longer comes from God and religion. This need is actually diluted for the reason mentioned earlier. It becomes more stringent by virtue of its secularization. It binds the individual in the spiritual area and in all areas of human life. We have in this passage an increase in the pressure on the individual.

This pressure increases even more as we move, according to Byung Chul Han, from a "disciplinary society" to a "performance society."[23] In the disciplinary society, the need, while secularized, still remained, for the most part, external to the individual. In the performance society, the exigency comes from within. The individual has internalized the norm. Even when there is no master, no system that constrains him, he has become the exploiter of himself.

In the performance society, guilt and success have been mixed. This sometimes produces satisfaction, sometimes guilt and depression. In either case, the common traits are the internal discomfort caused by guilt and the individualization of guilt or success. As in classical Christian Christocentrism, individualism and success, individualism and remorse overlap.

3. The Complexity of the Son: "Jesus" and "Emmanuel"[24]

Matthew 1:18-23

> "The birth of Jesus Christ took place in this way. Mary, his mother, had been betrothed to Joseph, and before they had come to be together, she found herself pregnant by the Holy Spirit. Joseph, her husband, who was a righteous man and did not want to expose her to infamy, proposed to leave her secretly."

---

23 *Ibid,* pp. 21-28.
24 J. Gnilka, *Vangelo di Matteo,* (*"Gospel of Matthew"*), vol. I, Theological Commentary on the New Testament, (Brescia: Paideia, 1990), pp. 40-66; R. Fabris, *Matteo,* ("Matthew"), (Roma: Borla, 1996), pp. 53-64; U. Luz, *Studies in Matthew,* (Grand Rapids: Eerdmans, 2005), pp. 83-96.

But while he had these things in his mind, an angel of the Lord appeared to him in a dream, saying, "Joseph, son of David, do not be afraid to take Mary, your wife, with you; for what is begotten in her is from the Holy Spirit. She shall bring forth a son, and you shall call his name Jesus, for it is he who will save his people from their sins." All this took place, so that what had been spoken by the Lord through the prophet would be fulfilled:
"The virgin shall be with child, and shall bring forth a son, to whom shall be put the name Emmanuel," which translated means, "God with us."

Joseph, when he arose from sleep, did as the angel of the Lord had commanded him and took his wife with him; and he had no conjugal relations with her until she had borne a son; and she named him Jesus."

Now let us turn our gaze to the Son to see what discourse the gospels elaborate on him. In the previous section, we briefly noted that the description of Christ's nature, profile and work in the New Testament is not clear or even complete. This is because the New Testament proceeds to a description by clues and by partial and incomplete hints.[25] It suggests themes but never expounds them in a comprehensive, synoptic and linear way. This way of proceeding depends on the object described, in this case Christ. It is also a function of the recipients, who must be from all ages and cultural affiliations. It must present a perspective and address that includes them all and is applicable to various contexts.[26] This kind of discourse, which is consequently or by its very nature

---

25 Theissen speaks of "basic features" from which not only later communities but the evangelists themselves reconstruct their image of Christ. G. Theissen, *Introduction to the New Testament*, (Minneapolis: Fortress Press, 2003), pp. 16-18. Bauckham, who chooses an intermediate path between understanding the gospels as direct transcripts and as expressions of faith communities by reconnecting with "eyewitnesses," also privileges the fragmentary nature of oral accounts of Jesus. R. Bauckham, *Jesus and the Eyewitnesses. The Gospels as Eyewitness Testimony*, (Grand Rapids: W. B. Eerdmans Publishing Company, 2006), pp. 114-147.

26 Luz speaks of "key words" because they are neither exhaustive nor complete even as a function of the communities that will take up and work those testimonies. U. Luz, *The Theology of the Gospel of Matthew*, (Cambridge: Cambridge University Press, 1995), pp. 3-5.

fragmentary, was sufficient to nourish faith and inform it of what is essential and central; however, it necessitated the interpretive intervention of the church.

A problem arose from the beginning. The intervention of the church, made necessary by the partial information about Jesus, simultaneously solved and complicated it. Like any interpretation, it made the figure of Christ clearer. It simultaneously distorted it because it interpreted it one-sidedly. The difference between descriptions deemed heretical about Christ (Arianism, Monophysitism) and those that were instead Orthodox (Nicaea I, Constantinople I, Ephesus, and Chalcedon) was often more a matter of proportion rather than nature. The Orthodox confessions were also fundamentally one-sided even though they were shared by many. They, too, tampered with the biblical material on Christ to make it more uniform and consistent.

Those justified clarifications and necessary specifications of the church should never have lost their provisionality and partiality. Instead, this is what happened. From provisional, they became definitive. From partial, they became totalizing. A return to the biblical sources is now necessary, not to deny the validity of these actualizations but to legitimize them through a flexibilization of them. This is what the passage from Matthew 1:18-23 will enable us to do.[27] By itself, this will not solve the Christological problem because it will deprive it of necessary specifications. But It will at least show an address that no historical Christological formula can do without. It will enable us to maintain the complexity of the Son. This is something that every Christological interpretation and formula must be able to safeguard.

The first chapter of Matthew, which is the first chapter of the New Testament, is perhaps the most neglected chapter because in it we are presented with an endless list of names. They are mostly unknown. We are not given even a minimum amount of information that would enable us to understand them better.

---

27 Luz will then discuss the value of what he calls "narrative Christology," which in Matthew's Gospel narrates by clues and not by total descriptions. U. Luz, *Studies...Op. cit.,* pp. 83-85.

Something of this first chapter is redeemable and still remains in our memory because in the second part we find the narrative of Jesus' birth, which, however, we take more as a Christmas anecdote than as an ontological reflection on Christ. In fact, this first chapter is heavily Christological. It articulates the logic of the entire New Testament and, founds the backbone of a new religion, Christianity, that will conquer the world. The New Testament could not begin any other way. It begins in a major tone. In a frontal, though sobering way, it immediately confronts us with the foundational and fundamental fact of the Christian faith: to believe is to confess that Christ is both human and divine.

This is the central chapter of the New Testament because it proposes in a concise, narrative and organized way the two statements of what Christ is and represents. In the genealogy we have the affirmation of his full humanity, while in the account of his birth we have the affirmation of his full divinity. Jesus is both human and divine. If he were only human he could not save us. If he were only divine he could not understand us.

The fact of its dual nature highlights how Jesus' being is not monolithic but heterogeneous and, at the same time, how it is unified and not shattered. That he is heterogeneous does not imply that he is a victim of ontological dispersiveness, just as that he is coherent does not mean that he is compact and homogeneous in his being. Jesus has a differentiated being; he is a polycentric unity. This fact that might seem exceptional is actually common to all human beings. This is not at the level of a dual nature like Jesus', certainly, but at the level of heterogeneous components that ground the complexity of each of us. We are all heterogeneous, complex beings. The difficulty, but also the greatness of our lives, consists in this. We would now like to briefly emphasize this plurality of dimensions in Jesus starting with two names given to him in this gospel passage: Jesus and Emmanuel.

4. "The Purity" of Jesus[28]

From a "Christological" point of view, God the Son is differentiated in his being into a human and a divine nature. From a "soteriological" point of view, in this passage, he appears differentiated by two names: "Jesus" because he saves and "Emmanuel" because he accompanies us.

The first name given to the Christ is that of Jesus. The text itself gives the transcription. Jesus means that he "saves the people from their sins." This is a "purist Jesus." We do not truly confess his name unless we allow ourselves to be saved by him, unless we agree to be the object of his ransom. By his grace he frees us from the spell and mirage of immobility, from that reassuring but inauspicious feeling of habit that prompts us to believe that we are well when we are bad. It frees us from the addiction to victimhood, from despair turned into virtue, and from suffering turned into cynicism. Where there is this "purist Jesus," evil, that which disturbs and destroys, cannot survive. He is a nonconformist toward downward laws, statistical averages, flattening fads, automatism and the mechanism of mediocrity.

The "purist Jesus" has the vocation of salvation. He delights in recomposing, in putting right. In this he never tires. He never loses the will or desire to heal. He is an inexhaustible source of health. There is no "purist Jesus" if at the same time there is no salvation. There is no salvation that is not guaranteed by the "purist Jesus." He alone is the mediator of redemption. We do not know him, or we know him only badly, if he does not become savior for us. We are his because he saves us. He saves us only if we become his. The "purist Jesus" is the guarantee of possible healing, its realization but also its imagination. Through the "purist Jesus" we dream and imagine a healing that in

---

28 A. Gesché, *Dio per pensare il Cristo*...Op. Cit., pp. 219-250; J. Gnilka, *Vangelo di Matteo*...Op. Cit., pp. 40-66; R. Fabris, *Matteo, Op. cit.*, pp. 53-64; U. Luz, Studies in Mattehw, *Op. cit.* pp. 83-96; J. Moltmann, *La via di Gesù Cristo*...*Op. Cit.*, pp. 166-170; O. CULLMANN, *The Christology of New Testament*, (Philadelphia: The Westminster Press, 1963), pp. 238-245; T. Hopko, *The Names of Jesus. Discovering the Person of Jesus Christ Through Scripture*, (Chesterton: Ancient Faith Publishing, 2015), pp. 24-32.

the moment is not there and is contradicted by the facts. The salvation of the "Purist Jesus" starts from reality but overwhelms it. It makes possible what seems impossible. He adjusts not us to reality but reality to the infinity of his grace. The "Purist Jesus" is an inexhaustible source of recomposition, restoration, and fulfillment.

In this first dimension of his ministry we catch two shades of his way of being. On the one hand, his generosity leads him to want to do the most for us, not settling for less. He does not just help us here and there. He is not satisfied with sporadically giving us a hand when we ask for it. His ambition is greater. It is to give his best to the point of fully transforming us. On the other hand, his eventual intransigence, his haste, his haste to save us, emerges slowly. As a "purist Jesus," he cannot be satisfied with less. He is restless when he sees sin. He is saddened when being able to go up, we go down instead. He is not pleased when we allow ourselves to be destroyed and, even less, when we destroy ourselves.

As a "purist Jesus," if we accept him, he will do his utmost. He will try to save us with all his might. He cannot leave unfinished what we have allowed him to start. If we sign the contract, he will be faithful beyond our expectations. He does not force us to accept it, but if we accept it he cannot stop and watch until he has accomplished his full salvation in us. In this sense we might speak of a purism of Jesus. He cannot stand sin and that is why he will not stop until he has wrested it completely from our lives. This absolute commitment to purity that eradicates all traces of sin is the explicit manifestation of his name: Jesus. However, in this he manifests his greatness but also one of his limitations.

5. "The Accompaniment" of "Emmanuel"[29]

To speak of a limit to the Savior's greatness sounds ungenerous and almost blasphemous. Can the "purist Jesus," the Savior, become dangerous to the human being? The answer is "yes." Even the

---

29   A. Gesché, *Dio per pensare il Cristo*...Op. Cit., pp. 253-279; J. Gnilka, *Vangelo di Matteo, Op. cit.,* pp. 40-66; R. Fabris, *Matteo, Op. cit.*, pp. 53-64; U. Luz, *Studies in Matthew... Op cit.*, pp. 83-96; J. Moltmann, *La via di Gesù Cristo...Op cit.,* pp. 133-138; O. Cullmann, *The Christology... Op cit., pp.* 137-191; T. Hopko, *The Names of Jesus...Op. cit.*, pp. 31-43.

greatest good can become the bearer and mediator of suffering. Virtue often exacerbates vice and goodness frequently awakens wickedness. The excessive desire for purity can easily destroy people. Good is also a matter of dosage and proportion. Evil many times is a disproportionate, unbalanced, out-of-proportion good. The paradox is that if Christ were just Jesus we would be pure, sinless, but probably distressed. Being and having to be before a Jesus who indulges in no sin easily becomes an unbearable and traumatic experience. The fear of being wrong paralyzes us. From a promise of salvation Jesus can easily become a nightmare. He can act as a form, so to speak, of soteriological stalking. The distortion of Jesus' name is easy and at hand for faith purists. There are numerous eras in the history of Christianity in which the anguish of guilt has worn down believers and led them to an obsession with purity because of a terroristic use of the name of Jesus. The gentleness, which the name of Jesus carries, has often made the situation worse. If it is the sweet and gentle Jesus himself who is asking you for a sinless life, how can you not try to follow him, even though you know you will be sicker?

This leads us to say that the very great name of Jesus, if names and words have any weight, expresses an essential component of Christology, but not all of Christology. The Christ is certainly Jesus but the name "Jesus" does not exhaust the richness of the Christ. What part of the Christ, then, is not visible in the name "Jesus"? Is not visible the fact that he is above and beyond sin. It is we who are obsessed with sin, not Christ. In some ways Christ is beyond "sin and virtue." Christ cannot be imprisoned in obsession with sin. Sin, in that case, would be greater than Christ. Christ thinks about life more than about sin. Christology is not reducible to soteriology and even less to "hamartology."[30] Christology is related to life. Christ is the God of life. He is not the God who is obsessed with sin and with the sinning of his own children.

This is what the alternative name of Emmanuel expresses. Emmanuel means accompaniment, "to be alongside," "to walk

---

30 Amartology is the study of the nature, manifestations and consequences of sin.

together with." The name Emmanuel immediately introduces a change of register in the understanding of Christ's interaction with human beings. There are two features of this change of register. At the outset, Emmanuel does not have a purist gaze. He does not look at our past, present, latent, possible sins. Not that they don't count: sins have value and express an abnormal wrinkle in our being. However, Emmanuel does not ask us to be sinless in order to walk with us, along with us. This is because life, every life, is greater than the sins that trap it. Emmanuel reminds us that life is beyond "good and evil," beyond "sin or holiness." A life is beautiful only by the fact that it is. As such it is already worthy of being lived. A life that is, is always worthy of accompaniment, beyond what that life does or does not do, what it succeeds or fails at, what it achieves or does not achieve. Virtue can destroy life as much as sin. Emmanuel is not a virtuous Christ; Emmanuel simply is. He is simply there, without medals, without titles, without virtue. He is with us only as a companion. He is always accompanying someone. His essence and joy are the act of accompanying. Emmanuel is not interested in the diagnosis of sin; he only wants to accompany. There is no adjustment or tactical cynicism in Emmanuel, only the joy of being close to us.

Further on, Emmanuel is horizontal while Jesus is vertical. There is a certain hidden paternalism in the name of Jesus. There is in a latent state that can only be controlled and balanced by the presence of Emmanuel. If Jesus remained Jesus alone, detached from Emmanuel, Jesus would easily become a deformed Jesus because he thirsts only for purity. This is purity that alienates and destroys. As in the parable of the tares (Mt 13:24-30), haste and zeal to eradicate sin cannot take over from the accompanying grace that is guaranteed by Emmanuel, who asks nothing of us.

The gospel is also good news because of the greatness of Emmanuel. This reminds us that the presence of the righteous and the unrighteous is a constant in the church itself and that we cannot anticipate the timing of the final judgment by trying to make the church pure. It also reminds us that the righteous themselves are actually a *corpus mixtum* of virtue and sin, indeed of virtue in sins and sin in virtues. This is why if Christ were Jesus alone, he would not be able to accompany anyone because we are all sinners and will be sinners until Christ returns, despite the claims of holiness and perfection made even in his name. Simul *peccator simul justus is* a formula that stands like smoke in the eyes of the purists of the faith who refer only to the name of Jesus. Instead, this anthropological and soteriological formula is at bottom also a fundamental Christological formula because it implicitly expresses the philosophy of Emmanuel. Emmanuel accompanies you without wondering and without asking whether you are righteous or sinful. Your life for him is above any moral or soteriological suspicion or evaluation.

6. From "Sinner" to "Person": Anthropological Rebirth[31]

This diversification of Christ's being as Jesus and Emmanuel affects what we Christians feel called to be. If we feel we are sinners, then we will only act as sinners. We will do this as active sinners, that is, sinners who still sin, or as sinners who do not want to sin, that is, potential sinners. The essential difference is minimal. There is only a small ethical advantage. Those who fear to sin have not yet sinned and therefore they are not liable to indictment. However, the anthropology that results from this fear of sinning is a poor anthropology because it is determined and conditioned by actual sin or potential sin. Can the record of sinfulness exhaust anthropology? Are we humans only beings who can do wrong? Should actual or potential sin determine the rhythm of our lives? If so, then structurally we are sinners even when we do not sin, because we allow the eventuality of sin to condition our lives and stiffen them in a cage of purity.

Different is the individual who, although aware of his sin, does not forget that he is a person. The sinner is a shrunken person because in order not to sin he does not live. A person, on the other hand, is someone who is aware of his sin. He is also aware that, because he has chosen to live, he will sin. But this does not block, does

---

31 A. Gesché, *Dio per pensare il Cristo... Op. cit.,* pp. 82-138; J. Gnilka, *Vangelo di Matteo... Op. cit.,* pp. 40-66; R. Fabris, *Matteo... Op. cit.,* pp. 53-64; U. Luz, *Studies in Matthew... Op. cit.,* pp. 83-96.

not paralyze his life. Every life is always greater than its sin. Birth happens for the believer, it is said, when from an unawareness of his sin, he learns to recognize it and confess it. True birth actually occurs when he is freed from the fear of sinning. Not because he no longer sins, but because the direction of his life is no longer conditioned by sin, but by his love for life. One is born for life and not to think about eventual sin. A person is always greater than his own sin. Emmanuel urges us to understand this fact and make it our own. It reminds us that evil is always smaller than good and that, in order to exist, evil needs to deform good. Any good intimidated by evil is shrunken and fails to germinate. That is why life is affirmation and restoration of the good from the good itself, and not as a function of evil.

With this anthropological rebirth of the sinner becoming a person, meaning itself is recovered. Meaning always starts from an intention, from the person who creates it. As in ethics, where action is always birthed by someone, in the same way meaning is always birthed by someone. If this someone is poor, the action will be poor; if the agent is rich, the action is very likely to be rich as well. The same rule applies to sense. It is always preceded by a motivation, by someone who gives rise to that motivation. If the agent of the sense is rich, the sense is very likely to be rich as well.

7. "The Exuberant and Sobering Grace of the Son": The Vulnerability of Meaning

(2 Co 13:13)[32]

Theology cannot remain the same if it properly understands the Christ of the gospel in the tension that grounds his "being," human and divine, in which his "action," Jesus and Emmanuel, is articulated. Christ is mediator not only in the sense of resolving the

---

32 R.P. Martin, *2 Corinthians,* Word Biblical Commentary, (Dallas: Word Incorporated, 1991), pp. 490-507; H.-D. Wendland, *Le lettere ai Corinti,* *("The Letters to the Corinthians"),* (Brescia: Paideia, 1976), pp. 472-476; F. Lang, *Le lettere ai Corinti,* *("The Letters to the Corinthians"),* (Brescia: Paideia, 2004), pp. 446-448; E. Best, *2 Corinzi,* *("2 Corinthians"),* (Turin: Claudiana, 2009), pp. 143-145.

tension that arises between God and man, between sin and purity or between present and future. He is also mediator in the sense of introducing tension when it has been ignored, minimized, made one-sided. Christ is tension and not just peace and reconciliation. There, where the allure of symbiosis and the counterfeit of an overly irenic reconciliation steeps in Christ reminds us that life is paradox, dialogue between opposites, convergence of differences and differentiation of convergences. The tension of life and in life is not the result of sin. The real sin is wanting to erase the tensions that guarantee the evolution of life. Taking away tension is tantamount to erasing life. The mirage of purity of life as a consistently homogeneous life is the usual Moloch of ancient perfectionists and modern puritans. They have tampered with and deformed the saving Christ.

Contrary to appearances, Jesus is a "theocentric name" that triggers in us an aspiration to purity. It is man who must rise, through the mediation of Christ, to the level of a holy God who remains the model to be reached. Emmanuel, on the other hand, is an "anthropocentric name". It is the "anthropophoric" name[33] of Christ because it validates human life in what it simply is. Emmanuel reminds us that if man is, he is already worthy of God's attention, to the point of awakening in God the desire to be with man. Emmanuel is not man aspiring to walk with God, but God desiring to walk with man. Emmanuel is not the cunning face of a Jesus who pretends to be a friend and then sets us up for salvation. Emmanuel is God's joy in being close to us as we humans are, regardless of our sinful condition.

This is the essence of grace that according to Paul distinguishes God the Son.

"The grace of Christ be with you all" (2 Co 13:13). Grace is not the ability to condone a sin. Grace cannot be reduced to forgiveness alone. Grace is not God's paternalistic charity. It is not God's commiseration. Grace cannot be confined to soteriology and the need to promote redemption. Grace cannot be the good image for clearing customs of a God obsessed with purity. Grace is the gift of a gaze that sees beyond sin. Grace is not the heroism of a God who

---

33 Anthropo-phoric, bearer of humanity, of man.

needs to save someone to feel he has fulfilled his mission. Grace is God's joy of being able to give himself as a gift to his creatures, without wanting or expecting repentance and purification in return. If God the Son is like this, the Bible as His Word cannot be any less. The Bible, through its sobriety and complexity, aims, like the Son, to make itself heroic in communicating urgent salvation. It also seeks mans as he is. This is beyond eventual salvific recompositing, because he is already in God's eyes a "pearl of great price" (Mt. 13:45,46). This is the essence of a biblical hermeneutic of paradox.

To sum up, in the specific case of the second person of the Trinity, the Son, which was the subject of reflection in this second chapter, we asked ourselves: How does the Son make possible life and consequently also the meaning of a text that tells us about human life and God's life? The answer is that it is possible through his "grace." The title of this chapter is "The Son's grace and the gratuitousness of meaning". It indicates that it is only through grace that the Son becomes incarnate in history, in a situation of vulnerability, in order to connect with trust with his Father and interact with trust with humanity. It is the Son's trust that breaks the mechanicity of exchanges between God and us humans and makes meaning possible. The possibility of meaning arises from the risk that the incarnation implies. If Christ had not become incarnate there would have been only a Christological tautology. It would have been only a communicative tautology of an ancient sense that is repeated identically in new times. Meaning always arises from a rupture, a differentiation, and the incarnation represents the rupture in the continuity of the Son's being. The rupture that the incarnation introduces creates the possibility and opportunity for the redemption of a humanity that has become dumb and meaningless. The possibility of meaning, as new meaning, requires, therefore, an anthropology of the freedom proper to a redeemed being and a theology of the risk faced by the Christ who decides to become incarnate in history.

It is possible to perceive all this in the Son's action through two characteristics belonging to the incarnate Son, which are parallel to the two characteristics that, in our hypothesis, also mark the Word of God (the Bible): "exuberance" and "sobriety."

a. *The Exuberance of the Son as Innovation*

The incarnation is an "exuberant" act of the Son. Exuberant grace distinguishes and marks the incarnation from its beginning. The incarnation is not a task, a well-arranged and well-executed plan. The incarnation is the articulation and affirmation of the confidence of a flourishing life, as Luke writes in his Gospel:

> "And Jesus grew in wisdom and stature and grace before God and men" (2:52).

This confidence in the free and light unfolding of a life, before God and man, characterizes Christ's being and acting throughout his existence. It marks the essence and perspective of his ministry. His ministry is a ministry of grace. It affirms life and the possibility that every life has to flourish. As John says in his Gospel:

> "The thief does not come except to steal, kill and destroy; I have come that they may have life and have it abundantly. I am the good shepherd; the good shepherd lays down his life for the sheep" (10:10,11)

Incarnation does not arise from the mechanics of a plan or the automaticity of the plan of salvation. Incarnation is not an experience undergone by the Son, who instead chooses it in conjunction with the Father's plan and will. The Son is charged with the Father's trust that sends him on a mission to humanity. The Son rejoices in this mission. He wants it and makes it his own with the exuberance of a life that spontaneously wants to flourish for others. The enthusiasm of the Son is grounded in the enthusiasm of the Father who, at the inauguration of the Son's earthly ministry, says, "This is my beloved Son, in whom I am well pleased" (Mt. 3:17). If the Father were not a happy, confident Father capable of enthusiasm, the incarnation of the Son would be like an escape, a sublimation, a martyrdom of one who dies in the virtue of a sacrifice without light and without hope.

The incarnation is not a beginning. It is a continuation of a Son who knows how to take up the enthusiasm and satisfaction from the Father and bring them to fulfillment. The incarnation is the mission that prolongs the Father's enthusiasm. Just as the Father believes and is content with the Son, so the Son in his "exuberance" believes and is content with humanity before saving it. The Incarnation is a story of a chain of enthusiasm that the Son takes up from the Father and delivers to us humans. He does this implicitly and without saying it in words, but by making it felt through his gaze and his way of being. The Son's exuberance is more lived than spoken, more implied than explicit, more upstream than downstream. The Son is not enthusiastic about humanity because he saves it; he saves humanity because he is enthusiastic about it previously. The Son does not make his enthusiasm dependent on the outcome of the mission. This is just as the Father was happy at the moment of baptism, at the beginning of the Son's mission, and not after the outcome of that mission.

If the Son were not exuberant, happy, enthusiastic for humanity before and regardless of salvation, he would be a poor, anxious, insecure Son. The mission of salvation would become a compulsion to try to value what is. The incarnation of the Son is a mission that cannot be reduced to salvation, to salvation from sin. The mission of the Son is exuberant because from the beginning it is a mission of life, for life. It aims to impart to us the joy and enthusiasm for life. A sinless life is not yet a life. A Christ who only saves from sin is not yet the Christ. To be such, Christ must be the exuberant Christ who conveys to us the enthusiasm of the Father.

In this sense Christ is the one who "begins." He is the initiator, the one who dares to begin. The Son is not only born of Mary and the Spirit; he is birth. Wherever the Son is, by virtue of this his exuberance, something is always born. He is the possibility of a new beginning. He is a new beginning because he transmits to us the joy of the Father and also because he transmits to us a new joy, his own joy, which is founded in that of the Father but goes beyond it. His joy is a new joy, distinct from the Father's, because Jesus, the perfect son, masterfully combines inheritance and innovation, dependence and autonomy, obedience and freedom. His exuberance is not conformist but creative. Jesus is birth, not prolongation. Jesus is a person other than the Father who, as a human, is born, introducing uniqueness into the world. As Son he is guarantor of the newness of each of us. Because of him, our uniqueness is possible as his was possible with respect to his Father.

This capacity to begin, which is nothing other than the capacity for creation made his own by his Father, makes Jesus a creator in all respects. Redemption is indeed a new creation. Just as forgiveness is a new birth and miracles are a new beginning. The Son is the teacher of a new beginning after a failure, a fall, an agony. His exuberance, then, is not a psychological trait, a salvation strategy, but an essential ontological trait of his. Jesus is vital because he is happy. This happiness of his founds and initiates a ministry of salvation that snatches us away from sin and its hypnotic gaze of death. This is messianism. It is the mission of the vital exuberance of the son. Messianism is the passion of the Son for what is possible.

b. *The Son's Sobriety as Renunciation*

The incarnation is a "sobering" act of the Son. As Paul writes in the Epistle to the Philippians:

> "but he stripped himself, taking on the condition of a servant and becoming like men; appearing in human form, he humbled himself by becoming obedient unto death and death on a cross" (2:7,8).

The Son brings with him an abundance of life. At the same time, he demonstrates self-limitation. The figure of the Son is inseparable from this emptying, this lowering. Incarnation is not at zero cost. This is the "kenotic" dimension of the Son. Most often, however, there is a dramatic and self-referential conception of it.

We are not faced here with suffering as virtue, or even suffering as resilience. Christ was virtuous and resilient, but that is not the point. The suffering of the incarnation is relational.

On the one hand, it is a suffering that gives birth to the other. On the other hand, it is a suffering that leads to the shrinking of self. Matthew 26:52,53 says:

> "Then Jesus said to him, "Put your sword back where it belongs, for everyone who takes the sword will perish by the sword. Do you think that I could not pray to my Father who would send me at this instant more than twelve legions of angels?""

Finally, it is not a sad suffering but a hopeful suffering linked to the emergence of the Other. Thus, *kenosis* is suffering; however, it is one that begins with a suffered self-restriction in order to make possible the presence of another and, therefore, of another sense. The is introduction of others sense, which is not mine as it would be if one resorted to the self-referentiality of a compact system. This another sense implies suffering. Sense is always a suffering sense because it implies self-limitation.

c. *The Vulnerability of Sense*

Incarnation is the recognition of the other as a place of enrichment for Christ Himself. This approach to a different place requires a "shrinking" (sobriety) of the Son. If the Son did not shrink, the other, that is, the human being, would feel violated in his own territory by a figure who does not recognize this otherness of his. This act of vulnerability of the Son makes possible the recognition of the other. It also makes possible its meaning, as a sense other. The other is indispensable for meaning. Sense is not given in a monolithic, closed, tautological system. Sense presupposes otherness, something new that is; however, it is inseparable from the actual presence of the other, as the incarnation guarantees. Incarnation is the introduction of Christ as an Other for man and of the human as a concrete Other for Christ. From this perspective, meaning is given only when there is an Other and the Other is given only when there is a narrowing of our own identity that makes it possible. Meaning is always vulnerable because it is linked to the sobriety and the capacity for narrowing and downsizing our own affirming identity. If meaning is the result of dialogue, meaning is the daughter of vulnerability. Without giving up the absolute claim of being completely myself, there can emerge no space for the other's voice. Dialogue turns into hidden a monologue, formally repeated by mechanical acts.

CHAPTER XI
THE VITALITY OF THE SPIRIT[1] AND THE RESILIENCE OF MEANING

As we did with God the Son in the previous chapter,[2] we will try in this chapter to read the complexity that characterizes the Third person of the Trinity, the Spirit, in connection with the complexity expressed in the Bible. We find ourselves in both cases before an interplay and tension between affirmation and flexibility, word and silence, action and passion, exposition and retraction, "ambivalence" and "paradox," "exuberance" and "sobriety." These are ways of expressing two characteristics of any complex identity that breaks with linear, atomistic and unidirectional logic and replaces it with the circular, relational, multidimensional and multidirectional logic that is typical of complex systems.[3]

In the case of the third person of the Trinity, we will ask: How does the Spirit make possible the meaning of life and consequently also the meaning of a text that tells us about human life and God's life? The answer is: through his "vitality." The title of this chapter is "The Vitality of the Spirit and the Resilience of Meaning," This indicates that the vitality of the Spirit makes possible the resilience

---

1 V. -M. Kärkkäinen, *Spirit and Salvation. A Constructive Christian Theology for a Pluralistic World,* vol. 4, (Grand Rapids: Eerdmans, 2016), pp. 7-31.
2 J. Moltmann, *Lo Spirito della vita. Per una pneumatologia integrale,* (*"The Spirit of Life. For an Integral Pneumatology"*), (Brescia: Queriniana, 1994), pp. 102-119. Cf. Y. Congar, *Credo nello Spirito Santo,* (*"I Believe in the Holy Spirit"*), vol. 2, (Brescia: Queriniana, 1998), pp. 195-433. J. Moltmann, *Nella storia del Dio trinitario. Contributi per una teologia trinitaria,* (*"In the History of the Trinitarian God. Contributions for a Trinitarian Theology"*), (Brescia: Queriniana, 1993), pp. 99-116.
3 G. Gembillo, A. Anselmo, *Filosofia della complessità,* (*"Philosophy of Complexity"*), (Florence: Le Lettere, 2017), pp. 19-33.

from human life and the resilience from God's life and brings them both into communion. Against abandonment and against giving up on living, against the mechanization and formalization of the drive to be, against the isolation and fragmentation of life, the Spirit creates perseverance and resilience. This is not blind and desperate stubbornness and obstinacy. It is light and spontaneous trust in the natural flow of life. Especially to the heroic but short-sighted thrusts of autonomous and partial pieces of life, the Spirit reminds us that life is connection and belonging. No life survives on its own. No being remains firm if it loses the sense of convergence and cooperation. Only in the communion fostered by the Spirit do legitimate individual forms of life find assurance of their own survival. Where there is the Spirit, there is resilience of life and drive toward the communion of lives. This is where the possibility of meaning arises. Meaning is life-affirming. The vitality of the Spirit recovers meaning and gives it a new opportunity.

Every sense, in the natural course of its evolution, goes through its own exhaustion, a natural decay. There is never an eternal sense. Sense is contingent by nature. It may be there as well as not. Calculus, on the other hand, is eternal. It is automatic. It has no hesitancy or interference or vicissitudes to interrupt its progressive and necessary manifestation. Sense is always a sense with a term, with an expiration date. It is always a specific sense that lives only in a specific context. Sense is by nature always a revitalized, resilient, reborn sense. Sense rebirth is not the exception, but the rule. The only way to remain in the sense is through its renewal. The contingency of sense makes its failure possible and its rebirth obligatory. Failure is possible. Sense can become senseless; however, right there, where sense has jammed irreversibly, vitality redeems it.

Sense is always a sense that, through resilience, has conquered a deadline, a term, a mechanism, a formalism. The reborn sense is a sense revitalized by the vitality of the Spirit. There is no sense without life. Sense is not an achievement, the product of an equation. It is not even the summation or multiplication of what is there. It comes to us by arising out of the unexpected through the gift of the Spirit. Sense is manifestation, not production. The possibility of meaning, as new meaning, requires an anthropology of vulnerability and a pneumatology of life from the perspective of a reborn life.

1. Pneumatological Positivism: "Sanctification"

We can begin to examine the complexity of the Spirit's being from the anomalies that emerged very early. As early as the second century, "monarchianism" had introduced a Christological subordinationism and a parallel pneumatological subordinationism to safeguard the supremacy of God the Father as the one and unitary God. The second type of "monarchianism," the so-called "modalist" type, known as "patripassianism" in the West and as Sabellianism in the East, reduced the trinitarian persons to mere "modes" or "manifestations" of the one God. This guaranteed the full divinity of Christ, thus securing and preserving the divinity of the second person of the Trinity. In the "adoptionist monarchianism" of Paul of Samosata, and in much of Eastern Christianity, including Origen, this was compromised. Pneumatology also came out the loser in both adoptionist and modalist monarchianism.

From the impact of monarchianism, pneumatology emerged halved and compromised. The real turning point for the structural affirmation of this pneumatological subordinationism, typical of Western Christianity, occured with the introduction of the theological formula of the *Filioque*.[4] Eastern Christianity contested this formula from the beginning.

The Latin expression *Filioque* means "and from the Son." In the context of the phrase *qui ex Patre Filioque procedit*[5] it expresses the

---

4   *Filioque* is the expression added by the Latin church to the Nicene-Constantinopolitan Creed, recited in the Mass, to better explain the procession (subordination) of the Holy Spirit (*qui ex Patre Filioque procedit*): it was one of the main causes of dissension and separation between the Greek-Latin churches and also one of the most controversial points at the Council of Florence (1439), which nevertheless ended up accepting it, considering it a legitimate and reasonable addition. Cf. J. Moltmann, Trinità e regno di Dio...*Op. cit.,* pp. 191-200.
5   "Which proceeds from the Father and the Son."

doctrine of the Catholic church for which the Holy Spirit proceeds from the Father and the Son jointly. This indicated the derivative and subordinate character[6] of the Spirit. This was subordination to both the Father, which had been affirmed previously, and to the Son which was affirmed from then on. This doctrine of the subordination of the Spirit was attested by some authors such as Tertullian as early as the end of the second century. In the third, fourth and fifth centuries, its affirmation in the West became massive through the testimonies of Novatian, Hilary of Poitiers, Ambrose of Milan, Jerome, Augustine and others.[7]

At a later stage, the *Filioque* achieved structural recognition and stability when it was included in the Nicene-Constantinopolitan Symbol during the Council of Toledo III in 589. It ordered that the Creed that included this formula be sung in Eucharistic liturgies. The effects of this inclusion of the *Filioque* with its structural pneumatological subordinationism had three consequences.

The first consequence occurred at the ecclesiological level. This *Filioque* formula caused a rupture between the churches of the East and the West.[8] Criticism, distrust and resentment covered the East for centuries. It continued until the formal rift that materialized in the Great Eastern Schism that occurred in 1054. The Patriarch of Constantinople deemed the *Filioque* heretical. It became the most emblematic, albeit not only, reason for this rupture.

At the Council of Lyon II (1274) an attempt was made to reach an agreement with the Eastern Church. The same thing happens at the Council of Florence (1439). It discussed but finally decided

---

6   This subordination will also be reinforced with the introduction of a binary trinitarian formula (Father, Son) as opposed to the classic ternary formula (Father, Son, Spirit). The binary formula is present in some texts (1 Co 8:6; 1 Ti 2:5,6) and will later become increasingly used. It will be used by Ignatius of Antioch, Polycarp of Smyrna, but also by Irenaeus of Lyons who used both formulas. Cf. B. Sesboüé, *Lo Spirito senza volto e senza voce. Breve storia della teologia dello Spirito Santo,* ("*The Faceless and Voiceless Spirit. A Brief History of the Theology of the Holy Spirit*"), (Milan: San Paolo, 2010), pp. 19-37.
7   Cf. K. Heussi, *Kompendium der Kirchengeschichte,* (Tübingen: J.C.B. Mohr, 1988), pp. 100-102.
8   Cf. B. Sesboüé, *Lo Spirito senza volto...Op. cit.*, pp. 39-52.

to accept the disputed *Filioque* formula in the liturgy as licit and reasonable. The *Filioque* is now part of the Creed which is recited in the liturgies of the Catholic Church. Protestant churches generally include the *Filioque* in the recitation of the Creed. The Anglican church also includes it in the Creed; however, it allows its omission on ecumenical occasions. Some steps have been taken to lower tensions. Some frontline Orthodox theologians, such as Sergius Bulgakov,[9] believe that the *Filioque* should be considered neither a dogma nor a heresy, but a *theologoumenon*, or permissible theological opinion. Both Karl Barth[10] and Yves Congar[11] believed that the view of the *Filioque* as a mere theological opinion was already shared by the majority of Orthodox theologians. However, not all Orthodox theologians hold it.[12]

The second consequence, less visible but in some ways more important, occurred within pneumatology itself as a theological problem. Pneumatological reductionism caused a theological homogenization within pneumatology itself by flattening it and making it overly dependent on ethical categories. This pragmatic deformation of pneumatology, reinforced and radicalized even more with the arrival of modernity, led to the nullification of the differences, tensions, alternatives, and asymmetries of the Spirit's presence and action. This obscured and eliminated its complexity by subordinating it to the overriding and ubiquitous category of

---

9 S. Bulgakov, *The Comforter,* (Grand Rapids: Eerdmans Publishing, 2004), p. 94.
10 K. Barth, *Church Dogmatics. The Doctrine of the Word of God*, Volume 1, Part 1, (Edinburgh: T & T Clark, 2004), p. 479.
11 Y. Congar, *After Nine Hundred Years. The Background of the Schism Between the Eastern and Western Churches*, (New York: Fordham University Press, 1998), pp. 147,148.
12 The double excommunication in 1054 between Cardinal Umberto and Patriarch Michael Cerularios would mark the final break between the Eastern and Western churches. The cardinal blames the East for removing the *Filioque* from the symbol of Faith, while the patriarch complains that he was excommunicated for refusing to alter the symbol. The double excommunication would not be lifted until 1965 in talks between Patriarch Athenagoras and Paul VI.

sanctification which reduces the Spirit to an agent of order, control, and stability.

Even in the New Testament at least two pneumatologies coexist: a "pneumatology of sanctification," partly linked to Paul[13] and the epistles in general, and a "pneumatology of life,"[14] present though in a hidden and implicit way in the gospels and the Acts of the Apostles. The fundamental difference is that the former links the Spirit predominantly to the ethical and ecclesiastical order while the latter links it to spiritual outpouring and ecstasy.[15] This primary difference concerns the conception of life.[16] Is the life introduced, fostered and enabled by the Spirit a life that, in order to preserve itself, organizes itself and gives itself an order of various kinds that it is bound to honor and respect? Or is it a life that precedes and exceeds and challenges any order and organizational scheme that tries to contain it? Two types of pneumatology were configured from different answers to these questions.

Excessive pneumatological pragmatism, with its corresponding theological reductionism, tends to privilege a "pneumatology of sanctification." Even when it perceives the alternative pneumatology, it tends to polarize them and make them mutually exclusive. This made the two pneumatologies rigidly sequential. This, in turn, created a temporal subordinationism that forced pneumatology to emerge only after Christ and only to reinforce what he did.[17] It forgot that "a pneumatology of life" describes a Spirit who both goes beyond

---

13 For example, Galatians 5:13-26, where the hallmark of the Spirit's presence is composure of life and control of the passions of the flesh.
14 The Spirit does not come after Christ; it precedes him. From this fact derives the equal value between Christology and pneumatology. This is the emphasis of the theology of the Orthodox church. Cf. P. Evdokimov, *L'Esprit dans la tradition Orthodoxe*, (Paris : Cerf, 1969), p. 72.
15 As described, for example, in Acts 2 in connection with speaking in tongues and spiritual ecstasy as a sign of the Spirit's presence.
16 J. Moltmann captures this central category in pneumatology well and describes the Spirit from it. J. Moltmann, *Lo spirito della vita...O.p ci.t,* pp. 102-119.
17 A number of texts are taken in this regard that suggest this. Among all of them mainly that of John 14:26: "And the spirit will remind you of everything I have told you."

what Christ did and precedes him.[18] In the Christological account of Matthew and Luke, Christ comes because he is preceded by the Spirit who makes his birth and incarnation possible.[19] Pneumatology is thus not only a consequence of Christology. It is also a condition and presupposition of every possible Christology.

The third consequence, even more hidden, has been sociocultural. Pneumatological reductionism that is based on a "pneumatology of sanctification" has led churches to resume an old purist pattern that perceives and judges the health of the faith by its order and non-contamination. This has bound the Spirit to the church and detached it from the world. The Spirit has become a reality that acts as an obstacle between the church and that which is outside the church. This has distorted a distinguishing characteristic of the pneumatology of life. In the pneumatology of life, the Spirit is not

---

18 In this regard Moltamann reverses the classical perspective in which the Spirit "strengthens" Christ to speak of another pneumatology where the Spirit precedes Christ and gives life to Jesus by bringing him into being. J. Moltmann, *La via di Gesù Cristo...Op. cit.,* pp. 97-106.

19 This is the formula that Paul Evdokimov proposes. The *Filioque* could correspond to a part of the relationship that the Bible describes between the Son and the Spirit, the proceeding of the Spirit from the Son, but provided that the reciprocity typical of true relationality is also emphasized. This reciprocity would be guaranteed, for example, by any *Spirituque* applied to the Son, according to which, the Son is also begotten of the Father and the Spirit. Evdokimov writes: "It is here that the formula *per filium* means and explains that the *Filioque* can be orthodox only if balanced by the corresponding formula of the *Spirituque* [...]. Thus the Son, in his generation, receives from the Father the Holy Spirit and therefore, in his being is eternally inseparable from the Holy Spirit; he is born *ex Patre Spirituque*. In the same way the Holy Spirit proceeds from and rests on the Son, and this corresponds to *Per Filium* and *ex Patre Filioque* [...]. The Father begets the Son with the participation of the Holy Spirit and breathes out the Spirit with the participation of the Son, and even his not being able to be born entails the participation of the Son and the Holy Spirit, who testify to this, coming from him as from their only Source. But these relations are not a production, but a correlation between the One who reveals Himself and those who reveal Him, the triune act of mutual Love between the Three." P. Evdokimov, *L'Esprit dans la tradition Orthodoxe,* (Paris : Cerf, 1969), pp. 71,72. Cf. also, B. Sesboüé, *Lo Spirito senza volto...Op. Cit.,* pp. 45-49.

ecclesiocentric but cosmo-centric. The scope of the Spirit's action is not centered on the church and faith, but on the human world and the cosmos in general. What distinguishes the Spirit of life is not only the mechanism but the space of his action which is universal because it is present everywhere, in every form of life. Beyond the Spirit's action, it is its universal presence that gives life to all. Wherever there is life, human and nonhuman, the Spirit is already present. This is so regardless of what religious, ethical or ideological confession one advocates. The Spirit of life decentralizes the role, the weight, the witness of religious communities. It does not do this to abolish them. It does this to center their work and witness on the kingdom of heaven and not on themselves.

2. *Sanctification and Regulation*

Religious sanctification continues to exert its great influence through one of its secularized forms, *regulation*. Sanctification aimed to make life orderly and governable from above. *Regulation* aims to make it orderly and governable from below. Christianity and the modern world are similar in their pursuit of order. This is the case even though Christianity looks askance at the secularized modern world and the modern world suspects Christianity of chronic and arbitrary heteronomism.

This search for and in some ways chronic obsession with order in the modern world is not immediately noticeable. Modernity appears as the historical period of freedom and spontaneity. In fact, the modern world has always struggled between *regulation* and *deregulation*. *Regulation* has been seen as necessary to ensure progress and efficiency. Typical forms of this *regulation were* embodied, for example, in the socialist state. This is a model which was prevalent especially in the first half of the 20th century in many parts of Europe. The value of *regulation* went beyond typical left-wing political alignments. The "Keynesian welfare state," which promoted substantial public intervention in economic and social matters after World War II as a mechanism to ensure development and progress in the developed countries of the West, is another example. Proposals for *deregulation* were equally important and remain so to this day.

This was the policy proposal, for example, of Robert Nozick.[20] The minimal state is, according to Nozick, a state that merely provides the minimum services, such as police service or the functioning of the Courts, to protect individuals from aggression and resolve wrongs. In contrast to the welfare state, the minimal state prefers to respect and safeguard private initiative. It as opposed to any attempt at state dirigisme.

Its present fundamental task, it is held, is not to pursue forms of substantive equality. It is to limit itself solely to those of formal equality. This is the idea of a lightened apparatus focused on the protection of a few essential rights capable of leaving maximum freedom to the initiative of individuals. The minimal state should guarantee services related to justice, law and protection. It would seem that in this *deregulation* has won over *regulation*, flexibilization over dirigisme. This is evidenced by the massive financialization of the economy with the parallel weakening of the state in the face of economic powers in our days.

In spite of extensive *deregulation* in some areas, such as economics and ethics, it can be said that the West and the cultural forms it has given birth to overwhelmingly favor the regulatory model. The West, from the most sophisticated to the most natural and immediate systems, is a culture of order. It is an order that makes everything predictable. Everything must be organized, planned, containing. It should limit surprises and unscheduled events as much as possible.

Sanctification created a limited order that somehow remained enchanted and full of mystery. *Regulation* as a secularization of Christian sanctification has not. Despite its dilution because order no longer descends from above, from a divine instance, but comes from below, it has increased the ordering effect. It has extended it to the whole of life while sanctification remained still limited to the spiritual realm. It has made it constant because it derived from a

---

20 Cf. R. Nozick, *Anarchia, stato ed utopia. I fondamenti filosofici dello stato minimo*, (*"Anarchy, State and Utopia. The Philosophical Foundations of the Minimal State")*, (Milan: Il Saggiatore, 2008), pp. 10-24.

human logic below. Let us now consider a passage from the Bible to see whether from a purely biblical point of view, in connection with sanctification, the primary work of the Spirit, this cross-continuous search for order is justified.

3. The Complexity of the Spirit: The "Spirit of Holiness" and the "Spirit of Life"[21]

Revelation 11:1-11

"Then a rod-like reed was given to me; and it was said to me, 'Arise and measure the temple of God and the altar and count those who worship there; but the outer court of the temple, leave it aside, and do not measure it, for it has been given to the nations, who will trample the holy city for forty-two months. I will grant My two witnesses to prophesy, and they shall prophesy clothed in sackcloth for one thousand two hundred and sixty days. These are the two olive trees and the two candlesticks that stand before the Lord of the earth. If anyone wishes to harm them, a fire will come out of their mouth and devour their enemies; and if anyone wishes to offend them they must be killed in this manner. They have the power to close the sky so that no rain falls, during the days of their prophecy. They also have power to turn water into blood and to smite the earth with any scourge, as many times as they will. And when they have finished their testimony, the beast that rises from the abyss will make war against them, overcome them and kill them. Their corpses will lie on the square of the great city, symbolically called Sodom and Egypt, where their Lord was also crucified. The men of the various peoples and tribes and languages and nations will see their corpses for three and a half days and will not let them be placed in graves. The inhabitants of the earth will rejoice over them and make merry and send gifts to one another, because these two prophets were the torment of the inhabitants of the earth. But after three and a half

---

21 R. H. Charles, *The Revelation of John. With Introduction, Notes and Indices,* vol. I, (Edinburgh: T&T Clark, 1963), pp. 281-292; M.E. Boring, *Apocalisse,* ("*Revelation*"), (Turin: Claudiana, 2008), pp. 171-177; D.E. Aune, *Revelation 6-16,* World Biblical Commentary, vol. 52B, (Nashville: Thomas Nelson, 1998), pp. 598-647; J. Moltmann, *Nella storia del Dio trinitario...Op. cit.,* pp. 117-144; J. Moltmann, *Lo spirito della vita...*Op. Cit., pp. 120-145.

days a Spirit of life proceeding from God came into them; they stood up, and great fear fell upon those who saw them."'"

We pause now to consider the profile of the Holy Spirit from a narrative point of view. In the previous section we noted that the description of the nature, profile and work of the Spirit is not clear or complete even in the Bible. The Bible proceeds and describes by clues and by partial and incomplete hints. It suggests themes but never expounds them in a comprehensive, synoptic and linear way. This way of proceeding depends not only on the object described, in this case the Spirit, but also according to the recipients who must be of all ages and cultural affiliations. A perspective and direction must be given that includes them all and is applicable to various contexts. Although this fragmentary discourse was sufficient to nourish faith and inform it of what is essential and central, it necessitated the interpretive intervention of the faith community.

A problem arose from the beginning. The community intervention, which the partial information about the Spirit made necessary, simultaneously solved and complicated it. It made the figure of the Spirit clearer. At the same time, it distorted it because it interpreted it one-sidedly. The difference between the descriptions considered heretical about the Spirit and those that were considered orthodox was many times a matter of proportion rather than nature. Even the orthodox confessions were one-sided though they were shared. They tampered with the biblical material on the Spirit by tending to make it uniform and homogeneous.

Those justified clarifications and necessary community specifications of the Spirit's being should never have lost their provisionality and partiality. Instead, this what happened. From provisional, they became definitive. From the partial they became totalizing. A return to the biblical sources is now necessary. This is not to deny the validity of these actualizations. It is to legitimize them through a flexibilization of them. This is what the passage in Revelation 11:1-11 will enable us to do. It alone will not solve the theological problem of who the Spirit is, because it will deprive it of necessary specifications; however, at least it will show an address that no historical pneumatological formula can do without. This is the maintenance of the complexity of the Spirit. This is something which every theological interpretation and formula must be able to safeguard.

The New Testament discourse on the Spirit is a differentiated and complex. The classical pneumatology of the epistles links the Spirit primarily to sanctification and control. By contrast, the gospels and Revelation offer a pneumatology of life. In Matthew, the birth of Christ is put before and dependent on the action of the Spirit. In Matthew the Spirit precedes Christ and gives him life.[22] In Revelation the churches are connected not only to Christ (past, present) but also to the Spirit in a future perspective.[23] In Revelation there is a pneumatological reversal that moves the Spirit from the church[24] to the world and history. The Spirit of God has a universal action. It is related to the church and spirituality. It is also related to the world and its history. The "seven Spirits of God, sent throughout the earth,"[25] act primarily outside the church. This different emphasis is qualitative as well as quantitative. It changes the very nature of the Spirit's action. This is what we will try to discern and focus on in the chosen passage, Revelation 11:1-11.

4. *"The Order" of the Spirit of Holiness."*[26]

Revelation 11:11 speaks of two witnesses. The identification of the two witnesses, in the history of the interpretation of this passage, is fluid. It fluctuates between an individual identification which is linked to a specific name and a corporate identification which is linked to a group. Tertullian, Irenaeus, and Hippolytus of Rome chose the first option. They identified the two witnesses with Enoch and Elijah, two prophets who did not know death. The *Geneva Bible,*

---

22 Matthew 1:18.
23 Revelation 1:4.
24 *Ibid.*
25 Revelation 5:6.
26 R.H. Charles, *The Revelation of John... Op. cit.,* pp. 281-292; M.E. Boring, *Revelation...Op. Cit.,* pp. 171-177; D.E. Aune, *Revelation 6-16, Op. cit.,* pp. 598-647.

which was translated by William Whittingham and the English exiles in Geneva in 1560, identified the two witnesses with the church. The corporate view identified the two witnesses with either the church, the Jews and Gentiles, the Bible, or the Old and New Testaments. We choose the latter option because it seems to somehow bring together all the others. This identifies the two witnesses with the Old and New Testaments. This is a classic interpretation of the Adventist church. It was articulated, for example, by one of its pioneers, E. G. White, who expressed herself in these terms:

> "About the two witnesses, the prophet declares, "these are the two olive trees and the two candlesticks that stand before the lord of the earth" (Rev. 11:4). "Your word," says the psalmist, "is a lamp to my foot and a light to my path" (PS 119:105). The two witnesses represent the Old and New Testament Scriptures. Both are important witnesses to the origin and perpetuity of God's law and plan of salvation."[27]

The essential underlying element in this passage is the prophetic witness that urges humanity to repent and test the spiritual steadfastness of one's faith experience. Witnessing is not an easy ministry. The two witnesses are opposed, threatened, hindered. Their witness is carried on with toil and suffering to the point of paying with death. The beast of the abyss wages war against them until it destroys them. Whether the two witnesses prophesy through individual figures, or through the church, or more fundamentally whether they represent the Old Testament and the New Testament, the subject acting behind that testimony is always the Holy Spirit.

The Holy Spirit is the real protagonist of this testimony. He is the one who makes possible the call to repentance uttered by the two witnesses. He is the impetus that spurs them toward contrition and conversion. Verse ten says that the death of the two witnesses, which neutralizes the prophetic word calling to repentance and holiness, curiously causes rejoicing among the people. The crowd is happy

---

27 E.G. White, *Il gran conflitto ("The Great Controversy")*, (Florence: Edizioni Adv, 2015), pp. 266-267. In fact, all of chapter fifteen of White's text comments on Revelation chapter 11 in light of the medieval period and the French Revolution.

because they are tired of the constant calls to holiness made by the two witnesses. The impatience of the people with the call to holiness by the two witnesses is actually resistance to the Holy Spirit.

The Holy Spirit is behind the two witnesses, the witnesses of holiness. He is the champion of the call to repentance. The incarnation of the compulsion to a sinless life. He does it in Jesus' name. The entire soteriological burden of Jesus is empowered by the Holy Spirit. It is he who prolongs, increases, spreads, expands, and makes fully universal the need for salvation and the realization of salvation included in Jesus' name. Were it not for the Spirit, people be invested with this desire for salvation only selectively and intermittently. They would have no awareness of their sin. Thanks to the Holy Spirit, everyone from below is moved to seek Jesus. Everyone is moved to repentance, to feeling uncomfortable with what they are and do, and moved to seek forgiveness, reconciliation, total healing.

Starting from each person's conscience, the Holy Spirit democratizes and makes universal the desire for perfection. The Holy Spirit has connected this desire to our every breath. He has democratized and secularized and thus extended this aspiration to everyone and everything. He has made it our own. He has internalized it and rooted it in us. He has woven it with our innermost fibers. Without this aspiration we feel that we are not whole, that we are not ourselves. What is external has made it internal. The aspiration for the good, the righteous, the holy, thanks to the Spirit germinates in us, in our innermost being. There is no place, no time, no heart where that desire to correct, to correct ourselves, is not invested by this desire fostered by the Spirit. Jesus said it clearly, "When he (the Spirit) has come, he will convince the world as to sin and righteousness and judgment" (Jn. 16:8). No one can say that they are not touched and crossed by this aspiration. This is why we can all be urged, held accountable and even accused of not being faithful and consistent with our own conscience. This the Spirit's inheritance in us.

The Holy Spirit, through the prophetic word of the two witnesses, is the promoter of a holiness without which no one can see God. The Holy Spirit is the guarantor of our sanctification. The two witnesses, the Old and New Testaments, are the prophetic voice that continually calls us to this holiness. The purpose of biblical hermeneutics is to promote and lead all people to holiness. Holiness is the goal of life. It is the goal of all life. "Be holy as I am holy, says the Lord' (Le 19:2; Mt 5:48). If he says so and the Spirit reiterates it, for us humans there is no other alternative. Holiness is our destiny.

This is how this passage and all the passages concerning the Spirit were read and so we moved forward. Here too, though, there is a problem. Lacking wisdom and a vision of the whole, always following this trail with determination and zeal, we ended up confusing the Spirit with one of its functions. This has resulted in a "pneumatology of holiness." The Spirit par excellence would be the Spirit of holiness, precisely named because of this the Holy Spirit. The Spirit can only be Holy. In holiness its profile would be exhausted. Everything it touches and crosses becomes pure and perfect. We urgently need holiness because everything in us is in compromise with sin. We have nothing completely pure. The bad things in us are condemnable in the beginning. Even the good things are never completely good. In every generous act, a biased interest is hidden. In every positive motivation, there is a passion that wears away. In every virtuous goal, there is a petty gain that haunts us. We need holiness, purity and clarity of life. We lack a clear separation between virtue and vice, good and evil, right and wrong, value and disvalue, sacred and profane, church and world. Only the Holy Spirit is able to bring to us this cathartic sense of clarity, that is, of holiness, to bring it in us, to bring it for us.

Such is the force and spread of this understanding, that for many Christians the Spirit has as its mission solely this, to bring holiness. The Spirit cannot be anything else, cannot bring anything else. The Spirit has been made a prisoner of his own holiness. As the prolonger of Jesus' work, the realization of that holiness in the lives of believers is expected of him. The Holy Spirit, as the prolonger of Christ's work, acts as a repeater of Christ's words to create a holy people through his memory. Christ's perfection and holiness are to be prolonged in the history of the church.

We are describing a pneumatology of the control of sin. The Holy Spirit seems to have become the policeman of the Trinity who watches over the containment of sin in the world. He is active in curbing and putting a limit on human wickedness, and this passage from Revelation would testify to that. The pneumatology of Christians today, almost across the board, has become only a pneumatology of holiness. Consequently, even the two witnesses, Old and New Testaments, that is, the Bible, have become a book promoting holiness. Hermeneutics has become hermeneutics of holiness. One who reads the Bible today must be able to become better, that is, holy. If one does not become holy, he has compressed nothing of either life or the Bible or God. This is a compact proof that the Spirit does not dwell in him.

5. "The Unpredictability" of the Spirit of Life[28]

The problem is that in the next verse (v. 11) of this chapter eleven of Revelation, a new register is introduced. A real break. What seems to characterize the two witnesses, beyond their call to holiness that "torments the inhabitants of the earth" (v. 10), is life and not holiness. The two witnesses from the dead are said to return to life. They do so by virtue of the "Spirit of life." It is as if the "Spirit of holiness" gives way to the "Spirit of life." That "Spirit of life," which proceeds directly from the God of life, has as its characteristic trait that of "giving life." At first it gives life to the very thing that should be alive, the Old Testament and the New Testament, but instead is dead. This passage describes two situations.

First, there is a possibility that the prophetic voice itself will be neutralized, that the Bible will die. The Bible dies not when it is physically erased but when it no longer conveys life. It is neutralized when its testimony has become irrelevant, harmless. It dies when it no longer produces any healing effect. This is perfectly possible. and It happens when one reads the letter of the Bible but does not derive

---

28 J. Moltmann, *Lo Spirito della vita...Op. cit.,* pp. 102-119. Cf. Y. Congar, *Credo nello Spirito Santo...Op. Cit.*, pp. 195-433. See also, R.H. Charles, *The Revelation of John... Op. cit.,* pp. 281-292; M E Boring, *Revelation... Op. Cit.*, pp. 171-177; D.E. Aune, *Revelation 6-16, Op. cit.,* pp. 598-647; J. Moltmann, *Lo Spirito della vita... Op. cit., pp.* 120-145.

life from it, the Spirit. This neutralization of the two witnesses, and thus of the Spirit, can occur through indifference. It can also happen through holiness, when the Spirit is only holy. Holiness can become the grave of the Spirit of life and of the Bible as witness of that life. The death of the Bible, its neutralization, is possible. It is possible in every historical season. This eventuality is not a fact of the past. The Bible, from being threatened in the Middle Ages, did not begin to live with modernity when it allowed the publication of endless translations, editions. The Bible does not begin to live when the draught of copies sold or freely distributed increases. The Bible does not begin to live when we find it in the room of every hotel, in the bookcase of every home, in the cell phone of every Christian. The period of dumbing down and silencing of the two witnesses is not over. It is always lurking. This is so more of some than others. Most often, it is not the enemies of faith who do this. Forgetting the life that the Bible conveys, believers themselves, are the ones who reduce the Bible to the letter rather than the Spirit.

This prophecy is still going on. In the Middle Ages, the two witnesses were neutralized and killed in their meaning by Christians who deprived people of owning the Bible and prohibited the reading of it. Today, Christians neutralize the Bible by spreading it and delivering it to everyone and everywhere. This coveys the letter of the Bible but not its spirit. Christians neutralize the Bible today because their reading of it, their hermeneutics, no longer produces and transmits life.

The Bible of Christians today is confessional, biased and partial. It defends only their side on issues and it defends only their truth. The truth in and of the Bible has killed life. It is the perfect crime because who would dare to impute anything to the truth? The biblical truth that won, however, is dead because the essence of genuine truth is life. The true and truthful Bible of Christians today is a small Bible. It is a negligible text. At best, it is only an ethical Bible; however, its ethics is only holiness turned secular. It is necessary but insufficient. Today, the Bible has become a cage life. It cages life with its truth and holiness.

In a second moment, the "Spirit of life" saves the two witnesses. It brings them back to life. The life of this testimony, the life that it procures, is more important than its form. The witnesses, the Bible, do not give life to the Spirit. The Spirit gives life to the witnesses. According to Jüergen Moltmann's reading, the Spirit as the source of life needs to be found again in order to give the Bible and the church a chance for rebirth.[29]

This is what, in our opinion, is missing in White's interpretation when she says the following about the Bible:

> "The two witnesses represent the Old and New Testament Scriptures. Both are important witnesses to the origin and perpetuity of God's law and plan of salvation."[30]

While we agree with White's identification of the two witnesses as the Old and New Testaments, we are critical of the restrictive meaning she gives them and to the overall scope of the entire chapter 11 of Revelation. She tends to narrow the nature of the Bible by focusing on God's "law," a typical leitmotif of Adventist thought. We think that, while it is important, God's law does not exhaust the scope of the Bible. This is the life that God conveys to us through the Bible. Life is the center of the two Testaments. It is also the center of pneumatology. White misses this in chapter eleven of Revelation. It is not about God's law. It is even less about the Bible as the guarantor of this law. This is chapter about the "Spirit of Life."

This is a pneumatological chapter par excellence. It suggests to us that the holiness fostered and enabled by the Holy Spirit is only one of the works of the Spirit. Rather than being a Spirit of Holiness it is a Spirit of life. It also suggests to us that the two witnesses, the two Testaments, are not guarantors of God's law. They are witnesses of the Spirit's life.

The Spirit gives life in his own way. This is a discreet and understated but decisive way. It is the Holy Spirit who is the real protagonist of this vital witness of the two resurrected witnesses. They return to life by the Spirit of life. The rebirth of the two witnesses is not relegated to the recent or remote past. It is ongoing. It is *in fieri*. It is played out in the realm of hermeneutics. An essential

---

29 J. Moltmann, *Lo Spirito della vita... Op. cit.*, pp. 34-37.
30 E.G. White, *Il gran conflitto...Op. cit.,* 266-267.

characteristic of the Spirit indirectly emerges here. This is its way of being and its way of intervening. Not all presences are equivalent and not all are articulated in the same way. The way of the Spirit is a type of presence that is not fashionable today. The prominence of human presence has been exacerbated by the individualistic, efficiency saturated and interventionist model of contemporary society. This presenteeism is required as moral proof of one's responsibility. One must appear, put one's face there. This is a sign of seriousness. It stigmatizes as disengagement and indifference the opposite of presenteeism which is hiding. Cleverness in hiding is a crime, a bad intention. He who hides, hides the worst. The virtue of anonymity has disappeared. All works, all productions must be signed. They are a monument to the vanity of the protagonists on duty. Narcissism is the virtue of our days.

This is not the Spirit's way of being and acting. The Spirit does not appear, does not intervene like this. Yet, he is there more than others. If the Spirit were not there, none of us would be there either. Yet, no credit is given to him. This is because we think that if we are there it is all because of us. The kind of presence the Spirit guarantees is not that of the protagonist of the creator God nor that of the evangelizing Jesus. The Spirit has a more discreet, more sober presence. His is a behind-the-scenes presence.[31] A supporting presence. The Spirit is the force of the parasympathetic nervous system of God. His presence makes the other presences possible. The Spirit is the presence of God as a condition of life. Every life presupposes her. All life is possible only because of her. This is the case of the two

---

31 This supportive presence, according to Bernard Sesboüé is a different kind of presence that essentially reveals itself in the anonymity of self and makes possible the speech of others. Sesboüé writes, "However, the proper of the Spirit is not to speak of himself, but to make men whom he inspires speak according to the thought of the Father and the Son," B. Sesboüé, *Lo spirito senza volto...Op. Cit.*, p. 15.

witnesses. The Old and New Testament,[32] are there by virtue of the Spirit infusing life into them in a universally inclusive sense.[33]

6. From "Holy" to "Vital": Anthropological Flourishing[34]

A different profile suddenly emerges for the believer. From being a morally reliable believer, that is, a holy one, he is called to become alive, that is, vital. Vital is someone who is alive himself and one who transmits life because he makes others live by what he does and says. Witnessing is not content-oriented. Not even pragmatic, it is attitudinal. The witness embodies in his or her way of being the life of which he or she speaks. The life of the witness does not stop with the witness but spreads from the witness to those who receive his or her witness.

One moves from orthodoxy of ideas and orthopraxis of behavior to orthopathy of emotions. The believer who becomes a witness is not the one who thinks well nor the one who acts well. It is the one who has healthy and living feelings. The truth of the witness is the life he conveys. Everything else is accompanying material, strategic support, support structure. Ideas and practices are not

---

32 B. Sesboüé writes on this subject, "The book of Acts mentions several times the initiative of the Spirit to make men speak.... "And they were all filled with the Holy Spirit and began to speak in other tongues as the Spirit gave them power to express themselves" (Acts 2:4). For Paul it is because of the Spirit that we can speak and confess our faith by saying "Abba, Father" (Ro 8:15) and "Jesus is Lord" (1 Co 12:3). For the word of the Spirit is on the side of the word of men who speak for God or who respond with all their human faith to God's gift," *Ibid*, p. 16.

33 There is a parallelism and conditioning between the spread of binary trinitarian formulas (Father, Son) and pneumatological subordinationism because these binary formulas simplify the faith and are affirmed in the sphere of teaching and mission. , it is in the missionary sphere that this subordinationism is affirmed. These binary formulas become typical of the Christian *kerygma* proclaimed in catechesis and evangelization. Cf. B. Sesboüé, *Ibid*, p. 22.

34 R.H. Charles, *The Revelation... Op. cit.*, pp. 281-292; M E Boring, *Revelation, Op. cit.*, pp. 171-177; D.E. Aune, *Revelation...Op. cit.*, pp. 598-647.

movable realities. If they become so, they become so by virtue of e-motions. The e-motions are the motions of life, body, witness, faith, interpretation. A testimony without e-motions is still a testimony, but a testimony that is dead. Life is e-motion and e-motion is life. The Spirit is life and the source of life because it moves itself and moves everything in the world. The Spirit makes others alive. The Spirit pushes everything forward. It is like the wind that moves and blows where and how it wants without any pattern that can contain it. Because it moves, life is always transgressive of the patterns that try to control it. The first fixed pattern that tries to control the Spirit of life is holiness.

The first task of the believer, the witness, is to be alive. In being alive one cannot merely preserve one's life. One who tries to preserve his own life loses it. One can only be a channel of life that comes to us from others and reaches others. Life comes to us only by contagion. It comes from being in contact with other living beings. Diligence, discipline, consistency or organization do not create and ensures the permanence of life. Only life creates life. The only way for the believer to stay alive is to connect to the upstream life and the downstream life of one's existence.

This growth of the believer from a saint to a vital person, thus someone who flourishes, also creates the possibility of a new sense that flourishes. Sense always starts from an intention, from the person who creates the sense. As in ethics, action is always birthed by someone. If this someone is poor, the action will be poor. If the agent is rich, the action is very likely to be so too. The same thing is true of sense. Sense is always preceded by a motivation, by someone who gives rise to that motivation. If the agent of sense is rich because it flourishes, the same thing will happen with sense. Sense will be a sense that flourishes.

7. "The Exuberant and Sobering Communion of the Spirit". The Miraculousness of Sense (2 Co 13:13)[35]

The reductionism of Spirit manifests itself in a dual form. On the one hand, we do not perceive it behind the forms of life around us. This occurs when we are oblivious to the fact that everything moves, not by its own motion, but by the motion initiated by the Spirit. Failure to recognize this fact leads us to idolize events and things. We idolize a form of life and neglect its foundation, we confuse the object with the subject, we take the letter of the Bible and not its vital Spirit.

On the other hand, this reductionism intervenes when we limit the Spirit to its holiness. Limiting it to its holiness means that we make the Spirit an instrument of curbing, containing and controlling life rather than an expander, propeller and promoter of it. The Spirit puts life where there is death, movement in inertia, aspiration in resignation, flowering in withering. Life is a more inclusive term than holiness. If the Spirit is life, the gospel of Christ has finally become universal. Holiness may belong to a few. Life, on the other hand, is everyone's. To be in the Spirit and of it is to accept life. Those who accept life are already in the Spirit. Those who fight for life and defend it are already followers of the Spirit.

The Spirit of life decentralizes the church and makes it a province of the world. All other provinces of the Spirit's realm are outside the church. The Spirit of life becomes the Spirit of all. It is the Spirit who is the true promoter of the universality of the gospel. He is the guarantor of the absolute inclusiveness of the kingdom of God that is the kingdom of the Spirit. Through the Spirit, membership in the kingdom of God is not a contingent, future goal. We are all already, through him, citizens of his kingdom of life.

This is the essence of fellowship that according to Paul distinguishes the Spirit. "The fellowship of the Spirit be with you all" (2 Co 13:13). That "fellowship" of the Spirit is not ours. It is not our fellowship

---

[35] R. P. Martin, *2 Corinthians*, Op. cit., pp. 490-507; H.-D. Wendland, *Le lettere ai corintis*, Op. cit., pp. 472-476; F. Lang, *Le lettere ai corinti*, Op. cit., pp. 446-448; E. Best, *2 Corinzi*, Op. cit., pp. 143-145.

around the Spirit. It is his fellowship, and consequently the Spirit puts in us whomever he wills. That "all of you" is not addressed only to us humans but to the whole community of creation. So that fellowship of the Spirit is not the fellowship of Christians, much less that of the saints.

The fellowship of the Spirit is the fellowship of those who believe and those who do not believe, those who reason and those who no longer reason, those who are close to me and those who are far from me, those who resemble me and those who are completely different. The fellowship of the Spirit is not a barrier but a porous membrane that attracts everyone and pushes them to enter the kingdom of life, the kingdom of God. This is why the kingdom of life, the kingdom of God, is necessarily polycentric. No life is forced to live against itself, in a hostile environment. This kingdom has an infinity of registers in which every life finds its own register of well-being and comfort.

The communion therefore proposed by the Spirit is not a "communion of saints" but a "communion of the living". The struggle and separation are not between those who are holy and those who are not. It is between those who are alive and those who are dead. One's political, social, religious, ethnic background is irrelevant. The fact does not exist. That is not what matters. Being in the group of life, among those who promote it, is what matters. The Spirit endorses the confessionalism of life and not the narrow doctrinal or ethical confessionalisms of churches and parties. Every life is welcomed by the Spirit. If a life is, it is already automatically worthy of being welcomed. If the Spirit is so, the Bible as its Word cannot be any less. The Bible through its sobriety and complexity aims, like the Spirit, not to make itself great but rather those who read it. This is the essence of a biblical hermeneutic of paradox. Paradox as the sign of life and life as the complexity of paradox.

The characteristics that distinguish the Bible and articulate its complexity and vitality, "exuberance" and "sobriety," are the same as those that distinguish the vitality of the Holy Spirit.

a. *The Exuberance of the Spirit as Communion*

The church is born out of an "exuberant" act of the Spirit. Says Luke in Acts of the Apostles 1:8.

> "But you will receive power when the Holy Spirit comes upon you,
> And you shall be my witnesses in Jerusalem, and in all Judea and Samaria,
> And to the ends of the earth."

The Spirit is exuberant and this exuberance infects it to others. Where the Spirit is present, people are empowered in their being and actions. The presence of the Spirit empowers their lives and propels them toward witnessing. This is not necessarily and solely a verbal or doctrinal witness. It is a witness of and for life. Believers expand and grow this witness for life, which is before and beyond words, wherever they go whether by choice or circumstances. Their birth in the Spirit bears the indelible mark of life in everything they do and everything they undertake. The ecclesiastical form, that is, the birth of the church from the power of the Spirit, is only one expression of this vitality.

Vitality is not a medal that is worn on the chest as a personal virtue. It is a committed, bonded vitality that aims to create communion. The Spirit of life is master in creating communion. The Spirit pushes toward communion, is communion. Communion, bonding, is the most suitable form for the permanence of life. Communion is the most distinctive sign of the Spirit's presence. Paul says of the Spirit in 1 Corinthians 12:4,7-11:

> "Now there is diversity of gifts, but there is one and the same Spirit... Now to each is given the manifestation of the Spirit for the common good. For to one is given, by the Spirit, word of wisdom; to another, word of knowledge, by the same Spirit; to another, faith, by the same Spirit; to another, gifts of healing, by the same Spirit; to another, power to work miracles; to another, prophecy; to another, discernment of spirits; to another, diversity of tongues; and to another, interpretation of tongues; but all these things that one and the same Spirit works them, distributing the gifts to each one in particular as he wills."

The Spirit creates connection between the various expressions of life inside and outside the church. It is as if the Spirit actually promotes two different but complementary experiences. First, there is differentiation. The Spirit does not push toward undifferentiated fusion. That would be an irreversible and therefore totalizing and totalitarian form of union. It would be a kind of symbiosis where one loses one's identity in the identity of the stronger. It would be a form of fusion that sees differences as obstacles to be overcome. It would be one which sees differences as only be transitory until a final homogeneous and irreversible convergence.

The Spirit of life is the experience of reversible convergence. A non-reversible convergence, contrary to what it appears, is not a good example of communion but of symbiosis. In the first movement, the Spirit promotes differentiation, in this second movement the Spirit promotes dialogue, confrontation, the coexistence of these differences and not their abatement or erasure. A symbiotic model would be a counterfeit union, an illusion of convergence. It is only in difference that communion can guarantee its own survival. This is why the exuberance of the Spirit as life force is a suffering but affirmative exuberance. It pushes toward these two horizons, differentiation and convergence, without yielding to the either.

This bonding vocation of the Spirit is not reducible to be an application of life. It is its essence. The Spirit is vital because it immediately creates vocation to bonding. It is communion because life manifests itself in network, in bonding with other lives. The exuberance of the Spirit is not the vitality as the resilience of a single life. It is life seeking other lives. No life can survive alone even in the midst of its vitality. Vitality is always solidarity of life. It comes to the defense of the lives of others. For if other lives end, mine will end as well. If I do everything possible for other lives to survive, mine will probably survive as well. The exuberant logic of the Spirit of life is the same as the logic of the Spirit of fellowship. It is only in the bonding of a networked life with other lives that life and its vitality can be guaranteed.

b. *The Sobriety of the Spirit as Anonymity*

The presence of the Spirit is always a "sober" presence. Sobriety is a rare quality in humans. This is probably because it is opposed to the need to survive. Every drive for life is thus at its base an act of bullying. Against the threat and danger that calls our lives into question, self-assertion necessarily appears as a bold and swaggering act. One cannot survive by apologizing for existing or by disturbing as little as possible. Life affirmation, if it is life, creates a problem for other lives, which then seek to stifle it or at least subordinate it. Life and its survival are always acts in a major tone. One cannot be born discreetly. Birth is always a rupture of a natural cycle. This overbearingness of single life in being born is simply protracted in the intent to survive. A sober life is almost a contradiction in terms. Life itself is impertinent and swaggering because it is unique and unpredictable.

If the Spirit is the embodiment of life, more vital than we humans, and if life is outpouring and vitality impertinent and uncomfortable, the Spirit consequently should be the most overbearing, swaggering and reckless of all beings. How can it be sober? How could the Spirit not be impetuous? If it is not impetuous, then it is not vital; but if it is vital, how can it be non-impetuous. In the mystery that inhabits the Trinity and the Spirit, these two drives to exuberance and sobriety coexist in tension. The Spirit is exuberantly vital but at the same time it is discreetly sober.

This sobriety is not a renouncing life. It is in virtue of life itself. Life is not only my life though. It is also the lives of others. If all lives were affirmed at the same time they would destroy each other. It is a law of the life of the Spirit, but also of life in general, that one must affirm the double bond of affirmation and sobriety. The virtue of sobriety, which resizes my affirmation, makes it possible for other lives to exist and find space for their expression.

The Spirit of life cannot be only the Spirit of life affirmation. It is also necessary for the Spirit of to be self-limiting to ensure that all lives have a space for manifestation. The Spirit's sobriety expresses its vocation to anonymity. The Spirit's vitality is a discrete vitality.

Mark in his Gospel (13:11) describes this unobtrusive vitality of the Spirit's presence, this behind-the-scenes presence that is both there and not there, as a continuous but not flashy presence of support:

> "When they lead you to place you in their hands, do not worry in advance about what you will say, but say what you will be given in that hour;
> For it is not you who speak, but the Holy Spirit."

The Spirit offers a guaranteeing presence for the presence of others. He remains in the background not to control, but to anonymously support the possibility of the manifestation of others, both humans and the Trinity.

Mark says again in chapter 3:16,17:

> "Jesus, as soon as he was baptized, went up out of the water; and behold, the heavens were opened, and he saw the Spirit of God descending like a dove and coming upon him. And behold, a voice from heaven said, 'This is my beloved Son, in whom I am well pleased.'"

The Spirit makes things possible through his discrete presence. He is the mediating and facilitating presence of the other persons within the Trinity. At the moment of Jesus' baptism, the crucial moment of Christ's earthly life, the leading role is not held by the Spirit. It is held by Jesus who begins his ministry. It is also held by the Father who makes himself felt in a major tone, anonymously guaranteeing and legitimizing the beginning of that Christic mission. The Spirit is there too. He has not disappeared. The sign and traces of his presence are perceptible. It is not a presence that clutters, intimidates or paralyzes. It is a presence that makes possible the presence of the Other. The Spirit is there at the moment of Jesus' baptism. It is heavily there. Both the manifestation of the Father and the beginning Jesus' mission are mediated by the power of the Spirit. He remains a sober and discreet presence so as not to steal prominence from the protagonists on duty.

The presence of the Spirit is a presence as a condition. It is the space that allows us to exist. No one would attribute an identity, an intention, to space. The Spirit is this space as a condition that allows us to exist because of its intention for life. The intentionality, personality and presence of Spirit, as the space that allows us to be, does not have the same configuration as human intentionality and personality. Human intentionality is explicit, protagonist and it tends to be exclusionary. Ontologically, human intentionality and personhood are only affirmative. It cannot be otherwise because the human path is marked by a structural contingency that one tries from the beginning to overcome. One never succeeds because the contingency always remains there. This concomitant contingency is what makes our lives a struggle. We are will, will for life and affirmation.

The intentionality and personhood of the Spirit do not have these characteristics. This is not to say that it is not intentionality and not personhood. The Spirit is both but in a different way. His presence is a presence as a condition. The Spirit binds, unites and guarantees in anonymity. His person, unlike ours, is not explicit, protagonist or exclusionary. His presence is a presence of assurance. This assurance is that in life, in events and in the intersection of what we are and do, there is an implicit, accompanying and inclusive presence.

This presence of the Spirit is typically kenotic. *Kenosis* is not a prerogative solely of the Son in the incarnation. It is not solely of the Father who creates by shrinking his space to accommodate the creatures he has created. It is also a characteristic of the Spirit that empties himself of what would be his legitimate way of being and asserting himself. He chooses the anonymity of someone who makes possible the life and manifestation of others instead.

Kenosis is not only a Christological act. It does not only have Christ as its protagonist. It is a Trinitarian act. This double movement of affirmation and limitation distinguishes whole Trinity. It is each person's capacity of "affirming itself" (exuberance), and "emptying itself" (sobriety) to allow the emergence of the Other. If the Spirit were not capable of *Kenosis*, human beings would have to deal with an unwieldy presence everywhere and always. This is because the Spirit by definition has the gift of ubiquity. Characteristic of the entire Trinity, *Kenosis* is an ontological movement of shrinking. It is visible before the incarnation of the Son, in the Father's creation and in the Spirit's continuous discrete and accompanying presence.

c. *The Miraculousness of Sense*

This "shrinking" (sobriety) of the Spirit opens to the Other. It also opens to sense, to the possibility of meaning. The Other is indispensable for meaning. Sense is not given in a monolithic, closed, tautological system. Sense presupposes otherness, something new that is inseparable from the actual presence of the Other. This is what the Spirit guarantees. Communion is the introduction of a concrete other for God through the Spirit. From this perspective, meaning is given only when there is an Other. The Other is only given when there is a narrowing of my own identity that makes it possible. The communion of the Spirit thus makes meaning possible. Convergence toward the Other does not exclude particularity or relative autonomy. The Spirit does not engulf them in a leveling symbiosis. In the communion created by the Spirit, the Spirit is not the one who predominates. He is the one who guarantees the diversity that, in that communion, converges by virtue of its own differences.

CHAPTER XII
READING THE BIBLE[1] FROM THE SOUTH
The Eros[2] of Interpretation[3]

We are at a crossroads. We can choose a minimalist perspective of meaning, whether it is purely rational and descriptive or innovative and spiritual, within a closed text. Or we can choose a sober but life-affirming sense through a text that pushes beyond itself as a guardian and witness to the passion for life itself. We have chosen the second option, which is the ontological perspective, from the beginning of our essay. It defends the text as a springboard that affects reality and life through the perception and empowerment of

---

1 D. Marguerat, Y. Bourquin, *Per leggere i racconti biblici...Op. cit.*, pp. 149-157.
2 W. Iser, *L'atto di lettura. Una teoria della risposta estetica*, (*"The Act of Reading. A Theory of Aesthetic Response"*), (Bologna: Il Mulino, 1996), pp. 6-21.
3 As remains clear by now after the previous chapter on the Holy Spirit, the renewal of hermeneutics and the construction of new meaning, possible through a different way of reading, starts from a rediscovery of pneumatology. The "Pneumatological *Turn*," to which we referred earlier, renews theology but is the basis for renewing culture and a new conception of meaning. This pneumatological renewal should not arouse suspicion in culture, apart from the just and legitimate scrutiny that must be exercised on every cultural form and proposal, because in pneumatology there is no intent of theological recovery of culture, because culture as such, without passing through religion, let alone "confessions," is in the Spirit, and through him, is legitimate as it is. The cultural, non-denominational register is for a register of the Spirit in its inclusive universality. This inclusive universality is present in the most recent studies of pneumatology. Cf. S. M. Studebaker, *From Pentecost to the Triune God. A Pentecostal Trinitarian Theology*, (Grand Rapids: Eerdmans, 2012), pp. 214-216; P. Althouse, *Spirit of the Last Days. Pentecostal Eschatology in Conversation with Jürgen Moltmann*, (New York: T & T Clark International), 2003, pp. 162-178.

textual projections. These are present in every text and they are able to propose alternative possible worlds.

Textual positivism is incarnated not only in that sense that remains imprisoned in the semantics of spoken or written words within a closed system but also in whatever sense which is unable to connect itself with reality and life despite the fact that it may even introduce some innovations. Reading can become the grave of meaning[4] or the place of its resurrection. It becomes a tomb when meanings follow one another uninterruptedly, but in an automatic, mechanical, predictable and tautological way. It becomes a tomb when reading becomes calculation, even sophisticated, but devoid of contingency. It becomes a tomb when the result excludes and erases surprise and mystery. It becomes a tomb when reading is pure ascertainment and from this derives nothing asymmetrical, no rupture and no paradox pointing forward.

It is the place of its resurrection when meanings are not automatic, but intermittent, unpredictable, fragile and fragmentary. It is the place of resurrection when reading becomes like childbirth, an experience marked by fatigue and suffering, but in the expectation of something new and unique.[5] That unique thing, though fragile, depends only in part on the reader. It is not entirely his though, because its emergence introduces something new into the world, an atypical, unexpected, better sense that the reader does not possess. He is only a witness and sentinel to its manifestation.

Like childbirth, every reading is a mixture of continuity and discontinuity, of connection and rupture. It is end and beginning, a place of hope par excellence. It is a space of waiting for conversion and change by virtue of a different, oblique and unplanned gaze. This is why reading demands vision and passion above all else rather

---

4   This is the crossroads at which we find ourselves culturally and hermeneutically. And religion, if articulated appropriately, can represent a space for the rebirth of meaning. See A. Gesché, *Le sens,* (Paris: Cerf, 2003), pp. 19-47.
5   It is what Willie Jennings calls the power of imagination to change the determinisms of a reality that is intended to be eternal and unchanging. Willie James Jennings, *The Christian Imagination. Theology and the Origins of Race,* Op. cit., pp. 32-43.

than precision and discipline.⁶ It is an erotic experience that sets the reader on the path to something that is both there and not there, seen and hidden, announced and retracted. It creates movement in the imagination and awakens curiosity and passion for a new meaning in the confidence of expectation and the surrender of control.

The relational thinking and logic of the Trinity have helped us discover the possibility of such a sense. It is open and flexible, announcing itself but concealing itself. It is a meaning that fades as soon as one tries to possess and program it. Yet, this powerful Trinitarian relational thinking has not been able to unhinge the hermeneutical and cultural positivism of our time. On the contrary, cultural positivism has overwhelmed it. "Cultural positivism" conditions and influences Christian hermeneutics and Christian Theology right at the core. This is at the level of the Trinity.

Not least because this cultural positivism has become chronic and resistant to correction, let us try to observe it from a different perspective. A typical mechanism of mutual reinforcement of cultural instances, which try to correct and renew themselves, takes hold and causes this resistance and chronicity. It resorts to foundational categories of reference that suffer from the same distortions. They do not provoke a correction or a change of direction but a radicalization of the anomaly itself, albeit in an updated and disguised in a new form. This is what we propaedeutically call "hermeneutic nihilism." It is the chronic stiffening and contortion of meaning which the very resolving strategies that seek to redeem it cause.

We have described in the last few chapters the nature of cultural positivism,⁷ in which "hermeneutic positivism" takes root. We have also discussed the dysfunctional Trinitarian theological perspective that serves as a foothold for its reinforcement and legitimization.

---

6   Theology is an act of resistance through imagination. An epistemic resistance as a condition for creating a rebirth. Cf. Jose Medina, *The Epistemology od Resistance. Gender and Racial Oppression, Epistemic Injustice, and Resistant Imagination*, (Oxford: Oxford University Press, 2012), pp. 12-35.

7   Cf. U. Galimberti, *Il tramonto dell'Occidente nella lettura di Heidegger e Jaspers*, ("*The Decline of the West in the Readings of Heidegger and Jaspers*"), (Milan: Feltrinelli, 2017), pp. 451-459.

Between this hermeneutic positivism and this "monolithic conception of the Trinity," there is a hidden but real relationship of dependence and mutual conditioning. This correlation between the Bible and the Trinity, between hermeneutics and theology, is not purely fortuitous. A basic theological presupposition or a foundational religious perspective, as in this case that of compactness and theological monolithism, necessarily ends up influencing all the primary categories of a faith community. This gives it a shared, well-typed ideological orientation.

The effect does not end here. After unifying the basic theological categories, the influence extends to the practical and concrete life of the community. A parallelism is born, a special synergy between the Bible and community, between hermeneutics and ecclesiology. It is not uncommon to see a strong and unwavering association between "biblical positivism" and "ecclesiological positivism." One almost always ends up attributing to one's church the qualities that belong only to the Bible and only to the foundational texts. One's church becomes as sacred, absolute, unchallengeable and untouchable as the Bible itself, and vice versa. The Bible, which by definition is a text of all and for all, becomes only the reflection and extension of a specific community and its narrow and limited interpretation.

The chain of effects triggered by this hermeneutic positivism does not stop here. It continues even beyond the churches until it takes shape as cultural orientation. Cultural positivism corresponds to biblical positivism and ecclesiological positivism which is transversal and widespread in our secularized Western societies. Because in a highly secularized age such as ours the impact of religion on culture is severely limited, doubt legitimately arises as to whether biblical positivism actually created cultural positivism. Or did cultural positivism influence and give birth to biblical positivism.

Every effort at theological reflection remains incomplete if it is not accompanied by a cultural reflection that is careful to discern the relationships, the cultural entrenchments and extensions, most often unconscious, that every theology implies and presupposes. Every theological endeavor and every religious stance arise in a given cultural context. Although they do not necessarily assume its explicit effects and choices, they do assume its implicit presuppositions.

These are embodied in the basic tools that configure the original categorical alphabet and primary reference point of every culture. This is not necessarily cultural determinism, nor is it a bad thing in itself. It is not a bad thing to be born Italian or German, medieval or modern. All of these are legitimate and noble cultural and historical configurations. In each of them, without exception, the gospel can descend and be encultured. At the same time, no one is destined to passively submit to his or her own culture, which can be corrected and even partially modified. To think that a theological choice remains neutral and is constructed independently of a particular and specific cultural context, without suffering some influence from it, is a pious illusion.

Although culture does not determine, it influences the theological and social configuration of all churches. Every church, like every theology, is culturally rooted and bears its specific historical name and surname. It is legitimate to think that modern Christianity is actually more modern than Christian. The proper connection and recall to the Bible and to original Christianity is still made starting from modern categories. Every theological reflection and configuration is always culturally mediated and a child of its own time.

Culture is not an object of conscious choice before us. It is an unconscious condition and presupposition behind us. It precedes us. We do not choose our culture. Our culture chooses us. It exists before us and it welcomes us into life and not the other way around. We modern Christians are modern and not medieval. Even the most traditionalist, the most anti-modernist and the most fundamentalist Christians today are all typical expressions of modernity. They often oppose modernity in the name of modernity. There is an aspect of modernity that they are unable to recognize which they project it into the Bible. They sacralize without their knowledge a part of modernity that they otherwise fight and detest.

The fact that linguistically we use the same categories as the ancients or of the men of the Bible, such as the categories of God, family, faith or work, does not mean that the meanings are the same. Cultural homonymy is a current phenomenon. We say we worship the same God as Abraham. It is true that nominally we are believers like Abraham, but substantively our God is a different God. Our God is a typically modern God. Our revival is a typical modern revival of Abraham. If Abraham were resurrected, he would be frightened by our individualistic, rational, functional and contractualist faith that nevertheless appeals to him. He would be more comfortable with the pagans of his time because he would see them, despite major theological ruptures and differences, as closer to him culturally. The same thing is true, for example, with the Sabbath, which Seventh-day Adventists passionately and convincingly defend as proof of their attachment to the Bible. Actually, for the reasons we have been discussing, Sabbath keeping today is more modern than Biblical. How, then, does modernity condition and impose on us Christians a certain kind of reductive and disenchanted relationship with meaning, with reading, with interpreting the Bible? Let us once again revisit textual positivism in its most recent and most resistant formulation which we call "hermeneutical nihilism."

1. *Chronicity and Persistence of Hermeneutic Nihilism*[8] *in Late Modernity*

Late modernity is characterized by a set of phenomena that we thought were events of the past but have returned to the scene, albeit in new forms and articulations. We have, for example, the return of religion and the cracking of the optimism that characterized early modernity. A kind of realism leads us to moderate the euphoria and

---

[8] Nihilism can be defined, as Bruno Forte does, as the erasure of the consciousness of otherness, referring to God, to one's neighbor, as we do in our text. In this particular case we also use it to refer to a hermeneutic with a mechanical and flat sense, that is, without otherness. Forte writes, "What the nihilist lacks is the consciousness of the Other, the recognition that he is not the whole, the exit from loneliness and the renunciation of communication. Surrender to nothingness remains the triumphant song of identity, its celebration in the highest presumption." B. Forte, *Trinità per atei. Con interventi di Massimo Cacciari, Giulio Giorello, Vincenzo Vitiello,* "(*Trinity for Atheists. With Contributions by Massimo Cacciari, Giulio Giorello, Vincenzo Vitiello"),* (Milan: Raffaello Cortina Editore, 1996), p. 17; U. Galimberti, *Il tramonto dell'Occidente nella lettura di Heidegger e Jaspers,* Op. Cit., pp. 531-561.

enthusiasm of early moderns who thought that everything would change with the introduction of shrewd, programmatic, and efficient reason. As we had a chance to briefly describe in Part I, the onset of so-called postmodernity marked the end of the great illusions founded on the great "meta-narratives" that sought to make overall and total sense of human experience. We prefer the term late modernity,[9] because the complex phenomena that ostensibly break with the past, initiating something new, actually radicalize trends that have long been present in modernity, albeit with important updates.

One such phenomenon that does not disappear with the transition from early to late modernity is cultural positivism and hermeneutic positivism. Cultural positivism does not retreat. Despite the ruptures of classical cultural paradigms that now occur clearly and evidently, its momentum remains and even comes out reinforced.[10] Cultural positivism[11] and hermeneutic positivism tamper with meaning and impoverish it, bringing it down to a level of total disenchantment.

---

9   While in Anglo-Saxon circles and in philosophy people more willingly speak of the arrival of a new era, postmodernity, in European circles and in the social sciences, especially in sociology, they prefer to speak of a second-modernity to identify this new historical period that has taken over roughly since the 1970s. Sociologists speak rather of late-modernity (Giddens), second-modernity (Beck, Tourraine), hypermodernity (Sebastien Charles). Cf. A. Tourraine, *Can We Live Together? Equality and Difference*, (Stanford: Stanford University Press, 2000), pp. 125-153.
10 Titus Perlini says that Horkheimer's critique of the Enlightenment, in his well-known book *Eclipse of Reason. Critique of Instrumental Reason* (1941) and continued in the equally well-known book he wrote with Adorno, *Dialectic of the Enlightenment* (1947), and it is a severe critique, but in light of the current situation it is a critique that errs on the side of defect rather than drasticness. T. Perlini, *Attraverso il nichilismo. Saggi di teoria critica, estetica e letteratura*, (*"Through Nihilism. Essays on Critical Theory, Aesthetics and Literature"*), (Turin: Aragno, 2015), pp. 10-25. See also, E. Cerasi, *Crisi del cristianesimo. Saggio su religione e modernità*, (*"Crisis of Christianity. Essay on Religion and Modernity"*), (Rome: Città Nuova Editrice, 2021), pp. 29,30.
11 E. Cerasi speaks of "positivistic rationality," meaning the same reductive phenomenon. Cerasi writes: "That instrumental and calculating rationality has spilled over into barbarism is what the obstinate apologists of positivistic and neorealistic rationality *à la Hitchens* just cannot get their heads around," E. Cerasi, *Crisi del cristianesimo...Op. cit.,* p. 29.

This clashes with the essence of religion and living culture. Eugen Drewermann writes the following about this cultural positivism embodied chronically in the modern way of reading the Bible:

> "... if this method, which is the only permissible form of approach to the fundamental texts of the Christian Hebrew tradition, and which is adopted in almost every chair of biblical sciences, were not in all respects an expression of that spiritual attitude which, conforming to the one-sidedness of nineteenth-century rationalistic thought, loved to consider historically real, of humanity and its history, only the world of objective facts. In its separateness from feeling, in its isolation from the subject, in its inability to consider inner, psychic reality as infinitely more real than the plane of external "facts," this form of "exegesis" is, in principle, atheistic, even though it often has the name of God on its lips."[12]

We are, according to Drewermann, faced with an interpretative anomaly and a true "theological nihilism." This nihilism is difficult to perceive and to correct because it takes on a double mode of presentation. For one thing, it disempowers meaning. Paradoxically, in a second way, it empowers it. The cultural positivism of the West, embodied in contemporary biblical hermeneutics, is structurally "atheistic" (to borrow Drewermann's own words) though it keeps multiplying and increasing its words and discourses about God. A disenchanted sense would attract no one and would not find its own legitimacy, let alone be able to persuade anyone. It must be disguised in a dress of efficiency and semantic power.

The rhythm of Western culture and corresponding biblical hermeneutics in recent centuries could be described by this unusual and paradoxical alternation and overlap of "disenchantment" and "empowerment." The West has been a constant and incredibly

---

12 Drewermann specifically refers in this passage to the historical-critical method. This is only one form of contemporary hermeneutic positivism. His words are applicable, as we are doing here, to the overall phenomenon we have called "cultural positivism." Cf. E. Drewermann, *Psicologia del profondo e esegesi. La verità delle forme. Sogno, mito, fiaba, saga e leggenda*, ("*Depth Psychology and Exegesis. The Truth of Forms. Dream, Myth, Fairy Tale, Saga and Legend*"), vol. 1, (Brescia: Queriniana, 1996), p. 8.

purposeful forge of new, unusual, and infinite meanings. Paradoxically, though, it arouses the suspicion of embodying the linear destiny of a compulsive race that tries to create meanings that it does not know and that always escape its hands.

The disenchanted meaning of the West's cultural positivism is a very effective meaning. It is forced to be. Because it depends on this compensation mechanism, modern efficiency is not all virtuous. Rather, it remains entrapped in a vicious circle. You try to make efficient a meaning that you have killed with your own hands. You try to make it only quantitatively great because you are no longer able to revive it. In this inflationary mechanism of meaning, as a compensatory mechanism for a meaning made poor, the West finds the measure of its greatness and its structural limitation and incapacity. At this point it is difficult to say whether disenchantment first occurred and then its correlated pragmatic enhancement. Or whether the pragmatic enhancement of meaning, produced by the obsession with clarity and precision, automatically disenchanted meaning. Both readings of the West's cultural positivism are possible and coexist.

This cultural positivism is composed of two anomalies. It is the perfect superposition of a "deficit" and an "excess."[13] It is a paradoxical mixture of a deficit of "enchantment" and an excess of "efficiency." This "excess" of efficiency, in its various possible forms, is given by the cult of precision. Number has replaced figure, measurement has swallowed complexity. Similarly, the "deficit" is the result of the now chronic inability to think and experience the symbol in its structural ambivalence and paradox. The failure of the simulacra of symbols that abound in today's marketplace of meaning, precisely as an intent to recapture a symbol that always eludes us, does not depend on their nature per se, but on the context and system that

---

13 This dual component will be called differently according to the perspective chosen by various authors. Massimo Cacciari speaks, for example, of "Paradise and Shipwreck" as characterizing the contemporary man already described by Musil. M. Cacciari, *Paradiso e naufragio. Saggio sull'Uomo senza qualità di Musil*, ("Paradise *and Shipwreck. Essay on Musil's Man Without Qualities")*, (Turin: Giulio Einaudi Editore, 2022), pp. 10-22.

behaves in effect as a shredder of meaning. The eventual existential and spiritual respite that indeed some symbols and myths try to create in us today is not functional for a change of perspective, a necessary cultural metanoia. It serves only as a moment of pause for an even more radical functioning of our pragmatic system, devoid of true symbols and metaphors. It swallows up and paralyzes any intent for new meaning.

It is what Eugenio Trias calls "the disease of the West."[14] The Spanish philosopher, a careful analyst of modernity and postmodernity, rightly and fairly recognizes the uniqueness of modern thought. Although it is unparalleled in its dynamism, he ends up categorizing it as structurally reductive thought. According to Trias, the limitation of this thought lies in its inability to mythicize. It sublimates this by presenting itself only as enlightened thought (*Enlightenment*). The symbolic and mythical defect is sold by modern and postmodern thought only as a virtue. Its inability to mythicize, which this chronic defect evidences, is a true form of cultural involution that Trias describes as the structural and unconscious disease of the West. The West is wise and well-informed. Yet, it is unable to be aware of its own discomfort and cognitive madness that it tries to sell as science to other peoples.

The unconscious mechanism of its articulation aggregates the problem. This superimposition of "deficit" and "excess" is its typical mode of dissimulation. Because it would be too humiliating to acknowledge that one has "killed the meaning" of God, nature, man, group, texts, one unconsciously proceeds to hide that defect behind an extraordinary "achievement," behind a cognitive virtue. One claims to know more when in fact one knows less. This mechanism of unconscious concealment occurs through what Freud called "reactive formation."[15] It is a defense as the mechanism of the self, of one's identity, of one's cultural pride, through a strategy of concealment.

---

14 Cf. E. Trias, *Pensar la religion*, (Barcelona: Galaxia Gutenberg, 2015), pp. 99-111.
15 Cf. N. McWilliams, *Psychoanalytic Diagnosis. Understanding Personality structure in the Clinical Process,* (New York: The Guilford Press, 2019), pp. 140-142.

In this secondary defense mechanism, an unmentionable thought is sublimated through the creation of a virtuous thought. A marked unmentionable sexual weakness, for example, is hidden unknowingly behind extreme purism and moral rigor. Similarly, the unmentionable chronic inability to create living, transformative meaning is covered up by scintillating analytical dexterity and quick, reactive thinking. It is what Christopher Bollas calls, in a more radical and provocative way, the "manic," inordinately alert, restless and compulsive component of the Western soul and thinking.[16] One is compelled to know more because one knows less and poorly.

Why should we describe this cultural positivism and related biblical positivism as hermeneutic nihilism? Because it results in an apathy and symbolic illiteracy that forces Western man to propose "empty forms" as resolutions which he erects as a universal parameter. It is like wanting to sell ice to Eskimos or "papas" (potatoes) to Peruvians. The West, through sophisticated informational, educational and advertising strategies, wants to teach the peoples of the South, how to group, how to manage nature, how to believe in God, how to read texts and how to know what symbols are. This is hermeneutical nihilism. It is emptiness presented as fullness, form as substance, quantity as quality, growth as development, complication as complexity, contract as gift or sense as meaning.

Hartmut Rosa describes this as social nihilism. It is hermeneutic nihilism at the cultural level. Concerned, even obsessed, with the resources, this social nihilism, detaches our experiences from the "meaning of life", which the author doesn't understand in a religious sense but from a purely social perspective. This cultural choice makes human groups socially dumb, without any social "resonance." Rosa perceives this nihilistic tendency in Western societies and in the very

---

16 Christopher Bollas makes, as a psychoanalyst, a psychological analysis of the cultural dysfunctions of the West, not by improperly extending individual clinical diagnoses to more general cultural situations, but by censoring parallels, similarities in the mechanisms that highlight the psychological component of the political, economic and cultural problems of the present, which is usually overlooked. Cf. C. Bollas, *Meaning and Melancholia. Life in the Age of Bewilderment*, (London: Routledge, 2018), pp. 7-13.

structure of modern sociology. It still behaves, albeit in a sublimated way, as a refined expression of cultural positivism:

> "Unfortunately, as indicated above, modern mainstream sociology, given its normative abstinence and its skepticism about psychophysical experiences has put itself in a situation (often quite unconsciously and unnoticed) in which it itself encourages this same fixation on resources and helps perpetuate the confusion of quantity of resources with quality of life. Beyond this, modernity's fixation on resources-promoted by happiness guides, happiness studies and the sociology of inequality- tends to be cemented by social philosophy as the discipline charged with addressing ethical questions of what is good and what is right. Because questions of happiness and the good life cannot be philosophically answered within the ethical horizon of modernity, debates in the field of political and practical philosophy in recent decades have focused largely, sometimes almost exclusively, on questions of distributive justice. Whether the discussion focuses on criteria of necessity, performance or equality, or on equality of opportunity versus equality of outcome, there is always an implicit assumption that any normative imperative should be calculated on the basis of the distribution of resources (material goods, rights and freedoms, or, more generally, personal latitude and opportunity) and that it is always better to have more resources than to have less."[17]

This cultural and social nihilism should have been corrected or at least curbed by Christianity. Instead, the opposite happened. Christianity prolonged this nihilism by giving it a theological-hermeneutical legitimacy. Modern religious positivism, whether biblical (Protestant) or ecclesiological (Catholic), has reduced the Bible and faith to a functional experience of clarity and functionality. It understands God the Father solely as an instance of authority and power, Christ solely as the mediator of salvation, and the Spirit solely as the guarantor of an ethical and political order. This has theologically legitimized this tendency toward cultural and social nihilism. Bible, Trinity and culture have in their modern version helped to create this cultural and religious positivism whose final form is nihilistic, denying meaning. To paraphrase Jacques Ellul,

---

17 H. Rosa, *Resonance. A sociology of Our Relationship to the World*, (Cambridge: Polity Press, 2019), pp. 23-25.

we live today in a time when "meaning has been humiliated." It has been humiliated by this positivist culture and by Christianity, which should have resisted it by proposing a true alternative.[18]

The West continues to propose, with a certain messianic compulsion, a sense that is nonsensical. It is an empty sense which does not intrigue, does not move, does not push forward. It is a sense that neither stirs nor heals. As Byung-Chul Han writes, it is a repetitive sense, blatant and without mystery in a society of exhibition where the obvious wins. It is the purely tautological pornographic transparency of a sense that is shameless and swaggering, recklessly decisive and overbearing. It is actually a tired, renunciatory, apathetic and orphaned sense of life.

> "Those who trace transparency solely to corruption and freedom of information misunderstand its scope. Transparency is a systemic compulsion that involves all social processes and subjects them to profound mutation. The social system now exposes all its processes to a transparency compulsion in order to standardize and accelerate them. The pressure of acceleration goes hand in hand with the dismantling of negativity... The negativity of otherness and foreignness or the resistance of the Other, disturbs and slows down the flat communication of the equal. Transparency stabilizes and accelerates the system by eliminating the Other or the Outsider. This systemic coercion makes the society of transparency a uni formed society. In this consists its totalitarian trait: "new name for uniformity: transparency." Transparent language is a formal rather purely mechanical, operational language that lacks all ambivalence."[19]

Late modernity is the time of the return of the religious post-secular society. It is also the time of the persistent assertion of

---

18 Jacques Ellul referred to the same phenomenon considered, however, from the perspective of the word using his well-known expression *La parole humiliée* (the humiliated word). In his analysis, the word has been humiliated by the positivism of images. Faced with the invasion of images, the word has been reduced to being only a commentary and caption of the prevailing image. See J. Ellul, *La parole humiliée*, (Paris: Seuil,, 1981), pp. 202-224.

19 B. -C. Han, *La società della trasparenza*, (*"The Society of Transparency"*), (Milan: Nottetempo, 2014), pp. 10,11.

cultural positivism. Cultural positivism becomes more insidious because it accepts a downsizing of itself. This includes the related recognition of religion as an indelible and even necessary reality as long as its survival is guaranteed in less transversal but more incisive forms. Cultural positivism in its most extreme and caricatured form has gone out of fashion; however, it survives, albeit halved, in more diluted, more chronic and cross-cutting forms. Cultural positivism is no longer a totalizing ideology. By coming to terms with religion in an implicit and forced tolerance, it gives birth to a "two-faced Janus." We now have a positivism that is halved but more powerful because it is implicit and transversal. Paradoxically, there is a religion that is pragmatic and identity-driven but impotent and culturally irrelevant because it is incapable of setting a new course for culture.

In the following two sections we will try to describe how the two theological categories we have described so far, the Bible and the Trinity, which should have stopped or at least curbed the impetuosity of this cultural positivism, did not. They were recovered and swallowed up by this positivism, which then deformed them and gave rise to dysfunctional cultural versions of both the Trinity[20] ("dysfunctional trinity") and the Bible (the "imprisoning canon").

2. *A Dysfunctional Trinity: The Death of Things*

This interplay of opposing forces, positivism and religiosity, pragmatism and mysticism, consumerism and faith, is deceptive because it suggests that positivism has actually been curbed. There is clear and indisputable data that decrees the death of a petulant and overbearing nineteenth-century positivism. Yet a positivism that we might call "mild" has survived smoothly in late modernity and blocks and paralyzes the meaning of texts and life more than the iron positivism of the 19th century. This is because it is an implicit, chronic and widespread positivism. This mild positivism is nurtured

---

20 Douglas F. Ottati through a different route points out these two themes as central to the construction of a new theology: a different understanding of the Trinity and the Bible. See especially the epilogue. Douglas F. Ottati, *A Theology for the Twenty-first Century*, Op. cit., pp. 390-420.

and reinforced by three cultural movements on which we would like to briefly dwell because of the synergy they create in neutralizing meaning. These are *atomism, globalization* and *regulation*. We describe these as the "dysfunctional trinity" in clear reference to a cultural deformation. As we have tried to describe in the first three chapters of this third section, in long and traverse ways it can be traced back to a one-sided and caricatured deformation of the true Trinity,

Late modernity is the scene of the persistent manifestation of this cultural positivism. It is also the convergence of various phenomena that condition each other. They do this by reinforcing in parallel, opposite and even contradictory ways, the same direction and tendency that neutralizes and depotentiates meaning in a chronic and paradoxical way.[21]

These parallel movements are difficult to describe because their linkage and mutual conditioning do not obey a causal or immediate and direct logic. These cultural movements condition themselves over long periods of time, in the slow cycles of history, where multiple causes predominate. These are not proximal but distal causes, not deterministic causes but conditioning influences, not linear but multidirectional processes. It is to three of these processes interacting in our culture today that we would like to refer briefly, with a view to grasping their complicity and convergence in the articulation and maintenance of this cultural positivism. These processes - atomism, globalization and *regulation* - are a kind of cultural trilogy. We venture the term of "dysfunctional trinity" to refer to them because they determine chronic cultural positivism as "dysfunctionality." We do this also because we qualify it as a sacred category (Trinity) in that it is implicitly ascribed with indisputable decisive power and relevance above any questioning.

---

21 The paradox of our culture can be seen from various points of view and also read in the opposite sense to ours not as a deficit of spirituality as the lack of a true secular society without the remorse and nostalgia for the old religious forms. See Joseph Blankholm, *The Secular Paradox: On the Religiosity of Not Religious,* (New York: *New* York University Press, 2022), pp. 23-41.

The parallel we try to draw between the biblical Trinity, as the guarantor of mystery and the possibility of meaning, and this "dysfunctional cultural trinity" that depotentiates and decapitates meaning, is part of a hypothesis. It is part of an experimental reading. This parallel is not a solid thesis, much less a definitive one. It nevertheless draws attention to a relationship as a clue, a trace, a coincidence. Our working hypothesis is that *globalization, atomism,* and *regulation,* typical cultural phenomena of our time, albeit by indirect and non-causal means, are the secularized extension of Trinitarian dysfunctionalities that Christianity has failed to correct and that initially emerged as theological-religious anomalies: "Monarchianism", "Christocentrism," and "Sanctification".

We would have in these three cultural phenomena the secularized version not of the Trinity but of three of its most typical dysfunctions. It is not that these cultural-historical tendencies appeared with Christianity and even less that they are based on the Trinity. We simply want to emphasize the fact that these various forms of cultural anomalies have received from Christianity and the Trinitarian thought, to which it refers, a special impetus and a suitable environment for their full development and manifestation, especially in modernity.

Carl Schmitt, in his "Political Theology,"[22] noted that all the most important concepts of modern state doctrine are secularized theological concepts. Following in Schmitt's wake, we could say that the most important cultural categories of the West are secularized theological concepts, in this case secularized Trinitarian categories.

The complicity and convergence of these three phenomena, described with a slightly different wording but in essence referring to the same events, is also the subject of Charles Taylor's reflection with reference to modernity. Taylor stresses the epochal value of three phenomena typical of modernity: the dynamism introduced by the individual, the force of organizational reason, and the

---

22 Cf. C. Schmitt, *Le categorie del politico,* (The Category of Politics"), (Bologna: Il Mulino, 2013), pp. 27-86; C. Galli, *Lo sguardo di Giano. Saggi su Carl Schmitt, ("Janus' Gaze. Essays on Carl Schmitt"),* (Bologna: Il Mulino, 2008), pp. 129-172.

mobilizing power of democracy pushing from below. His analysis stops at describing the side effects of these virtues that lead him to question the form that modern development has taken. Taylor pauses in his discussion of the chronic anomalies of modernity and its dysfunctions, to particularly describe three of them: self-referential individualism, instrumental reason, and mild despotism. Taylor writes the following:

> "These, then, are the three malaises about modernity that I want to deal with in this book. The first fear is about what we might call a loss of meaning, the fading of moral horizons. The second concerns the eclipse of ends in the face of rampant instrumental reason. And the third is about the loss of freedom."[23]

These three cultural dysfunctions, which Taylor calls the "Malaise of modernity," are superimposable on the three secularized Trinitarian dysfunctions which we listed earlier. Taylor is not alone in considering the simultaneity of different phenomena and trying to decipher their implicit convergence. Different cultural phenomena may share the same temporal and spatial setting. They may also trigger interactions that duplicate their effect. These would remain under-diagnosed if they were described in isolation. The synergy between contemporary phenomena, more often than not, is implicit and hidden. A special effort of attention, not without risk, must be made in order to bring out the mutual enhancement of their effects.

This is the diagnostic effort of the present that Giacomo Marramao[24] sees in the description of two different and contrasting phenomena such as the neoliberal thrust of contemporary economics and politics ("Western rationalism") and the opposing movement that seeks to counter it with a tight defense of identity ("cultural differentiation"). Also, and above all, he sees that their interaction creates a radical but sectorial change which results in the non-change of the system as a whole. There is a change in the overall paralysis of the system, which

---

23 C. Taylor, *Il disagio della modernità*...Op. cit., p. 10.
24 G. Marramao, *La passione del presente. Breve lessico della modernità-mondo*, (*"The Passion of the Present. A Brief Lexicon of Modernity-World"*), (Turin: Bollati Boringhieri, 2008), pp. 89-107.

becomes, by virtue of these contrasting phenomena, a radicalized bipolar system while remaining unchanged.

Likewise, Elena Pulcini, in her analysis of the contemporary world, does not reduce the situation of the present to the prevalence of one phenomenon, but to the interaction of different, conflicting, and even contrasting phenomena. Our present is for her, the radicalization of an "unlimited individualism," which coexists with and conditions nevertheless the strengthening of an opposite phenomenon; what she calls a diffuse and conquering "endogamic communitarianism."[25] So does sociologist Carlo Bordoni[26] in his analysis of contemporary European society. He stops to consider the interaction of three current phenomena such as "human distancing in post-society," the "discovery and radicalization of feelings," and "voluntary submission." The dysfunctional trilogy described by Bordoni overlaps with the one suggested by Taylor and can be related to what we have called the "dysfunctional trinity."

Returning to Taylor and his description of this "dysfunctional trinity," let us pause to briefly describe each of these three phenomena. On the first dysfunction, which he calls "ideology of authenticity" or "self-referential individualism," he writes:

> "Of course, the term "individualism" also names what many people consider the finest achievement of modern civilization. We live in a world where people have the right to choose for themselves their own pattern of life, to decide in conscience what convictions to espouse, to determine the shape of their lives in a whole host of ways that their ancestors couldn't control. And these rights are generally defended by our legal systems. In principle, people are no longer sacrificed to the demands of supposedly sacred orders that transcend them ... Modern freedom was won by our braking loose from older moral horizons. People used to see themselves as parts of a larger order. In some cases, this was a cosmic order, a 'great chain of Being', in which humans

---

25 E. Pulcini, *La cura del mondo. Paura e responsabilità nell'età globale*, (*"Caring for the World. Fear and Responsibility in the Global Age"*), (Turin: Bollati Boringhieri, 2009), pp. 29-112.
26 C. Bordoni, *Post-società. Il mondo dopo la fine della modernità*, (*"Post-Society. The World After the End of Modernity"*), (Rome: Luiss University Press, 2021), pp. 9-13.

figured in their proper place along with angels, heavenly bodies, and our fellow earthly creatures. This hierarchical ordering of the universe was reflected in the hierarchies of human society. People were often locked into a given place, a role and station that was properly theirs and from which it was almost unthinkable to deviate. Modern freedom came about through the discrediting of such orders."[27]

On the second dysfunction he calls "soft despotism," which is visible in democratic societies especially in the age of globalization, Taylor writes the following:

"This opens the danger of a new, specifically modern form of despotism, which Tocqueville calls 'soft' despotism. It will not be a tyranny of terror and oppression, as in the old days. The government will be mild and paternalistic. It may even keep democratic forms, with periodic elections. But, everything will be run by an "immense tutelary power," over which people will have very little control. The only defense against this, Tocqueville thinks, is a vigorous political culture in which participation is valued, at several levels of government and in voluntary associations as well. But the atomism of the self-absorbed individual militates against this. Once participation declines, once the lateral associations that were its vehicles wither away, the individual citizen is left alone in the face of the vast bureaucratic state, and feels, correctly, powerless. This demotivates the citizen even further, and we the vicious cycle of soft despotism is joined."[28]

Regarding the third dysfunction, which Taylor calls "instrumental reason," hyper-regulating especially in late modernity, he writes:

"By instrumental reason I mean the kind of rationality we draw on when we calculate the most economical application of available means to a given end. Maximum efficiency, the best cost-output ratio, is its measure of success... In one way, this change has been a liberating. But there is also a widespread unease that instrumental reason has enlarged its scope threatens to take over our lives. The fear is that things that ought to be determined by other criteria will be decided in terms of efficiency or cost-benefit analysis, that the independent ends that ought to be guiding our lives will be eclipsed by the demand to maximize

---

27 C. Taylor, *Il disagio della modernità, Op. cit.*, pp. 4,5.
28 C. Taylor, *Ibid,* p. 13.

output. There are lot of things one can point to that give substance to this worry: for instance, the ways the demands of economic growth are used to justify very unequal distribution of wealth and income, or the way these same demands make us insensitive to the needs of the environment, even to the point of potential disaster."[29]

Taylor considers the disenchanting effect and the anomalies of these three cultural phenomena on human life and experience.[30] Individualism, instrumental reason and soft despotism have as their common effect the mechanization of human life and its reduction to a programmable and predictable reality. This creates dynamism and efficiency in the system which is though short-lived because, in the long run, life is depowered. Life is reduced to its functionality and the results it produces. Taylor describes our culture as a typical form of cultural positivism whose main characteristic is the disenchantment of life and reality.

We started from a parallel analysis on the same phenomena, tracing them back to a theological matrix that does not create them but enhances them. The theological matrix that empowers them we identified with the heart of Christianity, that is, with the Trinity, a Trinity that is misread and misunderstood. First, we have linked atomism, of which social individualism is an expression, with the Christocentrism that serves in Christianity as a propeller. It is a lever that enhances the particular, the individual, consciousness, autonomy and personal responsibility, i. e. individualism. Second, we have connected globalization, of which economic-financial power is an expression, with the monarchianism of the one and compact God. Third, we have connected *regulation,* of which economic regulation is only one of its forms, with sanctification as a process of ordering, planning and rationalizing human life and behavior.

In addition to the disenchantment described by Taylor, we have emphasized the atomism of this dysfunctional cultural trinity. Disenchantment arises from an atomization of reality of which social individualism is only one manifestation. Atomism breaks

---

29 C. Taylor, *Ibid*, p. 8.
30 C. Taylor, *A Secular Age*, (Cambridge: Harvard University Press, 2007), p. 539.

down, disintegrates, separates and isolates in order to achieve more. This cultural anomaly that atomizes reality creates an apparent enchantment that is embodied in the efficiency and productivity of the system. This is why the disenchantment described by Taylor is actually a powerful but short-lived enchantment. It is an artificially inflated enchantment that immediately after its powerful initial effect sows only dispersion, detachment, isolation and emptiness. Similarly, the interaction of these three cultural dysfunctionalities (atomism, globalization and *regulation*) creates a very powerful but short-lived effect of success and gain. Immediately afterwards, it leaves apathy, emptiness and self-destruction. A compulsion to start over again sets in creating a clear cultural mechanism of dependence which pushes us to desperately search even more efficiency. We try to correct the distortions of too much efficiency with updated strategies of efficiency.

The ultimate effect of this dysfunctional trinity is the death of a culture. This is a strong and seemingly excessive statement. The fact is, though, that the disenchantment of the world produced by the radicalization of these three phenomena triggers a clear movement of sense-weariness that may well be described as a necrophilic drive.[31] It is not that all contemporary culture is necrophilic. In some ways it is vibrant and dynamic; however, it conveys a destructive drive that tends to cage life.

It tries to order life, to neutralize it. To the "death of God,"[32] as a symbol of transcendence, embodied in the typically modern motto *etsi deus non daretur*, we have added the "death of our neighbor."[33] As Luigi Zoja suggests, we have become chronically indifferent to the other, creating an individualistic lifestyle that may well be

---

31 This is the term used explicitly by Erich Fromm to characterize the direction of contemporary culture. E. Fromm, *The Heart of Man. Its Genius for Good and Evil*, (New York: Harper & Row, 1968), pp. 37-61.
32 According to the famous aphorism coined by Nietzsche. F. Nietzsche, *La gaia scienza e idilli di Messina*, (*"The Gay Science and Idylls of Messina"*), (Milan: Adelphi, 1977); G. Vahanian, *The Death of God. The Culture of Our Post-Christian Era*, (New York: George Braziller, 1961).
33 L. Zoja, *La morte del prossimo*, (*"The Death of the Neighbor"*), (Turin: Einaudi, 2018), pp. 12-31.

framed in the parallel motto *etsi homo non daretur*, as descriptive of this second narrowing of meaning and life. As if this were not enough, things have also become dead objects.[34] We have stopped experiencing the real.[35] It is possible to add a third parallel motto that describes the necrophilic tendency of contemporary societies this way: *etsi mundus non daretur*. In such a necrophilic context, meaning, the meaning of life and the meaning of texts can neither survive nor be reborn.

This necrophilic tendency is manifested today in the strong push to dematerialize things and the world. Things tend to lose consistency and become ethereal. This does not happen through the intervention of an external authoritarian force that prohibits us from enjoying things. Neither is it caused by an extreme idealism that, as in the past, privileged the intelligible world at the expense of the tangible world without denying it. Today, the evanescence of things occurs through an immanent phenomenon produced by ourselves, namely the information explosion. The power of information causes things to lose value and consistency. Information about things is now worth more than the things themselves. Digitization is dematerializing our world and our relationship with it. This is evidenced by the loss, for example, of memories, because memories are always memories of concrete things. Memory today has been replaced by data. We live in the age of the realm of data, and data is the prevalence of the information of things over things themselves.

This loss of things automatically drags with it a loss of the world, of its order and consistency. For the world is made, as Hannah Arendt recalled,[36] by things that give it stability. Only the things that stabilize life give consistency to the world. Today we tend to live more on "Google Earth" and the "Cloud" than on the real world. Information today tends to cover things and prevail over them.

---

34 R. Bodei, *La vita delle cose*, (*"The Life of Things"*), (Rome: Laterza, 2011).
35 B. -C. Han, *Le non cose. Come abbiamo smesso di vivere il reale*, (*"The Not Things. How We Stopped Experiencing the Real"*), (Turin: Einaudi, 2022), pp. 21-35.
36 H. Arendt, *Vita activa. La condizione umana*, (*"The Human Condition"*), (Milan: Bompiani, 2008), pp. 7-17.

It is to this intangible relationship with reality that a new kind of relationship with truth also belongs. Truth has always been a factual truth, a truth that is expressed and conquered in the world of things. The digital world puts an end to this kind of truth and gives rise to a post-factual truth. The information age is the age of a post-factual truth of which fake news is merely an extension and manifestation. Today's truth is a volatile truth, located and articulated above facts and independent of them. That is why the concreteness of things does not count today as corroboration of the truth claim exposed or defended. The only thing that counts is immediate and explosive effect of a truth without things. The effect and efficiency of truth has taken over, not its connection with the reality of things.

This realm of information that dispenses with things dispenses with the space of things as well. Things rooted in space which slow down our relationship with them also employ a particular kind of temporality. It is a fast and hurried temporality. The temporality of the new media and information is an accelerated temporality.

The realm of information deforms our relationship with space and time. It creates a space that is fast because it is aseptic of presences and things. Time that is fast is also aseptic and neutral because it is devoid of presences that contaminate it by slowing it down. The dematerialized world of information works with a caricature of space and time. Informational space and time are fast and performant because they are completely dissociated from things, the world and life.

The world of living things requires, as we shall see in the last section with respect to the categories of sabbath (space) and advent (time), a slow and contaminated space and time. This is what Marc Augé,[37] regarding space, calls "place," as opposed to a fast and aseptic space that he calls instead "non-place." At the same time, Marramao speaks of *kairos*,[38] as opposed to an accelerated time,

---

37 M. Augé, *Non-luoghi. Introduzione ad una antropologia della surmodernità*, ("*Non-Places. Introduction to an Anthropology of Surmodernity*"), (Milan: Eleuthera, 2005), pp. 20-31.
38 G. Marramao, *Kairos. Apologia del tempo debito*, ("*Kairos. Apology of Due Time*"), (Turin: Bollati Boringhieri, 2020), pp. 9-21.

which he defines, taking a phrase from Shakespeare's *Hamlet*,[39] "off-axis time" or "dromomania" or "hurry syndrome."[40]

The slow time and contaminated space of the world of things stabilize life and give it a framework that is the world of things. A different ethic is articulated here that values loyalty, commitment, promise, observances, obligations and resilience. In the world of information, all of this tends to disappear to be replaced by a valorization of efficiency, results, immediacy, speed, force of impact and strength of numbers. The world of information accelerates meaning and changes habits and attitudes. One takes note of the world's data without being able to know the world. One travels everywhere without experiencing the places one visits. One increases communication processes without being part of a community. One stores data without creating memories. One exponentially increases the number of friends without really discovering each other.

Passion and libidinal energies are also no longer oriented to things but to non-things, to information. Fetishism is reversed because it is no longer a fetishism of things but of data. Data are just a concentrate of information. Things and events are reduced to measurement. The infosphere,[41] a new reference reality, is the world of non-things, the world of data. These transparent data survive in functional and circumstantial connections. They do not create stories. Only narratives assemble and sew events into plots, into real stories. The digital, because it lives on the fragments of the world (data are fragments), does not create any story and it does not create memory. It gives birth to what Vilém Flusser[42] calls the parallel world of the worship of images, i.e., "idolatry," and the worship of

---

39 "The time is out of joint" in Hamlet's mouth. G. Marramao, *The Passion of the Present. A brief lexicon of modernity-world*...Op. cit., p. 101.
40 *Ibid*, p. 94.
41 L. Floridi, *Pensare l'infosfera. La filosofia come design concettuale*, (*"Thinking the Infosphere. Philosophy as Conceptual Design"*), (Turin: Bollati Boringhieri, 2020), pp. 12-23.
42 V. Flusser, *La cultura dei media*, (*"The Culture of the Media"*), (Milan: Bruno Mondadori, 2004), pp. 23-35.

text as a collection of data, i.e., "textolatry." The world of things has ceased to exist and we have entered the world of "non-things."[43]

In such a necrophilic context, the meaning of life and texts can neither survive, much less be reborn. There is a need for an *auferstehung*,[44] a cultural resurrection that will enable a resurrection of meaning.

3. A Dysfunctional Bible. The Canon Against the Spirit

One of the achievements of the Reformation was the new centrality it gave to the Bible as the primary reference point in the articulation and foundation of faith. It was embodied in the principle of *Sola Scriptura*. This is the assertion that only the Bible can and should be the ultimate rule of the Christian's faith and practice. No longer granting normative value to tradition, this formal principle of Protestantism detached it from Catholicism. The valorization of the Bible did not stop at a purely hermeneutical and interpretive level. It revolutionized Protestant anthropology and theology as well.

The Protestant movement revolutionized anthropology by functionally setting tradition aside. The reader-believer freed himself of a burden that conditioned and limited him in his religious and human experience. The individual believer would dare to propose meanings that would no longer have to be screened by either the magisterium or tradition, but solely by God in the forum of his personal conscience. Theologically, the medieval God remained subordinate to the sacramental power of the church. While aiming to bring God closer to the believer, the medieval church ended up imprisoning him and subjecting him to its own version of him and salvation. This medieval God was replaced by the Protestant God who remained sovereign in his Word. It replaced a God who is subject to the church with a church which is subject to God.

---

43 B. -C. Han, *The Not Things. How We Stopped Experiencing the Real*..Op. Cit., pp. 6-19.
44 "Resurrection" in German, for the additional and specific reference we will make to Gustav Mahler.

This achievement of Protestantism became over time no longer a guarantee of a renewal of the faith but rather a reason for its blockage and impoverishment. Both man and God ultimately became imprisoned in this Word which established a limit beyond which one could not go. The orthodoxy of the Bible took the place of the orthodoxy of the church against which it initially railed.

This normativity of the Bible which was proposed in the most radical and extreme way by the Reformers combined with the secular normativity of the "biblical canon." Formulated especially at the end of the fourth century of our era, it ended up imprisoning biblical meaning and severely limiting its impact. The Bible itself has functioned as a guarantor of modern cultural positivism. Biblical positivism is given by a particular kind of linear and fundamentalist reading of the Bible and by a certain understanding of the two Testaments and the biblical canon. Both the Bible and the biblical canon have functioned as a controlling and restraining element to reduce, tamper and subordinate reality and meaning.

Just as the map is not the territory, the canon is not reality. The canon, like the map, should function as a stimulus, as a ferrying element to go beyond the sacred text, and connect us with reality and with the true territory of life. Instead, the canon has functioned as a brake, as the ultimate reality beyond which reality cannot exist. By restricting the Word of God within the canon, one came to think that God spoke only in the canon, that outside the canon there are only confused and negligible human words. The canon was used against God Himself and His actual words. The dialogical flow between God and contemporary man was stopped.

This ambivalence was present in the Reformers and it is particularly visible in Luther's debate and confrontation with the "Schwärmer,"[45] of which Karlstadt was one of the most prominent leaders along with Thomas Münzer.

One of the crucial points of contention between Luther and these two Protestant theologians was the relationship between Bible and Spirit, between Word and mysticism, between stability and innovation of faith. Although the "Schwärmers" were Protestants

---

45 The "charismatics" or "enthusiastics."

like Luther, they felt that Luther was going too slowly in the reforms that they looked forward to with greater celerity. They felt that Luther excessively subordinated the Spirit to the Word. They felt that the Spirit, because it is still active in the world and in people's consciousness, revealed things that exceeded and went beyond the written Word. This strong and radical pneumatology challenged an overly domesticated Word (Bible) which was both a stabilization of faith and a legitimization of temporal power. It led Karlstadt and Thomas Münzer to break with Luther. Luther, in the name of a stability and order that the Bible creates, sided with the princes and the temporal power. This was to the detriment and against the German peasants who were accused of political sedition and destabilizing and dangerous religious mysticism.

The reading of Karlstadt, Thomas Münzer[46] and the German peasants of the 1500s is different in Ernst Bloch.[47] He describes them as the true custodians of the revolutionary utopia, who in the name of the Spirit dared to go beyond the limits that the written Word (Bible) prescribed. They also went beyond the limiting and unjust laws that, also abusing that Word, the protesting princes had built and defended to the bitter end as limits imposed by God himself (through his Word).

This use of the biblical canon to stop history did not occur only in Luther. It was a constant, especially with the Reformation's discovery of the centrality of the Bible. The limiting use of the canon was concomitant with a tampering with the Spirit. A reductive pneumatology, which conceives of the Spirit as a guarantor of ethical and even linguistic order and composure, which reduces it to being a normative instance rather than a propulsive and vital reality, ultimately resulted in a stiffening of the Bible, the Old and New Testaments, and the biblical canon as a whole.

Biblical and theological positivism is the result of this pneumatological loss. It is understandable only from this

---

46 E. Bloch, *Thomas Münzer teologo della rivoluzione*, (*"Thomas Münzer Theologian of Revolution"*), (Milan: Feltrinelli, 2009).
47 Especially see the last chapter of the book. E. Bloch, *Spirito dell'utopia*, (*"Spirit of Utopia"*), (Milan: Rizzoli, 2009), pp. 370-432.

forgetfulness. The loss of the flexibilizing, relational, sobering and vital presence of the Spirit stiffens, closes and mechanizes biblical hermeneutics and absolutizes both the Old and New Testaments. It makes them become self-referential, the yardstick and measure of all that can and must happen. The reality, however, is that where meaning does not flow, as with life itself, the Bible perishes. It implodes qualitatively by clinging to only a quantitative value of forms.

Without the Spirit, the relationship between the New and Old Testaments cannot be thought of in a balanced way. Without the Spirit, we easily fall into a relationship of "subordination" of the Old Testament to the New Testament or we fall into an "overcoming" of the Old Testament in the New. It is different if we look at them from the point of view of the "life of the Spirit." This Spirit is "comunion", as in maintaining differences, and not "symbiosis," as in overcoming them. This allows one Testament to express its specific particularity without affecting the specificity of the other Testament.

The "Spirit of life" is the real anonymous, behind-the-scenes actor and protagonist in the extraordinary and ordinary events of the Old and New Testaments. We see this, for example, in the most characterizing event of the Father as creator, when it is said that while creating, the Spirit was already present and acting in creation (Ge 1:2). In an even clearer and more obvious way it is the Spirit who mediates the Father's action in guiding and renewing his people, in the description of Ezekiel 37: 9,10:

> "Then he said to me, 'Prophesy to the Spirit, prophesy son of man, and say to the Spirit, "Thus speaks the Lord, God: 'Come from the four winds, O Spirit, blow on these slain, and let them come to life again!'" I prophesied, as he had commanded me, and the Spirit entered them: they came back to life and stood up; they were a great, great army."

The same thing happens in the New Testament. It is the Spirit who recognizes the special character of Jesus' mission during his baptism. It is the Spirit who leads Jesus into the wilderness to prepare him for his ministry. It is still in the name of the Spirit that Jesus formally begins his ministry in the Gospel version of Luke 4:18,19:

"The Spirit of the Lord is upon me, he has anointed me to evangelize the poor; he has sent me to proclaim release to the captives and recovery of sight to the blind; to set at liberty the oppressed, to proclaim the acceptable year of the Lord."

Just as the Spirit makes possible the validity and specificity of the Old and New Testaments, it also marks their limitation, their demise as unique and final realities. It does so by signaling the limit of the Old Testament when it brings forth Jesus as the axis and new protagonist in the economy of salvation, according to the description in Matthew 1:18:

"The birth of Jesus Christ took place in this way. Mary, his mother, had been betrothed to Joseph, and before they had come to be together, She found herself pregnant by the Holy Spirit."

It is still the Spirit who, through the description of extra-biblical events that occurred after the close of the canon, implicitly points out the limitations of even the New Testament according to Acts 2:17-21:

" 'It shall come to pass in the last days', says God, "that I will pour out my Spirit upon every person; your sons and daughters will prophesy, your young men will have visions, and your old men will dream dreams.
 On my servants and maidservants, too, I will pour out my Spirit in those days, and they will prophesy. I will do wonders up in the sky and signs down on the earth, blood and fire, and vapor of smoke. The sun will be changed into darkness and the moon into blood, before the great and glorious day of the Lord comes. And it shall come to pass that whosoever shall have called upon the name of the Lord shall be saved."

This last statement, which also finds limits in the new covenant and the New Testament, seems bold and reckless. It isn't because to describe the limits of a covenant or Testament is not to deny its past, present or future value. If a covenant of God in the past (Noah, Abraham, Moses) had been perfect and limitless, the history of humanity and salvation would have stopped at that historical point. Every covenant God has established with humanity has intrinsic value and structural limits. We Christians like to describe the limits of the first covenant and the Old Testament, thinking that the second covenant and the New Testament, being mediated by Christ, represent a perfect and definitive covenant.

Although the New Testament is a covenant that will never lapse, it does have limits. Most of today's problems, cultural or religious, are not addressable, much less solvable, by New Testament criteria. This is so for one obvious reason: the contemporary world is built on different sociocultural premises. This does not mean that the New Testament as revealed word is no longer valid. It is still valid as a revealed word in its calls for direction, for perspective, but not in the applications of prescriptions that in many cases would be anachronistic today.

The Spirit continues to act even after biblical times and after the closing of the canon. The Spirit highlights the perennial value and the structural limitations of the Old and New Testaments. In the Letter to the Hebrews we find one of the clearest statements on the structural limitations and imperfection of the Old Testament when the author in chapter 8:7,13 says:

> "For if that first covenant had been without defect, there would have been no need to replace it with a second."

> "By saying 'a new covenant,' he declared the first one old. Now, that which becomes old and aging is close to disappearing."

No one would doubt the validity of these statements with respect to the Old Testament. But, the author, taking the Old Testament as an example, is actually talking about the structural limits of every Testament. We find in this passage a phenomenology of the limits of every covenant. Although in this context the limitation applied to the Old Testament, it is also applicable to the New. Every Testament is marked by limits. Even the New Testament, while having Christ as its mediator, has these limits. Because it bases its religious legitimacy on it, each community (Israel or the Christian church) would like the reference to the Testament (Old or New) to be timeless. But the limits of the Old Testament did not indicate the erasure of the Father. They resulted in a relative displacement of the Father to make room for a new protagonist, namely Jesus. Similarly, the highlighting of the limits of the New Testament implies neither the demise of Jesus nor the abolition of his mediation. It is only the installation of a new, even more inclusive and universal actor, namely the Holy Spirit.

The Holy Spirit creates new life and new forms of religious faith by flexibilizing and relativizing previous forms of life that, if they remained final and definitive, would prevent the birth and emergence of new forms of life. The Spirit makes possible and guarantees life outside the Old and New Testaments. The Bible must not become the grave of life and spirituality in the name of transient forms improperly elevated to sacred and final ones. To use the Bible and the biblical canon to stop reality and, in the name of this ancient reality, to exclude current reality, is to make improper use of the vocation of the two Testaments and the biblical canon.

Biblical positivism is not related solely to a fundamentalist reading of the Bible, nor even to an inflexibility and self-referentiality in reading and interpreting it. It is related as well to the denial that meaningful, beautiful and spiritually generous things can happen outside the Bible. The Old Testament and the New Testament, unfortunately, are used across the board by all Christians today to downplay the validity and relevance of extra-biblical history in which God, through the Spirit of life, acts in an ongoing and resilient way.

The vocation and role of the canonical Bible is to recognize and appreciate the value of men's bibles. The biblical canon is not a boundary of overbearingness, of excluding other texts, but of self-limitation, of relinquishing control of others. Through the biblical canon God renounces invading the human word and gives himself as a task to dialogue with it by putting a boundary on his own Word. The canon is not a limit for the human word, lest it contaminate the divine word. The canon is a limit that God imposes on himself, on his Word, to prevent it from engulfing the human Word. The biblical canon expands the human word. It does this by reminding it that the desired and intended human word is a word preceded by God's word (canon). The biblical canon[48] is a sign of openness and not

---

48 B.M. Metzger, *Il canone del Nuovo Testamento*, (*"The New Testament Canon"*), (Brescia: Paideia, 1997), pp. 200-215.

closure. It is the sign that ennobles everything outside the Bible. This recognition of the value of all that is extra-canonical and extra-biblical, that is, human, becomes visible and articulated in the choice of human plurality, of which the Bible is only a part. To the intra-biblical plurality is added, by divine design choice, the extra-biblical plurality, without which the Bible would be limited to being just a sad piece of museum and history.

In modernity, the "biblical canon" has been secularized and broadened into the "Western canon" which has become the yardstick of all that is beautiful and culturally acceptable globally. Western culture has become the cultural canon for assessing and expressing the value of any cultural initiative and proposal in the world. Western culture has become the Bible of the world.

Harold Bloom defends the unique and absolute value of this cultural canon in his book titled *The Western Canon*.[49] It is an indirect take on the biblical canon and many of its stories, constructed from the West's most significant literary works. Although this canon proposed by Bloom is a faithful copy of the biblical canon and its absolute and overbearing normativity, it is culturally limited because it is reduced to the West. In addition, though, it has the narrow Anglophone flavor because, again according to Bloom, it has Shakespeare[50] and his works as its center. The idea is that the entire world should now limit itself to be the cultural extension of the *Commonwealth* where we are all forced to speak English. It is as poor a proposal as is locking the contemporary world into the Bible. Rightly read, the Bible does not stop history or imprison it in a particular pattern. Moved by the Spirit, it rejoices when the world moves forward and surpasses it in meaning and significance.

As it happened with the biblical canon, it also happens with the Western canon proposed by Harold Bloom. Born initially to make life possible, and to express it in its splendor and flourishing, it ends up killing it. It detaches it from other lives, from other peoples,

---

49 H. Bloom, *Il canone occidentale. I Libri e le scuole dell'Età*, ("*The Western Canon. The Books and Schools of the Age*"), (Milan: Bompiani, 2006), pp. 13-35.
50 *Ibid*, pp. 39-65.

from other knowledge, with an unstoppable involution of meaning. Where meaning is imprisoned, when it flows neither upstream nor downstream, it dies.

In such a necrophilic context, the meaning of life and the meaning of texts can neither survive nor even be reborn. There is an urgent need of an *Auferstehung*, a cultural resurrection that enables a resurrection of meaning.

4. *Auferstehung*[51] and the "Pneumatological Turn"[52]: Against the Necrophilia of Sense

How can we regain a lost hermeneutic and cultural meaning in a historical period like ours in which everything must be immediately efficient and immediately usable? A hermeneutic renewal is not enough. If hermeneutics were renewed while positivist culture remained the same, hermeneutic change would have short legs. It would immediately be swallowed up and manipulated. It would be used as an alibi to perpetuate the basic cultural direction that it timidly tries to challenge. This bewilderment of meaning cannot be reversed by a simple reform of the system, by a tweak or cosmetic trick.

A true cultural metanoia is needed. To use a figure and metaphor from Gustav Mahler, a true cultural *Auferstehung* (resurrection), a true rebirth of the Spirit, must take place.[53] Overthrowing a positivist

---

51 German word for "resurrection." Here it is used in clear reference to the Christian resurrection, but through Gustav Mahler's musical interpretation of this word in his second symphony, called *Auferstehung*.
52 This is the challenge of theology today according to Roberto Di Ceglie. If theology introduced new arguments while preserving the old language, nothing would change. Roberto Di Ceglie, *God the Good, and the Spiritual Turn in Epistemology,* (Cambridge: Cambridge University Press, 2022), pp. 24-35.
53 On the meaning of *Auferstehung* in Mahler there will be various interpretations. Martha Nussbaum will favor that of passage or rupture. Norman Lebrecht stands in the same wake as Nussbaum, but thinks that Mahler's symphonies, and the second one, represent a cultural turning point that changed the way we think about the world. Cf. N. Lebrecht,

culture that encloses life and meaning in the mechanism of a rational calculation and equation is possible only by a culture of life, by a change of language,[54] by a spiritual resurrection. This is why the Spirit of life must again become the center of a spiritual and cultural revival. This is not the Spirit of sanctification, the Spirit of the Bible or the Spirit of denominational or confessional commitment. The Spirit of life is the inclusive and universal Spirit whose horizon of action is not the narrow horizon of one denomination, one culture, one historical period, one territory, one party, one affiliation. It is the horizon that includes every form of life, human and non-human. The renewal of hermeneutics, the recovery of the meaning of life and biblical meaning, and, in a broader perspective, also the recovery of meaning in general, comes through the "penumatological turn." The change of language does not add a complement of meaning. It changes the sense and grounds it differently. It is what C. Geffré calls the "ilemorphic" property of language. It consists of a change of sense by changing the form of language. Geffré writes:

> "Language is the very locus of meaning, and when you change language, you change meaning. It is what I call an 'ilemorphic' conception of language: just as it is not given to dissociate the soul from the body, so one cannot dissociate the soul of language from its vehicle, its textual body."[55]

As previously contended in the chapter on the Holy Spirit, the renewal of hermeneutics and the construction of new meaning made

---

Why Mahler. How One Man and Ten Symphonies Changed the World, (London: Faber & Faber, 2011), pp. 72-80.

54 This is what Greffè suggests when he writes, "In any case, it must be known that there is no creation of a new language of faith without it leading to a reinterpretation of the Christian message." C. Geffré, *Credere e interpretare*...Op. cit., p. 56.

55 Geffré makes his own the typical "hilemorphic" Aristotelian conception that, unlike Plato who spoke of a sense (idea) independently of its container (body), every idea is linked to its form. C. Geffré, *Credere e interpretare...Op. cit.,* p. 57. Moreover, this close relationship between ideas and forms is also supported by P. Ricœur when he speaks of the indissolubility between "kerygmatic content" and "literary form." Cf. P. Ricœur, *Ermeneutica filosofica...*Op. cit., pp. 80-85.

possible by a different way of reading starts from a rediscovery of pneumatology. The "Pneumatological Turn," urges us to a change of language ("pneumatological language of life"). It simultaneously urges us to a revisit and reinterpret of the whole Christian message.[56] In this regard, Claude Geffré writes again:

> "So the search for a new language, for a reformulation of dogma is not simply 'adaptation' to the most common understanding of the faithful, it is a risky operation, it is an operation that leads to a reinterpretation of dogma."[57]

This "pneumatological turn," to which we referred earlier renews theology. It is also the basis of a new culture and of a new conception of meaning. This pneumatological renewal must not arouse suspicion in culture beyond the just and legitimate verification that must be exercised on every cultural form and proposal. The introduction of Pneumatology doesn't represent a hidden way of imposing a theological justification of culture. Culture, as such, without passing through religion, even less through "confessions," is already a manifestation of the true Spirit. The cultural, non-denominational is a register of the Spirit in its inclusive universality. This inclusive universality of pneumatology is present in the most recent studies of pneumatology.[58]

Why should we use such a strong metaphor as *Auferstehung*, moving it from its natural biblical-theological context and applying it to all of culture? This is so for several reasons; however, the one Martha Nussbaum suggests is especially important.[59] Commenting

---

56 Roberto Di Ceglie, *God the Good, and the Spiritual Turn in Epistemology*, Op. cit., pp. 56-76.
57 C. Geffré, *Credere e interpretare...Op. cit.,* p. 56.
58 Cf. S. M. Studebaker, *From Pentecost to the Triune God. A Pentecostal Trinitarian Theology*, (Grand Rapids: Eerdmans, 2012), pp. 214-216; P. Althouse, *Spirit of the Last Days. Pentecostal Eschatology in Conversation with Jürgen Moltmann*...Op. cit., pp. 162-178.
59 In her book on the intelligence of the emotions, Nussbaum actually discusses Mahler at various, even quantitatively important moments, but it is in the fourteenth chapter, devoted entirely to Mahler, that she analyzes and comments on Mahler's second symphony, *Auferstehung*. See M.

on Mahler's Second Symphony, she describes the real change today as one that must come from outside. After all, *Auferstehung*, unlike the immortality of the soul,[60] is a typical relational experience with the totally Other. One is not resurrected on one's own just as one is not born on one's own, through an exercise of one's own will and awareness. This happens solely through reliance on the intervention of an Other who comes to us from outside.

The rediscovery of meaning in the West cannot take place, according to Nussbaum, through refinement or innovation within the same modern system. This would lead to the perpetuation of the anomaly that is to be corrected. The system must be "broken" from the outside, through alternative forms of thinking that cause real telluric movements, epistemological shocks, earthquakes of thought. These other thoughts have as their common denominator the motivational, perspectival and symbolic force of emotions. The renewal of meaning can only take place through an *Auferstehung*, a resurrection of the symbolic forms of thought, which have been forgotten and stigmatized by the West in recent centuries.

The English title of Nussbaum's book, *Upheavals of Thought*,[61] conveys this sense of rupture, which is only presupposed and hidden in the Italian title, *L'intelligenza delle emozioni*.[62] Nussbaum describes five forms of thought which break the ordered but predictable linearity of the West's cultural positivism. These are: first, an ethics of pre-rational choices;[63] second, the empathically fast and immediate thinking of animals;[64] third, the slow and metaphorical thinking of non-Western peoples;[65] fourth, the non-

---

Nussbaum, *L'intelligenza delle emozioni*, ("Upheavals of Thought. *The Intelligence of the Emotions")*, (Bologna: Il Mulino, 2004), pp. 721-743.

60 Jürgen Moltmann reads the main difference between "immortality of the soul" and "resurrection" through the category of relationality, which in the former is missing while in the latter it is the heart of it. Cf. J. Moltmann, *L'avvento di Dio. Escatologia cristiana*, (*"The Advent of God. Christian Eschatology")*, (Brescia: Queriniana, 1998), pp. 71-92.
61 Literally in English, "earthquakes of thought."
62 M. Nussbaum, *L'intelligenza delle emozioni*, (Il Mulino, Bologna 2004).
63 *Ibid*, pp. 37-116.
64 *Ibid*, pp. 117-175.
65 *Ibid*, pp. 177-218.

sequential and instinctively trusting thinking of children;[66] fifth, the immaterial thinking and universally inclusive aesthetics of music.[67] In describing this fifth way, the musical way, Nussbaum comments on Mahler and his symphonic work. She presents it as an eventual prototype of a new kind of language which is capable of unhinging and overthrowing the cultural positivism we have so far tried to describe.

What do these alternative thoughts and languages provoke? It is not the empowerment of the one who knows. It is not the greater exhaustiveness of the cognitive process or reality of reference. It is not the individuation and greater sharpness of entities reduced to clear and distinct objects. It is not doctrinal reinforcement. It is not an the increase in confessional efficiency. It is the *Auferstehung* (resurrection) of the Other through "emotional intelligence." These alternative strategies of knowing are typical and classical strategies of "recognition"[68] of the Other which the West has misplaced and prematurely and cynically called "superstition. "

The epistemological anomaly represented by cultural positivism, which is a qualitative impoverishment of the West, began very early, through the loss of the Other. The West did not begin to configure itself as a culture of order and efficiency, and to orient itself in a massive way toward a new and different future, when it discovered a new epistemology. It began to envision a brighter future when it detached itself from "others" who were understood contemptuously then as different populations, as different species. This mechanism is a continuum in the history of modern Europe. It could not have been otherwise. I can create a clear and distinct epistemology, efficient and organized thinking, and a dynamic and continuously moving culture only when I detach myself from others and when I overlook and forget real people.

The presence of others always introduces an element of confusion, opacity and disorder, which prevents a perfect epistemological

---

66 *Ibid*, pp. 219-292.
67 *Ibid*, pp. 305-356.
68 This entire section, the first section of the book, is articulated on the pivotal category of "Recognition." See M. Nussbaum, *Ibid*, p. 35.

or social order. Others, whether people or other species, always slow our pace and act as disturbing elements and obstacles by the incommensurability and opacity of their mystery. In the narrative of modern man, this element is decidedly neglected. The drive for an orderly future and growth is seen exclusively as a virtue. Instead, it appears to us that this passion for an orderly and efficient world is the sign of an anthropological loss, the loss of the Other. The loss is marked by a structural ambiguity. It has given rise to an incredible organizational and creative dynamism, which is the basis of the West's progress. Its dark side from its beginning has been the minimization, discrediting and then oppression and exploitation of other peoples. Its dark side is even more the attrition and alienation of its own project of civilization.

Western epistemology is deeply tied to an anthropological problem because it is the thermometer of detachment and estrangement from other peoples, especially from the peoples of the Global South. This anomaly was present from the beginning, *in nuce*, as a latent reality, in the project itself, in its foundations, in the DNA of the West. Michel de Montaigne said in 1580 that Europe was being born as a new world under the sign of a new rationality and efficiency with two basic structural anomalies. In the "Apology of Raimond Sebond,"[69] the philosopher mentions a Europe breaking away from other peoples whom Europe contemptuously calls uncivilized and primitive. It is also a breaking away from nature, that is, from other species, in order to create, by manipulating them, wealth and progress. Montaigne envisioned the correlation of the two phenomena of "racism" and "speciesism." He managed to glimpse in the birth of Europe the seed of its perversion and self-destruction.

The *Auferstehung* of the Other, as a condition of social resonance, of a possible hermeneutic of meaning, necessarily requires and demands the introduction of a new language. The Other cannot be discovered and can't be said with our current and conventional languages. The Other cannot be thought of in its specificities with the same linguistic categories that deny it. Our common language

---

69 M. de Montaigne, *Saggi, ("Essays")*, (Milan: Bompiani, 2014), pp. 489-683. All of chapter XII of the second book.

is a positivist language that does not envisage the existence of the Other as such. It anonymizes it, objectifies it, neutralizes it. Mahler's music, in Nussbaum's interpretation, represents this intent to find another language that is able to recognize the Other as such. Nussbaum writes:

> "Mahler was rather dismissive of the visual arts, writing that they are hooked up with 'external appearances', rather than with 'getting to the bottom of things.' Music, by contrast, cuts beneath habit. It can shed a light that is, very , unseeable to the socially corrupted eye. Mahler uses the idea of "illumination" in describing both 'Urlicht' and the final experience of heavenly love. But I believe that it is, , an illumination unseeable, because musical, a light emanating from that inner world where the 'dark feelings hold sway.' This is fully compatible with, and a further specification of, the work's Jewish eschatology."[70]

Gustav Mahler's Symphony *No. 2 in C minor* for soloists, chorus and orchestra is a symphony of the *Auferstehung* (resurrection) of the Other. This is the first of Mahler's four symphonies for which the composer envisioned voices. It is also the first of the three *Wunderhorn* Symphonies in which texts from the collection of medieval German songs entitled "Des Knaben Wunderhorn" are set to music.[71] The first eight lines come from the poem "Die Auferstehung" ("The Resurrection") by Friedrich Gottlieb Klopstock, with the exclusion of its last four lines, which Mahler removed. The composer himself wrote most of the remaining text.

Why does Mahler speak of *Auferstehung*? Because Mahler perceives, in his own way, and with his own categories, the modern malaise that we have described as cultural positivism which is composed of this paradoxical overlap of "efficiency" and "symbolic deficit." In Nussbaum's words:

> "In Mahler the daily social routine is dead and deadening; the ascending artist, bitten by his own cry of disgust against this world,

---

70 M. Nussbaum, *L'intelligenza delle emozioni... Op. cit.*, p. 641.
71 In Italian "Il corno magico del fanciullo"; is a cycle of German poems and folk songs published in three volumes from 1805 to 1808 by Clemens Brentano and Achim von Arnim.

ascends to a creative realm in which love exists purified of the lapses of attention that make up much of our daily life."[72]

The fifth movement of the symphony *Auferstehung,*[73] the last, begins with an explosive recapitulation of the desperate weeping of the scherzo, followed by a repetition of material from the other movements, culminating in a tremendous *Dies Irae*; then a fast-developing section, in energetic allegro, offers us a grotesque funeral march, the procession of the dead, which once again results in the weeping of despair. Finally, mysterious and unexpected, an a cappella choir bursts in at the moment of the final recapitulation, accompanying the soprano in enunciating the saving message of the resurrection. Until we come to the long-awaited, liberating and sumptuous transition to the key of E-flat major: an excruciating sonic and emotional impact, like dying and being reborn to new life, like feeling God reaching out a hand from the heavens toward this unhappy and crooked world, and calling us to an encounter with eternity. Mahler reconstructed, from Klopstock's words, the Last Judgment as a moment of eschatological resurrection Christianly understood.

The intensity of the music and the words grow to almost unbearable peaks, in the shots of the solo alto, of the chorus with the two soloists, of the soloists in duet, until the triumphant, majestic free fugato of the chorus. Meanwhile, almost imperceptibly, there was a theological reversal. Klopstock's text, which elevated *Auferstehung* as a transcendent intervention in a typically Christian key, is interrupted and replaced by a text written by Mahler himself that introduces an immanent, human *Auferstehung*, produced by the earth itself. Nussbaum comments on this theological shift, in these words:

"Is there an otherworldly Christian salvation in this work? On the surface, there is. It is emphasized that there is no 'Last Judgment,' no

---

72 M. Nussbaum, *L'intelligenza delle emozioni...Op. cit.,* pp. 681, 682.
73 „Im Tempo des Scherzo. Wild herausfahrend. Langsam. Mysterious- "Aufersteh'n," Tempo di Scherzo. Wildly. Energetic allegro. Slow. Mysterious-"Rising").

assignment of static positions. Being and Love are the ends, and these ends are ends in this life and of this life. Mahler purposively omits portions of Klopstock's text referring to Jesus and heavenly peace, substituting his own romantic vision. Furthermore in order to be a salvation for the Self, the world of bliss must be a world of the heartbeat, of the body, of erotic striving, of continue receptivity and vulnerability -a world in which general compassion for human suffering yields a love as fully universal as music itself."[74]

Theological betrayal? Undue shift in perspective? Inappropriate secularization of a transcendent theological concept? None of this, Nussbaum replies. This theological move by Mahler is in perfect obedience to the Old Testament theology that Mahler has well in mind. Nussbaum writes:

"We can now note that in Jewish eschatology the afterlife is not a bright, but a shadowy place, rather like the Homeric underworld. And Judaism draws close to romanticism in its insistence on finding the worth and meaning of a life within history, in the choices and striving in this life. It seems not too bold to see here, then, a distinctively Jewish picture of the afterlife as in itself shadowy and uncertain, to be given light only by the achievements of the person within this life. Mahler's romanticism and his Jewishness are once again allied, in drawing attention to the light of wordly life, rather than to any *telos* beyond this world."[75]

This is not the *Auferstehung* of the "pantocrator" Christ,[76] of the almighty Christ. On the contrary, it presupposes a kenotic anthropology. As Nussbaum reminds us well, the possibility of the recognition of the Other, of others, presupposes a particular kind of anthropology. Not an anthropology of control but of "vulnerability," of need[77] and reliance, an anthropology that is kenotic.

The cultural positivism of the West is marked by an anthropological deficit caused by detachment from others, by the loss of the other. No

---

74 M. Nussbaum, *L'intelligenza delle emozioni...Op. cit.,* pp. 640, 641
75 *Ibid*, p. 750.
76 "Christ Pantocrator," is a depiction of Jesus in glory, typical of early Christianity and later Byzantine art.
77 *Ditto*.

recomposition of either hermeneutics or today's culture is possible if this primary loss is maintained or reinforced. The loss of meaning is a loss of the other. There is no meaning without the other just as there is no freedom. This strong relationship, between freedom and the other,[78] can be seen in the English words free and friend or in the German words *frei* (free), *freund* (friend) and *friede* (peace), all derived from the Indo-Germanic root *fri* meaning to love. To be free means to belong to friends or lovers. One is free only in bonding and there is bonding only in vulnerability.

The recovery of an anthropology of vulnerability is more essential to hermeneutics than one might think. This because the arrogance of man becomes the arrogance of his texts as well. Only an anthropology of vulnerability is able to give rise to a vulnerable hermeneutic, the bearer of a flexible and welcoming meaning, which opposes the presumption of hermeneutic and cultural positivism. Positivism is not reducible to Augusto Comte's "social physics" as an intent to program the human and society in a scientific key. Underlying it more significantly, it is the loss of this human and hermeneutic vulnerability.

This is the urgent and recurring call of Bernhard Waldenfels in his "Phenomenology of the Other."[79] The central feature of this discovery of the Other, according to Waldenfels, is not the relevance of our question. It is the vulnerability of our response, because our word is never primary. It is not initially configured as a question, but as a response to a voice that is there before us, that precedes us and

---

78 Byung-Chul Han expresses himself in this sense, saying that one is free only in belonging and in the perimeter of ties. He writes, "One feels free in a relationship of love and friendship. The bond, not the lack of it, makes one free. Freedom is then a relational term par excellence. Without a retainer there is also no freedom," in, B.-C. Han, *Il profumo del tempo. L'arte d'indugiare sulle cose*, (*"The Scent of Time. A Philosophical Essay on the Art of Lingering"*), (Milan: Vita e Pensiero, 2017), p. 41.
79 Waldenfels' entire oeuvre is traversed by this central motif of the Other. See the four volumes of his *Phenomenology of the Other*. B. Waldenfels, *Studien zur Phänomenologie des Fremdes*, vols. 1,2,3,4. See especially B. Waldenfels, *Topographie des Fremdes. Op. cit.*, vol. 1, pp. 16-53.

interpellates us.⁸⁰ When the Other resumes its place, we regain our vulnerability, the foundation of a possible relationality. Relationality is never the certainty of the self over the Other. It is the reliance on the Other of a vulnerable self. Such vulnerability does not make life precarious. It makes it full through the non-manipulation of the Other, who always remains a "stranger," not a threat, but a simultaneous source of "extraordinariness." The Other as "strange" "foreign," and "extraordinariness" determines the cornerstones of an anthropology of vulnerability.⁸¹

How can we hold it all together: resurrection of the Other, untampered sense, *kenosis,* vulnerability, earthly life? It is through the Spirit. Pneumatology makes possible the recomposition of meaning through the rediscovery of the Other who imposes himself on us through his *Auferstehung*. This is the most important passage in the Mahlerian interpretation of *Auferstehung*. This shift from a transcendent to an immanent resurrection, which represents Mahler's pneumatological interpretation, can be perceived in the full text that we quote below.⁸² In the first eight lines that Mahler takes from Klopstock, the first theological meaning of resurrection as transcendence, in typical Christian key, can be perceived: "life will give you the one who called you."

As the text develops, the second pneumatological meaning of the resurrection as a flowering from below comes to the fore when it says:
"With wings that I have won for myself, I will soar through the air! I must die to live!... What you fought for will bring you to God!"

We reproduce the full text below to perceive this important pneumatological passage in Mahler's reading.

---

80 B. Waldenfels, *Grundmotive einer Phänomenologie des Fremdes*, (Frankfurt am Main: Suhrkamp, 2018), pp. 56-67.
81 B. Waldenfels, *Estraneo, straniero, straordinario. Saggi di fenomenologia responsiva,* ("*Stranger, Foreigner, Extraordinary. Essays in Responsive Phenomenology"),* Turin: Rosenberg & Sellier, 2020, pp. 13-36.
82 T. Sacchi Lodispoto, *Gustav Mahler* - Vocal texts from Symphony No. 2 - The Resurrection, in, www.flaminioonline.it

(DEUTSCH)
Chor und Sopran
Aufersteh'n, ja aufersteh'n wirst du,
mein Staub,
nach kurzer Ruh'!
Unsterblich Leben! Unsterblich
Leben wird Der dich rief, dir geben.
Wieder aufzublüh'n wirst du gesät!
Der Her der Ernte geht
Und sammelt Garben
Uns ein, die starben!

Alt solo
O glaube, mein Herz, O glaube:
es geht dir nichts verloren!
Dein ist, dein, ja dein, was du gesehnt!
Dein, was du geliebt, was du
gestritten!

Sopran solo
O glaube: du wardst nicht umsonst
geboren!
Hast nicht umsonst gelebt, gelitten!

Chor und Alt
Was entstanden ist, das muß vergehen!
Was vergangen, aufersteh'n!
Hör' auf zu beben!
Bereite dich zu leben!

Sopran und Alt solo
O Schmerz! Du Alldurchdringer!
Dir bin ich entrungen!
O Tod! Du Allbezwinger!
Nun bist du bezwungen!
Mit Flügeln die ich mir errungen.
In Liebesstreben werd' ich
entschweben
Zum Licht zu dem kein Aug'
gedrungen.

(ENGLISH)
Chorus and soprano
You shall rise, yes you shall rise, my
dust,
after a short rest!
Immortal life! Immortal
life shall He who called you give you.
Again shalt thou be seed to blossom
again!
Goes the master of the harvest
and gathers sheaves
of us who died!

Contralto solo
Believe, my heart, believe:
nothing shall be lost to you!
Yours is, yours, so yours what you
yearned for!
Yours the one you loved, for whom
you fought!

Soprano solo
Only Believe, you were not born in
vain!
Not in vain have you lived, suffered!

Chorus and alto
That which is born must perish!
That which is past rise again!
Stop trembling!
Prepare to live!

Soprano and alto
Sorrow! You who pervade all!
I have escaped you!
Death! Thou who subjugates all!
Now are you subjugated!
With wings that I have won for myself
in lust of love I will soar through the
air
to the light that no eye has penetrated.

Chor	Chorus
Mit Flügeln die ich mir errungen,	With wings that I have won for myself
Werd ich entschweben!	I will soar
Sterben werd' ich, um zu leben!	through the air!
Aufersteh'n, ja aufersteh'n wirst du	I must die to live!
mein Herz, in einem Nu!	You will rise, yes you will rise
Was du geschlagen	my heart, in a moment!
Zu Gott wird es dich tragen!"	What you fought for
	will bring you to God!

Mahler's is not a pure romantic humanization of the resurrection. A pneumatological interpretation is central to hermeneutics because meaning not created by interpretive praxis is received through the recognition of the *Auferstehung* of the Other. It is the Other that guarantees the survival of sense and its persuasive power. It is the Spirit that is the guarantor of the Other and its sense other.

In a context such as ours, theological and hermeneutical revival necessarily passes through the articulation of a "pneumatology of life."[83] The Spirit, only transiently contains, disciplines, orders, stops. Its main impetus is drive, motivation, imagination, aspiration, sharing, bonding, communion and vocation for life. The Spirit is the

---

83 This "pneumatology of life" can also be described as the maternal side of the Spirit in a clear alternative reading of the Trinity, as Maria Zambrano does, for example, in a philosophical-theological key when she speaks of the "femininity of the Spirit." M. Zambrano, *Cartas de La pièce. Correspondencia con Augustin Andreu*, Pretextos, (Valencia: Universidad Politècnica de Valencia, 2002), p. 107. In this recovery of the feminine side of the Spirit, M. Zambrano relates to the work of Clement Alexandrinus, who believed that the Christian God, out of love for the world, also became a maternal God. Indeed, Clement Alexandrinus writes, "And while the ineffability of him is Father, compassion toward us has become mother. The Father because he loved, became feminine." C. AleSSANDRINO, *Quale ricco si salverà?* (*"What Rich Man Will Be Saved?"*), (Rome: Città Nuova, 1999), p. 37. See also, on Zambrano, L. Vantini, *La luce della perla. La scrittura di Maria Zambrano tra filosofia e teo-logia*, (*"The Light of the Pearl. Maria Zambrano's Writing Between Philosophy and Theo-logy"*), (Cantalupa: Effata Editrice, 2008), pp. 49-59.

Spirit of life.[84] It is connected to life beyond words. Not that words do not express life; they do express it and mightily so; but the life expressed by the Spirit is often ineffable, that is, expressible only beyond words. This is because the Spirit of life does not express or express itself only on the human level. It exists beyond the human in all those lives that have a nonverbal language of life.

This is the meaning of Bernard Sesboüé's reflection on the Holy Spirit. He conceives of the Holy Spirit as the Spirit of life. It is a "faceless and voiceless" Spirit because it is universally inclusive of all kinds of life. The Spirit's proper is not so much to speak, but to make others speak. Sesboüé writes about this:

> "However, the proper of the Spirit is not to speak of Himself, but to make men whom He inspires speak according to the thought of the Father and the Son."[85]

In the following two sections, we will try to describe how the two theological categories we have described so far, the Bible and the Trinity, can once again become ferrymen of living meaning. This is possible only if they do not try to hoard and stop meaning, but to make it fluid through a decentralization of their witness. Giving up being self-referential, and centered on them, transitively from them it aims to go beyond themselves to others.

"Beyond the Bible" and "beyond the West" is not a prevarication to the detriment of the Bible or the West. It is a fulfillment of them through the promotion of a meaning that has finally been set in motion and is beginning to transit and circulate in a reading that has become an erotics of life and for life.

---

84 J. Moltmann, *Lo Spirito della vita...Op. cit.,* pp. 120-145. Cf. Y. Congar, *Credo nello Spirito Santo...Op. Cit., pp. 34-45.*
85 B. Sesboüé, *Lo spirito senza volto...*Op. cit., p. 15.

5. Beyond the Bible. The Birth of a "Third Testament"[86]

The Spirit's affirmation, which also includes the revitalization of the Bible, entails the Bible's empowerment, its flexibilization. In the life of the Spirit there is no empowerment without flexibilization, exuberance without sobriety, presence without absence, affirmation without limitation, flourishing without *kenosis*. The Son experiences *chenosis* as the natural locus of his own identity. Like him, the Father and the Spirit, by virtue of their relational character, are also chemotic beings. They are capable of downsizing, emptying and relinquishing their more typical and more specific prerogatives by virtue of their dialogue and interaction with other lives.

Trinitarian *kenosis* is not a circumstantial concession or part of a communicative or promotional strategy. *Chenosis* is an ontological trait of the Trinity.[87] In *kenosis one* yields and resizes not as a secondary or peripheral trait of one's being. It is an important and central part of one's being which makes the presence of the other possible and real. Every true relationship involves the surrender and sacrifice of something important. What applies to the Trinity also applies to the Bible. The Bible cannot be just an affirmative book. Like the Trinity, the Bible is and should be a kenotic book.

---

[86] C. S. Keener, *Spirit Hermeneutics. Reading Scriptures in Light of Pentecost*, (Grand Rapids: Eerdmans, 2016), pp. 153-171; S.J. Land, *Pentecostal Spirituality. A Passion for the Kingdom,* (Cleveland: Ctp Press, 2010), pp. 191-208; D. Castelo, *Revisioning Pentecostal Ethics. The Epicletic Community,* (Cleveland: CPT Press, 2012), pp. 107-127; P. Althouse, *Spirit of the Last Days...Op. cit.,* pp. 162-169.

[87] It is in this self-limitation, true kenosis, that the Trinity becomes a paradigm of inclusiveness and welcome. Religious pluralism is not a drift or concession but represents the heart of the Trinity understood in this way, as a relational entity par excellence. Cf. Keith E. Johnson, *Rethinking the Trinity & Religious Pluralism. An Augustinian Assessment,* Op. cit., pp. 65-90. Cf. Amos Young, *The Spirit Poured Out on All Flesh: Pentecostalism and the Possibility of Global Theology*, (Grand Rapids: Baker Academic, 2005), pp. 12-24; Mark S. Heim, *The Depth of the Riches: A Trinitarian Theology of Religious Ends,* (Grand Rapids: Eerdmans, 2001), pp. 11-21; Jacques Dupuis, *Christianity and the Religions: From Confrontation to Dialogue,* (New York: Orbis, 2002), pp. 24-31.

There is no affirming Bible without a kenotic Bible. The *Kenotic Bible* renounces saying everything and the last word. In its kenotic momentum, the Bible envisions, indeed requires, the emergence of other words, the emergence of a third Testament.

The Bible, as the biblical canon, cannot be conceived as the end of God's Word but as its beginning. It is the initial Word of God that gives rise to other words of God that are beyond the canon.[88]

The task of biblical hermeneutics, in its effort to dismantle the persistent and varied biblical and cultural positivism, is to go beyond the Bible, in obedience to the Bible's own drive through the Spirit. We have described the centrifugal thrust of the Bible since the beginning of our essay and attributed it to the very type of language used by the Bible. This is articulated around the categories of ambivalence and paradox.

Biblical hermeneutics must go beyond the Bible because outside of it there are other human words of value which the Bible cannot disregard and which it must consider. The Bible does not have fixed meanings. It has meanings that are clear in its address from the beginning; however, they are flexible in their structure. The Bible, because of the kind of linguistic structure it possesses, is mostly made up of and constituted not of actual and present meanings. It is comprised of latent and potential meanings that would remain dormant and wasted if they were not resurrected and stimulated by non-Biblical words, narratives, events and stories. It is called upon to interact with these by virtue of possible application, but in accordance with its own flowering and empowerment.

Because life and truth are unavailable in the gaze of a single text, the Bible within itself gives voice to various versions of a single event, to various events uncontained in a single version. For this reason, it is incomprehensible that those who perceive plurality in the Bible reject the plurality of bibles. There is not just one Bible.

---

88 In this sense the strong Christocentrism of Karl Barth's theology runs parallel to his bibliocentrism as a limitation and obstacle to a more centrifugal dimension that instead characterizes the Bible and also a more relational Christology. K. Barth, *Dogmatica ecclesiale*, Antologia a cura di Helmut Gollwitzer, ("*Church Dogmatics*, Anthology edited by Helmut Gollwitzer"), (Bologna: Edb, 2013), pp. 12-34.

There are a variety of them. This variety is not the variety of different translations and even less the quantitative variety of different specimens. Every human word is a bible; it is sacred. It is sacred not canonically (canon), in its form, but in its essence.

One is the canonical Bible. One must remember that. But Many are the non-canonical Bibles. One must not forget that. We must resist the temptation to overestimate the canonical Bible and underestimate the bibles of men. Every human story, with its successes and failures, with its joys and sufferings, sometimes prolonged indefinitely, is a sacred story. It is a bible that God reads with emotion and attention. We must tenaciously resist the temptation to make the Bible an instrument that undervalues, minimizes the history of men. That is not its task.

The human words[89] of today are valid extra-biblical stories. They are words and events that enhance the Bible. And they are something more. These stories are also sacred. In the midst of them we also find God's words. They are expressions of God's interaction with the people of today who have taken over since the closing of the canon. They are not purely human words that common sense asks us to consider. They are divine words, which God Himself speaks today through the Spirit, with the intent to dialogue and interact with people today as He has always done.

God's word did not stop at Malachi, the last book of the Old Testament in the order given by the Septuagint. Neither did he stop at John's Revelation, last book of the New Testament. The stiffening of the Old Testament canon, which would like there to be no more God-inspired words after the *Tanak*, is matched by the parallel and equally pernicious Christian stiffening of the New Testament, which would like there to be no more God-inspired words after the book of Revelation.

Human and hermeneutical attention to human words that exist "beyond the Bible" can be linked to the dynamics of the Trinity

---

89 In this sense we should also take the Apostle Paul's words when he describes the lives of people who believe as true letters bearing witness of God through human affairs. Paul writes about this, "It is known that you are a letter from Christ" (2 Corinthians 3:3). The Bible does not contain all of God's holy letters.

itself. In the three biblical passages presented at the beginning of the third part of this essay, we emphasized the complexity and sobriety of the three persons of the Trinity in their dialogue and interaction with humanity. We have not considered their relationship and interaction at the intra-Trinitarian level, what is known by the name of "perichoresis."[90]

It is necessary to establish a difference in the trinitarian relationality. There is "ad extra" relationality and "ad intra" relationality. Relationality "ad extra" is that which God entertains with human beings. Relationality "ad intra" is that which God entertains within the Trinity. We cannot stop to consider the "ad intra" relatedness of the Trinity in detail because that would take us too far; however, we can briefly mention it because it has a bearing on understanding the scope of the Bible.

The Bible helps us to understand the Trinity as we have verified in the three Bible passages we commented on in this third part. The opposite should also happen. The Trinity should help us understand the Bible. The Trinity helps us to understand that the Bible is not monolithic. It helps us to understand that beyond the diversity of characters and styles there is a more structural diversity at the level of history. There is the history of the Father in the first covenant with its own written Testament (Old Testament). There is the history of the Son in the second covenant with its own written Testament (New Testament). There is the Spirit who seems to have neither a Testament nor even that it is canonical. Will the Spirit be a lesser God? Would we, as modern Christians, add to the classic "ontological subordinationism of the Spirit" also a "scriptural subordinationism of the Spirit"?[91]

---

90 *Perichoresis*, is the term (from Greek περιχώρησις, *pericóresis*, "penetration," a derivative of περιχωρέω, *pericoréo*, "to rotate," "circular movement") specific theological term to describe intra-trinitarian life and interaction, based on their unity of essence, according to the specificity of each.

91 In connection with this persistent pneumatological subordinationism, we can also refer to the work of Hans Urs Von Balthasar, as for example does Alessandra M. Turchi, who perceives the essence of Von Balthasar's theology in the Christological principle of Love. Cf. A.M. Turchi, *L'amore*

The essence of our essay on hermeneutics is embodied in the commitment to think, meditate and eventually overthrow this *"scriptural subordinationism of the Spirit."* Our "biblical *hermeneutics* of ambivalence and paradox" flows irreversibly into a *"pneumatological hermeneutics of life."* Paradox is not an end in itself. Biblical paradox is the hallmark of life and the Spirit is the source of life. Instead of proposing that the Spirit comes from outside to the Bible, we have chosen the opposite path. It is the very Bible that suggests a beyond itself, an overcoming of itself in the Spirit and toward the Spirit. This "beyond the text," without which the text would deny itself and its forward momentum, starts from the text itself.

This is the meaning of the phrase "beyond the text" which was present in the horizon of this Essay from the very beginning. Hermeneutics is never tautological. Its exuberance and sobriety, traits that distinguish it, are the appropriate and ideal mechanisms for making this going beyond itself possible. This "beyond the text" leitmotiv in this essay is a crypto-pneumatological motif. It expresses the claim that it is by virtue of the Spirit that all life exists and goes forward.

---

di Dio in Gesù Cristo come principio ermeneutico della vita cristiana nella teologia di Hans urs Von Balthasar, (*"The Love of God in Jesus Christ as a Hermeneutical Principle of Christian Life in the Theology of Hans urs Von Balthasar"*), (Milan: Glossa, 2021). Indeed, one may wonder whether in Von Balthasar, despite the enormous effort to construct a consistent pneumatology, this typical pneumatological subordinationism does not prevail despite himself. Indeed, Von Balthasar asks, "Can there be a pneumatology beyond Christology? ". Cf. H.U. von Balthasar, *Lo Spirito della verità,* (*"The Spirit of Truth"*), (Milan: Jaca Book, 1992), pp. 31-51. However, the doubt remains because on another side Von Balthasar emphasizes in the same work the freedom of the Spirit to go beyond all schemes and rules. With respect to this complexity in grasping the action of the Spirit, Von Balthasar writes: "The NT leaves free how to think more exactly and how to describe the powerful and life-giving power of God manifested in the Father's sending of Jesus, then in the Son's glorification and the Spirit's mission to the church. It is content to circumscribe the mysterious reality of the Spirit from many sides that often appear to be opposed," *Ibid.* p. 94.

The Bible exists only by virtue of the Spirit. This "beyond the text" is not a catch phrase to claim the relevance of culture or society, a way to leave Scripture behind. It is a way to claim the primacy of the motive and pneumatological foundation of every living entity. This primacy is not exhausted in the foundation of an event. It guarantees the flow of events and the genealogy and birthing of new events. The event that the Spirit claims as its own is the birth, relevance and validity of its own Testament, its Testament of life, a third Testament.

Will this concession be possible? Will it be possible to grant the Spirit this claim? Posing the problem in these terms is foolish because it is the Spirit who is guiding history and we should ask him if we can do this or do something else. This third Testament does not need to ask the other two Testaments for permission. This third Testament already exists. It is only a matter of us seeing it and recognizing it. The Spirit is amply active among us. The paperless record of its interaction with men is an irrepressible and inescapable reality to men of good will.

Pneumatological subordinationism, i.e., the inferiority, submission and queuing of the Spirit to Jesus and the Father, is especially typical of Western Christianity and it is embodied in the theological formula of the *Filioque*.[92] This formula, which is contested by Eastern Christianity, has its own biblical form. The Father has his own canonical testament (the Old Testament), the Son has his own canonical testament (the New Testament), the Spirit has neither his own testament nor canonicity. There is no theological *par condicio* here. Ontological subordinationism has created hermeneutical subordinationism.[93] One tries to compensate for this but in doing

---

92 *Filioque* is the expression added by the Latin church to the Nicene-Constantinopolitan Creed, recited in the Mass, to better explain the procession (subordination) of the Holy Spirit (*qui ex Patre Filioque procedit*); it was one of the main causes of the disagreement and separation between the Greek and Latin churches and also one of the most controversial points at the Council of Florence (1439), which nevertheless ended up accepting it, considering it a legitimate and reasonable addition. Cf. J. Moltmann, *Trinità e regno di Dio...Op. cit.*, pp. 191-200.
93 Von Balthasar highlights this "hermeneutical" dimension of the Spirit in the third volume of his *Theologica* trilogy devoted entirely to the Spirit. Typical of the Spirit would be this freedom of action described by John,

so one makes the situation worse. It is said that the Spirit is actually the one behind both the Old Testament and the New Testament. This "hermeneutical modalism," like "Trinitarian modalism,"[94] acknowledges the Spirit but depowers him. It makes the Spirit only a characteristic, a mode of God the Father.

The Testament of the Spirit[95] actually is composed of all the words, events, interactions, human that make up today's world.[96] This is not a secondary register. Like the first two Testaments, this third Testament is made up of divine and human words. There we find God and human experiences interwoven. The Word of God is not a Word of the past. Biblical times are not closed. Thanks to the Spirit,[97] biblical times are also our times. God continues to speak

---

Acts and Paul. Von Balthasar writes, " the Spirit has above all a characteristic freedom which in John is revealed in the elusiveness of his outpouring ("where he wills"), in Acts is manifested in his uncontrollable irruptions or imparting of certain commandments or prohibitions, in Paul in the believer's liberation from the bondage of sin such as begets the outward law and in enabling Christian love, in whose free superiority the whole law is fulfilled (Gl 5:13f.). Insofar as it is free and makes free, the Spirit cannot be defined legally. Another aspect that runs through it is the realization of a personal exchange through the Spirit. He accomplishes this insofar as he is, according to John, the exegete and the Interlocutor, in a much deeper sense than the sense of truth that one learns from a teacher, of which the Johannine 'formulas of immanence' testify," in H.U. von Balthasar, *Lo Spirito della verità, Op. cit.,* p. 94.

94 Modalism is the Christian theological conception according to which believing in one God in the Trinity of Persons and one Trinity of Persons in the unity of God means believing in one divine being who manifests himself for creatures (appears to them) in three different ways, namely as Father, as Son and as Holy Spirit.

95 Referring to the work of Hans Urs Von Balthasar, B. Sesboüé speaks of the Spirit as "The Spirit 'Exegete' of God." Cf. B. Sesboüé, *Lo spirito senza volto...Op. Cit.,* pp. 64-68.

96 This radical inclusiveness is typical of the Spirit, which means that opening up the scope of the Bible and the biblical canon necessarily pass through a reorientation of both in the perspective of the Spirit. Crf. B. Sesboüé, *Lo Spirito senza volto...Op. cit.,* pp. 13,14.

97 This dimension of the Spirit as the "inspirer" of new words, linked to new experiences that even today humans have of God, is highlighted in L. Bouyer's pneumatological reflection, according to which, the Spirit has

precious words in our midst. God's precious words are found in the Bible. They also exist today and it is good to know how to listen to them.

The Third Testament, as a Testament of the Spirit of life,[98] does not claim to be canonical. The Spirit, in fidelity to himself, to his discreet but vital way of acting, does not seek prominence and does not wish his testament to be canonized. Given its characteristics, it could not be this way. The Spirit is by nature always transgressive of the limits and censures, canons and schemes that try to imprison life. The Spirit is always outside and beyond the lines, stubbornly unpredictable, naturally asymmetrical. The word canon in itself is already a nonsense if applied to the Spirit.

The "canon of the Spirit" is an oxymoron. The Spirit demands that we at least acknowledge its Testament. It demands that we acknowledge the validity and relevance of its witness for life in the hearts of believers and non-believers, in churches and outside churches, in those who behave well and those who struggle with destruction, in human and non-human life. To the latent universality of the Old Testament, and the spiritual universality of the New Testament, the universality of the life of the third Testament of the Spirit is added. Because it is non-canonical, it is more inclusive and universal. This third Testament does not have Israel or the church as its living and articulating space. Its horizon and space is the "kingdom of the triune God" which every living being can call his or her own.

---

always prompted humans to create new words, new myths, outside the church, as new narrative experiences within. Cf. L. Bouyer, *Le Consolateur. Esprit Saint et vie de grâce,* (Paris : Cerf, 1980), pp. 218,219.

98 This connection of the Spirit with life is also very strong in the pneumatological reflection of François-Xavier Durrwell who speaks of the Spirit as the "generation" of life, reading the whole Trinity from this perspective but attributing the central role, in the generation of life, to the Spirit. He writes, "In God, there is the Parent, the Generate and the Generation. The Son and the Spirit both proceed from the Father, in his paternity: the one is begotten, the other is generating," in *L'Esprit du Père et du Fils,* (Montreal: Editions Paulines, 1988), p. 24.

6. Beyond the West[99]. On the Possibility of Alternative Knowledges

Why is it that an erotics of interpretation, made possible and triggered by the Spirit of life, urges us to go not only "beyond the Bible" but also "beyond the West"? Because between the Bible and the West an ironclad partnership has been forged. Even what is secularized and non-denominational in the Western world expresses this distorted biblical-Christian exclusivism which ignores or undermines the value present in other cultures. In many ways, secularization, which in the best of cases is a displacement and narrowing of the religious, and in its most radical form is not a denial of or detachment from religion, but a reformulation of it for modern use and consumption, does nothing more than displace the monolithism and compactness of religion in the political-cultural sphere. It appears, even with the contrasts, ruptures and juxtapositions it creates, to be a pure intra-system game, not creating a real alternative to the cultural monolithism and positivism of the West but rather reinforcing them.

Secularization intended to universalize meaning but, on the contrary, it has caused its narrowing. The paradox is that we are facing a second major failure. Western *hybris* has played wrong twice.

The first failure resides in the fact that Western Christianity wanted to contrast the benefits of its religious universalism with the limits and provincialism of paganism. Religion was supposed to reach everyone. It did reach everyone, but with the intent to subjugate them. It was a lazy universalism that erected a particular religion as universal. The religion of the West, namely Christianity in its various

---

99 Alberto Abruzzese, starting from a different perspective, calls for going beyond the West, in the sense that the classical representatives of Western culture, writers and readers, are no longer the center of new social processes, but rather a cultural barrier to be broken down. While we talk about other knowledge related to other peoples, he will instead speak for the new communicative codes present in the new media. Cf. A. Abruzzese, *Contro l'Occidente. Analfabeti di tutto il mondo uniamoci*, (*"Against the West. Illiterates of the World Let Us Unite"*), (Milan: Bevivino Editore, 2010), pp. 13-25.

forms and confessions, represents the failure of universalism and not its flowering.

The second failure came with secularization which was supposed to break the universalist claim of Western Christianity in order to really enlarge this universalism to all humanity. This was its scope. Just the opposite happened. With secularization the West did even worse because it made universal not a particular religion but a particular culture.

The same thing could be said of the West's political-cultural pluralism. This is in many ways a pluralism that perpetuates the same Western anomalies. This is because new strategies and ideas, even when they oppose each other, perpetuate the system and its basic orientation. True pluralism cannot only be a pluralism of different meanings, different schools or different ideas. True pluralism can only be a pluralism with different actors. The West is far from incarnating a true pluralism because it does not want different actors. It often cannot even recognize them as such. The only way forward is genuine dialogue with structurally different cultures. Only then there would be a pluralism of systems and not a pluralism within the same system.

We do not see this pluralism of systems on the horizon because the West has a historical rhythm that does not allow for dialogue and true sharing which are by nature slow and open. Non-Western cultures become in reaction identity-driven, self-referential, distrustful and, many times, even lazy. They expect others to come to them and not the other way around.

In some ways, the Christian Bible has had more effect outside the churches than in the churches because of a factor of proportion and number. Biblical closure, described in the previous paragraph, is prolonged in the West's closure to other human words and ways of thinking. It is not possible to liberate the Bible unless we liberate it also from the West. In our day, it would seem that the correct interpretation of the Bible is possible only in the West. This has been our critique of "liberation theology" which has *de facto* reinforced the West and its primordial cultural paradigms. Liberation Theology didn't propose truly alternative categories to think God, the earth and multiculturality.[100] The West cannot go by itself beyond the West. It's entrapped in its own cultural confessionalism. Only by cultural contamination, based in cultural incompleteness and humility, can the West welcome and enter in dialogue with real otherness incarnated in communities it has undervalued and despised in the past.

a. *A Chronic Cultural Closure*

The West's recovery and tampering with Christianity began very early. We find this in one of the founders of modernity, Thomas Hobbes. He was a diligent interpreter of the Bible. *Leviathan,*[101] his main work, and *De cive*[102] which precedes it only by a few years, are veritable exegetical-theological treatises. In these texts Hobbes achieves a true exegesis of the central texts of the Old and New Testaments. He does not aspire to give them a circumscribed, partial or outline idea. He embedded his analyses and penetrating reflections in a theological project with a clearly delineated and coherent outline. The result is not particularly sobering or self-critical of the project it tries to read from the Bible. From its formulation and for a few more centuries, Hobbes' reading and interpretation of the Bible will be original and spectacular. It succeeds in elaborating, from an ancient text, a project for a new and unprecedented historical era that is coming into being. Like any good interpretation, Hobbes' does not enslave its time to ancient patterns. He allows new times to receive the prospective thrust and legitimacy, at least partially, of an ancient text that serves as a propeller toward something new. This innovative thrust in reading the Bible is immediately visible in the two books just mentioned.

---

100 G. Gutierrez, *Teología della liberazione... Op. Cit.*, pp. 193-241. This is, according to Moltmann, the direction and emphasis of all liberation theologies, including non-Latin American ones. J. Moltmann, *Esperienze di pensiero teologico. Vie e forme della teologia cristiana,* (*"Experiences in Theology. Ways and Forms of Christian Theology"*), (Brescia: Queriniana, 2001), pp. 202-232.
101 T. Hobbes, *Leviathan...* Op. Cit.
102 T. Hobbes, *De Cive... Op. Cit.*

Hobbes gives birth to a new Christianity which is based on an innovative reading of the Bible (Old and New Testaments). This new Christianity is perfectly aligned with the modern state. It serves the logic of the modern state and only legitimizes and reinforces it. The Bible read by Hobbes,[103] and the Christianity derived from it, is a strange mixture of freedom and captivity.

By breaking with the deterministic logic of medieval, church-centered hermeneutics, Hobbessian biblical hermeneutics creates an innovative interpretation relative to an anthropology based on the individual and a modern state that is born with new characteristics and mechanisms. Unfortunately, it ends up chaining them both to the contract of a meaning that can only be put at the service of the state. The interpretation of the Bible is doomed to pander to Leviathan and to absolutely and exclusively legitimize its monopoly of political force for its own project.

The modern Christianity proposed by Hobbes is more modern than Christian. This is not a problem in itself because every Christian group in history interprets the Bible in accordance with its own historical context. This is inevitable. The problem arises when one wants to pass off as totally biblical an interpretation which is instead circumstantial. Above all, the problem arises when one wants it to be definitive even though we know that it is purely circumstantial and transitory because it is tied to a specific historical period.

We find the same problem of criticism that ends up legitimizing the West in liberation theology. Liberation theology has been, without a shadow of a doubt, the most characteristic, innovative and successful theological-cultural initiative that Latin America has given birth to in the past decades and with which it has contributed to contemporary world theological reflection. This has been possible by virtue of three characteristics that I would quickly like to highlight here.

First of all, liberation theology has reminded us that freedom is a never-ending experience, that liberation is a process that is

---

103 T. Hobbes, *Leviathan,* see especially Parts III and IV. Cf. *De Cive. Op. cit.,* see especially part III on religion, chapters 15 to 18.

always open and always in flux. Alienations never give up. They are continually recycled into new, ever more sophisticated alienations.

Second, liberation theology points out that faith, which should be the antidote against alienation, is frequently complicit in it and may very well generate oppression and exploitation. This is why faith, especially official faith, dogmas, and religious institutions, must be continuously monitored as much as vices and heresies.

Thirdly, liberation theology asserts that for faith to be genuine it must not make its internal coherence prevail as a guarantee of truth. This must be its relational dimension. It is only in the exercise of a close and current connection with the most immediate socio-political historical context that faith discloses the essence of its truth and its historical relevance. Liberation theology is a great experiment in contextual theology.

Liberation theology, while still necessary today, appears insufficient to give Latin America a sense of its own mission and future horizon. Here I would like to make three criticisms of the backbone of the liberation project of this theology.

The first is that liberation theology privileges one form of alienation, poverty, as the prototype of all alienation. In this it shows itself to be overly dependent on a Marxist analysis of society. It naively believes that when the poor have been liberated from their poverty automatically all other alienations will be vanquished and disarticulated. Reality shows otherwise. The liberated poor man often experiences no embarrassment in becoming the oppressor of his woman or the master father of his children.

The second is that liberation theology still describes liberation processes too linearly and homogeneously. As Homi Bhabha has well reminded us,[104] ambivalence irreversibly imbues every liberation process. The liberated person without any problem can simultaneously be an oppressor. His or her own liberation can even act as an alienating element for others.

The third criticism is that liberation theology, despite itself, is in an extreme extension of the typically modern, Western project of

---

104 H.K. Bhabha, *Interrogating Identity. Location of Culture,* (London: Routledge, 1994), pp. 57-93.

the struggle for freedom. Not wrongly, Jürgen Moltmann, a well-known theologian from Tübingen, in an open letter to José Miguez Bonino, asked three questions. The main one was: What is typically Latin American about liberation theology?[105] Despite its strength, especially in the 1980s and 1990s, liberation theology has not been a genuine alternative to the Western model. It has prolonged it.

b. *The Epistemicidal Effect*[106]

What effect has this Western monolithism had on other peoples and on the other knowledges expressed by those peoples? The answers to this question can be varied. It is possible to give a minimalist answer: nothing happened because the two realities developed in parallel ways. Or it is possible to give a maximalist answer: the influence was greater than it appears because it was only Western knowledge that gave other peoples the ability to organize, filter, and dynamize their own knowledge and make it more functional and effective.

Boaventura de Sousa Santos has a different opinion. He speaks of a perverse effect that the West has had on the world's other knowledge, most often unconsciously and implicitly, which he provocatively calls an "epistemicidal" effect.[107] By this he means the West's stigmatization, contempt and complete indifference of other peoples' knowledge. Epistemologically, the West has killed other world knowledges[108] by distancing itself from them by adopting a

---

105 J. Moltmann, *Esperienze di pensiero teologico...Op. cit.*, pp. 202-205.
106 Hanz Gutierrez, "The Invention of Blackness and the Anthropology of the Gospel. Between Cultural Insolence, Paradoxes, and the Resilience of Ambivalence," in, Maury D Jackson, Nathan Brown, *A House on Fire. How Adventist Faith Responds to Race and Racism*, (Warburton: Signs Publishing, 2022), pp. 193-208.
107 Hence the need to resist not militarily but culturally. Resistance understood from an epistemological perspective. Cf. Jose Medina, *The Epistemology od Resistance. Gender and Racial Oppression, Epistemic Injustice, and Resistant Imagination*, (Oxford: Oxford University Press, 2012), pp. 12-35.
108 B. de Sousa Santos, *Epistemologies of the South. Justice against Epistemicide*, (London: Paradigm Publishers, 2014), pp. 2-17.

pretended absolute knowledge and then by imposing this knowledge on other peoples as the only possibility.

The great controlling effect and conquest of other peoples did not occur militarily but epistemologically. Prior to the military and cultural colonialism that we know of and has been acknowledged and partly amended by the West, there has been an epistemological conquest that amounted to epistemic genocide. The knowledge of other peoples was forgotten, denigrated, minimized, asphyxiated and annihilated.

For Boaventura, this epistemicide Western culture was accomplished by three cognitive mechanisms that have rendered the alternative thoughts of the South invisible. The first mechanism is what Boaventura calls "abyssal thinking."[109] This is the Western thinking that establishes a dividing line between what is rational and justified and what is on the other side of the line, in the abyss of irrelevance, and nonexistence. "Abyssal thinking" sees, but it does not value other knowledges. It is a mechanism of non-recognition. Overly dependent on its own logic, it fails to value what it sees. Westerners have become unable to understand other knowledges which they have themselves discovered with curiosity and perseverance.

The second mechanism is what Boaventura calls "an epistemology of blindness."[110] The West, having rendered the knowledges of the Global South insignificant, at some point is no longer able to see them. They become disabused, lose their register, and finally these knowledges become invisible. This is not because they are not there but because Western logic is no longer able to perceive them. If the West no longer sees them, they no longer exist. From insignificance, those other knowledges have passed into nonexistence.

The third mechanism is what Boaventura calls "a lazy epistemology"[111] (Lazy Reason). The West no longer sees other knowledge and it does not even seek it out. The West becomes lazy, even though it passes itself off as dynamic and curious. The West

---

109 *Ibid*, pp. 118-135.
110 B. de Sousa Santos, *Epistemologies of the South...Op. cit.*, pp. 136-163.
111 *Ibid*, pp. 164-187.

no longer knows how to be curious about anything else; it is only concerned with itself. This structural laziness that it has built up by virtue of its inattention to the Other leads it to want to sublimate itself into the compulsiveness of restless, vigilant, dynamic but self-referential thinking. It is dynamic solely for its own creations and not for the creations of others.

c. *Provincializing Europe*

Going beyond the West in order to read the Bible in a new way is a moral imperative because the West's cultural monolithism and positivism are dangerous, self-destructive and contagious. Cultural positivism has destroyed other knowledge in the world. It has also destroyed the knowledge of the West itself which has become efficient but disenchanted and without eroticism. Without the other knowledges, even the reading of the Bible loses perspectives that would allow the enhancement of its own richness from new angles. This is why we urgently need to "provincialize" Europe, suggests Dipesh Chakrabarty. Europe (Western culture) is only one province of the world, he argues, not the whole world. For Dipesh Chakrabarty, going beyond Europe is not synonymous with destroying Europe or setting it aside. We need Europe, because of what Europe represents and has been able to do; however, we do not need it on the terms it imposes on us. Europe itself is unaware of its dysfunctions and the epistemicidal effect of what it exports and sells as cultural virtue.

Europe remains an important part of today's world. Yet is called upon them to interact with the rest of the world only as a province of the world and not as the entire world. It is called upon to interact with the equally important provinces of the same world, with their different and alternative knowledges. Provincializing Europe entails relativizing the West's pretensions to be unique. The point is not to erase these pretensions but to make Europe interact with other readings. Pluralism is not a pluralism of proposals, which could be traced back to a single actor. It must be a pluralism of actors.

Can history ask Europe to become a mediator and guarantor of other peoples? This is an urgent question because it would thereby reinforce a Eurocentrism that in other ways we want to unhinge.

We must distinguish between political strategy and cultural strategy. Europe cannot be asked to make a political sacrifice. Politically, Europe, like other regions of the world, must watch over its own interests, implement its own logics and strategies in order to ensure its own development. It must be able to agree, when necessary, on common policies with the various nations. It must be able to make concessions in the same terms as those which are imposed on other nation-states. But Europe cannot assume at the cultural level this legitimate self-referential political strategy either in the face of a past still laden with open questions or in the face of the present where the world has become polycentric.

d. A "Universalism of Differences"

How can we go beyond the West while leveraging the positive experience it created? Giacomo Marramao responds by saying that to do this we must go beyond the West's "abstract universalism." This is the European program elevated to a universal model in its two classical forms of assimilationism and multiculturalism. He calls for a movement toward what he calls a "universalism of difference." These two forms of integration, which start with a cultural monolithism, the Western one, have failed. This is not least because today's world has become even more heterogeneous and culturally polycentric. The failure of these Eurocentric models is evident in the coexistence of a radicalized "homogenizing" trend, especially of a consumerist nature, of which globalization is an example, and the differentiating counter-trend that reinforces and stiffens identities and their local rootedness. This opposition is present in the West and also on a planetary level.

Contemporary societies simultaneously move toward cultural global uniformity but also toward local and closed identities. There is homogenization, but there is also differentiation of culture. "Universalism of difference" means recognizing multiple actors in a polycentric world where the universal does not already exist. We need to create it by recognizing particular identities, which are both open and converging, in a dialogue that find elements of convergence not a priori but a posteriori. We are not in the *universum* but in the *pluriversum*, not in tolerance but in translation. The cultural convergence of the Roman Civitas was a good example because it did not require conformity to something already given. Roman identity always integrated elements of the conquered cultures, particularly their gods and goddesses.

e. *A Possible Cultural Mediation*

Bruno Latour also sees and contemplates the possibility and necessity of a mediating role of a culturally diverse Europe. This mediating role should arise from Europe's new awareness of itself from a revisitation of its history. He writes:

> "Europe is meaningless if it does not reflect on the abysses thrown wide open by modernization. That is the best sense that can be given to the idea of reflective modernization."[112]

Latour promotes a European presence, but in a different key. Referring to Dipesh Chakrabarty's proposal to limit European arrogance through a necessary process of provincialization, Latour responds positively.

> "It is said that Europe as a continent has sinned by being excessively ethnocentric and by pretending to dominate the world, and that it needs to be "provincialized", to be brought back to more just dimensions. But today it is this provincialization that can save it (Europe)."[113]

But this downsizing does not or should not mean a renunciation or abandonment.[114] If imperial arrogance were followed by Europe's

---

112 B. Latour, Tracciare la rotta...*Op. cit.*, p. 132.
113 *Ibid*, p. 130.
114 In this sense, Federico Rampini also believes that the West still has an important role to play in the international chessboard, albeit a diminished one. The West must not disappear either through the intervention of others or through its own annihilation. F. Rampini, *Il suicidio occidentale. Perché è sbagliato processare la nostra storia e cancellare i nostri valori,* (*"The Western Suicide. Why it is Wrong to Judge our History and Erase our Values"),* (Milan: Mondadori, 2021). In the same direction goes, though with considerations of a different nature, Roger Scruton. Cf. R.

anonymous and resigned presence, it would seemingly be better. In reality, it would amount to maintaining the same position, albeit reversed.

> "If Europe was dangerous when it believed itself capable of 'dominating' the world, but don't you think it would be even more dangerous if it shrank and tried, like a mouse, to hide from history? How could it escape its calling to recall, in all senses of the word "recall," the form of modernity it invented? Even because of the crimes she has committed, littleness is not for her."[115]

Latour does calls for a "going beyond the West." This leaves intact the possibility of Europe discovering its role as mediator of a different two-dimensional multiculturalism. The first is anthropological and multicultural and the second is ecological and political. Latour writes boldly about the first of these:

> "It is as if Europe has made a centuries-old pact with potential migrants: we came to you without asking you for anything; you will come to us without asking us for anything. *Quid pro quo*. From this there is no escape. Having invaded all peoples, all peoples return to you."[116]

On the second Latour reiterates the fact that the Earth problem is not a problem of environmentalists but of politics. Latour writes further:

> "The Earth that she had wanted to grasp as the Globe offers herself again as the Earthling, for a second chance that she has not at all deserved. Here is what befits the region of the world that bears the greatest responsibility in the history of ecological upheaval. Still a weakness it can turn to its advantage."[117]

Scruton, *Il suicidio dell'Occidente*, ("*The Suicide of the West*"), (Grassina: Le Lettere, 2021).
115 B. Latour, Tracciare la rotta...*Op. cit.*, p. 131.
116 B. Latour, *Ibid*, p. 133.
117 *Ibid*, p. 136.

Europe has already been a mediator of non-Eurocentric initiatives. It would be a matter of resuming the fine examples of non-self-affirming cultural mediation of recognition and empowerment of the other. We briefly report on two such initiatives which are evidence of what Europe has been able to create on the Latin American continent. Antonio Raimondi and Hans Maxime Kuczynski are two Europeans who arrived in South America and never returned to Europe. They contributed positively to development, in this case of Peru, by resorting to their European cultural background. They do not use this as an instrument of Eurocentric exploitation, but as a ferment of mediation to make the other flourish.

Antonio Raimondi[118] (Milan 1824 - San Pedro de Lloc 1890) was an Italian scientist who became a naturalized Peruvian. Even as a child he was noted for his irresistible attraction to the natural sciences. The choice of Peru as a destination for his research was conscious and emotional. The lack of scientific knowledge of the legendary land of the Incas was the first stimulus. The second was something that affected him deeply. This occurred when he witnessed, in the greenhouse of the Botanical Garden in Milan, the cutting of a giant cactus of Peruvian origin.

In 1848 he participated in the historic Five Days of Milan for the independence and unification of Italy. Afterwards, fleeing the horrors of war, he arrived at the port of Callao on July 28, 1850. He was received by the prestigious Peruvian physician Cayetano Heredia, director of the "Colegio medico de la Independencia" within the first university in the Americas which is the University of San Marcos. Heredia charged Raimondi with the classification and ordering of the zoological and mineralogical collections of the College itself. In 1851, when the chair of natural history became vacant, Heredia called Raimondi to fill that role because he recognized in the young Italian great scientific talent and exploration skills.

Raimondi belongs to the classic family of researchers of that era whom we might call encyclopedic naturalists. In them the motivation for learning knew no natural or human limits. Nothing was an

---

118 C. Estremadoyro Robles, "Antonio Raimondi," in *Diccionario historico biografico. Peruanos ilustres*, (Lima: A.F.A., 1999), pp. 599,600.

impediment to Raimondi's explorations and research. Neither the most rugged territory nor the most complex field of science could oppose his lust for knowledge. In his travels, Raimondi collected everything he could record of the natural and social landscapes he found on his way. He collected and systematically ordered plants, animals, insects and minerals while he made barometric measurements, meteorological observations and precise plans that completed the information about the different regions he explored.

He gathered abundant information on the coal deposits of the northern Peruvian littoral. He analyzed and quantified the guano of the Chincha Islands. He verified the saltpeter of Tarapacá. He traveled through the remote auriferous provinces of Carabaya and Sandia. He navigated the Marañon, Ucayali and Amazon, Peru's most important eastern rivers. He traced the plans of the cities of Cajamarca, Chachapoyas, and Huancavelica or of notable archaeological monuments, such as Huanuco Pampa or the Fortress of Paramonga. He discovered the Chavín Stele and the majestic Puya both of which bear his name in tribute to his work. It is striking how much respect and admiration men of science of other nationalities testified to him. This included explorers with a special interest in archaeology, such as the North American George E. Squier, or the Germans William Reiss and Adolph Stubel (the latter a teacher of Max Uhle). It included geologist George Kunz and paleontologists like Louis Agassiz and Gabb. It included travelers like the Frenchman W. Weiner, author of the well-known work *Peru and Bolivia*, and naturalists such as the Italian Pigorini, the Poles J. Stlzmann, K. Keiski and L. Taczanowski, the German Theodore Wolf. Even prestigious historiographers such as the Englishman Sir Clements Markham paid him the highest regard in his lifetime.

Undoubtedly Raimondi was, on his own merits, one of the most sought-after and cosmopolitan figures in Peru at that time. For his prestige and seriousness, he was recognized as a scientific adviser to the Peruvian state throughout his life. He died on October 26, 1890, tried by a long illness, assisted by his daughter Elvira in a land that had become his and for which he had given his best enthusiasm and skills.

Max Hans Kuczynski[119] (Berlin 1890 - Lima 1967) was a German physician who also became naturalized Peruvian. A bright, intelligent, polyglot boy born into a Jewish family, he grew up in the culturally prolific and scientifically intense Berlin of the early 20th century. He earned his first doctorate in natural sciences in 1913, with a research paper in parasitology, and his second doctorate in medicine in 1919. He began his scientific career at the Institute of Pathology of the University of Berlin and was also a visiting professor of pathology at the Institute of Medicine of the University of Omsk (Siberia). While there he led several medical and scientific expeditions to Central Asia (Soviet Union, Mongolia, China) to investigate the complex relationship between disease and sociocultural and geographical factors, particularly among the nomadic populations of the Asian steppes. His book, Steppe *and Man* (*Steppe und Mensch*, Leipzig 1925), where he described and studied the Kyrgyz nomads, became a classic in the social and geographical medicine of his time.

Just as his contemporary Albert Schweitzer had done a few years earlier, leaving Europe for Africa, Kuczynski traveled to Peru with his wife Madeleine Godard who was an aunt of French filmmaker Jean-Luc Godard of the "New Wave." He never to return to Europe. In Lima, he immediately contacted the Institute of Social Medicine at the National University of San Marcos. which was the oldest university in America, and began working with the eminent Dr. Carlos Enrique Paz Soldan. He did not stay in Lima. He chose to practice medicine in the rugged Peruvian jungle of Iquitos where he raised his two sons Michael and Pedro Pablo. This is where he began his fight against leprosy and the stigma that affected those with it. As chief physician of the San Pablo Leprosarium, where sufferers were kept in isolation and almost without medical care, he opened the gates and reorganized the sanitary and living conditions, both inside and outside and implementing innovative and visionary outpatient treatment.

---

119 M. Cueto, "Un medico aleman en los Andes. La visión medico-social de Maxime Kuczynski-Godard, in, *Allpanchis Puthurinqa*, (Revista de Estudios Andinos), Vol 32, Num. 56 (2000), pp. 39-74.

Max Hans also had strong civic and political convictions and became a Peruvian citizen. He later criticized the Peruvian ruling class, denouncing then-President Manuel Odria for his despotism and unilateral benefits he granted to wealthy Peruvian families at the expense of the poorer sections of the Peruvian population. As a result, he was imprisoned for nearly a year in 1948. Upon release he devoted himself to clinical practice in Lima, until his death in 1967, at the age of 77. He identified with a land that was not his and for which he had given his best. He died without thinking or in the least suspecting that fifty years later, his son Pedro Pablo Kuczynski, that little boy who had accompanied him into the jungle in his medical ministry on behalf of Peru's forgotten sick, would become president of the country that had welcomed him and that he had made his own.

f. *A Possible Cultural Contamination*

This role of possible mediation, articulated in new terms, in terms of sobriety and cultural empathy, glimpsed by Bruno Latour for today's Europe, needs to be accompanied by a parallel cultural contamination. Not in an exercise of procedural *par condicio* or cultural compensation, nor in the manner of a philanthropic concession to give the idea of being open to others when one can do everything oneself because others have nothing to give.

The cultural contamination of Europe today presents itself both as a cultural obligation and as a cultural opportunity. It is a cultural obligation because the undoubted validity of certain corrective proposals that Europe regularly proposes, to heal and straighten its historical path, emerge within itself in a typical example of self-medication. It ignores the fact that it is often not the idea or the proposal itself, but "the who," the agent who proposes it that has a determining and a correcting effect. It is cultural relationships with other different cultures that Europe needs as an exercise to break out of its chronic narcissism that leads it to think it can survive on its own, resorting to others only strategically and circumstantially. It is not the "what" but the "who" that Europe needs to discover.

Contamination also presents itself to Europe as a cultural opportunity because it is not true that Europe knows everything and that there are no things it needs to learn from other peoples. Despite all appearances, the lesson that Europe urgently needs to learn from the perspectives of a globalized world and of its own internal survival, is the immeasurable value of bonding. Without this conversion to bonding, which it cannot learn from itself, from a pure introspective exercise, Europe risks its self-destruction and the destruction of everything else.

Europe must learn or relearn bonding, which is important for life and for the possibility of meaning, from other peoples. Bonding, of which the Trinity is model and horizon, has a social form and a gnoseological form. The social form is the community and the gnoseological form is the symbol. This is why the cultural positivism of the West cannot solve its chronic problem of social disintegration nor its structural gnoseological nihilism unless it learns to interact with other peoples. All the bonding proposals spawned continuously by the West have created paradoxically more dispersion. It has produced a contractual bond that is short-lived.

Contractual bonding, which is a contradiction in terms, is not bonding because it points to the benefit of its exploitation. Contract perpetuates the atomistic assumption that wants the parties to be saved, regardless and apart from the group. The West embodies a typical example of cultural involution that has become chronic, manifesting itself in its inability to see bonding as the foundation of life.

This is what the German philosopher and biologist Andreas Weber suggests when he writes that we Westerners live by the pragmatic motto: "Try in every situation to survive at any cost." This is a typical individualist dogma. Indigenous people live instead by a different model that goes like this: "Everything lives, therefore try together with others to nurture life." This is what Weber calls *Indigenialität*[120] ("indi-geniality").[121]

"We are all indigenous," says Weber, making it clear that our civilization has colonized indigenous people and colonized them to our own way of thinking. Indigenous does not mean savage or

---

120 A. Weber, *Indigenialität*, (Berlin: NP & I, 2018), pp. 10-23.
121 A. Weber, *Ibid*, pp. 12-16.

primitive but having and cultivating the "genius" of seeing that life is a reality of relationships and relations. Life is relationship, and he who says relationship says trust. Trust is not a psychological or moral virtue that autonomizes the subject more. It is the experience that breaks the arrogance of wanting to do everything on our own and orients us confidently toward the other. Life is relationship and relationship is trust. The genius of indigenous[122] and non-Western peoples is, according to Weber, the ability to see life in relationship and relationship as life. This is something which non-Western peoples do not merely think about. They embody it in their way of life and relationship with others and with nature. This is why their civilization is not a civilization of "progress," but a civilization of "balance." The abandonment of relationships as the founding principle of life is what actually makes progress, understood as the apparent fulfillment of life, possible.

In a reversed reading, we must learn to see not what progress acquires but what it leaves out, namely relationship and life. For this reason, the recovery of relationship and life necessarily implies a scaling back of progress. It cannot be otherwise. Absolute progress and growth (GDP growth), no matter what, are incompatible with life understood as relationship and trust.

"Indi-geniality" is the defining thought of non-Western cultures that we have neglected and despised. It is time to re-establish an honest and open dialogue with the peoples of the Global South and non-Western peoples, to be positively contaminated by this relational and inclusive *ethos*. It is also time to urgently try to rediscover indigeniality within ourselves.

Avant-garde thinkers in physics, biology and other sciences have long been proposing a similar cultural shift that would make relationship, connection, networking and inclusiveness the central paradigm of a new kind of civilization. This is something that the

---

[122] The concept of true cultural alternatives is not elaborated by Andreas Weber alone. At the theological level, too, we are witnessing a reevaluation of non-Western contextual theologies that have been present for a number of years. Cf. Randy S. Woodley, *Indigenous Theology and the Western Worldview. A Decolonized Approach to Christian Doctrine*, (Grand Rapids: Baker Academic, 2022), pp. 53-88.

West cannot learn for itself as a new theory or cognitive perspective. The West must not delude itself into thinking that it is learning this in laboratories and research centers and spreading it through its books. Bonding and the vocation to bond can only be learned in deep relationship with real Others, with peoples other than ourselves.

7. The Resonance of Meaning: Sabbath, Advent and Unverfügbarkeit[123]

This section is not a confessional defence and apologetics of either the Sabbath or Advent. It is rather the opposite. It is a sharp and radical critique of them. Confessions that directly or indirectly relate to these two categories make the mistake of hiding their interpretive self-referentiality under concepts that by essence are universal, thus narrowing and limiting their scope.

The Sabbath expresses an "upstream universality," which reconnects us humans with the origin, with a good origin that finds its foundation in the abundance, joy and generosity of the Father. This origin cannot be seized or hoarded by any denomination. It belongs to all through the affirmation that we humans are born well in space, in a welcoming space contaminated by positive presences: that of the Creator, therefore that of his creatures as well.

We advocate a de-confessionalization of the Sabbath because the Sabbath expresses the universal right to feel and know happiness in a space of our own given to us by the Creator which guarantees our survival in a real way. Through the Sabbath, God loves us in the space of creation and declares us to be "spatiogenic" beings insofar as we are able to inhabit and enjoy the earth, transforming

---

[123] *Unverfügbarkeit*, German for "unavailability," is a technical term introduced by Hartmut Rosa in the context of a new understanding of society as a space not of efficiency but of vital resonance. We will use it in the context of cultural renewal because of a sense that it is such when it relinquishes control and becomes a witness to life. Particularly from it we will describe two important categories for the reconstruction of meaning, which are the Sabbath and the advent in a non-denominational nor religious, but human and cultural key.

it from an aseptic space into a place inhabited and contaminated by lives that dialogue with one another. The Sabbath is elegy and hymn, resilience and trust, of beings who become such only in their rootedness in space. The Sabbath is a praise of space as a place of life and humanity.

Advent expresses a "downstream universality," reconnecting us humans with the future, with a future that is good because it is connected to a God who is not afraid of surprises and who is curious about the alternative ways that the future brings, even when these push him to change his plans. A God who is faithful and confident in the future more than in his plans about the future. This good future cannot be seized or hoarded by any denomination. It belongs to everyone through the affirmation that we humans have a possible and happy future in time.

Happiness is the ability to gather the memories of the past and the experiences of the present and assemble them into a plot that flourishes by projecting it into the future. Through advent, God delivers and give us a specific future, a future of our own that guarantees our survival in a real way. He also declares us to be "futurogenic" beings, capable of creating new things. Advent is elegy and hymn, resilience and confidence, of beings who become such only by confidently following in the wake of time that blossoms into the future. Advent is a praise of the future as a place of life and humanity.

As we described at the beginning of this chapter, a necrophilic tendency has developed in our time. It is not that all contemporary culture is necrophiliic. In some ways it is a vibrant and dynamic culture; however, it conveys a destructive urge that tends to cage life and to neutralize it. To the "death of God,"[124] as a symbol of transcendence, we have added the "death of our neighbor,"[125] in that we have become chronically indifferent to the other. As if this were

---

124 According to the famous aphorism coined by Nietzsche. F. Nietzsche, *The Gay Science and Idylls of Messina*, Adelphi, Milan 1977; G. Vahanian, *The Death of God. The Culture of Our Post-Christian Era*, (New York: George Braziller, 1961).
125 L. Zoja, *La morte del prossimo, Op. cit.*, pp. 5-16.

not enough, even things have become dead objects,[126] ceasing to experience the real.[127]

In such a necrophilic context, meaning, the meaning of texts, can neither survive nor be reborn. For this reason there is an urgent need for *Auferstehung* (resurrection). Here is the context in which the Sabbath and Advent fit in as categories that reinforce the rebirth and recomposition of life.[128] Sabbath and Advent are places of Resurrection of life and meaning.

Today, in the realm of totalizing information, which dispenses with things and neutralizes the things of life and also the life of things, that is, our world, space and time are the first things to be deformed. The realm of information necessarily deforms our relationship with space and time. The time and space of information, the latest update of classical cultural positivism, create a space that is fast because it is aseptic of presences and things. It is also a time that is fast, also aseptic and neutral, because it is devoid of presences that contaminate it and, by contaminating it, slow it down. The dematerialized world of information works with a caricature of space and time. Informational space and time are fast and performant because they are completely dissociated from things and persons and from the world and from life.

The world of living things requires, as we shall see in this section on Sabbath (space) and advent (time), a slow time and a contaminated space. This is what Marc Augé[129] about space calls "place," as opposed to a fast and aseptic space that he calls instead "non-place." And this is what Marramao calls *kairos*,[130] as opposed to an accelerated time that he calls, borrowing a phrase from

---

126 R. Bodei, *La vita delle cose*...Op. cit., pp. 12-24.
127 B. -C. Han, *Le non cose*... *Op. cit.*, pp, 5-21.
128 In this sense, one could speak of Sabbath and Advent as rituals of meaning, characterized not by formalism but by the redemption of meaning through the inscription of meaning in the spaces of meaning that are rituals. B.-C. Han, *La scomparsa dei riti. Una topologia del presente*, ("*The Disappearance of Rituals. A Topology of the Present*"), (Milan: Nottetempo, 2021), pp. 53-65.
129 M. Augé, *Non-places. Introduction to an anthropology of surmodernity...* Op. Cit., pp. 9-23.
130 G. Marramao, *Kairos... Op. cit.*, pp. 8-18.

Shakespeare's Hamlet,[131] "off-axis time" or "dromomania" and also "hurry-up syndrome."[132]

The slow time and contaminated space of the world of things stabilize life and give it a framework that is the world of things in which a different ethic is also articulated that values fidelity, commitment, promise, observation, obligations and resilience. Time and space are warped by haste and no longer serve as rootedness and horizon, have become things that, along with others, punctuate the acceleration of our way of life. The only way to stop them is to rediscover the rituals that give meaning by slowing them down. The Spanish word "demora" (delay) and the Italian word "dimora" (home) highlight the close link between living at home and the slowing down that this implies. Without slowing down, the rituals that make a place and a moment lived and shared events disappear.[133]

The first two realities that must return to life are those on which life, events, and experiences rest: space and time. This is what we will try to do with respect to these two central categories of life: the space we will call Sabbath and the time we will call Advent. What distinguishes a living space and time is the contamination of these realities with the experiences, tragedies and concrete events of life. This contamination of space and time with concrete life is such by virtue of the bet on the value of relationships and bonds. It is the bet that relationships and not resources create, according to Hartmut Rosa, social resonance.

Hartmut Rosa reminds us that the hallmark of a true and meaningful bond is "resonance."[134] . Resonance is a bond that speaks, indeed sings. Beyond the almost mystical and heavenly register that the word resonance seems to evoke, Rosa wants to go beyond the purely functional register which we now try to describe as a successful life.

---

131 "The time is out of joint" in Hamlet's mouth. G. Marramao, *La passione del presente...Op. cit.*, p. 101.
132 *Ibid*, p. 94.
133 B.-C. Han, *L scomparsa dei riti, Op. cit.* pp. 11-27.
134 The entire third section of the fifth chapter summarizes his theory of "resonance." H. Rosa, *Resonance. A sociology of Our Relationship to the World*, (Cambridge: Polity Press, 2019), pp. 164-174.

Life is not successful only when it functions well and when it is efficient. Functionality and efficiency are inadequate registers for expressing the success of a life and they remain inadequate to what they want to express. Success still does not occur when a life remains only coordinated in itself, but separate from others. Full success occurs when the internal coordination of a life is expressed and witnessed in a perceptible way (resonance as expression), and when that success picks up and queues up with the success of other lives (resonance as harmonic network).

The atomized world of cultural positivism, though functional and efficient, is a dumb world. Resonance makes bonding fluid, moving, interactive, erotic, where eroticism means desire as openness *to* the Other, (I am able to desire the Other and the Other feels desired by me) and as openness *of* the Other (I am desired by the Other and the Other desires me). Resonance understands bonding not as a task, but as passion and gift, as a circular and nonlinear exchange not of a commodity that one controls, but of a prerational sound perceived as a gift and given back as such in an act of witnessing.

The best way to overcome cultural positivism of which alienation from others is the main sign, Rosa says, is resonance. Resonance is a way of life in which people feel touched, involved, and challenged by other people, places, and objects that previously produced no echo in us instead and which, in turn, we now touch and influence with the sound and meaning our actions, words, and presence produce.

From an existential point of view, we all know what it means to be touched by someone's gaze or voice, a piece of music we listen to, a book we read, or a place we visit. The ability to feel affected by something and, in turn, to develop an intrinsic interest in the part of the world that affects us, is a central element of any positive way of relating to the world. In contrast to alienation, which stops the flow of life, resonance recomposes this flow. It is defined by four crucial elements.

First from "a-ffection." This is not the ability to feel something, but rather the ability to welcome, to be touched (affected) by what comes to us from outside. From being numb to the voices of others, from the muteness of things and people that we had turned into manipulable and dumb objects, we become instead for the first time capable of being touched by voices that we stop manipulating. Affection is the afferent pathway that reaches us from the outside, creating a feeling that is not our own product, but simply the effect of others coming to us. The world is no longer indifferent to me but speaks to me.

Second, from "e-motion." This is not the ability to feel something closed in myself, but rather the momentum that starts from me toward others after I have been resurrected by their voice. E-emotion is the centrifugal movement that allows me for the first time, because I am alive, to offer something of myself to others. Emotion is the efferent way from me to others. I am no longer indifferent to the world but to this external world I am able to give something alive, which is my voice and my meaning.

Third, from "relationship." This doesn't mean controlling or being controlled by others. It is the act of trusting the Other that allows me to receive or give something in a fluid, vulnerable and non-automatic exchange. The muteness of others and the world was matched by my own muteness. Neither others nor the world was able to tell me anything, just as I was also unable to offer them anything. It was the parallel coexistence of two mutisms that thought they were sovereign because they were impervious to the voice of others. Relationship changes this situation and overwhelms it. It is others who give me back my voice and, as a result, I too become mutually capable of offering my voice to others. The lives of others make me alive, and I, as a living being, contribute to making the outside world and others alive.

Fourth, from "Unavailability. This is the *"Unverfügbarkeit"*[135] of the Other. This virtuous circuit is a fragile one, because the flow of the bond can run aground or break off easily at any time. It stumbles most often not because of indifference, disinterest or disaffection, but rather because of over-involvement and over-interest stifles the

---

135 This is an essential category in H. Rosa's theory. It is the recovery of it that enables the construction of a qualitatively different society oriented not to "resources" or growth but to "people" and flourishing (resonance). H. Rosa, *Resonance. A sociology of Our Relationship to the World*, Op. cit., pp. 184-191.

fragile voice of the Other. It is not indifference but rather the desire to control, the desire to program the voice of the Other that kills the Other.

For this reason, the Other, as much as the relationship and the bond, remains unavailable to us. However, this unavailability guarantees the bond and prevents it from becoming symbiotic. Bonding is neither a fate nor a necessity. The bond is vulnerable because it is contingent and chosen. Its unavailability is guaranteed by this opacity, this indelible ambivalence in any kind of identity, which is what allows the bond to exist. Resonance is not a monody repeated by various agents. It is a mysterious polyphony where each agent makes its own unique voice sound in a surprising convergence of musical perspectives and rhythms. Resonance is not symbiosis that erases differences. It is communion, by virtue of and because of those differences.

Where can we find together autonomy and dependence, difference and convergence, specificity and relationship, meaning and consensus? Two symbols and two reserves of this kind of bonding which is necessary for life and meaning are the Sabbath and Advent.

Sabbath and Advent are not just two doctrines, as certain confessional and ecclesiological positivism would have it, but two human experiences said with biblical symbolic categories. Just as the universal category of "nature" is said in the Bible to be "creation," similarly the category of "space" is said in the Bible to be "Sabbath" (origine/protology) and the category of "time" is said to be "advent" (future/escatology). Already the expression "biblical symbols," applied to Sabbath and advent, seems to dilute and water down their substance and halve their meaning, because the symbol is thought to be a halved and impoverished reality. It is actually the opposite. The symbol is more real because it also grasps the less visible and more hidden dimensions of reality and, as a result, gives us a more truthful record of all that exists and cannot be said in unambiguous languages.

Today, life and meaning have become a calculation and, as such, are without past and without future. The Sabbath, as a symbol of the past, and advent as a symbol of the future, aim to reconstruct the arc of human experience and the human arc, which is larger than the hermeneutic circle, and in which meaning is given. The theological or doctrinal formulas of Sabbath and Advent are of minor and secondary value compared to the human and cultural symbol that these two categories represent. Sabbath and advent are coordinates of life, space and time, as human archetypes, which we need to rediscover in order to articulate the experience of meaning. They are two rites of passage that help us discover the human and experiential character of time and space.

a. *The Sabbath:*[136] *a Space of Meaning and a Meaningful Space*

The first surprise comes from the universal significance of the Sabbath as a spatial category that reminds us that we are special beings because we are bound to a place[137] that precedes us and, by welcoming us, impels us to walk and go beyond in certainty and confidence because we are rooted in creation. The Sabbath is not a denominational category, as it seems, but a human one, regardless of the religious choice of individuals. Everybody is humanly blessed on the Sabbath by the mere fact of existence. There is no other condition.

The Sabbath is memorial to creation only to remind us that we are terrestrial. Creation and Sabbath are two biblical ways of saying that space is not neutral, but contaminated from the beginning with the biophilic presence of a benevolent Creator who calls all humans his children and, subsequently, with the presence of his creatures who feel loved by the Father because they receive from him a specific place they can call "their own."

---

136 Cf. J. Moltmann, *Dio nella creazione. Dottrina ecologica della creazione, ("God in Creation. A New Theology of Creation and the Spirit of God")*, (Brescia: Queriniana, 1992), pp. 318-341; A. Heschel, *Il sabato. Il suo significato per l'uomo moderno,* ("*The Sabbath. Its Meaning for Modern Man*"), (Milan: Garzanti, 2001), pp. 21-42; S. K. Tonstad, *The Lost Meaning of the Seventh Day,* (Berrien Springs: Andrews University Press, 2009), pp. 386-401.
137 R. Panikkar, *Spazio, tempo e scienza,* ("*Space, Time and Science*"), (Milan: Jaca Book, 2021), pp. 243-259.

Through space, of which the Sabbath is a symbol, we recognize ourselves as derivative beings in that we are created by the Creator and situated and rooted in a place that determines us in our identity and design. Through space we are particular, earthly beings, the negotiated expression of a territory, a place that imposes on us a specific profile, by virtue of which, however, we can be free and which we can also transgress by going beyond.

Freedom is always a going beyond, a transgressing a territory that allows us its transcending. Space is our ally because it is meant to be the stepping stone and not the grave of our freedom. Space is the territory that roots us but also allows us to fly. In order to fly and be free, we have to start from a place on which to rest our feet.

As happens in life and history, space from potential ally became enemy and danger for the ancients. Nature, which was the space in which, they lived and moved, seemed to distance itself from them making them feel like strangers as they perceived in it a constant threat. This was the birth of the first form of spatial alienation. This was a hidden and paradoxical alienation because nature became the object of conflicting feelings. The ancients felt it as a friend, in that it welcomed and nurtured them; however, being unpredictable and uncontrollable, it escaped their calculations and predictions, creating bewilderment among them with its force and impetuosity.

The ancients in their vulnerability and wisdom established a covenant with nature: they didn't spoil nor manipulate it and nature in return nurtured and homed them. Rhythms and customs were born, in the broad spectrum of human activities, all of which were marked by the cycles of nature. Human life stood in relation to nature and in relation to the rhythm that nature proposed and imposed. All ancient communities were cosmocentric; they had nature, the cosmos, as their point of reference. In this sense they were all spatial cultures because nature is space. The toll they though, had to pay to nature was high, because human life was not be able to follow its own momentum and design. It was only allowed to do so to the extent that these remained within the limits imposed by nature.

Human life became natural life through the daily patterns and recurring rituals that always led it back to nature. The result was a benefit, the tranquility and certainty of regular cycles. But the result was also a chronic and structural anguish in knowing that one is imprisoned and crushed by a natural space, which disregards the human and to which one must simply surrender. People make a virtue of necessity. One praised space and idolized it, worshipping it through divine figures that were all but extensions of natural space.

Ultimately, space became a place of scarcity, of attrition, of imprisonment. Instead of serving as a point of support, it became a point of subjugation. Space then absorbed, conditioned, transferred into the ancients the fear of freedom. It was better to give up freedom in order to have life guaranteed. The tyranny of space cast upon the ancients the allure of accommodation and conformity. Virtue lied in being able to be content and accept the place that nature entrusted and imposed on us.

All of this changed with the arrival of modernity. After long and complex transitions, modernity revolutionizes our relationship with space. It is not space that will impose its laws on us, but we humans who will manipulate space according to designs we choose. From being a home to be inhabited, nature becomes a material to be manipulated through experimentation. Humans move away from nature, and do so in a paradoxical way because, initially, they seem to recognize natural space as an autonomous space for the first time considered independently of humans.

Instead, the cosmos that had hitherto been considered and seen only in function of man, and was a large but friendly cosmos, becomes infinite and unlimited. For the first time there is a real measurement of the cosmos, but at the same time it is no longer a cosmos that man feels is his own. Yet, modern man describes in his autonomy that same cosmos which, by measuring it, he makes dependent on himself.

While the premodern cosmos was smaller and described on a human scale, it still remained outside human manipulation because it was inhabited by mystery and the presence of deities that we humans do not control. The modern cosmos, while autonomous, because it is first perceived in its true dimensions, because it is reduced to measurement, is actually depowered and made dependent on the measurer, that is, man.

Modern science is, from the very beginning, a strongly anthropocentric enterprise claiming on space, near and far, control and a strong hand. That nature has finally become the object of mathematical calculation, as it did with Galileo Galilei, means just that, that natural space has been neutralized.

This gives rise to the second form of spatial alienation, alienation that is typically modern, hidden and paradoxical, but of the opposite sign from the ancients. While in the ancients the patterns and rituals of life validated and respected nature, the modern ones, while appearing to respect it, are artificial and in essence anti-natural. The moderns' covenant is not a covenant with nature, but a covenant at the expense of nature. We thought it would not undermine it, much less destroy it or even destroy us. The environmental crisis, which is an unmistakable sign of an abnormal relationship with space, is also a human crisis, because the human cannot alienate itself from space. We are spatial beings.

The history of the last four or five centuries is the history of the deformation of space through the masking of a functional conception and control over it. Space by nature precedes us and we cannot expect to tamper with it and control it. It would be like wanting to be fathers of our parents. Of our fathers we can only be children who in the journey of life learn not to be subjected to their parents but rather know how to interact with them. We can't replace them and much less can we erase that symbolic precedence. Similarly, we can only be children of space which, in the troubled journey of life, we can learn not to suffer it, but to interact with it. Human life and life in general cannot be thought without space, not even with space controlled or manipulated.

The history of the West in recent centuries is the history of the tampering with space. This is the anthropocene according to the description made by Paul Crutzen.[138] We moderns thought for the first time in human history that we understood space and nature and

---

138 Paul Crutzen, *Benvenuti nell'Antropocene. L'uomo ha cambiato il clima, la Terra entra in una nuova era*, (*"Welcome to the Anthropocene. Man Has Changed the Climate. Earth Enters a New Era")*, (Milan: Mondadori, 2005), pp. 12-23.

that we knew more than other ages what needed to be done with space. This claim, in some ways incredibly creative and efficient for the positive results it brought, has unfortunately turned out to be an illusion of which the environmental crisis is an indisputable metaphor.

The two risks, that of sacralizing space and that of disenchanting it, have always existed but at the balance of results and effects, the second risk has produced the most negative results. This is the context that we moderns have created and in which we find ourselves today. A little "sacralization" of space does not hurt today, keeping in mind, however, that we should not overdo it. We otherwise risk creating a polarization between exploitation and sacralization, which, as in any polarization, gives the impression of improvement, leaving things as they are in reality. In our opinion, the Sabbath as a spatial symbol can act as a mediator between a necessary redemption of space and the rejection of its sacralization.

We believe that the Sabbath enables this recovery of space because it enchants but not sacralizes space by virtue of its relational character. We speak of relationship for three reasons.

First, because it is God's Sabbath, that is, it does not belong to us humans. It is not manipulable. The Sabbath is not based on what we do but rather on what God does and is. The Sabbath is God's rest; it is rest for him as well. This means pause but, above all, it means relationship. It is God's rest that we make our own.

Second, Sabbath is relational, because it is not a pure spatial category, but is related to time. It is a mixed category that even made us think it was only a temporal one. To a large extent, Sabbath is, on the contrary, an anti-temporal category because it splits time and does so from space.

Third, the Sabbath is relational because it is not conceived as a neutral space, but as a space contaminated by human events and experiences. The Sabbath is lived space. Lived by humans and other living beings. The Sabbath is God's but it is also one of the most typically human realities. It is by nature the Sabbath of humans.

The Sabbath is synonymous with creation; it is a memorial of it, a biblical term for space and nature. Nature is spatiality. There is no nature without space, and there is no space that is not expressed and configured as nature, as cosmos. The Sabbath comes into being with creation and as creation, and it ends and is configured as the Sabbath. The Sabbath is the crown of creation as lived and blessed spatiality. It is the celebration of the space that is known and felt to have been created by God. Creation and Sabbath are synonymous to express and say a nature that does not want to be autonomous but in relationship with its Creator.

The fact that the Bible calls nature "creation" or space "Sabbath," "sanctuary," or *Shekinah*, all spatial categories in the Bible, might seem like an intent to sacralize and confessionalize these purely human categories. To sacralize and to make partial what is instead human and everyone's remains a risk. The history of the Sabbath is the double story of an undue sacralization, confessionalization and spiritualization and of a narrowing and elitization of its meaning.

We find that the relational character of the Sabbath is not purely spiritual (man-God relationship) nor even merely human (man-man relationship). It expresses a cosmic relationality (man-nature relationship). In this sense, Sabbath is a perfect cosmotheandric symbol,[139] to use Raimon Panikkar's words, in that it relates God, humanity and the cosmos, and does so on a spatial level. The Sabbath tells us that humanity is not human if it is not corporeal, if it is not spatial. It tells us that the cosmos is not a real space if it is not inhabited by humans and God. It also tells us that God is not God if space does not touch him and if we do not regard the cosmos as God's body.[140]

The Sabbath is the biblical symbol for space, and it is so for three reasons.

---

139 In a new culture of bonding that tries to overcome an atomistic culture, bonding is given between agents within a single system, but between subjects of different systems. This is what Panikkar calls "cosmoteoandry," the bonding and dialogue between humanity, God and the cosmos. Cf. R. Panikkar, *Visione trinitaria e cosmoteandrica: Dio-Uomo-Cosmo,* (*"Trinitarian and Cosmotheandric Vision: God-Man-Cosmos"),* (Milan: Jaca Book, 2010), pp. 229-261.
140 S. Mcfague, *The Body of God. An Ecological Theology,* (Minneapolis: Fortress Press, 1993), pp. 65-97.

On a first level, because the Sabbath is a category that interrupts time and regularly breaks it every seven days. This is the deconstructive dimension of the Sabbath, breaking the linearity of chronological time. The Sabbath, as a memorial of creation, is a critical element of linear temporality. We might even describe it as a counter-temporal instance. This is not the most common meaning usually attributed to it. Abraham Heschel elaborates a reflection of the Sabbath in an entirely temporal key. According to him, the Sabbath in its essence is a strong temporal category.[141] We can discern the counter-temporal character of the Sabbath on the basis of the considerations we are making.

On a second level, the Sabbath, while presenting itself as a temporal category, as a rest stops time and imposes on it as a priority a non-temporal category or a category of a completely different temporality. This is one that is measured not chronologically but qualitatively. The Sabbath, being more than a chronological break, articulates a true ontological alternative, a different way of being and being in the world.

On a third level, the Sabbath more than being a temporal category is in effect a spatial category. It is synonymous with creation and with spatiality. The Sabbath is an explicit reference to the cosmos created beyond the temporal reference that inhabits it. He who says Sabbath says cosmos and space. The Sabbath is a praise of spatiality as an essential component of the identity of creatures. Creatures, in order to exist, beside having a specific history, need also a specific and proper space, which shapes their way of being in the world.

The Sabbath is a unique "place of resonance." The Sabbath transforms space into place[142] because it affirms and guarantees otherness, communion, mystery and the unavailability of life and meaning on a spatial level. The Sabbath is synonymous with rest, it is rest; however, there are two ways of conceiving rest. The first is pause, when a temporal sequence is transiently interrupted and then resumes the previous rhythm and preserves it in its essence.

---

141 A. Heschel, *Il sabato...Op. cit.,* pp. 21-42.
142 M. Augé, *Non-places...Op. cit.,* pp. 43-69.

The second presents us rest as reorientation, when the normal rhythm of the event is altered by it and the event, through rest, changes its essence. In the first case, rest as pause simply serves as a moment of respite, to leave temporality unchanged. In the second case, it acts as a transformative instance, because it conditions the whole temporal process by carrying it and pushing it toward a new configuration.

The Sabbath is a valuable source of spatial Unverfügbarkeit (unavailability), an essential component for articulating life and meaning. The *Unverfügbarkeit of the Sabbath* corrects the manipulative tendency of the cultural positivism of our time in three ways.

First, it reminds us that creation, and origin, is not the symbiotic moment where life forms are amalgamated into an undifferentiated whole. On the contrary, creation is the locus of differentiation as the presupposition and condition of life. Without differences and autonomy of entities, life is not possible. The Sabbath is the praise of the differences that ground the life created by God and that by virtue of this converges in Sabbath communion. Creation and Sabbath, then, are memorials of the goodness and nobility of the legitimate heterogeneity of the world of creatures.

Second, it reminds us that creation is corporeality. There is no creation without concreteness. The Sabbath as a memorial of creation is a memorial of the material concreteness of creation. The Sabbath, rather than being a temporal category is a spatial category. It is synonymous with creation and with spatiality. The Sabbath is an explicit reference to the created cosmos beyond the temporal reference that inhabits it.

He who says Sabbath says cosmos and space. Sabbath is a praise of spatiality as an essential component of the identity of creatures. Creatures, in order to exist need a specific and proper space that shapes their way of being in the world. Without this spatiality of which the Sabbath is memory, creatures would be only ideas, projects, abstract values, but ultimately nonexistent. It is only spatiality that grants creatures a particular and specific identity.

Third, it reminds us that the Sabbath is precedence and joy. It reveals God's refreshing presence as a reality that precedes what we do and what we are. Through the Sabbath our being is configured as a response to a word that is before us and who summons and challenges us. The Sabbath reminds us that we are derivative beings. We are preceded by a benevolent intention that grounds us and expresses the divine desire for life affirmation. The Sabbath is the assurance that we are all desired children, believers and nonbelievers, good people and morally untrustworthy people.

Thanks to the Sabbath we are all well-born beings before and regardless of what we may achieve, produce and accomplish professionally, ethically or religiously. The Sabbath belongs to neither Judaism nor Adventism. It is for everyone in a twofold sense: by creation and by election. It is enough to be an individual, of whatever origin, denomination and affiliation, to be blessed by the richness of the Sabbath. It is enough to be blessed in that primordial way to clearly perceive God's universal election. Through the Sabbath every created being is already an elected being. The Sabbath is the sign of God's universal election that includes all people.

b. *Advent:*[143] *a Time of Meaning and a Meaningful Time*

The second surprise comes from the human meaning of advent as a temporal category that reminds us that we are temporal beings because we are bound to a possible future. We are futuribles beings. We are Beings capable of innovation whose being is not meant for the mere reproduction of the past.

Advent is neither a religious nor denominational category as it might seem. It is a human category regardless of the religious choice of individuals. Everybody is blessed humanly in the Advent by the mere fact of existence. Through the Advent each of us is granted the possibility and the right to create future.[144] There is no other condition. Advent is the biblical way of saying the future, but to say

---

143 J. Moltmann, *L'avvento di Dio... Op. cit.*, pp. 13-60.
144 Chiara Giaccardi, Mauro Magatti, *Nella fine è l'inizio. In che modo vivremo*, (*"In the End is the Beginning. How we Will Live"*), (Bologna: Il Mulino, 2020), pp. 7-17.

it in a relational way.[145] Advent is the possibility of having a future in relationship with others, first with God, then with one's neighbor and finally with nature.

Advent dismantles the illusion that the best time is neutral time, a time devoid of presence and relationships. It disproves the idea that the future is only the scenario of an individual's perseverance and resilience. Advent is a future tainted with the gift of the presence of others who offer themselves to us as a free gift. Advent is the biblical way of saying that the future is not neutral. This is what the German philosopher and biologist Andreas Weber suggests when he writes that we Westerners live by the pragmatic motto: "Try in every situation to survive at any cost." This a typical individualist dogma. Indigenous people live by a different motto that goes like

---

145 The "ultimate" values must be lived in the "penultimate." The Sabbath, like the advent, are not ultimate but penultimate values, to borrow a terminology of Bonhoeffer in his Ethics, according to which what is absolute must be able to descend into the concrete of life and existence, which is not absolute (ultimate) but insofar as it is real and concrete (penultimate) gives meaning the possibility of expression because it is close to life. Cf. D. Bonhoeffer, *Ethics,* (New York: Macmillan Publishing, 1965), pp. 25-33; Salvatore Natoli also calls for care of the "penultimate." He writes: "Having said this, it is clear that we are always in a penultimate dimension because, since we do not have a radical expectation about the end, we are always in the penultimate. This is not to say that the penultimate excludes the idea of an ameliorability of the world, of a redemption of the evil that runs through the present, because radical incarnationalism, and consequently working in the penultimate, means: meanwhile let us try to reduce evil as much as possible through our work and our commitment, through the sense of our finiteness, which for me basically means reduction of the delusion of omnipotence, abandonment of *excessive* amor *sui*. Let us work in the penultimate because evil penetrates the present. We begin to work here and now, and on this basis we look at this present of ours "under the sign of redemption." the only dimension of the future is this: trying to leave to those who will come a world that is a little better than it is. Here the idea of continuity prevails over that of the end."-S. Natoli, F. Brancato, *Il mondo a venire. Dialogo sui novissimi, ("The World to Come. Dialogue on the Novissimi"),* (Bologna: Edb, 2021), pp. 22,23.

this: "Everything lives, therefore try together with others to nurture life." This is what Weber calls *Indigenialität*[146] ("indi-geniality").

"We are all indigenous," says Weber, making it clear that our civilization has colonized indigenous people and also our own way of thinking. Indigenous does not mean savage or primitive but having and cultivating the "genius" of seeing that life is a reality of relationships and relations. Life is relationship, and he who says relationship says trust. Trust is not a psychological or moral virtue that autonomizes the subject more, but rather, the experience that breaks the arrogance of wanting to do everything on our own and orient us confidently toward the other. Life is relationship and relationship is trust.

The genius of indigenous[147] and non-Western peoples is according to Weber, is the ability to see life in relationship and relationship as life. Non-Western peoples do not merely think about but embody it in their way of life and relationship with others and with nature. This is why their civilization is not a civilization of "progress," but a civilization of "balance." The abandonment of relationships as the founding principle of life, is what actually makes progress, understood as the apparent fulfillment of life, possible.

In a reversed reading, we must learn to see not what progress acquires, but what it leaves out, namely relationship and therefore life. For this reason, the recovery of relationship and life necessarily implies a scaling back of progress. It cannot be otherwise. Absolute progress and growth (GDP growth), no matter what, are incompatible with life understood as relationship and trust.

"Indi-geniality" therefore is the defining thought of non-Western cultures that we have not only neglected but also despised. It is time to re-establish an honest and open dialogue with the peoples of the Global South and non-Western peoples, to be positively contaminated by this relational and inclusive *ethos*. It is also time to

---

146 A. Weber, *Indigenialität*, Op. cit., pp. 10-23.
147 The concept of true cultural alternatives is certainly not elaborated by Andreas Weber alone. At the theological level, too, we are witnessing a reevaluation of non-Western contextual theologies that have been present for a number of years. Cf. Randy S. Woodley, *Indigenous Theology and the Western Worldview...Op.cit.*, pp. 53-88.

urgently try to rediscover indigeniality within ourselves which has been contaminated from the beginning with the biophilic presence of a benevolent God, who comes and calls all humans his children, no matter what they do.

Through time, of which advent is a symbol, we recognize ourselves as derivative beings.[148] The future toward which we are going is not the reproduction of the data of the present that we control, but the gift that comes to us from life and from God. Through the Advent we are particular beings, the negotiated expression of a chronology, a temporality that imposes a specific rhythm on us, by virtue of which we can be free and which we can also transgress, embodying it in a particular *kairos*. Through the Advent we introduce a new time by virtue of what we are, what comes to us from others and which we, in a uniquely way, are able to configure as new. Freedom is always a going beyond, a transgressing a standard time to create a new time. Freedom cannot subsist in a repetitive time.

Freedom is necessarily a temporal freedom that is articulated as innovation. Chronological time is our ally because it is meant to be the springboard and not the grave of our freedom. Time, does not imprison us. It allows us to fly. In order to fly and be free, we have to fit into a temporal wake that accompanies us and allows us to go further.

As happens in life and history, time from being a potential ally became, for the ancients, an enemy and a danger. The time that gave them a sense of growth and development seemed to backfire by making everything man did and touched transient. This sense of irreversible aging led them to regard it as an indomitable enemy.

This was the birth of the first form of temporal alienation. It was a hidden and paradoxical alienation because time became, for them, the object of conflicting feelings. The ancients felt it to be a friend, in that it brought to maturity the most significant events and experiences of life; however, being unpredictable and uncontrollable, it rendered transient and finite all that they sought to make eternal and immortal.

The ancients, in their vulnerability and wisdom, nevertheless thought of establishing a pact with time. They made time a friend,

---

148 R. Panikkar, *Spazio, tempo e scienza, Op. cit.* pp. 99-141.

privileging it in its past form. They applied to time a grand scheme, the cyclical scheme, which recognizes it and validates it, but at the same time nullifies it. The time resulting from this scheme was a tame, predictable time with no real future. What they called future was, in reality, a reproduction of the past. It had yet to manifest itself, which is why they await it. It was however, a weak expectation because in reality that expected future was already present, only it was hidden from their eyes. The future was only an expected unveiling of the eternal already present.

All ancient communities were cyclical, working with the cosmos as a reference point. It was space that swallowed up time. Theirs was a cosmic time, a stationary spatial time. That is why all moments for them were contemporary, just as all elements located in space are contemporary. Cyclical communities, by virtue of this covenant with time, were stable, orderly, predictable. Whether they were instinctive communities like the so-called barbarians and primitives or rational communities like the Greeks, this common stability derived to them from the spatial stability of the cosmos to which they always called upon and returned.

This advantage, however, took of them a very high toll because it made them repetitive communities, for better or worse. Life became a reproduction of the cosmos and history a set of events to be stabilized by copying the cosmic order in current events.

The cyclical time of the ancients knew not utopia,[149] but repetition. Not what can happen, but what has happened gathered and imprisoned all attention and interest. The goal was the "eternal return" of the same. Its sign was the ritual. Through ritual, traditional man surrendered to the eternal present, to the time that was, is and will always be the same. This time was a time without fractures, homogeneous and compact. By holding at bay, controlling and subduing the irregularities of life, that is, utopias, restlessness, dissatisfactions, and by aligning them with regular and eternal time, traditional man was reconciled with it and found happiness, peace and harmony with himself and nature. Time, the creator of false expectations and perennial emotional jitters, only needed to

---

149 A. Cavicchia Scalamonti, *La morte*,...Op. Cit., pp. 60-69.

be neutralized. Happiness cannot reside in it. Bliss was eternity, the abolition of time and its utopias.

In the ancient world there emerged, unexpectedly, a revolution at the temporal level. This was introduced by the Hebrews and it consisted in the dismissal of the cycle and the introduction of the line as a new temporal paradigm. The life of Abraham whose flourishing was not guaranteed by staying in his place of origin, but in the pilgrimage to a different goal, the promised land. The point of arrival no longer coincides with the point of departure. Consequently, each event is a unique and irreversible moment that drags forward.

Linear time, emerging with the Jewish tradition,[150] breaks with the tyranny of repetition.[151] Life, for this tradition, is in front not behind. It is task and quest, not confirmation and repetition. Every existence has a goal, a future without which it is impossible to achieve full meaning.[152] Not what one is, much less what one has been, but what one can be becomes important and makes a difference. It is forbidden to stop.

Everything must be new. Not contentment and fullness, but restlessness and dissatisfaction become a sign of health. Every moment in life is unique. It will never return. It is unrepeatable. It should not be wasted, but lived with the intention of creating something new, something that has never before existed. Not repetition, but innovation becomes the watchword. In this sense every moment is *kairos*, a qualitatively new and unique moment.[153]

Yet, Jewish history will remain a slow story. Why? Because the cosmos does not disappear in the Jewish religion. The linearity discovered in the spiritual realm will be balanced and tempered by

---

150 A. Neher, P. Ricœur, Unesco (eds), *Les cultures et le temps*, (Paris : Payot, 1975), pp. 171-191.
151 K. Loewith, *Significato e fine della storia. I presupposti teologici della filosofia della storia*, ("*Meaning and End of History. The Theological Presuppositions of the Philosophy of History*"), (Milan: Saggiatore, 2004), pp. 209-218.
152 G. Marramao, *Cielo e terra. Genealogia della secolarizzazione*, ("*Heaven and Earth. Geenalogy of Secularization*"), (Rome: Laterza, 1994), pp. 115,130.
153 A. Cavicchia Scalamonti, *La morte...Op. cit.*, pp. 69-80.

constant reference to the cosmos.[154] The only difference is that that cosmos, which for the surrounding peoples was divine and absolute, for the Jews it was a creature and a relative reality.

While it can be of some use, the division between cosmic and historical religions, can be misleading because the typical historical religions, Judaism, Christianity and Islam, were, at their inception and for a large part of their history, nonetheless cosmocentric religions. The proof of this is that the rhythm of life, of relationship in the group, of connection with work are strongly marked by continuous reference to nature. Even at the religious level, in Judaism, for example, the cosmos continues to play a large role as the created cosmos. Indeed, the two cycles of religious festivals in Israel, the spring festival cycle and the fall festival cycle, central to understanding the logic of Old Testament religiosity, are cosmic cycles, reread in light of God's intervention in history.

Ancient religions, pagan or biblical, move in slow time and in constant reference to the cosmos. There is a benefit to this. It is the tranquility and certainty of regular cycles, the feeling of not being fully free and adrift. One makes a virtue of necessity. One praises time, knowing, that it is a tamed time, with no real future. The resulting wisdom is a wisdom of accommodation. Temporal temperance is the virtue that looks askance at novelty and praises repetition.

All of this changed with the arrival of modernity. According to Aaron Gurevitch,[155] the modern world chooses time as its main category. The modern age, an age in which we still live, despite the proclamations of post-modernism, is characterized by its strong orientation toward the future. In this regard, it can and should be regarded as a true extension of Christian eschatology. Modernity is

---

154 This is the thesis of Mari Joerstad who sees in the Old Testament community not a community obsessed with time but very much rooted in nature and space. Mari Joerstad, *The Hebrew Bible and Environmental Ethics. Humans. Nonhumans, and the Living Landscape*, (New York: Cambridge University Press, 2021), pp. 1-14.

155 A.Y. Gourevitch, «Postface. Le temps comme problème d'histoire culturelle,» in, P. Ricœur, Unesco (eds), *Les cultures et le temps*, (Paris : Payot, 1975), pp. 257-276.

a secularized Christian eschatology. What does modernity innovate with respect to Christian eschatology, and in what does it prolong and confirm it?

The relationship between modernity and Christian eschatology can be read on a double level. First, on a level of contrast, modernity, while being a heterogeneous phenomenon, chose, on the whole, to set aside God as the guarantor of a future that until then had had a strong theological character. In other words, modernity introduced a discontinuity between God and the future by assigning this future no longer to God but to human activity.

On the second level, this relationship can be read under the banner of great continuity. This is because this future without God has become even more radicalized. It fulfilled, even more successfully, the Christian project of forward momentum by setting aside a God who until then served as an element of resistance and balance. Because there is no longer a God, modern man has become radically and dangerously eschatological because his future is now obstructed by no obstacles. The "anthropological turn," a typical trait of modernity, has various versions of its own that fuel and radicalize its project. Among these versions, the one concerning the future must be considered as decisive.

Corresponding to this radical forward momentum of modernity is a central distinctive psychological trait: confidence. Indeed, this new future was greeted with great enthusiasm and euphoria initially by a few, but later by increasingly large strata of the population. Modern man perceived for the first time that through total reliance on his reason and will, through calculation, planning, and discipline, life could be decidedly better and become what previous eras considered only a pipe dream. In the long run, this dream, came true.

Technical, economic and general welfare development, not for a few but for entire populations, now even on a planetary scale, when we take into account the access to welfare of important slices of people hitherto excluded from progress. This is the result of this secularized progressive eschatology which is confident in the performative capacities of human beings.

History is never linear. It always holds surprises, and even in this time, modernity has had to revise and reconsider its predictions. It escapes no one that this euphoric and confident modernity in the future is no longer there. At least it is no longer there as before. The great catastrophes of the 20th century, the world wars, the ecological crisis, the financial crises, etc., all the result of human activity and not attributable to natural causes, have significantly tempered if not completely erased this eschatological euphoria. The result is paradoxical. The forward rush, typical of modernity, has not stopped but continues even in a more pronounced form. At the same time, trust, the accompanying anthropological stratum, has undergone a strong modification. It has become distrust, indeed real pessimism about the future.

The soul of modern man has become divided, it has become schizoid. Contemporary man no longer has the belief that his innovations and creations will be able to qualitatively change his life and open up a better future for the next generation. He no longer has confidence in what he does; however, it is as if nothing has changed at the operational level[156] because he continues to do, ritually, the things he did before, when he still believed he could create a better future with his own hands. This sociological or cultural contradiction has also become a wearisome psychological contradiction.

The man of the first modernity, confident and hopeful about the future, is replaced by the man of the second modernity, emotionally apathetic and disillusioned about the future. Indeed, his confidence itself is divided. He continues to believe that he is technically capable of achieving what he plans but existentially he is convinced that that technically successful product will not change his life in the least. The man of the second modernity continues to invent futures with astonishing speed and regularity.

Technology is proof of this trend. Every year, every month, every week, technology puts new objects in our hands that make obsolete those we had only yesterday and did not even make time to learn about how they work. This incredible psychological protraction

---

[156] The concept of true cultural alternatives is certainly not elaborated by Andreas Weber alone. At the theological level, too, we are witnessing a reevaluation of non-Western contextual theologies that have been present for a number of years. Cf. Randy S. Woodley, *Indigenous Theology and the Western Worldview*... Op. cit., pp. 53-88.

forward into the future has become a real obsession, an attitude that is suspect because it is one-sided, overly linear. Underlying this obsession is uncertainty, apathy and lack of confidence. The man of the second modernity continues to create a future that he knows in advance will not qualitatively change his life. This period of strong technological innovation has also become the period of "sad passions."[157]

This gives rise to the second form of temporal alienation, alienation that is typically modern, hidden and paradoxical, but of the opposite sign from the ancients. While in the ancients the patterns and rituals of life validated and respected nature, the modern ones, while appearing to respect it, are artificial and in their essence anti-natural.

The covenant of moderns is not a covenant with nature, but a covenant at the expense of it. We thought that it would not undermine it, much less destroy it, and that it would not destroy us as well. The environmental crisis, which is an unmistakable sign of an abnormal relationship also with time, is also a human crisis, because humans cannot remain themselves while deforming time. We are temporal as much as spatial beings.

At this point, modern man must ask himself a central question: how is it that he has managed to create a non-future despite the protrusion of his future? It is because after setting aside God as a transcendent presence it was not difficult to also set aside his neighbor, others as historical presences, creating an illusion about the future.

This new future, without cumbersome presences, seemed more easily attainable. Yet the result turned out to be different. It was achieved, yes, but emptied of its essence, which is given by presences. From trust we passed to distrust, from promise to threat, from *adventus* to *futurum*. *Futurum is* purely quantitative, a sum of statistical predictions, inferences from present data. There are two things modern man must attempt in order to get back a real future, a future that restores his joy and hope.

The first is daring to repopulate his future with two presences: that of God and that of his neighbor. The second is to think differently

---

[157] See M. Benaseyag, G. Schmit, *L'epoca delle passioni tristi*, (*"The Age of Sad Passions"*), (Turin: Feltrinelli, 2005), pp. 9-23.

about his future, no longer as a product of his own efforts, but as a gift to be received from others. These two characteristics are at the heart of the future thought of as *adventus*. There is no need to renounce the future or even to sublimate it, making it a pure psychological desire, but to welcome it as possible in all its fragility in dialogue, love and interaction with others.

Advent is a place of resonance because it affirms and guarantees otherness, communion, mystery and the unavailability of life and meaning on a temporal level. European languages have two modes of expression for talking about tomorrow. The word *futurum* designates what becomes, what from the present extends forward; *adventus* designates what comes, what from the future comes to the present.

The *futurum* is an inference from what is in the present and consequently describes a present-future, a future tampered with. It is a future that is not really future. It only presents itself as such because of the morrow one wants to welcome has no surprise but only includes what is certain, what necessarily is to come as a result of what exists in the present.

Adventus corrects the future-projection, because it turns it from a "result" into a "gift." It welcomes surprise and, welcoming it, he waits for the next day with confidence, without overbearingness and impositions, and renouncing planning for it. It knows that what happens comes as a gift, beyond calculation. Advent is a valuable source of temporal Unverfügbarkeit (unavailability), an essential component in articulating life and meaning.

The *Unverfügbarkeit* of advent corrects the manipulative tendency of the cultural positivism of our time in three ways.

First, it reminds us that the future is neither achievement nor result, but gift and expectation. Western societies and political systems are, as never before, heavily already oriented toward the future. They appear as the expression of a secularized Christian eschatology (Marramao/Lowith). If for Christians the future still concealed uncertainty because only "God knows the times," by getting God out of the way, the future has lost its mystery and has become purely the result of human programming. The future should not be expected but planned. Instrumental reason, after manipulating nature, institutions, labor, and relationships, has ended up manipulating the future as well. The future we know and expect today is the result of inferences, projections, statistics, demographic surveys.

Is such a future still a future? Is it the bearer and generator of hope? According to Reinhardt Koselleck, no. Our future is actually a *vergangene zukunft*, a "past future,"[158] which is already born old, does not create newness or open new horizons. It is a fearful, self-focused future that knows only how to compulsively prolong the known present forward. It hates surprises and ends up generating an "age of sad passions" (Benaseyag). The typical instrumentarium of this already old future are the technical novelties that, as happened with the Iphone. After the initial enthusiasm and curiosity awakened by the latest version, it leave us as empty as before, without having generated even a simulacrum of hope.

Second it reminds us that the future is not a temporal mechanism but a way of being of the Other. There is no future without the Other. It is the Other who makes the future other and not an extension of myself. *Adventus* further corrects *futurum-projection* because it transforms it from an impersonal event into a person-centered event. The Latin term *adventus*-and even more so its Greek equivalent, *parousia*-designated the coming, the arrival of people. The anthropological correspondent of *adventus* is not programming, but trust, expectation, and the capacity to welcome the other.

The new future which we must relearn to welcome as a gift, is always connected to people. The new future is constituted by people themselves. For us today, in Italy and in Europe, this means assuming the moral duty of resuscitating, of guaranteeing the rebirth of that category of people who are called "young people" whom we are sacrificing in order to guarantee ourselves a myopic and petty welfare. To take Hans Jonas again, we are living at the expense of future generations, because we are consuming a heritage, even a temporal one, that does not belong to us.

Third, reminds us that the future belongs to everyone and goes beyond the particularist manipulation of narrow groups and self-

---

158 R. Koselleck, *Futuro passato. Per una semantica dei tempi storici,* (*"Future Past. For a Semantics of Historical Times"*), (Bologna: Clueb, 2007), pp. 11-29.

referential minorities. A*dventus* corrects *futurum-projection* because *adventus* means universality. The future, as *adventus*, is a democratizing event. It is not possible to work for a future that is only mine and not, at the same time, that of other peoples. The future is either everyone's or no one's.

The ecological crisis has reminded us that we inhabit the same earth. Pollution and global warming know no borders. The same is true for the future. The future is the possibility of a common horizon for all humans. A sectional future, only for some citizens, for some categories, for some states, for some communities, for some religions, is a perverse future, an idol that we must have the courage to tear down with our words and actions, with our imagination and hope.

Meaning today is a crushed sense. Actually, there is meaning today, even abundantly, but as quantitative, functional sense. It is sense reduced to calculation, to number and measurement. This is why meaning is in short supply today. This is not because it is not there. It is because there is too much of it as a muscular and resolving, transparent, evident sense.

Our culture and societies have become pornographic realities of an exhibitionist sense, without modesty and mystery. That is why there is an urgent need to restore its value and substance. It is this, however, that is misleading, because we think we can restore substance to it by increasing its presence, its quantity. The process of meaning today is a typical inflationary process because one wants to correct the lack of meaning by increasing its quantity but automatically decreasing its qualitative value.

Meaning has become data and information. From myth we moved to "dataism," from symbol to information. Even the concept has been disfigured. While promoting only clarity and precision, at least concepts still bound and put together. Concept implies judgment. It implies puting things together. Today, knowledge has become accumulation of isolated, plotless data. It has stopped narrating the world and creating it.

The infosphere and "Big data" have become the new reality that replaces the world of things, which had a mysterious and slow sense and forced us into thought, action, contemplation and collaboration.

Today, the more sense there is, the less operative and powerful it is. Sense has power but not potency, presence but not consistency. It says but does not speak, it lists but does not transform, it describes but does not inspire, it demands but does not attract, it pushes but does not motivate. It is a sense without enchantment. It has stopped provoking. It no longer seduces. It has lost its eroticism. It has become flat pornography.

The only way to enrich meaning is not to work on it again, but to connect it to what guarantees it, to life, to reality, to that which guarantees it upstream and downstream, to God. Meaning is always transitive and relational: it is either relationship or it dies. It indicates the successful relationship with life. There is a strong ontological deficit in the cultural positivism of our time,[159] which can only be resolved by connecting meaning with reality. This does not have to be the narrow reality of my system, but that which is beyond my system. It is in connecting with the other and other cultural, social and religious systems, however different, that meaning can return and begin to live again.

Connection with life, with others and with God, as a path to securing a living or true sense, rather than a functional sense, occurs only with that Other, with life, when I do not possess it but contemplate it, listen to it and well-talk about it, speak well of it without manipulating it, when in that Other I discover and recognize its unavailability. Meaning is guaranteed only by the Other who is unavailable.

The unavailability that marks the Other and the possibility of meaning is such only by virtue of its ambivalence and paradox, that is, its mystery and its capacity to surprise by virtue of that intrinsic complexity that one learns to recognize and respect. There is no

---

159 Umberto Galimberti writes in this regard, " because it happened in the oblivion of being, the philosophy that has developed in the West is in its depth anthropology, not in the sense that it is man who is doing philosophy or that philosophy is primarily concerned with man, but in the sense that man, instead of listening to being, has devised being, that is, has thought it to his own measure, exchanging the image, reported, with the face of being." U. Galimberti, *Il tramonto dell'Occidente nella lettura di Heidegger e Jaspers*…Op. cit., p. 282.

meaning without incompleteness, without partiality, without silence. The Sabbath and Advent are signs and witnesses of this. They are witnesses to the unavailability of time and space as the moment and place of the other, unmanipulable, as an opportunity for meaning. The absolute protagonist and mediator of this recomposition of meaning connected to life is the Spirit. As Yves Congar aptly suggests in the title of the third tome of his important book on the Holy Spirit, "The River of Life Flows in East and West" (cf., Rev. 22:1),[160] The Spirit is a recomposer of meaning, because it keeps meaning fluid and relational, like a river, because it unites and divides, dividing and uniting what must remain differentiated but in dialogue, like the river that separates the two banks that remain united by the flow of life and meaning. Meaning, as dialogue, is not the return of the undifferentiated symbiotic, but the respect of the Other in the flow and dialogue of communion and life.

Textual meaning cannot be reassembled without the recovery of the meaning of life. Meaning is always related to life as space and time. Meaning is a gift of life and God that we must learn to accept without manipulating it, but offering it and delivering it to the Other as it has been delivered to us in trust.

We need this meaning today in the texts we read and in the experiences we live. Our hearts long for it and yearn for it like the heart of Suzel, the farmer's daughter, in Pietro Mascagni's opera "L'amico Fritz";[161] The girl, flooded with love for Fritz Kobus, the wealthy landowner in late 19th century Alsace, for whom her family and her father work, asks in an ineffable voice, in front of Rabbi Daniel, who as a good mediator has done everything possible to bring meaning back into the lives of these two unlikely lovers: "Oh, parla, parla, imparadisa il cor!"[162]

We can well paraphrase this same proclamation of ineffable breath in connection with a new reading of the Bible and the texts, from the perspective of an erotics of interpretation that dares to restore

---

160 Y. Congar, *Credo nello Spirito Santo*, (*"I believe in the Holy Spirit"*), (Brescia: Queriniana, 1998), pp. 435-713.
161 *L'amico Fritz*, opera in three acts by Pietro Mascagni (1891).
162 "Oh speak, speak, make flourish (paradise) the heart". Central motto and *leitmotif* of the final duet of Act III entitled "Oh, say it for me that word".

passion to meaning and reading, with these words, "Oh, leggi, leggi, imparadisa il cor."[163]

Unlike Suzel and her legitimate personal aspiration to see her heart and life flourish through the biophilic and life-generating words uttered by Fritz, a "hermeneutics of life," of which the "hermeneutics of the South" are an expression, aims to articulate meaning at a broader and more inclusive level which is embodied in life as a community of creation, from an ecological, multicultural and cosmic perspective.

In this broader perspective of a meaning beyond personal flourishing, and paraphrasing Wang Lung, who instead links meaning to life and the earth, in Pearl S. Buck's text,[164] cited in the introduction of our essay, we can also say, from the perspective of a hermeneutics of the South, that when we become detached from the earth, from rootedness and embodiment in the earth, life ends and so do the texts that are all, in one way or another, in their complementarity and tension, witnesses to this rootedness. Text and reader, meaning and perspective, reading and interpretation, others and other, Being and rootedness, bonding and autonomy, reason and emotions, world and things, orthopraxis and orthopathy, truth and holiness, earth and cosmos, complexity and paradox, mystery and wonder;[165] here are the extremes of a hermeneutics of life that finds a possible and concrete trace in the fragile and vulnerable, yet real, witness of the hermeneutics of the South.[166]

---

163 "Oh read, read, make flourish (paradise) the heart".
164 Wang Lung in an ecological perspective of meaning says, "When you start selling land...it is the end of a family." See P. S. Buck, La buona terra (*"The Good Earth")*, (Milan: Mondadori, 2021), p. 334.
165 A hermeneutics of life presupposes the non-manipulation of the real through the discovery of wonder. See K. L. Schmitz, *"The Recovery Of Wonder. The New Freedom and the Asceticism of Power,* (Montreal: McGill-Queen's University Press, 2005).
166 With respect to the churches of the South, see in particular the entire fifth chapter of Ph. Jenkins' book, *La terza chiesa. Il cristianesimo nel XXI secolo...Op. cit.*, pp. 115-145. Jenkins interprets this new Southern Christianity as a dynamic, inclusive movement, however, with a reductive and fundamentalist hermeneutic. The Southern churches are very heterogeneous, indeed in many this hermeneutic criticized by Jenkins

This hermeneutics of life is strongly linked to the rediscovery of the Trinity[167] and the model of relationality that it presupposes and proposes as a horizon, and which finds its center in the action of the Holy Spirit[168] ("pneumatological turn").[169] This hermeneutic of life generates and makes possible a new spirituality that is not focused and limited to humans and less so only to their reason and awareness. With respect to this new spirituality, Jürgen Moltmann writes:

> "True spirituality is regeneration of love for life: full and undivided love. The first experiences one has of the Holy Spirit are those of an unconditional Yes to life and an unreserved love for all that lives. *That is why since ancient times the 'ruah Jahweh' has been called Fons vitae.*"[170]

---

predominates. If, however, one considers their reading of the Bible but their understanding of life in general, the conclusions differ. Cf. P. Jenkins, *I nuovi volti del cristianesimo*...Op. cit., pp. 13-35.

167 See the entire third part of our essay entitled "Trinity, Mystery and the Unavailability of Meaning." See Douglas F. Ottati, *A Theology for the Twenty-first Century*, (Grand Rapids: William B. Eerdmans, 2021), pp. 350-396.

168 V. -M. Kärkkäinen, *Pneumatology: The Holy Spirit in Ecumenical, International and Contextual Perspective*, (Grand Rapids: Baker Academic, 2002), pp. 8-25.

169 "Pneumatological turn," an ongoing theological and cultural movement in clear and radical contestation of the anthropocentrism of our culture, secular and religious, and in equal rupture with the confessionalism and ecclesiocentrism of faith communities across the religious spectrum; is the recognition of the centrality of the person and action of the Holy Spirit within the Trinity, as an element that enhances the profile of the Father and the Son and their interaction (perichoresis), outside the Trinity in human history and () in the church, through its ability to promote life, in its autonomy and differentiation, but at the same time in its convergence and communion, from a discrete and anonymous profile, all aimed solely at making others flourish and free for relationship and convergence (communion). See, for example, R. R. Rodriguez, *Dogmatics After Babel. Beyond the Theologies of Word and Culture*, (Louisville: Westminster John Knox Press, 2018), pp. 145-195.

170 J. Moltmann, *La fonte della vita*...*Op. cit.*, pp. 107-109.

The new "true spirituality" of love for life, promoted by Moltmann, cannot stop being a "liberating spirituality," according to a recurrent and typical aspiration of Southern hermeneutics, as expressed by Ruben Rosario Rodriguez:

> "A spirituality of liberation emphasizes life as possible only in communion, marked by concrete works that tend toward and aspire to universal human liberation. Consequently, the imperative arises to identify guidelines in Scripture that promote 'life in communion,' and in this fact the inherently political character of theological thought is manifested."[171]

From nihilism to life, from non-being to Being, from the denial of meaning to the possibility of meaning, this is what is made possible by a hermeneutics of life and the hermeneutics of the South and what Luis G. Pedraja describes as the transition from the meaninglessness and cultural and linguistic monolithism of "Babel" to the flourishing and multiculturalism of "Pentecost," in his book *Jesus Is My Uncle*.[172] He argues that language, speech, texts and reading, are essential to creating a community of faith. No community can be reborn by using the language of others or by remaining imprisoned in the languages of the past. A new theology, like a new affirmation of life, necessarily passes through a new hermeneutic that elaborates a new way of speaking about God and the world and does so in the plural, in recognition of the linguistic and theological specificity of each participant in the dialogue. Pedraja writes about the inseparable relationship between meaning, community and pluralism:

> "In Pentecost, the opposite happens: God creates true community from diversity. Unlike Babel, where people try to build community from a common language, in Pentecost, community is built by the sharing of God's Spirit. Through the Holy Spirit, God affirms our different languages and cultures without imposing one language on others. The miracle of Pentecost is not the creation of a single language that

---

171 R.R. Rodriguez, *Dogmatics After Babel...Op. cit.,* p. 187.
172 L. G. Pedraja, *Jesus Is My Uncle: Christology from a Hispanic Perspective,* (Nashville: Abingdon Press, 1999), pp. 101,111.

everyone understands. The miracle of Pentecost consists in everyone being able to hear God's words in their own language (Acts 2:1-11)."[173]

This is why a hermeneutic of life, multicultural and ecological in an irreversibly plural world, as Veli-Matti Kärkkäinen reminds us in his five-volume systematic theology entitled *A Constructive Christian Theology for a Pluralistic World*,[174] is necessarily a hermeneutic centered on the Holy Spirit. Ruben Rosario Rodriguez, from a perspective of Southern hermeneutics, reworks the same thought, linking life, pluralism, cultural specificity and community around the centrality of the Spirit's work, when he writes on the subject:

> "Specifically, the work of the Spirit in preserving the inherent dignity of humanity created in the image of God is the foundation for authentic community, the basis of hope in the face of despair and, the perfect model of unity in plurality in establishing a bridge between our differences without dissolving them. Not the forced unity of Babel nor the confusion of tongues in the aftermath of God's punishment, but a community made possible through the work of the Spirit in which unity is maintained through respect and affirmation of particularities and differences. However this new community may be defined elsewhere, the prophetic witness of the Bible is clear in affirming that a Spirit-led community embodies the divine imperative to expand compassion, justice, and hospitality to all, but especially to those most in need... Who is our neighbor? Those who need our help and whom we find deflecting, going out of our way."[175]

The hermeneutics of the South,[176] of which we have tried to trace a possible outline, which already exists in the present as traces but

---

173 L. G. Pedraja, *Jesus Is My Uncle...Op. cit.,* p. 112.
174 V. -M. Kärkkäinen, *A Constructive Christian Theology for a Pluralistic World,* vols. 1-5, (Grand Rapids: Eerdmans, 2013, 2014, 2015, 2016, 2017).
175 R. R. Rodriguez, *Dogmatics After Babel...Op. cit.,* pp. 194, 195.
176 Hermeneutics that remain plural and intension with the West and its theology with each other. Cf. Randy S. Woodley, *Indigenous Theology and the Western Worldview...* Op. cit., pp. 89-117. See also François Julien, *Essere o vivere. Il pensiero occidentale e il pensiero cinese in venti*

at the same time do not yet exist because they are still on the way, can in their witness remain persuasive only under two conditions. First, if they remain aware of their fragility and partiality and make these their beacon and motivation. Second, if they remain witnesses to life, its complexity, ambivalence and paradox, as a sign of its mystery and unavailability, in listening and obeying the guidance of the Holy Spirit, who is the Spirit of life.[177]

---

contrasti, (*"Being or Living. Western Thought and Chinese Thought in Twenty Contrasts"),* (Milan: Feltrinelli, 2016), pp. 11-26.
177 G. Gutierrez, *Il Dio della vita, Op. cit.,* 241-246.

BIBLIOGRAPHY

Abruzzese A., *Contro l'Occidente. Analfabeti di tutto il mondo uniamoci,* (*"Against the West. Illiterates of the World Let Us Unite"*), (Milano: Bevivino Editore, 2010).
Adorno T.W., Horkheimer M., *Dialectic of Enlightenment,* (New York: Verso, 2016).
Agostino, *Confessioni,* I, 1,1.
Al-Azmeh A., *Islam and Modernities,* (New York: Verso, 2009).
Alessandrino C., *Quale ricco si salverà?* (*"What Rich Man Will Be Saved?"*), (Roma: Citta Nuova, 1999).
Alter R., *L'arte della narrativa biblica,* (Brescia: Queriniana, 1990).
Alter R., *L'arte della poesia biblica,* (Milano: San Paolo Edizioni, 2011).
Alter R., *The Art of Biblical Narrative,* (London: George Allen & Unwin, 1981).
Alter R., *The Art of Biblical Poetry,* Edinburgh: (T&T Clark, 2000).
Althouse P., *Spirit of the Last Days. Pentecostal Eschatology in Conversation with Jürgen Moltmann,* (New York: T & T Clark International, 2003).
Anders G., *L'uomo è antiquato. Sulla distruzione della vita nell'epoca della terza rivoluzione industriale,* vol. I, (*"Man is Outdated. Considerations on the Soul of the Age of the Second Industrial Revolution"*), (Torino: Bollati Boringhieri, 2003).
Anselmo A., Gembillo G., *Filosofia della complessità,* (Firenze: Le Lettere, 2017).
Appadurai A., *Modernity at Large. Cultural Dimensions of Globalization,* (Minneapolis: University of Minnesota Press, 2010).
Appadurai A., *The Future as Cultural Fact. Essays on the Global Condition,* (New York: Verso, 2013).
Arendt H., *Vita activa. La condizione umana,* (*"The Human Condition"*), (Milan: Bompiani, 2008).
Aristotele (*Metafisica* IV, 1005b, 19-20).

Asad T., *Genealogies of Religion. Discipline and Reasons of Power in Christianity and Islam*, (Baltimore: The Johns Hopkins University Press, 1997).
Audi R., *Epistemologia. Un'introduzione alla teoria della conoscenza*, (*"Epistemology. An Introduction to the Theory of Knowledge"*), (Macerata: Quodlibet, 2016).
Auerbach E., *Mimesis. Il realismo nella letteratura occidentale*, (Torino: Einaudi, 2000).
Auerbach Erich, *Mimesis. The Representation of Reality in Western Literature*, (Princeton: Princeton University Press, 2003).
Augé M., *Genio del paganesimo*, (*"Genius of Paganism"*), (Torino: Bollati Boringhieri, 2002).
Augé M., *Non-luoghi. Introduzione ad una antropologia della surmodernità*, (*"Non-Places. Introduction to an Anthropology of Surmodernity"*), Milan: Eleuthera, 2005.

Aune D.E., *Revelation 6-16*, World Biblical Commentary, vol. 52 B, (Nashville: Thomas Nelson, 1998).
Bacchiocchi S., *From Sabbath to Sunday. A Historical Investigation of the Rise of the Sunday Observance in Early Christianity,* (Rome: The Pontifical Gregorian University Press, 1977).
Barker C., Jane E.A., *Cultural Studies. Theory and Practice*, Sage, (London, Sage, 2016).
Barr J., *Old and New in Interpretation: A Study of the Two Testaments*, London: SMC, 1966.
Barr J., *The Semantics of Biblical Language*, Xpress, (London: Xpress, 1983).
Barth K., *Anselm: Fides Quaerens Intellectum. Anselm's Proof of the Existence of God in the Context of His Theological Scheme*, (Pittsburg: Pickwick Publications, 2004).
Barth K., *Der Römerbrief*, (Zürich: Theologischer Verlag, 1922).
Barth K., *Protestant Theology in the Nineteenth Century. Its Background and History*, (Grand Rapids Eerdmans, 2001).
Battaglia L., *Bioetica senza dogmi*, (Roma: Rubbettino, 2009).
Battaglia L., *Bioetica*, (Milano: Editrice Bibliografica, 2022).
Battaglia L. (ed), *Uomo, natura, animali. Per una bioetica della complessità*, (Pavia: Altravista, 2016).
Bauckham R., *Jesus and the Eyewitnesses. The Gospels as Eyewitness Testimony,* (Grand Rapids: W. B. Eerdmans Publishing Company, 2006).

Bellinger Jr. W.H., Brueggemann W., *Psalms*, New Cambridge Bible Commentary, (New York: Cambridge University Press, 2014).
Benasayag M., Schmit G., *L'epoca delle passioni tristi*, (*"The Age of Sad Passions"*), (Torino: Feltrinelli, 2005).
Benedict R., *Il crisantemo e la spada. Modelli di cultura giapponesi*, (*"The Chrysanthemum and the Sword. Patterns of Japanese Culture"*), (Roma: Laterza, 2010).
Benjamin W., *L'opera d'arte nell'epoca della sua riproducibilità tecnica*, (*"The Work of Art in the Age of its Technical Reproducibility"*), (Torino: Einaudi, 2014).
Benveniste É., *Problemi di linguistica generale*, (Milano: Il Saggiatore, 1973).
Berkhof L., *The History of Christian Doctrines*, (Grand Rapids: Baker Book House, 1992).
Besnier J.-M., *Teorie della conoscenza*, ("Theories of Knowledge"), (Soveria-Mannelli: Rubbettino, 2013).
Best E., *2 Corinzi*, (*"2 Corinthians"*), (Torino: Claudiana, 2009).
Bettelheim B., *Un genitore quasi perfetto*, ("A *Good Enough Parent. A A Book on Child-Rearing"*), (Milano: Feltrinelli, 2013).
Bettini M., *Elogio del politeismo. Quello che possiamo imparare dalle religioni antiche*, (*"In Praise of Polytheism. What We Can learn From Ancients Religions"*), (Bologna: Il Mulino, 2014).
Bhabha H.K., *The Location of Culture*, (London: Routledge, 2007).
Blankholm J., *The Secular Paradox: On the Religiosity of Not Religious*, (New York: New York University Press, 2022).
Bloch E., *Thomas Münzer teologo della rivoluzione*, (*"Thomas Münzer Theologian of Revolution"*), (Milano: Feltrinelli, 2009).
Bloch E., *Spirito dell'utopia*, (*"Spirit of Utopia"*), (Milan: Rizzoli, 2009).
Bloesch D.G., *Holy Scripture. Revelation, Inspiration & Interpretation, Christian Foundations*, (Downers Grove: IVP Academic, 1994).
Bloom H., *Il canone occidentale. I Libri e le scuole dell'Età*, (*"The Western Canon. The Books and Schools of the Age"*), (Milano: Bompiani, 2006).
Bock D.L., *Luke (2) 9:51-24:53* (Baker Exegetical Commentary On the New Testament), (Ada: Baker Academic, 2010).
Bodei R., *La vita delle cose*, (*"The Life of Things"*), (Roma: Laterza, 2011).
Bollas C., *L'età dello smarrimento. Senso e malinconia*, (*"Meaning and Melancholy. Life in the Age of Bewilderment"*), (Milano: Raffaello Cortina Editore, 2018).
Bonhoeffer D., *Ethics*, (New York: MacMillan, 1965).

Bonhoeffer D., *Pregare i salmi con Cristo. Il libro di preghiera della Bibbia*, ("*Praying the Psalms with Christ. The Prayer Book of the Bible*"), (Brescia: Queriniana, 2019).
Bonomi A., Frege G., (a cura di), *La struttura del linguaggio*, (Milano: Bompiani, 1973).
Bordoni C., *Società digitali. Mutamento culturale e nuovi media*, ("*Digital Societies. Cultural Change and New Media*"), (Napoli: Liguori Editori, 2007).
Bordoni C., *Post-società. Il mondo dopo la fine della modernità*, ("*Post-Society. The World After the End of Modernity*"), (Rome: Luiss University Press, 2021).
Boring M.E., *Apocalisse*, (Torino: Claudiana, 2008).
Bourquin Y., Marguerat D., *Per leggere i racconti biblici. La Bibbia si racconta. Iniziazione all'analisi narrativa*, ("*To Read Biblical Narratives. The Bible Narrates Itself. Initiation to Narrative Analysis*") (Roma: Borla, 2011).
Bouyer L., *Le Consolateur. Esprit Saint et vie de Grâce*, (Paris : Cerf, 1980).
Brancato F., Natoli S., *Il mondo a venire. Dialogo sui novissimi*, (Bologna: EDB, 2021).
Bravo Aragon J.M., Schökel L.A., *Appunti di ermeneutica. Comprendere e interpretare i testi biblici e letterari*, (Bologna: EDB, 2014).
Brueggemann W., Bellinger Jr W.H., *Psalms*, New Cambridge Bible Commentary, (New York: Cambridge University Press, 2014).
Brugiatelli V., *La relazione tra linguaggio ed essere in Ricoeur*, ("*The Relation Between Language and Being in Ricœur*"), (Trento: Uni Service, 2009).
Buck P.S., *La buona terra*, ("*The Good Earth*"), (Milano: Mondadori, 2021).
Bulgakov S., *The Comforter*, (Grand Rapids: Eerdmans Publishing, 2004).
Bultmann R., *Foi et Compréhension. Eschatologie et démythologisation*, (Paris : Seuil, 1969).
Cacciari M., *Paradiso e naufragio. Saggio sull'Uomo senza qualità di Musil*, ("*Paradise and Shipwreck. Essay on Musil's Man Without Qualities*"), (Torino: Giulio Einaudi Editore, 2022).
Calvin J., *Commentary on The Psalms*, (Carlisle: The Banner of Truth Trust, 2009).
Campbell M.W., *1919: The Untold Story of Adventism's Struggle with Fundamentalism*, (Nampa: Pacific Press Publishing Association, 2019).

Canclini N.G., *Hybrid Cultures. Strategies for Entering and Leaving Modernity*, (Minneapolis: University of Minnesota Press, 1995).
Carniti C., Schökel L.A., *Salmos,* vol. I, (Navarra: Verbo Divino, 1992).
Cassirer E., *The Individual and the Cosmos in the Renaissance Philosophy*, (New York: Angelico Press, 1963).
Castelo D., *Revisioning Pentecostal Ethics. The Epicletic Community*, (Cleveland: CPT Press, 2012).
Cavicchia Scalamonti A., *La morte. Quattro variazioni sul tema*, (*"Death. Four Variations on the Theme")*, (S. Maria Capua Vetere: Ipermedium, 2007).
Celocanti G., F. Di Iorio, E. Di Nuoscio, "Dalla filosofia alla scienza, e ritorno: l'analisi della conoscenza tra epistemologia e scienze cognitive", (*"From Philosophy to Science, and Back: The Analysis of Knowledge Between Philosophy and Cognitive Science"*), in, J.-M. Besnier, *Teorie della conoscenza*, (*"Theories of Knowledge")*, (Soveria-Mannelli: Rubbettino, 2013).
Cerasi E., *Dire quasi la verità. Per una filosofia del linguaggio religioso*, (*"Saying Almost the Truth. For a Philosophy of Religious Language")*, (Roma: Città Nuova Editrice, 2014).
Cerasi E., *Il mito del cristianesimo. Per una fondazione metaforica della teologia*, , (*"The Myth of Christianity. For a Metaphorical Foundation of Theology")*, (Roma: Città Nuova Editrice, 2011).
Cerasi, *Crisi del cristianesimo. Saggio su religione e modernità*, (*"Crisis of Christianity. Essay on Religion and Modernity")*, Rome: Città Nuova Editrice, 2021.
Ceruti M., *Il tempo della complessità. Prefazione di Edgar Morin*, (*"The Time of Complexity. Preface by Edgar Morin")*, (Milano: Raffaello Cortina, 2018).
Chakrabarty D., *Provincializing Europe. Postcolonial Thought and Historical Difference*, (Princeton: Princeton University Press, 2000).
Chakravorty Spivak G., *A Critique of Postcolonial Reason. Toward a History of the Vanishing Present*, (Cambridge-Massachusetts: Harvard University Press, 2003).
Chanady A. (ed*)*, *Latin American Identity and Constructions of Difference*, (Minneapolis: University of Minnesota Press, 1994).
Charles R.H., *The Revelation of John. With Introduction, Notes and Indices*, vol. I, (Edinburgh: T&T Clark, 1963).
Charles S., *L'hypermoderne expliqué aux enfants*, (Montréal : Liber, 2017).
Child B.S., *Biblical Theology of the Old and New Testaments. Theological Reflection on the Christian Bible*, (London: Xpress, 1996).

Cole R., Petersen P. (eds), *Hermeneutics, Intertextuality and the Contemporary Meaning of Scripture,* (Cooranbong: Avondale Academic Press, 2014).

Conradie E. M., "What on Earth is an Ecological Hermeneutics? Some Broad Parameters," in, David G. Horrell, Cherryl Hunt, Christopher Southgate, Francesca Stavrakopoulou (Eds), *Ecological Hermeneutics. Biblical, Historical and Theological Perspectives,* (New York: T & T Clark, 2010).

Congar Y., *Jésus-Christ,* (Paris : Edition du Cerf, 1965).

Congar Y., *Credo nello Spirito Santo, ("I Believe in the Holy Spirit"),* vol. 2, (Brescia: Queriniana, 1998).

Craddock F.B., *Luca,* ("Luke"), (Torino: Claudiana, 2002).

Croce B., *La storia come pensiero e come azione, ("History as Thought and Action"),* (Napoli: Bibliopolis, 2002).

Crocombe J., Cole R., Petersen P. (eds), *Hermeneutics, Intertextuality and the Contemporary Meaning of Scripture,* (Adelaide: Avondale Academic Press, 2014).

Crutzen P.J., *Benvenuti nell'Antropocene. L'uomo ha cambiato il clima. La terra entra in una nuova era, ("Welcome to the Anthropocene. Man has Changed the Climate. The Earth Enters a New Era"),* (Milano: Mondadori, 2005).

Cueto M., "Un medico aleman en los Andes. La visión medico-social de Maxime Kuczynski-Godard, in, *Allpanchis Puthurinqa,* (Revista de Estudios Andinos), Vol 32, Num. 56 (2000), pp. 39-74.

Cullmann O., *Il Nuovo Testamento, ("The New Testament"),* (Bologna: Il Mulino, 1968).

Cullmann O., *Le salut dans l'histoire. L'existence chrétienne selon le Nouveau Testament,* (Neuchatel : Delachaux et Niestlé, 1966).

Cullmann O., *The Christology of New Testament,* (Philadelphia: The Westminster Press, 1963).

D'Aquino T., *Somma contro i Gentili. Libro primo e secondo,* (Bologna: Edizioni Studio Domenicano, 2000).

Davidson R.M., "Biblical Interpretation", in, R. Dederen (Ed), *Handbook of Seventh-day Adventist Theology,* (Hagerstown:MD, 2000), pp. 58-104.

D'Ippona A., *Confessioni,* I, 1,1.

D'Ippona A., *De doctrina christiana.*

De Certeau M., *L'écriture de l'histoire,* (Paris : Gallimard, 1995).

De Lubac H., *Exégèse médiévale: Les quatre sens de l'Ecriture,* (Paris : Aubier, 1959).

De Montaigne M., *Saggi*, (Milano: Bompiani, 2014).
De Saussure F., *Corso di linguistica generale*, ("Course of Linguistics"), (Roma: Laterza, 2009).
De Sousa Santos B., *Epistemologies of the South. Justice against Epistemicide*, (London: Paradigm Publishers, 2014).
De Tocqueville A., *La democrazia in America*, (*"Democracy in America"*), (Milano: Utet, 2019).
Dederen R. (Ed), *Handbook of Seventh-day Adventist Theology*, (Hagerstown: MD, 2000).
Delitzsch F. & Keil C.F., *Ezra, Nehemiah, Esther, Job*, (Peabody: Hendrickson Publishers, 1989).
Della Stella I., *Sermoni*, vol. II, (Milano: Edizioni Paoline, 2007).
Derrida J., *Della grammatologia*, ("Of Grammatology"), (Milano: Jaca Book, 1968).
Descartes R., *Meditazioni metafisiche*, (*"Metaphysical Meditations"*), (Roma: Laterza, 1997).
Descola Ph., *L'écologie des autres. L'anthropologie et la question de la nature*, (Paris : Quae, 2016).
Descola Ph., *Par-delà nature et culture*, Paris: Gallimard, 2005).
Di Ceglie R., *God the Good, and the Spiritual Turn in Epistemology*, (Cambridge: Cambridge University Press, 2022).
Di Paola M., Pellegrino G., *Nell'Antropocene. Etica e politica alla fine di un mondo*, (Roma: Habitus, 2018).
di Sante C., *Dentro la Bibbia. La teologia alternativa di Armido Rizzi*, (*"Inside the Bible. The Alternative Theology of Armido Rizzi"*), (Verona: Gabrielli, 2018).
Diotallevi L., *Fine corsa. La crisi del cristianesimo come religione confessionale*, (*"End of the Race. The Crisis of Christianity as a Confessional Religion"*), (Bologna: EDB, 2017).
Drewermann E., *Heilende Religion. Überwindung der Angst*, (Freiburg: Herder, 2013).
Drewermann E., *Psicologia del profondo ed esegesi. La verità delle forme. Sogno, mito, fiaba, saga e leggenda* (1), (*"Depth Psychology and Exegesis. The Ttruth of Forms. Dream, Myth, Fairy Tale, Saga and Legend,* 1"), (Brescia: Queriniana, 1996).
Drewermann E., *Wozu Religion? Sinnfindung in Zeiten der Gier nach Macht und Geld. Im Gesprach mit Juergen Hoeren*, (Freiburg: Herder, 2012).

Dumont L., *Saggi sull'individualismo. Una prospettiva antropologica sull'ideologia moderna*, (*"Essays on Individualism. An Anthropological Perspective on Modern Ideology"*), (Milano: Adelphi, 1983).
Dupuis J., *Christianity and the Religions: From Confrontation to Dialogue*, (New York: Orbis, 2002).
Durrwell F.-X., in *L'Esprit du Père et du Fils*, (Montreal : Editions Paulines, 1988).
Eco U., *Lector in fabula. La cooperazione interpretativa nei testi narrativi*, (*"Lector in Fabula. Interpretive Cooperation in Narrative Tetxs",)* (Milano: Bompiani, 2006).
Ellul J., *La parole humiliée*, (Paris: Seuil, 1981).
Eraclito, *Frammenti*, Francesco Fronterotta (curatore), (Milano: Rizzoli, 2013).
Ehrenberg A., *The Weariness of the Self. Diagnosing the History of Depression in the Contemporary Age*, (Montreal & Kingston: McGill-Queen's University Press, 2016).
Erickon M.J., *Christian theology*, (Grand Rapids: Baker Academic, 2013).
Estremadoyro Robles C., "Antonio Raimondi", in *Diccionario historico biografico. Peruanos ilustres*, (Lima: A.F.A., 1999).
Etzioni A., *The Spirit of Community. The Reinvention of American Society*, (New York: Touchstone Book, 1993).
Evdokimov P., *L'Esprit dans la tradition Orthodoxe*, (Paris : Cerf, 1969).
Fabris R., *Luca*, (*"Luke"*), (Assisi: Cittadella, 2003).
Fabris R., *Matteo*, ("Matthew"), (Roma: Borla, 1996).
Ferraris M., *L'ermeneutica*, ("Hermeneutics"), (Roma: Laterza, 1998).
Ferraris M., *Storia dell'ermeneutica*, (*"History of Hermeneutics"*), (Milano: Bompiani, 1997).
Feuerbach L., *Fondamenti della filosofia dell'avvenire*, (Forlì: Clinamen, 2020).
Finkielkraut A., *Noi, i moderni*, (*"We, the Moderns"*), (Torino: Lindau, 2006).
Floridi L., *Pensare l'infosfera. La filosofia come design concettuale*, (*"Thinking the Infosphere. Philosophy as Conceptual Design"*), (Torino: Bollati Boringhieri, 2020).
Flusser V., *La cultura dei media*, (*"The Culture of the Media"*), (Milano: Bruno Mondadori, 2004).
Forte Bruno, "Sacra scrittura e teologia", in, *Adventus* (Facoltà avventista di teologia, Firenze), n. 22/2012, pp. 30-42.
Forte B., *Dove va il cristianesimo?*, (*"Where is Christianity Going?"*), (Brescia: Queriniana, 2001).

Forte B., *Trinità per atei. Con interventi di Massimo Cacciari, Giulio Giorello, Vincenzo Vitiello*, "(*Trinity for Atheists. With Contributions by Massimo Cacciari, Giulio Giorello, Vincenzo Vitiello*"), (Milan: Raffaello Cortina Editore, 1996).
Fosnot C.T., *Constructivism. Theory, Perspectives and Practice*, (New York: Teachers College Press, 2005).
Foucault M., *Le parole e le cose. Un'archeologia delle scienze umane*, ("*The Order of Things: An Archeology of the Human Sciences*"), (Milano: BUR, 1978).
Frege G., in, A. Bonomi (a cura di), *La struttura del linguaggio*, ("*The Structure of Language*"), (Milano: Bompiani, 1973).
Fromm E., *L'arte di amare*, ("*The Art of Loving*"), (Milano: Mondadori, 1996).
Fry P.H., *Theory of Literature*, (Yale: Yale University Press, 2012).
Funk R.W., *Language, Hermeneutic and the Word of God*, (New York: Harper & Row, 1966).
Gadamer H.G., *Verità e metodo*, ("*Truth and Method*"), (Milano: Bompiani, 2000).
Galimberti U., *Cristianesimo. La religione del cielo vuoto*, ("*Christianity. The Religion of the Empty Sky*"), (Milano: Feltrinelli, 2012).
Galimberti U., *Il corpo*, ("The Body"), (Milano: Feltrinelli, 2002).
Galimberti U., *Il tramonto dell'Occidente nella lettura di Heidegger e Jaspers*, ("The Decline of the West in the Readings of Heidegger and Jaspers"), (Milano: Feltrinelli, 2017).
Galimberti U., *Orme del sacro. Il cristianesimo e la desacralizzazione del sacro*, ("*Footsteps of the Sacred. Christianity and the Desacralization fo the Sacred*"), (Milano: Feltrinelli, 2000).
Galimberti U., *Psiche e techne. L'uomo nell'età della tecnica*, ("*Psyche and Techne. Man in the Age of Technology*"), (Milano: Feltrinelli, 2004).
Galli C., *Contingenza e necessità nella ragione politica moderna*, ("*Contingency and Necessity in Modern Political Reason*"), (Roma: Laterza, 2009).
Galli C., *Lo sguardo di Giano. Saggi su Carl Schmitt*, ("*Janus' Gaze. Essays on Carl Schmitt*"), (Bologna: Il Mulino, 2008).
Gauchet M., *Il disincanto del mondo*, ("*The Disenchantment of the World*"), (Torino: Einaudi, 1992).
Geffré C., *Credere e interpretare. La svolta ermeneutica della teologia*, ("*Believing and Interpreting. The Hermeneutical Turn in Theology*"), (Brescia: Queriniana, 2002).

Gembillo G., Anselmo A., *Filosofia della complessità*, *("Philosophy of Complexity")*, (Firenze: Le Lettere, 2017).
Geshé A., *Dieu,* (Paris : Cerf, 2010).
Geshé A., *Dio per pensare il Cristo, ("God to Think Christ")*, (Milan: San Paolo, 2003),
Gettier E., Is Justified True Belief Knowledge? JTB, 1963.
Giaccardi C., Magatti M., *Nella fine è l'inizio. In che modo vivremo*, *("In the End is the Beginning. How We Will Live")*, (Bologna: Il Mulino, 2020).
Giovanni Paolo II, *Evangelium Vitae*, 25 marzo1995.
Gisel P., *Verité et Histoire. La théologie dans la modernité. Ernst Käsmann*, (Paris: Beauchesne, 1985).
Gnilka J., *Vangelo di Matteo, ("Gospel of Matthew")*, vol. I, Commentario teologico del Nuovo Testamento, (Brescia: Paideia, 1990).
Gonzalez Casanova P., *Las Nuevas Ciencias y las Humanidades. De la Academia a la Política*, (The New Sciences and Humanities. From Academia to Politics), (Barcelona: Anthropos, 2005).
Gonzalez J.L., *Christian Thought Revisited. Three Types of Theology*, (Nashville: Abingdon Press, 1989).
Gourevitch A.J., *La naissance de l'individu dans l'Europe médiévale*, (Paris : Seuil, 1997).
Grondin J., *Introduction to Philosophical Hermeneutics*, (Yale: Yale University Press 1994).
Gutierrez G., *Il Dio della vita, ("The God of Life")*, (Brescia: Queriniana, 1992).
Gutierrez G., *Teologia della liberazione. Prospettive, ("Liberation Theology. Perspectives")*, (Brescia: Queriniana, 1992).
Gutierrez H., "The Invention of Blackness and the Anthropology of the Gospel. Between Cultural Insolence, Paradoxes, and the Resilience of Ambivalence," in, Maury D Jackson, Nathan Brown, *A House on Fire. How Adventist Faith Responds to Race and Racism*, (Warburton: Signs Publishing, 2022),
Han B.-C., *Il profumo del tempo. L'arte d'indugiare sulle cose, ("The Scent of Time. A Philosophical Essay in the Art of Lingering")*, (Milano: Vita e Pensiero, 2017).
Han B.-C., *L'espulsione dell'altro. Società, percezione e comunicazione oggi*, *("The Expulsion of the Other. Society, Perception and Communication Today")*, (Milano: Nottetempo, 2017).
Han B.-C., *La società della trasparenza*, *("The Transparency Society")*, (Milano: Nottetempo, 2014).

Han B.-C., *Società della stanchezza*, ("The *Burn out Society*"), (Roma: Nottetempo, 2012).
Han B.-C., *Le non cose. Come abbiamo smesso di vivere il reale*, ("*The Not Things. How We Stopped Experiencing the Real*"), (Turin: Einaudi, 2022).
Han B.-C, *La scomparsa dei riti. Una topologia del presente*, ("*The Disappearance of Rituals. A Topology of the Present*"), (Milan: Nottetempo, 202).
Hasel F.M., *Biblical Hermeneutics: An Adventist Approach*, vol. 3, (Silver Spring: Biblical Research Institute, 2021).
Hasel F.M. e Hasel M.G., *How to Interpret Scripture*, (Oakland: Pacific Press Publishing Association, 2020).
Heidegger M., *Basic Writings*, David Farrell Krell (ed.), (San Francisco: Harper, 1992).
Heidegger M., *Essere e tempo*, ("*Being and Time*"), (Milano: Longanesi, 1976).
Heidegger M., *Hermeneutics and the Human Sciences*, (Cambridge: Cambridge University Press, 2016).
Heim M.S., *The Depth of the Riches: A Trinitarian Theology of Religious Ends*, (Grand Rapids: Eerdmans, 2001).
Heschel A.J., *Il messaggio dei profeti*, ("*The Message of the Prophets*"), (Roma: Borla, 1993).
Heschel A.J., *Il sabato. Il suo significato per l'uomo moderno*, ("*The Sabbath. Its meaning for Modern Man*"), (Milan: Garzanti, 2001).
Heussi K., *Kompendium der Kirchengeschichte*, (Tübingen: J.C.B. Mohr, 1988).
Hillman J., *Re-Visione della psicologia*, (Milano: Adelphi, 2008).
Hjelmslev L.T., *Essais linguistiques*, (Copenhague : Cercle linguistique de Copenhague, 1959).
Hobbes Th., *De Cive. Elementi filosofici sul cittadino*, ("*De Cive. Philosophical Elements on the Citizen*"), (Roma: Editori riuniti, 2014).
Hobbes Th., *Leviatano*, ("*Leviathan*"), (Milano: Rizzoli, 2013).
Hopko T., *The Names of Jesus. Discovering the Person of Jesus Christ Through Scripture*, (Chesterton: Ancient Faith Publishing, 2015).
Horkheimer M., Adorno T., *Dialectic of Enlightenment*, (New York: Verso, 2016).
Huanacuni Mamani F., *Vivir bien, buen vivir. Filosofía, políticas, estrategias y experiencias de los pueblos ancestrales*, (Lima: Caoi, 2010).
Iser W, *L'atto di lettura. Una teoria della risposta estetica*, ("*The Act of Reading. A Theory of Aesthetic Response*"), (Bologna: Il Mulino, 1996).

Jackson M.D., Brown N., *A House on Fire. How Adventist Faith Responds to Race and Racism*, (Warburton: Signs Publishing, 2022).
Janowski B., *Konfliktgespräche mit Gott. Eine anthropologie der psalmen*, (Neukircher-Vluyn: Neukirchener Verlag, 2003).
Jeanrond W.G., *L'ermeneutica teologica. Sviluppo e significato, ("Theological Hermeneutics. Development and Meaning")*, (Brescia: Queriniana, 1994).
Jenkins Ph., *I nuovi volti del cristianesimo, ("The New Faces of Christianity. Believing the Bible in the Global South")*, (Milano: Vita e pensiero, 2007).
Jenkins Ph., *La terza chiesa. Il cristianesimo nel XXI secolo, ("The Next Christendom. The Coming of Global Christianity")*, (Roma: Fazi, 2004).
Jenkins Ph., *The Next Christendom. The Coming of the Global Christianity*, (Oxford: Oxford University Press, 2002).
Jenkins Ph., *The New Faces of Christianity. Believing the Bible in the Global South*, (Oxford: Oxford University Press, 2006).
Jennings W.J., *The Christian Imagination. Theology and the Origins of Race,* (Yale: Yale University Press, 2011).
Jensen A.S., *Theological Hermeneutics*, (London: SCM Press, 2007).
Jeremias J., *Gesù e il suo annuncio, ("Jesus and His Proclamation")*, (Brescia: Paideia, 1993).
Jeremias J., *Teologia del Nuovo Testamento. La predicazione di Gesù* (1), *("New Testament Theology. The Preaching of Jesus")*, (Brescia: Paideia, 2000).
Jeremias J., *The Parables of Jesus*, (New York: SCM Press, 1963).
Joerstad M., *The Hebrew Bible and Environmental Ethics. Humans. Nonhumans, and the Living Landscape*, (New York: Cambridge University Press, 2021).
Johnson K.E., *Rethinking the Trinity & Religious Pluralism. An Augustinian Assessment,* (Downers Grove: IVP Academic, 2011).
Jullien F., *Essere o vivere. Il pensiero occidentale e il pensiero cinese in venti contrasti*, (Milano: Feltrinelli, 2016).
Jung C.G., *Psychologische Typen*, (Dusseldorf: Walter-Verlag, 1995).
Kant I., *Prolegomeni a ogni futura metafisica che potrà presentarsi come scienza, ("Prolegomena to Any Future Metaphysics That Would Be Able To Present Itself as a Science")*, (Roma: Laterza, 1996).
Kärkkäinen V.-M., *A Constructive Christian Theology for a Pluralistic World,* vol. 1-5, (Grand Rapids: Eerdmans, 2013, 2014, 2015, 2016, 2017).

Kärkkäinen V.-M., *Christian Theology for a Pluralistic World. A Global Introduction*, (Grand Rapids: Eerdmans, 2019).
Kärkkäinen V.-M., *Trinity and Religious Pluralism. The Doctrine of the Trinity in Christian Theology of religions,* (London: Routledge, 2004).
Keener C.S., *Spirit Hermeneutics. Reading Scriptures in Light of Pentecost,* (Grand Rapids: Eerdmans, 2016).
Keil C.F. & Delitzsch Franz, *Ezra, Nehemiah, Esther, Job*, (Peabody: Hendrickson Publishers, 1989).
Kierkegaard S., *Timore e tremore*, (*"Fear and Trembling"),* (Milano: Mondadori, 2016).
Koselleck R., *Futuro passato. Per una semantica dei tempi storici,* (*"Future Past. For a Semantics of Historical Times"),* (Bologna: Clueb, 2007).
Kraus H.J., *L'Antico Testamento nella ricerca storico-critica dalla Riforma a oggi, ("The Old Testament in Historical-Critical Research From the Reformation to the Present"),* (Bologna: Il Mulino, 1975).
Kümmel W.G., *Il Nuovo Testamento. Storia dell'indagine scientifica sul problema neotestamentario,* (*"The New Testament. History of the Scholarly Investigation of the New Testament Problem")*, (Bologna: Il Mulino, 1976).
Kuhn Th.S., *The Structures of Scientific Revolutions*, (Chicago: University of Chicago Press, 1996).
Kundera M., *L'arte del romanzo*, ("The *Art of the Novel")*, (Milano: Adelphi, 1988).
Lakoff G. and Johnson M., *Metaphors We Live By*, (Chicago: Chicago University Press, 1981).
Lancellotti A., *I Salmi*. Versione, introduzione, note, *("The Psalms*. Version, introduction, notes"), (Milano: San Paolo, 1987).
Land S.J., *Pentecostal Spirituality. A Passion for the Kingdom,* (Cleveland: CTP Press, 2010).
Lane T., *A concise History of Christian Thought*, (Grand Rapids: Baker Academic, 2006).
Lang F., *Le lettere ai Corinti,* (*"The Letters to the Corinthians"),* (Brescia: Paideia, 2004).
Lasch Ch., *The Culture of Narcissism. American Life in an Age of Diminishing Expectations,* (New York: Warner Books, 1979).
Latour B., *Dove sono? Lezioni di filosofia per un pianeta che cambia, ("Where Are They? Lessons in Philosophy For a Changing Planet")*, (Torino: Einaudi, 2021).
Latour B., *La sfida di Gaia. Il nuovo regime climatico,* (*"The Gaia Challenge. The New Climate Regime"),* (Milano: Meltemi, 2020).

Latour B., *Tracciare la rotta. Come orientarsi in politica*, ("Charting the Course. How to Orient Oneself in Politics"), (Milano: Raffaello Cortina Editore, 2018).
Le Goff J., *La civilisation de l'Occident médiéval*, (Paris : Flammarion, 2008).
Le Goff J., *Le Dieu du Moyen Âge. Entretiens avec Jean-Luc Pouthier*, (Paris : Bayard, 2003).
Le Goff Jacques, *Pour un autre Moyen Âge. Temps, travail et culture en Occident*, (Paris : Gallimard, 1977).
Lebrecht N., *Why Mahler. How One Man and Ten Symphonies Changed the World*, (London: Faber & Faber, 2011).
Levinas E., *L'au-delà du verset. Lectures et discours talmudiques,* (Paris : Minuit, 1982).
Lewis J., *Cultural Studies. The Basics*, (London: Sage, 2008).
Lindbeck G.A., *La natura della dottrina. Religione e teologia in un'epoca post-liberale*, (Torino: Claudiana, 2004).
Lindbeck G.A., *The Nature of Doctrine. Religion and Theology in a Postliberal Age*, (Philadelphia: The Westminster Press, 1984).
Löwith K., *Significato e fine della storia. I presupposti teologici della filosofia della storia*, (Milano: Saggiatore, 2004).
Luther M., *Reading the Psalms with Luther*, (Saint Louis: Concordia Publishing House, 2007).
Luther M., *Degli ebrei e delle loro menzogne*, ("*Of the Jews and Their Lies*"), (Turin: Einaudi, 2008).
Luz U., *Studies in Matthew*, (Grand Rapids: Eerdmans, 2005).
MacIntyre A., *Whose Justice? Which Rationality*, (Notre Dame: Notre Dame University Press, 1988).
Magno Gregorio, *Commento morale a Giobbe 20,1,1*: Ogm I/3, 86,87.
Mahmood S., *Religious Difference in a Secular Age. A Minority Report*, (Princeton: Princeton University Press, 2016).
Marguerat D., Bourquin Y., *Per leggere i racconti biblici. La Bibbia si racconta. Iniziazione all'analisi narrativa*, ("*To Read Biblical Narratives. The Bible Narrates Itself. Initiation to Narrative Analysis*"), (Roma: Borla, 2011).
Marramao G., *La passione del presente. Breve lessico della modernità-mondo*, ("*The Passion of the Present. A Brief Lexicon of Modernity-World*"), (Torino: Bollati Boringhieri, 2008).
Marramao G., *Cielo e terra. Genealogia della secolarizzazione*, ("*Heaven and Earth. Geenalogy of Secularization*"), (Rome: Laterza, 1994).

Marramao, *Kairos. Apologia del tempo debito*, ("*Kairos. Apology of Due Time*"), (Turin: Bollati Boringhieri, 2020).
Martin R.P., *2 Corinthians,* Word Biblical Commentary, (Dallas: Word Incorporated, 1991).
Massarenti A., *Il filosofo tascabile. Dai presocratici a Wittgenstein. 44 ritratti per una storia del pensiero in miniatura*, ("*The Pocket Philosopher. From the Presocratics to Wittgenstein. 44 Portraits for a History of Thought in Miniature*"), (Parma: Ugo Guanda Editore, 2010).
Mbembe A., *Critique de la raison nègre*, (Paris : La Découverte, 2013).
Mcfague S., *The body of God. An Ecological Theology,* (Minneapolis: Fortress Press, 1993).
McLuhan M., *La galassia Gütenberg. La nascita dell'uomo tipografico*, (Roma: Armando editori, 2011).
McLuhan M., *The Gütenberg Galaxy. The Making of Typographic Man*, (New York: Signet Books, 1969).
McLuhan M., *Understanding Media. The Extensions of Man*, (New York: Signet, 1964).
McWilliams N., *Psychoanalytic Diagnosis. Understanding Personality structure in the Clinical Process*, (New York: The Guilford Press, 2019).
Medina J., *Suma Qamaña. Por una convivialidad postindustrial*, (La Paz: PBCC, 2000).
Medina J., *The Epistemology od Resistance. Gender and Racial Oppression, Epistemic Injustice, and Resistant Imagination*, (Oxford: Oxford University Press, 2012).
Melanchton Ph., *Loci Communes*, 1521, Werke, R. (Gütersloh: Stupperich, 1952).
Metzger B.M., *Il canone del Nuovo Testamento. Origine, sviluppo e significato*, ("*The New Testament Canon. Origin, Developement and Meaning*"), (Brescia: Paideia, 1997).
Metzger B.M., *Il testo del Nuovo Testamento*, ("*The Text of the New Testament*"), (Brescia: Paideia, 1996).
Mignolo W.D., Tlostanova M.V., *Encounters*, vol. 1, n. 1, Fall, 2009.
Mignolo W.D., *The Darker Side of Western Modernity. Global Futures, Decolonial Options*, (Durham: Duke University Press, 2011).
Moltmann J., *Dio nella creazione. Dottrina ecologica della creazione,* ("*God in Creation. A New Theology of Creation and the Spirit of God*"), (Brescia: Queriniana, 1986).
Moltmann J., *La via di Gesù Cristo. Cristologia in dimensioni messianiche,* ("*The Way of Jesus Christ. Christology in Messianic Dimensions*"), (Brescia: Queriniana, 1993).

Moltmann J., *La fonte della vita. Lo Spirito Santo e la teologia della vita,* *("The Spirit of Life. The Holy Spirit and the Theology of Life"),* (Brescia: Queriniana, 1998).
Moltmann J., *Lo spirito della vita. Per una pneumatologia integrale, ("The Spirit of Life. For an Integral Pneumatology"),* (Brescia: Queriniana, 1994).
Moltmann J., *Trinità e regno di Dio. La dottrina su Dio, ("Trinity and the Kingdom of God. The Doctrine on God"),* (Brescia: Queriniana, 1983).
Moltmann J., *Nella storia del Dio trinitario. Contributi per una teologia trinitaria, ("In the History of the Trinitarian God. Contributions for a Trinitarian Theology"),* (Brescia: Queriniana, 1993).
Moltmann J., *La chiesa nella forza dello Spirito. Contributo per una ecclesiologia messianica, ("The Church in the Power of the Spirit. Contribution to a Messianic Ecclesiology"),* (Brescia: Queriniana, 1976).
Moltmann, *Esperienze di pensiero teologico. Vie e forme della teologia cristiana, ("Experiences in Theology. Ways and Forms of Christian Theology"),* (Brescia: Queriniana, 2001).
Mura G., *Ermeneutica e verità. Storia e problemi della filosofia dell'interpretazione, ("Hermeneutics and Truth. History and Problems of the Philosophy of Interpretation"),* (Roma: Città Nuova Editrice, 1990).
Müller-Fahrenholz G. Erwecke die Welt. Unsere Glaube an Gottes Geist in dieser bedrohten Zeit (*"Awaken the World. Our Faith in God's Spirit in this endangered Time"),* (Gütersloh: Gütersloher Verlagshaus, 1993).
Natoli S., *La felicità. Saggio di teoria degli affetti, ("Happiness. Essay on a Theory of Affection"),* (Milano: Feltrinelli, 2017).
Natoli S., Il linguaggio della verità. Logica ermeneutica, (*"The Language of Truth. Hermeneutic Logic"),* (Brescia: Morcelliana, 2014).
Natoli S., F. Brancato, *Il mondo a venire. Dialogo sui novissimi, ("The World to Come. Dialogue on the Novissimi"),* (Bologna: Edb, 2021).
Neher A., Ricoeur P., Unesco (eds), *Les cultures et le temps,* (Paris : Payot, 1975).
Nietzsche F., *La gaia scienza e idilli di Messina, ("The Gay Science and Idylls of Messina"),* (Milano: Adelphi, 1977).
Nitti S., *Lutero,* (Roma: Salerno editrice, 2017).
Nolland J., *Luke 1-9:20,* Word Biblical Commentary, (Dallas: Word Books, 1989).

Nozick R., *Anarchia, stato ed utopia. I fondamenti filosofici dello stato minimo*, (*"Anarchy, State and Utopia. The Philosophical Foundations of the Minimal State"*), (Milano: Il Saggiatore, 2008).
Nussbaum M., *L'intelligenza delle emozioni*, (*"Upheavals of Thought. The Intelligence of Emotions)*, (Bologna: Il Mulino, 2004).
Nussbaum Martha, *Le nuove frontiere della giustizia. Disabilità, nazionalità, appartenenza di specie*, (*"Frontiers of Justice: Disability, Nationality, Species Membership"*), (Bologna: Il Mulino, 2007).
O'Brien D., *Theory of Knowledge*, (Cambridge: Polity Press, 2017).
Ong W.J., *Orality and Literacy*, (New York: Routledge, 2012).
Ottati F., *A Theology for the Twenty-first Century*, (Grand Rapids: William B. Eerdmans, 2021).
Otto R., *Il sacro*, (*"The Sacred"*), (Milano: Se, 2014).
Palmer R.E., *Hermeneutics. Interpretation Theory in Schleiermacher, Dilthey, Heidegger and Gadamer*, (Evanston: Northwestern University Press, 1969).
Panikkar R., *Mito, fede, ermeneutica. Il triplice velo della realtà*, (*"Myth, Faith, Hermeneutics. The Triple Veil of Reality"*), (Milano: Jaca Book, 2000).
Panikkar R., *Mito, simbolo, culto, Mistero ed ermeneutica*, vol. I, (*"Myth, Symbol, Cult. Mystery and Hermeneutics"*), (Milano: Jaca Book, 2008).
Panikkar R., *Spazio, tempo e scienza*, (*"Space, Time and Science"*), (Milan: Jaca Book, 2021).
Panikkar R., *Visione trinitaria e cosmoteandrica: Dio-Uomo-Cosmo*, (*"Trinitarian and Cosmotheandric Vision: God-Man-Cosmos"*), Milan: Jaca Book, 2010
Pannenberg W., *Fondamenti dell'etica. Prospettive filosofico-teologiche*, (*"Foundations of Ethics. Philosophical-Theological Perspectives"*), (Brescia: Queriniana, 1998).
Pannenberg W., *Storia e problemi della teologia evangelica contemporanea in Germania. Da Schleiermacher fino a Barth e Tillich*, (*"History and Problems of Contemporary Evangelical Theology in Germany. From Schleiermacher Until Barth and Tillich"*), (Brescia: Queriniana, 2000).
Pascal B., *Pensieri*, (Milano: Rizzoli, 1999).
Pedraja L.G., *Jesus Is My Uncle: Christology from a Hispanic Perspective*, (Nashville: Abingdon Press, 1999).
Pellegrino G., Di Paola M., *Nell'antropocene. Etica e politica alla fine di un mondo*, (*"In the Antropocene. Ethics and Politics at the End of a World"*), (Roma: Habitus, 2018).

Perlini T., *Attraverso il nichilismo. Saggi di teoria critica, estetica e letteratura*, (*"Through Nihilism. Essays on Critical Theory, Aesthetics and Literature"*), (Torino: Aragno, 2015).

Piazza T., *Che cos'è la conoscenza*, (*"What is Knowledge"*), (Roma: Carocci, 2019).

Platone, *Repubblica*, Libro VI, 509d-511e.

Platone, *Simposio*, pp. 202-210.

Prosperi A., *Lutero. Gli anni della fede e della libertà*, (*"Luther. The Years of Faith and Freedom"*), (Milano: Mondadori, 2017).

Pulcini E., *La cura del mondo. Paura e responsabilità nell'età globale*, (*"Caring for the World. Fear and Responsibility in the Global Age"*), (Torino: Bollati Boringhieri, 2009).

Pulcini Elena, *Tra cura e giustizia. Le passioni come risorsa sociale*, (*"Between Care and Justice. Passions as a Social Resource"*), (Torino: Bollati Boringhieri, 2009).

Rampini F., *Il suicidio occidentale. Perché è sbagliato processare la nostra storia e cancellare i nostri valori*, (*"The Western Suicide. Why it is Wrong to Judge our History and Erase our Values"*), (Milano: Mondadori, 2021).

Rasmussen L. L., *Earth Community. Earth Ethics*, (New York: Orbis Books, 2000).

Ravasi G., *Il libro dei salmi. Commento e attualizzazione*, vol. I, (*"The Book of Psalms. Commentary and actualization"*), (Bologna: Edizioni Dehoniane, 1999).

Reid G.W. (ed), *Understanding Scripture. An Adventist Approach*, (Hagerstown: Review and Herald Publishing Association 2006); Latest Edition, (Silver Spring: Biblical Research Institute, 2021).

Remotti F., *Cultura. Dalla complessità all'impoverimento*, (*"Culture. From Complexity to Impoverishment"*), (Roma: Laterza, 2011).

Rengstorf K.H., *Il Vangelo secondo Luca*, (*"The Gospel according to Luke"*), (Brescia: Paideia, 1980).

Ricœur P., *Dal testo all'azione. Saggi di ermeneutica*, (*"From Text to Action. Essays in Hermeneutics II"*), (Milano: Jaca Book, 1994).

Ricœur P., *Ermeneutica filosofica ed ermeneutica biblica*, (*"Philosophical Hermeneutics and Theological Hermeneutics"*), (Brescia: Paideia, 1983).

Ricœur P., *Finitude et culpabilité. Philosophie de la volonté*, vol. II, (Paris: Aubier, 1988).

Ricœur P., *Hermeneutics and the Human Sciences*, (Cambridge: Cambridge University Press, 2016).

Ricœur P., *Il conflitto delle interpretazioni*, ("*The Conflict of Interpretation. Essays in Hermeneutics*"), (Milano: Jaca Book, 1995).
Ricœur P., *Interpretations Theory. Discourse and the Surplus of Meaning*, (Forth Worth: TCU Press, 1976).
Ricœur P., *Le Volontaire e l'Involontaire. Philosophie de la volonté*, vol. I, (Paris: Aubier, 1988).
Ricœur P., *Sé come un altro*, ("*Self as Another*"), (Milano: Jaca Book, 2005).
Rieff Ph., *The Triumph of the Therapeutic. Uses of Faith After Freud*, (Wilmington: ISI Books, 2006).
Rizzi A., *Pensare dentro la Bibbia*, (Roma: LAS, 2010).
Robbins R.H., *Cultural Anthropology. A Problem-Based Approach*, (Belmont: Wadsworth, 2013).
Rodriguez R.R., *Dogmatics After Babel. Beyond the Theologies of Word and Culture*, (Louisville: Westminster John Knox Press, 2018).
Rosa H., *Resonance. A sociology of Our Relationship to the World*, (Cambridge: Polity Press, 2019).
Sacchi Lodispoto T., *Gustav Mahler* - Testi vocali della Sinfonia n. 2 - La risurrezione, su www.flaminioonline.it
Sandel M.J., *Justice. What's the Right Thing to Do?* (New York: Farrar, Straus and Giroux, 2009).
Schleiermacher F., *Sulla religione. Discorsi a quegli intellettuali che la disprezzano*, ("*On Religion. Discourses to Those Intellectuals Who Despise It*"), (Brescia: Queriniana, 2017).
Schmitz K.L., *The Recovery Of Wonder. The New Freedom and the Asceticism of Power*, (Montreal: McGill-Queen's University Press, 2005).
Schökel L.A., Bravo Aragon J.M., *Appunti di ermeneutica. Comprendere e interpretare i testi biblici e letterari*, ("*Notes on Hermeneutics. Understanding and Interpreting Biblical and Literary Texts*"), (Bologna: EDB, 2014).
Schökel L.A., Carniti C., *Salmos,* vol. I, (Navarra: Verbo Divino, 1992).
Scholem G., *Die jüdische Mystik in ihren Hauptströmungen,* (Frankfurt: Suhrkamp, 2009).
Scholem G., *Schöpfung aus Nichts und Selbstverschränkung Gottes,* Eranos-Jahrbuch, 1956.
Scholem G., *Concetti fondamentali dell'Ebraismo*, ("*Fundamental Concepts of Judaism*"), (Milano: Marietti, 1820, 1986).
Schürmann H., *Il Vangelo di Luca* (1) *1-9:50*, ("*The Gospel of Luke* (1) *1-9:50*"), (Brescia: Paideia, 1983).

Sciolla L., *Sociologia dei processi culturali*, (*"Sociology of Cultural Processes"*), (Bologna: Il Mulino, 2007).
Scruton R., *Il suicidio dell'Occidente*, (Grassina FI: Le Lettere, 2021).
Sesboüé B., *Lo Spirito senza volto e senza voce. Breve storia della teologia dello Spirito Santo*, (*"The Faceless and Voiceless Spirit. A Brief History of the Theology of the Holy Spirit"*), (Milano: San Paolo, 2010).
Solon P., *¿Es posible el Vivir Bien? Reflexiones a quema ropa sobre alternativas sistémica*, (La Paz: Solon, 2016).
Spinoza B., *Tractatus theologico-politicus* (1670).
Subilia V., *La nuova cattolicità del Cattolicesimo. Una valutazione protestante del Concilio vaticano Secondo*, (*"The New Catholicity of Catholicism. A Protestant Evaluation of the Second Vatican Council"*), (Turin: Claudiana, 1967).
Tannehill R.C., *Luke*, Abingdon New Testament Commentaries, (Nashville: Abingdon Press, 1996).
Taylor Ch., *A Secular Age*, (Cambridge: Harvard University Press, 2007).
Taylor Ch., *Il disagio della modernità*, (*"The Malaise of Modernity"*), (Roma: Laterza, 2003).
Taylor Ch., *Sources of the Self*, (Massachusetts-Cambridge: Harvard University Press, 1989).
Theissen G., *Introduction to the New Testament*, (Minneapolis: Fortress Press, 2003).
Thomas Aquinas, *Somma contro i gentili. Libro primo e secondo*, (*"Sum Against the Gentiles. Book One and Two"*), (Bologna: Edizioni Studio Domenicano, 2000).
Throntveit M.A., *Esdra e Neemia*, (*"Ezra and Nehemiah"*), (Torino: Claudiana, 2011).
Tillich P., *A History of Christian Thought. From Its Judaic and Hellenistic Origins to Existentialism*, (New York: Touchstone, 1972).
Tillich P., *The Courage to Be*, (Glasgow: Collins, 1979).
Tonstad S.K., *The Lost Meaning of the Seventh Day*, (Berrien Springs: Andrews University Press, 2009).
Toulmin S., *Cosmopolis. The Hidden Agenda of Modernity*, (Chicago: University of Chicago Press, 1990).
Trementozzi D., *Salvation in the Flesh. Understanding How Embodiment Shapes Christian Faith*, (Eugene: Pickwick Publications, 2018).
Trias E., *Pensar la religion*, (Barcelona: Galaxia Gutenberg, 2015).
Turchi A.M., *L'amore di Dio in Gesù Cristo come principio ermeneutico della vita cristiana nella teologia di Hans Urs von Balthasar*, (*"The Love

of God in Jesus Christ as a Hermeneutical Principle of Christian Life in the Theology of Hans urs Von Balthasar"), (Milano: Glossa, 2021).
Ullmann W., *Individuo e società nel medioevo, ("Individual and Society in the Middle Ages")*, (Roma: Laterza, 1974).
Vahanian G., *The Death of God. The Culture of Our Post-christian Era*, (New York: George Braziller, 1961).
Vantini L., *La luce della perla. La scrittura di Maria Zambrano tra filosofia e teologia*, (*"The Light of the Pearl. Maria Zambrano's Writing Between Philosophy and Theo-logy")*, (Cantalupa: Effatà Editrice, 2008).
Varicalla V. (ed), *Animali ed ecologia in una rilettura del mondo al femminile*, (Bologna: Alberto Perdisa, 2009).
Varicalla V., *Natura e cultura Occidentale. Tra mondo antico ed età moderna*, (Bologna: Alberto Perdisa, 2002).
Vassallo N., *Teoria della conoscenza*, (*"Theory of Knowledge")*, (Roma: Laterza, 2015).
Vattimo G., *Essere e dintorni*, (*"Being and Surroundings")*, (Milano: La nave di Teseo, 2018).
von Balthasar H. U., *Lo Spirito della verità*, (*"The Spirit of Truth")*, (Milan: Jaca Book, 1992)
Von Harnack Adolf, *Marcione. Il vangelo del Dio straniero*, (*"Marcion. The Gospel of the Foreign God")*, (Turin: Marietti 1820, 2008).

Waldenfels B., *Studien zur Phänomenologie des Fremdes*, voll. 1,2,3,4. (Frankfurt am Main: Suhrkamp, 2001, 2016, 2013, 2015).
Ward G., *Barth, Derrida and the Language of Theology*, (Cambridge: Cambridge University Press, 1998).
Weber A., *Indigenialität*, Berlin: NP & I, 2018.
Weber M., *La scienza come professione*, (*"Science as a Profession")*, (Torino: Einaudi, 2004).
Welker M., *Lo Spirito di Dio. Teologia dello Spirito Santo*, (*"The Spirit of God. Theology of the Holy Spirit")*, (Brescia: Queriniana, 1995).
Wendland H.-D., *Le lettere ai Corinti*, (*"The Letters to the Corinthians")*, (Brescia: Paideia, 1976).
White E.G., *Il gran conflitto*, (*"The Great Controversy")*, (Firenze: Edizioni Adv, 2015).
Wittgenstein L., *Ricerche filosofiche*, (PhilosophicaInvestigations"), (Torino: Einaudi, 2021).
Wittgenstein L., *Tractatus Logico-Philosophicus*, (Milano: Feltrinelli, 2022).

Woodley R.S., *Indigenous Theology and the Western Worldview. A Decolonized Approach to Christian Doctrine*, (Grand Rapids: Baker Academic, 2022).

Young A., *The Spirit Poured Out on All Flesh: Pentecostalism and the Possibility of Global Theology*, (Grand Rapids: Baker Academic, 2005).

Zambrano M., *Cartas de la pièce. Correspondencia con Augustin Andreu*, Pretextos, (Valencia: Universidad Politècnica de Valencia, 2002).

Zimmermann J.G., *Hermeneutics. A Very Short Introduction*, (Oxford: Oxford University Press, 2015).

Žižek S., *Il cuore perverso del cristianesimo*, (*"The Perverse Heart of Christianity"*), (Roma: Meltemi, 2006).

Zoja L., *Contro Ismene. Considerazioni sulla violenza*, (*"Against Ismene. Considerations on Violence"*), (Torino: Bollati Boringhieri, 2009).

Zoja, *La morte del prossimo*, (*"The Death of the Neighbor"*), (Turin: Einaudi, 2018).

INDEX

ABRUZZESE Alberto 467
ADORNO Theodor 274,419
AL-AZMEH Aziz 31,457
ALESSANDRINO Clemente 391
ALTER Robert 196,203
ALTHOUSE Peter 413,447,459
ANDERS Günther 312
ANSELMO Annamaria 333,357,383
APPADURAI Arjun 31
ARENDT Hannah 313,314,434
ARISTOTELE 136,160,200-212,226,293
ASAD Talal 31
AUDI Robert 61
AUERBACH Erich 198,199
AUGÉ Marc 242,435,486,497
AUNE David E. 392,394,398,402

BACCHIOCCI Samuele 361
BAIER Annette 40
BARKER Chris 158
BARR James 72,200
BARTH Karl 104,105,235,288,387,460
BARTHES Roland 114
BATTAGLIA Luisella, 11
BAUCKHAM Richard 368
BECK Ulrich 112,419
BELLINGER Jr. William H. 258,340
BENASAYAG Miguel 508,510
BENEDICT Ruth 365,366
BENJAMIN Walter 134
BENVENISTE Émile 145,190,226,323

BERKELEY George 160,308
BERKHOF Louis 93,94,333
BESNIER Jean-Michel 61
BEST Ernst 348,376,404
BETTELHEIM Bruno 281
BETTINI Maurizio 120
BHABHA Homi K. 291,471
BLANKHOLM Joseph 427
BLOCH Ernst 439
BLOESCH Donald G. 191
BLOOM Harold 444
BOCK Darrell L. 91,143,167,172
BODEI Remo 434,486
BOLLAS Christopher, 37,423
BONHOEFFER Dietrich, 43,254,340,500
BONINO José Miguez 472
BONOMI Andrea 145,323
BORDONI Carlo 132,430
BORING Eugene M. 392,394,398,402
BOURQUIN Yvan 21,127,153,196,323,413
BOUYER Louis 465,466
BRANCATO Francesco 500
BRAVO ARAGON José Maria 18,28,68,165,169,171,195,196
BRUEGGEMANN Walter 258,340
BRUGIATELLI Vereno 27,323
BUCK Pearl S. 46,47,514
BULGAKOV Sergius 387
BULTMANN Rudolf 191-193

VON BALTHASAR Hanz U. 462-465

CACCIARI Massimo 418,421
CALVIN John 250
CAMPBELL Michael W. 123,285
CANCLINI Nestor Garcia 31
CARNITI Cecilia 248,250,252,254,256,258,340,503,504
CASSIRER Ernst 82
CASTELO Daniel 459
CAVICCHIA SCALAMONTI Antonio 82,133,134,301,303
CERASI Enrico 208,232,419
CERUTI Mauro 333
CHAKRABARTY Dipesh 291,474,476
CHAKRAVORTY SPIVAK Gayatri 291
CHANADY Amaryll 31
CHARLES Robert H. 392,394,398,402
CHARLES Sebastien 112,113,419
CHILD Brevard S. 200,205
COLE Reece 123
COMTE Augusto 454
CONGAR Yves 362,383,387,398,458,513
CONRADIE Ernst M. 46
CRADDOCK Fred B. 91
CROCE Benedetto 82
CROCOMBE Jeff 285
CRUTZEN Paul J. 316,494
CUETO Marcos 480
CULLMANN Oscar 192,200,357,371,372

DAVIDSON Richard M. 285
DE CERTEAU Michel 82
DE LUBAC Henri 95
DE MONTAIGNE Michel 450
DE SAUSSURE Ferdinand 145,158,189,225
DE SOUZA SANTOS Boaventura 31

DE TOCQUEVILLE Alexis 35,337,338
DEDEREN Raoul 285
DELITZSCH Franz 88
DELLA MIRANDOLA Pico 301
DELLA STELLA Isacco 220
DERRIDA Jaques 214,235
DESCARTES René 82-85,160,278,291,308
DESCOLA Philippe 36,45
DI CEGLIE Roberto 445,447
DI IORIO Francesco 61
DI MOPSUESTIA Teodoro 94
DI NUOSCIO Enzo 61
DI PAOLA Marcello 316
DI SAMOSATA Paolo 333,334,385
DI SANTE Carmine 192,204,218
DILTHEY Wilhelm 99,103,105-107,322
DIOTALLEVI Luca 364
DONDEYNE Albert 332
DORNISCH Loretta 196
DREWERMANN Eugen 232,233,294,420
DUMONT Louis 301
DUPUIS Jaques 459
DURRWELL François-Xavier 466

ECO Umberto, 20,21,114,159,160
EHRENBERG Alain 307
ELLUL Jacques 424,425
ERASMO da Rotterdam 96,101
ERICKSON Millard J. 191,282
ESTREMADOYRO ROBLES Camilla 478
ETZIONI Amitai 310
EVDOKIMOV Paul 388,389

FABRIS Rinaldo 140,164,367,371,372,375
FERRARIS Maurizio 64,66,106,107,109,132

FEUERBACH Ludwig 186,187
FINKIELKRAUT Alain 301
FISH Stanley 114,209,224
FLORIDI Luciano 436
FLUSSER Vilém 436
FORTE Bruno 28,38,418
FOSNOT TWOMEY Catherine 159
FOUCAULT Michel 187,366
FREGE Gottlob 145,323,331
FROMM Erich 180,211,293,433
FRY Paul H.114,128
FUNK Robert W. 196

GADAMER Hans G. 11,17,99,103,104, 107,109,110,188,323
GALIMBERTI Umberto 24,25,231,232,236, 240-242,261,274,312,415,418,512
GALLI Carlo 135,136,428
GAUCHET Marcel 133
GEFFRÉ Claude 17,59,60,69,72,78,115,122,446,447
GEMBILLO Giuseppe 333,357,383
GESHÉ Adolphe 331,359
GETTIER Edmund 61
GIACCARDI Chiara 499
GIDDENS Anthony 112,419
GISEL Pierre 211
GNILKA Joachim 367,371,372,375
GONZALEZ CASANOVA P. 31
GONZALEZ Justo L. 93,94
GOUREVITCH Aron J. 82,505
GRONDIN Jean 59,103,105,107,109
GOUREVITCH Aaron Y.82,505
GUTIERREZ Gustavo 35,36,469,518

HAN Byung-Chul 26,39,278,312,366, 367,425,434,437,454,486,487
HARNACK Adolf von 288,362
HASEL Frank M. 285

HASEL Michael G. 285
HEGEL Georg W.F.186
HEIDEGGER Martin 17,25-27,42,99,103, 107-110,274,415,418,512
HEIM Mark S. 459
HELD Virginia 40
HERRMANN Wilhelm 288
HESCHEL Abraham J.354,491,497
HEUSSI Karl 93,101,386
HILLMAN James 232,276,277,366
HJELMSLEV Louis T. 145,189,225
HOBBES Thomas 135-137,292,469,470
HOLLAND Norman 114
HOPKO Thomas 371,372
HORKHEIMER Max 274,419
HORRELL David G. 46
HUANACUNI MAMANI Fernando 43
HUME David 40
HUNT Cherryl 46

ISER Wolfgang 114,331,413

JACKSON Maury D. 472
JANE Emma A. 158
JANOWSKI Bernd 256,340
JAUSS Hans-R. 114
JEANROND Werner G. 64,65,70,73,80, 94-96, 100,104,127,129,153,155,170, 174,191,195
JENKINS Philip 31,48,123,514,515
JENNINGS Isaac 37
JENNINGS Willie J. 169,414
JENSEN Alexander S. 74,75,79, 100-103,105,107,109,114
JEREMIAS Joachim 202,203
JOHNSON Keith E.,459
JOHNSON Mark 213
JUNG Carl Gustav 178,276-278

KANT Immanuel 160,161,187
KÄRKKÄINEN Veli-Matti 48,115,326,331,357,383,515,517
KEENER Craig S. 459
KEIL Carl F. 88
KIERKEGAARD Søren 104,240
KITTAY Eva 40
KLOPSTOCK Friedrich G. 451-453,455
KOSELLECK Reinhart 510
KRAUS Hans J. 102
KUCZYŃSKI Maxime Hans 478,480,481
KÜMMEL Werner G. 102
KUHN Thomas 122
KUNDERA Milan 196
KYUNG Chung Hyun 32

LAKOFF George 213
LANCELLOTTI Angelo 342
LAND Steven J. 459
LANE Tony 93,94,100,101
LANG Friedrich 348,376,404
LASCH Christopher 307
LATOUR Bruno 36,37,316,476,477,481
LE GOFF Jacques 82,97
LEBRECHT Norman 445
LESSING Gottohold E. 102
LÉVI STRAUSS Claude 21
LEVINAS Emmanuel 89
LEWIS Jeff 158
LINDBECK George A. 213,232,237,238
LONERGAN Bernard 237
LÖWITH Karl 509
LUNG Wang 47,514
LURIA Isaak 354
LUTHER Martin 100,101,248,362,438,439
LUZ Ulrich 367-369,371,372,375

MACINTYRE Alasdair 310
MAGATTI Mauro 499
MAGNO Gregorio 220
MAHLER Gustav 437,445-449,451-453,455,457
MAHMOOD Saba 31
MARCIONE 362
MARGUERAT Daniel 21,127,153,196,323,413
MARRAMAO Giacomo 291,305-307,429, 435,436,475,486,487,504,509
MARTIN Ralph P. 348,376,404
MARX Karl 313,431
MASSARENTI Armando 239
MBEMBE Achille 31,37
MCFAGUE Sallie 496
MCLUHAN Marshall 128,133,201
MCWILLIAMS Nancy 272,422
MEDINA Javier 43
MEDINA José 415,472
METZGER Bruce M. 134,152,205,443
MIGNOLO Walter D. 31,41
MILBANK John 235
MOLTMANN Jürgen 32,46,48,49,331, 334,335,340,350,354,357,363,364, 371,372,383,385,388,389,392,398, 400,413,447,448,458,464,469,472, 491,499,515,516,
MORIN Edgar 333
MÜLLER-FAHRENHOLZ Geiko 32
MÜNZER Thomas 438,439
MURA Gaspare 96,207
MUSIL Robert 421

NATOLI Salvatore 43,329,500
NEEMIA (Sacre Scritture) 87
NEHER André 504
NIETZSCHE Friedrich 453,485
NITTI Silvana 100

NOLLAND John 140,164
NOZICK Robert 391
NUSSBAUM Martha 14,40,445,447-449,451-453

O'BRIEN Dan 61
ONG Walter J. 58,82,132,158,159
ORIGENE 93,94,385
OTTATI Douglas F. 28,29,426,515
OTTO Rudolf 241

PALMER Richard E. 99,103,105,107,109,
PANIKKAR Raimon, 40-42,491,496,502
PANNENBERG Wolfhart 33,288
PASCAL Blaise 61
PEDRAJA Luis G. 516,517
PELLEGRINO Gianfranco 316
PERLINI Tito 419
PETERSEN Peter 123
PIAZZA Tommaso 61
PICKSTOCK Catherine 235
PLATONE 62,63,93,94
PROSPERI Adriano 101
PROTAGORA 307
PULCINI Elena, 40,124,301,430

RAHNER Karl 237
RAIMONDI Antonio 478,479
RAMPINI Federico 476
RAMSEY Iam 232
RASMUSSEN Larry L. 46
RAVASI Gianfranco 248,250,252,340,343,344,346,
REID George W. 123,285
REMOTTI Francesco, 42-44
RENGSTORF Karl H. 146,169
RICŒUR Paul 22,23,27,33,41,54,56 ,57,63,64,85,103,107,118,127,129, 132,134,138,139,141,144,145,154, 162,163,165,168,170,185,189,192, 193,196,201,202,226,232,252,321-324,446,504,505
RIEFF Philip 262
RITSCHL Albert 288
RIZZI Armido 128,192,198,315
ROBBINS Robert H. 158
RODRIGUEZ Ruben Rosario 48,515-517
ROSA Hartmut 423,424,484,487,488,489

SACCHI LODISPOTO Teresa 455
SANDEL Michael J. 310
SCHLEIERMACHER Friedrich, 38,83,99, 100,102, 103-105,107,110,113,237, 288,302
SCHMIT Gerard 508
SCHMITT Carl 428
SCHMITZ Kenneth L. 47,514
SCHÖKEL Luis Alonso 18,28,68,165, 169,171,194-196,248,250,252,254, 256,258,340
SCHOLEM Gershom 354
SCHÜRMANN Heinz 143,167,172
SCHWEITZER Albert 480
SCIOLLA Loredana 158
SCRUTON Roger 476,477
SEBOND Raimond 450
SESBOÜÉ Bernard 386,389,401,402,458,465
SMITH Adam 40
SOLON Pablo 43
SOUTHGATE Christopher 46
SPINOZA Baruch 102
STAVRAKOPOULOU Francesca 46
STUDEBAKER Steven M. 413,447
SUBILIA Vittorio 360

TANNEHILL Robert C. 90,146,169
TAYLOR Charles 299,301,303,304,339, 365,428-433
TERTULLIANO Fiorente 333,386,394
THEISSEN Gerd 368
THRONTVEIT Mark A. 87
TILLICH Paul 93,94,179,180,288
TLOSTANOVA Madina V. 41
TONSTAD Sigve K. 491
TOULMIN Stephen 274
TREMENTOZZI David 38
TRIAS Eugenio 192,422
TRONTO Joan C. 40
TURCHI Alessandra M. 462

ULLMANN Walter 82

VAHANIAN Gabriel 433,485
VANTINI Lucia 457
VASSALLO Nicla 61
VATTIMO Gianni 109,329

WALDENFELS Bernhard 454,455
WARD Graham 235
WEBER Andreas, 44,45,482,483,500,501,507
WEBER Max 121,294,304
WELKER Michael 32
WENDLAND Heinz-Dietrich 348,376,404
WHITE Ellen G. 395,400
WHITTINGHAM William 395
WITTGENSTEIN Ludwig 238-240
WOODLEY Randy S. 483,501,507,517

YOUNG Amos 459

ZAMBRANO Maria 457
ZIMMERMANN Jens 57
ŽIŽEK Slavoj 235-237
ZOJA Luigi 274,276-278,282,433,485

MIMESIS GROUP
www.mimesis-group.com

MIMESIS INTERNATIONAL
www.mimesisinternational.com
info@mimesisinternational.com

MIMESIS EDIZIONI
www.mimesisedizioni.it
mimesis@mimesisedizioni.it

ÉDITIONS MIMÉSIS
www.editionsmimesis.fr
info@editionsmimesis.fr

MIMESIS COMMUNICATION
www.mim-c.net

MIMESIS EU
www.mim-eu.com

Printed by
Rotomail Italia S.p.A.
October 2023

www.ingramcontent.com/pod-product-compliance
Lightning Source LLC
Chambersburg PA
CBHW021413300426
44114CB00010B/480